Math 87

An Incremental Development

Second Edition

Math 87

An Incremental Development

Second Edition

Stephen Hake

John Saxon

Saxon Publishers, Inc.

Math 87: An Incremental Development
Second Edition

Teacher's Edition

Printed in the United States of America.

ISBN: 1-56577-187-7

Prepress Manager: J. Travis Rose

Production Coordinator: Joan Coleman

Second printing: June 1999

Printed on recycled paper.

┌─ *Reaching us via the Internet* ─┐
WWW: http://www.saxonpub.com
E-mail: info@saxonpub.com

Saxon Publishers, Inc.
2450 John Saxon Blvd.
Norman, OK 73071

Contents

Preface

To The Teacher

This book grew out of years of intense classroom interaction with students in which the goal was for students to learn and **remember** the foundational skills of mathematics. The term "foundational" is appropriate because mathematics, perhaps more than any other subject, is a cognitive structure that builds upon prior learning. The ultimate height and stability of the mathematical structure within each individual are determined by the strength of the foundation. This book, as well as each book that precedes or follows it, provides the student with the time and opportunities necessary to build a rock-solid foundation in beginning mathematics. **For this to occur it is essential that all practice problems and all problem sets be completed by the student.**

How To Use This Book

This book consists of a series of daily lessons and investigations that are carefully sequenced to incrementally develop a spectrum of skills and concepts. Each daily lesson has four components as described below.

First is a collection of warm-up activities that includes facts practice, mental math practice, and a problem-solving opportunity. The masters for the suggested facts practice speed tests are presented in the *Math 87 Test Masters* and need to be reproduced for students. We suggest beginning class with this activity, having students race to improve their personal performance on each facts practice sheet. Emphasizing speed helps to automate the recall of basic facts. Confine this activity to five minutes or less. The back of the facts practice paper may be used to record mental math answers and problem solving work. The suggested mental math questions may be orally posed by the teacher or read by the students. The students record their answers on paper while performing the calculations "in their heads." Class discussion of various mental calculation strategies is helpful. The problem-solving activity is intended to be a whole-group effort. Eager students often work ahead on these problems. However, the goal is to provide a problem-solving experience for all students without intimidating those who are more hesitant. The three warm-up activities should be completed in 10 to 12 minutes.

The second component of the daily lesson is an explanation of the new increment. Example problems are included to illustrate the day's topic. The presentation of the new increment should be brief and lead promptly to the practice problems.

The practice problems, the third component of the daily lesson, are designed to provide massed, guided practice on the new skill or concept. Closely monitor student work on the practice questions to provide immediate feedback. An asterisk after the word "practice" in a lesson indicates that additional practice for that lesson can be found in the appendix. This supplemental practice is intended for remedial use only. Most students do not require the additional practice to acquire the skills and concepts presented.

The fourth and most important component of the daily lesson is the problem set. The problem set provides distributed practice on previously presented skills and concepts. The conscientious completion of the daily problem set is essential for student success in this program. The majority of class time should be devoted to student work on the problem set. To focus students on the problem set, some teachers choose to begin class each day with five selected problems from the new problem set. This is an acceptable variation from beginning class with facts practice, which then moves to a later portion of the class period. Students should deliberately work on the more difficult problems in the set while they are in class and save the easier problems for homework. Designating student tutors and cooperative groups to assist students who are having difficulty can help all students be successful.

Following every ten lessons is an investigation which is an expanded lesson that is likely to take an entire class period to cover. Investigations are designed to be teacher-led and often include activities that require some preparation. Since an investigation consumes a full class period, a problem set is not included. Each investigation presents essential content that is included in subsequent problem sets.

Assessment

The *Math 87 Test Masters* booklet contains two forms of tests for every five lessons. The second test form may be used for make-up testing. The testing program begins following Lesson 10 and continues every five lessons thereafter. Students will make excellent progress if they are able to score 80% or better on the tests. Students who fall below the 80% level should be given remedial attention immediately. A facts practice test as a component of assessment is suggested at the top of each test.

Activity Masters for selected lessons and investigations are also included in the *Math 87 Test Masters*. Activities requiring hands-on materials occur throughout the text. We encourage teachers to plan a few lessons ahead of the students to anticipate the material needs of future lessons.

Stephen Hake *John Saxon*
Temple City, California *Norman, Oklahoma*

Acknowledgments

We thank Shirley McQuade Davis for her ideas on teaching word problem thinking patterns. We would also like to thank the following people for their contributions in the production of this revision: Coen Barnes, Chris Braun, Wendy Chitwood, Serena Freeberg, Angela Johnson, Anthony Lawson, David LeBlanc, Sherri Little, Matt Maloney, Adriana Maxwell, Erin McCain, Tonea Morrow, Dan O'Connor, Brian Rice, Travis Southern, Letha Steinbron, and Jan Stratton.

Arithmetic with Whole Numbers and Money

Mental Math:
a. 60
b. 80
c. 87
d. 6
e. 24
f. 48
g. 5
Problem Solving:
21, 28, 36

Facts Practice: 64 Multiplication Facts (Test A in Test Masters)[†]

Mental Math: A score is 20. Two score and 4 is 44. How many is

    a. 3 score   **b.** 4 score   **c.** 4 score and 7

    d. Half a dozen   **e.** 2 dozen   **f.** 4 dozen

    g. Start with a score, and add a dozen. Divide by 4, add 2, then divide by 2. What is the answer?

Problem Solving:

  What are the next three numbers in this pattern?

$$1, 3, 6, 10, 15, \ldots$$

The numbers we say when we count are called **counting numbers** or **natural numbers.** We may show the set of counting numbers this way.

$$\{1, 2, 3, 4, 5, \ldots\}$$

The three dots, called an *ellipsis*, mean that the list is infinite (goes on without end). The symbols { } are called **braces.** One use of braces is to designate a set. Including zero with the set of counting numbers forms the set of **whole numbers.**

$$\{0, 1, 2, 3, 4, \ldots\}$$

Whole numbers include all the counting numbers and zero. Whole numbers do not include numbers less than zero or any numbers between 0 and 1 or between any consecutive counting numbers.

The four fundamental **operations of arithmetic** are addition, subtraction, multiplication, and division. In this lesson we will review the operations of arithmetic with whole numbers and with money. Amounts of money are sometimes indicated with a dollar sign ($) or with a cent sign (¢), but not both. We may show 50 cents either of these two ways:

$$\$0.50 \qquad \text{or} \qquad 50¢$$

[†]For instructions on how to use the boxed activities, please consult the preface.

Occasionally we will see a dollar sign or cent sign used incorrectly.

Soft Drinks
0.50¢
each

This sign is incorrect because it uses a decimal point with a cent sign. This incorrect sign literally means that soft drinks cost not half a dollar but half a cent! Take care to express amounts of money in the proper form when performing arithmetic with money.

In addition, the numbers that are added are called **addends** and the result is the **sum.**

$$\text{addend} + \text{addend} = \text{sum}$$

Example 1 (a) 36 + 472 + 3614

(b) $1.45 + $6 + 8¢

Solution (a) We align the digits in the ones' place and add in columns. Looking for combinations of digits that total 10 may speed the work.

$$\begin{array}{r} {}^{111} \\ 36 \\ 472 \\ + \ 3614 \\ \hline 4122 \end{array}$$

(b) We write each amount of money with a dollar sign and two places to the right of the decimal point. We align the decimal points and add.

$$\begin{array}{r} {}^{1} \\ \$1.45 \\ \$6.00 \\ + \ \$0.08 \\ \hline \$7.53 \end{array}$$

In subtraction we subtract the **subtrahend** from the **minuend.** The result is the **difference.**

$$\text{minuend} - \text{subtrahend} = \text{difference}$$

Example 2 (a) 5207 − 948

(b) $5 − 25¢

Solution (a) We align the digits in the ones' place. We must follow the correct order of subtraction by writing the minuend (first number) above the subtrahend (second number).

$$\begin{array}{r} {}^{4}{}^{1}9{}_{1} \\ \cancel{5}\cancel{2}\cancel{0}7 \\ - \ \ 948 \\ \hline 4259 \end{array}$$

(b) We write each amount in dollar form. We align decimal points and subtract.

$$\begin{array}{r} {}^{4}\ {}^{9}{}_{1} \\ \$\cancel{5}.\cancel{0}0 \\ -\ \$0.25 \\ \hline \$4.75 \end{array}$$

Numbers that are multiplied are called **factors.** The result is the **product.**

$$\text{factor} \times \text{factor} = \text{product}$$

We can indicate multiplication with a times sign, a center dot, or by writing numbers next to each other with no sign between them.

$$4 \times 5 \qquad 4 \cdot 5 \qquad 4(5) \qquad ab$$

The parentheses in 4(5) clarify that 5 is a quantity separate from 4 and that the two digits do not represent the number 45. The expression ab means a times b.

Example 3   (a) $164 \cdot 23$

(b) $\$4.68 \times 20$

(c) $5(29¢)$

Solution   (a) We usually write the number with the most digits on top. We first multiply by the 3 of 23, then by the 20 of 23. We add the partial products to find the final product.

$$\begin{array}{r} 164 \\ \times\ \ 23 \\ \hline 492 \\ 328\ \ \\ \hline 3772 \end{array}$$

(b) We may let the zero in 20 "hang out" to the right. We write zero below the line then multiply by the 2 of 20. We write the product with a dollar sign and two decimal places.

$$\begin{array}{r} \$4.68 \\ \times\ \ \ \ \ 20 \\ \hline \$93.60 \end{array}$$

(c) We may multiply 29¢ by 5 or write 29¢ as $0.29 first. Since the product is greater than $1, we use a dollar sign to write the answer.

$$\begin{array}{r} 29¢ \\ \times\ \ 5 \\ \hline 145¢ = \textbf{\$1.45} \end{array}$$

When we divide, we divide the **dividend** by the **divisor.** The result is the **quotient.** We may indicate division with a division sign (÷), a division box ($\overline{)\ \ }$), or a division bar (–).

$$\text{dividend} \div \text{divisor} = \text{quotient}$$

$$\text{divisor}\overline{)\text{dividend}}^{\text{quotient}} \qquad \frac{\text{dividend}}{\text{divisor}} = \text{quotient}$$

Example 4 (a) 1234 ÷ 56

(b) $\dfrac{\$12.60}{5}$

Solution (a) In this division there is a remainder. Other methods for dealing with a remainder will be considered later.

$$
\begin{array}{r}
22\ \text{r}\ 2 \\
56\overline{)1234} \\
112 \\
\hline
114 \\
112 \\
\hline
2
\end{array}
$$

(b) We write the quotient with a dollar sign. The decimal point in the answer is directly above the decimal point in the dividend.

$$
\begin{array}{r}
\$2.52 \\
5\overline{)\$12.60} \\
10 \\
\hline
2\ 6 \\
2\ 5 \\
\hline
10 \\
10 \\
\hline
0
\end{array}
$$

Practice **a.** This sign is incorrect. Show two ways to correct the sign.
$0.45 per glass; 45¢ per glass

Lemonade
0.45¢
per glass

b. Name a whole number that is not a counting number. 0

c. When the product of 4 and 4 is divided by the sum of 4 and 4, what is the quotient? 2

Simplify by adding, subtracting, multiplying, or dividing as indicated:

d. $1.75 + 60¢ + $3 $5.35

e. $2 − 47¢ $1.53

f. 5(65¢) $3.25

g. 250 · 24 6000

h. $24.00 ÷ 5 $4.80

i. $\dfrac{234}{18}$ 13

Problem set
1

1. When the sum of 5 and 6 is subtracted from the product of 5 and 6, what is the difference? 19

2. If the subtrahend is 9 and the difference is 8, what is the minuend? 17

3. If the divisor is 4 and the quotient is 8, what is the dividend? 32

4. When the product of 6 and 6 is divided by the sum of 6 and 6, what is the quotient? 3

5. Name the four fundamental operations of arithmetic. addition, subtraction, multiplication, and division

6. If the sum is 12 and one addend is 4, what is the other addend? 8

Simplify by adding, subtracting, multiplying, or dividing, as indicated:

7.
$$\begin{array}{r} \$43.74 \\ - \ \$16.59 \\ \hline \$27.15 \end{array}$$

8.
$$\begin{array}{r} 64 \\ \times \ 37 \\ \hline 2368 \end{array}$$

9.
$$\begin{array}{r} 7 \\ 8 \\ 4 \\ 6 \\ 9 \\ 3 \\ 5 \\ + \ 7 \\ \hline 49 \end{array}$$

10. 364 + 52 + 867 + 9 1292

11. 4000 − 3625 375

12. (316)(18) 5688

13. $43.60 ÷ 20 $2.18

14. 300 · 40 12,000

15. 8 · 12 · 0 0

16. 3708 ÷ 12 309

17. 365 × 20 7300

18. $25\overline{)767}$ 30 r 17

19. 30(40) 1200

20. $10 − $2.34 $7.66

21. 4017 − 3952 65

22. $2.50 × 80 $200.00

23. 20($2.50) $50.00

24. $\dfrac{560}{14}$ 40

25. $\dfrac{\$10.00}{8}$ $1.25

26. What is another name for counting numbers? natural numbers

27. Write 25 cents twice, once with a dollar sign and once with a cent sign. $0.25; 25¢

28. Which counting numbers are also whole numbers? All counting numbers are whole numbers.

29. What is the name for the answer to a division problem?
quotient

30. Here we use a plus sign and an equals sign to show the relationship of addends and their sum.

$$\text{addend} + \text{addend} = \text{sum}$$

Use a minus sign and an equals sign to show the relationship between the numbers in subtraction using the words difference, subtrahend, and minuend.
minuend − subtrahend = difference

LESSON 2

Properties of Operations • Sequences

Mental Math:
a. 48
b. 18
c. 50
d. 900
e. 6000
f. 600
g. 0
Problem Solving:
55

Facts Practice: 64 Multiplication Facts (Test A in Test Masters)

Mental Math:

  a. 2 score and 8   **b.** $1\frac{1}{2}$ dozen   **c.** Half of 100

  d. 400 + 500   **e.** 9000 − 3000   **f.** 20 × 30

  g. Start with a dozen and divide by 2. Multiply by 4, add 1, divide by 5, then subtract 5. What is the answer?

Problem Solving:

When we add 1, 2, 3, and 4, the sum is 10. What is the sum when we add 1, 2, 3, 4, 5, 6, 7, 8, 9, and 10? (Try pairing numbers to make equal sums.)

Properties of operations

Addition and subtraction are **inverse operations.** We can "undo" an addition by subtracting one addend from the sum.

$$2 + 3 = 5 \qquad 5 - 3 = 2$$

The numbers 2, 3, and 5 together are an addition-subtraction **fact family.** With these numbers we can write two addition facts and two subtraction facts.

$$2 + 3 = 5 \qquad 5 - 3 = 2$$
$$3 + 2 = 5 \qquad 5 - 2 = 3$$

We see that both 2 + 3 and 3 + 2 equal 5. Changing the order of addends does not change the sum. This characteristic of addition is known as the **commutative property of addition** and is often stated in equation form using letters, called **variables,** that can stand for any number.

$$a + b = b + a$$

Since changing the order of numbers in subtraction may change the result, subtraction is not commutative.

Addition is commutative.

$$2 + 3 = 3 + 2$$

Subtraction is not commutative.

$$5 - 3 \neq 3 - 5$$

($\neq$ means "is not equal to")

The **identity property of addition** states that when zero is added to a given number, the sum is equal to the given number.

$$a + 0 = a$$

Thus, zero is the **additive identity.**

Multiplication and division are also inverse operations. Dividing a product by one of its factors "undoes" the multiplication.

$$4 \times 5 = 20 \qquad 20 \div 5 = 4$$

The numbers 4, 5, and 20 together are a multiplication-division fact family that can be arranged into two multiplication facts and two division facts.

$$4 \times 5 = 20 \qquad 20 \div 5 = 4$$
$$5 \times 4 = 20 \qquad 20 \div 4 = 5$$

Changing the order of the factors does not change the product. This characteristic of multiplication is known as the **commutative property of multiplication.**

$$a \times b = b \times a$$

Changing the order of division may change the quotient so division is not commutative.

Multiplication is commutative.

$$4 \times 5 = 5 \times 4$$

Division is not commutative.

$$20 \div 5 \neq 5 \div 20$$

The **identity property of multiplication** states that when a given number is multiplied by one, the result equals the given number. Thus, one is the **multiplicative identity.**

$$a \times 1 = a$$

The **property of zero for multiplication** states that when a number is multiplied by zero, the product is zero.

$$a \times 0 = 0$$

The operations of arithmetic are **binary,** which means that we only work with two numbers in one step. If we wish to add

$$2 + 3 + 4$$

we can add two of the numbers and then add the other number. The **parentheses** around $2 + 3$ in the expression below show that $2 + 3$ should be treated as a single quantity. Therefore 2 and 3 should be added before 4 is added to their sum.

$$(2 + 3) + 4 \qquad \text{Add 2 and 3 first}$$
$$5 + 4 \qquad \text{Then add 5 and 4}$$
$$9 \qquad \text{Sum}$$

Notice that the sum is the same if 3 and 4 are added first.

$$2 + (3 + 4) \qquad \text{Add 3 and 4 first}$$
$$2 + 7 \qquad \text{Then add 2 and 7}$$
$$9 \qquad \text{Sum}$$

We see that how we group the addends does not affect the sum. This addition illustrates the **associative property of addition.**

$$(2 + 3) + 4 = 2 + (3 + 4)$$

The associative property of addition is often stated as an equation using variables.

$$(a + b) + c = a + (b + c)$$

The **associative property of multiplication** states that the grouping of factors does not change the product.

$$(a \times b) \times c = a \times (b \times c)$$

The grouping of numbers in subtraction and division does affect the result, as we see in the following expressions. Thus, there is no associative property of subtraction, and there is no associative property of division.

$$(8 - 4) - 2 \neq 8 - (4 - 2)$$
$$(8 \div 4) \div 2 \neq 8 \div (4 \div 2)$$

Example 1   Name each property illustrated.

(a) $5 \cdot 3 = 3 \cdot 5$

(b) $(3 + 4) + 5 = 3 + (4 + 5)$

(c) $6 + 0 = 6$

(d) $6 \cdot 0 = 0$

Solution   (a) **Commutative property of multiplication**

(b) **Associative property of addition**

(c) **Identity property of addition**

(d) **Property of zero for multiplication**

Example 2   Which property can you use to find each missing number?

(a) $8 + ? = 8$

(b) $1 \times ? = 9$

(c) $10 \times ? = 0$

Solution   (a) **Identity property of addition**

(b) **Identity property of multiplication**

(c) **Property of zero for multiplication**

Sequences   A **sequence** is an ordered list of numbers that follow a certain pattern or rule. A list of the whole numbers is an example of a sequence.

$$0, 1, 2, 3, 4, \ldots$$

If we wish to make a list of the **even** or **odd** whole numbers, we could write these sequences.

Even Whole Numbers	Odd Whole Numbers
$0, 2, 4, 6, 8, \ldots$	$1, 3, 5, 7, 9, \ldots$

A rule for both of these sequences is to add two to one term in the sequence to find the next term. However the lists are different because the starting numbers of the sequences are different. To continue a sequence, we study the sequence to understand its pattern or rule, then we apply the rule to find additional numbers in the sequence.

Example 3   Find the next three numbers in this sequence.

$$1, 4, 9, 16, \ldots$$

Solution   We will describe two solutions. First we see that the numbers increase in size by a larger amount as we move to the right in the sequence.

$$\overset{+3}{\frown}\ \overset{+5}{\frown}\ \overset{+7}{\frown}$$
$$1,\quad 4,\quad 9,\quad 16, \ldots$$

The increase itself forms a sequence we may recognize: 3, 5, 7, 9, 11, …. We will continue the sequence by adding successively larger odd numbers.

$$\overset{+3}{\frown}\ \overset{+5}{\frown}\ \overset{+7}{\frown}\ \overset{+9}{\frown}\ \overset{+11}{\frown}\ \overset{+13}{\frown}$$
$$1,\quad 4,\quad 9,\quad 16,\quad 25,\quad 36,\quad 49, \ldots$$

We find that the next three numbers in the sequence are **25, 36,** and **49.**

Another solution to the problem is to recognize the sequence as a list of **perfect squares.** When we multiply a counting number by itself, the product is a perfect square.

$$1 \cdot 1 = 1 \qquad 2 \cdot 2 = 4 \qquad 3 \cdot 3 = 9 \qquad 4 \cdot 4 = 16$$

So we can solve this problem by finding the next three perfect squares.

$$5 \cdot 5 = 25 \qquad 6 \cdot 6 = 36 \qquad 7 \cdot 7 = 49$$

The next three terms of the sequence are **25, 36,** and **49.**

$$1, 4, 9, 16, 25, 36, 49, \ldots$$

Practice   **a.** Which number is known as the additive identity, and which number is the multiplicative identity?
The additive identity is 0. The multiplicative identity is 1.

b. Which operation is the inverse operation of multiplication? division

c. Use the letters x, y, and z to write an equation that illustrates the associative property of addition. Then write an example using counting numbers of your choosing.
$(x + y) + z = x + (y + z)$; Numerical answers will vary.

d. Name the property you can use to find the missing number in this equation. commutative property of multiplication

$$5 \times ? = 8 \times 5$$

Add, subtract, multiply, or divide as indicated to simplify ε expression. Remember to work within the parentheses first.

e. (5 + 4) + 3   12

f. 5 + (4 + 3)   12

g. (10 − 5) − 3   2

h. 10 − (5 − 3)   8

i. (6 · 2) · 5   60

j. 6 · (2 · 5)   60

k. (12 ÷ 6) ÷ 2   1

l. 12 ÷ (6 ÷ 2)   4

Find the next three terms of each sequence.

m. 1, 2, 4, 8, ...   16, 32, 64

n. 1, 4, 9, 16, 25, 36, 49, ...
64, 81, 100

Problem set 2

†1. When the product of 2 and 3 is subtracted from the sum
(1) of 4 and 5, what is the difference?   3

2. Write four cents (a) with a cent sign and (b) with a
(1) dollar sign.   (a) 4¢   (b) $0.04

3. The sign shown is incorrect. Show
(1) two ways to correct this sign.
75¢ per glass; $0.75 per glass

Orange Juice
0.75¢
per glass

4. Which operation of arithmetic is the inverse operation of
(2) addition?   subtraction

5. If the dividend is 60 and the divisor is 4, what is the
(1) quotient?   15

6. For the fact family 3, 4, and 7, we can write two addition
(2) facts and two subtraction facts.

$$3 + 4 = 7 \qquad 7 - 4 = 3$$
$$4 + 3 = 7 \qquad 7 - 3 = 4$$

3 × 5 = 15, 5 × 3 = 15, 15 ÷ 3 = 5, 15 ÷ 5 = 3

For the fact family 3, 5, and 15, write two multiplication
facts and two division facts.

---

†The italicized numbers within parentheses underneath each problem number
are called *lesson reference numbers*. These numbers refer to the lesson(s) in
which the major concept of that particular problem is introduced. If additional
assistance is needed, reference should be made to the discussion, examples,
practice, or problem set of that lesson.

Simplify:

7. $42.47
(1) + $63.89
———
$106.36

8. $20.00
(1) − $14.79
———
$5.21

9. $1.54
(1) × 7
———
$10.78

10. $30.00
(1) ——
8
$3.75

11. $4.36 + 75¢ + $12 + 6¢ $17.17
(1)

12. $10.00 − ($4.89 + 74¢) $4.37
(2)

13.
(1)
```
   8
   5
   4
   6
   5
   4
   3
   7
   2
   4
   1
 + 8
 ———
  57
```

14. 3105 ÷ 15 207
(1)

15. 40)‾1630‾ 40 r 30
(1)

16. 81 ÷ (9 ÷ 3) 27
(2)

17. (81 ÷ 9) ÷ 3 3
(2)

18. (10)($3.75) $37.50
(1)

19. 3167 − (450 − 78) 2795
(2)

20. (3167 − 450) − 78 2639
(2)

21. $20.00 ÷ 16 $1.25
(1)

22. 70 · 800 56,000
(1)

23. $10 − $8.45 $1.55
(1)

24. 3714 + 268 + 47 + 9
(1) 4038

25. 5 · 4 · 3 · 2 · 1 120
(1)

26. $20 − ($1.47 + $8)
(2) $10.53

27. $75.00 ÷ 12 $6.25
(1)

28. 30 × 45¢ $13.50
(1)

29. Zero is called
the additive
identity because
when zero is
added to another
number, the sum
is identical to
that number.

29. Why is 0 called the additive identity?
(2)

30. Here we show the relationship between factors and their
(1) product.

$$\text{factor} \times \text{factor} = \text{product}$$

Use a division and an equals sign to show the relationship
between numbers in division using the words dividend,
quotient, and divisor. dividend ÷ divisor = quotient

LESSON
3

Missing Numbers in Addition, Subtraction, Multiplication, and Division

Mental Math:
a. 66
b. 30
c. 500
d. 1500
e. 250
f. 900
g. 7
Problem Solving:
  39 seats

**LESSON
3**

Facts Practice: 64 Multiplication Facts (Test A in Test Masters)

Mental Math:

a. 3 score and 6	**b.** $2\frac{1}{2}$ dozen	**c.** Half of 1000
d. 1200 + 300	**e.** 750 − 500	**f.** 30 × 30

  g. Start with the number of minutes in an hour and divide by 2. Subtract 5, double that number, subtract 1, then divide by 7. What is the answer?

Problem Solving:

  In one section of a theater there are 12 rows of seats. In the first row there are 6 seats, in the second row there are 9 seats, and in the third row there are 12 seats. If the pattern continues, how many seats are in the twelfth row?

An **equation** is a statement that two quantities are equal. Here we show two equations.

$$3 + 4 = 7 \qquad 5 + A = 9$$

The equation on the right contains a letter, called a variable, that stands for an unknown number. In this lesson we will practice finding the value of variables in addition, subtraction, multiplication, and division equations.

Missing numbers in addition

Sometimes we encounter addition problems in which the sum is missing. Sometimes we encounter addition problems in which an addend is missing. We can use a letter to represent a missing number. The letter may be uppercase or lowercase.

Missing Sum	Missing Addend	Missing Addend
2	2	B
+ 3	+ A	+ 3
N	5	5

If we know two of the three numbers, we can find the missing number. We can find a missing addend by subtracting the known addend from the sum. If there are more than two addends, we subtract all the known addends from the sum.

For example, to find n in this problem

$$3 + 4 + n + 7 + 8 = 40$$

we subtract 3, 4, 7, and 8 from 40. To do this we may add the known addends and subtract their sum from the final sum.

Example 1   Find each missing number:

(a)
$$\begin{array}{r} N \\ + \ 53 \\ \hline 75 \end{array}$$

(b) $26 + A = 61$

(c) $3 + 4 + n + 7 + 8 = 40$

Solution   In both (a) and (b) we can find each missing addend by subtracting the known addend from the sum. Then we check.

(a) Subtract.   Try it.

$$\begin{array}{r} 75 \\ - \ 53 \\ \hline 22 \end{array} \qquad \begin{array}{r} 22 \\ + \ 53 \\ \hline 75 \end{array} \text{ check}$$

So the missing number in (a) is **22.**

(b) Subtract.   Try it.

$$\begin{array}{r} 61 \\ - \ 26 \\ \hline 35 \end{array} \qquad \begin{array}{r} 26 \\ + \ 35 \\ \hline 61 \end{array} \text{ check}$$

So the missing number in (b) is **35.**

(c) We add the known addends.

$$3 + 4 + 7 + 8 = 22$$

Then we subtract their sum, 22, from 40.

$$40 - 22 = \mathbf{18}$$

We use the answer in the original problem for a check.

$$3 + 4 + 18 + 7 + 8 = 40 \quad \text{check}$$

Missing numbers in subtraction

There are three numbers in a subtraction problem. If one of the three numbers is missing, we can find the missing number.

MISSING MINUEND	MISSING SUBTRAHEND	MISSING DIFFERENCE
$\begin{array}{r} N \\ - \ 3 \\ \hline 2 \end{array}$	$\begin{array}{r} 5 \\ - \ X \\ \hline 2 \end{array}$	$\begin{array}{r} 5 \\ - \ 3 \\ \hline M \end{array}$

To find a missing minuend, we add the other two numbers. To find a missing subtrahend or difference, we subtract.

Example 2   Find each missing number: (a)
$$\begin{array}{r} P \\ - \ 24 \\ \hline 17 \end{array}$$
(b) $32 - x = 14$

Solution   (a) To find the top number in a subtraction problem, we add the other two numbers. We find that the missing number in (a) is **41.**

$$
\begin{array}{cc}
\text{Add.} & \text{Try it.}
\end{array}
$$

	Add.	Try it.

$$
\begin{array}{cc}
17 & 41 \\
+\ 24 & -\ 24 \\
\hline
41 & 17 \quad \text{check}
\end{array}
$$

(b) To find a subtrahend, we subtract the difference from the minuend. So the missing number in (b) is **18.**

$$
\begin{array}{cc}
\text{Subtract.} & \text{Try it.} \\
32 & 32 \\
-\ 14 & -\ 18 \\
\hline
18 & 14 \quad \text{check}
\end{array}
$$

Missing numbers in multiplication   A multiplication problem is composed of factors and a product. If any one of the numbers is missing, we can figure out what it is.

$$
\begin{array}{ccc}
\text{MISSING PRODUCT} & \text{MISSING FACTOR} & \text{MISSING FACTOR} \\[4pt]
3 & 3 & R \\
\times\ 2 & \times\ F & \times\ 2 \\
\hline
P & 6 & 6
\end{array}
$$

To find a missing product, we multiply the factors. To find a missing factor, we divide the product by the known factor(s).

Example 3   Find each missing number:

(a)
$$
\begin{array}{c}
12 \\
\times\ N \\
\hline
168
\end{array}
$$

(b) $7K = 105$

(c) $2 \cdot 3a = 30$

Solution   In both (a) and (b) the missing number is one of the two factors. Notice that $7K$ means 7 times K. We can find a missing factor by dividing the product by the known factor.

(a) Divide. Try it.

$$
\begin{array}{r}
14 \\
12\overline{)168} \\
12 \\
\hline
48 \\
48 \\
\hline
0
\end{array}
\qquad
\begin{array}{r}
12 \\
\times\ 14 \\
\hline
48 \\
12 \\
\hline
168 \quad \text{check}
\end{array}
$$

So the missing number in (a) is **14.**

(b) Divide. Try it.

$$
\begin{array}{r}
15 \\
7\overline{)105} \\
7 \\
\hline
35 \\
35 \\
\hline
0
\end{array}
\qquad
\begin{array}{r}
15 \\
\times\ 7 \\
\hline
105 \quad \text{check}
\end{array}
$$

So the missing number in (b) is **15.**

In (c) there are three factors shown, 2, 3, and a. One way to find a is to divide the product, 30, by one of the known factors and then divide that result by the other known factor.

$$\frac{30}{2} = 15 \qquad \frac{15}{3} = 5$$

Another way to find a is to divide 30 by the product of the known factors. Since the product of 2 and 3 is 6, we divide 30 by 6.

$$\frac{30}{6} = 5$$

We check our answer, 5, in the original problem.

$$2 \cdot 3(5) = 30 \quad \text{check}$$

Missing numbers in division
If we know two of the three numbers in a division problem, we can figure out the missing number.

MISSING QUOTIENT	MISSING DIVISOR	MISSING DIVIDEND
$\dfrac{24}{3} = N$	$\dfrac{24}{M} = 8$	$\dfrac{P}{3} = 8$

To find a missing quotient or divisor, we divide the known dividend by the known quotient or divisor. To find a missing dividend, we multiply the known quotient by the known divisor.

Example 4 Find each missing number:

(a) $A \div 3 = 15$

(b) $\dfrac{64}{B} = 4$

Solution (a) To find a missing dividend we multiply the quotient and divisor.

$$3 \times 15 = \mathbf{45} \qquad \text{try it} \qquad 45 \div 3 = 15 \quad \text{check}$$

(b) To find a missing divisor, divide the dividend by the quotient.

$$\begin{array}{r} \mathbf{16} \\ 4\overline{)64} \end{array} \qquad \text{try it} \qquad \frac{64}{16} = 4 \quad \text{check}$$

Practice*† Find each missing number:

a.
$$\begin{array}{r} A \quad 19 \\ +\ 12 \\ \hline 31 \end{array}$$

b.
$$\begin{array}{r} B \quad 39 \\ -\ 24 \\ \hline 15 \end{array}$$

c.
$$\begin{array}{r} C \quad 12 \\ \times\ 15 \\ \hline 180 \end{array}$$

---

†The asterisk after "Practice" indicates that additional practice questions intended for remediation are available in the appendix.

d. $\dfrac{R}{8} = 12$ 96

e. $14e = 420$ 30

f. $26 + f = 43$ 17

g. $51 - g = 20$ 31

h. $364 \div h = 7$ 52

i. $3 + 6 + m + 12 + 5 = 30$ 4

Problem set 3

1. When the product of 4 and 4 is divided by the sum of 4 and 4, what is the quotient? 2
(1)

2. If you know the subtrahend and the difference, how can you find the minuend? Write a complete sentence to answer the question.
(1,3)
Add the subtrahend and difference to find the minuend.

3. Which property of addition is stated by this equation?
(2)

$$(a + b) + c = a + (b + c)$$

associative property of addition

4. If one addend is 7 and the sum is 21, what is the other addend? 14
(3)

5. Use the numbers 3 and 4 to illustrate the commutative property of multiplication. Use a center dot to indicate multiplication. $3 \cdot 4 = 4 \cdot 3$
(2)

6. If the product of two identical factors is 36, what is each factor? 6
(3)

Find each missing number:

7. X 29
(3) $+\ 83$
     $\overline{112}$

8. 96
(3) $-\ R$ 69
     $\overline{27}$

9. $7K = 119$ 17
(3)

10. 127
(3) $+\ \ \ Z$ 173
     $\overline{300}$

11. M 868
(3) $-\ 137$
     $\overline{731}$

12. 25
(3) $\times\ N$ 16
     $\overline{400}$

13. $625 \div W = 25$ 25
(3)

14. $\dfrac{X}{60} = 700$ 42,000
(3)

Simplify:

15. 96 ÷ (16 ÷ 2) *12*
(2)

16. (96 ÷ 16) ÷ 2 *3*
(2)

17.
(1)

$$
\begin{array}{r}
8 \\
5 \\
6 \\
1 \\
8 \\
7 \\
4 \\
3 \\
5 \\
8 \\
5 \\
+ \ 3 \\
\hline
63
\end{array}
$$

18. $16.47 + $15 + 63¢ *$32.10*
(1)

19. $50.00 − ($6.48 + $31.75) *$11.77*
(2)

20.
(1)
$$
\begin{array}{r}
47 \\
\times \ 39 \\
\hline
1833
\end{array}
$$

21.
(1)
$$
\begin{array}{r}
\$8.79 \\
\times \ \ \ \ 80 \\
\hline
\$703.20
\end{array}
$$

22. $\dfrac{4740}{30}$ *158*
(1)

23. 1100 − (374 − 87) *813*
(2)

24. (1100 − 374) − 87 *639*
(2)

25. 4736 + 271 + 9 + 88 *5104*
(1)

26. 30,145 − 4,299 *25,846*
(1)

27. 35)‾2104 *60 r 4*
(1)

28. $\dfrac{\$40.00}{32}$ *$1.25*
(1)

29.
(1)
$$
\begin{array}{r}
\$0.48 \\
\times \ \ \ \ 40 \\
\hline
\$19.20
\end{array}
$$

30. Why is 1 called the multiplicative identity?
(2) One is the multiplicative identity because when any number is multiplied by 1, the product is identical to that number.

LESSON
4

Number Line

Facts Practice: 64 Multiplication Facts (Test A in Test Masters)

Mental Math:

  a. Five score   **b.** Ten dozen   **c.** Half of 500

  d. 350 + 400   **e.** 50 × 50   **f.** 400 ÷ 10

  g. Start with the number of feet in a yard and multiply by 12. Divide by 6, add 4, double that number, add 5, double that number, then double that number. What is the answer?

Problem Solving:

Simon held a die (number cube) so that he could see the dots on three of the faces. Simon said he could see 7 dots. How many dots could he not see?

A **number line** can be used to help us arrange numbers in order. Each number corresponds to a unique point on the number line. The zero point of a number line is called the **origin**. The numbers to the right of the origin are called **positive numbers**, and they are all **greater than zero**. Every positive number has an **opposite** that is the same distance to the left of the origin.

The numbers to the left of the origin are called **negative numbers.** The negative numbers are all **less than zero.** Zero is neither positive nor negative.

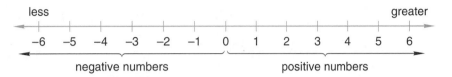

On this number line the tick marks indicate the location of **integers.** Integers include all of the counting numbers as well as their opposites—their negatives—and the number zero. Integers do not include fractions and other numbers between the whole numbers or their opposites.

Integers

$$\{..., -3, -2, -1, 0, 1, 2, 3, ...\}$$

The ellipses to the left and the right indicate that the number of negative and positive integers is infinite. Notice that the negative numbers are written with a negative sign. For −5 we say "negative five." Positive numbers may be written with or without a positive sign. Both +5 and 5 are positive and equal to each other.

As we move to the right on a number line, the numbers become greater and greater. As we move to the left on a number line, the numbers become less and less. A number is greater than another number if it is farther to the right on a number line.

We **compare** two numbers by determining whether one number is greater than another number or whether the two numbers are equal. We place a **comparison symbol** between two numbers to show the comparison. The comparison symbols are the equals sign (=) and the greater than/less than symbol (> or <). The greater than/less than symbol may point in either direction. We write this symbol so that the smaller end (the point) points to the "smaller" number. Below we show three comparisons.

$$-5 < 4 \qquad\qquad 3 + 2 = 5 \qquad\qquad 5 > -6$$

−5 is less than 4   3 plus 2 equals 5   5 is greater than −6

Example 1 Arrange these numbers in order from least to greatest:

$$0, 1, -2$$

Solution We arrange the numbers in the order in which they appear on a number line.

−2, 0, 1

Example 2   Rewrite this expression by replacing the circle with the correct comparison symbol. Then use words to write the comparison.

$$-5 \bigcirc 3$$

Solution   Since –5 is less than 3, we write

$$\mathbf{-5 \: < \: 3}$$

Negative five is less than three.

We can use a number line to help us add and subtract. We will use arrows to show addition and subtraction. To add, we let the arrow point to the right. To subtract, we let the arrow point to the left.

Example 3   Show this addition problem on a number line: 3 + 2

Solution   First we sketch a number line. Next we start at the origin (at zero) and draw an arrow 3 units long that points to the right. From this arrowhead we draw a second arrow 2 units long that points to the right.

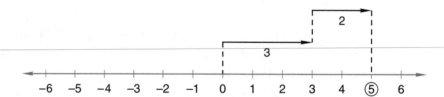

The second arrow ends at 5. This shows that 3 + 2 = **5.**

Example 4   Show this subtraction problem on a number line: 5 – 3

Solution   We sketch a number line. Then, starting at the origin, we draw an arrow 5 units long that points to the right. To subtract, we draw a second arrow 3 units long that points to the left. Remember to draw the second arrow from the arrowhead.

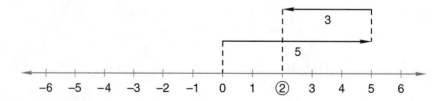

The second arrow ends at 2. This shows that 5 – 3 = **2.**

Example 5   Show this subtraction problem on a number line: 3 – 5

Solution   We take the numbers in the order given. We always begin at the origin. Starting from the origin, we draw an arrow 3 units long that points to the right. From this arrowhead we draw a second arrow 5 units long that points to the left. The second arrow ends to the left of zero which illustrates that the result of the subtraction is a negative number.

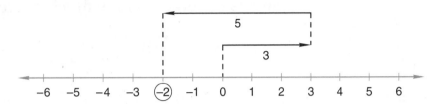

The second arrow ends at –2. This shows that **3 – 5 = –2.**

Together, Examples 4 and 5 graphically show that subtraction is not commutative, that order affects the outcome in subtraction.

Notice that reversing the order of subtraction results in the opposite difference.

$$5 - 3 = 2$$
$$3 - 5 = -2$$

We may use this characteristic of subtraction to help us with subtraction problems like the next example.

Example 6   Simplify: 376 – 840

Solution   We see that the result will be negative. We reverse the order of the numbers to perform the subtraction.

$$
\begin{array}{r}
840 \\
- 376 \\
\hline
464
\end{array}
$$

The answer to the original problem is the opposite of 464 which is **–464.**

Practice   Use arrows to show each addition or subtraction problem on a number line.

a. 4 + 2   **b.** 4 – 2   **c.** 2 – 4

d. Arrange these numbers in order from least to greatest.

0, –1, –2, –3   –3, –2, –1, 0

e. Use digits and other symbols to write "the sum of 2 and 3 is less than the product of 2 and 3." $2 + 3 < 2 \times 3$

Replace each circle with the proper comparison symbol.

f. $3 \gtrless -4$

g. $2 \cdot 2 \bumpeq 2 + 2$

h. Where is the origin on the number line? 0

i. Simplify: $436 - 630$ -194

Problem set 4

1. What is the difference when the sum of 5 and 4 is subtracted from the product of 3 and 3? 0
(1)

2. If the minuend is 27 and the difference is 9, what is the subtrahend? 18
(1,3)

3. What is the name for numbers that are greater than zero? positive numbers
(4)

4. The sign shown is incorrect. Show two ways to correct this sign. 15¢ each; $0.15 each
(1)

Grapefruit

0.15¢ each

5. Use digits and other symbols to write "the product of 5 and 2 is greater than the sum of 5 and 2." $5 \cdot 2 > 5 + 2$
(4)

6. Arrange these numbers in order from least to greatest:
(4)
$$-2, 1, 0, -1 \quad -2, -1, 0, 1$$

7. Replace each circle with the proper comparison symbol.
(4)

(a) $3 \cdot 4 \bumpeq 2(6)$

(b) $-3 \lessgtr -2$

(c) $3 - 5 \lessgtr 5 - 3$

8. If you know the divisor and quotient, how can you find the dividend? Write a complete sentence to answer the question. Multiply the divisor and quotient to find the dividend.
(3)

9. Show this subtraction problem on a number line: $2 - 3$
(4)

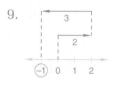

Find each missing number:

10. $12X = 12$ 1
(3)

11. $4 + 8 + N + 6 = 30$ 12
(3)

12. $Z - 123 = 654$ *777*
(3)

13. $1000 - M = 101$ *899*
(3)

14. $\begin{array}{r} P \\ + \$1.45 \\ \hline \$4.95 \end{array}$ P *$3.50*
(3)

15. $\begin{array}{r} 32 \\ \times \ K \\ \hline 224 \end{array}$ *7*
(3)

16. $\dfrac{R}{8} = 24$ *192*
(3)

Simplify:

17. $\$3.67 + 14¢ + \$52.75$
(1) *$56.56*

18. $\$100.00 - \$36.49$ *$63.51*
(1)

19. $48(36¢)$ *$17.28*
(1)

20. $5 \cdot 6 \cdot 7$ *210*
(1)

21. $9900 \div 18$ *550*
(1)

22. $30(20)(40)$ *24,000*
(1)

23. $(130 - 57) + 9$ *82*
(2)

24. $1987 - 2014$ *−27*
(1)

25. $\$68.60 \div 7$ *$9.80*
(1)

26. $46¢ + 64¢$ *$1.10*
(1)

27. $\dfrac{4640}{80}$ *58*
(1)

28. $\begin{array}{r} \$3.75 \\ \times \quad 30 \\ \hline \$112.50 \end{array}$
(1)

29. Use the numbers 2, 3, and 6 to illustrate the associative
(2) property of multiplication.
  Answers may vary. One answer is $(2 \times 3) \times 6 = 2 \times (3 \times 6)$.

30. Use the numbers 10, 20, and 30 to write two addition
(2) facts and two subtraction facts.
  $10 + 20 = 30$, $20 + 10 = 30$, $30 - 10 = 20$, $30 - 20 = 10$

LESSON 5

Place Value through Hundred Trillions • Reading and Writing Whole Numbers

Mental Math:
a. 10
b. 144
c. 1000
d. 275
e. 500
f. 500
g. 15
Problem Solving:

$$\begin{array}{r} 7520 \\ -\ 2607 \\ \hline 4913 \end{array}$$

Facts Practice: 64 Multiplication Facts (Test A in Test Masters)

Mental Math:

  a. Half a score   **b.** Twelve dozen   **c.** Ten hundreds

  d. 475 − 200   **e.** 25 × 20   **f.** 5000 ÷ 10

  g. Start with the number of years in a century, subtract 1, and divide by 9. Add 1, multiply by 3, subtract 1, divide by 5, multiply by 4, add 2, then find half of that number. What is the answer?

Problem Solving:

Copy this problem and fill in the missing digits.

$$\begin{array}{r} 75\_0 \\ -\ \_60\_ \\ \hline 4\_13 \end{array}$$

Place value through hundred trillions

In our number system the value of a digit depends upon its position within a number. The value of each position is its **place value.** The chart below shows place values from the ones' place to the hundred-trillions' place.

Whole Number Place Values

hundred trillions, ten trillions, trillions, hundred billions, ten billions, billions, hundred millions, ten millions, millions, hundred thousands, ten thousands, thousands, hundreds, tens, ones, decimal point

— — — , — — — , — — — , — — — , — — — .

Example 1 (a) Which digit is in the trillions' place in the number 32,567,890,000,000?

(b) In 12,457,697,380,000, what is the place value of the digit 4?

Solution (a) The digit in the trillions' place is **2.**

(b) The place value of the digit 4 is **hundred billions.**

We write a number in **expanded notation** by writing each nonzero digit times its place value. We write 5280 in expanded notation this way.

$$(5 \times 1000) + (2 \times 100) + (8 \times 10)$$

Example 2 Write 25,000 in expanded notation.

Solution **$(2 \times 10{,}000) + (5 \times 1000)$**

Reading and writing whole numbers

Whole numbers with more than three digits are often written with commas to make the numbers easier to read. Commas help us read large numbers by marking the end of the trillions', billions', millions', and thousands' places. We need only to read the three-digit number in front of each comma and then say "trillion," "billion," "million," or "thousand" when we reach the comma.

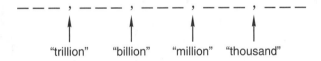

We will use the following guidelines when writing out numbers.

1. Put commas after the words trillion, billion, million, and thousand.
2. Hyphenate numbers between 20 and 100 that do not end in zero. For example, 52, 76, and 95 are written fifty-two, seventy-six, and ninety-five.

Example 3 Use words to write 1,380,000,050,200.

Solution **One trillion, three hundred eighty billion, fifty thousand, two hundred.**

Note: Since there are no millions, we do not read the millions' comma.

Example 4 Use words to write 3406521.

Solution First we start on the right and insert commas every three places as we move to the left.

3,406,521

Three million, four hundred six thousand, five hundred twenty-one.

Example 5 Use digits to write twenty trillion, five hundred ten million.

Solution It may be helpful to draw a "skeleton" of the number. We see that the number is more than one trillion, so we draw this skeleton.

The letters below the commas stand for trillion, billion, million, and thousand. We will read to a comma, then pause to write what we have read. We read "twenty trillion." We write:

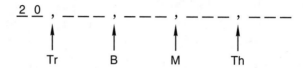

Next we read "five hundred ten million." We write 510 before the **millions'** comma.

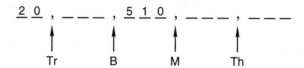

Since there are **no billions,** we write zeros in the three places before the billions' comma.

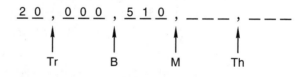

To hold place values we write zeros in the remaining places. Now we omit the dashes and write the number.

20,000,510,000,000

Large numbers that end with many zeros are often named using a combination of digits and words such as $3 billion for $3,000,000,000.

Example 6 Use only digits to write 25 million.

Solution **25,000,000**

Example 7 Sam said he drove twenty-four hundred miles on his trip. Use digits to write that number.

Solution Counting up by hundreds some people say eight hundred, nine hundred, ten hundred, eleven hundred, and so on, for 800, 900, 1000, 1100, ...

In this example Sam said "twenty-four hundred" for 2400, which is actually two thousand, four hundred. Four digit whole numbers are often written without commas, so either of these forms is correct, **2400** or **2,400**.

Practice   **a.** In 217,534,896,000,000, which digit is in the ten-billions' place? 3

b. In 9,876,543,210,000, what is the place value of the digit 6? billions' place

c. Write 2500 in expanded notation. (2 × 1000) + (5 × 100)

Use words to write each number.

d. 36427580 thirty-six million, four hundred twenty-seven thousand, five hundred eighty

e. 40302010 forty million, three hundred two thousand, ten

Use digits to write each number.

f. Twenty-five million, two hundred six thousand, forty 25,206,040

g. Fifty billion, four hundred two million, one hundred thousand 50,402,100,000

h. $15 billion $15,000,000,000

Problem set 5

1. What is the sum of six hundred seven and two thousand, three hundred ninety-three? 3000
(5)

2. Use digits and other symbols to write "one hundred one thousand is greater than one thousand, one hundred."
(4,5) 101,000 > 1,100

3. Use words to write 50,574,006.
(5) fifty million, five hundred seventy-four thousand, six

4. Which digit is in the trillions' place in the number 12,345,678,900,000? 2
(5)

5. Use digits to write two hundred fifty million, five thousand, seventy. 250,005,070
(5)

6. Replace the circle with the proper comparison symbol. Then use words to write the comparison.
(4)

$$-12 \; \bigodot \; -15$$

Negative twelve is greater than negative fifteen.

7. Arrange these numbers in order from least to greatest:
(4)

$$-1, 4, -7, 0, 5, 7 \quad -7, -1, 0, 4, 5, 7$$

8. Sketch a number line. Start at zero and draw an arrow 5 units long to the right. From this point draw an arrow 4 units long to the left. The second arrow ends at 1 showing that 5 − 4 is 1.

8. Describe how to show this subtraction problem on a number line: 5 − 4
(4)

9. How many units is it from negative 5 to positive 2 on the number line? 7 units
(4)

Find each missing number:

10. 2 · 3 · 5 · N = 960 32
(3)

11. A − 1367 = 2500 3867
(3)

12. B + 5 + 17 = 50 28
(3)

13. $25.00 − K = $18.70 $6.30
(3)

14.   6,400
(3)   +   D 3,600
         ‾‾‾‾‾‾‾‾‾
          10,000

15. $\dfrac{144}{F} = 8$ 18
(3)

16. Write 750,000 in expanded notation.
(5) $(7 \times 100,000) + (5 \times 10,000)$

Simplify:

17.   37,428
(1)   + 59,775
        ‾‾‾‾‾‾‾‾
         97,203

18.   31,014
(1)   − 24,767
        ‾‾‾‾‾‾‾‾
          6,247

19. 45 + 362 + 7 + 4319 4733
(1)

20. $64.59 + $124 + $6.30 + 37¢ $195.26
(1)

21. 144 ÷ (12 ÷ 3) 36
(2)

22. (144 ÷ 12) ÷ 3 4
(2)

23. 40(500) 20,000
(1)

24. $20\overline{)1000}$ 50
(1)

25. $10 − ($4.60 − 39¢)
(2) $5.79

26. 29¢ × 36 $10.44
(1)

27. 8505 ÷ 21 405
(1)

28. Find the next three numbers in this sequence.
(2)

                10, 8, 6, 4, 2, ... 0, −2, −4

29. Name each set of numbers illustrated.
(1,4)

    (a) {1, 2, 3, 4, ...} counting numbers or natural numbers

    (b) {0, 1, 2, 3, ...} whole numbers

    (c) {..., −2, −1, 0, 1, 2, ...} integers

30. Use braces, an ellipsis, and digits to illustrate the set of
(1,4) negative even numbers. {..., −6, −4, −2}

LESSON
6

Factors • Divisibility

Facts Practice: 30 Equations (Test B in Test Masters)

Mental Math:

   a. $5.00 + $2.50   **b.** $1.50 × 10   **c.** $1.00 − $0.45

   d. 450 + 35   **e.** 675 − 50   **f.** 750 ÷ 10

   g. 9 × 5, − 1, ÷ 4, + 1, ÷ 4, × 5, + 1, ÷ 4[†]

Problem Solving:

If there are twelve glubs in a lorn and four lorns in a dort, then how many glubs are in half a dort?

Mental Math:
a. $7.50
b. $15.00
c. $0.55
d. 485
e. 625
f. 75
g. 4
Problem Solving:
  24 glubs

Factors Recall that a factor is one of the numbers multiplied to form a product.

In 3 × 5 = 15,   the factors are 3 and 5, so both 3 and 5 are factors of 15.

In 1 × 15 = 15, the factors are 1 and 15, so both 1 and 15 are factors of 15.

Therefore, any of the numbers 1, 3, 5, and 15 can serve as a factor of 15.

Notice that 15 can be divided by 1, 3, 5, and 15 without a remainder. This leads us to another definition of factor.

> A *factor* is a whole number that divides another whole number without a remainder.

For example, the numbers 1, 2, 5, and 10 are factors of 10 because each divides 10 without a remainder (that is, with a remainder of zero).

$$
\begin{array}{r} 10 \\ 1\overline{)10} \\ \underline{10} \\ 0 \end{array} \qquad
\begin{array}{r} 5 \\ 2\overline{)10} \\ \underline{10} \\ 0 \end{array} \qquad
\begin{array}{r} 2 \\ 5\overline{)10} \\ \underline{10} \\ 0 \end{array} \qquad
\begin{array}{r} 1 \\ 10\overline{)10} \\ \underline{10} \\ 0 \end{array}
$$

Example 1 List the whole numbers that are factors of 12.

Solution The factors of 12 are the whole numbers that divide 12 with no remainder. They are **1, 2, 3, 4, 6,** and **12.**

[†]As a shorthand, we will use commas to separate operations to be performed sequentially from left to right. This is not standard mathematical notation.

Example 2   List the factors of 51.

Solution   As we try to think of whole numbers that divide 51 with no remainder, we may think that 51 has only two factors, 1 and 51. However there are actually four factors of 51. Notice that 3 and 17 are also factors of 51.

$$\begin{array}{r} 17 \\ 3\overline{)51} \end{array}$$

17 is a factor of 51

3 is a factor of 51

Since $3 \cdot 17$ equals 51, both 3 and 17 are factors of 51. Thus, the four factors of 51 are **1, 3, 17,** and **51.**

From Examples 1 and 2 we see that 12 and 51 have two common factors, 1 and 3. The **greatest common factor (GCF)** of 12 and 51 is 3 because it is the largest factor of both numbers.

Example 3   Find the greatest common factor of 18 and 30.

Solution   We are asked to find the largest factor (divisor) of both 18 and 30. Here we list the factors of both numbers, circling the common factors.

Factors of 18: ①,②,③,⑥, 9, 18
Factors of 30: ①,②,③, 5,⑥, 10, 15, 30

The greatest common factor is **6.**

Divisibility   As we saw in Example 2, 51 **can be divided** by 1, 3, 17, and 51, and the remainder is zero. The capability of a whole number to be divided by another whole number with no remainder is called **divisibility.** Thus, 51 is **divisible** by 1, 3, 17, and 51.

There are several methods for testing the divisibility of a number without actually performing the division. Below are listed some methods for testing whether a number is divisible by 2, 3, 4, 5, 6, 8, 9, and 10.

TESTS FOR DIVISIBILITY

A number can be divided by...
2   if the last digit is even.
4   if the last two digits can be divided by 4.
8   if the last three digits can be divided by 8.
5   if the last digit is 0 or 5.
10   if the last digit is 0.
3   if the **sum of the digits** can be divided by 3.
6   if the number can be divided by 2 **and** by 3.
9   if the **sum of the digits** can be divided by 9.

Note: Whole numbers ending in one zero are divisible by 2; those ending in two zeros are divisible by 2 and 4; and those ending in three zeros are divisible by 2, 4, and 8.

Example 4 Which whole numbers from 1 through 10 are divisors of 9060?

Solution In the sense used in this problem, a **divisor** is a **factor.** The number 1 is a divisor of any whole number. As we apply the tests for divisibility, we find that 9060 passes the tests for 2, 4, 5, and 10. The sum of its digits (9 + 0 + 6 + 0) is 15, which can be divided by 3 but not by 9. Since 9060 is divisible by both 2 and 3, it is also divisible by 6. The only whole number from 1 to 10 we have not tried is 7, for which we have no simple test. We divide 9060 by 7 to find out if 7 is a divisor. It is not. We find that the numbers from 1 to 10 that are divisors of 9060 are **1, 2, 3, 4, 5, 6,** and **10.**

Practice* List the whole numbers that are factors of each number.

    a. 25   1, 5, 25   **b.** 24   **c.** 23   1, 23

                    1, 2, 3, 4, 6, 8, 12, 24

List the whole numbers from 1 to 10 that are factors of each number.

    d. 1260   **e.** 73,500   **f.** 3600

    1, 2, 3, 4, 5, 6, 7, 9, 10   1, 2, 3, 4, 5, 6, 7, 10   1, 2, 3, 4, 5, 6, 8, 9, 10

    g. List the single-digit divisors of 1356.   1, 2, 3, 4, 6

    h. The number 7000 is divisible by which single-digit numbers?   1, 2, 4, 5, 7, 8

    i. List all the common factors of 12 and 20.   1, 2, 4

    j. Find the greatest common factor (GCF) of 24 and 40.   8

Problem set 6

    1. If the product of 10 and 20 is divided by the sum of 20 (1) and 30, what is the quotient?   4

    2. (a) List all the common factors of 30 and 40.   1, 2, 5, 10 (6)

          (b) Find the greatest common factor of 30 and 40.   10

    3. Use braces, an ellipsis, and digits to illustrate the set of (4) negative odd numbers.   {..., –5, –3, –1}

    4. Use digits to write four hundred seven million, six (5) thousand, nine hundred sixty-two.   407,006,962

    5. List the whole numbers from 1 to 10 that are divisors of (6) 12,300.   1, 2, 3, 4, 5, 6, 10

6. Replace the circle with the proper comparison symbol.
(4) Then use words to state the same comparison.

$$-7 \, \textcircled{>} \, -11$$

Negative seven is greater than negative eleven.

7. The number 3456 is divisible by which single-digit
(6) numbers? 1, 2, 3, 4, 6, 8, 9

8. Show this subtraction problem on a number line: 2 − 5
(4)

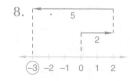

9. Write 6400 in expanded notation. $(6 \times 1000) + (4 \times 100)$
(5)

Find each missing number:

10. X $5.40
(3)
$$+ \, \$4.60$$
$$\overline{\quad \$10.00 \quad}$$

11. P 8350
(3)
$$- \, 3850$$
$$\overline{\quad 4500 \quad}$$

12.   7
(3)
     4
     8
     6
     2
     1
     6
     8
     9

13. Z $6.25
(3)
$$\times \, 8$$
$$\overline{\quad \$50.00 \quad}$$

14.   1426
(3)
$$- \quad\quad K \text{ 1339}$$
$$\overline{\quad\quad 87 \quad}$$

     $+ \, N$ 9
$$\overline{\quad 60 \quad}$$

15. $\dfrac{990}{P} = 45$ 22
(3)

16. $\dfrac{Z}{8} = 32$ 256
(3)

Simplify:

17. $\dfrac{1225}{35}$ 35
(1)

18.   800
(1)
$$\times \quad 50$$
$$\overline{\quad 40,000 \quad}$$

19. $100.00
(1)
$$- \quad \$48.37$$
$$\overline{\quad \$51.63 \quad}$$

20.   46,302
(1)
$$+ \, 49,998$$
$$\overline{\quad 96,300 \quad}$$

21. $45.00 ÷ 20 $2.25
(1)

22. 7 · 11 · 13 1001
(1)

23. 9)43,271
(1)
        4,807 r 8

24. 3625 + 59 + 570 + 8
(1) 4262

25. 48¢ + $8.49 + $14
(1) $22.97

26. 1000 − (430 − 58)
(2) 628

27. 140(16) 2240
(1)

28.   25¢
(1)
$$\times \, 24$$
$$\overline{\quad \$6.00 \quad}$$

29. $\dfrac{\$43.50}{10}$ $4.35
(1)

30. Name the property illustrated by this equation.
(2) commutative property
     of multiplication

$$x \cdot 5 = 5x$$

Describe the meaning of this property.

The order of factors can be changed without changing the product.

LESSON
7

Lines and Angles

Mental Math:
a. −5
b. $25.00
c. 65¢
d. 365
e. 265
f. 48
g. 6
Problem Solving:
10 × 21 = 210

Facts Practice: 30 Equations (Test B in Test Masters)

Mental Math:

a. 5 − 10   **b.** $2.50 × 10   **c.** $1.00 − 35¢

d. 340 + 25   **e.** 565 − 300   **f.** 480 ÷ 10

g. Start with the number of years in a decade, × 7, + 5, ÷ 3, − 1, ÷ 4.

Problem Solving:

The sum of the counting numbers from 1 through 4 is 10. What is the sum of the counting numbers from 1 through 20?

We live in a world of three dimensions called **space.** We can measure the length, width, and depth of objects in space. We may imagine a two-dimensional world called a **plane,** a flat world having length and width but not depth. Occupants of a two-dimensional world could not pass over or under objects because, without depth, over and under would not exist. A one-dimensional world, a **line,** has length but not width or depth. Occupants of a one-dimensional world could not move left or right, over or under.

In **geometry** we study figures that have one dimension, two dimensions, and three dimensions, but we begin with a **point** which has no dimensions. A point is an exact location in space, unmeasurably small. We represent points with dots and usually name them with uppercase letters. Here we show point A.

A **line** is an infinite number of points extending in opposite directions without end. A line has one dimension, length. A line has no thickness. We may represent a line by sketching part of a line with two arrowheads. We may identify a line by naming two points on the line in either order. Here we show line AB (also line BA).

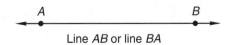

Line AB or line BA

The symbols $\overleftrightarrow{AB}$ and $\overleftrightarrow{BA}$ (read "line AB and line BA") also can be used to refer to this line.

A **ray** is part of a line with one endpoint. We may name a ray with the endpoint and one other point. Here we show ray AB $(\overrightarrow{AB})$.

Ray *AB*

A **segment** is part of a line with two endpoints. We identify a segment by naming the two endpoints in either order. Here we show segment AB $(\overline{AB})$.

A   B

Segment *AB* or segment *BA*

A segment has a specific length. We may refer to the length of segment AB by writing $m\overline{AB}$, which means the measure of segment AB, or by writing the letters AB without an overbar. Thus, both AB and $m\overline{AB}$ refer to the distance from point A to point B. We use this notation in the figure below to state that the sum of the lengths of the shorter segments equals the length of the longest segment.

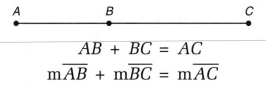

$$AB + BC = AC$$
$$m\overline{AB} + m\overline{BC} = m\overline{AC}$$

Example 1 For this figure use symbols to name a line, two rays, and a segment.

Solution The line is $\overleftrightarrow{AB}$ (or $\overleftrightarrow{BA}$). The rays are $\overrightarrow{AB}$ and $\overrightarrow{BA}$. The segment is $\overline{AB}$ (or $\overline{BA}$).

Example 2 In this figure AB is 3 cm and AC is 7 cm. Find BC.

Solution BC means the length of segment BC. We are given that AB is 3 cm and AC is 7 cm. From the figure above we see that $AB + BC = AC$. Therefore, we find that BC is **4 cm.**

A plane is a flat surface that has no boundaries. A plane has two dimensions, length and width. A desktop occupies a part of a plane.

Two lines in the same plane either cross once or they do not cross at all. If two lines cross, we say that they **intersect.** They intersect at one point. Two lines on a plane that do not intersect remain the same distance apart and are called **parallel lines.**

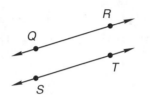

Line *AB* intersects line *CD* at point *M*.

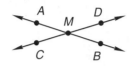

In this figure, line *QR* is parallel to line *ST*. This statement can be written with symbols, as we show here:

$$\overleftrightarrow{QR} \parallel \overleftrightarrow{ST}$$

Lines that intersect and form "square corners" are **perpendicular.** The small square in the figure below indicates a "square corner."

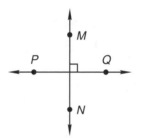

In this figure, line *MN* is perpendicular to line *PQ*. This statement can be written with symbols, as we show here:

$$\overleftrightarrow{MN} \perp \overleftrightarrow{PQ}$$

An **angle** is formed by two rays that have a common endpoint. Angle *DMB* is formed by the two rays $\overrightarrow{MD}$ and $\overrightarrow{MB}$. The common endpoint is *M*. Ray *MD* and ray *MB* are the **sides** of the angle. Point *M* is the **vertex** of the angle. Angles can be named in several ways.

Angles may be named by using three letters in this order: a point on one ray, the vertex, then a point on the other ray.

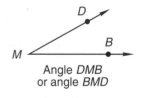

Angle *DMB*
or angle *BMD*

When there is no chance of confusion, an angle may be named with only one letter: the letter at the vertex.

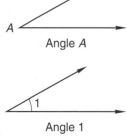

Angle *A*

An angle may be named by placing a small letter or number near the vertex and between the rays (in the interior of the angle).

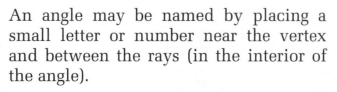

Angle 1

The symbol ∠ is often used instead of the word "angle." Thus, the three angles just named could be referred to as:

∠DMB   read as "angle DMB"

∠A   read as "angle A"

∠1   read as "angle 1"

Angles are classified by their size. An angle that is formed by perpendicular rays is a **right angle.** An angle smaller than a right angle is an **acute angle.** An angle that forms a straight line is a **straight angle.** An angle that is smaller than a straight angle but larger than a right angle is an **obtuse angle.**

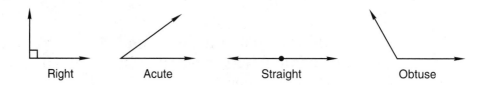

Right	Acute	Straight	Obtuse

Example 3 (a) Which line is parallel to line AB?

(b) Which line is perpendicular to line AB?

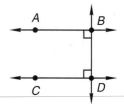

Solution (a) **Line CD** (or **DC⃡**) is parallel to line AB.

(b) **Line BD** (or **DB⃡**) is perpendicular to line AB.

Example 4 There are several angles in this figure.

(a) Name the straight angle.

(b) Name the obtuse angle.

(c) Name two right angles.

(d) Name two acute angles.

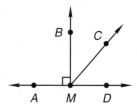

Solution (a) ∠**AMD** (or ∠**DMA**)

(b) ∠**AMC** (or ∠**CMA**)

(c) 1. ∠**AMB** (or ∠**BMA**)
   2. ∠**BMD** (or ∠**DMB**)

(d) 1. ∠**BMC** (or ∠**CMB**)
   2. ∠**CMD** (or ∠**DMC**)

Practice   **a.** Name a point on this figure that is not on ray BC.   point A

b. In this figure XZ is 10 cm and YZ is 6 cm. Find XY.   4 cm

c. Draw two parallel lines.

d.

d. Draw two perpendicular lines.

e. Draw two lines that intersect but are not perpendicular.

e.

f. Draw a right angle.

g. Draw an acute angle.

h. Draw an obtuse angle.

Problem set 7

1. If the product of two one-digit whole numbers is 35, what
(3) is the sum of the same two numbers?   12

2. Name the property illustrated by this equation.
(2)

$$-5 \cdot 1 = -5$$

identity property of multiplication

3. List the whole number divisors of 50.   1, 2, 5, 10, 25, 50
(6)

4. Use digits and symbols to write "two minus five equals
(4) negative three." $2 - 5 = -3$

5. Use only digits to write 90 million.   90,000,000
(5)

6. List the single-digit whole numbers that are factors of
(6) 924.   1, 2, 3, 4, 6, 7

7. Arrange these numbers in order from least to greatest:
(4)

$$-10, 5, -7, 8, 0, -2 \quad -10, -7, -2, 0, 5, 8$$

8. Find the next three numbers in this sequence.
(2)

$$49, 64, 81, 100, \ldots \quad 121, 144, 169$$

9. (a) List the common factors of 24 and 32. 1, 2, 4, 8
(6)
  (b) Find the greatest common factor of 24 and 32. 8

10. How many units is it from 3 to −4 on a number line?
(4) 7 units

Find each missing number:

11. $6 \cdot 6 \cdot Z = 1224$ 34
(3)

12. $\$100.00 - K = \$17.54$
(3) $82.46

13. $W - 98 = 432$ 530
(3)

14. $20X = \$36.00$ $1.80
(3)

15. $\dfrac{W}{20} = 200$ 4000
(3)

16. $\dfrac{300}{X} = 30$ 10
(3)

17. There is no remainder (the remainder is zero). A number is divisible by 9 if the sum of its digits is divisible by 9. The sum of the digits in 4554 is 18, which is divisible by 9.

17. Does the quotient of $4554 \div 9$ have a remainder? How can you tell without dividing?
(6)

Simplify:

18. $\begin{array}{r} 36{,}475 \\ + \ 55{,}984 \\ \hline 92{,}459 \end{array}$
(1)

19. $\begin{array}{r} 476 \\ \times \quad 38 \\ \hline 18{,}088 \end{array}$
(1)

20. $\$80.00 - \$72.45$ $7.55
(1)

21. $49 + 387 + 1579 + 98$ 2113
(1)

22. Compare: $4000 \div (200 \div 10)$ (>) $(4000 \div 200) \div 10$
(2,4)

23. $(200)(400)$ 80,000
(1)

24. $\$68.00 \div 40$ $1.70
(1)

25. $8 \cdot 7 \cdot 5$ 280
(1)

26. $\$1.25 \times 38$ $47.50
(1)

27. Refer to this figure to answer questions (a) and (b).
(7)

∠BMC (or ∠CMB) (a) Which angle is an acute angle?

∠AMC (or ∠CMA) (b) Which angle is a straight angle?

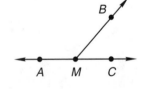

28. What type of angles are formed by perpendicular lines?
(7) right angles

Refer to this figure to answer problems 29 and 30.

29. Name three segments in this figure. $\overline{XY}, \overline{YZ}, \overline{XZ}$
(7)

30. If you knew m$\overline{XY}$ and m$\overline{YZ}$, describe how you would find m$\overline{XZ}$. Add m$\overline{XY}$ and m$\overline{YZ}$ to find m$\overline{XZ}$.
(7)

**LESSON
8**

Fractions and Percents • Inch Ruler

Facts Practice: 64 Multiplication Facts (Test A in Test Masters)

Mental Math:

a. 4 − 10	**b.** $0.25 × 10	**c.** $1.00 − 65¢
d. 325 + 50	**e.** 347 − 30	**f.** 200 × 10

g. Start with a score, + 1, ÷ 3, × 5, + 1, ÷ 4, + 1, ÷ 2, × 6, + 3, ÷ 3.

Problem Solving:

The smallest three-digit number that contains 2, 3, and 5 is 235, and the largest is 532. List in order from least to greatest all the three-digit numbers that contain 2, 3, and 5.

Fractions and percents

Fractions and **percents** are commonly used to name parts of a whole or parts of a group.

Here we use a whole circle to represent 1. The circle is divided into four equal parts with one part shaded. One fourth $\left(\frac{1}{4}\right)$ of the circle is shaded, and $\frac{3}{4}$ of the circle is not shaded.

Since the whole circle also represents 100% of the circle, we may divide 100% by 4 to find the percent of the circle that is shaded.

$$100\% \div 4 = 25\%$$

We find that 25% of the circle is shaded, so 75% of the circle is not shaded.

A common fraction is written with two numbers and a division bar. The number below the bar is the **denominator** and shows how many equal parts are in the whole. The number above the bar is the **numerator** and shows how many of the parts have been selected.

$$\text{numerator} \longrightarrow \frac{1}{4} \longleftarrow \text{division bar}$$
$$\text{denominator} \longrightarrow$$

A percent describes a whole as though there were 100 parts, even though the whole may not actually contain 100 parts. Thus the "denominator" of a percent is always 100.

$$25 \text{ percent means } \frac{25}{100}$$

Instead of writing the denominator, 100, we use the word "percent" or the percent symbol, %.

A whole number plus a fraction is a **mixed number.** To name the number of circles shaded below, we use the mixed number $2\frac{3}{4}$. We see that $2\frac{3}{4}$ means $2 + \frac{3}{4}$. To read a mixed number, we first say the whole number, then we say "and," and then we say the fraction.

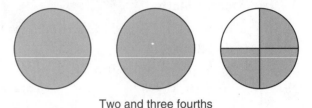

Two and three fourths

It is possible for a percent to be greater than 100% in certain situations. If we were to write $2\frac{3}{4}$ as a percent, we would write 275%.

Example 1   Name the shaded part of the circle as a fraction and as a percent.

Solution   Two of the five equal parts are shaded so the fraction that is shaded is $\frac{2}{5}$.

Since the whole circle (100%) is divided into five equal parts, each part is 20%.

$$100\% \div 5 = 20\%$$

Two of the parts are shaded. So $2 \times 20\%$ is shaded, which is **40%.**

Example 2   Which of the following could describe the portion of this rectangle that is shaded?

A. $\frac{1}{2}$ B. 40%   C. 60%

Solution   There is a shaded and an unshaded part of this rectangle, but the parts are not equal. More than $\frac{1}{2}$ of the rectangle is shaded, so the answer is not A. Half of a whole is 50%.

$$100\% \div 2 = 50\%$$

Since more than 50% of the rectangle is shaded the correct choice is **C. 60%.**

Between the points on a number line that represent whole numbers are many points that represent fractions and mixed numbers. To identify the fraction or mixed number associated with a point on a number line, it is first necessary to discover the number of segments into which each length has been divided.

Example 3 Point *A* represents what mixed number on this number line?

Solution We see that point *A* represents a number greater than 8 but less than 9. It represents 8 plus a fraction. To find the fraction, we first notice that the segment from 8 to 9 has been divided into 5 smaller segments. From 8 to point *A* is 2 of the 5 segments. Thus, point *A* represents the mixed number **$8\frac{2}{5}$.**

> **Note:** It is important to focus on the *number of segments* and not on the number of vertical tick marks. The four vertical tick marks divide the space between 8 and 9 into 5 segments, just as four cuts divide a candy bar into 5 pieces.

Inch ruler A ruler is a practical use of a number line. The units on a ruler are of a standard length. The units of an inch ruler are often divided successively in half. That is, inches are divided in half to half inches. Then half inches are divided in half to quarter inches, and so on to eighths, sixteenths, and even thirty-seconds and sixty-fourths. In this book we will practice measuring and drawing segments to the nearest sixteenth of an inch.

Here we show a magnified view of an inch ruler with divisions to $\frac{1}{16}$ of an inch. We have labeled each division for reference.

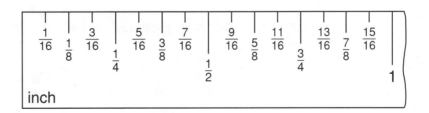

It is important to bear in mind that all measure is approximate. The quality of a measurement depends upon many conditions including the care taken in performing the measurement and the precision of the measuring instrument. The finer the gradations are on the instrument, the more precise the measurement can be.

Example 4 Use an inch ruler to find *AB*, *BC*, and *AC* to the nearest sixteenth of an inch.

Solution From point *A* we find *AB* and *AC*. We measure from the center of one dot to the center of the other dot. **AB is about** $\frac{7}{8}$ **in. and AC is about** $2\frac{1}{2}$ **in.**

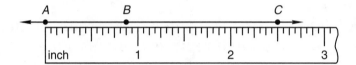

We move the zero mark on the ruler to *B* to measure *BC*. We find **BC is about** $1\frac{5}{8}$ **in.**

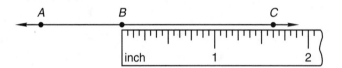

Practice **a.** What fraction of this circle is not shaded? $\frac{3}{5}$

b. What percent of this circle is not shaded? 60%

c. Half of a whole is what percent of the whole? 50%

Draw and shade circles to illustrate each fraction, mixed number, or percent.

d. $\frac{2}{3}$ **e.** 75% **f.** $2\frac{3}{4}$

Points **g.** and **h.** represent what mixed numbers on these number lines?

g. $4\frac{2}{3}$

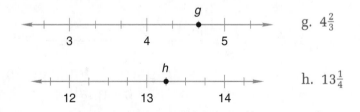

h. $13\frac{1}{4}$

i. Find *XZ* to the nearest sixteenth of an inch. $3\frac{5}{16}$ in.

Problem set 8

1. Use digits and a comparison symbol to write "one and
(4,8) three fourths is greater than one and three fifths."
$1\frac{3}{4} > 1\frac{3}{5}$

2. Refer to practice i. Use your ruler to find XY and YZ.
(8) XY is $2\frac{1}{4}$ in.; YZ is $1\frac{1}{16}$ in.

3. What is the quotient when the product of 20 and 20 is
(1)   divided by the sum of 10 and 10?   20

4. List the single-digit whole numbers that are divisors of
(6)   1680.   1, 2, 3, 4, 5, 6, 7, 8

5. Point A represents what mixed number on this number
(8)   line? $3\frac{4}{5}$

6. (a) Replace the circle with the proper comparison symbol.
(2,4)
$$3 + 2 \bigcirc 2 + 3$$

(b) What property of addition is illustrated by this
comparison?   commutative property of addition

7. Use words to write 32500000000.
(5)   thirty-two billion, five hundred million

8. (a) What fraction of the circle is
(8)   shaded? $\frac{3}{8}$

(b) What fraction of the circle is not
shaded? $\frac{5}{8}$

9. (a) What percent of the rectangle is
(8)   shaded?   20%

(b) What percent of the rectangle is
not shaded?   80%

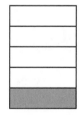

10. What is the name of the number of a fraction that
(8)   indicates the number of parts in the whole?   denominator

Find each missing number:

11. $A - \$4.70 = \$2.35$
(3) $7.05

12. $B + \$25.48 = \$60.00$
(3) $34.52

13. $8C = \$60.00$ $7.50
(3)

14. $10,000 - D = 5,420$
(3)   4,580

15. $\dfrac{E}{15} = 15$ 225
(3)

16. $\dfrac{196}{F} = 14$ 14
(3)

17. $8 + 9 + 8 + 8 + 9 + 8 + N = 60$ 10
(3)

Simplify:

18. $\begin{array}{r} 400 \\ \times\ 500 \\ \hline 200{,}000 \end{array}$
(1)

19. $\begin{array}{r} \$50.00 \\ -\ \$48.79 \\ \hline \$1.21 \end{array}$
(1)

20. $3625 + 431 + 687$ 4743
(1)

21. $6000 \div 50$ 120
(1)

22. $20 \cdot 10 \cdot 5$ 1000
(1)

23. $\$27.00 \div 18$ $1.50
(1)

24. $1000 - 11$ 989
(1)

25. $\dfrac{3456}{6}$ 576
(1)

26. $\begin{array}{r} 79¢ \\ \times\ 30 \\ \hline \$23.70 \end{array}$
(1)

27. Compare: $416 - (86 + 119) \enspace \textcircled{<} \enspace (416 - 86) + 119$
(2,4)

Refer to this figure to answer problems 28 and 29.

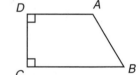

28. Name the acute, obtuse, and right angles.
(7)

28. acute: $\angle CBA$ (or $\angle ABC$); obtuse: $\angle DAB$ (or $\angle BAD$); right: $\angle CDA$ (or $\angle ADC$), $\angle DCB$ (or $\angle BCD$)

29. (a) Name a segment parallel to $\overline{DA}$. $\overline{CB}$
(7)
    (b) Name a segment perpendicular to $\overline{DA}$. $\overline{DC}$

30. $\overline{QR}$ identifies the segment QR, while QR refers to the distance from Q to R. So $\overline{QR}$ is a segment and QR is a length.

30. Referring to this figure, what is the difference in meaning between the notations $\overline{QR}$ and QR?
(7)

LESSON 9

Adding, Subtracting, and Multiplying Fractions • Reciprocals

Mental Math:
a. −2
b. $3.90
c. 71¢
d. 542
e. 540
f. 10
g. 15

Problem Solving:
$\dfrac{5}{16}, \dfrac{3}{8}, \dfrac{7}{16}, \dfrac{1}{2}$

Facts Practice: 30 Equations (Test B in Test Masters)

Mental Math:

a. $3 - 5$
b. $\$0.39 \times 10$
c. $\$1.00 - 29¢$
d. $342 + 200$
e. $580 - 40$
f. $500 \div 50$
g. Start with half a dozen, + 1, × 6, − 2, ÷ 2, + 4, ÷ 4, − 5, × 15.

Problem Solving:

Find the next four numbers in this sequence.

$$\frac{1}{16}, \frac{1}{8}, \frac{3}{16}, \frac{1}{4}, \cdots$$

Adding fractions On the line below, AB is $1\frac{3}{8}$ in. and BC is $1\frac{4}{8}$ in. We can find AC by measuring or by adding $1\frac{3}{8}$ in. and $1\frac{4}{8}$ in.

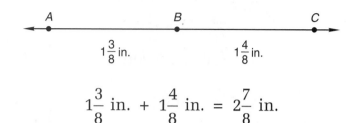

$$1\frac{3}{8} \text{ in.} + 1\frac{4}{8} \text{ in.} = 2\frac{7}{8} \text{ in.}$$

When adding fractions that have the same denominators, we add the numerators and write the sum over the same denominator.

Example 1 Find each sum.

(a) $\dfrac{1}{7} + \dfrac{2}{7} + \dfrac{3}{7}$

(b) $33\dfrac{1}{3}\% + 33\dfrac{1}{3}\%$

Solution (a) $\dfrac{1}{7} + \dfrac{2}{7} + \dfrac{3}{7} = \mathbf{\dfrac{6}{7}}$

(b) $33\dfrac{1}{3}\% + 33\dfrac{1}{3}\% = \mathbf{66\dfrac{2}{3}\%}$

When the numerator and denominator of a fraction are equal (but not zero), the fraction is equal to 1. The illustration shows $\frac{4}{4}$ of a circle which is one whole circle.

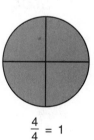

$\frac{4}{4} = 1$

Example 2 Add: $\dfrac{3}{5} + \dfrac{2}{5}$

Solution $\dfrac{3}{5} + \dfrac{2}{5} = \dfrac{5}{5} = \mathbf{1}$

Subtracting fractions To subtract fractions with the same denominators we write the difference of the numerators over the same denominator.

Example 3 Find each difference.

(a) $3\dfrac{5}{9} - 1\dfrac{1}{9}$

(b) $\dfrac{3}{5} - \dfrac{3}{5}$

Solution (a) $3\dfrac{5}{9} - 1\dfrac{1}{9} = \mathbf{2\dfrac{4}{9}}$

(b) $\dfrac{3}{5} - \dfrac{3}{5} = \mathbf{0}$

Multiplying fractions The first illustration shows $\frac{1}{2}$ of a circle. The second illustration shows $\frac{1}{2}$ of $\frac{1}{2}$ of a circle. We see that $\frac{1}{2}$ of $\frac{1}{2}$ is $\frac{1}{4}$. We find $\frac{1}{2}$ of $\frac{1}{2}$ by multiplying.

$\frac{1}{2}$

$\frac{1}{2}$ of $\frac{1}{2}$

$$\frac{1}{2} \text{ of } \frac{1}{2} \text{ becomes } \frac{1}{2} \times \frac{1}{2}$$

We translate the word "of" into a multiplication symbol. To multiply fractions we multiply the numerators to find the numerator of the product, and we multiply the denominators to find the denominator of the product. Notice that the product of two positive fractions that are less than 1 is less than either factor.

$\frac{1}{2}$ of $\frac{1}{2}$

$$\downarrow$$

$$\frac{1}{2} \times \frac{1}{2} = \frac{1}{4}$$

Example 4 Find each product.

(a) $\frac{1}{2}$ of $\frac{1}{3}$

(b) $\frac{1}{2} \cdot \frac{3}{4} \cdot \frac{1}{5}$

Solution (a) $\frac{1}{2} \times \frac{1}{3} = \frac{1}{6}$

(b) $\frac{1}{2} \cdot \frac{3}{4} \cdot \frac{1}{5} = \frac{3}{40}$

Reciprocals If we reverse the terms of a fraction, we form the **reciprocal** of the fraction.

The reciprocal of $\frac{4}{3}$ is $\frac{3}{4}$.

The reciprocal of $\frac{3}{4}$ is $\frac{4}{3}$.

The reciprocal of $\frac{1}{4}$ is $\frac{4}{1}$, which is 4.

The reciprocal of 4 $\left(\text{or } \frac{4}{1}\right)$ is $\frac{1}{4}$.

Note this very important property of reciprocals.

> **The product of a fraction and its reciprocal is 1.**

$$\frac{4}{3} \cdot \frac{3}{4} = \frac{12}{12} = 1$$

$$\frac{1}{4} \cdot \frac{4}{1} = \frac{4}{4} = 1$$

Example 5   Find the reciprocal of each number.

(a) $\dfrac{3}{5}$ (b) 3

Solution   (a) The reciprocal of $\frac{3}{5}$ is $\frac{5}{3}$.

(b) The reciprocal of 3, which is 3 "wholes" or $\frac{3}{1}$, is $\frac{1}{3}$.

Example 6   Find the missing number: $\dfrac{3}{4}n = 1$

Solution   The expression $\frac{3}{4}n$ means $\frac{3}{4}$ times n. Since the product of $\frac{3}{4}$ and n is 1, the missing number must be the reciprocal of $\frac{3}{4}$, which is $\frac{4}{3}$.

$$\frac{3}{4} \cdot \frac{4}{3} = \frac{12}{12} = 1 \quad \text{check}$$

Example 7   How many $\frac{3}{4}$'s are in 1?

Solution   The answer is the reciprocal of $\frac{3}{4}$, which is $\frac{4}{3}$.

In Lesson 2 we noted that although multiplication is commutative ($6 \times 3 = 3 \times 6$), division is not commutative ($6 \div 3 \neq 3 \div 6$). Reversing the order of division results in the reciprocal quotient.

$$6 \div 3 = 2$$

$$3 \div 6 = \frac{1}{2}$$

Practice   **a.** $\dfrac{5}{6} + \dfrac{1}{6}$ 1 **b.** $\dfrac{4}{5} - \dfrac{3}{5}$ $\frac{1}{5}$ **c.** $\dfrac{3}{5} \times \dfrac{1}{2} \times \dfrac{3}{4}$ $\frac{9}{40}$

d. $\dfrac{3}{10} + \dfrac{3}{10} + \dfrac{3}{10}$ $\frac{9}{10}$ **e.** $\dfrac{4}{7} \times \dfrac{2}{3}$ $\frac{8}{21}$ **f.** $\dfrac{5}{8} - \dfrac{5}{8}$ 0

g. $14\dfrac{2}{7}\% + 14\dfrac{2}{7}\%$ $28\frac{4}{7}\%$ **h.** $87\dfrac{1}{2}\% - 12\dfrac{1}{2}\%$ 75%

Write the reciprocal of each number.

i. $\dfrac{4}{5}$ $\frac{5}{4}$ **j.** $\dfrac{8}{7}$ $\frac{7}{8}$ **k.** 5 $\frac{1}{5}$

Find each missing number.

l. $\dfrac{5}{8}a = 1$ $\frac{8}{5}$ **m.** $6m = 1$ $\frac{1}{6}$

n. How many $\frac{2}{3}$'s are in 1? $\frac{3}{2}$

o. If $a \div b$ equals 4, what does $b \div a$ equal? $\frac{1}{4}$

Problem set 9

1. What is the quotient when the sum of 1, 2, and 3 is divided by the product of 1, 2, and 3?   1
_(1)_

2. This sign is incorrect. Show two ways to correct this sign.
_(1)_   45¢ per pound; $0.45 per pound

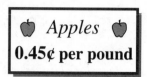

3. Replace each circle with the proper comparison symbol. Then use words to write the same comparison.
_(4,9)_

3.(a) One half is greater than one half times one half.

(a) $\dfrac{1}{2}$ $\bigodot{>}$ $\dfrac{1}{2} \cdot \dfrac{1}{2}$

(b) -2 $\bigodot{>}$ -4
Negative two is greater than negative four.

4. Write twenty-six thousand in expanded notation.
_(5)_ $(2 \times 10{,}000) + (6 \times 1000)$

5. (a) A dime is what fraction of a dollar? $\frac{1}{10}$
_(8)_

   (b) A dime is what percent of a dollar?   10%

6. (a) What fraction of the square is shaded? $\frac{5}{9}$
_(8)_

   (b) What fraction of the square is not shaded? $\frac{4}{9}$

7. Is an imaginary "line" from Earth to the Moon a line, a ray, or a segment? Why?
_(7)_
It is a segment because it has two endpoints.

8. Use an inch ruler to find *LM*, *MN*, and *LN* to the nearest sixteenth of an inch.   *LM* is $1\frac{1}{4}$ in.;   *MN* is $1\frac{1}{4}$ in.;   *LN* is $2\frac{1}{2}$ in.
_(8)_

9. (a) List the factors of 18.   1, 2, 3, 6, 9, 18
_(6)_

   (b) List the factors of 24.   1, 2, 3, 4, 6, 8, 12, 24

   (c) Which numbers are factors of both 18 and 24?   1, 2, 3, 6

   (d) Which number is the GCF of 18 and 24?   6

Find each missing number:

10.   4315
(3)   − ___A   2158
         ——————
         2157

11.   85,000
(3)   + ___B   115,000
         ——————
         200,000

12. $\dfrac{900}{C}$ = 60   15
(3)

13.   D $14.40
(3)   + $5.60
      ——————
      $20.00

14.   E $2.50
(3)   × 12
      ——————
      $30.00

15.   F $110.50
(3)   − $98.03
      ——————
      $12.47

16. 5 + 7 + 5 + 7 + 6 + N + 1 + 2 + 3 + 4 = 40   0
(3)

Simplify:

17. $3\dfrac{11}{15} - 1\dfrac{3}{15}$ $2\frac{8}{15}$
(9)

18. $1\dfrac{3}{8} + 1\dfrac{4}{8}$ $2\frac{7}{8}$
(9)

19. $\dfrac{3}{4} \times \dfrac{1}{4}$ $\frac{3}{16}$
(9)

20. $\dfrac{1802}{17}$ 106
(1)

21. $8.97 + $110 + 53¢ $119.50
(1)

22. $60.00
(1)   − $49.49
      ——————
       $10.51

23.   607
(1)   × 78
      ——————
      47,346

24. $0.09 × 56 $5.04
(1)

25. 50 · 60 · 70   210,000
(1)

26. $\dfrac{4}{5} \times \dfrac{2}{3} \times \dfrac{1}{3}$ $\frac{8}{45}$
(9)

27. $\dfrac{1}{9} + \dfrac{2}{9} + \dfrac{4}{9}$ $\frac{7}{9}$
(9)

28. Refer to this figure to answer questions
(7) (a) and (b).

   (a) Which angles are acute?   ∠A and ∠B

   (b) Which segment is perpendicular
       to $\overline{CB}$? $\overline{AC}$

29. What's the next number in this sequence?
(2,8)

$$1, \frac{1}{2}, \frac{1}{4}, \frac{1}{8}, \dots \quad \frac{1}{16}$$

30. How many $\frac{2}{5}$'s are in 1? $\frac{5}{2}$
(9)

LESSON 10

Writing Division Answers as Mixed Numbers • Improper Fractions

Facts Practice: 64 Multiplication Facts (Test A in Test Masters)

Mental Math:

   a. 7 − 10   **b.** $1.25 × 10   **c.** $1.00 − 82¢

   d. 384 + 110   **e.** 649 − 200   **f.** 300 ÷ 30

   g. 3 × 6, ÷ 2, × 5, + 3, ÷ 6, − 3, × 4, + 1, ÷ 3

Problem Solving:

   Copy this problem and fill in the missing digits.

$$\begin{array}{r} \_37\_ \\ -\ 2\_65 \\ \hline 59\_7 \end{array}$$

Writing division answers as mixed numbers

Alex cut a 25-inch ribbon into four equal lengths. How long was each of the shorter pieces of ribbon?

To find the answer to this question we divide. However, expressing the answer with a remainder does not answer the question.

$$\begin{array}{r} 6 \text{ r } 1 \\ 4\overline{)25} \\ \underline{24} \\ 1 \end{array}$$

The answer 6 r 1 means that each of the four pieces of ribbon was 6 inches long with a piece remaining that was 1 inch long. That makes five pieces of ribbon!

Instead of writing the answer with a remainder, we will write the answer as a mixed number. The remainder becomes the numerator of the fraction and the divisor is the denominator.

$$\begin{array}{r} 6\frac{1}{4} \\ 4\overline{)25} \\ \underline{24} \\ 1 \end{array}$$

This answer means that each piece of ribbon was $6\frac{1}{4}$ inches long, which is the correct answer to the question.

Example 1   What percent of the circle is shaded?

Solution   One third of the circle is shaded, so we divide 100% by 3.

$$\begin{array}{r} 33\frac{1}{3}\% \\ 3\overline{)100\%} \\ \underline{9} \\ 10 \\ \underline{9} \\ 1 \end{array}$$

We find that $33\frac{1}{3}\%$ of the circle is shaded.

Improper fractions   A fraction is equal to 1 if the numerator and denominator are equal (and are not zero). Here we show four fractions equal to 1.

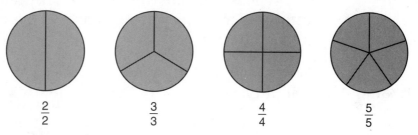

A fraction that is equal to 1 or is greater than 1 is called an **improper fraction.** Improper fractions can be rewritten either as whole numbers or as mixed numbers. To convert an improper fraction to a whole number or to a mixed number, we divide the numerator by the denominator.

Example 2   Convert each improper fraction to either a whole number or a mixed number.

(a) $\dfrac{5}{3}$ (b) $\dfrac{6}{3}$

Solution   We perform the division indicated by each fraction. A remainder is written as the numerator of a fraction with the same denominator.

(a) $\dfrac{5}{3} \longrightarrow 3\overline{)5} \longrightarrow 1\dfrac{2}{3}$ (b) $\dfrac{6}{3} \longrightarrow 3\overline{)6}$
$\phantom{(a)\ \dfrac{5}{3} \longrightarrow}\ \underline{3}$
$\phantom{(a)\ \dfrac{5}{3} \longrightarrow 3}\ 2$

This picture illustrates that $\frac{5}{3}$ is equivalent to $1\frac{2}{3}$. By shading the remaining section we could illustrate that $\frac{6}{3}$ equals 2.

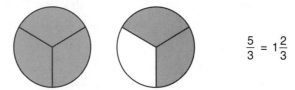

$$\frac{5}{3} = 1\frac{2}{3}$$

Example 3   Rewrite $3\frac{7}{5}$ with a proper fraction.

Solution   The mixed number $3\frac{7}{5}$ means $3 + \frac{7}{5}$. The fraction $\frac{7}{5}$ converts to $1\frac{2}{5}$.

$$\frac{7}{5} = 1\frac{2}{5}$$

Now we combine 3 and $1\frac{2}{5}$.

$$3 + 1\frac{2}{5} = \mathbf{4\frac{2}{5}}$$

When the answer to an arithmetic problem is an improper fraction, we may convert the improper fraction to a mixed number.

Example 4   Simplify: (a) $\frac{4}{5} + \frac{4}{5}$ (b) $\frac{5}{2} \times \frac{3}{4}$ (c) $1\frac{3}{5} + 1\frac{3}{5}$

Solution   (a) $\frac{4}{5} + \frac{4}{5} = \frac{8}{5} = \mathbf{1\frac{3}{5}}$ (b) $\frac{5}{2} \times \frac{3}{4} = \frac{15}{8} = \mathbf{1\frac{7}{8}}$

(c) $1\frac{3}{5} + 1\frac{3}{5} = 2\frac{6}{5} = \mathbf{3\frac{1}{5}}$

Sometimes we need to convert a mixed number to an improper fraction. The illustration below shows $3\frac{1}{4}$ converted to the improper fraction $\frac{13}{4}$.

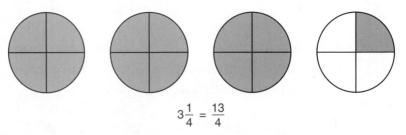

$$3\frac{1}{4} = \frac{13}{4}$$

We see that every whole circle equals $\frac{4}{4}$. So three whole circles is $\frac{12}{4}$, and $\frac{1}{4}$ more makes $\frac{13}{4}$. A quick way to convert $3\frac{1}{4}$ to an improper fraction is to multiply the whole number, 3, by the denominator, 4, and then add the numerator of the fraction, 1. This gives us the numerator of the improper fraction. The denominator of the improper fraction equals the denominator of the fractional part of the mixed number.

$$3\frac{1}{4} \longrightarrow \overset{+1}{\underset{\times 4}{③\frac{1}{4}}} = \frac{(4 \times 3) + 1}{4} = \frac{13}{4}$$

Example 5 Write each mixed number as an improper fraction.

(a) $3\dfrac{1}{3}$ (b) $2\dfrac{3}{4}$ (c) $12\dfrac{1}{2}$

Solution In each case we multiply the whole number by the denominator and then add the numerator to find the numerator of the improper fraction.

(a) $3\dfrac{1}{3} = \dfrac{10}{3}$ (b) $2\dfrac{3}{4} = \dfrac{11}{4}$ (c) $12\dfrac{1}{2} = \dfrac{25}{2}$

Practice **a.** Alex cut a 35-inch ribbon into four equal lengths. How long was each of the shorter pieces of ribbon? $8\frac{3}{4}$ inches

b. One day is what percent of one week? $14\frac{2}{7}\%$

Convert each improper fraction to either a whole number or a mixed number.

c. $\dfrac{12}{5}$ $2\frac{2}{5}$ **d.** $\dfrac{12}{6}$ 2 **e.** $2\dfrac{12}{7}$ $3\frac{5}{7}$

f. Draw and shade circles to illustrate that $2\frac{1}{4} = \frac{9}{4}$.

Simplify:

g. $\dfrac{2}{3} + \dfrac{2}{3} + \dfrac{2}{3}$ 2 **h.** $\dfrac{7}{3} \times \dfrac{2}{3}$ $1\frac{5}{9}$ **i.** $1\dfrac{2}{3} + 1\dfrac{2}{3}$ $3\frac{1}{3}$

Convert each mixed number to an improper fraction.

j. $1\dfrac{2}{3}$ $\frac{5}{3}$ **k.** $3\dfrac{5}{6}$ $\frac{23}{6}$ **l.** $4\dfrac{3}{4}$ $\frac{19}{4}$

Problem set 10 **1.** Write an equation using the fractions $\frac{1}{2}$, $\frac{1}{3}$, and $\frac{1}{6}$ that
$^{(2,9)}$ illustrates the associative property of multiplication.
Answers may vary. One answer is $\left(\frac{1}{2} \cdot \frac{1}{3}\right) \cdot \frac{1}{6} = \frac{1}{2} \cdot \left(\frac{1}{3} \cdot \frac{1}{6}\right)$.

2. Use the words "perpendicular" and "parallel" to complete
$^{(7)}$ the following sentence: (a) parallel (b) perpendicular

In a rectangle, opposite sides are (a) , and
adjacent sides are (b) .

3. What is the difference when the sum of 2, 3, and 4 is
$^{(1)}$ subtracted from the product of 2, 3, and 4? 15

4. (a) What percent of the rectangle is shaded? 30%
₍₈₎

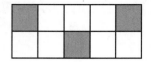

(b) What percent of the rectangle is not shaded? 70%

5. Write $3\frac{2}{3}$ as an improper fraction. $\frac{11}{3}$
₍₁₀₎

6. Replace each circle with the proper comparison symbol.
_(4,9)

(a) $2 - 2 \ \textcircled{<} \ 2 \div 2$ (b) $\frac{1}{2} + \frac{1}{2} \ \textcircled{>} \ \frac{1}{2} \times \frac{1}{2}$

7. Point M represents what mixed number on this number line? $9\frac{5}{6}$
₍₈₎

8. Draw and shade circles to show that $1\frac{3}{5} = \frac{8}{5}$.
₍₁₀₎

9. List the single-digit numbers that are divisors of 420.
₍₆₎ 1, 2, 3, 4, 5, 6, 7

Find each missing number:

10. $12{,}500 + X = 36{,}275$
₍₃₎ 23,775

11. $18Y = 396$ 22
₍₃₎

12. $77{,}000 - Z = 39{,}400$
₍₃₎ 37,600

13. $\frac{A}{8} = \$1.25$ $10.00
₍₃₎

14.
₍₃₎
$$\begin{array}{r} B \ \$25.00 \\ - \ \$16.25 \\ \hline \$8.75 \end{array}$$

15.
₍₃₎
$$\begin{array}{r} C \ \$37.50 \\ + \ \$37.50 \\ \hline \$75.00 \end{array}$$

16. $8 + 7 + 5 + 6 + 4 + N + 3 + 7 = 50$ 10
₍₃₎

17. $\frac{5}{2} \times \frac{5}{4}$ $3\frac{1}{8}$
₍₁₀₎

18. $\frac{5}{8} - \frac{5}{8}$ 0
₍₉₎

19. $\frac{11}{20} + \frac{18}{20}$ $1\frac{9}{20}$
₍₁₀₎

20. $2000 - (680 - 59)$ 1379
₍₂₎

21. $100\% \div 9$ $11\frac{1}{9}\%$
₍₁₀₎

22. $89\cent + 57\cent + \$15.74$
₍₁₎ $17.20

23. 800×300 240,000
₍₁₎

24. $2\frac{2}{3} + 2\frac{2}{3}$ $5\frac{1}{3}$
₍₁₀₎

25. $\frac{2}{3} \cdot \frac{2}{3} \cdot \frac{2}{3}$ $\frac{8}{27}$
₍₉₎

26. Describe each figure as a line, ray, or segment. Then use a
(7) symbol and letters to name each figure.

(a) M ——● C ——→
ray; $\overrightarrow{MC}$

(b) P
line; $\overleftrightarrow{PM}$ (or $\overleftrightarrow{MP}$)

(c) F ●——————● H
segment; $\overline{FH}$ (or $\overline{HF}$)

27. How many $\frac{5}{9}$'s are in 1? $\frac{9}{5}$
(9)

28. What are the next three numbers in this sequence?
(2,8)
$$32, 16, 8, 4, 2, \dots \quad 1, \tfrac{1}{2}, \tfrac{1}{4}$$

29. Which of these numbers is not an integer?   C. $\frac{1}{2}$
(4)

A. -1 B. 0 C. $\dfrac{1}{2}$ D. 1

30. (a) If $a - b = 5$, then what does $b - a$ equal? -5
(4,9)
     (b) If $\frac{w}{x} = 3$, then what does $\frac{x}{w}$ equal? $\frac{1}{3}$

INVESTIGATION 1

Investigating Fractions and Percents with Manipulatives

In this investigation students will make a set of fraction manipulatives to use in solving problems with fractions.

Materials needed:

- Each student needs a copy of both "Activity Master 1" and "Activity Master 2" (available in the *Math 87 Test Masters*).

- Scissors

- Envelopes or locking plastic bags if fraction pieces will be stored for later use.

- Colored pencils or markers if the fraction manipulatives are to be color-coded.

Note: Color-coding the fraction manipulatives makes sorting easier. If you wish to color-code the manipulatives, agree upon a different color for each fraction circle. Students may lightly color the front and back of each circle before cutting. Following the activity, each student may store the fraction manipulatives in an envelope or plastic bag for use in later lessons.

Preparation for activities:

- Distribute materials. Have students color-code the manipulatives if desired. Then have students separate the fraction manipulatives by cutting out the fraction circles and cutting apart the fraction slices along the lines. After the activities, the manipulatives may be stored for later use.

Working in groups of two or three students, use your fraction manipulatives to help you with the following activities and questions:

1. What fraction is half of $\frac{1}{2}$? $\frac{1}{4}$

2. What fraction is half of $\frac{1}{4}$? $\frac{1}{8}$

3. What fraction is half of $\frac{1}{3}$? $\frac{1}{6}$

4. What fraction is half of $\frac{1}{6}$? $\frac{1}{12}$

5. What fraction is $\frac{1}{3}$ of $\frac{1}{2}$? $\frac{1}{6}$

6. What fraction is $\frac{1}{3}$ of $\frac{1}{4}$? $\frac{1}{12}$

7. How many $\frac{1}{12}$'s equal $\frac{1}{2}$? 6

8. Find a single fraction piece that equals $\frac{3}{12}$. $\frac{1}{4}$

9. Find a single fraction piece that equals $\frac{4}{8}$. $\frac{1}{2}$

10. Find a single fraction piece that equals $\frac{4}{12}$. $\frac{1}{3}$

11. How many sixths equal $\frac{2}{3}$? 4

12. How many twelfths equal $\frac{3}{4}$? 9

13. With a partner assemble five $\frac{1}{3}$ pieces to illustrate a mixed number. Draw a picture of your work. Then write an equation that relates the improper fraction to the mixed number. ; $\frac{5}{3} = 1\frac{2}{3}$

14. Find a single fraction piece that equals $\frac{3}{6}$. $\frac{1}{2}$

15. With a partner assemble nine $\frac{1}{6}$ pieces to form $\frac{5}{6}$ of a circle and $\frac{4}{6}$ of a circle. Then demonstrate the addition of $\frac{5}{6}$ and $\frac{4}{6}$ by recombining the pieces to make $1\frac{1}{2}$ circles. Draw a picture to illustrate your work.

16. Two $\frac{1}{4}$ pieces form $\frac{1}{2}$ of a circle. Which two different manipulative pieces also form $\frac{1}{2}$ of a circle? $\frac{1}{3}$ and $\frac{1}{6}$

Find a fraction to complete each equation.

17. $\frac{1}{2} + \frac{1}{3} + a = 1$ $\frac{1}{6}$

18. $\frac{1}{6} + b = \frac{1}{4}$ $\frac{1}{12}$

19. $\frac{1}{2} + c = \frac{3}{4}$ $\frac{1}{4}$

20. $\frac{1}{4} + d = \frac{1}{3}$ $\frac{1}{12}$

Find each percent.

21. What percent of a circle is $\frac{2}{3}$ of a circle? $66\frac{2}{3}\%$

22. What percent of a circle is $\frac{3}{12}$ of a circle? 25%

23. What percent of a circle is $\frac{3}{8}$ of a circle? $37\frac{1}{2}\%$

24. What percent of a circle is $\frac{3}{6}$ of a circle? 50%

25. What percent of a circle is $\frac{1}{4} + \frac{1}{12}$? $33\frac{1}{3}\%$

26. Use four $\frac{1}{4}$'s to demonstrate the subtraction $1 - \frac{1}{4}$ and write the answer.   Remove $\frac{1}{4}$; $1 - \frac{1}{4} = \frac{3}{4}$

27. What two equal fraction pieces together cover $\frac{4}{6}$ of a circle? $\frac{1}{3}$

28. What three equal fraction pieces together cover $\frac{6}{8}$ of a circle? $\frac{1}{4}$

30. $\frac{2}{4} = \frac{1}{2}, \frac{3}{6} = \frac{1}{2},$
$\frac{4}{8} = \frac{1}{2}, \frac{6}{12} = \frac{1}{2},$
$\frac{1}{3} + \frac{1}{6} = \frac{1}{2},$
$\frac{1}{3} + \frac{2}{12} = \frac{1}{2},$
$\frac{2}{12} + \frac{2}{6} = \frac{1}{2},$
$\frac{4}{12} + \frac{1}{6} = \frac{1}{2},$
$\frac{1}{4} + \frac{2}{8} = \frac{1}{2},$
$\frac{3}{12} + \frac{2}{8} = \frac{1}{2},$
$\frac{3}{12} + \frac{1}{4} = \frac{1}{2}$

29. If you subtract $\frac{1}{12}$ of a circle from $\frac{1}{3}$ of a circle, what fraction is left? $\frac{1}{4}$

30. Using these fraction manipulatives, find as many ways as you can to make half of a circle using two or more smaller pieces. Write an equation for each way you find. For example, $\frac{2}{4} = \frac{1}{2}$ and $\frac{1}{3} + \frac{1}{6} = \frac{1}{2}$.

Extension   Write new problems for other groups to answer.

LESSON 11

"Some and Some More" and "Some Went Away" Word Problems

Facts Practice: 30 Improper Fractions and Mixed Numbers
(Test C in Test Masters)

Mental Math:

  a. $7.50 + 75¢   **b.** $40.00 ÷ 10   **c.** $10.00 − $5.50

  d. $(3 \times 20) + (3 \times 5)$ **e.** 250 − 1000   **f.** $\frac{1}{2}$ of 28

  g. Start with the number of hours in a day, ÷ 2, × 3, ÷ 4, × 5, + 4, ÷ 7.

Problem Solving:

  Letha has 7 coins in her hands totaling 50¢. What are the coins?

"Some and some more" word problems

In this lesson we will begin solving one-step story problems. There are hundreds of different story problems but only a few different patterns. One common story problem is that someone has some and then gets some more. A **"some and some more"** story has an **addition pattern.**

$$\text{some} + \text{some more} = \text{total}$$

There are three (or more) numbers in this pattern. Any one of the numbers may be missing. If the missing number is an addend we subtract the known addend from the sum to find the missing addend. Although we may employ subtraction to answer a "some and some more" problem, it is important to recognize that a "some and some more" problem has an addition pattern.

We will follow these four steps when solving story problems.

Step 1: Read and recognize the problem type.

Step 2: Write an equation for the given information.

Step 3: Find the number that solves the equation.

Step 4: Review and answer the question.

We will follow these steps as we consider some examples.

Example 1 At the end of the first day of camp, Marissa counted 47 mosquito bites. The next morning she counted 114 mosquito bites. How many new bites did she get?

Solution **Step 1:** We recognize this as a "some and some more" problem. She had some bites and then she got some more bites.

Step 2: We write an equation for the given information. She had 47 bites. She got some more bites. Then she had a total of 114 bites. We will use B in the equation to stand for the number of new bites.

$$47 + B = 114$$

Step 3: We find B, the missing number. We find a missing addend by subtracting. We subtract, then check our work.

$$
\begin{array}{r}
114 \\
-\ 47 \\
\hline
67
\end{array}
\qquad
\begin{array}{r}
47 \text{ bites} \\
+\ 67 \text{ bites} \\
\hline
114 \text{ bites} \quad \text{check}
\end{array}
$$

Step 4: Now we review the question and write our answer. Marissa got **67 new bites.**

Example 2 The first scout troop encamped in the ravine. A second troop of 137 scouts joined them, making a total of 312 scouts. How many scouts were in the first troop?

Solution **Step 1:** We recognize this problem as a "some and some more" story. There were some scouts. Then some more scouts came.

Step 2: We write an equation using S to stand for the number of scouts in the first group.

$$S + 137 = 312$$

Step 3: We find S, the missing number. To find the first or second number in an addition pattern, we subtract. Then we check our answer.

$$
\begin{array}{r}
312 \\
-\ 137 \\
\hline
175
\end{array}
\qquad
\begin{array}{r}
175 \text{ scouts} \\
+\ 137 \text{ scouts} \\
\hline
312 \text{ scouts} \quad \text{check}
\end{array}
$$

Step 4: Now we review and answer the question. There were **175 scouts** in the first troop.

"Some went away" word problems

Another type of story problem is a **"some went away"** story. A "some went away" story has a **subtraction pattern.**

some − some went away = what is left

There are three numbers in this pattern. Any one of the three numbers may be missing in the problem. To solve the problem, we find the missing number. Then we answer the question in the problem. Thus, we follow the same four steps we followed in solving "some and some more" problems.

Example 3 Tim baked 4 dozen cookies. While they were cooling, he went to answer the phone. When he came back, only 32 cookies remained. His dog was nearby, licking her chops. How many cookies did the dog eat while Tim was answering the phone?

Solution **Step 1:** We recognize that this problem is a "some went away" story.

Step 2: We write an equation using 48 for 4 dozen cookies and C for the number of cookies that went away.

$$48 - C = 32$$

Step 3: We find the missing number. To find the second number in a subtraction pattern, we subtract. Then we check our work.

$$
\begin{array}{r}
48 \\
- 32 \\
\hline
16
\end{array}
\qquad
\begin{array}{r}
48 \text{ cookies} \\
- 16 \text{ cookies} \\
\hline
32 \text{ cookies} \quad \text{check}
\end{array}
$$

Step 4: Now we review and answer the question. While Tim was answering the phone, his dog ate **16 cookies.**

Example 4 The room was full of boxes when Sharon began. Then she shipped out 56 boxes. Only 88 boxes were left. How many boxes were in the room when Sharon began?

Solution **Step 1:** We recognize that this problem is a "some went away" problem.

Step 2: We write an equation using B to stand for the number of boxes in the room when Sharon began.

$$B - 56 = 88$$

Step 3: We find the missing number. To find the first number in a subtraction pattern, we add the other two numbers. Then we check the solution.

$$
\begin{array}{r}
88 \\
+ 56 \\
\hline
144
\end{array}
\qquad
\begin{array}{r}
144 \text{ boxes} \\
- 56 \text{ boxes} \\
\hline
88 \text{ boxes} \quad \text{check}
\end{array}
$$

Step 4: Now we answer the question. There were **144 boxes** in the room when Sharon began.

Practice Follow the four-step method shown in this lesson for each problem.

a. Billy stood on the scales. Billy weighed 118 pounds. Then Nathan and Billy stood on the scales. Together they weighed 230 pounds. How much did Nathan weigh?
118 + *N* = 230; 112 pounds

b. Tim cranked for a number of turns. Then Dawn gave the crank 216 turns. If the total number of turns was 400, how many turns did Tim give the crank?
T + 216 = 400; 184 turns

c. At dawn 254 horses were in the corral. Later that morning, Tex found the gate open and saw that only 126 horses remained. How many horses got away?
254 − *H* = 126; 128 horses

d. Cynthia had a lot of paper. After using 36 sheets for a report, only 164 sheets remained. How many sheets of paper did she have at first? *P* − 36 = 164; 200 sheets

Problem set 11

1. As the day of the festival drew near, there were 200,000
(11) people in the city. If the usual population of the city was 85,000, how many visitors had come to the city?
85,000 + *V* = 200,000; 115,000 visitors

2. Syd returned from the store with $12.47. He had spent
(11) $98.03 on groceries. How much money did he have when he went to the store? *M* − $98.03 = $12.47; $110.50

3. Exactly 10,000 runners began the marathon. If only 5,420
(11) runners finished the marathon, how many dropped out along the way? 10,000 − *D* = 5,420; 4,580 runners dropped out

4. (a) What fraction of the group is
(8,10) shaded? $\frac{7}{8}$

(b) What fraction of the group is not shaded? $\frac{1}{8}$

(c) What percent of the group is not shaded? $12\frac{1}{2}\%$

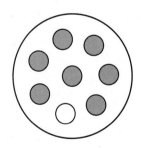

5. (a) Arrange these numbers in order from least to greatest:
(4,8)

$$\frac{1}{2}, 0, -2, 1 \quad -2, 0, \tfrac{1}{2}, 1$$

(b) Which of these numbers is not an integer? $\frac{1}{2}$

6. A 35-inch ribbon was cut into 8 equal lengths. How long
(10) was each of the smaller ribbons? $4\frac{3}{8}$ inches

7. Use digits and symbols to write "the product of one and
(4) two is less than the sum of one and two." $1 \cdot 2 < 1 + 2$

8. Subtract 89 million from 100 million. Use words to write
(5) the difference. eleven million

9. (a) List the factors of 16. 1, 2, 4, 8, 16
(6)

  (b) List the factors of 24. 1, 2, 3, 4, 6, 8, 12, 24

  (c) Which numbers are factors of both 16 and 24? 1, 2, 4, 8

  (d) What is the GCF of 16 and 24? 8

Find each missing number:

10. $8000 - K = 5340$ 2660
(3)

11. $1320 + M = 1760$ 440
(3)

12. $4 \cdot 9 \cdot N = 720$ 20
(3)

13. $\$126 + R = \$375$ $249
(3)

14. $\dfrac{169}{S} = 13$ 13
(3)

15. $\dfrac{T}{40} = \$25.00$ $1000.00
(3)

16. Compare: $100 - (5 \times 20)$ ⊘ $(100 - 5) \times 20$
(2,4)

Simplify:

17. $1\dfrac{5}{9} + 1\dfrac{5}{9}$ $3\frac{1}{9}$
(10)

18. $\dfrac{5}{3} \times \dfrac{2}{3}$ $1\frac{1}{9}$
(10)

19. $\begin{array}{r} 135 \\ \times\ 72 \\ \hline 9720 \end{array}$
(1)

20. $\dfrac{1000}{40}$ 25
(1)

21. $30(\$1.49)$ $44.70
(1)

22. $\$140.70 \div 35$ $4.02
(1)

23. $\dfrac{5}{9} \cdot \dfrac{1}{3} \cdot \dfrac{1}{2}$ $\frac{5}{54}$
(9)

24. $\dfrac{5}{8} + \left(\dfrac{3}{8} - \dfrac{1}{8}\right)$ $\frac{7}{8}$
(9)

25. Write $3\frac{3}{4}$ as an improper fraction. $\frac{15}{4}$
(10)

26. Which choice below is the best esti-
(8) mate of the portion of the rectangle
that is shaded? C. 40%

A. $\dfrac{1}{4}$ B. $\dfrac{1}{2}$ C. 40%   D. 60%

27. What are the next four numbers in this sequence?
(2,8)

$$\frac{1}{8}, \frac{1}{4}, \frac{3}{8}, \frac{1}{2}, \dots \quad \tfrac{5}{8}, \tfrac{3}{4}, \tfrac{7}{8}, 1$$

28. Refer to this figure to answer questions
(7) (a) and (b).

   (a) Which angles appear to be acute angles? $\angle 1, \angle 3$

   (b) Which angles appear to be obtuse angles? $\angle 2, \angle 4$

29. Use an inch ruler to draw segment AC $3\frac{1}{2}$ inches long. On
(8) $\overline{AC}$ mark point B so that AB is $1\frac{7}{8}$ inches. Now find BC.

A —————————————— B ———————— C; $1\frac{5}{8}$ inches

30. If $n \div m$ equals $\frac{7}{8}$, what does $m \div n$ equal? $\frac{8}{7}$
(9)

LESSON 12

"Larger-Smaller-Difference" Word Problems • Time Problems

Mental Math:
a. $7.10
b. $12.90
c. $7.50
d. 92
e. −1500
f. 32
g. 22
Problem Solving:
$\frac{3}{4}$ in.

Facts Practice: 30 Improper Fractions and Mixed Numbers
(Test C in Test Masters)

Mental Math:

   a. $6.50 + 60¢   **b.** $1.29 × 10   **c.** $10.00 − $2.50
   d. (4 × 20) + (4 × 3)   **e.** 500 − 2000   **f.** $\frac{1}{2}$ of 64
   g. Start with three score, ÷ 2, + 2, ÷ 2, + 2, ÷ 2, + 2, × 2.

Problem Solving:

   The diameter of a circle or a circular object is the distance across a circle through its center. Find the approximate diameter of this penny.

"Larger-smaller-difference" word problems

In the previous lesson we practiced solving "some went away" problems. A "some went away" problem has a subtraction pattern.

   Another type of problem that has a subtraction pattern is a **"larger-smaller-difference"** problem. In "larger-smaller-difference" problems we are asked to **compare** two numbers.

In these problems we not only decide which number is greater and which number is less, but also **how much** greater or **how much** less. The number that describes how much greater or how much less is called the difference. We follow this pattern when writing an equation for a "larger-smaller-difference" problem.

$$\text{larger} - \text{smaller} = \text{difference}$$

Example 1   During the day, 1320 employees worked at the toy factory. At night, 897 employees worked there. How many more employees worked at the factory during the day than at night?

Solution   **Step 1:** Questions such as "How many more?" or "How many fewer?" indicate that the problem is a "larger-smaller-difference" problem.

Step 2: We write an equation for the given information. We use the letter E in the equation to stand for how many more employees worked at the factory during the day than at night.

$$1320 - 897 = E$$

Step 3: We find the missing number in the pattern by subtracting.

$$
\begin{array}{r}
1320 \text{ employees} \\
- \ 897 \text{ employees} \\
\hline
423 \text{ employees}
\end{array}
$$

Step 4: We review and answer the question: **423 more employees** work at the factory during the day than work there at night.

Example 2   The number 620,000 is how much less than 1,000,000?

Solution   **Step 1:** The words "how much less" indicate that this problem is a "larger-smaller-difference" problem.

Step 2: We write an equation using D to stand for the **difference** between the two numbers.

$$1{,}000{,}000 - 620{,}000 = D$$

Step 3: We subtract to find the missing number.

$$
\begin{array}{r}
1{,}000{,}000 \\
- \ 620{,}000 \\
\hline
380{,}000
\end{array}
$$

Step 4: The difference is "how much less." We answer the question. Six hundred twenty thousand is **380,000 less than one million.**

Time problems Time problems are like "larger-smaller-difference" problems. We arrange the times in this order: **"later-earlier-difference."** At this point we will consider time problems involving only years A.D.

Example 3 How many years were there from 1492 to 1776?

Solution **Step 1:** We recognize that this problem is a "later-earlier-difference" problem.

Step 2: We write an equation for the pattern. The year 1776 is later than 1492. We use Y for the number of years between 1492 and 1776.

$$1776 - 1492 = Y$$

Step 3: We subtract to find the missing number.

$$
\begin{array}{r}
1776 \\
- 1492 \\
\hline
284
\end{array}
$$

Step 4: Now we answer the question. There were **284 years** from 1492 to 1776.

Example 4 Abraham Lincoln died in 1865 at the age of 56. In what year was he born?

Solution **Step 1:** This is a time problem. Time problems are "later-earlier-difference" problems.

Step 2: Age is the difference between the date of birth (earlier) and the date of death (later). We write an equation using B to stand for the year of Lincoln's birth.

$$1865 - B = 56$$

Step 3: To find the subtrahend in a subtraction pattern, we subtract the difference from the minuend.

$$
\begin{array}{r}
1865 \\
- 56 \\
\hline
1809
\end{array}
\qquad
\begin{array}{r}
1865 \\
- 1809 \\
\hline
56 \quad \text{check}
\end{array}
$$

Step 4: Now we answer the question. Abraham Lincoln was born in **1809.**

Practice   **a.** The number 1,000,000,000 is how much greater than 25,000,000? 1,000,000,000 − 25,000,000 = G; 975,000,000

b. How many years were there from 1215 to 1791?
1791 − 1215 = Y; 576 years

c. John F. Kennedy died in 1963 at the age of 46. In what year was he born? 1963 − B = 46; 1917

Problem set 12

1. Seventy-seven thousand fans filled the stadium. As the fourth quarter began, only thirty-nine thousand, four hundred remained. How many fans left before the fourth quarter began? 77,000 − L = 39,400; 37,600 fans
(11)

2. Mary purchased 18 bananas at the store. When she got home, she discovered that she already had some bananas. If she now has 31 bananas, how many did she have before she went to the store? B + 18 = 31; 13 bananas
(11)

3. How many years were there from 1066 to 1215?
(12) 1215 − 1066 = Y; 149 years

4. The first week 77,000 fans came to the stadium. Only 49,600 came the second week. How many fewer fans came to the stadium the second week?
(12) 77,000 − 49,600 = F; 27,400 fewer fans

5. Draw and shade circles to show that $2\frac{1}{4}$ equals $\frac{9}{4}$.
(10)

6. What property is illustrated by this equation?
(2)

$$\frac{1}{2} \times 1 = \frac{1}{2}$$

identity property of multiplication

7. Twenty-three thousand is how much less than one million? Use words to write your answer.
(5,12) 1,000,000 − 23,000 = d; nine hundred seventy-seven thousand

8. Replace each circle with the proper comparison symbol.
(4,8)

(a) 2 − 3 Ⓐ −1   (b) $\frac{1}{2}$ Ⓐ $\frac{1}{3}$

9. Name three segments in this figure in order of length from shortest to longest. $\overline{PQ}, \overline{QR}, \overline{PR}$
(7)

10. (a) What fraction of the triangle is
(8)   shaded? $\frac{3}{4}$

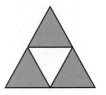

   (b) What percent of the triangle is
       not shaded? 25%

11. The number 100 is divisible by which whole numbers?
(6) 1, 2, 4, 5, 10, 20, 25, 50, 100

Find each missing number:

12. X 42
(3)   × 15
    ─────
       630

13. Y 6315
(3)   − 2714
    ─────
       3601

14.   5
(3)   8
       4
       7
       6
       5
       7
     N 6
       4
    + 6
    ─────
      58

15.   2900
(3) − P 2836
    ─────
        64

16. $1.53
(3) + Q $3.47
    ─────
      $5.00

17.   20
(3) × R 60
    ─────
     1200

18. $\frac{M}{14} = 16$ 224
(3)

Simplify:

19.   72,112
(1) − 64,309
    ─────
      7,803

20.   453,978
(1) + 386,864
    ─────
      840,842

21. $\frac{8}{9} - \left(\frac{3}{9} + \frac{5}{9}\right)$ 0
(9)

22. $\left(\frac{8}{9} - \frac{3}{9}\right) + \frac{5}{9}$ $1\frac{1}{9}$
(10)

23. $\frac{9}{2} \times \frac{3}{5}$ $2\frac{7}{10}$
(10)

24. $37.20 ÷ 15 $2.48
(1)

25. Divide 42,847 by 9 and express the quotient as a mixed
(10) number. $4760\frac{7}{9}$

26. $4.36 + $15.96 + 76¢ + $35 $56.08
(1)

27. Find the next three numbers in this sequence.
(2,8)

$$\frac{1}{4}, \frac{1}{2}, \frac{3}{4}, \ldots \quad 1, 1\frac{1}{4}, 1\frac{1}{2}$$

28. How many $\frac{2}{3}$'s are in 1? $\frac{3}{2}$
(9)

29. Write $1\frac{2}{3}$ as an improper fraction and multiply the
$^{(10)}$ improper fraction by $\frac{1}{2}$. What is the product? $\frac{5}{3} \times \frac{1}{2} = \frac{5}{6}$

30.

30. Using a ruler, draw a triangle that has two perpendicular
$^{(7,8)}$ sides that are $\frac{3}{4}$ in. long and 1 in. long. What is the
measure of the third side?

LESSON 13

"Equal Groups" Word Problems

Mental Math:
a. $7.20
b. $2.50
c. $3.25
d. 165
e. −250
f. 43
g. 9
Problem Solving:
6

Facts Practice: 30 Improper Fractions and Mixed Numbers
(Test C in Test Masters)

Mental Math:

a. $8.00 − $0.80   b. $25.00 ÷ 10   c. $10.00 − $6.75
d. $(5 \times 30) + (5 \times 3)$ e. $250 − 500$ f. $\frac{1}{2}$ of 86
g. $7 \times 8, + 4, ÷ 3, + 1, ÷ 3, + 8, \times 2, − 3, ÷ 3$

Problem Solving:

Joe, Moe, and Larry stood side-by-side for a picture. Then they
rearranged themselves in the order Moe, Joe, and Larry, and took
another picture. Altogether, how many different side-by-side
arrangements are possible?

We have used both the addition pattern and the subtraction
pattern to solve word problems. In this lesson we will use a
multiplication pattern to solve word problems. Consider this
problem:

*Willie packed 25 marbles in each box. If he filled 32
boxes, how many marbles did he pack in all?*

This problem has a pattern that is different from the addition
pattern or subtraction pattern. This problem is an **"equal
groups"** problem and has a **multiplication pattern.**

> number of groups × number in group = total

To find an unknown factor, we divide. We will consider three
examples.

Example 1   Willie packed 25 marbles in each box. If he filled 32 boxes,
how many marbles did he pack in all?

Solution   **Step 1:** The words "in each" are a clue to help us recognize
that this is an "equal groups" problem.

Step 2: We write an equation using T for the total number of marbles. There are 32 groups with 25 marbles in each group.

$$32 \times 25 = T$$

Step 3: To find the missing product, we multiply the factors.

Step 4: We answer the question. Willie packed **800 marbles** in all.

$$\begin{array}{r} 32 \\ \times\ 25 \\ \hline 160 \\ 64 \\ \hline 800 \end{array}$$

Example 2   Movie tickets sold for $5 each. The total ticket sales were $820. How many tickets were sold?

Solution   **Step 1:** The word "each" is a clue that this is an "equal groups" problem.

Step 2: We write an equation. We use T in the equation for the number of tickets.

$$T \times \$5 = \$820$$

Step 3: To find a missing factor, we divide the product by the known factor.

$$\begin{array}{r} 164 \\ 5\overline{)820} \end{array} \qquad 164 \times \$5 = \$820 \quad \text{check}$$

Step 4: We answer the question: **164 tickets** were sold.

Example 3   Every truck carried the same number of cars. Six hundred new cars were delivered to the dealer by 40 trucks. How many cars were delivered by each truck?

Solution   **Step 1:** An equal number of cars were grouped on each truck. This problem is an "equal groups" problem.

Step 2: We write an equation using C to stand for the number of cars on each truck.

$$40 \times C = 600$$

Step 3: To find a missing factor, we divide.

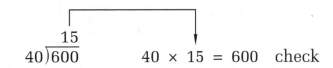

$$\begin{array}{r} 15 \\ 40\overline{)600} \end{array} \qquad 40 \times 15 = 600 \quad \text{check}$$

Step 4: We answer the question: **15 cars** were delivered by each truck.

Practice   **a.** Beverly bought 2 dozen juice bars for 18¢ each. How much did she pay for all the juice bars? 24 × 18¢ = M; $4.32

b. Johnny planted a total of 375 trees with 25 trees in each row. How many rows of trees did he plant?
R × 25 = 375; 15 rows

c. Every day Arnold did the same number of push-ups. If he did 1225 push-ups in one week, then how many push-ups did he do each day? 7P = 1225; 175 push-ups

Problem set 13

1. In 1980, the population of Ashton was 64,309. By the
(12) 1990 census, the population had increased to 72,112. The population of Ashton in 1990 was how much greater than the population in 1980? 72,112 − 64,309 = I; 7,803

2. Huck had 5 dozen night crawlers in his pockets. He was
(11) unhappy when all but 17 escaped through holes in his pockets. How many night crawlers had escaped?
60 − N = 17; 43 night crawlers

3. President Franklin D. Roosevelt died in office in 1945 at
(12) the age of 63. In what year was he born?
1945 − B = 63; 1882

4. The beach balls were packed 12 in each case. If 75 cases
(13) were delivered, how many beach balls were there in all?
75 × 12 = B; 900 beach balls

5. The product of 5 and 8 is how much greater than the sum
(1,12) of 5 and 8? 27

6. (a) Three quarters is what fraction of a dollar? $\frac{3}{4}$
(8)
(b) Three quarters is what percent of a dollar? 75%

7. How many units is it from −5 to +5 on the number line?
(4) 10 units

8. Write 10400
(5)
(a) with words. ten thousand, four hundred

(b) in expanded notation. (1 × 10,000) + (4 × 100)

9. Describe each figure as a line, a ray, or a segment. Then
(7) use a symbol and letters to name each figure.

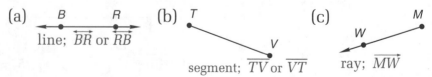

(a) $\begin{array}{cc} B & R \end{array}$ (b) T (c) M
line; $\overleftrightarrow{BR}$ or $\overleftrightarrow{RB}$ W

                                    V
                        segment; $\overline{TV}$ or $\overline{VT}$ ray; $\overrightarrow{MW}$

10. (a) What whole numbers are factors of both 24 and 36?
(6) 1, 2, 3, 4, 6, 12
(b) What is the GCF of 24 and 36? 12

11. (a) What fractions or mixed numbers are represented by
(8)   points A and B on this number line? A: $\frac{6}{7}$; B: $1\frac{4}{7}$

   (b) Find AB. $\frac{5}{7}$

Find each missing number:

12. $36C = 1800$ 50   **13.** $F - \$1.64 = \$3.77$ \$5.41
(3)   (3)

14. $\dfrac{D}{7} = 28$ 196   **15.** $\dfrac{4500}{E} = 30$ 150   **16.**
(3)   (3)   (3)

$$
\begin{array}{r}
4 \\
7 \\
6 \\
8 \\
4 \\
5 \\
5 \\
7 \\
9 \\
6 \\
N \ 6 \\
+ \ \ 8 \\
\hline
75
\end{array}
$$

17. $3674 - A = 2159$ 1515
(3)

18. $4610 + B = 5179$ 569
(3)

Simplify:

19. $363 + 4579 + 86 + 7$ 5035
(1)

20. $(5 \cdot 4) \div (3 + 2)$ 4
(2)

21. $\$63.75 \div 5$ **22.** $3\dfrac{4}{5} - \left(\dfrac{2}{5} + 1\dfrac{1}{5}\right)$ $2\frac{1}{5}$
(1) \$12.75   (9)

23. $\dfrac{600}{25}$ 24   **24.** $\dfrac{5}{3} \cdot \dfrac{5}{2}$ $4\frac{1}{6}$ **25.**
(1)   (10)   (1)

$$
\begin{array}{r}
600 \\
\times \ \ 25 \\
\hline
15{,}000
\end{array}
$$

26. Compare: $1000 \div (100 \div 10)$ $\gtrdot$ $(1000 \div 100) \div 10$
(2,4)

27. Write $2\frac{1}{2}$ as an improper fraction. Then multiply the
(10) improper fraction by $\frac{1}{3}$. What is the product? $\frac{5}{2} \cdot \frac{1}{3} = \frac{5}{6}$

28. What is the product of $\frac{11}{12}$ and its reciprocal?   1
(9)

Refer to the figure to answer problems 29
and 30.

29. Name the obtuse, acute, and right
(7) angles.   obtuse: $\angle D$; acute: $\angle A$;
    right: $\angle B$ and $\angle C$.

30. (a) $\overline{AB}$ $\parallel$ which segment? $\overline{DC}$
(7)

    (b) $\overline{AB}$ $\perp$ which segment? $\overline{CB}$

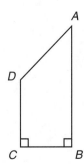

LESSON 14

"Part-Part-Whole" Word Problems

Facts Practice: 30 Equations (Test B in Test Masters)

Mental Math:

a. $7.50 − 75¢   b. $0.63 × 10   c. $10.00 − $8.25
d. (6 × 20) + (6 × 4)   e. 625 − 500   f. $\frac{1}{2}$ of 36
g. Start with three dozen, ÷ 2, + 2, ÷ 2, + 2, ÷ 2, + 2, ÷ 2, + 2, ÷ 2.

Problem Solving:

Terry folded a square piece of paper in half diagonally to form a triangle and then folded the triangle in half as shown, making a smaller triangle. With scissors Terry cut off the upper corner of the triangle. What will the paper look like when it is unfolded?

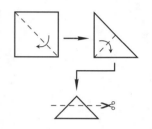

We remember that a "some and some more" problem has an addition pattern. Another type of problem that has an addition pattern is the **"part-part-whole"** problem.

$$\text{part} + \text{part} = \text{whole}$$

Sometimes the parts are expressed as fractions or percents.

Example 1   One third of the students earned a B on the test. What fraction of the students did not earn a B on the test?

Solution   We are not given the number of students. We are given only the fraction of students in the whole class who earned a B on the test. A drawing may help us to visualize the problem.

All students

Step 1: We recognize this as a "part-part-whole" problem.

Step 2: We write an equation for the given information. It may seem as though we are given only one number, $\frac{1}{3}$. The drawing should remind us that the whole class of students is $\frac{3}{3}$. We will use N_B to stand for "not B" students.

$$\frac{1}{3} + N_B = \frac{3}{3}$$

Step 3: We find the missing number, N_B, by subtracting. Then we complete the pattern.

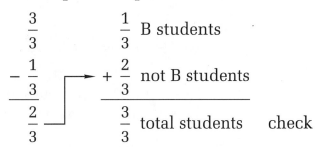

Step 4: Then we review and answer the question. The fraction of the students that did not earn a B on the test is $\frac{2}{3}$.

Example 2   Shemp was excited that 61% of his answers were correct. What percent of Shemp's answers were not correct?

Solution   **Step 1:** Part of Shemp's answers were correct, and part were not correct. This is a "part-part-whole" problem.

Step 2: We write an equation. The total is 100%. We use N_C in the equation to stand for the percent not correct.

$$61\% + N_C = 100\%$$

Step 3: We find the missing number, N_C, by subtracting. Then we check our work.

$$100\% - 61\% = 39\%$$

$$61\% + 39\% = 100\% \quad \text{check}$$

Step 4: We review and answer the question. Of Shemp's answers, **39% were not correct.**

Practice   Use the four-step method described in this lesson to solve the following problems.

 a. Only 39% of the lights were on. What percent of the lights were off? 39% + N = 100%; 61% of the lights were off.

 b. Two fifths of the pioneers did not survive the journey. What fraction of the pioneers did survive the journey? $\frac{2}{5} + S = \frac{5}{5}$; $\frac{3}{5}$ of the pioneers

Problem set 14

1. Beth fed the baby 65 grams of cereal. The baby wanted to
(11) eat 142 grams of cereal. How many additional grams of
cereal did Beth need to feed the baby?
$65 + C = 142$; 77 grams of cereal

2. Seven tenths of the new recruits did not like their first
(14) haircut. What fraction of the new recruits did like their
first haircut? $\frac{7}{10} + W = \frac{10}{10}$; $\frac{3}{10}$ of the recruits

3. How many years were there from 1776 to 1789?
(12) $1789 - 1776 = Y$; 13 years

4. One hundred twenty poles were needed to construct the
(13) new pier. If each truckload contained eight poles, how
many truckloads were needed? $T \times 8 = 120$; 15 truckloads

5. If 24% of the students earned an A on the test, what
(14) percent of the students did not earn an A?
$24\% + N_A = 100\%$; 76% did not earn an A.

6.

6. Draw and shade circles to show that $3\frac{1}{3} = \frac{10}{3}$.
(10)

7. Use digits to write four hundred seven million, forty-two
(5) thousand, six hundred three. 407,042,603

8. What property is illustrated by this equation?
(2)
$$3 \cdot 2 \cdot 1 \cdot 0 = 0$$
zero property of multiplication

9. (a) List the common factors of 40 and 72. 1, 2, 4, 8
(6)

(b) What is the greatest common factor of 40 and 72? 8

10. Name three segments in this figure in order of length
(7) from shortest to longest. $\overline{XY}, \overline{WX}, \overline{WY}$

11. Count the
number in the
group, which
is 12. Use this
as the denomi-
nator. Count
the number
that are shad-
ed, which is 5.
Use this as the
numerator. $\frac{5}{12}$

11. Describe how to find the fraction of the group that is
(8) shaded.

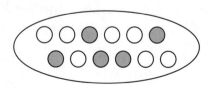

Find each missing number:

12. $B - 407 = 623$ 1030
(3)

13. $\$20 - E = \$3.47$ $16.53
(3)

14. $7 \cdot 5F = 7070$ **15.** $\dfrac{M}{25} = 25$ 625   **16.**
(3) 202   (3)   (3)

17. $A + 295 = 1000$ 705
(3)

Simplify:

18. $3\dfrac{3}{5} + 2\dfrac{4}{5}$ $6\frac{2}{5}$ **19.** $\dfrac{5}{2} \cdot \dfrac{3}{2}$ $3\frac{3}{4}$
(10)   (10)

20. $\$3.63 + \$0.87 + 96¢$ $5.46
(1)

21. $5 \cdot 4 \cdot 3 \cdot 2 \cdot 1$ 120
(1)

22. $\dfrac{2}{3} \cdot \dfrac{2}{3} \cdot \dfrac{2}{3}$ $\frac{8}{27}$ **23.** $\dfrac{900}{20}$ 45
(9)   (1)

24.   145   **25.** $30(65¢)$ $19.50
(1) $\times$ 74   (1)
       10,730

26. $(5)(5 + 5)$ 50   **27.** $9,714 - 13,456$ $-3,742$
(2)   (4)

28. Compare: $(1000 - 100) - 10$ $\underset{<}{\bigcirc}$ $1000 - (100 - 10)$
(2,4)

29. Name each type of angle illustrated.
(7)

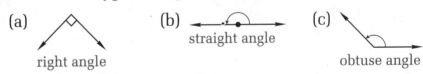

(a) right angle   (b) straight angle   (c) obtuse angle

30. How many $\frac{4}{5}$'s are in 1? $\frac{5}{4}$
(9)

5
8
7
6
5
9
4
3
6
4
7
8
5
N 6
$+$ 6
89

LESSON 15

Equivalent Fractions • Reducing Fractions, Part 1

Mental Math:
a. $5.25
b. $0.40
c. $5.02
d. 224
e. 75
f. 26
g. 5
Problem Solving:

```
    36
  × 15
  ----
   180
    36
  ----
   540
```

Facts Practice: 30 Improper Fractions and Mixed Numbers
(Test C in Test Masters)

Mental Math:

  a. $3.50 + $1.75   **b.** $4.00 ÷ 10   **c.** $10.00 − $4.98

  d. (7 × 30) + (7 × 2) **e.** 125 − 50   **f.** $\frac{1}{2}$ of 52

  g. 10 − 9, + 8, − 7, + 6, − 5, + 4, − 3, + 2, − 1

Problem Solving:

  Copy this problem and fill in the missing digits.

```
       36
     × __
     ----
     __0
     _6
     ----
     ---
```

Equivalent fractions

Different fractions that name the same number are called **equivalent fractions.** Here we show four equivalent fractions.

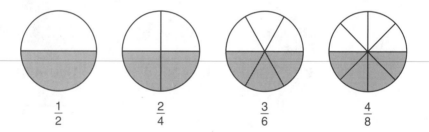

$$\frac{1}{2} \qquad \frac{2}{4} \qquad \frac{3}{6} \qquad \frac{4}{8}$$

Equivalent fractions have the same value.

$$\frac{1}{2} = \frac{2}{4} = \frac{3}{6} = \frac{4}{8}$$

We can form equivalent fractions by multiplying a fraction by a fraction equal to 1. Here we multiply $\frac{1}{2}$ by $\frac{2}{2}$, $\frac{3}{3}$, and $\frac{4}{4}$ to form fractions equivalent to $\frac{1}{2}$.

$$\frac{1}{2} \times \frac{2}{2} = \frac{2}{4} \qquad \frac{1}{2} \times \frac{3}{3} = \frac{3}{6} \qquad \frac{1}{2} \times \frac{4}{4} = \frac{4}{8}$$

Example 1 Find an equivalent fraction for $\frac{2}{3}$ that has a denominator of 12.

Solution The denominator of $\frac{2}{3}$ is 3. To make an equivalent fraction with a denominator of 12 we multiply by $\frac{4}{4}$.

$$\frac{2}{3} \times \frac{4}{4} = \frac{8}{12}$$

Example 2 Find a fraction equivalent to $\frac{1}{3}$ that has a denominator of 6. Next find a fraction equivalent to $\frac{1}{2}$ with a denominator of 6. Then add the two fractions you found.

Solution We multiply $\frac{1}{3}$ by $\frac{2}{2}$, and we multiply $\frac{1}{2}$ by $\frac{3}{3}$ to find the equivalent fractions that have denominators of 6. Then we add $\frac{2}{6}$ and $\frac{3}{6}$.

$$
\begin{aligned}
\frac{1}{3} \times \frac{2}{2} &= \frac{2}{6} \\
+ \quad \frac{1}{2} \times \frac{3}{3} &= \frac{3}{6} \\
\hline
&\quad\; \frac{5}{6}
\end{aligned}
$$

Reducing fractions, part 1 Here is another example of equivalent fractions. The segment in the figure below is $\frac{1}{2}$ inch long. By counting the tick marks on the ruler we see that there are several equivalent names for $\frac{1}{2}$ inch.

$$ \frac{1}{2}\text{ in.} = \frac{2}{4}\text{ in.} = \frac{4}{8}\text{ in.} = \frac{8}{16}\text{ in.} $$

The fractions $\frac{2}{4}$, $\frac{4}{8}$, and $\frac{8}{16}$ each reduce to $\frac{1}{2}$. We can reduce some fractions by dividing the fraction to be reduced by a fraction equal to 1.

$$ \frac{4}{8} \div \frac{4}{4} = \frac{1}{2} \quad \begin{array}{l}(4 \div 4 = 1)\\(8 \div 4 = 2)\end{array} $$

By dividing $\frac{4}{8}$ by $\frac{4}{4}$ we have reduced $\frac{4}{8}$ to $\frac{1}{2}$.

The numbers we use when we write a fraction are called the **terms** of the fraction. To reduce a fraction, we divide both terms of the fraction by a factor of both terms. In some cases the terms of a fraction are divisible by more than one number. For example, 4 and 8 are both divisible by 2 and by 4.

$$ \frac{4}{8} \div \frac{2}{2} = \frac{2}{4} \qquad \frac{4}{8} \div \frac{4}{4} = \frac{1}{2} $$

Dividing $\frac{4}{8}$ by $\frac{4}{4}$ instead of by $\frac{2}{2}$ results in a fraction with lower terms, since the terms of $\frac{1}{2}$ are lower than the terms of $\frac{2}{4}$. It is customary to reduce fractions to **lowest terms.** We can reduce fractions to lowest terms in one step by dividing the terms of the fraction by the greatest common factor of the terms.

Example 3   Reduce $\frac{18}{24}$ to lowest terms.

Solution   Both 18 and 24 are divisible by 2, so we divide both terms by 2.

$$\frac{18}{24} \div \frac{2}{2} = \frac{9}{12}$$

This is not in lowest terms because 9 and 12 are divisible by 3.

$$\frac{9}{12} \div \frac{3}{3} = \frac{\mathbf{3}}{\mathbf{4}}$$

We could have used just one step had we noticed that the greatest common factor of 18 and 24 is 6.

$$\frac{18}{24} \div \frac{6}{6} = \frac{\mathbf{3}}{\mathbf{4}}$$

Both methods are correct. One method took two steps, and the other took just one step.

Example 4   Reduce $3\frac{8}{12}$ to lowest terms.

Solution   To reduce a mixed number, we reduce the fraction and leave the whole number unchanged.

$$\frac{8}{12} \div \frac{4}{4} = \frac{2}{3}$$

$$3\frac{8}{12} = \mathbf{3\frac{2}{3}}$$

Example 5   Write $\frac{12}{9}$ as a mixed number with the fraction reduced.

Solution   There are two steps to reduce and convert to a mixed number. Either step may be taken first.

REDUCE FIRST   CONVERT FIRST

Reduce: $\frac{12}{9} = \frac{4}{3}$ Convert: $\frac{12}{9} = 1\frac{3}{9}$

Convert: $\frac{4}{3} = 1\frac{\mathbf{1}}{\mathbf{3}}$ Reduce: $1\frac{3}{9} = 1\frac{\mathbf{1}}{\mathbf{3}}$

Example 6   Simplify: $\frac{7}{9} - \frac{1}{9}$

Solution First we subtract. Then we reduce.

SUBTRACT   REDUCE

$$\frac{7}{9} - \frac{1}{9} = \frac{6}{9}$$ $$\frac{6}{9} \div \frac{3}{3} = \frac{2}{3}$$

Example 7 Write 70% as a reduced fraction.

Solution Recall that a percent is a fraction with a denominator of 100.

$$70\% = \frac{70}{100}$$

We can reduce the fraction by dividing each term by 10.

$$\frac{70}{100} \div \frac{10}{10} = \frac{7}{10}$$

Practice* **a.** Form three equivalent fractions for $\frac{3}{4}$ by multiplying by $\frac{5}{5}$, $\frac{7}{7}$, and $\frac{3}{3}$. $\frac{15}{20}, \frac{21}{28}, \frac{9}{12}$

b. Find an equivalent fraction for $\frac{3}{4}$ that has a denominator of 16. $\frac{12}{16}$

Find the number that makes these fractions equivalent fractions.

c. $\frac{4}{5} = \frac{?}{20}$ 16   **d.** $\frac{3}{8} = \frac{9}{?}$ 24

e. Find a fraction equivalent to $\frac{3}{5}$ that has a denominator of 10. Next find a fraction equivalent to $\frac{1}{2}$ with a denominator of 10. Then subtract the second fraction you found from the first fraction. $\frac{6}{10} - \frac{5}{10} = \frac{1}{10}$

Reduce each fraction to lowest terms.

f. $\frac{3}{6}$ $\frac{1}{2}$ **g.** $\frac{8}{10}$ $\frac{4}{5}$ **h.** $\frac{8}{16}$ $\frac{1}{2}$ **i.** $\frac{12}{16}$ $\frac{3}{4}$

j. $4\frac{4}{8}$ $4\frac{1}{2}$ **k.** $6\frac{9}{12}$ $6\frac{3}{4}$ **l.** $12\frac{8}{15}$ $12\frac{8}{15}$ **m.** $8\frac{16}{24}$ $8\frac{2}{3}$

Perform each indicated operation and reduce the result.

n. $\frac{5}{12} + \frac{5}{12}$ $\frac{5}{6}$ **o.** $3\frac{7}{10} - 1\frac{1}{10}$ $2\frac{3}{5}$ **p.** $\frac{5}{8} \cdot \frac{2}{3}$ $\frac{5}{12}$

Write each percent as a reduced fraction.

q. 90% $\frac{9}{10}$ **r.** 75% $\frac{3}{4}$ **s.** 5% $\frac{1}{20}$

t. Find a fraction equivalent to $\frac{2}{3}$ that has a denominator of 6. Subtract $\frac{1}{6}$ from the fraction you found and reduce the answer. $\frac{4}{6} - \frac{1}{6} = \frac{3}{6}$; $\frac{3}{6}$ reduces to $\frac{1}{2}$.

Problem set 15

1. Great-grandpa celebrated his seventy-fifth birthday in
(12) 1998. In what year was he born? $1998 - b = 75$; 1923

2. Austin watched the geese fly south. He counted 27 in the
(11) first flock, 38 in the second flock, and 56 in the third flock. How many geese did Austin see in all three flocks?
$27 + 38 + 56 = t$; 121 geese

3. If 40% of the eggs were cracked, what fraction of the eggs
(15) were cracked? $\frac{2}{5}$ of the eggs were cracked.

4. The farmer harvested 9000 bushels of grain from 60 acres.
(13) The crop produced an average of how many bushels of grain for each acre? $60c = 9000$; 150 bushels

5. With your ruler draw a segment $2\frac{1}{2}$ inches long. Draw a
(8) second segment $1\frac{7}{8}$ inches long. The first segment is how much longer than the second segment?

_____ ; $\frac{5}{8}$ in. longer

6. Use digits and symbols to write "the product of three and
(4) five is greater than the sum of three and five."
$3 \cdot 5 > 3 + 5$

7. List the single-digit divisors of 2100. 1, 2, 3, 4, 5, 6, 7
(6)

8. Reduce each fraction or mixed number.
(15)

(a) $\frac{6}{8}$ $\frac{3}{4}$ (b) $2\frac{6}{10}$ $2\frac{3}{5}$

9. Make three equivalent fractions for $\frac{2}{3}$ by multiplying by $\frac{3}{3}$,
(15) $\frac{5}{5}$, and $\frac{6}{6}$. $\frac{6}{9}, \frac{10}{15}, \frac{12}{18}$

10. For each fraction find an equivalent fraction that has a
(15) denominator of 20.

(a) $\frac{3}{5}$ $\frac{12}{20}$ (b) $\frac{1}{2}$ $\frac{10}{20}$ (c) $\frac{3}{4}$ $\frac{15}{20}$

11. Refer to this figure to answer (a), (b), and (c).
(7)

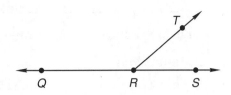

(a) Name the line. $\overleftrightarrow{QS}$ or $\overleftrightarrow{QR}$ or $\overleftrightarrow{RS}$ (or $\overleftrightarrow{SQ}$ or $\overleftrightarrow{RQ}$ or $\overleftrightarrow{SR}$)

(b) Name three rays originating at point R. $\overrightarrow{RT}, \overrightarrow{RQ}, \overrightarrow{RS}$

(c) Name an acute angle. $\angle TRS$ (or $\angle SRT$)

12. Convert each fraction to either a whole number or a
(10) mixed number.

(a) $\dfrac{11}{3}$ $3\frac{2}{3}$ (b) $\dfrac{12}{3}$ 4   (c) $\dfrac{13}{3}$ $4\frac{1}{3}$

Find each missing number:

13. $39 + B = 50$ **14.** $6A = 300$ 50   **15.**
(3) 11   (3)   (3)

16. $C - \$5 = 5¢$ **17.** $\dfrac{W}{35} = 35$ 1225
(3) \$5.05   (3)

Write each percent as a reduced fraction:

18. 80% $\frac{4}{5}$ **19.** 35% $\frac{7}{20}$
(15)   (15)

20. How many $\frac{1}{8}$'s are in 1? 8
(9)

Simplify:

21. $\dfrac{2}{5} + \dfrac{3}{5} + \dfrac{4}{5}$ $1\frac{4}{5}$ **22.** $3\dfrac{5}{8} - 1\dfrac{3}{8}$ $2\frac{1}{4}$
(10)   (15)

	5
	21
	30
	6
	8
	4
	7
	6
	9
	5
	21
+	N 12
	134

23. $\dfrac{4}{3} \cdot \dfrac{3}{4}$ 1   **24.** $\dfrac{3}{4} + \dfrac{3}{4}$ $1\frac{1}{2}$ **25.** $\dfrac{7}{5} + \dfrac{8}{5}$ 3
(9)   (15)   (10)

26. $\dfrac{11}{12} - \dfrac{1}{12}$ $\frac{5}{6}$ **27.** $\dfrac{5}{6} \cdot \dfrac{2}{3}$ $\frac{5}{9}$ **28.** $(11)(6 + 7)$
(15)   (15)   (2) 143

29.
$\frac{2}{6} + \frac{1}{6} = \frac{3}{6} = \frac{1}{2}$

29. Find a fraction equal to $\frac{1}{3}$ that has a denominator of 6.
(15) Add the fraction to $\frac{1}{6}$ and reduce the answer.

30.
$\frac{8}{3} \cdot \frac{1}{4} = \frac{8}{12} = \frac{2}{3}$

30. Write $2\frac{2}{3}$ as an improper fraction. Then multiply the
(10,15) improper fraction by $\frac{1}{4}$ and reduce the product.

LESSON 16

U.S. Customary System

Facts Practice: 40 Fractions to Reduce (Test D in Test Masters)

Mental Math:

a. 10 − 20   b. 15¢ × 10   c. $1.00 − 18¢

d. 4 × 23   e. 875 − 750   f. $\frac{1}{2}$ of $\frac{1}{3}$

g. Start with 2 score and 10, ÷ 2, × 3, − 3, ÷ 9, + 2, ÷ 5.

Problem Solving:

Brenda has 8 coins totaling 50¢. What combinations of coins could Brenda have?

Mental Math:
a. −10
b. $1.50
c. 82¢
d. 92
e. 125
f. $\frac{1}{6}$
g. 2
Problem Solving:
5 pennies, 2 dimes, 1 quarter, or 6 nickels and 2 dimes

One of the characteristics of a civilization is the use of an agreed-upon system of measurement. The fair exchange of goods and services requires consistent units of weight, volume, and length. In a technological society the necessity for a standard system of measurement is even greater.

There are two systems of measurement currently used in the United States. The traditional system of measurement, with units such as feet, gallons, and pounds, was adopted from England. This system used to be known as the English system, but is now referred to as the **U.S. Customary System.**

The second system of measurement used in the United States is the system used in the rest of the world. It is known as the **International System** (or SI, for *Système international*) or the **metric system.** The metric system has units such as meters, liters, and kilograms.

We will consider both systems of measurement over many lessons. In this lesson we will consider units of the U.S. Customary System. We can measure many characteristics of objects including their dimensions, weight, volume, and temperature. Each type of measurement has a set of units. The following tables show units of length, weight, liquid measure, and temperature in the U.S. system. We should remember the equivalent measures, have a "feel" for the units so that we can estimate measures, and be able to use tools and read scales when measuring.

UNITS OF WEIGHT

16 ounces (oz) = 1 pound (lb)
2000 pounds = 1 ton (t)

Example 1   What is the load capacity in pounds of a $\frac{1}{2}$-ton pick-up truck?

Solution   A $\frac{1}{2}$-ton pick-up truck can carry a load of $\frac{1}{2}$ of a ton. Since a ton is 2000 pounds, half of a ton is **1000 pounds.**

The following table and examples demonstrate using units of length.

UNITS OF LENGTH

12 inches (in.) = 1 foot (ft)
3 feet = 1 yard (yd)
1760 yards = 1 mile (mi)
5280 feet = 1 mile

Example 2   One yard is how many inches?

Solution   One yard is 3 feet long. One foot is 12 inches long. Thus, 1 yard is 36 inches long.

$$1 \text{ yard} = 3 \times 12 \text{ inches} = \textbf{36 inches}$$

Example 3   A mountain bicycle is about how many feet long?

Solution   We should develop a feel for various units of measure. Most mountain bicycles are about $5\frac{1}{2}$ feet long, so a good estimate would be **about 5 or 6 feet.**

Just as an inch ruler is divided successively in half, so units of liquid measure are divided successively in half. Half of a gallon is a half gallon. Half of a half gallon is a quart. Half of a quart is a pint. Half of a pint is a cup.

The capacity of each of these containers is half the capacity of the next larger container.

The following table and example demonstrates using units of liquid measure.

UNITS OF LIQUID MEASURE

8 ounces (oz) = 1 cup (c)
2 cups = 1 pint (pt)
2 pints = 1 quart (qt)
4 quarts = 1 gallon (gal)

Example 4   Steve always drinks at least 8 cups of water every day. How many quarts is that?

Solution   Two cups is a pint, so 8 cups is 4 pints. Two pints is a quart, so 4 pints is **2 quarts.**

The following table and example demonstrate using units of temperature.

Fahrenheit Temperature Scale

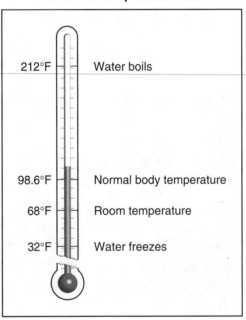

Example 5   How many Fahrenheit degrees are between the freezing and boiling temperatures of water?

Solution   212°F − 32°F = **180°F**

Practice   **a.** A tall man may be over how many yards tall?   2 yards

b. How many quarts is half a gallon?   2 quarts

c. When Chad was born, he weighed 8 lb, 7 oz. Is that weight closer to 8 lb or closer to 9 lb? 8 lb

Simplify:

d. $\frac{3}{8}$ in. + $\frac{5}{8}$ in. 1 in.   **e.** 32°F + 180°F 212°F

f. 2(3 ft + 4 ft) 14 ft

Problem set 16

1. $^{(14)}$ Thirty-five of the one hundred eighteen students who took the test earned an A. How many of the students did not earn an A on the test? $35 + n = 118$; 83 students

2. $^{(13)}$ At Henry's egg ranch 18 eggs are packaged in each carton. How many cartons would be needed to package 4500 eggs?
$18c = 4500$; 250 cartons

3. $^{(11)}$ Three hundred twenty-four ducks floated peacefully on the lake. As the first shot rang out, all but twenty-seven of the ducks flew away. How many ducks flew away?
$324 - f = 27$; 297 ducks

4. $^{(5)}$ Write the integer 250 in expanded notation.
$(2 \times 100) + (5 \times 10)$

5. $^{(10,15)}$ Replace each circle with the proper comparison symbol.

(a) $\frac{8}{10}$ ⃝= $\frac{4}{5}$ (b) $\frac{8}{5}$ ⃝> $1\frac{2}{5}$

6. $^{(8)}$ Use an inch ruler to find *AB*, *CB*, and *CA* to the nearest sixteenth of an inch. *AB* is $1\frac{3}{8}$ in.; *CB* is $1\frac{3}{8}$ in.; *CA* is $2\frac{3}{4}$ in.

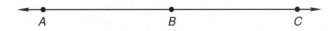

7. $^{(15)}$ Write each number as a reduced fraction or mixed number.

(a) $\frac{8}{12}$ $\frac{2}{3}$ (b) 40% $\frac{2}{5}$ (c) $6\frac{10}{12}$ $6\frac{5}{6}$

8. $^{(10)}$ Draw and shade circles to show that $3\frac{1}{3}$ equals $\frac{10}{3}$.

8.

9. $^{(15)}$ For each fraction, find an equivalent fraction that has a denominator of 24.

(a) $\frac{5}{6}$ $\frac{20}{24}$ (b) $\frac{3}{8}$ $\frac{9}{24}$ (c) $\frac{1}{4}$ $\frac{6}{24}$

10. (a) What percent of a yard is a foot? $33\frac{1}{3}\%$
(16)

(b) What fraction of a gallon is a quart? $\frac{1}{4}$

11. The number 630 is divisible by which single-digit
(6) numbers? $1, 2, 3, 5, 6, 7, 9$

12. Convert each fraction to either a whole number or a
(10) mixed number.

(a) $\dfrac{16}{7}$ $2\frac{2}{7}$ (b) $3\dfrac{16}{8}$ 5 (c) $2\dfrac{16}{9}$ $3\frac{7}{9}$

Find each missing number:

13.
(3)
$\begin{array}{r} M \\ -\ 1776 \\ \hline 87 \end{array}$ 1863

14. $\dfrac{1001}{M} = 13$ 77
(3)

15.
(3)
$\begin{array}{r} 43 \\ 7 \\ 86 \\ 24 \\ 7 \\ 6 \\ +\ N \\ \hline 175 \end{array}$ 2

16.
(3)
$\begin{array}{r} \$16.25 \\ -\ \ \ \ \ B \\ \hline \$10.15 \end{array}$ $\$6.10$

17.
(3)
$\begin{array}{r} 42 \\ \times\ \ D \\ \hline 1764 \end{array}$ 42

Simplify:

18. $3\dfrac{3}{4} - 1\dfrac{1}{4}$ $2\frac{1}{2}$
(15)

19. $\dfrac{3}{10}$ in. $+ \dfrac{8}{10}$ in. $1\frac{1}{10}$ in.
(10,16)

20. $\dfrac{3}{4} \times \dfrac{1}{3}$ $\frac{1}{4}$
(15)

21. $\dfrac{4}{3} \cdot \dfrac{3}{2}$ 2
(10)

22. $\dfrac{10,000}{16}$ 625
(1)

23. $\dfrac{100\%}{8}$ $12\frac{1}{2}\%$
(10,15)

24. $9\overline{)70,000}$ $7,777\frac{7}{9}$
(10)

25. $45 \cdot 45$ 2025
(1)

26. Find the next three numbers in this sequence.
(2,8)

$$\frac{1}{16}, \frac{1}{8}, \frac{3}{16}, \dots$$ $\frac{1}{4}, \frac{5}{16}, \frac{3}{8}$

27. If two intersecting lines are not perpendicular, then they
(7) form which two types of angles? acute angle, obtuse angle

28. Convert $2\frac{1}{2}$ and $1\frac{2}{3}$ to improper fractions and multiply the
(10) improper fractions. Then convert the product to a mixed
number. $\frac{5}{2} \times \frac{5}{3} = \frac{25}{6} = 4\frac{1}{6}$

29. Find a fraction equivalent to $\frac{2}{3}$ that has a denominator of 6.
$^{(15)}$ Then add that fraction to $\frac{1}{6}$. What is the sum? $\frac{4}{6} + \frac{1}{6} = \frac{5}{6}$

30. How many $\frac{3}{8}$'s are in 1?
$^{(9)}$

LESSON
17

Measuring Angles with a Protractor

Facts Practice: 40 Fractions to Reduce (Test D in Test Masters)

Mental Math:

    a. $3.50 + $1.50   **b.** $3.60 ÷ 10   **c.** $10.00 − $6.40

    d. 5 × 33   **e.** 250 − 125   **f.** $\frac{1}{2}$ of 32

    g. Start with 3 score and 15, ÷ 3, × 2, ÷ 5, × 10, ÷ 2, − 25, ÷ 5.

Problem Solving:

    Nelson held a die (number cube) between two fingers that covered opposite faces of the die. On two of the faces that Nelson could see were 3 dots and 5 dots. How many dots were on each of the two faces his fingers covered?

Materials needed:

- Protractors for students
- "Activity Master 3" from the *Math 87 Test Masters*

In Lesson 7 we discussed angles and classified them as acute, right, obtuse, or straight. In this lesson we will begin measuring angles.

Angles are commonly measured in units called **degrees.** The abbreviation for degrees is a small circle written above and to the right of the number. One full rotation, a full circle, measures 360 degrees.

A full circle measures 360°.

A half circle measures half of 360°, which is 180°.

A half circle measures 180°.

One fourth of a full rotation is a right angle. A right angle measures one fourth of 360°, which is 90°.

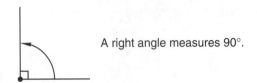

A right angle measures 90°.

Thus, the measure of an acute angle is less than 90°, and the measure of an obtuse angle is greater than 90° but less than 180°. An angle that measures 180° is a straight angle. The chart below summarizes the types of angles and their measures.

Type of Angle	Measure
Acute angle	Greater than 0° but less than 90°
Right angle	Exactly 90°
Obtuse angle	Greater than 90° but less than 180°
Straight angle	Exactly 180°

A **protractor** may be used to measure angles. The protractor is placed on the angle to be measured so that the vertex is under the dot, circle, or cross-mark of the protractor, and one side of the angle is under the zero mark at either end of the scale of the protractor.

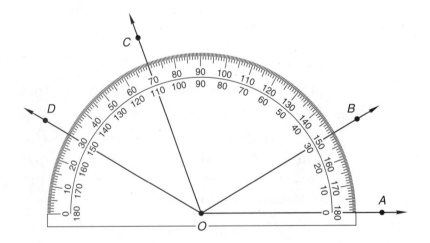

The measures of the three angles shown are as follows:

$$\angle AOB = 30° \qquad \angle AOC = 110° \qquad \angle AOD = 150°$$

Notice that there are two scales on a protractor, one starting from the left side, the other from the right. One way to check whether you are reading from the correct scale is to consider whether you are measuring an acute angle or an obtuse angle.

Example 1   Find the measure of each angle.

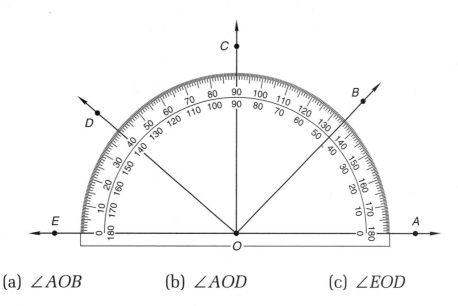

(a) ∠AOB   (b) ∠AOD   (c) ∠EOD

Solution   (a) ∠AOB is an acute angle. We use the scale with the numbers less than 90. Ray OB passes through the mark halfway between 40 and 50. Thus, the measure of ∠AOB is **45°**.

(b) ∠AOD is an obtuse angle. We read from the scale with numbers greater than 90. The measure of ∠AOD is **140°**.

(c) ∠EOD is an acute angle. The measure of ∠EOD is **40°**.

Example 2   Use a protractor to draw a 60° angle.

Solution   We use a ruler or the straight edge of the protractor to draw a ray. Our sketch of the ray should be longer than half the diameter of the protractor. Then we carefully position the protractor so that it is centered over the endpoint of the ray, with the ray extending through either the left or right 0° mark.

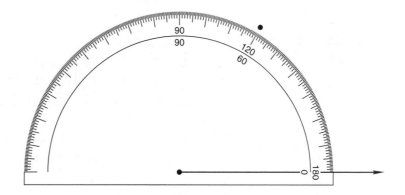

From the zero mark we follow the curve of the protractor to the 60 degree mark and make a dot on the paper at that mark.

Then we remove the protractor and draw the second ray of the angle from the endpoint of the first ray through the dot we made at the 60° mark. This completes the 60° angle.

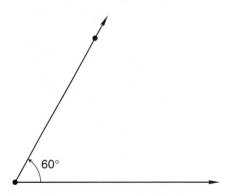

60°

Practice   Find the measure of each angle.

For additional practice using a protractor to measure angles, see "Activity Master 3" in the *Math 87 Test Masters*.

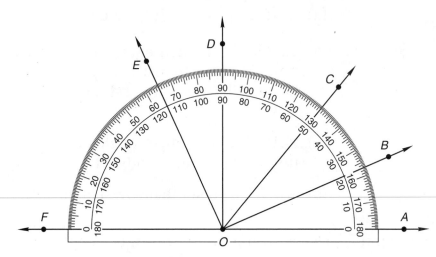

a. ∠AOD 90°   **b.** ∠AOC 50°   **c.** ∠AOE 115°

d. ∠FOE 65°   **e.** ∠FOC 130°   **f.** ∠AOB 23°

Use your protractor to draw each of these angles.

g. 45° 45°   **h.** 120° 120°   **i.** 100° 100°   **j.** 80° 80°

Problem set   **1.** Prince Caspian assembled his soldiers at the bank of the
17 (11) river. Two thousand, four hundred twenty had gathered by noon. An additional five thousand, ninety arrived after noon. How many soldiers arrived in all?
2420 + 5090 = *t*; 7510 soldiers

2. Three twentieths of the test answers were incorrect. What
(14) fraction of the answers were correct? $\frac{3}{20}$ + *f* = $\frac{20}{20}$; $\frac{17}{20}$ of the answers

3. There are 210 students in the first-year physical education
(13) class. If they are equally divided into 15 squads, how many students will be in each squad? 15*s* = 210; 14 students

4. How many years were there from 1492 to 1620?
(12) $1620 - 1492 = d$; 128 years

5. Which of the following does not equal $1\frac{1}{3}$?   C. $\frac{5}{3}$
(10,15)

A. $\frac{4}{3}$ B. $1\frac{2}{6}$ C. $\frac{5}{3}$ D. $1\frac{4}{12}$

6. Refer to this figure to answer the
(7,17) following questions:

6.(a) $\overleftrightarrow{QR}$ (or $\overleftrightarrow{RQ}$)

(b) $\overleftrightarrow{RT}$ (or $\overleftrightarrow{TR}$)

(a) Which line is parallel to $\overleftrightarrow{ST}$?

(b) Which line is perpendicular to $\overleftrightarrow{ST}$?

(c) Angle QRT measures how many degrees?   90°

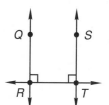

7. Write each number as a reduced fraction or mixed number.
(15)

(a) $\frac{12}{16}$ $\frac{3}{4}$ (b) $3\frac{12}{18}$ $3\frac{2}{3}$ (c) 25% $\frac{1}{4}$

8. How many ounces is 2 lb, 8 oz?   40 oz
(16)

9. Complete each equivalent fraction.
(15)

(a) $\frac{2}{9} = \frac{?}{18}$ 4   (b) $\frac{1}{3} = \frac{?}{18}$ 6   (c) $\frac{5}{6} = \frac{?}{18}$ 15

10. Use your protractor to draw a 30° angle.
(17)

11. (a) What factors of 20 are also factors of 50?   1, 2, 5, 10
(6)

(b) What is the GCF of 20 and 50?   10

12.

12. Draw $\overline{RS}$ $1\frac{3}{4}$ in. long. Then draw ray ST perpendicular
(7,8) to $\overline{RS}$.

Find each missing number:

13. $X - 231 = 141$
(3)   372

14. $\$6.30 + y = \$25$
(3) $18.70

15. $8W = \$30.00$
(3) $3.75

16. $\dfrac{100\%}{M} = 20\%$
(3)   5

17.
(3)

$$\begin{array}{r} 58 \\ 4 \\ 2 \\ 62 \\ N \\ + \quad 6 \\ \hline 143 \end{array}$$ 11

Simplify:

18. $3\frac{5}{6} - 1\frac{1}{6}$ $2\frac{2}{3}$
(15)

19. $\frac{1}{2} \cdot \frac{2}{3}$ $\frac{1}{3}$
(15)

20. $\dfrac{\$100.00}{40}$ $2.50
(1)

21. $55 \cdot 55$ 3025
(1)

22. $2(8 \text{ in.} + 6 \text{ in.})$ 28 in.
(2,16)

23. $\dfrac{3}{4}$ in. $+ \dfrac{3}{4}$ in. $1\frac{1}{2}$ in.
(15,16)

24. $\dfrac{15}{16}$ in. $- \dfrac{3}{16}$ in. $\frac{3}{4}$ in.
(15,16)

25. $\dfrac{1}{2} \cdot \dfrac{4}{3} \cdot \dfrac{9}{2}$ 3
(10)

26. The bill was $15.17. Nathan gave the cashier a $20 bill
(1) and a quarter. Name the coins and bills he probably got
back in change. $5 bill, 1 nickel, 3 pennies

27. (a) Compare: $\left(\dfrac{1}{2} \cdot \dfrac{3}{4}\right) \cdot \dfrac{2}{3}$ ⊜ $\dfrac{1}{2}\left(\dfrac{3}{4} \cdot \dfrac{2}{3}\right)$
(2,9)

(b) What property is illustrated by this comparison?
associative property of multiplication

28. What percent of a dollar is a nickel? 5%
(8)

29. Write $3\frac{3}{4}$ as an improper fraction. Then write its reciprocal.
(9,10) $\frac{15}{4}$, $\frac{4}{15}$

30. Find a fraction equal to $\frac{3}{4}$ with a denominator of 8. Add the
(15) fraction to $\frac{5}{8}$. Write the sum as a mixed number.
$\frac{6}{8} + \frac{5}{8} = \frac{11}{8} = 1\frac{3}{8}$

LESSON
18

Polygons •
Similar and Congruent

Mental Math:
a. $5.50
b. $16.50
c. $7.50
d. 144
e. 125
f. $\frac{1}{8}$
g. 7
Problem Solving:
8-17-32
8-32-17
17-8-32
17-32-8
32-8-17
32-17-8

Facts Practice: 40 Fractions to Reduce (Test D in Test Masters)

Mental Math:

a. $3.75 + $1.75   b. $1.65 × 10   c. $20.00 − $12.50
d. 6 × 24   e. 375 − 250   f. $\frac{1}{2}$ of $\frac{1}{4}$
g. Start with two score, × 2, + 1, ÷ 9, × 3, + 1, ÷ 4.

Problem Solving:

Sarah remembered that the three numbers to her combination
lock were 17, 32, and 8, but she could not remember the order.
She knew to turn the dial clockwise, then counterclockwise, then
clockwise. List all possible combinations for Sarah's lock.

Polygons When three or more line segments are connected to enclose a portion of a plane, a **polygon** is formed. The word *polygon* comes from the ancient Greeks and means "many angles." The name of a polygon tells how many angles and sides the polygon has.

Names of Polygons

Name of Polygon	Number of Sides	Name of Polygon	Number of Sides
Triangle	3	Octagon	8
Quadrilateral	4	Nonagon	9
Pentagon	5	Decagon	10
Hexagon	6	Undecagon	11
Heptagon	7	Dodecagon	12
A polygon with more than 12 sides may be referred to as an *n*-gon, with *n* being the number of sides. Thus, a polygon with 15 sides is a 15-gon.			

Two sides of a polygon meet at a point called the vertex. (The plural of vertex is **vertices.**) A particular polygon may be identified by naming the letters of its vertices in order. Any letter may be first. The rest of the letters can be named clockwise or counterclockwise. This polygon has eight names, which are listed here.

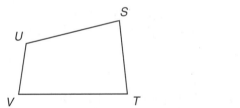

USTV	*TSUV*
UVTS	*TVUS*
STVU	*VTSU*
SUVT	*VUST*

If all the sides of a polygon have the same length and all the angles have the same measure, then the polygon is a **regular polygon.**

Regular and Irregular Polygons

Type	Regular	Irregular
Triangle	△	◁
Quadrilateral	□	▱
Pentagon	⬠	⬠
Hexagon	⬡	⬡

Similar and congruent Two figures are **similar** if they are the same shape even though they may vary in size. In the illustration below, triangles I, II, and III are similar. Imagine enlarging (dilating) triangle II as though you were looking through a magnifying glass. By enlarging triangle II, it could become the same size and shape as triangle I. Likewise, triangle III could be reduced in size. As it shrinks it could become the same size as triangle I.

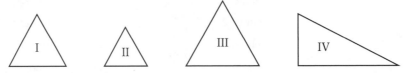

Although triangle IV is a triangle, it is not similar to the other three triangles because its shape is different. Viewing triangle IV through a reducing or enlarging lens will change its size but not its shape.

Figures that are the same shape and size are not only similar, they are also **congruent.** All three of the triangles below are similar, but only triangles *ABC* and *DEF* are congruent. Note that figures may be "flipped" or "turned" without affecting their similarity or congruence.

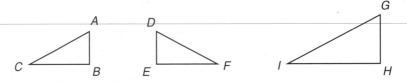

When inspecting polygons to determine if they are similar or congruent, we compare their **corresponding parts.** A triangle has six parts—three sides and three angles. If the six parts of one triangle have the same measures as the six corresponding parts of another triangle, the triangles are congruent. Referring back to the illustration of triangle *ABC* ($\triangle ABC$) and triangle *DEF* ($\triangle DEF$), we identify the following corresponding parts:

$$\angle A \text{ corresponds to } \angle D$$
$$\angle B \text{ corresponds to } \angle E$$
$$\angle C \text{ corresponds to } \angle F$$
$$\overline{AB} \text{ corresponds to } \overline{DE}$$
$$\overline{BC} \text{ corresponds to } \overline{EF}$$
$$\overline{CA} \text{ corresponds to } \overline{FD}$$

Notice that the corresponding angles of similar figures have the same measure, even though the corresponding sides may be different lengths.

Example 1 (a) Name this polygon.

(b) Is the polygon regular or irregular?

Solution (a) **pentagon** (b) **irregular**

Example 2 (a) Which of these quadrilaterals appear to be similar?

(b) Which of these quadrilaterals appear to be congruent?

Solution (a) **I, II, IV** (b) **I, IV**

Example 3 (a) Which angle in △XYZ corresponds to ∠A in △ABC?

(b) Which side in △XYZ corresponds to $\overline{BC}$ in △ABC?

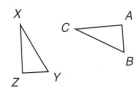

Solution (a) **∠Z** (b) **$\overline{YX}$**

Practice **a.** What is the shape of a stop sign? octagon

b. What do we usually call a regular quadrilateral? square

c. What kind of angle is each angle of a regular triangle? acute angle

d. Are all squares similar? yes

e. Are all squares congruent? no

f. Referring to Example 3, which angle in △ABC corresponds to ∠Y in △XYZ? ∠B

g. Referring to Example 2, are the angles in figure II larger in measure, smaller in measure, or equal in measure to the corresponding angles in figure I? equal in measure

Problem set 18

1. The Collins family completed the 3300-mile coast-to-coast
$^{(13)}$ drive in 6 days. They traveled an average of how many miles each day? $6d = 3300$; 550 miles

2. On their return trip, the Collins family drove four
$^{(11)}$ hundred fifty-six miles the first day and five hundred seventeen miles the second day. How far did they travel on the first two days of their return trip?
$456 + 517 = t$; 973 miles

3. Albert ran 3977 meters of the 5000-meter race, but
(14) walked the rest of the way. How many meters of the race
did Albert walk? 3977 + W = 5000; 1023 meters

4. One billion is how much greater than ten million? Use
(5,12) words to write the answer.
1,000,000,000 − 10,000,000 = d; nine hundred ninety million

5. (a) Arrange these numbers in order from least to greatest:
(4,10)

$$\frac{5}{3}, -1, \frac{3}{4}, 0, 1 \quad -1, 0, \frac{3}{4}, 1, \frac{5}{3}$$

(b) Which of these numbers are not positive? −1, 0

6. In rectangle *ABCD*, which side is
(7) parallel to side *BC*? side *AD*

7. Refer to this number line to answer questions (a) and (b).
(4)

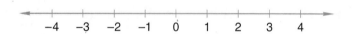

(a) What integer is two units to the left of the origin? −2

(b) What integer is seven units to the right of −3? 4

8. Write each number as a reduced fraction or mixed
(15) number.

(a) 2% $\frac{1}{50}$ (b) $\frac{12}{20}$ $\frac{3}{5}$ (c) $6\frac{15}{20}$ $6\frac{3}{4}$

9. For each fraction find an equivalent fraction that has a
(15) denominator of 30.

(a) $\frac{4}{5}$ $\frac{24}{30}$ (b) $\frac{2}{3}$ $\frac{20}{30}$ (c) $\frac{1}{6}$ $\frac{5}{30}$

10. An octagon has how many more sides than a pentagon?
(18) 3 sides

11.(a)

11. (a) Draw a triangle that has one obtuse angle.
(7,18)

(b) What kind of angles are the other two angles of the
triangle? acute angles

12. (a) What percent of the circle is
(8,15) shaded? 25%

(b) What fraction of the circle is not
shaded? $\frac{3}{4}$

Find each missing number:

13. $x - \dfrac{3}{8} = \dfrac{5}{8}$ **14.** $y + \dfrac{3}{10} = \dfrac{7}{10}$ **15.**
(9) $\frac{8}{8}$ or 1   (9,15) $\frac{4}{10}$ or $\frac{2}{5}$ (3)

$$\begin{array}{r} 4 \\ 7 \\ 8 \\ 15 \\ 4 \\ 6 \\ 5 \\ 7 \\ 8 \\ 21 \\ + \ N \\ \hline 93 \end{array}$$

16. $\dfrac{5}{6} - m = \dfrac{1}{6}$ **17.** $\dfrac{3}{4}x = 1$ $\frac{4}{3}$
(9,15) $\frac{4}{6}$ or $\frac{2}{3}$ (9)

Simplify:

18. $5\dfrac{7}{10} - \dfrac{3}{10}$ $5\frac{2}{5}$ **19.** $\dfrac{3}{2} \cdot \dfrac{2}{4}$ $\frac{3}{4}$
(15)   (15)

20. $\dfrac{2025}{45}$ 45   **21.** $\begin{array}{r} 750 \\ \times \ \ 80 \\ \hline 60{,}000 \end{array}$
(1)   (1)   N 8

22. $21 \cdot 21$ 441   **23.** $2(50 \text{ in.} + 40 \text{ in.})$ 180 in.
(1)   (2,16)

24. What percent of a pound is 8 ounces?   50%
(16)

25. (a) How many degrees is $\frac{1}{4}$ of a circle or $\frac{1}{4}$ of a full turn?
(17)   90°
    (b) How many degrees is $\frac{1}{6}$ of a circle or $\frac{1}{6}$ of a full turn?
       60°

26. (a) Use a protractor to draw a 135° angle.   135°
(17)

    (b) A 135° angle is how many degrees less than a straight
       angle?   45°

27. Refer to these triangles to answer questions (a), (b), and (c).
(18)

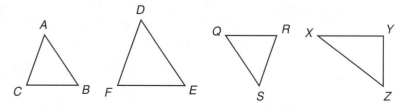

27.(a) $\triangle SQR$ (a) Which triangle appears to be congruent to $\triangle ABC$?

               (b) Which triangle is not similar to $\triangle ABC$? $\triangle XYZ$

               (c) Which angle in $\triangle DEF$ corresponds to $\angle R$ in $\triangle SQR$? $\angle F$

28. Write a fraction equal to $\frac{1}{2}$ with a denominator of 6, and a
(15) fraction equal to $\frac{1}{3}$ with a denominator of 6. Then add the
fractions. $\frac{3}{6} + \frac{2}{6} = \frac{5}{6}$

29. Write $2\frac{1}{4}$ as an improper fraction and multiply the
(9,10) improper fraction by the reciprocal of $\frac{3}{4}$. $\frac{9}{4} \cdot \frac{4}{3} = \frac{36}{12} = 3$

30.

1 in.   1 in.

1 in.

30. Use your ruler to draw a triangle with each side 1 inch
(8,18) long. Is the triangle regular or irregular? regular

LESSON 19

Perimeter

Facts Practice: 30 Improper Fractions and Mixed Numbers
(Test C in Test Masters)

Mental Math:

   a. $8.25 + $1.75   **b.** $12.00 ÷ 10   **c.** $1.00 − 76¢

   d. 7 × 32   **e.** 625 − 250   **f.** $\frac{1}{2}$ of 120

   g. Start with 4 dozen, ÷ 6, × 5, + 2, ÷ 6, × 7, + 1, ÷ 2, − 1, ÷ 2.

Problem Solving:

   Billy has 25 tickets, Bobby has 12 tickets, and Mary has 8 tickets.
How many tickets does Billy need to give to Bobby and give to
Mary so that they all have the same number of tickets?

Mental Math:
a. $10.00
b. $1.20
c. 24¢
d. 224
e. 375
f. 60
g. 12

Problem Solving:
Billy gives Bobby 3 tickets and Mary 7 tickets. (Then they each have 15.)

The distance around a polygon is the **perimeter** of the
polygon. To find the perimeter of a polygon, we add the
lengths of its sides.

Example 1   What is the perimeter of this rectangle?

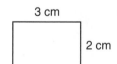
3 cm

2 cm

Solution   The opposite sides of a rectangle are equal
in length. Tracing around the rectangle,
our pencil travels 3 cm, then 2 cm, then
3 cm, then 2 cm. Thus, the perimeter is

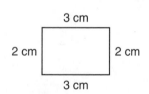
3 cm

2 cm   2 cm

3 cm

   3 cm + 2 cm + 3 cm + 2 cm = **10 cm**

Example 2   What is the perimeter of this regular
hexagon?

8 mm

Solution   All sides of a regular polygon are equal in length. Thus the perimeter of this hexagon is

8 mm + 8 mm + 8 mm + 8 mm + 8 mm + 8 mm = **48 mm**

or

6 × 8 mm = **48 mm**

Example 3   Find the perimeter of this polygon. All angles are right angles. Dimensions are in feet.

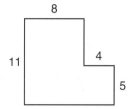

Solution   We will use the letters a and b to refer to the unmarked sides. Notice that side a plus the side marked 5 totals 11 feet.

$a + 5 = 11$ So side a is 6 ft.

Also notice that side b equals the total lengths of the sides marked 8 and 4.

$8 + 4 = b$ So side b is 12 ft.

The perimeter of the figure in feet is

8 ft + 6 ft + 4 ft + 5 ft + 12 ft + 11 ft = **46 ft**

Example 4   The perimeter of a square is 48 ft. How long is each side of the square?

Solution   A square has four sides whose lengths are equal. The sum of the four lengths is 48 ft. Here are two ways to think about this problem:

1. The sum of what 4 identical addends is 48?

_____ + _____ + _____ + _____ = 48 ft

2. What number multiplied by 4 equals 48?

4 × _____ = 48 ft

As we think about the problem the second way, we can see that we can divide 48 ft by 4 to find the length of each side.

$$\frac{12}{4\overline{)48}}$$

The length of each side of the square is **12 ft.**

Example 5　Ray wants to fence some grazing land for his sheep. He made this sketch of his pasture. How many feet of wire fence does he need?

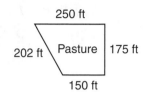

250 ft

202 ft　Pasture　175 ft

150 ft

Solution　We add the lengths of the sides to find how many feet of fence Ray needs.

$$250 \text{ ft} + 175 \text{ ft} + 150 \text{ ft} + 202 \text{ ft} = 777 \text{ ft}$$

We see that Ray needs **777 ft** of wire fence.

Practice*　**a.** What is the perimeter of this quadrilateral? 13 in.

3 in.　　3 in.　　2 in.　　5 in.

b. What is the perimeter of this regular pentagon? 25 cm

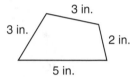

5 cm

c. If each side of a regular octagon is 12 inches, what is its perimeter? 96 inches

d. What is the perimeter of this hexagon? 30 in.

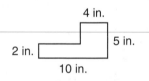

4 in.

2 in.　　5 in.

10 in.

e. MacGregor has 100 feet of wire fence that he plans to use to surround a square garden. Each side of his garden will be how many feet long? 25 feet

Problem set 19

1. One eighth of the students in the class were left-handed.
(14) What fraction of the students were not left-handed?
$\frac{1}{8} + d = \frac{8}{8}$; $\frac{7}{8}$ of the students

2. The theater was full when the horror film began. Seventy-
(11) six people left before the movie ended. One hundred twenty-four people remained. How many people were in the theater when it was full? $f - 76 = 124$; 200 people

3. The Pie King restaurant cuts each pie into 6 slices. The
(13) restaurant served 84 pies one week. How many slices of pie were served? $84 \times 6 = t$; 504 slices of pie

4. President Lincoln began his speech, "Four score and
(1) seven years ago ..." How many years is four score and seven? 87 years

5.(a) eighteen million, seven hundred thousand

5. (a) Use words to write 18700000.
(5)
    (b) Write 874 in expanded notation.
        $(8 \times 100) + (7 \times 10) + (4 \times 1)$

6. Use digits and other symbols to write "three minus seven
(4) equals negative four." $3 - 7 = -4$

7. At what temperatures on the Fahrenheit scale does water
(16) freeze and boil?   freezes at 32°F; boils at 212°F

8. Find the perimeter of this rectangle.
(19) 28 cm

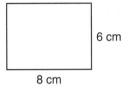
6 cm

8 cm

9. Write each number as a reduced fraction or mixed number.
(15)

    (a) $3\dfrac{16}{24}$ $3\frac{2}{3}$ (b) $\dfrac{15}{24}$ $\frac{5}{8}$ (c) 4% $\frac{1}{25}$

10. Find *a* and *b* to complete each equivalent fraction.
(15)

    (a) $\dfrac{3}{4} = \dfrac{a}{36}$ 27   (b) $\dfrac{4}{9} = \dfrac{b}{36}$ 16

11. Draw a sketch of a regular pentagon.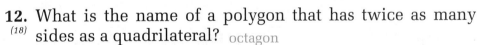
(18)

12. What is the name of a polygon that has twice as many
(18) sides as a quadrilateral? octagon

13. (a) Each angle of a rectangle measures how many degrees?
(17)   90°
    (b) The four angles of a rectangle total how many degrees?
     360°

Find each missing number:

14.
(3)
$$\begin{array}{r} A \quad 7451 \\ +\ 1547 \\ \hline 8998 \end{array}$$

15.
(3)
$$\begin{array}{r} B \quad \$1.37 \\ \times\ 30 \\ \hline \$41.10 \end{array}$$

16.
(3)
$$\begin{array}{r} 4 \\ 8 \\ 7 \\ 29 \\ 4 \\ 6 \\ 8 \\ N \quad 7 \\ +\ 5 \\ \hline 78 \end{array}$$

17.
(3)
$$\begin{array}{r} \$0.32 \\ \times \qquad C \quad 23 \\ \hline \$7.36 \end{array}$$

18.
(3)
$$\begin{array}{r} \$26.57 \\ +\qquad D \quad \$3.53 \\ \hline \$30.10 \end{array}$$

Simplify:

19. $\dfrac{2}{3} + \dfrac{2}{3} + \dfrac{2}{3}$ 2   **20.** $3\dfrac{7}{8} - \dfrac{5}{8}$ $3\frac{1}{4}$
(10)   *(15)*

21. $\dfrac{2}{3} \cdot \dfrac{3}{7}$ $\frac{2}{7}$
(15)

22. $3\dfrac{7}{8} + \dfrac{5}{8}$ $4\frac{1}{2}$
(15)

23. $50 \cdot 50$ 2500
(1)

24. $\dfrac{100,100}{11}$ 9,100
(1)

25. (a) How many $\frac{1}{2}$'s are in 1?   2
(9)

    (b) Use the answer to part (a) to find the number of $\frac{1}{2}$'s in 5.
    10

26.

$2\frac{1}{2}$ in. C 2 in.

A $1\frac{1}{2}$ in. B

26. Use your ruler to draw segment AB $1\frac{1}{2}$ in. long. Then draw
(7,8) $\overline{BC}$ perpendicular to $\overline{AB}$ 2 in. long. Draw a segment from point A to point C to complete $\triangle ABC$. What is the length of segment AC?

27. Write $3\frac{1}{3}$ as a mixed number and multiply it by the
(9,10) reciprocal of $\frac{2}{3}$. $\frac{10}{3} \cdot \frac{3}{2} = \frac{30}{6} = 5$

28. Find a fraction equal to $\frac{1}{2}$ that has a denominator of 10.
(15) Subtract this fraction from $\frac{9}{10}$. Write the difference as a reduced fraction. $\frac{9}{10} - \frac{5}{10} = \frac{4}{10} = \frac{2}{5}$

29. What percent of a yard is a foot? $33\frac{1}{3}\%$
(8,16)

30. What is the perimeter of this hexagon?
(19) 34 in.

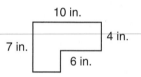

10 in.

7 in.   4 in.

6 in.

**LESSON
20**

Exponents • Rectangular Area, Part 1 • Square Root

Mental Math:
a. $7.25
b. $3.60
c. $0.68
d. 215
e. 500
f. $\frac{3}{8}$
g. 1

Problem Solving:

$\begin{array}{r} 116 \\ 8\overline{)928} \\ \underline{8} \\ 12 \\ \underline{8} \\ 48 \\ \underline{48} \\ 0 \end{array}$

Facts Practice: 40 Fractions to Reduce (Test D in Test Masters)

Mental Math:

  a. $4.75 + $2.50   **b.** 36¢ × 10   **c.** $5.00 − $4.32
  d. 5 × 43   **e.** 625 − 125   **f.** $\frac{1}{2}$ of $\frac{3}{4}$
  g. 10 × 10, − 10, ÷ 10, + 1, − 10, × 10, + 10, ÷ 10

Problem Solving:

  Copy this problem and fill in the missing digits.

$\begin{array}{r} \overline{=\,=\,=} \\ 8\overline{)\,\_\,\_\,\_} \\ = \\ \_\,\_ \\ \overline{=} \\ 4\,\_ \\ \underline{\_\,8} \\ 0 \end{array}$

Exponents We remember that we can show repeated addition by using multiplication.

$$5 + 5 + 5 + 5 \quad \text{has the same value as} \quad 4 \times 5$$

There is also a way to show repeated multiplication. We can show repeated multiplication by using an **exponent.**

$$5 \cdot 5 \cdot 5 \cdot 5 = 5^4$$

In the expression 5^4, the 4 is the exponent and the 5 is the base. The exponent shows how many times the base is to be used as a factor.

$$\text{base} \longrightarrow 5^4 \longleftarrow \text{exponent}$$

The following examples show how we read expressions with exponents, which we call **exponential expressions.**

4^2 "four squared" or "four to the second power"

2^3 "two cubed" or "two to the third power"

5^4 "five to the fourth power"

10^5 "ten to the fifth power"

To find the value of an expression with an exponent, we use the base as a factor the number of times shown by the exponent.

$$5^4 = 5 \cdot 5 \cdot 5 \cdot 5 = 625$$

Example 1 Simplify:

(a) 4^2 (b) 2^3 (c) 10^5 (d) $\left(\dfrac{2}{3}\right)^2$

Solution (a) $4^2 = 4 \cdot 4 = \mathbf{16}$

(b) $2^3 = 2 \cdot 2 \cdot 2 = \mathbf{8}$

(c) $10^5 = 10 \cdot 10 \cdot 10 \cdot 10 \cdot 10 = \mathbf{100{,}000}$

(d) $\left(\dfrac{2}{3}\right)^2 = \dfrac{2}{3} \cdot \dfrac{2}{3} = \dfrac{\mathbf{4}}{\mathbf{9}}$

Example 2 Simplify: $4^2 - 2^3$

Solution We first find the value of each exponential expression. Then we subtract.

$$4^2 - 2^3$$
$$16 - 8 = \mathbf{8}$$

We may use exponents to indicate that units have been multiplied. Recall that when we add or subtract measures with like units, the units do not change.

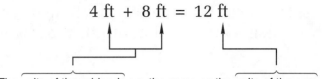

$$4 \text{ ft} + 8 \text{ ft} = 12 \text{ ft}$$

The units of the addends are the same as the units of the sum.

However, when we multiply or divide measures, the units do change.

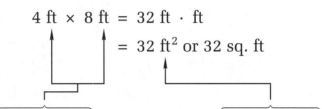

$$4 \text{ ft} \times 8 \text{ ft} = 32 \text{ ft} \cdot \text{ ft}$$
$$= 32 \text{ ft}^2 \text{ or } 32 \text{ sq. ft}$$

The units of the factors are not the same as the units of the product.

The result of multiplying feet and feet is square feet, which we may abbreviate sq. ft or ft^2. Square feet are units used to measure area, as we see in the next section of this lesson.

Rectangular area, part 1   The diagram below represents the floor of a hallway that has been covered with square floor tiles that are 1 foot on each side. How many 1-ft square tiles does it take to cover the floor of the hallway?

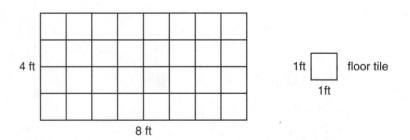

We see that there are 8 floor tiles in each row and 4 rows. So there are 32 1-ft square tiles.

The floor tiles cover the **area** of the hallway. Area is an amount of surface. Floors, ceilings, walls, sheets of paper, and polygons all have areas. If a square is 1 foot on each side, it is a **square foot.** Thus the area of the hallway is 32 square feet.

Other standard square units in the U.S. system include square inches, square yards, and square miles. It is important to distinguish between a unit of length and a unit of area.

Units of length, such as an inch or a foot, are used for measuring distances, not for measuring areas. To measure area, we use units that take up area. Square inches and square feet take up area and are used to measure area. We include the word "square" or the exponent 2 when we designate units of area.

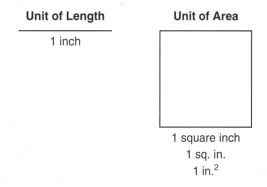

Unit of Length

1 inch

Unit of Area

1 square inch
1 sq. in.
1 in.^{2}

Notice that the area of the rectangular hallway equals the length of the hallway times the width.

> **Area of a rectangle = length × width**

We often abbreviate this formula as

$$A = lw$$

Example 3   What is the area of this rectangle?

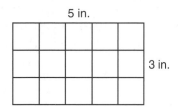

5 in.

3 in.   3 in.

5 in.

Solution   The area of the rectangle is the number of square inches needed to cover the rectangle.

5 in.

3 in.

We can find this number by multiplying the length (5 in.) times the width (3 in.).

$$\text{Area of rectangle} = 5 \text{ in.} \cdot 3 \text{ in.}$$
$$= \mathbf{15 \, in.^2}$$

Example 4   The perimeter of a certain square is 12 inches. What is the area of the square?

Solution   To find the area of the square, we first need to know the length of the sides. The sides of a square are equal in length, so we divide 12 inches by 4 and find that each side is 3 inches. Then we multiply the length (3 in.) by the width (3 in.) to find the area.

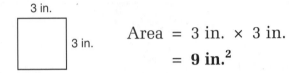

3 in.

3 in.

Area = 3 in. × 3 in.

= **9 in.²**

Example 5   Dickerson Ranch is a level plot of land 4 miles square. The area of Dickerson Ranch is how many square miles?

Solution   Four miles square does not mean 4 square miles. A plot of land that is 4 miles square is square and has sides 4 miles long. So the area is

4 mi × 4 mi = **16 mi²**

Square root   The area of a square and the length of its side are related by "squaring." If we know the length of a side of a square, we square the length to find the area.

3 units squared is 9 square units.

If we know the area of a square, we can find the length of a side by finding the **square root** of the area.

The square root of 9 square units is 3 units.

We often indicate square root with the radical symbol, $\sqrt{}$. Here we show "the square root of 9 equals 3."

$$\sqrt{9} = 3$$

Example 6   Simplify:

(a) $\sqrt{121}$ (b) $\sqrt{8^2}$

Solution   (a) To find the square root of 121 we may think, "What number multiplied by itself equals 121?" Since 10×10 equals 100, we try 11×11 and find that $11^2 = 121$. Therefore, $\sqrt{121}$ equals **11.**

(b) Squaring and finding a square root are inverse operations, so one operation "undoes" the other operation.

$$\sqrt{8^2} = \sqrt{64} = 8$$

Practice* Use words to show how each exponential expression is read. Then find the value of each expression.

a. 4^3 four cubed; 64

b. $\left(\dfrac{1}{2}\right)^2$ one half squared; $\frac{1}{4}$

c. 10^6 ten to the sixth power; 1,000,000

d. In the expression 10^3, what number is the base and what number is the exponent? base is 10; exponent is 3

Find each square root.

e. $\sqrt{100}$ 10   **f.** $\sqrt{400}$ 20   **g.** $\sqrt{15^2}$ 15

Find the area of each rectangle.

h. 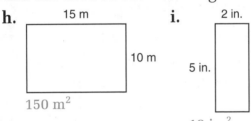   **i.**   **j.**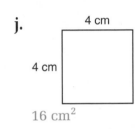

150 m²   10 in.²   16 cm²

k. If the perimeter of a square is 20 cm, what is its area?
25 cm²

l. What is the area of a park that is 100 yards square?
10,000 square yards

**Problem set
20**

1. There were 628 students in 4 dormitories. Each dormitory
(13) housed the same number of students. How many students were housed in each dormitory? $4d = 628$; 157 students

2. Thirty-six bright green parrots flew away while 46 parrots
(11) remained in the tree. How many parrots were in the tree before the 36 parrots flew away? $p - 36 = 46$; 82 parrots

3. Two hundred twenty-five of the six hundred fish in the
(14) lake were trout. How many of the fish were not trout?
$225 + f = 600$; 375 fish

4. Twenty-one thousand, fifty swarmed in through the front
(11) door. Forty-eight thousand, nine hundred seventy-two swarmed in through the back door. Altogether, how many swarmed in through both doors? $21,050 + 48,972 = t$; 70,022

5. This sign is written incorrectly. Show
(1) two ways to correct this sign.
20¢ each; $0.20 each

6. (a) Arrange these numbers in order from least to greatest:
(4,8)

$$\frac{1}{3}, -2, 1, -\frac{1}{2}, 0 \quad -2, -\frac{1}{2}, 0, \frac{1}{3}, 1$$

(b) Which of these numbers are not integers? $\frac{1}{3}$ and $-\frac{1}{2}$

7. Which is the best estimate of how
(8) much of this rectangle is shaded?
B. $33\frac{1}{3}\%$

A. 50%   B. $33\frac{1}{3}\%$ C. 25%   D. 60%

8. Each angle of a rectangle is a right
(7) angle. Which two sides are perpendicular to side *BC*?   sides *DC* and *AB*

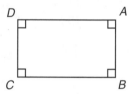

9. Simplify:
(20)

(a) $\left(\frac{1}{3}\right)^3$ $\frac{1}{27}$ (b) 10^4 10,000   (c) $\sqrt{12^2}$ 12

10. For each fraction find an equivalent fraction that has a
(15) denominator of 36.

(a) $\frac{2}{9}$ $\frac{8}{36}$ (b) $\frac{3}{4}$ $\frac{27}{36}$

11. List the factors of each number.
(6)
     (a) 10   1, 2, 5, 10   (b) 7   1, 7   (c) 1   1

12. The perimeter of a certain square is 2 feet. How many
(16,19) inches long is each side of the square?   6 inches

Solve each equation:

13. $36 + a = 54$ 18   **14.** $46 - w = 20$ 26
(3)   (3)

15. $5x = 60$ 12   **16.** $100 = m + 64$ 36
(3)   (3)

17. $y - 14 = 30$ 44   **18.** $\dfrac{60}{y} = 4$ 15
(3)   (3)

Simplify:

19. $3\dfrac{9}{10} - 1\dfrac{3}{10}$ $2\frac{3}{5}$ **20.** $1\dfrac{8}{9} + 1\dfrac{7}{9}$ $3\frac{2}{3}$ **21.** $\dfrac{5}{2} \cdot \dfrac{5}{6}$ $2\frac{1}{12}$

(15)   (10,15)   (10)

22. $\dfrac{6345}{9}$ 705

(1)

23.   360

(1) $\times$ 25

        9000

24. $\dfrac{3}{4} - \left(\dfrac{1}{4} + \dfrac{2}{4} \right)$ 0

(9)

25. $\left(\dfrac{3}{4} - \dfrac{1}{4} \right) + \dfrac{2}{4}$ 1

(10)

26. Find a fraction equivalent to $\frac{1}{2}$ that has a denominator of

(15) 10. Add $\frac{3}{10}$ to that fraction and reduce the sum.

$\frac{5}{10} + \frac{3}{10} = \frac{8}{10} = \frac{4}{5}$

27. Write $1\frac{4}{5}$ as an improper fraction. Then multiply the

(10,15) improper fraction by $\frac{1}{3}$ and reduce the product.

$\frac{9}{5} \cdot \frac{1}{3} = \frac{9}{15} = \frac{3}{5}$

28. Which property is illustrated by this equation?

(2,15)

$$\dfrac{1}{2} \times \dfrac{3}{3} = \dfrac{3}{6}$$

identity property of multiplication

29. A common floor tile is 12 inches square.

(19,20)

    (a) What is the perimeter of a common floor tile?

       48 in. or 4 ft

    (b) What is the area of a common floor tile?

       144 in.² or 1 ft²

30. What is the perimeter of this figure?

(19) 36 in.

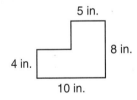

5 in.

8 in.

4 in.

10 in.

INVESTIGATION 2

Using a Compass and Straight Edge, Part 1

Materials needed:

- Compass

- Ruler or straight edge

- Protractor

A **compass** is a tool used to draw **circles** and portions of circles called **arcs.** Compasses are manufactured in various forms. Here we show two forms.

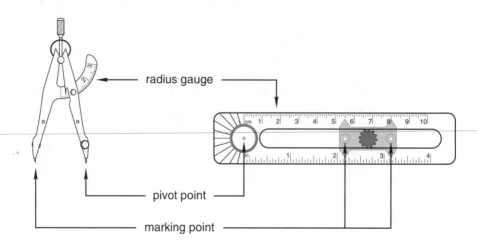

A compass has a pivot point which is placed at the center of the desired circle or arc. The marking point is the pencil point that draws the circle or arc. The radius gauge is a guide for determining the size of the circle by setting the **radius** (plural, **radii**), which is the distance from the center to the circle. The distance between the pivot point and marking point determines the radius of the circle or arc. In this investigation we will construct circles and other geometric figures using a compass and straight edge.

Concentric circles

Concentric circles are two or more circles with a common center. When a pebble is dropped into a quiet pool of water, waves forming concentric circles can be seen. A "bull's-eye" target is another example of a concentric circle.

To draw concentric circles with a compass, we begin by swinging the compass a full turn to make one circle. Then we make additional circles using the same center, changing the radius for each new circle. Practice drawing several concentric circles. See student work.

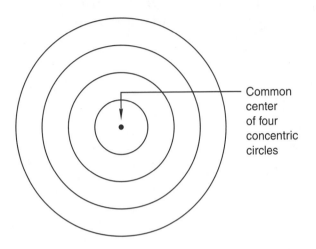

Common center of four concentric circles

Regular hexagon and regular triangle

Recall that all the sides of a regular polygon are equal in length, and all the angles are equal in measure. Due to their uniform shape, regular polygons can be **inscribed** in circles. A polygon is inscribed in a circle if all of its vertices are on the circle and all of the other points of the polygon are within the circle. We will inscribe a regular hexagon and a regular triangle.

First we fix the compass at a comfortable setting and do not change the compass until the project is finished. We swing the compass a full turn to make a circle. Then we lift the compass without changing the radius and place the pivot point anywhere on the circle. With the pivot point on the circle we swing a small arc that intersects the circle as shown here.

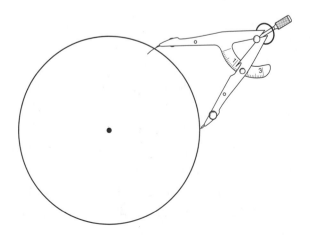

Again we lift the compass without changing the radius and place the pivot point at the point where the arc intersects the circle. From this location we swing another small arc that intersects the circle. We continue by moving the pivot point to where each new arc intersects the circle, until six small arcs are drawn. We find that the six small arcs are equally spaced around the circle.

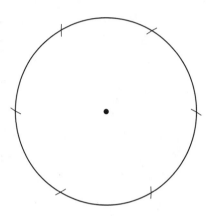

Now, to inscribe a regular hexagon, we draw line segments connecting each point where an arc intersects the circle to the next point where an arc intersects the circle. Use a compass and straight edge to inscribe a regular hexagon in a circle.

See student work.

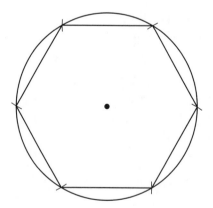

To inscribe a regular triangle we will start the process over again. We swing a circle with the compass. Then, without resetting the radius, we swing six small arcs around the circle. A triangle has three vertices, but there are six points around the circle where the small arcs intersect the circle. Therefore, to inscribe a regular triangle we draw segments between *every other* point of intersection. In other words, we

skip one point of intersection for each side of the triangle. Use your tools to inscribe a regular triangle in a circle.
See student work.

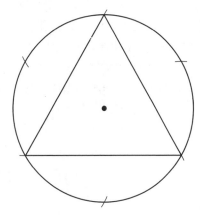

With a protractor we can measure each angle of the triangle. Extend the rays of each angle if necessary to perform the angle measurements. Since the vertex of each angle is on the circle and the angle opens to the interior of the circle, the angle is called an **inscribed** angle.

1. What is the measure of each inscribed angle? 60°

2. What is the sum of the measures of all three angles of the triangle? 180°

3. What shape will we make if we now draw segments between the remaining three points of intersection?
   a six-point star with a regular hexagon inside

Dividing a circle into sectors We can use a compass and straight edge to divide a circle into equal parts. First we swing a compass a full turn to make a circle. Next we draw a segment across the circle through the center of the circle. A segment with both endpoints on a circle is a **chord.** The longest chord of a circle passes through the center and is called a **diameter** of the circle. Notice that the diameter equals two radii. Thus the diameter of a circle is twice the length of the radius. The **circumference** is the distance around the circle and is determined by the length of the radius and diameter as we will see in a later lesson.

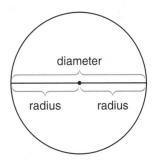

A diameter divides a circle into two half circles called **semicircles.**

To divide a circle into thirds we begin with the process we used to inscribe a hexagon. We draw a circle and swing six small arcs. Then we draw three segments from the center of the circle to *every other* point where an arc intersects the circle. These segments divide the circle into three congruent **sectors.** A sector of a circle is a portion of a circle bordered by part of the circumference (an arc) and two radii. A model of a sector is a slice of pie. Use a compass and straight edge to draw a circle and to divide the circle into thirds. See student work.

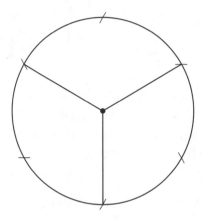

The segments we drew from the center to the circle formed angles. Each angle which has its vertex at the center of the circle is a **central angle.** We can measure a central angle with a protractor. We may extend the rays of the central angle if necessary in order to use the protractor.

4. What is the measure of each central angle of a circle divided into thirds? 120°

5. Each sector of this circle occupies what percent of the area of the whole circle? $33\frac{1}{3}\%$

To divide a circle into sixths we again begin with the process we used to inscribe a hexagon. We divide the circle by drawing a segment from the center of the circle to the point of intersection of each small arc.

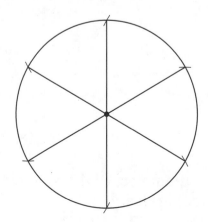

6. What is the measure of each central angle of a circle divided into sixths? 60°

7. Each sector of this circle occupies what percent of the area of the whole circle? $16\frac{2}{3}$%

In exercises 8–20, we provide the definition of terms presented in this investigation. Find the term for each definition:

8. The distance around a circle circumference

9. The distance across a circle through its center diameter

10. The distance from the center of a circle to the circle radius

11. Part of the circumference of a circle arc

12. A section of a circle bordered by a portion of the circumference and two radii sector

13. Two or more circles with the same center concentric circles

14. A segment that passes through the interior of a circle and has its endpoints on the circle chord

15. A polygon drawn within a circle, all of whose vertices are on the circumference of the circle inscribed polygon

16. A half circle semicircle

17. An angle whose vertex is the center of a circle central angle

18. The distance between the pivot point and marking point of a compass when drawing a circle radius

19. The name of the point that is the same distance from any point on the circle center of the circle

20. An angle with its vertex on the circumference of the circle that opens to the interior of the circle inscribed angle

The following paragraphs summarize important facts about circles. A copy of this summary is available as "Facts Practice Test E" in the *Math 87 Test Masters*.

The distance around a circle is its circumference. Every point on the circumference is the same distance from the center of the circle. The distance from the center to the circumference is the radius. The distance across the circle through the center is the diameter, which equals two radii. A diameter divides a circle into two half circles called semicircles. A diameter and any other segment between two points on a circle is a chord of the circle. Two or more circles with the same center are concentric circles.

An angle formed by two radii of a circle is called a central angle. A central angle opens to a portion of a circle called an arc, which is part of the circumference of a circle. The region enclosed by an arc and its central angle is called a sector.

An angle whose vertex is on the circumference of a circle and whose sides are chords of the circle is an inscribed angle. A polygon is inscribed in a circle if all of its vertices are on the circumference of the circle.

LESSON 21

Prime and Composite Numbers • Prime Factorization

Facts Practice: Circles (Test E in Test Masters)

Mental Math:

  a. $1.25 + 99¢   **b.** $6.50 ÷ 10   **c.** $20.00 − $15.75

  d. 6 × 34   **e.** $1\frac{2}{3} + 2\frac{1}{3}$ **f.** $\frac{1}{3}$ of 36

  g. Start with the number of sides of a hexagon, × 5, + 2, ÷ 8, + 1, ÷ 5.

Problem Solving:

  If Sam can read 20 pages in 30 minutes, how many hours will it take Sam to read 200 pages?

Prime and composite numbers

We remember that the counting numbers (or natural numbers) are the numbers we use to count. They are

$$1, 2, 3, 4, 5, 6, 7, 8, 9, 10, \ldots$$

Counting numbers greater than 1 are either **prime numbers** or **composite numbers**.

We define a prime number as follows.

> **A *prime number* is a counting number greater than 1 whose only factors are 1 and the number itself.**

A prime number has exactly two different factors. The number 1 does not have two different factors, so the number 1 is not a prime number. Composite numbers have three or more factors. The following table lists the factors of the first ten counting numbers.

Factors of Counting Numbers 1-10

Number	Factors
1	1
2	1, 2
3	1, 3
4	1, 2, 4
5	1, 5
6	1, 2, 3, 6
7	1, 7
8	1, 2, 4, 8
9	1, 3, 9
10	1, 2, 5, 10

From this table we can see that 2, 3, 5, and 7 are prime numbers, while 4, 6, 8, 9, and 10 are composite numbers. Notice that each **composite number** is divisible by a number other than 1 and itself. In other words, a composite number has three or more factors.

Example 1 Make a list of the prime numbers that are less than 16.

Solution First we list the counting numbers from 1 through 15.

1, 2, 3, 4, 5, 6, 7, 8, 9, 10, 11, 12, 13, 14, 15

A prime number must be greater than 1, so we cross out 1. The next number, 2, has only two divisors, so 2 is a prime number. However, all the even numbers greater than 2 are divisible by 2, so they are not prime. We cross these out.

1̸, 2, 3, 4̸, 5, 6̸, 7, 8̸, 9, 1̸0̸, 11, 1̸2̸, 13, 1̸4̸, 15

The numbers that are left are

2, 3, 5, 7, 9, 11, 13, 15

The numbers 9 and 15 are divisible by 3 so we cross them out.

2, 3, 5, 7, 9̸, 11, 13, 1̸5̸

The only divisors of **2, 3, 5, 7, 11,** and **13** are 1 and the numbers themselves. So these are the prime numbers less than 16.

Example 2 List the composite numbers between 40 and 50.

Solution First we write the counting numbers between 40 and 50.

41, 42, 43, 44, 45, 46, 47, 48, 49

Any number in this list that is divisible by a number besides 1 and itself is composite. All the even numbers in this list are composite since they are divisible by 2. That leaves the odd numbers to consider. Of these, 45 is divisible by 3 and by 5 and 49 is divisible by 7. So both 45 and 49 are composite. The remaining numbers, 41, 43, and 47, are prime. The composite numbers are **42, 44, 45, 46, 48,** and **49.**

Prime factorization Every composite number can be formed or *composed* by multiplying two or more prime numbers. Here we show each of the first nine composite numbers written as a product of prime number factors.

$$4 = 2 \cdot 2 \qquad 6 = 2 \cdot 3 \qquad 8 = 2 \cdot 2 \cdot 2$$
$$9 = 3 \cdot 3 \qquad 10 = 2 \cdot 5 \qquad 12 = 2 \cdot 2 \cdot 3$$
$$14 = 2 \cdot 7 \qquad 15 = 3 \cdot 5 \qquad 16 = 2 \cdot 2 \cdot 2 \cdot 2$$

Notice that we factor 8 as $2 \cdot 2 \cdot 2$ and not $2 \cdot 4$ because 4 is not prime.

When we write a composite number as a product of prime numbers, we have written the **prime factorization** of the number.

Example 3 Write the prime factorization of each number.
(a) 30   (b) 81   (c) 420

Solution We will write each number as the product of two or more prime numbers.

(a) $30 = \mathbf{2 \cdot 3 \cdot 5}$ We do not use $5 \cdot 6$ or $3 \cdot 10$ because neither 6 nor 10 is prime.

(b) $81 = \mathbf{3 \cdot 3 \cdot 3 \cdot 3}$ We do not use $9 \cdot 9$ because 9 is not prime.

(c) $420 = \mathbf{2 \cdot 2 \cdot 3 \cdot 5 \cdot 7}$ Two methods for doing this one are shown after Example 4.

Example 4 Write the prime factorization of 100 and of $\sqrt{100}$.

Solution The prime factorization of 100 is **2 · 2 · 5 · 5.** We find that $\sqrt{100}$ is 10, and the prime factorization of 10 is **2 · 5.** Notice that 100 and $\sqrt{100}$ have the same factors, 2 and 5, but the prime factorization of $\sqrt{100}$ has half as many factors as the prime factorization of 100.

There are two commonly used methods for factoring composite numbers. One method uses a factor tree. The other method uses division by primes. We will factor 420 using both methods.

Factor tree To factor a number using a factor tree, we write the number, and below the number we write any two whole numbers greater than 1 that multiply to equal the number. If these numbers are not prime, then we continue the process until there is a prime number at the end of each "branch" of the factor tree. These numbers are the prime factors of the original number.

Factor Tree

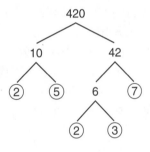

$$420 = 2 \cdot 2 \cdot 3 \cdot 5 \cdot 7$$

Division by primes To factor a number using division by primes, we write the number in a division box and begin dividing by the smallest prime number that is a factor. Then we divide the answer by the smallest prime number that is a factor. We repeat this process until the quotient is 1[†]. The divisors are the prime factors of the number.

Division by Primes

$$
\begin{array}{r}
1 \\
7\overline{)7} \\
5\overline{)35} \\
3\overline{)105} \\
2\overline{)210} \\
2\overline{)420} \\
\end{array}
$$

$$420 = 2 \cdot 2 \cdot 3 \cdot 5 \cdot 7$$

[†]Some people prefer to divide until the quotient is a prime number. In this case, the final quotient is included in the list of prime factors.

Practice*　　**a.** List the first 10 prime numbers.　2, 3, 5, 7, 11, 13, 17, 19, 23, 29

b. If a whole number greater than 1 is not prime, then what kind of number is it?　composite number

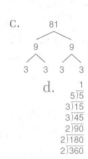
c.

c. Write the prime factorization of 81 using a factor tree.

$81 = 3 \cdot 3 \cdot 3 \cdot 3$

d.
```
    1
  5)5
 3)15
 3)45
 2)90
2)180
2)360
```

d. Write the prime factorization of 360 using division by primes.　$360 = 2 \cdot 2 \cdot 2 \cdot 3 \cdot 3 \cdot 5$

e. Write the prime factorization of 64 and $\sqrt{64}$.

$64 = 2 \cdot 2 \cdot 2 \cdot 2 \cdot 2 \cdot 2$; $\sqrt{64} = 8 = 2 \cdot 2 \cdot 2$

Problem set 21

1. Two thirds of the students wore green on St. Patrick's Day. What fraction of the students did not wear green on St. Patrick's Day?　$\frac{2}{3} + n = \frac{3}{3}$; $\frac{1}{3}$ of the students
(14)

2. There were 343 quills carefully placed into 7 compartments. If each compartment held the same number of quills, how many quills were in each compartment?
(13)
$7q = 343$; 49 quills

3. How much less than 2 billion is 21 million? Use words to write the answer.　$2{,}000{,}000{,}000 - 21{,}000{,}000 = d$;
(5,12)
one billion, nine hundred seventy-nine million

4. Last year the price was \$14,289. This year the price has been increased \$824. What is the price this year?
(11)
\$14,289 + \$824 = N; \$15,113

5. Write each number as a reduced fraction or mixed number.
(15)

(a) $3\dfrac{12}{21}$　$3\frac{4}{7}$　　　(b) $\dfrac{12}{48}$　$\frac{1}{4}$　　　(c) 12%　$\frac{3}{25}$

6. List the prime numbers between 50 and 60.　53, 59
(21)

7. Write the prime factorization of each number.
(21)

(a) 50　$2 \cdot 5 \cdot 5$　　(b) 60　$2 \cdot 2 \cdot 3 \cdot 5$　(c) 300

$2 \cdot 2 \cdot 3 \cdot 5 \cdot 5$

8. *C.* The tick mark between *B* and *C* is halfway between 1000 and 2000, which is 1500, so choices *A* and *B* are eliminated. *C* is closer to 1500 than to 2000 so *C* is the best choice.

8. Which point could represent 1610 on this number line? How did you decide?
(4)

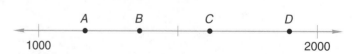

9. Complete each equivalent fraction.
(15)

(a) $\dfrac{2}{3} = \dfrac{?}{15}$　10　　(b) $\dfrac{3}{5} = \dfrac{?}{15}$　9　　(c) $\dfrac{?}{3} = \dfrac{8}{12}$　2

10. (a) How many $\frac{1}{3}$'s are in 1? 3
(9)

(b) How many $\frac{1}{3}$'s are in 3? 9

11. The perimeter of a regular quadrilateral is 12 inches.
(20) What is its area? 9 square inches

12.

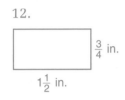

$\frac{3}{4}$ in.

$1\frac{1}{2}$ in.

12. Use your ruler to draw a rectangle that is $\frac{3}{4}$ in. wide and
(8,19) twice as long as it is wide.

(a) How long is the rectangle? $1\frac{1}{2}$ in.

(b) What is the perimeter of the rectangle? $4\frac{1}{2}$ in.

13. Find the perimeter of this hexagon. 46 in.
(19)

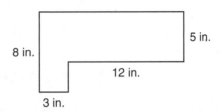

8 in.

5 in.

12 in.

3 in.

Solve:

14. $p + \dfrac{3}{5} = 1\frac{2}{5}$ **15.** $\dfrac{3}{5}q = 1\frac{5}{3}$ **16.**
(9)   (9)   (3)

17. $\dfrac{W}{25} = 50$ 1250   **18.** $\dfrac{1}{6} + f = \dfrac{5}{6}$
(3)   (9,15)
$\frac{4}{6}$ or $\frac{2}{3}$

19. $M - 3\dfrac{2}{3} = 1\dfrac{2}{3}$ **20.** $51 = 3C$ 17
(10)   (3)
$5\frac{1}{3}$

Simplify:

21. $\dfrac{2}{3} + \dfrac{2}{3} + \dfrac{2}{3}$ 2   **22.** $\left(\dfrac{2}{3}\right)^3$ $\frac{8}{27}$
(9)   (20)

$$
\begin{array}{r}
5 \\
7 \\
8 \\
4 \\
6 \\
3 \\
7 \\
4 \\
9 \\
8 \\
N \ \ 4 \\
+ \ 6 \\
\hline
71
\end{array}
$$

24. If we divide
the numerator
and denominator
of a fraction by
their GCF, we
reduce the
fraction to lowest
terms in one step.

23. (a) Write the prime factorization of 225. $225 = 3 \cdot 3 \cdot 5 \cdot 5$
(21)

(b) Find $\sqrt{225}$ and write its prime factorization.
$\sqrt{225} = 15 = 3 \cdot 5$

24. Describe how finding the greatest common factor of the
(15) numerator and denominator of a fraction can help us
reduce the fraction.

25.

$2\frac{1}{2}$ in.

A $2\frac{1}{2}$ in. B

m∠A = 45°

25. Draw $\overline{AB}$ $2\frac{1}{2}$ inches long. Then draw $\overline{BC}$ perpendicular to
(17) $\overline{AB}$ also $2\frac{1}{2}$ inches long. Complete the triangle by drawing
$\overline{AC}$. Use a protractor to find the measure of ∠A.

26. Write $1\frac{3}{4}$ as an improper fraction. Multiply the improper
(9,10) fraction by the reciprocal of $\frac{2}{3}$. Then write the product as
a mixed number. $\frac{7}{4} \times \frac{3}{2} = \frac{21}{8} = 2\frac{5}{8}$

27. Refer to this circle with center at
(Inv. 2) point M to answer questions (a)–(d).

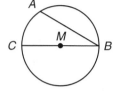

  (a) Which segment is a diameter? $\overline{CB}$

  (b) Which segment is a chord but not
     a diameter? $\overline{AB}$

  (c) Which two segments are radii? $\overline{MC}$ and $\overline{MB}$

  (d) Which angle is an inscribed angle?   ∠ABC

28. A quart is what percent of a gallon?   25%
(16)

29. How many $\frac{3}{10}$'s are in 1? $\frac{10}{3}$
(9)

30. Refer to these triangles to answer questions (a), (b), and (c).
(18)

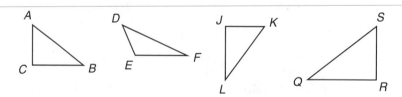

  (a) Which triangle appears to be congruent to △ABC?
     △KLJ
  (b) Which triangle is not similar to △ABC?   △DEF

  (c) Which angle in △QRS corresponds to ∠A in △ABC?
     ∠S

LESSON
22

Fraction-of-a-Group Problems

Mental Math:
a. $2.53
b. $8.00
c. $2.11
d. 371
e. 5
f. 6
g. octagon
Problem Solving:
64 inches

Facts Practice: Circles (Test E in Test Masters)

Mental Math:

   a. $1.54 + 99¢   **b.** 8¢ × 100   **c.** $10.00 − $7.89
   d. 7 × 53   **e.** $3\frac{3}{4} + 1\frac{1}{4}$ **f.** $\frac{1}{4}$ of 24

   g. Start with the number of years in half a century, add the number of inches in half a foot, divide by the number of days in a week. What is the name of the polygon with this number of sides?

Problem Solving:

   How many inches longer than $2\frac{2}{3}$ feet is $2\frac{2}{3}$ yards?

One way to describe part of a group is by using a fraction. Consider this statement:

> *Two thirds of the students in the class wore green on St. Patrick's Day.*

We can draw a diagram of this statement. We will use a rectangle to represent all the students in the class. Next we will divide the rectangle into 3 equal parts. Then we describe the parts.

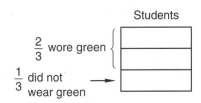

If we know how many students are in the class, we can figure out how many students are in each part.

> *Two thirds of the 27 students in the class wore green on St. Patrick's Day.*

There are 27 students in all. If we divide 27 students into 3 equal parts, there will be 9 students in each part. We write these numbers on our diagram.

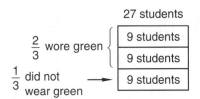

Since $\frac{2}{3}$ of the students wore green, we add 2 of the parts and find that 18 students wore green. Since $\frac{1}{3}$ of the students did not wear green, we find that 9 students did not wear green.

Example 1   Draw a diagram of this statement. Then answer the questions that follow.

Two fifths of the 30 students in the class are boys.

(a) How many boys are in the class?

(b) How many girls are in the class?

Solution   We draw a rectangle to represent all 30 students. Since the statement uses fifths to describe a part of the class, we divide the 30 students into 5 equal parts with 6 students in each part. Then we describe the parts.

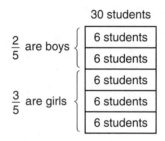

Now we answer the questions.

(a) Two of the five parts are boys. Since there are 6 students in each part, there are **12 boys.**

(b) Since 2 of the 5 parts are boys, 3 of the 5 parts must be girls. Thus, there are **18 girls.**

Another way to find the answer to (b) after finding the answer to (a) is to subtract. Since 12 of the 30 students are boys, the rest of the students (30 − 12 = 18) are girls.

Example 2   Change the percent to a fraction. Then draw a diagram of the statement and answer the questions that follow.

Britt correctly answered 80% of the 40 questions.

(a) What fraction of the questions did Britt answer correctly?

(b) How many questions did Britt answer correctly?

Solution   We write 80% as 80 over 100 and reduce.

$$\frac{80}{100} \div \frac{20}{20} = \frac{4}{5}$$

So 80% is equivalent to the fraction $\frac{4}{5}$.

Now we sketch a rectangle to represent all 40 questions, dividing the rectangle into 5 parts. Since 40 ÷ 5 is 8, there are 8 questions in each part.

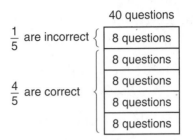

Now we answer the questions.

(a) Britt answered $\frac{4}{5}$ of the questions correctly.

(b) Britt correctly answered 4 × 8 questions, which is **32 questions.**

Practice Draw a diagram of each statement. Then answer the questions that follow.

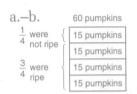

First statement:

Three fourths of the 60 pumpkins were ripe.

a. How many pumpkins were ripe? 45 pumpkins

b. How many pumpkins were not ripe? 15 pumpkins

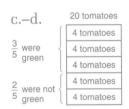

Second statement:

Sixty percent of the 20 tomatoes were green.

c. What fraction of the tomatoes were not green? $\frac{2}{5}$

d. How many tomatoes were green? 12 tomatoes

Problem set 22

1. In Room 7 there are 28 students. In Room 9 there are 30 students. In Room 11 there are 23 students. Altogether, how many students are in all three rooms?
(11) 28 + 30 + 23 = t; 81 students

2. If all the students in problem 1 were equally divided among three rooms, how many students would be in each room?
(13) 3r = 81; 27 students

3. One hundred twenty-six thousand scurried through the colony before the edentate attacked. Afterward only seventy-nine thousand remained. How many were lost when the edentate attacked?
(11) 126,000 − L = 79,000; 47,000 were lost.

4. Two thousand, seven hundred is how much less than ten
(5,12) thousand, three hundred thirteen? Use words to write the answer.

10,313 − 2,700 = d; seven thousand, six hundred thirteen

5.

36 spectators

| 4 spectators |
| 4 spectators |
| 4 spectators |
| 4 spectators |
| 4 spectators |
| 4 spectators |
| 4 spectators |
| 4 spectators |
| 4 spectators |

$\frac{5}{9}$ were happy

$\frac{4}{9}$ were not happy

5. Draw a diagram of this statement. Then answer the
(22) questions that follow.

Five ninths of the 36 spectators were happy with the outcome.

(a) How many spectators were happy with the outcome?
20 spectators

(b) How many spectators were not happy with the outcome?   16 spectators

6.

36 eggs

$\frac{3}{4}$ were not cracked

| 9 eggs |
| 9 eggs |
| 9 eggs |
| 9 eggs |

$\frac{1}{4}$ were cracked

6. Change the percent to a reduced fraction. Then draw a
(22) diagram of this statement and answer the questions.

Twenty-five percent of the three dozen eggs were cracked.

(a) What fraction of the eggs were not cracked? $\frac{3}{4}$

(b) How many eggs were not cracked?   27 eggs

7. (a) What fraction of the rectangle is
(15)   shaded? $\frac{2}{5}$

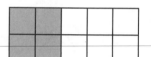

(b) What percent of the rectangle is not shaded?   60%

8. (a) How many $\frac{1}{4}$'s are in 1?   4
(9)

(b) Use the answer to part (a) to find the number of $\frac{1}{4}$'s in 3.
12

9. (a) Multiply: 6 · 5 · 4 · 3 · 2 · 1 · 0   0
(2)

(b) What property is illustrated by the multiplication in part (a)?   zero property of multiplication

10. Simplify and compare: $\frac{3}{3} - \left(\frac{1}{3} \cdot \frac{3}{1}\right) \bigcirc \left(\frac{3}{3} - \frac{1}{3}\right) \cdot \frac{3}{1}$
(9)   0 < 2

11.

11. Draw a rectangle *ABCD* so that *AB* is 2 in. and *BC* is 1 in.
(19,20)

(a) What is the perimeter of rectangle *ABCD*?   6 in.

(b) What is the area of the rectangle?   2 in.²

(c) What is the sum of the measures of all four angles of the rectangle?   360°

12. Write the prime factorization of each number.
(21)

(a) 32   (b) 900   (c) $\sqrt{900}$
2 · 2 · 2 · 2 · 2   2 · 2 · 3 · 3 · 5 · 5   30 = 2 · 3 · 5

13. For each fraction, write an equivalent fraction that has a
(15) denominator of 60.

(a) $\dfrac{5}{6}$ $\frac{50}{60}$ (b) $\dfrac{3}{5}$ $\frac{36}{60}$ (c) $\dfrac{7}{12}$ $\frac{35}{60}$

14. Add the three fractions with denominators of 60 from
(10) problem 13 and write their sum as a mixed number. $2\frac{1}{60}$

15. (a) Arrange these numbers in order from least to greatest:
(4,10)

$$0, -\frac{2}{3}, 1, \frac{3}{2}, -2 \quad -2, -\frac{2}{3}, 0, 1, \frac{3}{2}$$

(b) Which of these numbers are positive? 1 and $\frac{3}{2}$

Solve:

16. $\dfrac{5}{12} + a = \dfrac{11}{12}$ **17.** $\dfrac{900}{c} = 90$ 10 **18.**
(9,15)   (3)   (3)
$\frac{6}{12}$ or $\frac{1}{2}$

19. $121 = 11x$ 11 **20.** $2\dfrac{2}{3} = y - 1\dfrac{1}{3}$ 4
(3)   (10)

Simplify:

21. $\dfrac{5}{6} + \dfrac{5}{6} + \dfrac{5}{6}$ $2\frac{1}{2}$ **22.** $\dfrac{15}{2} \cdot \dfrac{10}{3}$ 25
(15)   (10)

4
7
8
21
4
6
7
3
8
N 7
+ 6
81

23. $\left(\dfrac{5}{6}\right)^2$ $\frac{25}{36}$ **24.** $\sqrt{30^2}$ 30
(20)   (20)

25. How many $\frac{5}{9}$'s are in 1? $\frac{9}{5}$
(9)

26. Write $1\frac{1}{2}$ and $1\frac{2}{3}$ as improper fractions. Then multiply the
(10,15) improper fractions and write the product as a mixed
number. $\frac{3}{2} \times \frac{5}{3} = \frac{15}{6} = 2\frac{1}{2}$

27. A package that weighs 1 lb, 5 oz weighs how many
(16) ounces? 21 oz

28. 45°

28. Use a protractor to draw a 45° angle.
(17)

29. Find the next number in this sequence.
(2,9)

$$100, 10, 1, \frac{1}{10}, \ldots \quad \frac{1}{100}$$

30. Write an odd negative integer greater than −3.   −1
(4)

LESSON
23

Subtracting Mixed Numbers with Regrouping

Facts Practice: Circles (Test E in Test Masters)

Mental Math:

  a. $3.65 + 98¢   **b.** $25.00 ÷ 100   **c.** 449 − 500
  d. 8 × 62   **e.** $1\frac{1}{2} + 2\frac{1}{2}$ **f.** $\frac{1}{2}$ of 76
  g. 8 × 8, − 1, ÷ 9, × 4, − 1, ÷ 3, × 2, + 2, ÷ 4

Problem Solving:

There are two routes Tricia can take to school. There are three routes Samantha can take to school. If Tricia is going from her house to school and then on to Samantha's house, how many different routes is it possible for Tricia to take?

In this lesson we will practice subtracting mixed numbers that require regrouping.

Example 1 There are $3\frac{1}{5}$ pies on the shelf. If the baker takes away $1\frac{2}{5}$ pies, how many pies will be on the shelf?

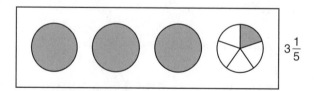

$3\frac{1}{5}$

Solution To answer this question, we subtract $1\frac{2}{5}$ from $3\frac{1}{5}$. However, before we subtract we will look at the picture again to see how the baker solves the problem.

In order for the baker to remove $1\frac{2}{5}$ pies, it will be necessary to slice one of the whole pies into fifths. After cutting one pie into fifths, there are 2 whole pies plus $\frac{5}{5}$ plus $\frac{1}{5}$, which is $2\frac{6}{5}$ pies. Then the baker can remove $1\frac{2}{5}$ pies, as we illustrate. This leaves $1\frac{4}{5}$ pies still on the shelf.

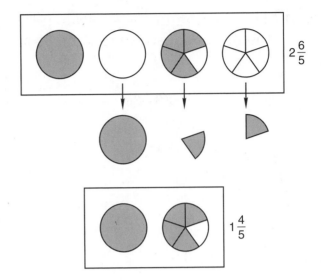

To perform the subtraction on paper, we first rename $3\frac{1}{5}$ as $2\frac{6}{5}$, as we show. Then we can subtract.

$$
\begin{array}{r}
3\frac{1}{5} \\
- 1\frac{2}{5} \\
\hline
\end{array}
\xrightarrow{\;2 + \frac{5}{5} + \frac{1}{5}\;}
\begin{array}{r}
2\frac{6}{5} \\
- 1\frac{2}{5} \\
\hline
1\frac{4}{5}
\end{array}
$$

There will be **$1\frac{4}{5}$ pies** left on the shelf.

Example 2   Simplify: $3\dfrac{5}{8} - 1\dfrac{7}{8}$

Solution   We need to regroup in order to subtract. The mixed number $3\frac{5}{8}$ equals $2 + 1 + \frac{5}{8}$, which equals $2 + \frac{8}{8} + \frac{5}{8}$. Combining $\frac{8}{8}$ and $\frac{5}{8}$ gives us $\frac{13}{8}$, so we use $2\frac{13}{8}$. Now we can subtract.

$$
\begin{array}{r}
3\frac{5}{8} \\
- 1\frac{7}{8} \\
\hline
\end{array}
\xrightarrow{\;2 + \frac{8}{8} + \frac{5}{8}\;}
\begin{array}{r}
2\frac{13}{8} \\
- 1\frac{7}{8} \\
\hline
1\frac{6}{8} = 1\frac{3}{4}
\end{array}
$$

The difference is $1\frac{6}{8}$, which reduces to $1\frac{3}{4}$.

Example 3 Simplify: $83\frac{1}{3}\% - 41\frac{2}{3}\%$

Solution The fraction in the subtrahend is greater than the fraction in the minuend, so we rename $83\frac{1}{3}\%$.

$$83\frac{1}{3}\% \quad \xrightarrow{\left[82 + \frac{3}{3} + \frac{1}{3}\right]\%} \quad 82\frac{4}{3}\%$$

$$- 41\frac{2}{3}\% \qquad\qquad\qquad - 41\frac{2}{3}\%$$

$$\overline{} \qquad\qquad\qquad \overline{\;\;41\frac{2}{3}\%}$$

Example 4 Simplify: $6 - 1\frac{3}{4}$

Solution We rewrite 6 as a mixed number with a denominator of 4. Then we subtract.

$$6 \quad \longrightarrow \quad 5\frac{4}{4}$$

$$- 1\frac{3}{4} \qquad\qquad - 1\frac{3}{4}$$

$$\overline{} \qquad\qquad \overline{\;\;4\frac{1}{4}}$$

Example 5 Simplify: $100\% - 16\frac{2}{3}\%$

Solution We rename 100% as $99\frac{3}{3}\%$ and subtract.

$$100\% \quad \longrightarrow \quad 99\frac{3}{3}\%$$

$$- 16\frac{2}{3}\% \qquad\qquad - 16\frac{2}{3}\%$$

$$\overline{} \qquad\qquad \overline{\;\;83\frac{1}{3}\%}$$

Practice* Subtract as indicated. Then simplify the answer if possible.

a. $7 - 2\frac{1}{3}$ $4\frac{2}{3}$

b. $6\frac{2}{5} - 1\frac{4}{5}$ $4\frac{3}{5}$

c. $5\frac{1}{6} - 1\frac{5}{6}$ $3\frac{1}{3}$

d. $100\% - 12\frac{1}{2}\%$ $87\frac{1}{2}\%$

e. $83\frac{1}{3}\% - 16\frac{2}{3}\%$ $66\frac{2}{3}\%$

Problem set 23

2. $50,000,000 -$
$250,000 = d;$
forty-nine
million, seven
hundred fifty
thousand

5.

56 restaurants

| 7 restaurants |
| 7 restaurants |
| 7 restaurants |
| 7 restaurants |
| 7 restaurants |
| 7 restaurants |
| 7 restaurants |
| 7 restaurants |

$\frac{3}{8}$ were closed

$\frac{5}{8}$ were open

6.

30 students

| 6 students |
| 6 students |
| 6 students |
| 6 students |
| 6 students |

$\frac{3}{5}$ were girls

$\frac{2}{5}$ were boys

9. Express the mixed number as an improper fraction. Then make a new fraction, reversing the numerator and the denominator.

1. Willie shot eighteen rolls of film for the school annual. If
(13) there were thirty-six exposures in each roll, how many exposures were there in all? $18 \times 36 = E$; **648 exposures**

2. Fifty million is how much greater than two hundred fifty
(5,12) thousand? Use words to write your answer.

3. There were 259 people who attended on opening night.
(11) On the second night 269 attended, and 307 attended on the third night. How many people attended on the first three nights? $259 + 269 + 307 = t$; **835 people**

4. The 16-pound turkey cost $14.24. What was the price for
(13) each pound? $16p = \$14.24$; **89¢ per pound**

5. Draw a diagram of this statement. Then answer the
(22) questions that follow.

> *Three eighths of the 56 restaurants in town were closed on Monday.*

(a) How many of the restaurants in town were closed on Monday? **21 restaurants**

(b) How many of the restaurants in town were open on Monday? **35 restaurants**

6. Write the percent as a fraction. Then draw a diagram of
(22) the statement and answer the questions.

> *Forty percent of the 30 students in the class were boys.*

(a) How many boys were in the class? **12 boys**

(b) How many girls were in the class? **18 girls**

7. After contact was made, the spheroid sailed four thousand,
(16) one hundred forty inches. How many yards did the spheroid sail after contact was made? **115 yards**

8. (a) How many $\frac{1}{5}$'s are in 1? **5**
(9)
    (b) How many $\frac{1}{5}$'s are in 3? **15**

9. Describe how to find the reciprocal of a mixed number.
(9,10)

10. Replace each circle with the proper comparison symbol.
(15)

(a) $\frac{2}{3} \cdot \frac{3}{2} \enspace \textcircled{=} \enspace \frac{5}{5}$

(b) $\frac{12}{36} \enspace \textcircled{<} \enspace \frac{12}{24}$

11. Write $2\frac{1}{4}$ and $3\frac{1}{3}$ as improper fractions. Then multiply the
(10,15) improper fractions and write the product as a reduced mixed number. $\frac{9}{4} \times \frac{10}{3} = \frac{90}{12} = 7\frac{1}{2}$

12. Complete each equivalent fraction.
(15)

(a) $\frac{3}{4} = \frac{?}{40}$ 30   (b) $\frac{2}{5} = \frac{?}{40}$ 16   (c) $\frac{?}{8} = \frac{15}{40}$ 3

13. The prime factorization of 100 is 2 · 2 · 5 · 5. We can
(21) write the prime factorization of 100 using exponents this way:

$$2^2 \cdot 5^2$$

(a) Write the prime factorization of 400 using exponents.
$400 = 2^4 \cdot 5^2$
(b) Write the prime factorization of $\sqrt{400}$ using exponents. $\sqrt{400} = 20 = 2^2 \cdot 5$

14. Refer to this figure to answer the
(7) following questions:

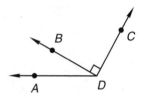

14.(a) acute angle
(b) right angle

(a) What type of angle is $\angle ADB$?

(b) What type of angle is $\angle BDC$?

(c) What type of angle is $\angle ADC$? obtuse angle

(d) Which ray is perpendicular to $\overrightarrow{DB}$? $\overrightarrow{DC}$

Solve:

15. $\frac{105}{W} = 7$ 15   **16.** $2x = 10^2$ 50   **17.**
(3)   (3,20)   (3)

18. $x + 1\frac{1}{4} = 6\frac{3}{4}$ $5\frac{2}{4}$ or $5\frac{1}{2}$
(9,15)

19. $m - 4\frac{1}{8} = 1\frac{5}{8}$ $5\frac{6}{8}$ or $5\frac{3}{4}$
(9,15)

Simplify:

20. $5 - 3\frac{1}{3}$ $1\frac{2}{3}$ **21.** $83\frac{1}{3}\% - 66\frac{2}{3}\%$
(23)   (23)
                                        $16\frac{2}{3}\%$

22. $\frac{2}{3}$ **22.** $\frac{7}{12} + \left(\frac{1}{4} \cdot \frac{1}{3}\right)$ **23.** $\frac{7}{8} - \left(\frac{3}{4} \cdot \frac{1}{2}\right)$ $\frac{1}{2}$
         (9,15)   (9,15)

```
    4
    7
    8
    2
    6
    4
    9
    5
    8
    7
    4
    1
N   9
+   3
───────
   77
```

24.

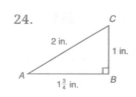

24. Draw $\overline{AB}$ $1\frac{3}{4}$ inches long. Then draw $\overline{BC}$ perpendicular to
(19) $\overline{AB}$ 1 inch long. Complete the triangle by drawing $\overline{AC}$. Use your ruler to find the approximate length of $\overline{AC}$. Use that length to help you calculate the perimeter of $\triangle ABC$.
The perimeter is about $4\frac{3}{4}$ inches.

25. Use a protractor to find the measure of $\angle A$ in $\triangle ABC$
(17) (problem 24). You may extend the rays if necessary to measure the angle. **m$\angle A$ is about 30°.**

26. Mary wants to apply a strip of wallpaper along the walls
(19) of the dining room just below the ceiling. If the room is a 14 ft by 12 ft rectangle, then the strip of wallpaper needs to be at least how long? **52 ft**

27. Multiply $\frac{3}{4}$ by the reciprocal of 3 and reduce the product.
(9,15) $\frac{3}{4} \times \frac{1}{3} = \frac{3}{12} = \frac{1}{4}$

28. Find fractions equivalent to $\frac{3}{4}$ and $\frac{2}{3}$ with denominators of
(15) 12. Then subtract the smaller fraction from the larger fraction. $\frac{9}{12} - \frac{8}{12} = \frac{1}{12}$

29. A sequence of perfect cubes may be written as in (a) or as
(20) in (b). Find the next two terms in both sequences.

(a) $1^3, 2^3, 3^3, \ldots$ $4^3, 5^3$

(b) $1, 8, 27, \ldots$ **64, 125**

30. The figure shows a circle with the
(Inv. 2) center at M.

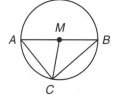

(a) Which chord is a diameter? $\overline{AB}$

(b) Which central angle appears to be obtuse? $\angle CMB$

(c) Name an inscribed angle that appears to be a right angle. $\angle ACB$

LESSON 24

Reducing Fractions, Part 2

Facts Practice: 40 Fractions to Reduce (Test D in Test Masters)

Mental Math:

a. $5.74 + 98¢   b. $1.50 × 10   c. $1.00 − 36¢

d. 4 × 65   e. $3\frac{1}{3} + 1\frac{2}{3}$ f. $\frac{1}{3}$ of 24

g. What number is 3 more than half the product of 4 and 6?

Problem Solving:

A card with a triangle on it in the position shown is rotated 90° clockwise three times. Sketch the pattern shown and draw the triangle in the correct position.

We have been practicing reducing fractions by dividing the numerator and the denominator by a common factor. In this lesson we will practice a method of reducing fractions that uses prime factorization to find the common factors of the terms. If we write the prime factorization of the numerator and of the denominator, we can see how to reduce a fraction easily.

Example 1   (a) Use prime factorization to reduce $\frac{420}{1050}$.

(b) Find the greatest common factor of 420 and 1050.

Solution   (a) We rewrite the numerator and the denominator as products of prime numbers.

$$\frac{420}{1050} = \frac{2 \cdot 2 \cdot 3 \cdot 5 \cdot 7}{2 \cdot 3 \cdot 5 \cdot 5 \cdot 7}$$

Next we look for pairs of factors that equal 1. A fraction equals 1 if the numerator and denominator are equal. In this fraction there are four pairs of factors that equal 1. They are $\frac{2}{2}, \frac{3}{3}, \frac{5}{5}$, and $\frac{7}{7}$. Below we have indicated each of these pairs.

$$\frac{2 \cdot 2 \cdot 3 \cdot 5 \cdot 7}{2 \cdot 3 \cdot 5 \cdot 5 \cdot 7}$$

Each pair of factors reduces to $\frac{1}{1}$.

$$\frac{\overset{1}{\cancel{2}} \cdot 2 \cdot \overset{1}{\cancel{3}} \cdot \overset{1}{\cancel{5}} \cdot \overset{1}{\cancel{7}}}{\underset{1}{\cancel{2}} \cdot \underset{1}{\cancel{3}} \cdot 5 \cdot \underset{1}{\cancel{5}} \cdot \underset{1}{\cancel{7}}}$$

The reduced fraction equals $1 \cdot 1 \cdot 1 \cdot 1 \cdot \frac{2}{5}$, which is $\frac{2}{5}$.

(b) In part (a) we found the common factors of 420 and 1050. The common factors are 2, 3, 5, and 7. The product of these common factors is the greatest common factor of 420 and 1050.

$$2 \cdot 3 \cdot 5 \cdot 7 = \mathbf{210}$$

Reducing before multiplying The terms of fractions may be reduced before they are multiplied. Reducing before multiplying is also known as **canceling.** Consider this multiplication:

$$\frac{3}{8} \cdot \frac{2}{3} = \frac{6}{24} \qquad \frac{6}{24} \text{ reduces to } \frac{1}{4}$$

We see that neither $\frac{3}{8}$ nor $\frac{2}{3}$ can be reduced. The product, $\frac{6}{24}$, can be reduced. We can avoid reducing after we multiply by reducing before we multiply. To reduce, any numerator may be paired with any denominator. Below we have paired the 3 with 3 and the 2 with 8.

Then we reduce these pairs: $\frac{3}{3}$ reduces to $\frac{1}{1}$, and $\frac{2}{8}$ reduces to $\frac{1}{4}$, as we show below. Then we multiply the reduced terms.

$$\frac{\overset{1}{\cancel{3}}}{\underset{4}{\cancel{8}}} \cdot \frac{\overset{1}{\cancel{2}}}{\underset{1}{\cancel{3}}} = \frac{1}{4}$$

Example 2 Simplify: $\dfrac{9}{16} \cdot \dfrac{2}{3}$

Solution Before multiplying, we pair 9 with 3 and 2 with 16 and reduce these pairs. Then we multiply the reduced terms.

$$\frac{\overset{3}{\cancel{9}}}{\underset{8}{\cancel{16}}} \cdot \frac{\overset{1}{\cancel{2}}}{\underset{1}{\cancel{3}}} = \frac{3}{8}$$

Example 3   Simplify: $\dfrac{8}{9} \cdot \dfrac{3}{10} \cdot \dfrac{5}{4}$

Solution   We mentally pair 8 with 4, 3 with 9, and 5 with 10 and reduce.

$$\dfrac{\overset{2}{\cancel{8}}}{\underset{3}{\cancel{9}}} \cdot \dfrac{\overset{1}{\cancel{3}}}{\underset{2}{\cancel{10}}} \cdot \dfrac{\overset{1}{\cancel{5}}}{\underset{1}{\cancel{4}}}$$

We can still reduce by pairing 2 with 2. Then we multiply.

$$\dfrac{\overset{\overset{1}{\cancel{2}}}{\cancel{8}}}{\underset{3}{\cancel{9}}} \cdot \dfrac{\overset{1}{\cancel{3}}}{\underset{\underset{1}{\cancel{2}}}{\cancel{10}}} \cdot \dfrac{\overset{1}{\cancel{5}}}{\underset{1}{\cancel{4}}} = \dfrac{1}{3}$$

Example 4   Simplify: $\dfrac{27}{32} \cdot \dfrac{20}{63}$

Solution   To give us easier numbers to work with we may factor the terms of the fractions before we reduce and multiply.

$$\dfrac{3 \cdot \overset{1}{\cancel{3}} \cdot \overset{1}{\cancel{3}}}{2 \cdot 2 \cdot 2 \cdot \underset{1}{\cancel{2}} \cdot \underset{1}{\cancel{2}}} \cdot \dfrac{\overset{1}{\cancel{2}} \cdot \overset{1}{\cancel{2}} \cdot 5}{\underset{1}{\cancel{3}} \cdot \underset{1}{\cancel{3}} \cdot 7} = \dfrac{15}{56}$$

Practice   Use prime factorization to reduce each fraction.

a. $\dfrac{48}{144}$ $\frac{1}{3}$

b. $\dfrac{90}{324}$ $\frac{5}{18}$

c. Find the greatest common factor of 90 and 324.   **18**

Reduce before multiplying.

d. $\dfrac{5}{8} \cdot \dfrac{3}{10}$ $\frac{3}{16}$

e. $\dfrac{8}{15} \cdot \dfrac{5}{12} \cdot \dfrac{9}{10}$ $\frac{1}{5}$

f. $\dfrac{8}{3} \cdot \dfrac{6}{7} \cdot \dfrac{5}{16}$ $\frac{5}{7}$

g. Factor and reduce before multiplying: $\dfrac{36}{45} \cdot \dfrac{25}{24}$

$\dfrac{2 \cdot 2 \cdot 3 \cdot 3}{3 \cdot 3 \cdot 5} \cdot \dfrac{5 \cdot 5}{2 \cdot 2 \cdot 2 \cdot 3} = \frac{5}{6}$

Problem set 24

1. From Hartford to Los Angeles is two thousand, eight
(12) hundred ninety-five miles. From Hartford to Portland is
three thousand, twenty-six miles. The distance from
Hartford to Portland is how much greater than the
distance from Hartford to Los Angeles?
$3026 - 2895 = d$; **131 miles**

2. Hal ordered 15 boxes of microprocessors. If each box
(13) contained two dozen microprocessors, how many
microprocessors did Hal order?
$15 \times 24 = m$; **360 microprocessors**

3.
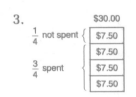

3. Write the percent as a fraction. Then draw a diagram of
(22) this statement and answer the questions.

> *Jill went to the store with $30.00 and spent 75%*
> *of the money.*

(a) What fraction of her money did she spend? $\frac{3}{4}$

(b) How much money did she spend? **$22.50**

4. If the diameter of a wheel is one yard, then its radius is
(Inv. 2) how many inches? **18 inches**

5. Nancy descended the 30 steps that led to the floor of the
(22) cellar. One third of the way down she paused. How many
more steps were there to the cellar floor? **20 steps**

6. (a) How many $\frac{1}{8}$'s are in 1? **8**
(9)
(b) How many $\frac{1}{8}$'s are in 3? **24**

7. (a) Write the reciprocal of 3. $\frac{1}{3}$
(9)
(b) What fraction of 3 is 1? $\frac{1}{3}$

8. (a) Use prime factorization to reduce $\frac{540}{600}$. $\frac{9}{10}$
(24)
(b) What is the greatest common factor of 540 and 600?
60

9. What type of angle is formed by the hands of a clock at
(17)
(a) 2 o'clock?   (b) 3 o'clock?   (c) 4 o'clock?
acute angle   right angle   obtuse angle

10. Describe how to complete this equivalent fraction.
(15)

$$\frac{3}{5} = \frac{?}{30}$$

10. Equivalent fractions are formed by multiplying or dividing a fraction by a fraction equal to 1. To change from 5ths to 30ths we multiply $\frac{3}{5}$ by $\frac{6}{6}$.

11. The prime factorization of 1000 using exponents is
(21) $2^3 \cdot 5^3$.

    (a) Write the prime factorization of 10,000 using exponents. **10,000 = $2^4 \cdot 5^4$**

    (b) Write the prime factorization of $\sqrt{10,000}$ using exponents. **$\sqrt{10,000}$ = 100 = $2^2 \cdot 5^2$**

12.(a)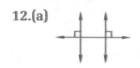

12. (a) Draw two parallel lines that are intersected by a third
(7)   line that is perpendicular to the parallel lines.

    (b) What type of angles are formed? **right angles**

13. The perimeter of a square is one yard.
(20)

    (a) How many inches long is each side of the square?
    9 inches
    (b) What is the area of the square in square inches?
    81 square inches

14. This equation illustrates that which property does not
(2) apply to division? **commutative property**

$$10 \div 5 \neq 5 \div 10$$

Solve:

15. $4\dfrac{7}{12} = x + 1\dfrac{1}{12}$ **$3\frac{1}{2}$**
(9,15)

16. $w - 3\dfrac{3}{4} = 2\dfrac{3}{4}$ **$6\frac{1}{2}$**
(9,15)

17. $8m = 100$ **$12\frac{1}{2}$**
(3,10)

18. $\dfrac{n}{12} = 28\text{¢}$ **$3.36**
(3)

Simplify:

19. $10^5 \div 10^2$ **10^3 or 1000**
(20)

20. $\sqrt{9} - \sqrt{4^2}$ **−1**
(20)

21. $100\% - 66\dfrac{2}{3}\%$ **$33\frac{1}{3}\%$**
(23)

22. $5\dfrac{1}{8} - 1\dfrac{7}{8}$ **$3\frac{1}{4}$**
(23)

23. $\left(\dfrac{5}{6}\right)^2$ **$\frac{25}{36}$**
(20)

24. $\dfrac{3}{4} \cdot \dfrac{1}{2} \cdot \dfrac{8}{9}$ **$\frac{1}{3}$**
(24)

25. Solve mentally: **8**
(3)

    $4 + 7 + 6 + 3 + 5 + 8 + 14 + 7 + 16 + N = 78$

26. Write twenty-four thousand in expanded notation.
(5) **(2 × 10,000) + (4 × 1000)**

27. Find the perimeter of this figure.
⁽¹⁹⁾ Dimensions are in yards and all
angles are right angles. **90 yards**

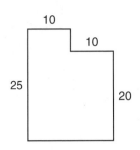

28. Find equivalent fractions for $\frac{1}{4}$ and $\frac{1}{6}$ that have
⁽¹⁵⁾ denominators of 12 and add them. $\frac{3}{12} + \frac{2}{12} = \frac{5}{12}$

29. Segment *AC* divides rectangle *ABCD*
⁽¹⁸⁾ into two congruent triangles. Angle
ADC corresponds to $\angle CBA$. Name
two more pairs of corresponding
angles.
$\angle DAC$ and $\angle BCA$; $\angle DCA$ and $\angle BAC$

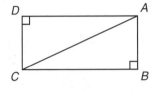

30. (a) Arrange these numbers in order from least to greatest.
^(4,9)

$$0, 1, -1, \frac{1}{2}, -\frac{1}{2} \quad -1, -\tfrac{1}{2}, 0, \tfrac{1}{2}, 1$$

(b) The ordered numbers in the answer to question (a)
form a sequence. What are the next three positive
numbers in the sequence? $1\tfrac{1}{2}, 2, 2\tfrac{1}{2}$

LESSON
25

Dividing Fractions

Facts Practice: Lines, Angles, Polygons (Test F in Test Masters)

Mental Math:

a. $2.65 + $1.99   b. $60.00 ÷ 10   c. $2.00 − $1.24

d. 7 × 36   e. $1\frac{3}{4} + 4\frac{1}{4}$ f. $\frac{1}{4}$ of 36

g. What number is 3 less than half the sum of 8 and 12?

Problem Solving:

Copy this problem and fill in the missing digits.

$$\begin{array}{r} \_\,6 \\ \times\ \_\,\_ \\ \hline \_\,\_ \\ \_\,\_\ \ \\ \hline 2\,\_\,6 \end{array}$$

When we ask the question "How many $\frac{1}{4}$'s are in 1?" we are asking a division question that can be expressed by writing:

$$1 \div \frac{1}{4}$$

The question can also be modeled with fraction manipulatives.

How many are in ?

With manipulatives we see that the answer is 4. Recall that 4 $\left(\text{or } \frac{4}{1}\right)$ is the reciprocal of $\frac{1}{4}$.

Likewise, when we ask the second question, "How many $\frac{1}{4}$'s are in 3?" we are again asking a division question.

$$3 \div \frac{1}{4}$$

How many are in ?

We may use the answer to the first question to help us answer the second question. There are *four* $\frac{1}{4}$'s in 1, so there must be *three times as many* $\frac{1}{4}$'s in 3. Thus, we find the answer to the second question by multiplying 3 times 4, that is, 3 *times the reciprocal of* $\frac{1}{4}$. We will follow this line of thinking with the following examples.

Example 1 (a) How many $\frac{2}{3}$'s are in 1? $\left(1 \div \frac{2}{3}\right)$

(b) How many $\frac{2}{3}$'s are in 3? $\left(3 \div \frac{2}{3}\right)$

Solution (a) We may model the question with manipulatives.

How many are in ?

We see that the answer is more than 1 but less than 2. From our work with reciprocals we know that the answer is $\frac{3}{2}$ (which equals $1\frac{1}{2}$).

(b) We use the answer to (a) to help us answer (b). There are $\frac{3}{2}$ (or $1\frac{1}{2}$) $\frac{2}{3}$'s in 1, so there are 3 times as many $\frac{2}{3}$'s in 3.

Thus, to answer the question, we multiply 3 times $\frac{3}{2}$ (or 3 times $1\frac{1}{2}$).

$$3 \times \frac{3}{2} = \frac{9}{2} \qquad\qquad 3 \times 1\frac{1}{2} = 1\frac{1}{2} + 1\frac{1}{2} + 1\frac{1}{2}$$

$$= 4\frac{1}{2} \qquad\qquad\qquad\qquad = 4\frac{1}{2}$$

We found the answer by multiplying 3 times the reciprocal of $\frac{2}{3}$.

Example 2   (a) $1 \div \frac{2}{5}$ (b) $\frac{3}{4} \div \frac{2}{5}$

Solution   (a) The problem $1 \div \frac{2}{5}$ means, "How many $\frac{2}{5}$'s are in 1?" The answer is the reciprocal of $\frac{2}{5}$, which is $\frac{5}{2}$.

$$1 \div \frac{2}{5} = \frac{5}{2}$$

(b) We use the answer to (a) to help us answer (b). There are $\frac{5}{2}$ (or $2\frac{1}{2}$) $\frac{2}{5}$'s in 1, so there are $\frac{3}{4}$ times as many $\frac{2}{5}$'s in $\frac{3}{4}$. Thus we multiply $\frac{3}{4}$ times $\frac{5}{2}$.

$$\frac{3}{4} \times \frac{5}{2} = \frac{15}{8}$$

$$= 1\frac{7}{8}$$

The number of $\frac{2}{5}$'s in $\frac{3}{4}$ is **$1\frac{7}{8}$**. We found the answer by multiplying $\frac{3}{4}$ times the reciprocal of $\frac{2}{5}$.

Example 3 $\frac{2}{3} \div \frac{3}{4}$

Solution   To find how many $\frac{3}{4}$'s are in $\frac{2}{3}$, we take two steps. First we find how many $\frac{3}{4}$'s are in 1. The answer is the reciprocal of $\frac{3}{4}$.

$$1 \div \frac{3}{4} = \frac{4}{3}$$

Then we use the reciprocal of $\frac{3}{4}$ to find the number of $\frac{3}{4}$'s in $\frac{2}{3}$. The number of $\frac{3}{4}$'s in $\frac{2}{3}$ is $\frac{2}{3}$ times as many $\frac{3}{4}$'s in 1. So we multiply $\frac{2}{3}$ times $\frac{4}{3}$.

$$\frac{2}{3} \times \frac{4}{3} = \frac{8}{9}$$

The answer $\frac{8}{9}$ means there is slightly less than one $\frac{3}{4}$ in $\frac{2}{3}$. We found the answer by multiplying $\frac{2}{3}$ times the reciprocal of $\frac{3}{4}$.

Example 4 $\dfrac{3}{4} \div \dfrac{9}{10}$

Solution   Here we show the original problem and the two-step solution.

Original problem: $\dfrac{3}{4} \div \dfrac{9}{10}$

Step 1: Find the number of $\frac{9}{10}$'s in 1. $1 \div \dfrac{9}{10} = \dfrac{10}{9}$

Step 2: Use the number of $\frac{9}{10}$'s in 1 to find the number of $\frac{9}{10}$'s in $\frac{3}{4}$. $\dfrac{\overset{1}{\cancel{3}}}{\underset{2}{\cancel{4}}} \times \dfrac{\overset{5}{\cancel{10}}}{\underset{3}{\cancel{9}}} = \dfrac{5}{6}$

Working on paper we often move from the original problem directly to step 2 by multiplying the dividend (first number) by the reciprocal of the divisor (second number).

$$\dfrac{3}{4} \div \dfrac{9}{10}$$

$$\dfrac{\overset{1}{\cancel{3}}}{\underset{2}{\cancel{4}}} \times \dfrac{\overset{5}{\cancel{10}}}{\underset{3}{\cancel{9}}} = \dfrac{5}{6}$$

 The reciprocal function on a calculator is the 1/x key. Pressing this key changes the previously entered number to its reciprocal (in decimal form). If we press 2 then 1/x, the calculator display changes from 2 to 0.5, which is the decimal form of $\frac{1}{2}$, the reciprocal of 2. Using the 1/x key is sometimes helpful when performing division. For example, assume you had this division to calculate.

$$144\overline{)\$10,461.60}$$

The divisor is 144. You could choose to divide $10,461.60 by 144, or to multiply $10,461.60 by the reciprocal of 144. Since multiplication is commutative, using the reciprocal of 144 allows you to enter the numbers in either order. The following multiplication entry yields the answer even though the entry begins with the divisor.

1 4 4 1/x × 1 0 4 6 1 . 6 =

Whether we choose to divide 10,461.6 by 144 or multiply by the reciprocal of 144, either way the answer is $72.65.

Practice   **a.** How many $\frac{2}{3}$'s are in 1, and how many $\frac{2}{3}$'s are in $\frac{3}{4}$? $\frac{3}{2}$; $1\frac{1}{8}$

b. How many $\frac{3}{4}$'s are in 3? 4

c. Describe how to use the reciprocal of the divisor to find the answer to a division question. Instead of dividing by the divisor, multiply by the reciprocal of the divisor.

d. Pressing this key changes the number previously entered to its reciprocal (in decimal form).

d. Describe the function of the $\boxed{1/x}$ key on a calculator.

Use the two-step method described in this lesson to find each quotient:

e. $\dfrac{3}{5} \div \dfrac{2}{3}$ $\frac{9}{10}$

f. $\dfrac{7}{8} \div \dfrac{1}{4}$ $3\frac{1}{2}$

g. $\dfrac{5}{6} \div \dfrac{2}{3}$ $1\frac{1}{4}$

Problem set 25

1. Three hundred twenty-four students were treated to ice cream for receiving A's in citizenship. If each box of ice cream contained a half dozen ice-cream bars, how many boxes of ice cream were needed? $6b = 324$; 54 boxes
(13)

2.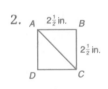

2. Use a ruler to draw square $ABCD$ with sides $2\frac{1}{2}$ in. long. Then divide the square into two congruent triangles by drawing $\overline{AC}$.
(17,19)

(a) What is the perimeter of square $ABCD$? 10 in.

(b) What is the measure of each angle of the square? 90°

(c) What is the measure of each acute angle in $\triangle ABC$? 45°

(d) What is the sum of the measures of the three angles of $\triangle ABC$? 180°

Use this information to answer problems 3–5.

The family picnic was a success, as 56 relatives attended. Half of those who attended played in the big game. However, the number of players on the two teams was not equal since one team had only 7 players.

3. How many relatives played the game? 28 relatives
(22)

4. If one team had 7 players, how many players did the other team have? 21 players
(11)

5. If the teams were rearranged so that the number of players on each team was equal, how many players would be on each team? 14 players
(13)

6.

310 pages

31 pages
31 pages
31 pages

$\frac{7}{10}$ have been read

31 pages
31 pages
31 pages
31 pages

31 pages

$\frac{3}{10}$ have not been read

31 pages
31 pages

6. Write the percent as a reduced fraction. Then draw a
(22) diagram of this statement and answer the questions that
follow.

Jason has read 70% of the 310 pages in the book.

(a) How many pages has Jason read? **217 pages**

(b) How many pages has Jason not read? **93 pages**

7. (a) How many $\frac{3}{4}$'s are in 1? $\frac{4}{3}$
(25)

(b) How many $\frac{3}{4}$'s are in $\frac{7}{8}$? $1\frac{1}{6}$

8. C. $\frac{2}{5}$. A little
less than half is
shaded. We
eliminate $\frac{2}{3}$,
which is more
than $\frac{1}{2}$. Since $\frac{2}{4}$
equals $\frac{1}{2}$, and $\frac{2}{5}$ is a
little less than $\frac{1}{2}$,
we choose $\frac{2}{5}$.

8. Which is the best estimate of how
(8) much of this rectangle is shaded?
Why?

A. $\frac{2}{3}$ B. $\frac{2}{4}$ C. $\frac{2}{5}$

9. Write 84 and 210 as products of prime numbers. Then
(24) reduce $\frac{84}{210}$. 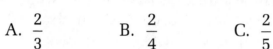 $= \frac{2}{5}$

10. Write the reciprocal of each number.
(9,10)

(a) $\frac{9}{10}$ $\frac{10}{9}$ (b) 8 $\frac{1}{8}$ (c) $2\frac{3}{8}$ $\frac{8}{19}$

11. Find fractions equivalent to $\frac{3}{4}$ and $\frac{4}{5}$ that have 20 as their
(15) denominator. Then add the two fractions you found and
write the sum as a mixed number. $\frac{15}{20} + \frac{16}{20} = \frac{31}{20} = 1\frac{11}{20}$

12. The prime factorization of 40 is $2^3 \cdot 5$. Write the prime
(21) factorization of 640 using exponents. **640 = $2^7 \cdot 5$**

13. Write $2\frac{2}{3}$ and $2\frac{1}{4}$ as improper fractions. Then find the
(10,24) product of the improper fractions. $\frac{8}{3} \cdot \frac{9}{4} = 6$

14. (a) Points A and B represent what mixed numbers on this
(8,15)   number line? $A: 4\frac{2}{3}; B: 5\frac{1}{2}$

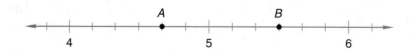

(b) Find the difference between the numbers represented
     by points A and B. $\frac{5}{6}$

15.(a)

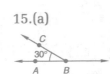

15. (a) Draw line *AB*. Then draw ray *BC* so that $\angle ABC$
(17)   measures 30°. (Use a protractor.)

(b) What kind of angle is $\angle ABC$? acute angle

Solve:

16. $1\dfrac{7}{12} + y = 3$ $1\frac{5}{12}$
(23)

17. $5\dfrac{7}{8} = x - 4\dfrac{5}{8}$ $10\frac{1}{2}$
(9,15)

18. $8n = 360°$ 45°
(3)

19. $\dfrac{4}{3}m = 1^3$ $3\frac{3}{4}$
(9,20)

Simplify:

20. $6\dfrac{1}{6} + 1\dfrac{5}{6}$ 8
(10)

21. $\dfrac{3}{4} \cdot \dfrac{5}{9} \cdot \dfrac{8}{15}$ $\frac{2}{9}$
(24)

22. $\dfrac{4}{5} \div \dfrac{2}{1}$ $\frac{2}{5}$
(25)

23. $\dfrac{8}{5} \div \dfrac{6}{5}$ $1\frac{1}{3}$
(25)

24. $\dfrac{3}{7} \div \dfrac{5}{6}$ $\frac{18}{35}$
(25)

25. $\dfrac{100\%}{8}$ $12\frac{1}{2}\%$
(10)

26. In the problem $5 \div \frac{3}{5}$, instead of dividing 5 by $\frac{3}{5}$, we can
(25) find the answer by multiplying 5 by what number? $\frac{5}{3}$ or $1\frac{2}{3}$

27. (a) Simplify and compare: $4 \cdot 8 = 8 \cdot 4$ or $32 = 32$
(20)
$$2^2 \cdot 2^3 \bigcirc 2^3 \cdot 2^2$$

(b) Simplify: $\sqrt{2^2}$ 2

28. A regular hexagon is inscribed in a
(19) circle. If one side of the hexagon is 6
inches long, then the perimeter of the
hexagon is how many feet? 3 feet

29. A 2 in. square was cut from a 4 in.
(19) square as shown in the figure. What
is the perimeter of the resulting
polygon? 16 in.

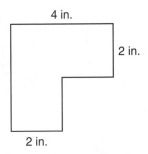

30. Which negative integer is the opposite of the third prime
(4,21) number? −5

LESSON
26

Multiplying and Dividing
Mixed Numbers

Facts Practice: Lines, Angles, Polygons (Test F in Test Masters)

Mental Math:

  a. $8.56 + 98¢   **b.** 30¢ × 100   **c.** $1.00 − 7¢

  d. 3 × 74   **e.** $\frac{2}{3} + \frac{2}{3}$ **f.** $\frac{2}{3}$ of 24

  g. 7 × 7, + 1, × 2, ÷ 5, + 5, ÷ 5, − 5, × 5

Problem Solving:

  The restaurant bill was $20.00. Nelda left a tip equal to $\frac{1}{5}$ of the bill. What was the total cost including the bill and the tip?

One way to multiply or divide mixed numbers is to first rewrite the mixed numbers as improper fractions. Then we multiply or divide the improper fractions as indicated.

Example 1   Simplify: $3 \times 2\frac{1}{2}$

Solution   We will show two ways to find the answer. One way is to recognize that $3 \times 2\frac{1}{2}$ equals three $2\frac{1}{2}$'s. Then we add.

$$3 \times 2\frac{1}{2} = 2\frac{1}{2} + 2\frac{1}{2} + 2\frac{1}{2}$$

$$= 7\frac{1}{2}$$

Another way to find the product is to write 3 and $2\frac{1}{2}$ as improper fractions and multiply. We may write 3 as $\frac{3}{1}$, since 3 divided by 1 is 3.

$$3 \times 2\frac{1}{2}$$
$$\downarrow \quad \downarrow$$
$$\frac{3}{1} \times \frac{5}{2} = \frac{15}{2}$$
$$= 7\frac{1}{2}$$

Example 2   Simplify:

    (a) $3\frac{2}{3} \times 1\frac{1}{2}$ (b) $\left(1\frac{1}{2}\right)^2$

Solution (a) We first rewrite $3\frac{2}{3}$ as $\frac{11}{3}$ and $1\frac{1}{2}$ as $\frac{3}{2}$. Then we multiply and simplify.

$$\frac{11}{\cancel{3}_1} \times \frac{\cancel{3}^1}{2} = \frac{11}{2}$$

$$= 5\frac{1}{2}$$

(b) The expression $\left(1\frac{1}{2}\right)^2$ means $1\frac{1}{2} \times 1\frac{1}{2}$. We write each factor as an improper fraction and multiply.

$$1\frac{1}{2} \times 1\frac{1}{2}$$
$$\downarrow \qquad \downarrow$$
$$\frac{3}{2} \times \frac{3}{2} = \frac{9}{4}$$

$$= 2\frac{1}{4}$$

Example 3 Simplify: $3\frac{2}{3} \div 2$

Solution As we think about the problem, we see that by dividing $3\frac{2}{3}$ by 2, we will be finding *half of* $3\frac{2}{3}$. We can find half of a number either by dividing by 2 or multiplying by $\frac{1}{2}$.

These are equivalent expressions.

$$3\frac{2}{3} \div 2 \qquad 3\frac{2}{3} \times \frac{1}{2}$$

Notice that instead of dividing by 2 we may multiply by the reciprocal of 2. We will write $3\frac{2}{3}$ as an improper fraction and multiply by $\frac{1}{2}$.

$$3\frac{2}{3} \times \frac{1}{2}$$
$$\downarrow$$
$$\frac{11}{3} \times \frac{1}{2} = \frac{11}{6}$$

$$= 1\frac{5}{6}$$

Example 4 Simplify: $3\frac{1}{3} \div 2\frac{1}{2}$

Solution First we write $3\frac{1}{3}$ and $2\frac{1}{2}$ as improper fractions. Then we multiply by the reciprocal of the divisor and simplify.

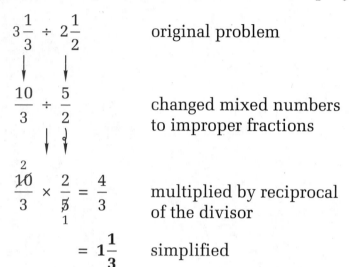

$$3\frac{1}{3} \div 2\frac{1}{2} \qquad \text{original problem}$$

$$\frac{10}{3} \div \frac{5}{2} \qquad \text{changed mixed numbers to improper fractions}$$

$$\frac{\overset{2}{\cancel{10}}}{3} \times \frac{2}{\underset{1}{\cancel{5}}} = \frac{4}{3} \qquad \text{multiplied by reciprocal of the divisor}$$

$$= 1\frac{1}{3} \qquad \text{simplified}$$

Practice* Simplify:

a. $6\frac{2}{3} \times \frac{3}{5}$ 4

b. $2\frac{1}{3} \times 3\frac{1}{2}$ $8\frac{1}{6}$

c. $3 \times 3\frac{3}{4}$ $11\frac{1}{4}$

d. $1\frac{2}{3} \div 3$ $\frac{5}{9}$

e. $2\frac{1}{2} \div 3\frac{1}{3}$ $\frac{3}{4}$

f. $5 \div \frac{2}{3}$ $7\frac{1}{2}$

g. $2\frac{2}{3} \div 1\frac{1}{3}$ 2

h. $1\frac{1}{3} \div 2\frac{2}{3}$ $\frac{1}{2}$

i. $4\frac{1}{2} \times 1\frac{2}{3}$ $7\frac{1}{2}$

Problem set 26

1. After the first hour of the monsoon, 23 millimeters of
(11) precipitation had fallen. After the second hour, a total of 61 millimeters of precipitation had fallen. How many millimeters of precipitation fell during the second hour? **$23 + M = 61$; 38 millimeters**

2. Each enlargement cost 85¢ and Willie needed 26 enlarge-
(13) ments. What was the total cost of the enlargements Willie needed? **$26 \times 85¢ = t$; $22.10**

3. The Byzantine Empire lasted from 330 to 1453. How
(12) many years did the Byzantine Empire last? **$1453 - 330 = B$; 1123 years**

4. Dolores went to the theater with $20 and came home with
(11) $11.25. How much money did Dolores spend at the theater? **$20.00 - S = $11.25; $8.75**

5. A gross is a dozen dozens. A gross of pencils is how many
(13) pencils? 12 × 12 = P; 144 pencils

6. Draw a diagram of this statement and answer the questions
(22) that follow. Begin by changing the percent to a reduced fraction.

> *Forty percent of the 60 marbles in the bag were blue.*

6.(a) 24 marbles

(a) How many of the marbles in the bag were blue?

(b) How many of the marbles in the bag were not blue?
36 marbles

7. Roan estimated that the weight of the water in a full
(16) bathtub is a quarter ton. How many pounds is a quarter of a ton? 500 pounds

8. (a) What fraction of this square is shaded? $\frac{3}{100}$
(8)

(b) What percent of this square is not shaded? 97%

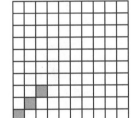

9. (a) Write 210 and 252 as products of prime numbers.
(24) Then reduce $\frac{210}{252}$. $\frac{2 \cdot 3 \cdot 5 \cdot 7}{2 \cdot 2 \cdot 3 \cdot 3 \cdot 7} = \frac{5}{6}$

(b) Find the GCF of 210 and 252. 42

10. Write the reciprocal of each number.
(9,10)

(a) $\frac{5}{9}$ $\frac{9}{5}$ (b) $5\frac{3}{4}$ $\frac{4}{23}$ (c) 7 $\frac{1}{7}$

11. Find each equivalent fraction in (a) and (b).
(15)

(a) $\frac{5}{8} = \frac{?}{24}$ $\frac{15}{24}$ (b) $\frac{5}{12} = \frac{?}{24}$ $\frac{10}{24}$

(c) Add the fractions you found in (a) and (b).
$\frac{15}{24} + \frac{10}{24} = \frac{25}{24} = 1\frac{1}{24}$

12. Write fifteen million in expanded notation.
(5) (1 × 10,000,000) + (5 × 1,000,000)

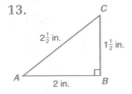

13. Draw segment *AB* 2 in. long. Then draw $\overline{BC}$ $1\frac{1}{2}$ in. long
(8) perpendicular to $\overline{AB}$. Complete triangle *ABC* by drawing $\overline{AC}$. How long is $\overline{AC}$?

14. (a) Arrange these numbers in order from least to greatest:
(4,10)

$$1, -3, \frac{5}{6}, 0, \frac{4}{3} \quad -3, 0, \frac{5}{6}, 1, \frac{4}{3}$$

(b) Which of these numbers are whole numbers?   **0, 1**

Solve:

15. $x - 8\frac{11}{12} = 6\frac{5}{12}$ $15\frac{1}{3}$
(10,15)

16. $180 - y = 75$ **105**
(3)

17. $12w = 360°$ **30°**
(3)

18. $w + 58\frac{1}{3} = 100$ $41\frac{2}{3}$
(23)

19.(a) 100 in.²   **19.** (a) Find the area of the square.
(20)

(b) Find the area of the shaded part of the square.   **50 in.²**

10 in.

Simplify:

20. $9\frac{1}{9} - 4\frac{4}{9}$ $4\frac{2}{3}$
(23)

21. $\frac{5}{8} \cdot \frac{3}{10} \cdot \frac{1}{6}$ $\frac{1}{32}$
(24)

22. $\left(2\frac{1}{2}\right)^2$ $6\frac{1}{4}$
(26)

23. $1\frac{3}{5} \div 2\frac{2}{3}$ $\frac{3}{5}$
(26)

24. $3\frac{1}{3} \div 4$ $\frac{5}{6}$
(26)

25. $5 \cdot 1\frac{3}{4}$ $8\frac{3}{4}$
(26)

26. $\sqrt{10^2 \cdot 10^4}$ **10³ or 1000**
(20)

27. $\frac{16,524}{36}$ **459**
(1)

28. $100 - (78¢ \times 48)$
(1,2)   **$62.56**

29. $80(64)(25)$ **128,000**
(1)

30. The central angle of a half circle is
(Inv. 2)   180°. The central angle of a quarter circle is 90°. How many degrees is the central angle of $\frac{1}{8}$ of a circle?   **45°**

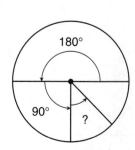

**LESSON
27**

**Multiples •
Least Common Multiple •
Equivalent Division Problems**

Mental Math:
a. $5.73
b. $12.50
c. 420
d. 210
e. $1\frac{1}{2}$
f. 18
g. 0

Problem Solving:
It is not true that
the total is 8.
Although 5, 2, and
1 totals 8, 5 and 2
are on opposite
faces. Also 4, 3,
and 1 totals 8, but
4 and 3 are on
opposite faces.

Facts Practice: Circles (Test E in Test Masters)

Mental Math:

   a. $3.75 + $1.98   **b.** $125.00 ÷ 10   **c.** 10 × 42

   d. 5 × 42   **e.** $\frac{3}{4} + \frac{3}{4}$ **f.** $\frac{3}{4}$ of 24

   g. Start with a score, add a dozen, then add the number of feet in a yard. Divide by half the number of years in a decade, then subtract the number of days in a week. What is the answer?

Problem Solving:

Simon held a die so that he could see the dots on three adjoining faces. Simon said he could see a total of 8 dots. Could Simon be telling the truth? Why or why not?

Multiples

The **multiples** of a number are the numbers that are produced by multiplying the number by 1, by 2, by 3, by 4, and so on. Thus the multiples of 4 are

$$4, 8, 12, 16, 20, 24, 28, 32, 36, \ldots$$

The multiples of 6 are

$$6, 12, 18, 24, 30, 36, 42, 48, 54, \ldots$$

If we inspect these two lists, we see that some of the numbers in both lists are the same. A number that appears in both of these lists is a **common multiple** of 4 and 6. Here we have circled some of the common multiples of 4 and 6.

Multiples of 4: 4, 8, ⑫, 16, 20, ㉔, 28, 32, ㊱, …

Multiples of 6: 6, ⑫, 18, ㉔, 30, ㊱, 42, 48, 54, …

We see that 12, 24, and 36 are common multiples of 4 and 6. If we continued both lists, we would find many more common multiples.

Least common multiple

Of particular interest is the least (smallest) of the common multiples. The **least common multiple** of 4 and 6 is 12. It is the smallest number that is a multiple of both 4 and 6. The term "least common multiple" is often abbreviated **LCM.**

Example 1   Find the least common multiple of 6 and 8.

Solution   We will list some multiples of 6 and of 8 and circle common multiples.

Multiples of 6: 6, 12, 18, (24), 30, 36, 42, (48), ...

Multiples of 8: 8, 16, (24), 32, 40, (48), 56, 64, ...

The least common multiple of 6 and 8 is **24.**

It is not necessary to list the multiples each time. Often the search for the least common multiple can be conducted mentally.

Example 2   Find the LCM of 3, 4, and 6.

Solution   To find the least common multiple of 3, 4, and 6 we may mentally search for the smallest number divisible by 3, 4, and 6. We may conduct the search by first thinking of multiples of the largest number, 6.

6, 12, 18, 24, ...

Then we mentally test these multiples for divisibility by 3 and by 4. We find that 6 is divisible by 3 but not by 4, while 12 is divisible by 3 and 4. Thus the LCM of 3, 4, and 6 is **12.**

We may use prime factorization to help us find the least common multiple of a set of numbers. The LCM of a set of numbers contains *only the factors necessary to form any number in the set.*

Example 3   Use prime factorization to help you find the LCM of 18 and 24.

Solution   We write the prime factorization of 18 and 24.

$$18 = 2 \cdot 3 \cdot 3 \qquad 24 = 2 \cdot 2 \cdot 2 \cdot 3$$

The prime factors of 18 and 24 are 2's and 3's. The number of 2's needed to form either number is three. The number of 3's needed to form either number is two. So the LCM of 18 and 24 is the product of three 2's and two 3's.

$$\text{LCM of 18 and 24} = 2 \cdot 2 \cdot 2 \cdot 3 \cdot 3$$
$$= \textbf{72}$$

**Equivalent
division
problems**

Tricia's teacher asked this question.

> *If sixteen popsicles cost $4.00, what was the price for
> each popsicle?*

Tricia quickly gave the correct answer, 25¢, and then explained how she found the answer.

> *I knew I had to divide $4.00 by 16, but I did not know
> the answer. So I mentally found half of each number,
> which made the problem $2.00 divided by 8. I still
> couldn't think of the answer, so I found half of those
> numbers. That made the problem $1.00 divided by 4,
> and I knew the answer was 25 cents.*

How does Tricia's mental calculation technique work? Recall from Lesson 15 that we can form equivalent fractions by multiplying or dividing a fraction by a fraction name for 1.

$$\frac{3}{4} \times \frac{10}{10} = \frac{30}{40} \qquad \frac{6}{9} \div \frac{3}{3} = \frac{2}{3}$$

We can form equivalent division problems in a similar way. We multiply (or divide) the dividend and divisor by the same number to form a new division problem with the same quotient that is easier to mentally calculate.

$$\frac{\$4.00 \div 2}{16 \div 2} = \frac{\$2.00}{8} \qquad \frac{\$2.00 \div 2}{8 \div 2} = \frac{\$1.00}{4}$$

Example 4   Instead of dividing 220 by 5, double both numbers and mentally calculate the quotient.

Solution   We double the two numbers in 220 ÷ 5 and get 440 ÷ 10. We mentally calculate the new quotient to be **44,** which is also the quotient of the original problem.

Example 5   Instead of dividing 6000 by 200, divide both numbers by 100 and then mentally calculate the quotient.

Solution   We mentally divide by 100 by removing two places (two zeros) from each number which forms the equivalent division problem 60 ÷ 2. We mentally calculate the quotient as **30.**

Practice   Find the least common multiple (LCM) of each pair or group of numbers.

   a. 8 and 10   40

   b. 4, 6, and 10   60

Use prime factorization to help you find the LCM of these pairs of numbers.

   c. 24 and 40   120

   d. 30 and 75   150

   e. Instead of dividing $7\frac{1}{2}$ by $1\frac{1}{2}$, double each number and mentally calculate the quotient.   5

Find an equivalent division problem for each of these division problems and mentally calculate the quotient. Discuss your strategy with the class.

   f. 24,000 ÷ 400
   $240 \div 4 = 60$

   g. $6.00 ÷ 12
   $\frac{\$6.00 \div 6}{12 \div 6} = \frac{\$1.00}{2} = 50¢$

   h. 140 ÷ 5
   $280 \div 10 = 28$

Problem set 27

1. There were three towns in the valley. The population of Brenton was 11,460. The population of Elton was 9,420. The population of Jennings was 8,916. What was the total population of the three towns in the valley?
(11)
$11,460 + 9,420 + 8,916 = P;$ **29,796**

2. Norman is 6 feet tall. How many inches tall is Norman?
$(13,16)$ $6 \cdot 12 = I;$ **72 inches**

3. $0.15 per egg; Some equivalent division problems:
$0.90 ÷ 6
$0.60 ÷ 4
$0.45 ÷ 3
$0.30 ÷ 2

3. If the cost of one dozen eggs was $1.80, what was the cost per egg? Write an equivalent division problem that is easier to calculate mentally and find the quotient.
(27)

4. 1,000,000,000 − 10,900,000 = d; nine hundred eighty-nine million, one hundred thousand

4. One billion is how much greater than ten million, nine hundred thousand? Use words to write your answer.
$(5,12)$

5.
712 students

89 students

$\frac{3}{8}$ bought their lunch

$\frac{5}{8}$ did not buy their lunch

5. Draw a diagram of this statement. Then answer the questions that follow.
(22)

   Three eighths of the 712 students bought their lunch.

   (a) How many students bought their lunch?   **267 students**

   (b) How many students did not buy their lunch?
   445 students

6. The perimeter of this rectangle is 30 inches.
$(19,20)$

6 in.

   (a) What is the length of the rectangle?   **9 in.**

   (b) What is the area of the rectangle?   **54 in.²**

7. Use prime factorization to help find the least common
(27) multiple of 25 and 45. **225**

8. What number is halfway between 3000 and 4000? **3500**
(4)

9. (a) Write 24% as a reduced fraction. $\frac{6}{25}$
(15,24)

   (b) Use prime factorization to help you reduce $\frac{36}{180}$. $\frac{1}{5}$

10. It was a "scorcher." The temperature was 102°F in the
(16) shade.

   (a) The temperature was how many degrees above the
       freezing point of water? **70°F**

   (b) The temperature was how many degrees below the
       boiling point of water? **110°F**

11. For each fraction, write an equivalent fraction that has a
(15) denominator of 36.

   (a) $\dfrac{5}{12}$ $\frac{15}{36}$ (b) $\dfrac{1}{6}$ $\frac{6}{36}$ (c) $\dfrac{7}{9}$ $\frac{28}{36}$

   (d) What property do we use when we find equivalent
       fractions? **identity property of multiplication**

12.(a)
$576 = 2^6 \cdot 3^2$

12. (a) Write the prime factorization of 576 using exponents.
(21)

   (b) Find $\sqrt{576}$. **24**

13. Write $5\frac{5}{6}$ and $6\frac{6}{7}$ as improper fractions and find their
(26) product. $\dfrac{\overset{5}{\cancel{35}}}{\underset{1}{\cancel{6}}} \times \dfrac{\overset{8}{\cancel{48}}}{\underset{1}{\cancel{7}}} = 40$

Figures *ABCF* and *FCDE* are squares. Refer to this figure to
answer problems 14, 15, and 16.

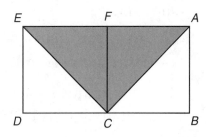

14. (a) What kind of angle is $\angle ACD$? obtuse angle
(7)
   (b) Name two segments parallel to $\overline{FC}$. $\overline{AB}$ and $\overline{ED}$

15. (a) What fraction of square $CDEF$ is shaded? $\frac{1}{2}$
(8)
   (b) What fraction of square $ABCF$ is shaded? $\frac{1}{2}$

   (c) What fraction of rectangle $ABDE$ is shaded? $\frac{1}{2}$

16. If AB is 3 ft,
(19,20)
   (a) what is the perimeter of rectangle $ABDE$? 18 ft

   (b) what is the area of rectangle $ABDE$? 18 ft²

Solve:

17. $10y = 360°$ 36°
(3)

18. $p + 2^4 = 12^2$ 128
(3,20)

19. $5\frac{1}{8} - n = 1\frac{3}{8}$ $3\frac{3}{4}$
(23)

20. $m - 6\frac{2}{3} = 4\frac{1}{3}$ 11
(10)

Simplify:

21. $10 - 1\frac{3}{5}$ $8\frac{2}{5}$
(23)

22. $5\frac{1}{3} \cdot 1\frac{1}{2}$ 8
(26)

23. $3\frac{1}{3} \div \frac{5}{6}$ 4
(26)

24. $5\frac{1}{4} \div 3$ $1\frac{3}{4}$
(26)

25. $\frac{5}{6} \cdot \frac{9}{8} \cdot \frac{4}{15}$ $\frac{1}{4}$
(24)

26. $\frac{8}{9} - \left(\frac{7}{9} - \frac{5}{9}\right)$ $\frac{2}{3}$
(9,15)

27. If the diameter of a circle is half of a yard, then its radius
(Inv. 2) is how many inches? 9 inches

28. Divide $12.00 by 16 or find the quotient of an equivalent
(27) division problem. 75¢

29. A 3 in. by 3 in. paper square is cut
(19,20) from a 5 in. by 5 in. paper square as
   shown.

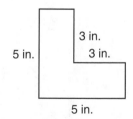

   (a) What is the perimeter of the
      resulting polygon? 20 in.

   (b) How many square inches of the
      5 in. by 5 in. square remain? 16 in.²

30. Refer to this circle with center at point M to answer
(Inv. 2) questions (a)–(e).

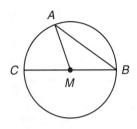

(a) Which chord is a diameter? $\overline{CB}$ (or $\overline{BC}$)

(b) Which chord is not a diameter? $\overline{AB}$ (or $\overline{BA}$)

(c) What angle is an acute central angle? $\angle AMC$ (or $\angle CMA$)

(d) Which angles are inscribed angles? $\angle ABC$ and $\angle BAM$

(e) Which two sides of triangle AMB are equal in length?
$\overline{MA}$ and $\overline{MB}$

LESSON 28

Two-Step Word Problems • Average, Part 1

Facts Practice: Lines, Angles, Polygons (Test F in Test Masters)

Mental Math:

a. $6.23 + $2.99   **b.** $1.75 × 100   **c.** $5.00 − $1.29

d. 8 × 53   **e.** $\frac{5}{8} + \frac{5}{8}$ **f.** $\frac{2}{5}$ of 25

g. Think of an easier equivalent division for $56.00 ÷ 14 and find the quotient.

Problem Solving:

When Bill, Phil, Jill, and Gil entered the room they found four chairs waiting for them, so they each took a seat. One minute later they traded seats. Then they traded seats again and again. If they don't move the chairs but only move themselves, how many seating arrangements are possible?

Two-step word problems

We have considered five types of one-step word problems thus far.

1. "Some and some more"
2. "Some went away"
3. "Larger-smaller-difference"
4. "Equal groups"
5. "Part-part-whole"

Word problems often require more than one step to solve. In this lesson we will begin practicing problems that require two or more steps to solve, involving a combination of the one-step problems we have practiced.

Example 1   Julie went to the store with $20. If she bought 8 cans of dog food for 67 cents per can, how much money did she have left?

Solution   This is a two-step problem. First we find out how much Julie spent. This first step is an "equal groups" problem.

$$
\begin{array}{rl}
\text{Number in group} \longrightarrow & \$0.67 \quad \text{each can} \\
\text{Number of groups} \longrightarrow \times & 8 \quad\quad \text{cans} \\
\hline
\text{Total} \longrightarrow & \$5.36
\end{array}
$$

Now we can find out how much money Julie had left. This second step is a "some went away" problem.

$$
\begin{array}{r}
\$20.00 \\
- \quad \$5.36 \\
\hline
\$14.64
\end{array}
$$

After spending $5.36 of her $20 on dog food, Julie had **$14.64** left.

Average, part 1   Calculating an average is often a two-step process. As an example consider these five stacks of coins.

There are 15 coins in all. If we made all the stacks the same size, there would be 3 coins in each stack.

We say that the average number of coins in each stack is 3. Now look at the following problem:

There are 4 squads in the physical education class. Squad A has 7 players, squad B has 9 players, squad C has 6 players, and squad D has 10 players. What is the average number of players in a squad?

The average number of players in a squad is the number of players that would be on each squad if all of the squads had the same number of players. To find the average of a group of numbers, we begin by finding the sum of the numbers.

$$
\begin{array}{r}
7 \text{ players} \\
9 \text{ players} \\
6 \text{ players} \\
+ \ 10 \text{ players} \\
\hline
32 \text{ players}
\end{array}
$$

Then we divide the sum of the numbers by the number of numbers. There are 4 squads, so we divide by 4.

$$
\frac{\text{sum of numbers}}{\text{number of numbers}} = \frac{32 \text{ players}}{4 \text{ squads}}
$$

$$
= 8 \text{ players per squad}
$$

Finding the average took two steps. First we added the numbers to find the total. Then we divided the total to make equal groups.

Example 2   When people were seated, there were 3 in the first row, 7 in the second row, and 20 in the third row. What was the average number of people in each of the first 3 rows?

Solution   The average number of people in the first 3 rows is the number of people that would be in each row if the number in each row were equal. First we add to find the total number of people.

$$
\begin{array}{r}
3 \text{ people} \\
7 \text{ people} \\
+ \ 20 \text{ people} \\
\hline
30 \text{ people}
\end{array}
$$

Then we divide by 3 to separate the total into 3 equal groups.

$$
\frac{30 \text{ people}}{3 \text{ rows}} = 10 \text{ people per row}
$$

The average was **10 people** in each of the first 3 rows. *Notice that the average of a set of numbers is greater than the smallest number in the set but less than the largest number in the set.*

Another name for the average is the **mean**. We find the mean of a set of numbers by adding the numbers and then dividing the sum by the number of numbers.

Example 3 On the last test five students in the class scored 100, four scored 95, six scored 90, and five scored 80. What was the mean of the scores?

Solution First we find the total of the scores.

$$
\begin{array}{rcl}
5 \times 100 &=& 500 \\
4 \times 95 &=& 380 \\
6 \times 90 &=& 540 \\
5 \times 80 &=& \underline{400} \\
&& 1820
\end{array}
$$

Next we divide the total by 20 because there were 20 scores in all.

$$
\frac{\text{sum of numbers}}{\text{number of numbers}} = \frac{1820}{20} = 91
$$

We find that the mean of the scores was **91**.

Practice Work each problem as a two-step problem.

a. Jody went to the store with $20 and returned home with $5.36. If all she bought was 3 bags of dog food, how much did she pay for each bag? $4.88

b. Three eighths of the 32 students were girls. How many boys were in the class? 20 boys

c. In Room 1 there were 28 students, in Room 2 there were 29 students, in Room 3 there were 30 students, and in Room 4 there were 25 students. What was the average number of students in the 4 rooms? 28 students

d. What is the mean of 46, 37, 34, 31, 29, and 24? $33\frac{1}{2}$

e. What is the average of 40 and 70? What number is halfway between 40 and 70? 55; 55

f. Dan has taken eight tests. His lowest score was 80 and his highest score was 95. Which of the following *could be* his average test score? B. 84

A. 80   B. 84   C. 95   D. 96

Problem set 28 (28)

1. The 5 players on the front line weighed 242 pounds, 236 pounds, 248 pounds, 268 pounds, and 226 pounds. What was the average weight of the players on the front line? **244 pounds**

2. Matt ran a mile in 5 minutes, 14 seconds. How many seconds did it take Matt to run a mile? **314 seconds** (28)

3. Ginger bought a pair of pants for $24.95 and 3 blouses for $15.99 each. Altogether, how much did she spend? **$72.92** (28)

4. The Italian navigator Christopher Columbus was 41 years old when he reached the Americas in 1492. In what year was he born? **1451** (12)

5.

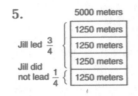

5. Change the percent to a fraction. Then draw a diagram of this statement and answer the questions that follow. (22)

Jill led for 75% of the 5000-meter race.

(a) Jill led the race for how many meters? **3750 meters**

(b) Jill did not lead the race for how many meters? **1250 meters**

6. This rectangle is twice as long as it is wide. (19,20)

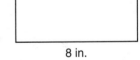

8 in.

(a) What is the perimeter of the rectangle? **24 in.**

(b) What is the area of the rectangle? **32 in.²**

7. (a) List the first six multiples of 3. **3, 6, 9, 12, 15, 18** (27)

(b) List the first six multiples of 4. **4, 8, 12, 16, 20, 24**

(c) What is the LCM of 3 and 4? **12**

(d) Use prime factorization to help find the least common multiple of 27 and 36. **108**

8. On this number line, 283 is closest to (27)

(a) which multiple of 10? **280**

(b) which multiple of 100? **300**

9. Write 56 and 240 as products of prime numbers. Then
(24) reduce $\frac{56}{240}$.   2·2·2·7 / 2·2·2·2·3·5 = $\frac{2·7}{2·3·5}$ = $\frac{7}{30}$

10. A mile is five thousand, two hundred eighty feet. Write
(5) that number in expanded notation.
$(5 \times 1000) + (2 \times 100) + (8 \times 10)$ feet

11. For (a) and (b), find an equivalent fraction that has a
(15) denominator of 24.

   (a) $\frac{7}{8}$ $\frac{21}{24}$ (b) $\frac{11}{12}$ $\frac{22}{24}$

   (c) Add the two fractions you found. $\frac{21}{24} + \frac{22}{24} = \frac{43}{24} = 1\frac{19}{24}$

12.(a) **3600** =
$2^4 · 3^2 · 5^2$

12. (a) Write the prime factorization of 3600 using exponents.
(21)
   (b) Find $\sqrt{3600}$.   **60**

13. Describe how to find the mean of 45, 36, 42, 29, 16, and 24.
(28) **Add the six numbers. Then divide the sum by 6.**

14.

14. (a) Draw square $ABCD$ so that each side is 1 inch long.
(8,20)   What is the area of the square?   **1 square inch**

   (b) Draw segments AC and BD. Label the point at which
       they intersect point E.

   (c) Shade triangle CDE.

   (d) What percent of the area of the square did you shade?
       25%

15. (a) Arrange these numbers in order from least to greatest:
(4,10)

$$-1, \frac{1}{10}, 1, \frac{11}{10}, 0 \quad -1, 0, \tfrac{1}{10}, 1, \tfrac{11}{10}$$

   (b) Which of these numbers are odd integers?   **−1 and 1**

Solve:

16. $12y = 360°$ **17.** $10^2 = m + 8^2$ **18.** $\dfrac{180}{w} = 60$ **3**
(3)   **30°**   (3,20)   **36**   (3)

Simplify:

19. $4\dfrac{5}{12} - 1\dfrac{1}{12}$ $3\frac{1}{3}$ **20.** $8\dfrac{7}{8} + 3\dfrac{3}{8}$ $12\frac{1}{4}$
(9,15)   (10,15)

21. $12 - 8\dfrac{1}{8}$ $3\frac{7}{8}$ **22.** $6\dfrac{2}{3} · 1\dfrac{1}{5}$ **8**
(23)   (26)

23. $\left(1\frac{1}{2}\right)^2 \div 7\frac{1}{2}$ $\frac{3}{10}$
(26)

24. $8 \div 2\frac{2}{3}$ 3
(26)

25. $\dfrac{10,000}{80}$ 125
(1)

26. $\dfrac{3}{4} - \left(\dfrac{1}{2} \div \dfrac{2}{3}\right)$ 0
(25)

27. $47.63
(1) $78.49
     + $35.24
     ─────────
     $161.36

28. $4.56
(1)   × ___9
     ─────────
     $41.04

29. In this figure the two triangles are congruent.
(18)

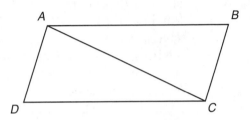

29.(a) $\angle ACD$
   (b) $\overline{CB}$

(a) Which angle in $\triangle ACD$ corresponds to $\angle CAB$ in $\triangle ABC$?

(b) Which segment in $\triangle ABC$ corresponds to $\overline{AD}$ in $\triangle ACD$?

(c) If the area of $\triangle ABC$ is $7\frac{1}{2}$ in.^{2}, what is the area of figure $ABCD$?   15 in.^{2}

30.

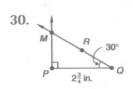

30. With a ruler draw $\overline{PQ}$ $2\frac{3}{4}$ in. long. Then with a protractor
(17) draw ray QR so that $\angle PQR$ measures 30°. Then draw a ray from point P perpendicular to $\overline{PQ}$ that intersects ray QR (extending ray QR if necessary for the rays to intersect). Label the point where this ray intersects ray QR point M. Use your protractor to measure $\angle PMQ$. $\angle PMQ$ measures 60°.

LESSON 29

Rounding Whole Numbers • Rounding Mixed Numbers • Estimating Answers

Facts Practice: Circles (Test E in Test Masters)

Mental Math:

a. $4.32 + $2.98   b. $12.50 ÷ 10   c. $10.00 − $8.98

d. 9 × 22   e. $\frac{5}{6} + \frac{5}{6}$ f. $\frac{3}{5}$ of 20

g. 6 × 6, ÷ 4, × 3, + 1, ÷ 4, × 8, − 1, ÷ 5, × 2, − 2, ÷ 2

Problem Solving:

Huck followed the directions on the treasure map. Starting at the big tree, he walked 6 paces north, turned left, and took seven paces. He turned left and went five paces, turned left again, and walked four paces. He then turned right and took one pace. In which direction was Huck facing, and how far was he from the big tree?

Rounding whole numbers

The first sentence below uses an exact number to state the size of a crowd. The second sentence uses a rounded number.

There were 3947 fans at the game.
There were about 4000 fans at the game.

Round numbers are often used instead of exact numbers. One way to round numbers is to consider where the number is located on the number line.

Example 1 Use a number line to

(a) round 283 to the nearest hundred.

(b) round 283 to the nearest ten.

Solution (a) We draw a number line and mark the location of the hundreds as well as the estimated location of 283.

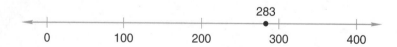

We see that 283 is between 200 and 300 and is closer to 300. To the nearest hundred, 283 rounds to **300.**

(b) We draw a number line and mark the location of the tens from 200 to 300 as well as the estimated location of 283.

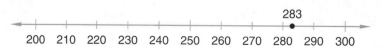

We see that 283 is between 280 and 290 and is closer to 280. To the nearest ten, 283 rounds to **280.**

Sometimes we are asked to round a number to a certain place value. We can use a circle and an arrow to help us do this. We will circle the digit in the place to which we are rounding, and we will draw an arrow above the next place to the right. Then we will follow these rules.

1. If the arrow-marked digit is 5 or more, we increase the circled digit by 1. If the arrow-marked digit is less than 5, we leave the circled digit unchanged.
2. We change the arrow-marked digit and all digits to the right of the arrow-marked digit to zero.

This rounding strategy is sometimes called the "4-5 split," because if the arrow-marked digit is 4 or less we round down, and if it is 5 or more we round up.

Example 2 (a) Round 283 to the nearest hundred.

(b) Round 283 to the nearest ten.

Solution (a) We circle the 2 since it is in the hundreds' place. Then we draw an arrow over the digit to its right.

Since the arrow-marked digit is 5 or more, we increase the circled digit 2 to 3. Then we change the arrow-marked digit and all digits to its right to zero and get

300

(b) Since we are rounding to the nearest ten, we circle the tens' digit and mark the digit to its right with an arrow.

Since the arrow-marked digit is less than 5, we leave the 8 unchanged. Then we change the 3 to zero and get

280

Example 3 Round 5280 so that there is one nonzero digit.

Solution We round the number so that all but one of the digits are zeros. In this case we round to the nearest thousand. So 5280 rounds to **5000.**

Example 4   Round 93,167,000 to the nearest million.

Solution   To the nearest million, 9③,167,000 rounds to **93,000,000**.

Rounding mixed numbers   When rounding a mixed number to a whole number we need to determine if the fraction part of the mixed number is more or less than $\frac{1}{2}$. If the fraction is more than or equal to $\frac{1}{2}$, the mixed number rounds up to the next whole number. If the fraction is less than $\frac{1}{2}$, the mixed number rounds down.

A fraction is more than $\frac{1}{2}$ if the numerator of the fraction is more than half of the denominator. A fraction is less than $\frac{1}{2}$ if the numerator is less than half of the denominator.

Example 5   Round $14\frac{7}{12}$ to the nearest whole number.

Solution   The mixed number $14\frac{7}{12}$ is between the consecutive whole numbers 14 and 15. We study the fraction to decide which is nearer. The fraction $\frac{7}{12}$ is more than $\frac{1}{2}$ because 7 is more than half of 12. So $14\frac{7}{12}$ rounds to **15.**

Estimating answers   Rounding can help us estimate the answers to arithmetic problems. Estimating is a quick and easy way to get close to an exact answer. Sometimes a close answer is "good enough," but even when an exact answer is necessary, estimating can help us decide if our exact answer is reasonable. One way to estimate is to round the numbers before performing the calculations.

Example 6   Mentally estimate:

(a) $5\frac{7}{10} \times 3\frac{1}{3}$ (b) 396×312 (c) $4160 \div 19$

Solution   (a) We round both mixed numbers to the nearest whole number before we multiply.

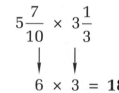

$$6 \times 3 = 18$$

(b) We may round each number to the nearest ten or to the nearest hundred.

Problem	Rounded to tens	Rounded to hundreds
396	400	400
× 312	× 310	× 300

When mentally estimating we often round the numbers to one nonzero digit so that it is easier to perform the calculations. In this case we would round to the nearest hundred.

$$
\begin{array}{r}
400 \\
\times\ 300 \\
\hline
\mathbf{120,000}
\end{array}
$$

(c) We round each number so there is one nonzero digit before we divide.

$$
\frac{4160}{19} \longrightarrow \frac{4000}{20} = \mathbf{200}
$$

Performing a quick mental estimate helps us determine if the result of a more complicated calculation is reasonable.

Practice   **a.** Round 1760 to the nearest hundred. **1800**

b. Round 5489 to the nearest thousand. **5000**

c. Round 186,282 to the nearest thousand. **186,000**

Estimate each answer.

d. 7986 − 3074 **5000**

e. 297 × 31 **9000**

f. 5860 ÷ 19 **300**

g. $12\dfrac{1}{4} \div 3\dfrac{7}{8}$ **3**

Problem set 29 **1.** Larry jumped 16 feet, 8 inches on his first try. How many
(16,28) inches did he jump on his first try? **200 inches**

2. If 8 pounds of bananas cost $3.68, how can we find the
(13) cost per pound? **The cost per pound means the cost for each pound. We divide $3.68, which is the cost for 8 pounds, by 8.**

3. On her first six tests Sandra's scores were 75, 70, 80, 80, 85,
(28) and 90. What was her average score on her first six tests? **80**

4. Two hundred nineteen billion, eight hundred million is
(5,12) how much less than one trillion? Use words to write your answer. **seven hundred eighty billion, two hundred million**

5.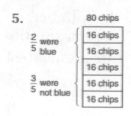

5. Change the percent to a fraction. Then draw a diagram of
(22) this statement and answer the questions that follow.

Forty percent of the 80 chips were blue.

(a) How many of the chips were blue? **32 chips**

(b) How many of the chips were not blue? **48 chips**

6. (a) What is the least common multiple (LCM) of 4, 6,
(27) and 8? **24**

(b) Use prime factorization to help find the LCM of 16
and 36. **144**

7. (a) What is the perimeter of this
(19,20) square? **3 in.**

(b) What is the area of this square?
$\frac{9}{16}$ in.^{2}

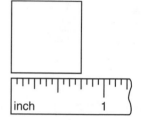

8. (a) Round 366 to the nearest hundred. **400**
(29)

(b) Round 366 to the nearest ten. **370**

9. Mentally estimate the sum of 6143 and 4952 by rounding
(29) each number to the nearest thousand before adding.
11,000

10. (a) Mentally estimate the following product by rounding
(26,29) each number to the nearest whole number before
multiplying. **5**

$$\frac{3}{4} \cdot 5\frac{1}{3} \cdot 1\frac{1}{8}$$

(b) Find the product of these fractions and mixed
numbers by performing the calculations. $4\frac{1}{2}$

11. Complete each equivalent fraction.
(15)

(a) $\frac{2}{3} = \frac{?}{30}$ **20**

(b) $\frac{?}{6} = \frac{25}{30}$ **5**

12. The prime factorization of 1000 is $2^3 \cdot 5^3$. Write the
(21) prime factorization of one billion using exponents.
$1,000,000,000 = 2^9 \cdot 5^9$

In this figure, quadrilaterals *ACDF*, *ABEF*, and *BCDE* are rectangles. Problems 13, 14, and 15 refer to this figure.

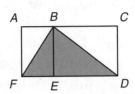

13. (a) What percent of rectangle *ABEF* is shaded? **50%**
(8)
   (b) What percent of rectangle *BCDE* is shaded? **50%**

   (c) What percent of rectangle *ACDF* is shaded? **50%**

14. The relationship between the lengths of the sides of the
(19,20) rectangles is the following:

$$AB + FE = BC$$
$$AF + CD = AC$$
$$AB = 2 \text{ in.}$$

   (a) Find the perimeter of rectangle *ABEF*. **10 in.**

   (b) Find the area of rectangle *BCDE*. **12 in.²**

15. Triangle *ABF* is congruent to △*EFB*.
(18)
   (a) Which angle in △*ABF* corresponds to ∠*EBF* in △*EFB*?
   ∠*AFB*
   (b) What is the measure of ∠*A*? **90°**

Solve:

16. $8^2 = 4m$ **16**
(3,20)

17. $x + 4\frac{4}{9} = 15$
(23) $10\frac{5}{9}$

18. $3\frac{5}{9} = n - 4\frac{7}{9}$
(10,15)
   $8\frac{1}{3}$

Simplify:

19. $6\frac{1}{3} - 5\frac{2}{3}$ $\frac{2}{3}$
(23)

20. $6\frac{2}{3} \div 5$ $1\frac{1}{3}$
(26)

21. $1\frac{2}{3} \div 3\frac{1}{2}$ $\frac{10}{21}$
(26)

22. 7.49×24 **$179.76**
(1)

23. $\frac{2}{5} + \left(\frac{4}{5} \div \frac{1}{2} \right)$ **2**
(25)

24. Mentally find this quotient by first
(27) multiplying both numbers by 4, then
   dividing both of those numbers by
   100. **160,000**

   $\dfrac{4,000,000}{25}$

25. (a) Write the prime factorization of 4,000,000 using
(21)   exponents. 4,000,000 = $2^8 \cdot 5^6$

(b) Find $\sqrt{4,000,000}$. 2,000

26. Recall how you inscribed a regular
(Inv. 2) hexagon in a circle in Investigation 2.
If the radius of this circle is one inch,

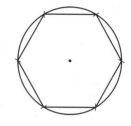

(a) what is the diameter of the circle?
2 inches

(b) what is the perimeter of the
hexagon? 6 inches

27. Find fractions equivalent to $\frac{2}{3}$ and $\frac{1}{2}$ with denominators
(15) of 6. Subtract the smaller fraction you found from the
larger fraction. $\frac{4}{6} - \frac{3}{6} = \frac{1}{6}$

28. What type of angle is
(7)

(a) $\angle RQS$? acute angle

(b) $\angle PQR$? obtuse angle

(c) $\angle PQS$? straight angle

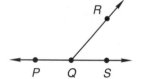

29. If two full cups of water are poured from a full quart
(16) container, how many ounces of water would be left in the
quart container? 16 ounces

30. Find the perimeter of this hexagon.
(19) 34 in.

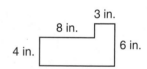

LESSON 30

Common Denominators • Adding and Subtracting Fractions with Different Denominators

Mental Math:
a. $3.98
b. $150.00
c. 9
d. 420
e. $4\frac{1}{3}$
f. 15
g. 6
Problem Solving:

$$\begin{array}{r} 32 \\ 53\overline{)1696} \\ \underline{159} \\ 106 \\ \underline{106} \\ 0 \end{array}$$

Facts Practice: Lines, Angles, Polygons (Test F in Test Masters)

Mental Math:

  a. $1.99 + $1.99   b. $0.15 × 1000   c. $\frac{3}{4} = \frac{?}{12}$

  d. 5 × 84   e. $1\frac{2}{3} + 2\frac{2}{3}$ f. $\frac{3}{4}$ of 20

  g. Find $\frac{1}{2}$ of 88, + 4, ÷ 8, × 5, − 5, double it, − 2, ÷ 2, ÷ 2, ÷ 2.

Problem Solving:

  Copy this problem and fill in the missing digits.

$$\begin{array}{r} 3\_ \\ \_3\overline{)\_6\_6} \\ \underline{1\_\_} \\ \_0\_ \\ \overline{} \\ 0 \end{array}$$

Common denominators

When two fractions have the same denominator, we say they have **common denominators**.

$$\frac{3}{8} \qquad \frac{6}{8} \qquad\qquad\qquad \frac{3}{8} \qquad \frac{3}{4}$$

These two fractions have common denominators.

These two fractions do not have common denominators.

If two fractions do not have common denominators, then one or both fractions can be renamed so both fractions do have common denominators. We remember that we can rename a fraction by multiplying the fraction by a fraction equal to 1. Thus we can rename $\frac{3}{4}$ so that it has a denominator of 8 by multiplying by $\frac{2}{2}$.

$$\frac{3}{4} \cdot \frac{2}{2} = \frac{6}{8}$$

Example 1 Rename $\frac{2}{3}$ and $\frac{1}{4}$ so that they have common denominators.

Solution The denominators are 3 and 4. A common denominator for these two fractions would be any common multiple of 3 and 4. The lowest common denominator would be the least common multiple of 3 and 4, which is 12. We want to rename each fraction so that the denominator is 12.

$$\frac{2}{3} = \frac{}{12} \qquad \frac{1}{4} = \frac{}{12}$$

We multiply $\frac{2}{3}$ by $\frac{4}{4}$ and multiply $\frac{1}{4}$ by $\frac{3}{3}$.

$$\frac{2}{3} \cdot \frac{4}{4} = \frac{8}{12} \qquad \frac{1}{4} \cdot \frac{3}{3} = \frac{3}{12}$$

Thus $\frac{2}{3}$ and $\frac{1}{4}$ can be written with common denominators as

$$\frac{8}{12} \quad \text{and} \quad \frac{3}{12}$$

Fractions written with common denominators can be compared by simply comparing the numerators.

Example 2 Write these fractions with common denominators and then compare them.

$$\frac{5}{6} \bigcirc \frac{7}{9}$$

Solution The common denominator for these fractions is the LCM of 6 and 9, which is 18.

$$\frac{5}{6} \cdot \frac{3}{3} = \frac{15}{18} \qquad \frac{7}{9} \cdot \frac{2}{2} = \frac{14}{18}$$

So, in place of $\frac{5}{6}$ we may write $\frac{15}{18}$, and in place of $\frac{7}{9}$ we may write $\frac{14}{18}$. Then we compare the renamed fractions.

$$\frac{15}{18} \bigcirc \frac{14}{18} \qquad \text{renamed}$$

$$\frac{15}{18} > \frac{14}{18} \qquad \text{compared}$$

Adding and subtracting fractions with different denominators To add or subtract two fractions that do not have common denominators, we first rename one or both fractions so that they do have common denominators. Then we can add or subtract.

Example 3 Add: $\frac{3}{4} + \frac{3}{8}$

Solution First we write the fractions with common denominators. The denominators are 4 and 8. The least common multiple of 4 and 8 is 8. We rename $\frac{3}{4}$ so that the denominator is 8 by multiplying by $\frac{2}{2}$. We do not need to rename $\frac{3}{8}$. Then we add the fractions and simplify.

$$\frac{3}{4} \cdot \frac{2}{2} = \frac{6}{8} \qquad \text{renamed } \frac{3}{4}$$
$$+ \frac{3}{8} \qquad = \frac{3}{8}$$
$$\overline{\qquad\qquad \frac{9}{8}} \qquad \text{added}$$

We finish by simplifying $\frac{9}{8}$.

$$\frac{9}{8} = 1\frac{1}{8}$$

Example 4 Subtract: $\dfrac{5}{6} - \dfrac{3}{4}$

Solution First we write the fractions with common denominators. The LCM of 6 and 4 is 12. We multiply $\frac{5}{6}$ by $\frac{2}{2}$ and multiply $\frac{3}{4}$ by $\frac{3}{3}$ so that both denominators are 12. Then we subtract the renamed fractions.

$$\frac{5}{6} \cdot \frac{2}{2} = \frac{10}{12} \qquad \text{renamed } \frac{5}{6}$$
$$- \frac{3}{4} \cdot \frac{3}{3} = \frac{9}{12} \qquad \text{renamed } \frac{3}{4}$$
$$\overline{\qquad\qquad \frac{1}{12}} \qquad \text{subtracted}$$

Example 5 Subtract: $8\dfrac{2}{3} - 5\dfrac{1}{6}$

Solution We first write the fractions with common denominators. The LCM of 3 and 6 is 6. We multiply $\frac{2}{3}$ by $\frac{2}{2}$ so that the denominator is 6. Then we subtract and simplify.

$$8\frac{2}{3} = 8\frac{4}{6} \qquad \text{renamed } 8\frac{2}{3}$$
$$- 5\frac{1}{6} = 5\frac{1}{6}$$
$$\overline{\qquad\qquad 3\frac{3}{6} = 3\frac{1}{2}} \qquad \text{subtracted and simplified}$$

Example 6   Add: $\dfrac{1}{2} + \dfrac{2}{3} + \dfrac{3}{4}$

Solution   The denominators are 2, 3, and 4. The LCM of 2, 3, and 4 is 12. We rename each fraction so that the denominator is 12. Then we add and simplify.

$$\dfrac{1}{2} \cdot \dfrac{6}{6} = \dfrac{6}{12} \qquad \text{renamed}$$

$$\dfrac{2}{3} \cdot \dfrac{4}{4} = \dfrac{8}{12} \qquad \text{renamed}$$

$$+\dfrac{3}{4} \cdot \dfrac{3}{3} = \dfrac{9}{12} \qquad \text{renamed}$$

$$\dfrac{23}{12} = 1\dfrac{11}{12} \qquad \text{added and simplified}$$

Example 7   Use prime factorization to help you add these fractions.

$$\dfrac{5}{32} + \dfrac{7}{24}$$

Solution   We write the prime factorization of the denominators of both fractions.

$$\dfrac{5}{32} = \dfrac{5}{2 \cdot 2 \cdot 2 \cdot 2 \cdot 2} \qquad \dfrac{7}{24} = \dfrac{7}{2 \cdot 2 \cdot 2 \cdot 3}$$

The lowest common denominator of the two fractions is the least common multiple of the denominators. So the lowest common denominator is

$$2 \cdot 2 \cdot 2 \cdot 2 \cdot 2 \cdot 3 = 96$$

To rename the fractions with common denominators we multiply $\frac{5}{32}$ by $\frac{3}{3}$, and we multiply $\frac{7}{24}$ by $\frac{2 \cdot 2}{2 \cdot 2}$.

$$\dfrac{5}{32} \cdot \dfrac{3}{3} = \dfrac{15}{96}$$

$$+\dfrac{7}{24} \cdot \dfrac{2 \cdot 2}{2 \cdot 2} = \dfrac{28}{96}$$

$$\mathbf{\dfrac{43}{96}}$$

Practice*   Write the fractions with common denominators and then compare them.

a. $\dfrac{3}{5} \bigcirc \dfrac{7}{10}$ $\frac{6}{10} < \frac{7}{10}$

b. $\dfrac{5}{12} \bigcirc \dfrac{7}{15}$ $\frac{25}{60} < \frac{28}{60}$

Add or subtract.

c. $\dfrac{3}{4} + \dfrac{5}{6} + \dfrac{3}{8}$ $1\frac{23}{24}$

d. $7\dfrac{5}{6} - 2\dfrac{1}{2}$ $5\frac{1}{3}$

e. $4\dfrac{3}{4} + 5\dfrac{5}{8}$ $10\frac{3}{8}$

f. $4\dfrac{1}{6} - 2\dfrac{5}{9}$ $1\frac{11}{18}$

g. Use prime factorization to help you subtract these fractions. $\frac{17}{225}$

$$\frac{3}{25} - \frac{2}{45}$$

Problem set 30

1. The 5 starters on the basketball team were tall. Their
(28) heights were 76 inches, 77 inches, 77 inches, 78 inches, and 82 inches. What was the average height of the 5 starters? **78 inches**

2. Marie bought 6 pounds of apples for $0.87 per pound and
(28) paid for them with a $10 bill. How much did she get back in change? **$4.78**

3. On the first day of their 2479-mile trip, the Curtis family
(11) drove 497 miles. How many more miles do they have to drive until they complete their trip? **1982 miles**

4. One hundred forty of the two hundred sixty students in
(14) the auditorium were boys. What fraction of the students in the auditorium were girls? $\frac{6}{13}$ **of the students**

5.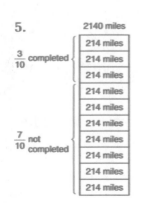

5. Change the percent to a fraction. Then draw a diagram of
(22) this statement and answer the questions that follow.

   The Daltons completed 30% of their 2140-mile trip the first day.

   (a) How many miles did they travel the first day? **642 miles**

   (b) How many miles of their trip do they still have to travel? **1498 miles**

6. If the perimeter of a square is 5 feet, how many inches
(19) long is each side of the square? **15 inches**

7. Use prime factorization to help you subtract these
(30) fractions. $\frac{1}{45}$

$$\frac{1}{18} - \frac{1}{30}$$

8. (a) Round 36,467 to the nearest thousand. 36,000
(29)

    (b) Round 36,467 to the nearest hundred. 36,500

9. Mentally estimate the quotient when 29,376 is divided
(29) by 49. 600

10. (a) Write 32% as a reduced fraction. $\frac{8}{25}$
(15,24)

    (b) Use prime factorization to help in reducing $\frac{48}{72}$. $\frac{2}{3}$

11. Write these fractions with common denominators. Then
(30) compare them. $\frac{20}{24} < \frac{21}{24}$

$$\frac{5}{6} \bigcirc \frac{7}{8}$$

In this figure, a 3 in. by 3 in. square is joined to a 4 in. by 4 in.
square. Refer to this figure to answer problems 12 and 13.

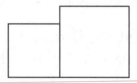

12. (a) What is the area of the smaller square? 9 in.²
(20)

    (b) What is the area of the larger square? 16 in.²

    (c) What is the total area of the figure? 25 in.²

13.(b) The
perimeter of the
hexagon is 6 in.
less than the
combined
perimeter of the
squares because a
3 in. side of the
smaller square
and the adjoining
3 in. portion of a
side of the larger
square are not
part of the
perimeter of the
hexagon.

13. (a) What is the perimeter of the hexagon that is formed
(19) by joining the two squares? 22 in.

    (b) The perimeter of the hexagon is how many inches less
than the combined perimeter of the two squares? Why?

14. (a) Write the prime factorization of 5184 using exponents.
(21) $5184 = 2^6 \cdot 3^4$

    (b) Use the answer to (a) to help you find $\sqrt{5184}$.
$2^3 \cdot 3^2 = 72$

15. What is the mean of 5, 7, 9, 11, 12, 13, 24, 25, 26, and 28?
(28) 16

16. List the single-digit divisors of 5670. 1, 2, 3, 5, 6, 7, 9
(6)

Solve:

17. $6w = 6^3$ **36**
(3,20)

18. $90° + 30° + a = 180°$
(3) **60°**

19. $45.00 = 36p$ **$1.25**
(3)

20. $\dfrac{t}{32} = \$3.75$ **$120.00**
(3)

Simplify:

21. $\dfrac{1}{2} + \dfrac{1}{3}$ $\frac{5}{6}$
(30)

22. $\dfrac{3}{4} - \dfrac{1}{3}$ $\frac{5}{12}$
(30)

23. $2\dfrac{5}{6} - 1\dfrac{1}{2}$ $1\frac{1}{3}$
(30)

24. $\dfrac{4}{5} \cdot 1\dfrac{2}{3} \cdot 1\dfrac{1}{8}$ $1\frac{1}{2}$
(26)

25. $1\dfrac{3}{4} \div 2\dfrac{2}{3}$ $\frac{21}{32}$
(26)

26. $3 \div 1\dfrac{7}{8}$ $1\frac{3}{5}$
(26)

27. $3\dfrac{2}{3} + 1\dfrac{5}{6}$ $5\frac{1}{2}$
(30)

28. $5\dfrac{1}{8} - 1\dfrac{3}{4}$ $3\frac{3}{8}$
(23,30)

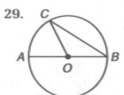

29. Draw a circle with a compass and label the center point O.
(Inv. 2) Draw chord AB through O. Draw chord CB not through O.
Draw segment CO. **See student work. One possibility is shown.**

30. Refer to the figure drawn in problem 29 to answer
(Inv. 2) questions (a)–(c).

  (a) Which chord is a diameter? $\overline{AB}$

  (b) Which segments are radii? $\overline{OA}, \overline{OB}, \overline{OC}$

  (c) Which central angle is an angle of $\triangle OBC$?
     $\angle BOC$

INVESTIGATION 3

Coordinate Plane

By drawing two perpendicular number lines and extending the marks, we can create a grid over an entire plane called the **coordinate plane.** We can identify any point on the coordinate plane with two numbers.

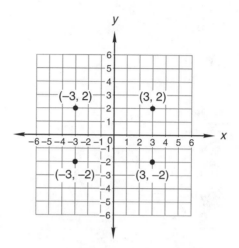

The horizontal number line is called the **x-axis.** The vertical number line is called the **y-axis.** The point at which the x-axis and the y-axis intersect is called the **origin.** The two numbers that indicate the location of a point are the **coordinates** of the point. The coordinates are written as a pair of numbers in parentheses, such as (3, 2). The first number shows the horizontal (↔) direction and distance from the origin. The second number shows the vertical (↕) direction and distance from the origin. The sign of the number indicates the direction. Positive coordinates are to the right or up. Negative coordinates are to the left or down. The origin is at point (0, 0).

The two axes divide the plane into four regions called **quadrants,** which are numbered counterclockwise beginning with the upper right as first, second, third, and fourth. The signs of the coordinates of each quadrant are shown below. Every point on a plane is either in a quadrant or on an axis.

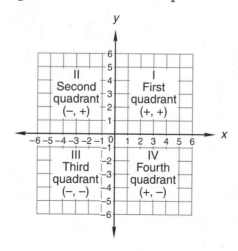

Example 1 Find the coordinates for points *A*, *B*, and *C* on this coordinate plane.

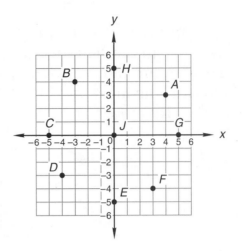

Solution We first find the point on the *x*-axis that is directly above or below the designated point. That is the first coordinate. Then we determine how many units above or below the *x*-axis the point is. That is the second coordinate.

Point *A* **(4, 3)**

Point *B* **(–3, 4)**

Point *C* **(–5, 0)**

===

Activity: Coordinate Plane[†]

Materials needed:

- Graph paper or copies of "Activity Master 4" (available in the *Math 87 Test Masters*) for each student.

- Straight edge

- Protractor

We suggest students work in pairs or in small groups. If using graph paper instead of "Activity Master 4," begin by drawing an *x*-axis and *y*-axis by darkening two perpendicular lines on the graph paper. For this activity we will let the distance between adjacent lines on the graph paper represent a distance of one unit. Perform each of the examples on a coordinate plane before going on to the practice exercises.

[†]Double lines indicate the beginning or ending of an activity.

Example 2   Graph the following points on a coordinate plane:

(a) (3, 4)   (b) (2, −3)   (c) (−1, 2)   (d) (0, −4)

Solution   To graph each point, we begin at the origin. To graph (3, 4), we move to the right (positive) 3 units along the *x*-axis. **From there** we turn and move up (positive) 4 units and make a dot. We label the location (3, 4). We follow a similar procedure for each point.

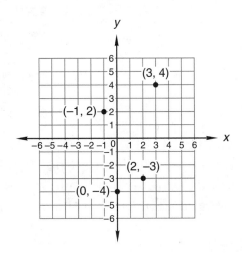

Example 3   The vertices of a square are located at (2, 2), (2, −1), (−1, −1), and (−1, 2). Draw the square and find its perimeter and area.

Solution   We graph the vertices and draw the square.

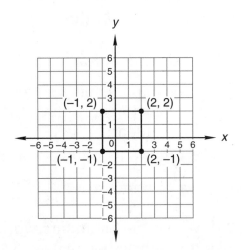

We find that each side of the square is 3 units long. So its perimeter is **12 units** and its area is **9 square units.**

Example 4   Three vertices of a rectangle are located at (2, 1), (2, −1), and (−2, −1). Find the coordinates of the fourth vertex and the perimeter and area of the rectangle.

Solution   We graph the given coordinates.

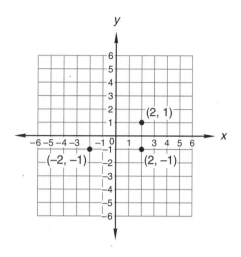

We see that the location of the fourth vertex is **(–2, 1),** which we graph. Then we draw the rectangle and find that it is 4 units long and 2 units wide. So its perimeter is **12 units** and its area is **8 square units.**

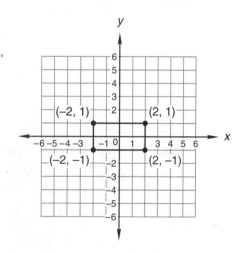

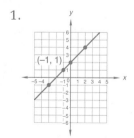

1. Graph these three points: (2, 4), (0, 2), and (–3, –1). Then draw a line that passes through these points. Name a point in the second quadrant that is on the line.

2. One vertex of a square is the origin. Two other vertices are located at (–2, 0) and (0, –2). What are the coordinates of the fourth vertex?   (–2, –2)

3. Find the perimeter and area of a rectangle whose vertices are located at (3, –1), (–2, –1), (–2, –4), and (3, –4).
16 units; 15 units^2

4. Points (4, 4), (4, 0), and (0, 0) are the vertices of a triangle. The triangle encloses whole squares and half squares on the grid. Determine the area of the triangle by counting the whole squares and the half squares. (Two half squares count for one square unit.)

Six whole squares plus 4 half squares totals 8 square units.

5. Draw a ray from the origin through the point at (10, 10). Draw another ray from the origin through (10, 0). Then use a protractor to measure the angle. 45°

6. Name the quadrant that contains each of these points.

(a) (−15, −20) (b) (12, 1)   (c) (20, −20)   (d) (−3, 5)
  3rd   1st   4th   2nd

7. Draw $\triangle ABC$ with vertices at A (0, 0), B (8, −8), and C (−8, −8). Use a protractor to find the measure of each angle of the triangle. m$\angle A$ = 90°; m$\angle B$ = 45°; m$\angle C$ = 45°

8.

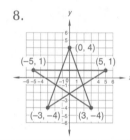

8. Shae wrote these directions for a dot-to-dot drawing. To complete the drawing, draw segments from point to point in the order given.

1. (0, 4)   2. (−3, −4)

3. (5, 1)   4. (−5, 1)

5. (3, −4)   6. (0, 4)

9. Plan and create a straight-segment drawing on graph paper. Determine the coordinates of the vertices. Then write directions for completing the dot-to-dot drawing for your other classmates to follow. Include the directions "lift pencil" between consecutive coordinates of points not to be connected. See student work.

10. Graph a dot-to-dot design created by a classmate.
See student work.

LESSON
31

Mental Math:
a. $3.01
b. $2.45
c. 8
d. $\frac{3}{4}$
e. 19
f. 45
g. 3
Problem Solving:
  169, 196, 225

Facts Practice: $+ - \times \div$ Fractions (Test G in Test Masters)

Mental Math:

  a. $4.00 - 99¢   **b.** $7 \times 35¢$ **c.** $\frac{2}{3} = \frac{?}{12}$

  d. Reduce $\frac{18}{24}$ **e.** $\sqrt{100} + 3^2$ **f.** $\frac{3}{4}$ of 60

  g. Start with the number of degrees in a right angle, $\div 2$, $+ 5$, $\div 5$, $- 1$, find the square root.

Problem Solving:

  Find the next three numbers in this sequence.

$$..., 100, 121, 144, ...$$

We have used fractions and percents to name parts of a whole. We remember that a fraction has a numerator and a denominator. The denominator indicates the number of equal parts in the whole. The numerator indicates the number of parts that are being selected.

$$\frac{\text{Number of parts selected}}{\text{Number of equal parts in the whole}} = \frac{3}{10}$$

Parts of a whole can also be named by using **decimal fractions.** In a decimal fraction we can see the numerator, but we cannot see the denominator. **The denominator of a decimal fraction is indicated by place value.** Here is the decimal fraction three tenths. The denominator, 10, is indicated by one place to the right of the decimal point.

$$0.3$$

The decimal fraction 0.3 and the common fraction $\frac{3}{10}$ are equivalent. Both are read, "three tenths."

$$0.3 = \frac{3}{10} \qquad \text{three tenths}$$

A decimal fraction written with two digits after the decimal point (two decimal places) is understood to have a denominator of 100, as we show here.

$$0.03 = \frac{3}{100} \qquad \text{three hundredths}$$

$$0.21 = \frac{21}{100} \qquad \text{twenty-one hundredths}$$

A number that contains a decimal fraction is called a **decimal number** or just a **decimal.**

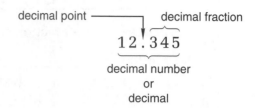

$$
\underset{\text{decimal number}}{\underset{\text{or}}{\underset{\text{decimal}}{\underbrace{12\underset{\uparrow}{.}\overbrace{345}^{\text{decimal fraction}}}}}}
$$

decimal point ⟶ ⬑ decimal fraction

Example 1 Write seven tenths (a) as a fraction and (b) as a decimal.

Solution (a) $\dfrac{7}{10}$ (b) **0.7**

Example 2 Name the shaded part of this square

(a) as a fraction.

(b) as a decimal.

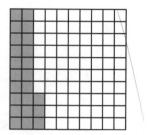

Solution (a) $\dfrac{23}{100}$ (b) **0.23**

In our number system the place a digit occupies has a value, called **place value.** We remember that places to the left of the decimal point have values of 1, 10, 100, 1000, and so on, becoming greater and greater. Places to the right of the decimal point have values of $\frac{1}{10}$, $\frac{1}{100}$, $\frac{1}{1000}$, and so on, becoming less and less. This chart shows decimal place values from the millions' place through the millionths' place.

Decimal Place Values

millions		hundred thousands	ten thousands	thousands		hundreds	tens	ones	decimal point	tenths	hundredths	thousandths	ten thousandths	hundred thousandths	millionths
1,000,000	,	100,000	10,000	1000	,	100	10	1	.	$\frac{1}{10}$	$\frac{1}{100}$	$\frac{1}{1000}$	$\frac{1}{10,000}$	$\frac{1}{100,000}$	$\frac{1}{1,000,000}$

Example 3   In the number 12.34579, which digit is in the thousandths' place?

Solution   The thousandths' place is the third place to the right of the decimal point and is occupied by the **5.**

Example 4   Name the place occupied by the 7 in 4.63471.

Solution   The 7 is in the fourth place to the right of the decimal point. This is the **ten-thousandths' place.**

To read a decimal number, we first read the whole number part, then we read the fraction part. To read the fraction part of a decimal number, we read the digits to the right of the decimal point as though we were reading a whole number. This number is the numerator of the decimal fraction. Then we say the name of the last decimal place. This number is the denominator of the decimal fraction.

Example 5   Read this decimal number: 123.123

Solution   First we read the whole number part. *When we come to the decimal point, we say "and."* Then we read the fraction part, ending with the name of the last decimal place.

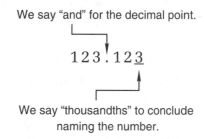

We say "and" for the decimal point.

123.123

We say "thousandths" to conclude
naming the number.

One hundred twenty-three and one hundred twenty-three thousandths

Example 6   Use digits to write these decimal numbers.

(a) Seventy-five thousandths

(b) One hundred and eleven hundredths

Solution   (a) The last word tells us the last place in the decimal number. "Thousandths" means there are three places to the right of the decimal point.

. _ _ _

We fit the digits of 75 into the places so the 5 is in the last place. We write zero in the remaining place.

. <u>0</u> <u>7</u> <u>5</u>

Decimal numbers without a whole number part are usually written with a zero in the ones' place.

0.075

(b) To write one hundred and eleven hundredths, we remember that the word "and" separates the whole number part of the number from the fraction part. First we write the whole number part followed by a decimal point for "and."

100.

Then we write the fraction part. We shift our attention to the last word to find out how many decimal places there are. "Hundredths" means there are two decimal places.

100. __ __

Now we fit 11 into the two decimal places.

100.11

Practice*

a. Write three hundredths as a fraction. Then write three hundredths as a decimal. $\frac{3}{100}$; 0.03

b. Name the shaded part of this circle both as a fraction and as a decimal. $\frac{3}{10}$; 0.3

c. In the number 16.57349, which digit is in the thousandths' place? 3

d. The number 36.4375 has how many decimal places? 4

Use words to write each decimal number.

e. 25.134 twenty-five and one hundred thirty-four thousandths

f. 100.01 one hundred and one hundredth

Use digits to write each decimal number.

g. One hundred two and three tenths 102.3

h. One hundred twenty-five ten thousandths 0.0125

i. Three hundred and seventy-five thousandths 300.075

Problem set 31

1. James and his brother are putting their money together to
(28) buy a radio that costs $89.89. James has $26.47. His brother has $32.54. How much more money do they need to buy the radio? $30.88

2. Norton read 4 books during his vacation. The first book
(28) was 326 pages, the second was 288 pages, the third was 349 pages, and the fourth was 401 pages. What was the average number of pages of the 4 books he read? 341 pages

3. A one-year subscription to the monthly magazine costs
(13) $15.96. At this price, what is the cost for each issue? $1.33

4. The settlement at Jamestown began in 1607. This was
(12) how many years after Columbus reached the Americas in 1492? 115 years

5. Divide the perimeter of the square by 4 to find the length of a side. Then multiply the length of a side by 6 to find the perimeter of the hexagon.

5. A square and a regular hexagon share
(19) a common side. The perimeter of the square is 24 in. Describe how to find the perimeter of the hexagon.

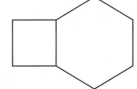

6.

20 questions	
$\frac{4}{5}$ were correct	4 questions
	4 questions
	4 questions
	4 questions
$\frac{1}{5}$ were incorrect	4 questions

6. Change the percent to a fraction. Then draw a diagram of
(22) this statement and answer the questions that follow.

Nelson correctly answered 80% of the 20 questions on the test.

(a) How many questions did Nelson answer correctly?
16 questions

(b) How many questions did Nelson answer incorrectly?
4 questions

7. Round 481,462
(29)

(a) to the nearest hundred thousand. 500,000

(b) to the nearest thousand. 481,000

8. Mentally estimate the difference between 49,623 and
(29) 20,162. 30,000

9. Name the shaded part of this square
(31)

(a) as a fraction. $\frac{7}{100}$

(b) as a decimal. 0.07

(c) as a percent. 7%

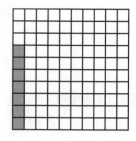

10. In the number 9.87654, which digit is in the hundredths'
(31) place? 7

11. Replace each circle with the proper comparison symbol.
(31)

(a) $\frac{3}{10}$ ⊜ 0.3

(b) $\frac{3}{100}$ ⓒ 0.3

12. The vertices of a square are located at (3, 3), (3, −3),
(Inv. 3) (−3, −3), and (−3, 3).

(a) What is the perimeter of the square? 24 units

(b) What is the area of the square? 36 units²

13. Complete each equivalent fraction.
(15)

(a) $\frac{5}{?} = \frac{15}{24}$ 8

(b) $\frac{7}{12} = \frac{?}{24}$ 14

(c) $\frac{?}{6} = \frac{4}{24}$ 1

14.(a) 2025
= 3⁴ · 5²

14. (a) Write the prime factorization of 2025 using exponents.
(21)
(b) Find $\sqrt{2025}$. 45

15.

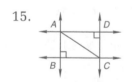

15. Draw two parallel lines. Then draw two more parallel
(18) lines that are perpendicular to the first pair of lines. Label
the points of intersection A, B, C, and D consecutively in
a counterclockwise direction. Draw segment AC. Refer to
this figure to answer the following questions:

(a) What kind of quadrilateral is figure $ABCD$? rectangle

(b) Triangles ABC and CDA are congruent. Which angle
in $\triangle ABC$ corresponds to $\angle DAC$ in $\triangle CDA$? $\angle BCA$

Solve:

16. $9n = 6 \cdot 12$ 8
(3)

17. $90° + 45° + b = 180°$
(3) 45°

18. $\$98.75 + W = \$220.15$
(3) $121.40

19. $\frac{m}{48} = \$4.65$ $223.20
(3)

Simplify:

20. $\frac{1}{2} + \frac{2}{3}$ $1\frac{1}{6}$
(30)

21. $\frac{3}{4} - \frac{2}{3}$ $\frac{1}{12}$
(30)

22. $3\frac{5}{6} - \frac{1}{3}$ $3\frac{1}{2}$
(30)

23. $\frac{5}{8} \cdot 2\frac{2}{5} \cdot \frac{4}{9}$ $\frac{2}{3}$
(26)

24. $2\frac{2}{3} \div 1\frac{3}{4}$ $1\frac{11}{21}$
(26)

25. $1\frac{7}{8} \div 3$ $\frac{5}{8}$
(26)

26. $3\frac{1}{2} + 1\frac{5}{6}$ $5\frac{1}{3}$
(30)

27. $5\frac{1}{4} - 1\frac{5}{8}$ $3\frac{5}{8}$
(23,30)

28. $\frac{1}{2} - \left(\frac{3}{4} \cdot \frac{2}{3} \right)$ 0
(9,24)

29. $\frac{9}{14} \cdot \frac{7}{12} \cdot \frac{8}{15} \cdot \frac{5}{2}$ $\frac{1}{2}$
(24)

30. (a) A half circle or half turn measures
(17)   how many degrees? 180°

(b) A quarter of a circle measures how many degrees? 90°

(c) An eighth of a circle measures how many degrees? 45°

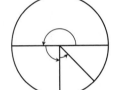

LESSON
32

Mental Math:
a. $2.77
b. $2.00
c. 20
d. $\frac{3}{5}$
e. 25
f. 12
g. 2
Problem Solving:
  16 pennies

Facts Practice: $+ - \times \div$ Fractions (Test G in Test Masters)

Mental Math:

  a. $3.76 − 99¢   b. 8 × 25¢   c. $\frac{5}{6} = \frac{?}{24}$
  d. Reduce $\frac{12}{20}$ e. $3^2 + 4^2$ f. $\frac{2}{5}$ of 30

  g. Start with the number of sides of an octagon, × 5, + 2, ÷ 6, × 5, + 1, $\sqrt{\ }$, ÷ 3.

Problem Solving:

  The diameter of a penny is $\frac{3}{4}$ in. How many pennies placed side-by-side would it take to make a row of pennies one foot long?

The U.S. Customary System of measurement with units like inches, feet, miles, pounds, and gallons, was once used throughout the former British Empire, and was known as the English system. Over the years countries have converted to the metric system of measurement which is now the International System (or SI for *Système international*). The metric system has several advantages over the U.S. Customary System, two of which are that the metric system is a decimal system and that the units of one category of measurement are linked to units of other categories of measurement.

The metric system is a decimal system in that units within a category of measurement differ by a factor of 10 or a power of 10. The U.S. Customary System is not a decimal system so converting between units is more difficult. Here we show some equivalent measures of length in the metric system.

UNITS OF LENGTH

10 millimeters (mm) = 1 centimeter (cm)

1000 millimeters (mm) = 1 meter (m)

100 centimeters (cm) = 1 meter (m)

1000 meters (m) = 1 kilometer (km)

Notice that the basic unit of length in the metric system is the meter. Units larger than a meter or smaller than a meter are indicated by prefixes that are consistent across the categories of measurement. These prefixes are shown in the table below with their numerical relationship to the basic unit.

Examples of Metric Prefixes

Unit	Relationship
kilometer (km)	1000 meters
hectometer (hm)	100 meters
dekameter (dkm)	10 meters
meter (m)	
decimeter (dm)	$\frac{1}{10}$ meter
centimeter (cm)	$\frac{1}{100}$ meter
millimeter (mm)	$\frac{1}{1000}$ meter

As we move up the table the units become larger so fewer units are needed to describe a length.

$$1000 \text{ mm} = 100 \text{ cm} = 10 \text{ dm} = 1 \text{ m}$$

As we move down the table the units become smaller, so the number of units required to describe a length increases.

$$1 \text{ km} = 10 \text{ hm} = 100 \text{ dkm} = 1000 \text{ m}$$

Note that a meter is about 3 inches longer than a yard, and an inch is exactly 2.54 centimeters.

Example 1   (a) Five kilometers is how many meters?

(b) Three hundred centimeters is how many meters?

Solution   (a) Every kilometer is 1000 meters, so 5 kilometers is **5000 meters.**

(b) A centimeter is $\frac{1}{100}$ of a meter (just as a cent is $\frac{1}{100}$ of a dollar). One hundred centimeters equals a meter, so 300 centimeters equals **3 meters.**

The liter is the basic unit of capacity in the metric system. We are familiar with 2-liter beverage bottles which contain a little more than a half gallon of soft drink. So a liter is a little more than a quart. A milliliter is $\frac{1}{1000}$ of a liter.

UNITS OF LIQUID MEASURE

> 1000 milliliters (mL) = 1 liter (L)

Example 2   A 2-liter beverage bottle contains how many milliliters of beverage?

Solution   Each liter is 1000 mL, so 2 L is **2000 mL.**

We distinguish between mass and weight. The weight of an object varies with the gravitational force, while its mass does not vary. The weight of an object on the Moon is about $\frac{1}{6}$ of its weight on Earth, yet its mass is the same. The mass of this book is about one kilogram. A gram is $\frac{1}{1000}$ of a kilogram—about the mass of a paperclip. A milligram, $\frac{1}{1000}$ of a gram and one millionth of a kilogram, is a unit used for measuring the mass of smaller quantities of matter such as the amount of vitamins in the food we eat.

UNITS OF MASS/WEIGHT

> 1000 grams (g) = 1 kilogram (kg)
>
> 1000 milligrams (mg) = 1 gram

Although a kilogram is a unit for measuring mass anywhere in the universe, here on Earth shopkeepers use kilograms to measure the weights of the goods they buy and sell. A kilogram mass weighs about 2.2 pounds.

Example 3   How many 250 mg tablets of Vitamin C equal one gram of Vitamin C?

Solution   A gram is 1000 mg, so **four** 250 mg tablets of Vitamin C total one gram of Vitamin C.

The **Celsius** and **Kelvin** scales are used by scientists to measure temperature. Both are **centigrade** scales because there are 100 gradations, or degrees, between the freezing and boiling temperatures of water. The Celsius scale places 0°C at the freezing point of water. The Kelvin scale places 0 K at *absolute zero*, which is 273 centigrade degrees below the freezing temperature of water (−273°C). The Celsius scale is more commonly used by the general population. Below we show frequently referenced temperatures on the Celsius scale.

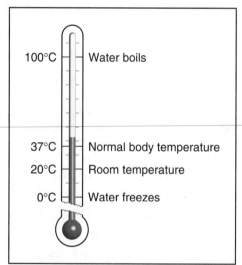

Celsius Temperature Scale

Example 4   An increase in temperature of 100°C on the Celsius scale is equivalent to an increase of how many degrees on the Fahrenheit scale?

Solution   The Celsius and Fahrenheit scales are different scales. An increase of one degree on one scale is not equivalent to an increase of one degree on the other scale. An increase of 100° on the Celsius scale is equivalent to an increase in temperature from the freezing temperature of water to the boiling temperature of water. On the Fahrenheit scale that is an increase from 32°F to 212°F, an increase of 180°F. So an increase of 100°C on the Celsius scale is equivalent to an increase of **180°F** on the Fahrenheit scale.

Practice   **a.** The closet door is 2 meters tall. How many centimeters is that?   200 centimeters

b. A gallon bottle can hold a little less than four liters. (Have students check the label on a gallon bottle; 3.78 liters.)

b. A one-gallon milk bottle can hold about how many liters of milk?

c. A metric ton is 1000 kilograms, so a metric ton is about how many pounds?   1000 × 2.2 pounds is about 2200 pounds

d. An increase in temperature of 10 degrees on the Celsius scale is equivalent to an increase of how many degrees on the Fahrenheit scale? (See Example 4.)   18°F

Problem set 32

1. There were 3 towns on the mountain. The population of Hazelhurst was 4248. The population of Baxley was 3584. The population of Jesup was 9418. What was the average population of the 3 towns on the mountain?   5750
(28)

2. The film was a long one, lasting 206 minutes. How many hours and minutes long was the film?   3 hours, 26 minutes
(28)

3. A mile is 1760 yards. Claudia ran 440 yards. What fraction of a mile did she run? $\frac{1}{4}$ mile
(14)

4. A square and a regular pentagon share a common side. The perimeter of the square is 20 cm. What is the perimeter of the pentagon?   25 cm
(19)

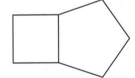

5. Round 3,197,270
(29)

    (a) to the nearest million.   3,000,000

    (b) to the nearest hundred thousand.   3,200,000

6. Mentally estimate the product of 313 and 489.   150,000
(29)

7.

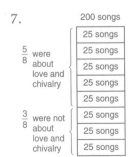

7. Draw a diagram of this statement. Then answer the questions that follow.
(22)

Five eighths of the troubadour's 200 songs were about love and chivalry.

    (a) How many of the songs were about love and chivalry?   125 songs

    (b) How many of the songs were not about love and chivalry?   75 songs

8. (a) What fraction of the rectangle is
(31)   not shaded? $\frac{9}{10}$

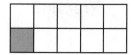

(b) What decimal part of the rectangle
is not shaded? 0.9

(c) What percent of the rectangle is not shaded? 90%

9. Use words to write 3.025. three and twenty-five thousandths
(31)

10. Use digits to write the decimal number seventy-six and
(31) five hundredths. 76.05

11. Instead of dividing $15.00 by $2\frac{1}{2}$, double both numbers
(27) and then find the quotient. $30.00 ÷ 5 = $6.00

12.(a) (2 × 1000)   **12.** (a) Write 2500 in expanded notation.
    + (5 × 100) (5,21)
(b) 2500   (b) Write the prime factorization of 2500 using exponents.
  = 2² · 5⁴
                     (c) Find $\sqrt{2500}$. 50

13. If 35 liters of petrol cost $21.00, what is the price per liter?
(13) $0.60 per liter

14.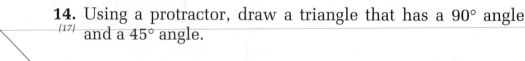

14. Using a protractor, draw a triangle that has a 90° angle
(17) and a 45° angle.

In this figure a 6 cm by 6 cm square is joined to an 8 cm by
8 cm square. Refer to this figure to answer problems 15 and 16.

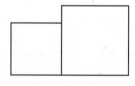

15. (a) What is the area of the smaller square? 36 cm²
(20)
(b) What is the area of the larger square? 64 cm²

(c) What is the total area of the figure? 100 cm²

16. What is the perimeter of the hexagon that is formed by
(19) joining the squares? 44 cm

Solve:

17. 10 · 6 = 4w 15   **18.** 180° − S = 65° 115°
(3)   (3)

Simplify:

19.
(30) $\dfrac{1}{4} + \dfrac{3}{8} + \dfrac{1}{2}$ $1\frac{1}{8}$

20.
(30) $\dfrac{5}{6} - \dfrac{3}{4}$ $\frac{1}{12}$

21.
(30) $\dfrac{5}{16} - \dfrac{3}{20}$ $\frac{13}{80}$

22.
(26) $\dfrac{8}{9} \cdot 1\dfrac{1}{5} \cdot 10$ $10\frac{2}{3}$

23.
(26) $5\dfrac{2}{5} \div \dfrac{9}{10}$ 6

24.
(30) $4\dfrac{5}{8} + 1\dfrac{1}{2}$ $6\frac{1}{8}$

25.
(30) $7\dfrac{3}{4} + 1\dfrac{7}{8}$ $9\frac{5}{8}$

26.
(23,30) $6\dfrac{1}{6} - 2\dfrac{1}{2}$ $3\frac{2}{3}$

27.
(25) $\dfrac{2}{3} + \left(\dfrac{2}{3} \div \dfrac{1}{2} \right)$ 2

28.
(24) $\dfrac{25}{36} \cdot \dfrac{9}{10} \cdot \dfrac{8}{15}$ $\frac{1}{3}$

29. The coordinates of three vertices of a rectangle are (−5, 3),
(Inv. 3) (−5, −2), and (2, −2).

(a) What are the coordinates of the fourth vertex? (2, 3)

(b) What is the area of the rectangle? 35 units²

30. Refer to the figure to answer questions (a)–(c).
(Inv. 2)

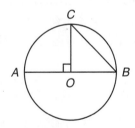

(a) Which chord is not a diameter? $\overline{BC}$

(b) Name a central angle that is a right angle.
∠AOC or ∠BOC

(c) Name an inscribed angle. ∠ABC or ∠BCO

LESSON 33

Comparing Decimals • Rounding Decimals

Mental Math:
a. $1.85
b. $3.30
c. 9
d. $\frac{4}{5}$
e. 20
f. 25
g. 12
Problem Solving:

6 handshakes

Facts Practice: Lines, Angles, Polygons (Test F in Test Masters)

Mental Math:

    a. $2.84 − 99¢   **b.** 6 × 55¢   **c.** $\frac{3}{8} = \frac{?}{24}$

    d. Reduce $\frac{24}{30}$ **e.** $5^2 − \sqrt{25}$ **f.** $\frac{5}{6}$ of 30

    g. Think of an equivalent division problem for 600 ÷ 50 and then find the quotient.

Problem Solving:

When Bill, Phil, Jill, and Gil entered the room they all shook hands with each other. How many handshakes were there in all? Draw a diagram that illustrates the problem. (Four students may act out the story.)

Comparing decimals

When comparing decimal numbers it is necessary to consider place value. The value of a place is determined by its position with respect to the decimal point. Terminal zeros to the right of the decimal point have no value.

$$1.3 = 1.30 = 1.300 = 1.3000$$

When we compare decimal numbers, it is helpful to insert terminal zeros so that both numbers will have the same number of digits to the right of the decimal point.

Example 1   Compare: 0.12 ◯ 0.012

Solution   So that each number has the same number of decimal places, we insert a terminal zero in the number on the left and get

$$0.120 \bigcirc 0.012$$

One hundred twenty thousandths is greater than twelve thousandths, so we write our answer this way.

$$\textbf{0.12} > \textbf{0.012}$$

Example 2   Compare: 0.4 ◯ 0.400

Solution   We may delete two terminal zeros from the number on the right and get

$$0.4 = 0.4$$

We could have added terminal zeros to the number on the left to get

$$0.400 = 0.400$$

We write our answer this way.

0.4 = 0.400

Example 3 Compare: 1.232 $\bigcirc$ 1.23185

Solution We insert two terminal zeros in the number on the left and get

1.23200 $\bigcirc$ 1.23185

Since 1.23200 is greater than 1.23185, we write

1.232 > 1.23185

Rounding decimals To round decimal numbers, we can use the same circle and arrow procedure that we use to round whole numbers.

Example 4 Round 3.14159 to the nearest hundredth.

Solution The hundredths' place is two places to the right of the decimal point. We circle the digit in that place and mark the digit to its right with an arrow.

$$\downarrow$$
$$3.1④159$$

Since the arrow-marked digit is less than 5, we leave the circled digit unchanged. Then we change all digits to the right of the circled digit to zero.

3.14000

Terminal zeros to the right of the decimal point do not serve as placeholders as they do in whole numbers. After rounding decimal numbers, we should remove terminal zeros to the right of the decimal point.

3.14~~000~~ ⟶ **3.14**

Note that a calculator simplifies decimal numbers by omitting from the display extraneous (unnecessary) zeros. For example, enter the following sequence of keystrokes:

1 0 . 2 0 3 0 0

Notice that all entered digits are displayed. Now press the = key and the unnecessary zeros are removed from the display.

Example 5 Round 4396.4315 to the nearest hundred.

Solution We are rounding to the nearest hundred, not to the nearest hundredth.

$$4\textcircled{3}\overset{\downarrow}{9}6.4315$$

Since the arrow-marked digit is 5 or more, we increase the circled digit by 1. All of the following digits become zeros.

4400.0000

Zeros at the end of a whole number are needed as placeholders. Terminal zeros to the right of the decimal point are not needed as placeholders. We remove these zeros.

4400.~~0000~~ → **4400**

Example 6 Round 38.62 to the nearest whole number.

Solution To round a number to the nearest whole number, we round to the ones' place.

$$3\textcircled{8}.\overset{\downarrow}{6}2 \rightarrow 39.\cancel{00} \rightarrow \mathbf{39}$$

Example 7 Estimate the product of 12.21 and 4.9 by rounding each number to the nearest whole number before multiplying.

Solution We round 12.21 to 12 and 4.9 to 5. Then we multiply 12 and 5 and find that the estimated product is **60.**

Practice* Compare:

a. 10.30 (=) 10.3

b. 5.06 (<) 5.60

c. 1.1 (>) 1.099

d. Round 3.14159 to the nearest ten thousandth. 3.1416

e. Round 365.2418 to the nearest hundred. 400

f. Round 57.432 to the nearest whole number. 57

g. Simplify 10.2000 by removing extraneous zeros.   10.2

h.
$$\begin{array}{r} 9 \\ 22 \\ + \ 11 \\ \hline 42 \end{array}$$

h. Estimate the sum of 8.65, 21.7, and 11.038 by rounding each decimal number to the nearest whole number before adding.

Problem set 33

1. We multiply 5 times 12 inches to find the number of inches in 5 feet. Then we add 8 inches to find the total number of inches in 5 feet, 8 inches.

1. The high jumper set a new school record when she cleared 5 feet, 8 inches. How can we find how many inches high 5 feet, 8 inches is?
(28)

2. During the first week of November the high daily temperatures in degrees Fahrenheit were 42°F, 43°F, 38°F, 47°F, 51°F, 52°F, and 49°F. What was the average high daily temperature during the first week of November?   46°F
(28)

3. In 10 years the population increased from 87,196 to 120,310. By how many people did the population increase in 10 years?   33,114 people
(11)

4. Find the next two numbers in this sequence.
(2)

120, 105, 90, 75, ...   60, 45

5. A regular hexagon and a regular octagon share a common side. If the perimeter of the hexagon is 24 cm, what is the perimeter of the octagon?   32 cm
(19)

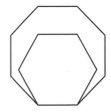

6.

	60 questions
$\frac{2}{3}$ were not T-F	20 questions
	20 questions
$\frac{1}{3}$ were T-F	20 questions

6. Draw a diagram of this statement. Then answer the questions that follow.
(22)

One third of the 60 questions on the test were true-false.

(a) How many of the questions on the test were true-false?   20 questions

(b) How many of the questions on the test were not true-false?   40 questions

(c) What percent of the questions were true-false? $33\frac{1}{3}\%$

7. Find the area of a square whose vertices have the coordinates (3, 6), (3, 1), (−2, 1), and (−2, 6).   25 units²
(Inv. 3)

8. (a) Round 15.73591 to the nearest hundredth. 15.74
(33)

(b) Estimate the product of 15.73591 and 3.14 by rounding each decimal number to the nearest whole number before multiplying. 16 × 3 = 48

9. Use words to write each of these decimal numbers.
(31)

(a) 150.035 one hundred fifty and thirty-five thousandths

(b) 0.0015 fifteen ten thousandths

10. Use digits to write each of these decimal numbers.
(31)

(a) One hundred twenty-five thousandths 0.125

(b) One hundred and twenty-five thousandths 100.025

11. Replace each circle with the proper comparison symbol.
(33)

(a) 0.128 ⊂< 0.14   (b) 0.03 ⊃> 0.0015

12. Find the length of this segment
(32)

(a) in centimeters. 4 cm

(b) in millimeters. 40 mm

13.

13. Draw the straight angle *AOC*. Then use a protractor to draw a ray *OD* so that ∠*COD* measures 60°.
(17)

14. If we multiply one integer by another integer that is a whole number but not a counting number, what is the product? $N \cdot 0 = 0$
(2)

15. Use prime factorization to help find the least common multiple of 63 and 49. 441
(27)

Solve:

16. $8m = 4 \cdot 18$ 9   **17.** $135° + a = 180°$ 45°
(3)   (3)

18. (a) Solve: $54 = 54 + y$ 0
(2)

(b) What property is illustrated by the equation in (a)?
identity property of addition

Simplify:

19. $\frac{3}{4} + \frac{5}{8} + \frac{1}{2}$ $\;1\frac{7}{8}$
(30)

20. $\frac{3}{4} - \frac{1}{6}$ $\;\frac{7}{12}$
(30)

21. $4\frac{1}{2} - \frac{3}{8}$ $\;4\frac{1}{8}$
(30)

22. $\frac{3}{8} \cdot 2\frac{2}{5} \cdot 3\frac{1}{3}$ $\;3$
(26)

23. $2\frac{7}{10} \div 5\frac{2}{5}$ $\;\frac{1}{2}$
(26)

24. $5 \div 4\frac{1}{6}$ $\;1\frac{1}{5}$
(26)

25. $8\frac{5}{8} + 5\frac{3}{4}$ $\;14\frac{3}{8}$
(30)

26. $6\frac{1}{2} - 2\frac{5}{6}$ $\;3\frac{2}{3}$
(23,30)

27. $\frac{3}{4} + \left(\frac{1}{2} \div \frac{2}{3} \right)$ $\;1\frac{1}{2}$
(25)

28.
(1)
$$\begin{array}{r} \$7.40 \\ \times \quad 800 \\ \hline \$5920.00 \end{array}$$

29. $\$40.00 \div 16$ $\;\$2.50$
(1)

30.
(17)
30. Use a protractor to help you draw a triangle that has a 30° angle and a 60° angle.

LESSON
34

Decimal Numbers on the Number Line

Facts Practice: $+ - \times \div$ Fractions (Test G in Test Masters)

Mental Math:

  a. $6.48 - 98¢   **b.** $5 \times 48¢$ **c.** $\frac{3}{5} = \frac{?}{30}$

  d. Reduce $\frac{16}{24}$ **e.** $\sqrt{36} \cdot \sqrt{49}$ **f.** $\frac{2}{3}$ of 36

  g. Square the number of sides on a pentagon, double that number, $- 1$, $\sqrt{}$, $\times 4$, $- 1$, $\div 3$, $\sqrt{}$.

Problem Solving:

Jamaal glued 27 small blocks together to make this cube. Then Jamaal painted the six faces of the cube. Later the cube broke apart into 27 blocks. How many of the small blocks had 3 painted faces, 2 painted faces, 1 painted face, no painted faces?

If the distance between consecutive numbers on a number line is divided into 10 equal segments, then numbers corresponding to these marks can be named using decimal numbers with one decimal place. An example of this kind of number line is a centimeter ruler.

If each centimeter segment on a centimeter scale is divided into 10 equal segments, then each segment is 1 millimeter long. Each segment is also one tenth of a centimeter long.

Example 1 Find the length of this segment

(a) in millimeters.

(b) in centimeters.

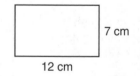

Solution (a) Each centimeter is 10 mm. Thus, each small segment on the scale is 1 mm. The length of the segment is **23 mm.**

(b) Each centimeter on the scale has been divided into 10 equal parts. The length of the segment is 2 centimeters plus three tenths of a centimeter. In the metric system we use decimals rather than common fractions to indicate parts of a unit. The length of the segment is **2.3 cm.**

If the distance between consecutive whole numbers on a number line is divided into 100 equal units, then numbers corresponding to the marks on the number line can be named using two decimal places. For instance, a meter is 100 cm. So each centimeter segment on a meter stick is 0.01 $\left(\text{or } \frac{1}{100}\right)$ of the length of the meter stick. This means that an object 25 cm long is also 0.25 m long.

Example 2 Find the perimeter of this rectangle in meters.

7 cm

12 cm

Solution The perimeter of the rectangle is 38 cm. Each centimeter is $\frac{1}{100}$ of a meter. So 38 cm is $\frac{38}{100}$ of a meter, which we write as **0.38 m.**

Example 3 Find the number on the number line indicated by each arrow.

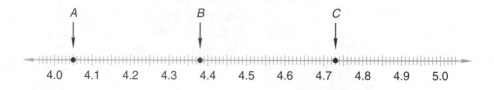

Solution We are considering a portion of the number line from 4 to 5. The distance from 4 to 5 has been divided into 100 equal segments. Tenths have been identified. The point 4.1 is one tenth of the distance from 4 to 5. However, it is also ten hundredths of the distance from 4 to 5, so 4.1 equals 4.10.

Arrow *A* indicates **4.05.**

Arrow *B* indicates **4.38.**

Arrow *C* indicates **4.73.**

Practice **a.** Find the length of this segment in centimeters. 1.6 cm

b. Seventy-five centimeters is how many meters? 0.75 meter

c. Alfredo is 1.57 meters tall. How many centimeters tall is Alfredo? 157 centimeters

d. What point on a number line is halfway between 2.6 and 2.7? 2.65

e. What decimal number names the point marked by *A* on this number line? 10.01

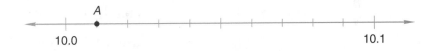

Problem set 34 **1.** In 3 boxes of cereal Jeff counted 188 raisins, 212 raisins,
(28) and 203 raisins. What was the average number of raisins in each box of cereal? 201 raisins

2. The pollen count had increased from 497 parts per
(11) million to 1032 parts per million. By how much had the pollen count increased? 535 parts per million

3. Sylvia spent $3.95 for lunch but still had $12.55. How
(11) much money did she have before she bought lunch? $16.50

4. In 1903 the Wright brothers made the first powered
(12) airplane flight. Just 66 years later astronauts first landed on the Moon. In what year did astronauts first land on the Moon? 1969

5. The perimeter of the square equals
(19) the perimeter of the regular hexagon. If each side of the hexagon is 6 inches long, how long is each side of the square? 9 inches

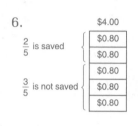

6.

$4.00

$\frac{2}{5}$ is saved

$\frac{3}{5}$ is not saved

| $0.80 |
| $0.80 |
| $0.80 |
| $0.80 |
| $0.80 |

6. Write the percent as a fraction. Then draw a diagram of
(22) this statement and answer the questions that follow.

Each week Jessica saves 40% of her $4.00 allowance.

(a) How much allowance money does she save each week? $1.60

(b) How much allowance money does she not save each week? $2.40

7. Describe how to estimate the product of 396 and 71.
(29) First round 396 to 400 and 71 to 70. Then multiply 400 and 70.

8. Round 7.49362 to the nearest thousandth. 7.494
(33)

9. Use words to write each of these decimal numbers.
(31)

(a) 200.02   two hundred and two hundredths

(b) 0.001625   one thousand, six hundred twenty-five millionths

10. Use digits to write each of these decimal numbers.
(31)

(a) One hundred seventy-five millionths   0.000175

(b) Three thousand, thirty and three hundredths   3030.03

11. Replace each circle with the proper comparison symbol.
(33)

(a) 6.174 $\bigcirc$< 6.17401   (b) 14.276 $\bigcirc$> 1.4276

12. Find the length of this segment
(34)

(a) in centimeters.   2.7 cm

(b) in millimeters.   27 mm

13. What decimal number names the point marked X on this
(34) number line? 8.25

14. The coordinates of three vertices of a square are (0, 0),
(Inv. 3) (0, 3), and (3, 3).

    (a) What are the coordinates of the fourth vertex? (3, 0)

    (b) What is the area of the square? 9 units²

15. (a) What decimal number is halfway between 7 and 8?
(34)   7.5
    (b) What number is halfway between 0.7 and 0.8? 0.75

Solve:

16. $15 \cdot 20 = 12y$ 25
(3)

17. $180° = 74° + c$ 106°
(3)

18. Which is equivalent to $2^2 \cdot 2^3$? A. 2^5
(20)

    A. 2^5 B. 2^6 C. 12   D. 24

Simplify:

19. $\dfrac{5}{6} + \dfrac{2}{3} + \dfrac{1}{2}$ 2
(30)

20. $\dfrac{5}{36} - \dfrac{1}{24}$ $\frac{7}{72}$
(30)

21. $3\dfrac{11}{12} - 1\dfrac{1}{4}$ $2\frac{2}{3}$
(30)

22. $\dfrac{1}{10} \cdot 2\dfrac{2}{3} \cdot 3\dfrac{3}{4}$ 1
(26)

23. $5\dfrac{1}{4} \div 1\dfrac{2}{3}$ $3\frac{3}{20}$
(26)

24. $3\dfrac{1}{5} \div 4$ $\frac{4}{5}$
(26)

25. $6\dfrac{7}{8} + 4\dfrac{1}{4}$ $11\frac{1}{8}$
(30)

26. $5\dfrac{1}{6} - 1\dfrac{2}{3}$ $3\frac{1}{2}$
(23,30)

27. $\dfrac{1}{8} + \left(\dfrac{5}{6} \cdot \dfrac{3}{4} \right)$ $\frac{3}{4}$
(9,24)

28. $\dfrac{90,900}{18}$ 5,050
(1)

29. $36 + $3.60 + 36¢ $39.96
(1)

30.
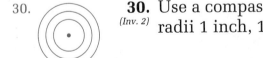
Note: Not actual size.

30. Use a compass to draw three concentric circles. Make the
(Inv. 2) radii 1 inch, $1\frac{1}{2}$ inches, and 2 inches.

LESSON 35

Adding, Subtracting, Multiplying, and Dividing Decimal Numbers

Mental Math:
a. $5.51
b. $3.20
c. 27
d. $\frac{5}{8}$
e. 14
f. 10
g. decade
Problem Solving:

$$
\begin{array}{r}
1231 \text{ r } 5 \\
8\overline{)9853} \\
\underline{8} \\
18 \\
\underline{16} \\
25 \\
\underline{24} \\
13 \\
\underline{8} \\
5
\end{array}
$$

Facts Practice: Measurement Facts (Test H in Test Masters)

Mental Math:

a. $7.50 − $1.99   b. 5 × 64¢   c. $\frac{9}{10} = \frac{?}{30}$

d. Reduce $\frac{15}{24}$ e. $4^2 − \sqrt{4}$ f. $\frac{5}{12}$ of 24

g. Start with the number of inches in two feet, + 1, × 4, $\sqrt{\ }$. What do we call this many years?

Problem Solving:

Copy this problem and fill in the missing digits.

$$
\begin{array}{r}
\underline{} \text{ r } 5 \\
\_\overline{)\_\_\_\_} \\
8 \\
\overline{--} \\
16 \\
\overline{--} \\
24 \\
\overline{--} \\
\overline{=} \\
-
\end{array}
$$

Adding and subtracting decimal numbers

Adding and subtracting decimal numbers is similar to adding and subtracting money. We align the decimal points to assure that we are adding or subtracting digits that have the same place value.

Example 1 Add: 3.6 + 0.36 + 36

Solution We align the decimal points vertically. A number written without a decimal point is a whole number, so the decimal point is to the right of 36.

$$
\begin{array}{r}
3.6 \\
0.36 \\
+\ 36. \\
\hline
\mathbf{39.96}
\end{array}
$$

Example 2 Add: 0.1 + 0.2 + 0.3 + 0.4

Solution We align the decimal points vertically and add. We record only one digit in each column. The sum is 1.0, not 0.10. Since 1.0 equals 1, we can simplify the answer to 1.

$$
\begin{array}{r}
0.1 \\
0.2 \\
0.3 \\
+\ 0.4 \\
\hline
1.0 = 1
\end{array}
$$

Example 3   Subtract: $12.3 - 4.567$

Solution   We write the first number above the second number, aligning the decimal points. We write zeros in the empty places and subtract.

$$\begin{array}{r} \overset{0}{\cancel{1}}\overset{1}{1}\,\overset{1}{2}\,\overset{1}{9}\,{}_1 \\ \cancel{1}2.3\cancel{0}0 \\ -\ \ 4.567 \\ \hline \mathbf{7.733} \end{array}$$

Example 4   Subtract: $5 - 4.32$

Solution   We write the whole number 5 with a decimal point and write zeros in the two empty decimal places. Then we subtract.

$$\begin{array}{r} \overset{4}{}\,\overset{9}{}{}_1 \\ 5.00 \\ -\ 4.32 \\ \hline \mathbf{0.68} \end{array}$$

Multiplying decimal numbers   If we multiply the fractions three tenths and seven tenths, the product is twenty-one hundredths.

$$\frac{3}{10} \times \frac{7}{10} = \frac{21}{100}$$

Likewise if we multiply the decimal numbers three tenths and seven tenths, the product is twenty-one hundredths.

$$0.3 \times 0.7 = 0.21$$

Notice that the factors each have one decimal place and the product has two decimal places. When we multiply decimal numbers the product has as many decimal places as there are in all the factors combined.

Example 5   Multiply: $(0.23)(0.4)$

Solution   We need not align decimal points to multiply. We set up the problem as though we were multiplying whole numbers, and then we multiply. After multiplying, we count the number of decimal places in both factors. There are a total of three decimal places, so we write the product with three decimal places. We count from right to left, writing one or more zeros in front as necessary. The product of 0.23 and 0.4 is **0.092.**

$$\begin{array}{r} 0.23 \\ \times\ \ 0.4 \\ \hline 92 \end{array}$$

$$\begin{array}{rl} 0.23 & \text{2 places} \\ \times\ \ 0.4 & \text{1 place} \\ \hline 0.092 & \text{3 places} \end{array}$$

Example 6 Multiply: 35×0.4

Solution We set up the problem as though we were multiplying whole numbers. After multiplying, we count the total number of decimal places in the factors. Then we place a decimal point in the product so that the product has the same number of decimal places as there are in the factors combined. After placing the decimal point, we simplify the result.

$$\begin{array}{rl} 35 & \text{0 places} \\ \times\ 0.4 & \text{1 place} \\ \hline 14.0 & \text{1 place} \end{array}$$

$$14.0 = \mathbf{14}$$

Example 7 Multiply: $(0.2)(0.3)(0.04)$

Solution Sometimes we can perform the multiplication mentally. First we multiply as though we were multiplying whole numbers: $2 \cdot 3 \cdot 4 = 24$. Then we count decimal places. There are four decimal places in the three factors. Starting from the right side of 24, we count to the left four places. We write zeros in the empty places.

$$24 \longrightarrow \mathbf{0.0024}$$

Dividing decimal numbers Dividing a decimal number by a whole number is like dividing money. The decimal point in the answer is straight up from the decimal point in the division box.

Example 8 Divide: $3.425 \div 5$

Solution We rewrite the problem with a division box. We place a decimal point in the answer directly above the decimal point in the division box. Then we divide as though we were dividing whole numbers. The answer is **0.685**.

$$\begin{array}{r} 0.685 \\ 5\overline{)3.425} \\ \underline{3\ 0} \\ 42 \\ \underline{40} \\ 25 \\ \underline{25} \\ 0 \end{array}$$

Example 9 Divide: $0.0144 \div 8$

Solution We place the decimal point in the answer directly above the decimal point inside the division box. We write a digit in every place following the decimal point until the division is completed. If we cannot perform a division, we write a zero in that place. The answer is **0.0018**.

$$\begin{array}{r} 0.0018 \\ 8\overline{)0.0144} \\ \underline{8} \\ 64 \\ \underline{64} \\ 0 \end{array}$$

Example 10   Divide: 1.2 ÷ 5

Solution   We do not write a decimal division
answer with a remainder. Since a
decimal point fixes place values, we may
write a zero in the next decimal place.
This zero does not change the value of
the number, but it does let us continue
dividing. The answer is **0.24.**

$$\begin{array}{r} 0.24 \\ 5\overline{)1.20} \\ \underline{1\,0} \\ 20 \\ \underline{20} \\ 0 \end{array}$$

Practice*   Simplify:

a. 1.2 + 3.45 + 23.6 28.25

b. 4.5 + 0.51 + 6 + 12.4
23.41

c. 0.2 + 0.4 + 0.6 + 0.8 2

d. 36.274 − 5.39 30.884

e. 16.7 − 1.936 14.764

f. 12 − 0.875 11.125

g. 4.2 × 0.24 1.008

h. (0.12)(0.06) 0.0072

i. 5.4 × 7 37.8

j. 0.3 × 0.2 × 0.1 0.006

k. (0.04)(10) 0.4

l. 0.045 × 0.6 0.027

m. 14.4 ÷ 6 2.4

n. 0.048 ÷ 8 0.006

o. 3.4 ÷ 5 0.68

p. 0.3 ÷ 6 0.05

**Problem set
35**

1. In the first six months of the year the Montgomerys'
(28) monthly electric bills were $128.45, $131.50, $112.30,
$96.25, $81.70, and $71.70. How can the Montgomerys
find their average monthly electric bill during the first six
months of the year? Add all the bills together and divide by 6.

2. There were $2\frac{1}{2}$ gallons of milk in the refrigerator before
(23,30) breakfast. There were $1\frac{3}{4}$ gallons after dinner. How many
gallons of milk were consumed during the day? $\frac{3}{4}$ gallon

3. A 1-year subscription to a monthly magazine costs $15.60.
(28) The regular newsstand price is $1.75 per issue. How much
is saved per issue by paying the subscription price? $0.45

4. Carlos ran one lap in 1 minute, 3 seconds. Orlando ran
(28) one lap 5 seconds faster than Carlos. How many seconds
did it take Orlando to run one lap? 58 seconds

5. The perimeter of the square equals
(19) the perimeter of the regular pentagon.
Each side of the pentagon is 16 cm
long. How long is each side of the
square? 20 cm

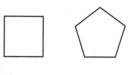

6.

54 fish

$\frac{2}{9}$ were guppies {
| 6 fish |
| 6 fish |

| 6 fish |
| 6 fish |
| 6 fish |

$\frac{7}{9}$ were not guppies {
| 6 fish |
| 6 fish |
| 6 fish |
| 6 fish |

6. Draw a diagram of this statement. Then answer the
(22) questions that follow.

Two ninths of the 54 fish in the tank were guppies.

(a) How many fish were guppies? 12 fish

(b) How many of the fish were not guppies? 42 fish

7. A 6 cm by 6 cm square is cut from a 10 cm by 10 cm
(20) square sheet of paper as shown. Refer to this figure to
answer questions (a), (b), and (c).

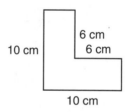

(a) What was the area of the original square? 100 cm²

(b) What was the area of the square that was cut out?
36 cm²

(c) What is the area of the remaining figure? 64 cm²

8. (a) What fraction of this square is not
(31)   shaded? $\frac{99}{100}$

(b) What decimal part of this square
is not shaded? 0.99

(c) What percent of this square is not
shaded? 99%

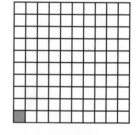

9. The coordinates of three vertices of a rectangle are (−3, 2),
(Inv. 3) (3, −2), and (−3, −2).

(a) What are the coordinates of the fourth vertex? (3, 2)

(b) What is the area of the rectangle? 24 units²

10.(a) one
hundred and
seventy-five
thousandths

10. (a) Use words to write 100.075.
(31)

(b) Use digits to write twenty-five hundred thousandths.
0.00025

11. Find the length of this segment
(34)

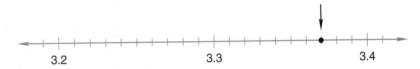

   (a) in centimeters. 3.5 centimeters

   (b) in millimeters. 35 millimeters

12. $\begin{array}{r} \$1.50 \\ \times \quad 12 \\ \hline \$18.00 \end{array}$ **12.** Mr. Edwards bought 11.92 gallons of gasoline at 1.49\frac{9}{10}$
                    (33) per gallon. Estimate how much he paid for the gasoline.

13. What decimal number names the point marked with an
(34) arrow on this number line? 3.37

$$\xleftarrow{\qquad} \;\; \underset{3.2}{|} \;\;\;\;\;\;\;\;\;\; \underset{3.3}{|} \;\;\;\;\;\;\;\; \bullet \;\;\; \underset{3.4}{|} \;\; \xrightarrow{\qquad}$$

14. Instead of dividing 24 by $1\frac{1}{2}$, make an equivalent division
(27) problem by doubling both numbers and then dividing.
$48 \div 3 = 16$

15. What decimal number is halfway between 1.2 and 1.3?
(34) 1.25

Solve:

16. $15x = 9 \cdot 10$ 6
(3)

17. $f + 4.6 = 5.83$ 1.23
(35)

18. $8y = 46.4$ 5.8
(35)

Simplify:

19. $3.4 + 5.63 + 15$ 24.03
(35)

20. $3.65 + 0.9 + 8 + 15.23$
(35) 27.78

21. $36.45 - 4.912$ 31.538
(35)

22. $15 - 4.29$ 10.71
(35)

23. $1\frac{1}{2} + 2\frac{2}{3} + 3\frac{3}{4}$ $7\frac{11}{12}$
(30)

24. $1\frac{1}{2} \cdot 2\frac{2}{3} \cdot 3\frac{3}{4}$ 15
(26)

25. $1\frac{1}{6} - \left(\frac{1}{2} + \frac{1}{3} \right)$ $\frac{1}{3}$
(23,30)

26. $3\frac{1}{12} - 1\frac{3}{4}$ $1\frac{1}{3}$
(23,30)

27. $1.2 \div 10$ 0.12
(35)

28. $(0.3)(0.4)(0.5)$ 0.06
(35)

29. $\left(3\frac{1}{2} + 1\frac{3}{4} \right) \div \left(4 - 3\frac{1}{8} \right)$ 6
(26,30)

30. Use a protractor to help you draw a triangle that has two
(17) 45° angles.

LESSON
36

Ratio • Simple Probability

Facts Practice: $+ - \times \div$ Fractions (Test G in Test Masters)

Mental Math:

a. 1.45×10 b. $4 \times \$1.50$ c. $\frac{4}{5} = \frac{?}{20}$

d. Reduce $\frac{24}{30}$ e. $\sqrt{144} - 3^2$ f. $\frac{9}{10}$ of 40

g. Find the square root of three dozen, $\times$ 5, $\div$ 3, square that number, $- 20$, $+ 1$, $\sqrt{\ }$.

Problem Solving:

In the four class periods before lunch Matt has math, English, science, and history, though not necessarily in that order. If each class is offered during each period, how many different orders are possible?

Ratio   A **ratio** is a way to describe a relationship between two numbers. For instance, if there are 12 boys and 16 girls in the classroom, the ratio of boys to girls is 12 to 16 which reduces to 3 to 4. The ratio 3 to 4 can be written several ways.

with the word "to"	3 to 4
as a fraction	$\dfrac{3}{4}$
as a decimal number	0.75
with a colon	3:4

The numbers used to express a ratio are stated in the same order as the items are named. If the boy-girl ratio is 3 to 4, then the girl-boy ratio is 4 to 3. Note that we reduce ratios, but we do not express them as mixed numbers.

Most ratios involve three numbers even though only two numbers may be stated. When the ratio of boys to girls is 3 to 4, then the unstated number is the total, which is 7.

$$
\begin{array}{r}
3 \text{ boys} \\
+ \ 4 \text{ girls} \\
\hline
7 \text{ total}
\end{array}
$$

Sometimes the total is given and one of the parts is unstated as we show in the following two examples.

Example 1   In a class of 28 students there are 12 boys.

(a) What is the boy-girl ratio?

(b) What is the girl-boy ratio?

Solution We will begin by writing all three ratio numbers.

$$
\begin{array}{r}
\text{12 boys} \\
+\ \ \text{? girls} \\
\hline
\text{28 total}
\end{array}
\longrightarrow
\begin{array}{r}
\text{12 boys} \\
+\ \text{16 girls} \\
\hline
\text{28 total}
\end{array}
$$

Now we can write the answers.

(a) The boy-girl ratio is $\frac{12}{16}$, which reduces to $\frac{3}{4}$, a ratio of 3 to 4.

(b) The girl-boy ratio is $\frac{16}{12}$, which reduces to $\frac{4}{3}$, a ratio of 4 to 3. Remember, we do not change the ratio to a mixed number.

Example 2 The team won $\frac{4}{7}$ of its games and lost the rest. What was the team's won-lost ratio?

Solution We are not told how many games the team played. However, we are told that the team won $\frac{4}{7}$ of its games. Therefore, the team lost $\frac{3}{7}$ of its games. Thus, on the average, the team won 4 out of every 7 games. So the three ratio numbers are

$$
\begin{array}{r}
\text{4 won} \\
+\ \text{3 lost} \\
\hline
\text{7 total}
\end{array}
$$

The won-lost ratio was 4 to 3, which we write as $\frac{4}{3}$.

Example 3 In the bag were red marbles and green marbles. If the ratio of red marbles to green marbles was 4 to 5, what fraction of the marbles was red?

Solution First we write all three ratio numbers.

$$
\begin{array}{r}
\text{4 red} \\
+\ \text{5 green} \\
\hline
\text{? total}
\end{array}
\longrightarrow
\begin{array}{r}
\text{4 red} \\
+\ \text{5 green} \\
\hline
\text{9 total}
\end{array}
$$

The question was what fraction of the marbles was red. There were 4 red marbles and a total of 9 marbles so the fraction that was red was $\frac{4}{9}$.

Simple probability **Probability** is the likelihood that a particular event will occur. Probability is often written as a ratio.

$$
\text{Probability} = \frac{\text{number of favorable outcomes}}{\text{number of possible outcomes}}
$$

If we know a bag contains 4 red marbles and 5 green marbles, we can calculate the probability—the likelihood—of drawing a marble of a specified color from the bag. If one marble is to be drawn from the bag without looking, then the probability that the marble will be ...

$$\text{red is} \quad \frac{\text{number of red}}{\text{number of marbles}} = \frac{4}{9} \ (4 \text{ in } 9)$$

$$\text{green is} \quad \frac{\text{number of green}}{\text{number of marbles}} = \frac{5}{9} \ (5 \text{ in } 9)$$

$$\text{blue is} \quad \frac{\text{number of blue}}{\text{number of marbles}} = \frac{0}{9} = 0$$

A probability of 0 means that the event cannot occur. A probability of 1 means that the event is certain to occur. A probability of $\frac{1}{2}$ means that the event is as likely to occur as it is not to occur.

Example 4   A single die is rolled. What is the probability of rolling

(a) a 4?

(b) a number greater than 4?

(c) a number greater than 6?

(d) a number less than 7?

Solution   There are 6 different faces on a die, so there are 6 equally likely outcomes. Thus, 6 will be the bottom number of each probability ratio.

(a) There is only one way to roll a 4 with one die, so the probability of rolling a 4 is one chance in six, $\frac{1}{6}$.

(b) The numbers greater than 4 on a die are 5 and 6, so there are 2 ways to roll a number greater than 4. Thus the probability is two in six, $\frac{2}{6}$, which we reduce to $\frac{1}{3}$.

(c) On a die, there are no numbers greater than 6, so there is no way to roll a number greater than 6. Thus the probability is $\frac{0}{6}$, which is **0**. An event that cannot happen has a probability of 0.

(d) On a die, there are 6 numbers less than 7, so there are 6 ways to roll a number less than 7. Thus the probability is six out of six, $\frac{6}{6}$, which is **1**. An event that is certain to happen has a probability of 1.

Example 5   The face of a spinner is divided into five equal sectors and is numbered as shown. If this spinner is spun, what is the probability of the spinner

(a) stopping on 3?

(b) not stopping on 3?

Solution   There are 5 equally likely outcomes, so 5 is the bottom number of each ratio.

(a) There is one way for the spinner to stop on 3, so the probability is one chance in five, $\frac{1}{5}$.

(b) There are 4 ways for the spinner not to stop on 3, so the probability is four out of five, $\frac{4}{5}$.

Notice that the probability of an event happening plus the probability of the event not happening is 1.

Example 6   The face of a spinner is divided into one half and two quarters as shown. What is the probability of this spinner stopping on 3?

Solution   There are 3 possible outcomes, but the outcomes are not equally likely. Since region 1 occupies half the area, the probability of the spinner stopping in region 1 is $\frac{1}{2}$. Regions 2 and 3 each occupy $\frac{1}{4}$ of the area, so the probability of the spinner stopping on 2 is $\frac{1}{4}$ and on 3 is $\frac{1}{4}$.

Practice   **a.** In the pond were 240 little fish and 90 big fish. What was the ratio of big fish to little fish? $\frac{3}{8}$

b. Fourteen of the 30 students in the class were girls. What was the boy-girl ratio in the class? $\frac{8}{7}$

c. The team won $\frac{3}{8}$ of its games and lost the rest. What was the team's won-lost ratio? $\frac{3}{5}$

d. The bag contained red marbles and blue marbles. If the ratio of red marbles to blue marbles was 5 to 3, what fraction of the marbles was blue? $\frac{3}{8}$

e. What is the probability of rolling a number less than 4 with one roll of a die? $\frac{1}{2}$

The face of this spinner is divided into four equal parts.

f. What is the probability of this spinner stopping on 3? $\frac{1}{4}$

g. What is the probability of this spinner stopping on 5? 0

h. What is the probability of this spinner stopping on a number less than 6? 1

The face of this spinner is divided into one half and two fourths.

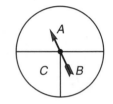

i. What is the probability of this spinner stopping on A? $\frac{1}{2}$

j. What is the probability of this spinner not stopping on B? $\frac{3}{4}$

Problem set 36

1. Fourteen of the 32 students in the class were girls. What
$^{(36)}$ was the ratio of boys to girls in the class? $\frac{9}{7}$

2. During the last 3 years the annual rainfall has been
$^{(28)}$ 23 inches, 21 inches, and 16 inches. What has been the average (mean) annual rainfall during the last 3 years?
20 inches

3. Sean reads 35 pages each night. How many pages does
$^{(13)}$ Sean read in a week? 245 pages

4. Shannon swam 100 meters in 56.24 seconds. Donna swam
$^{(35)}$ 100 meters in 59.48 seconds. Donna took how many seconds longer to swim 100 meters than Shannon?
3.24 seconds

5.

5. Change the percent to a fraction. Then draw a diagram of
$^{(22,36)}$ this statement and answer the questions that follow.

Forty percent of the 30 players in the game had never played rugby before.

(a) How many of the players had never played rugby before? 12 players

(b) What was the ratio of those who had played rugby to those who had not played rugby? $\frac{3}{2}$

6. *AB* is 4 cm. *AC* is 9.5 cm. Describe how to find *BC* in
(34) millimeters. One way to find *BC* in millimeters is to first convert
AB to 40 mm and *AC* to 95 mm. Then subtract 40 mm from 95 mm.

7. The length of the rectangle is 5 cm
(19,20) greater than its width.

(a) What is the area of the rectangle?
104 cm^2
(b) What is the perimeter of the rectangle? 42 cm

8. Estimate the sum of 3624, 2889, and 896 by rounding each
(29) number to the nearest hundred before adding.
3600 + 2900 + 900 = 7400

9. (a) Round 6.857142 to three decimal places. 6.857
(33)

(b) Estimate the product of 6.8571420 and 1.9870 by
rounding each number to the nearest whole number
before multiplying. 7 × 2 = 14

10. Use digits to write each number.
(31)

(a) Twelve million 12,000,000

(b) Twelve millionths 0.000012

11. A bag contained 3 red marbles, 4 white marbles, and 5
(36) blue marbles. If one marble is drawn from the bag, what
is the probability that the marble will be

(a) red? $\frac{1}{4}$ (b) white? $\frac{1}{3}$ (c) blue? $\frac{5}{12}$ (d) green? 0

12. Find the length of this segment
(34)

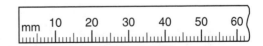

(a) in centimeters. 4.2 cm

(b) in millimeters. 42 mm

13. What decimal number names the point marked *M* on this
(34) number line? 13.56

14. (a) Write 85% as a reduced fraction. $\frac{17}{20}$
(24)

14.(b) $\frac{\cancel{2}\cdot\cancel{2}\cdot\cancel{2}\cdot 2\cdot\cancel{3}\cdot 3}{\cancel{2}\cdot\cancel{2}\cdot\cancel{2}\cdot\cancel{3}\cdot 5\cdot 5}$

$= \frac{6}{25}$

(b) Write the prime factorization and reduce: $\frac{144}{600}$

15. Alba worked for 6 hr, 45 min at $7.90 per hour. What
(29) numbers could she use to estimate how much money she
earned? Make an estimate and state whether you think
the exact answer is a little more or a little less than your
estimate.

$6\frac{3}{4}$ hr or 7 hr and $8 per hour. She earned a little less than $56.

16. In this figure, which angle is
(7)

(a) a right angle? $\angle MPN$

(b) an acute angle? $\angle LPM$

(c) an obtuse angle? $\angle LPN$

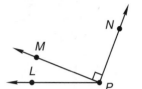

Solve:

17. $8y = 12^2$ 18
(20)

18. $\dfrac{W}{4} = 1.2$ 4.8
(35)

Simplify:

19. $4.27 + 16.3 + 10$ 30.57
(35)

20. $4.2 - 0.42$ 3.78
(35)

21. $3\dfrac{1}{2} + 1\dfrac{1}{3} + 2\dfrac{1}{4}$ $7\frac{1}{12}$
(30)

22. $3\dfrac{1}{2} \cdot 1\dfrac{1}{3} \cdot 2\dfrac{1}{4}$ $10\frac{1}{2}$
(26)

23. $3\dfrac{5}{6} - \left(\dfrac{2}{3} - \dfrac{1}{2}\right)$ $3\frac{2}{3}$
(30)

24. $8\dfrac{5}{12} - 3\dfrac{2}{3}$ $4\frac{3}{4}$
(23,30)

25. $2\dfrac{3}{4} \div 4\dfrac{1}{2}$ $\frac{11}{18}$
(26)

26. $5 - \left(\dfrac{2}{3} \div \dfrac{1}{2}\right)$ $3\frac{2}{3}$
(23,25)

27. (a) 12.25×10 122.5
(35)

(b) $12.25 \div 10$ 1.225

28. $1.4 \div 8$ 0.175
(35)

29. $(0.2)(0.3)(0.4)$ 0.024
(35)

30. On a coordinate plane, draw a square that has an area of
(Inv. 3) 25 units^2. Then write the coordinates of the vertices of
the square on your paper. See student work.

LESSON
37

Area of a Triangle •
Rectangular Area, Part 2

Mental Math:
a. $4.65
b. $6.25
c. 21
d. $\frac{3}{5}$
e. 2
f. 18
g. 30
Problem Solving:
   9

Facts Practice: Measurement Facts (Test H in Test Masters)

Mental Math:

   a. $3.67 + $0.98   **b.** 5 × $1.25   **c.** $\frac{7}{8} = \frac{?}{24}$

   d. Reduce $\frac{18}{30}$ **e.** $\frac{\sqrt{144}}{\sqrt{36}}$ **f.** $\frac{3}{10}$ of 60

   g. What number is 5 less than the sum of 5^2 and $\sqrt{100}$?

Problem Solving:

   If the last page of a section of a large newspaper is page 36, what is the fewest number of sheets of paper that could be in that section?

Area of a triangle

A triangle has a **base** and a **height** (or **altitude**).

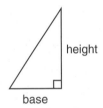

The base is one of the sides of the triangle. The height (or altitude) is the perpendicular distance between the base (or baseline) and the opposite vertex of the triangle. Since a triangle has three sides, and any side can be the base, a triangle may have three base-height orientations, as we show by rotating this triangle.

One Right Triangle Rotated to Three Positions

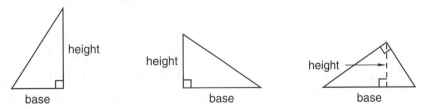

If one angle of a triangle is a right angle, the height may be a side of the triangle, as we see above. If none of the angles of a triangle are right angles, then the height will not be a side of the triangle, and will be shown as a series of dashes perpendicular to the base. If one angle of a triangle is an obtuse angle, then the height is shown outside of the triangle in two of the three orientations as we see here.

One Obtuse Triangle Rotated to Three Positions

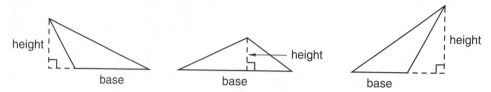

The area of a triangle is half the area of a rectangle with the same base and height, as is illustrated by the following activity.

Activity: Area of a Triangle

Materials needed:

- Ruler

- Protractor

- Scissors

Use a ruler or straight edge to draw a triangle. Determine which side of the triangle is the longest side. The longest side will be the base of the triangle for this activity. To represent the height (altitude) of the triangle draw a series of dashes from the vertex of the triangle to the base. Make sure the row of dashes is perpendicular to the base, as shown below.

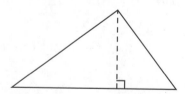

Now we draw a rectangle that just contains the triangle. The base of the triangle is one side of the rectangle. The height of the triangle equals the height (width) of the rectangle.

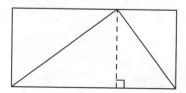

Cut out the rectangle and set the scraps aside. Next carefully cut out the triangle you drew from the rectangle. Save all three pieces.

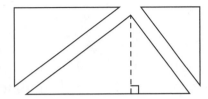

Rotate the two smaller pieces and fit them together to make a triangle congruent to the triangle you drew.

Notice that each of the congruent triangles is half the area of the rectangle with the same base and height (length and width).

When we multiply two perpendicular dimensions, the product is the area of a rectangle with those dimensions.

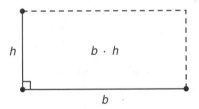

The product *b · h* equals the area of a *b* by *h* rectangle.

One formula multiplies the product of the base and height by $\frac{1}{2}$, and the other divides the product by 2. The result is the same because multiplying by $\frac{1}{2}$ and dividing by 2 are equivalent operations.

To find the area of a triangle with a base of *b* and a height of *h*, we find half of the product of *b* and *h*. We show two formulas for finding the area of a triangle. How are the formulas different? Why do both formulas yield the same result?

$$\text{Area of a triangle} = \frac{1}{2}bh$$

$$\text{Area of a triangle} = \frac{bh}{2}$$

Example 1   Find the area of this triangle.
(Use $A = \frac{bh}{2}$.)

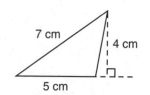

Solution   We find the area of the triangle by multiplying the base and height then dividing the product by 2. The base and height are perpendicular dimensions. In this figure the base is 5 cm and the height is 4 cm.

$$\text{Area} = \frac{5 \text{ cm} \times 4 \text{ cm}}{2}$$

$$= \frac{20 \text{ cm}^2}{2}$$

$$= \mathbf{10 \text{ cm}^2}$$

Example 2   Find the area of this triangle.
(Use $A = \frac{1}{2}bh$.)

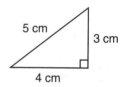

Solution   The base and height are perpendicular dimensions. Since one angle of this triangle is a right angle, the base and height are the perpendicular sides which are 4 cm and 3 cm long.

$$\text{Area} = \frac{1}{2} \cdot 4 \text{ cm} \cdot 3 \text{ cm}$$

$$= \mathbf{6 \text{ cm}^2}$$

Rectangular area, part 2   We have practiced finding the areas of rectangles. Sometimes we can find the area of a more complex shape by dividing the shape into rectangular parts. We find the area of each part and then add the areas of the parts to find the total area.

Example 3   Find the area of this figure. Dimensions are in centimeters. All angles are right angles.

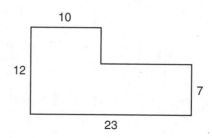

Solution   We show two ways to solve this problem.

SOLUTION 1

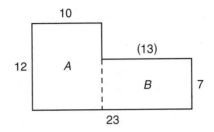

Total area = area A + area B

$$\text{Area } A = 10 \text{ cm} \cdot 12 \text{ cm} = 120 \text{ cm}^2$$

$$\underline{+ \text{ Area } B = 13 \text{ cm} \cdot 7 \text{ cm} = 91 \text{ cm}^2}$$

$$\text{Total area} = \textbf{211 cm}^2$$

SOLUTION 2

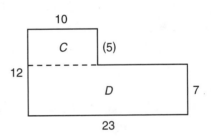

Total area = area C + area D

$$\text{Area } C = 10 \text{ cm} \cdot 5 \text{ cm} = 50 \text{ cm}^2$$

$$\underline{+ \text{ Area } D = 23 \text{ cm} \cdot 7 \text{ cm} = 161 \text{ cm}^2}$$

$$\text{Total area} = \textbf{211 cm}^2$$

Example 4   Find the area of this figure. Dimensions are in meters. All angles are right angles.

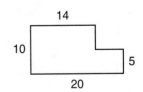

Solution   This time we will imagine this figure as a large rectangle with a small rectangular piece removed. If we find the area of the large rectangle and then *subtract* the area of the small rectangle, the answer will be the area of the figure shown above.

Here we show the figure redrawn and the calculations:

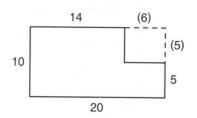

Area of figure = area of large rectangle − area of small rectangle

Area of large rectangle = 20 m · 10 m = 200 m²
− Area of small rectangle = 6 m · 5 m = 30 m²
Area of figure = **170 m²**

We did not need to use subtraction to find this area. We could have added the areas of two smaller rectangles as we did in Example 3. However, sometimes subtraction is easier.

Practice*   Find the area of each triangle. Dimensions are in centimeters.

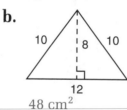

a. 13, 5, 12, 30 cm²

b. 10, 8, 10, 12, 48 cm²

c. 6, 6, 18 cm²

d.

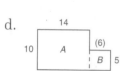

14, 10, A, (6), B, 5

Area A = 140 m²
+ Area B = 30 m²
Total = 170 m²

or

14, C, (5), D, 5, 20

Area C = 70 m²
+ Area D = 100 m²
Total = 170 m²

e.

12, (13), (5), 23

Large = 276 cm²
− Small = 65 cm²
Figure = 211 cm²

g. $A = \frac{1}{2}bh$;
$A = \frac{bh}{2}$

d. Sketch the figure in Example 4 and find its area by dividing the shape into two rectangles and adding the areas.

e. Sketch the figure in Example 3. Imagine that a small rectangle was cut out of a large rectangle to make this shape. Use dashes to complete the outline of these rectangles. Then find the area of both the smaller rectangle and the larger rectangle. Subtract the area of the smaller rectangle from the area of the larger rectangle to find the area of the remaining figure.

f. Find the area of this figure. Dimensions are in inches. All angles are right angles.   256 in.²

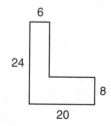

6, 24, 8, 20

g. Write two formulas for finding the area of a triangle.

Problem set 37

1. The team won $\frac{2}{3}$ of its games and lost the rest. What was the team's won-lost ratio? $\frac{2}{1}$
   (36)

2. During the first six months of the year, the car dealership sold 47 cars, 53 cars, 62 cars, 56 cars, 46 cars, and 48 cars. What was the average number of cars sold during the first six months of the year? 52 cars
   (28)

3. The relay team carried the baton around the track. Darren ran his part in eleven and six tenths seconds. Robert ran his part in eleven and three tenths seconds. Orlando ran his part in eleven and two tenths seconds. Claude ran his part in ten and nine tenths seconds. What was the team's total time? 45 seconds
   (35)

4. Subtract $1.30 from $10 to find how much the 3 gallons of milk cost. Then divide that number by 3 to find how much each gallon cost.

4. Jenny went to the store with $10 and returned home with 3 gallons of milk and $1.30 in change. How can she find the cost of each gallon of milk?
   (28)

5.

18 holes	
$\frac{2}{3}$ were par holes {	6 holes
	6 holes
$\frac{1}{3}$ were not { par holes	6 holes

5. Draw a diagram of this statement. Then answer the questions that follow.
   (22)

   Kevin shot par on two thirds of the 18 holes.

   (a) On how many holes did Kevin shoot par? 12 holes

   (b) On how many holes did Kevin not shoot par? 6 holes

Sketch this hexagon on your paper and find the length of each unmarked side. Dimensions are in inches. All angles are right angles. Refer to the figure to answer problems 6 and 7.

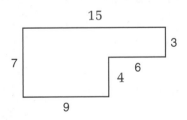

6. What is the perimeter of the hexagon? 44 in.
   (19)

7. What is the area of the hexagon? 81 in.²
   (37)

8. Complete each equivalent fraction.
   (15)

   (a) $\dfrac{5}{6} = \dfrac{?}{18}$ 15   (b) $\dfrac{?}{8} = \dfrac{9}{24}$ 3   (c) $\dfrac{3}{4} = \dfrac{15}{?}$ 20

9. (a) What decimal part of this square is shaded? 0.49
(31)

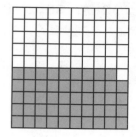

(b) What decimal part of this square is not shaded? 0.51

(c) What percent of this square is not shaded? 51%

10. Round 3184.5641
(33)

(a) to two decimal places. 3184.56

(b) to the nearest hundred. 3200

11. (a) Name 0.00025. twenty-five hundred thousandths
(31)
(b) Use digits to write sixty and seven hundredths. 60.07

12. (a) Write 2% as a reduced fraction. $\frac{1}{50}$
(24)
(b) Reduce $\frac{720}{1080}$. $\frac{2}{3}$

13. Find the length of segment *BC*. $1\frac{1}{8}$ in.
(8)

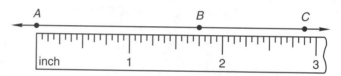

14. One possibility

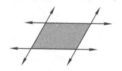

14. Draw a pair of parallel lines. Next draw another pair of
(7) parallel lines that intersect the first pair of lines but are not perpendicular to them. Then shade the region enclosed by the intersecting pairs of lines.

15. Refer to this triangle to answer questions (a) and (b).
(37)

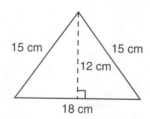

15 cm   15 cm   12 cm   18 cm

(a) What is the perimeter of the triangle? 48 cm

(b) What is the area of the triangle? 108 cm²

16. Simplify and compare: 0.2 + 0.3 ◯ 0.2 × 0.3   0.5 > 0.06
(33,35)

17. What is the probability of tossing heads on one toss of a
(36) fair coin? $\frac{1}{2}$

Solve:

18. $7 \cdot 8 = 4x$ 14
(3)

19. $4.2 = 1.7 + y$ 2.5
(35)

20. $m - 3.6 = 0.45$ 4.05
(35)

21. $\dfrac{4.5}{W} = 3$ 1.5
(35)

Simplify:

22. $\dfrac{3}{5} \cdot 12 \cdot 4\dfrac{1}{6}$ 30
(26)

23. $\dfrac{5}{6} + 1\dfrac{3}{4} + 2\dfrac{1}{2}$ $5\frac{1}{12}$
(30)

24. $\dfrac{5}{8} + \left(\dfrac{1}{2} + \dfrac{3}{8} \right)$ $1\frac{1}{2}$
(30)

25. $3\dfrac{9}{20} - 1\dfrac{5}{12}$ $2\frac{1}{30}$
(30)

26. $3\dfrac{1}{3} \div 5$ $\frac{2}{3}$
(26)

27. $4 - \left(\dfrac{3}{2} \div \dfrac{2}{3} \right)$ $1\frac{3}{4}$
(23,25)

28. (a) 0.25×10 2.5
(35)

(b) $0.25 \div 10$ 0.025

29.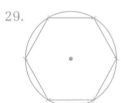

29. Use a compass to draw a circle. Then use the compass
(Inv. 2) and a straight edge to inscribe a regular hexagon.

30. A point with the coordinates (3, –3) lies in which quadrant
(Inv. 3) of the coordinate plane? fourth quadrant

LESSON
38

Interpreting Graphs

Facts Practice: $+ - \times \div$ Fractions (Test G in Test Masters)

Mental Math:

a. $7.43 − $0.99   **b.** 3 × $2.50   **c.** $\dfrac{5}{6} = \dfrac{?}{30}$
d. Reduce $\dfrac{18}{36}$ **e.** $\sqrt{121} + 7^2$ **f.** $\dfrac{7}{10}$ of 50
g. 8 × 4, − 2, ÷ 3, × 4, ÷ 5, + 1, $\sqrt{}$, × 6, + 2, × 2, + 2, ÷ 6,
   × 5, + 1, $\sqrt{}$

Problem Solving:

Javier used a one-yard length of string to make a rectangle that was
twice as long as it was wide. What was the area of the rectangle in
square feet?

We use **graphs** to help us understand quantitative information. A graph may use pictures, bars, lines, or parts of circles
to help the reader visualize comparisons or changes. In this
lesson we will practice interpreting graphs.

Example 1   Use the information in this pictograph to answer the following questions.

Doughnut Sales

Jan.	○ ○ ○ ○
Feb.	○ ○ ○ ○ ○ ○
Mar.	○ ○ ○ ○ ○ (

(○) Represents 10,000 doughnuts

(a) About how many doughnuts were sold in March?

(b) About how many doughnuts were sold in the first 3 months of the year?

Solution   The key at the bottom of the graph shows us that each picture of a doughnut represents 10,000 doughnuts.

(a) For March we see 5 whole doughnuts, which represents 50,000 doughnuts, and half a doughnut, which represents 5,000 doughnuts. Thus, the $5\frac{1}{2}$ doughnuts pictured mean that **about 55,000 doughnuts** were sold in March.

(b) We see a total of $15\frac{1}{2}$ doughnuts pictured for the first 3 months of the year. Fifteen times 10,000 is 150,000. Half of 10,000 is 5,000. Thus, **about 155,000 doughnuts** were sold in the first 3 months of the year.

Example 2   Use the information in this bar graph to answer the following questions.

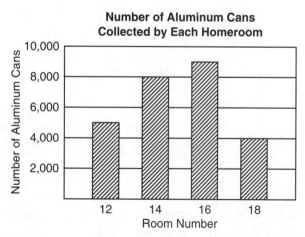

(a) About how many cans were collected by the students in Room 14?

(b) The students in Room 16 collected about as many cans as what other two homerooms combined?

Solution We look at the scale on the left side of the graph. We see that the distance between two horizontal lines on the scale represents 2000 cans. Thus, halfway from one line to the next represents 1000 cans.

(a) The students in Room 14 collected **about 8000 cans.**

(b) The students in Room 16 collected about 9000 cans. This was about as many cans as **Room 12** and **Room 18** combined.

Example 3 This line graph shows how Paul's test scores have changed during the year.

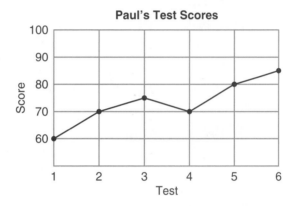

(a) What was Paul's score on Test 3?

(b) In general, are Paul's scores improving or getting worse?

Solution (a) We find Test 3 on the scale across the bottom of the graph and go up to the point that represents Paul's score. We see that the point is halfway between the lines that represent 70 and 80. Thus, on Test 3, Paul's score was about **75.**

(b) With only one exception, Paul scored higher on each succeeding test. So, in general, Paul's scores are **improving.**

Example 4 Use the information in this circle graph to answer the following questions:

(a) Altogether, how many hours are included in this graph?

(b) What fraction of Dina's day is spent at school?

Solution   A circle graph (sometimes called a pie graph) shows the relationship between parts of a whole. This graph shows parts of a whole day.

(a) This graph includes **24 hours,** one whole day.

(b) Dina spends 8 of the 24 hours at school. We reduce $\frac{8}{24}$ to $\frac{1}{3}$.

Practice   Use the information from the graphs in this lesson to answer each question.

a. How many more doughnuts were sold in February than in January? 20,000 doughnuts

b. How many aluminum cans were collected by all four homerooms? 26,000 cans

c. On which test was Paul's score lower than his score on the previous test? Test 4

d. What fraction of Dina's day was spent somewhere other than at home or at school? $\frac{1}{6}$

Problem set 38

1. The ratio of soldiers to civilians at the outpost was 3 to 7.
   (36) What fraction of the people at the outpost were soldiers?
   $\frac{3}{10}$

2. Denise read a 345-page book in 3 days. What was the
   (28) average number of pages she read each day? 115 pages

3. Christine ran a mile in 5 minutes, 52 seconds. How many
   (28) seconds did it take Christine to run a mile? 352 seconds

Refer to the graphs in this lesson to answer problems 4, 5, and 6.

4. How many fewer cans were collected by the students in
   (12,38) Room 18 than by the students in Room 16? 5000 cans

5. If Paul scores 85 on Test 7, what will be his test score
   (28,38) average for all 7 tests? 75

6. Use the information in the graph in Example 3 to write a
   (12,38) "larger-smaller-difference" type problem. See student work.

7.

Mira read $\frac{3}{8}$

384 pages
48 pages
48 pages
48 pages
48 pages
48 pages
48 pages
48 pages
48 pages

Mira did not read $\frac{5}{8}$

7. Draw a diagram for this statement. Then answer the
(22) questions that follow.

> *Mira read three eighths of the 384-page book
> before she could put it down.*

(a) How many pages did she read? 144 pages

(b) How many more pages does she need to read to be
halfway through the book? 48 pages

8. Refer to this figure to answer (a) and
(37) (b). Angles are right angles. Dimensions are in inches.

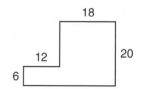

(a) What is the area of the hexagon?
432 in.^{2}

(b) What is the perimeter of the hexagon? 100 in.

9. Complete each equivalent fraction.
(15)

(a) $\dfrac{7}{9} = \dfrac{?}{18}$ 14   (b) $\dfrac{?}{9} = \dfrac{20}{36}$ 5   (c) $\dfrac{4}{5} = \dfrac{24}{?}$ 30

10. Round 2986.34157
(33)

(a) to the nearest thousand. 3000

(b) to three decimal places. 2986.342

11. The face of this spinner is divided
(36) into eight congruent sectors. If the
spinner is spun once, on which
number is it

(a) most likely to stop? 1

(b) least likely to stop? 4

12. Find the next three numbers in this sequence.
(2,35)

$$2.1,\ 1.8,\ 1.5,\ 1.2,\ \ldots$$ 0.9, 0.6, 0.3

13. Find the length of this segment
(34)

(a) in centimeters. 1.2 cm

(b) in millimeters. 12 mm

14. The number
3.4 is between 3
and 4 and is
nearly halfway
between. Point *B*
is too close to 3 to
be 3.4. So the best
choice is *C*.

14. Which point marked on this number line could represent
(34) 3.4? Why?

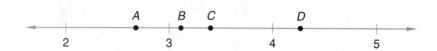

In this figure, diagonal *AC* divided quadrilateral *ABCD* into two congruent triangles. Refer to this figure to answer problems 15 and 16.

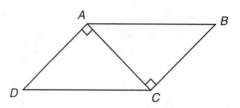

15. (a) Which segment is perpendicular to $\overline{AD}$? $\overline{AC}$
(7)

(b) Which segment appears to be parallel to $\overline{AD}$? $\overline{BC}$

16. The perpendicular sides of $\triangle ACD$ are 6 cm and 6 cm.
(37)

(a) What is the area of $\triangle ACD$? 18 cm²

(b) What is the area of $\triangle CAB$? 18 cm²

(c) What is the area of the quadrilateral? 36 cm²

Solve:

17. $4.3 + a = 6.7$ 2.4
(35)

18. $m - 3.6 = 4.7$ 8.3
(35)

19. $10w = 4.5$ 0.45
(35)

20. $\dfrac{x}{2.5} = 2.5$ 6.25
(35)

Simplify:

21. $5.37 + 27.7 + 4$ 37.07
(35)

22. $1.25 \div 5$ 0.25
(35)

23. $\dfrac{5}{9} \cdot 6 \cdot 2\dfrac{1}{10}$ 7
(26)

24. $\dfrac{5}{8} + \dfrac{3}{4} + \dfrac{1}{2}$ $1\frac{7}{8}$
(30)

25. $5 \div 3\dfrac{1}{3}$ $1\frac{1}{2}$
(26)

26. $\dfrac{3}{10} - \left(\dfrac{1}{2} - \dfrac{1}{5}\right)$ 0
(30)

27. Which is equivalent to $2^2 \cdot 2^4$? A. $4 \cdot 4^2$
(20)

A. $4 \cdot 4^2$ B. 2^8 C. 4^8 D. 4^6

28. About how many milliliters of liquid
(32) are in this container?   125 mL

29. Five books on the library shelf were in this order. Which
(33) two books need to be reversed so that they are in the
correct order?   reverse 916.42 and 916.37

916.3   916.35   916.42   916.37   916.5

30.

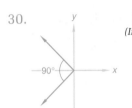

30. On graph paper draw a ray from the origin through the
(Inv. 3) point at (–10, –10). Then draw a ray from the origin
through the point at (–10, 10). Use a protractor to measure
the angle formed by the two rays and write the measure
on the graph paper.

LESSON
39

Proportions

Mental Math:
a. $2.45
b. $7.20
c. 35
d. $\frac{3}{4}$
e. 16
f. 32
g. 0
Problem Solving:
  Even, 2–4–6, yes
  Odd, 1–3–5, yes

Facts Practice: Measurement Facts (Test H in Test Masters)

Mental Math:

  a. $24.50 ÷ 10   **b.** 6 × $1.20   **c.** $\frac{7}{12} = \frac{?}{60}$

  d. Reduce $\frac{24}{32}$ **e.** $5^2 - \sqrt{81}$ **f.** $\frac{4}{5}$ of 40

  g. Start with the number of degrees in a straight angle, and
    subtract the number of years in a century. Add the number of
    years in a decade, and subtract the number of degrees in a
    right angle. What is the answer?

Problem Solving:

  Is it possible to hold a die in a position that the three adjoining
  faces that can be seen each have an even number of dots? An odd
  number of dots?

A **proportion** is a statement that two ratios are equal.

$$\frac{16}{20} = \frac{4}{5}$$

We may test if two ratios are equal by comparing their cross products. If we multiply the upper term of one ratio by the lower term of the other ratio, we form a **cross product.** The cross products of equal ratios are equal. We illustrate by finding the cross products of this proportion:

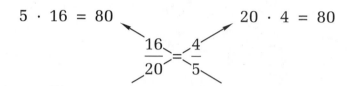

$$5 \cdot 16 = 80 \qquad\qquad 20 \cdot 4 = 80$$

We find that both cross products equal 80. If the cross products are equal, the ratios are equal. We will use cross products to help us find the missing terms in proportions.

We will follow a two-step process.

Step 1: Find the cross products.

Step 2: Divide the known product by the known factor.

Example 1 Solve the proportion: $\dfrac{12}{20} = \dfrac{n}{30}$

Solution We solve a proportion by finding the missing term.

Step 1: First we find the cross products. Since we are completing a proportion, the cross products are equal.

$$\frac{12}{20} = \frac{n}{30}$$

$$20 \cdot n = 30 \cdot 12 \qquad \text{equal cross products}$$
$$20n = 360 \qquad\qquad \text{simplified}$$

Step 2: Divide the known product (360) by the known factor (20). The result is the missing term.

$$n = \frac{360}{20} \qquad \text{divided by 20}$$

$$n = \textbf{18} \qquad \text{simplified}$$

Example 2 Solve: $\dfrac{15}{x} = \dfrac{20}{32}$

Solution **Step 1:** $20x = 480$ equal cross products

Step 2: $x = \mathbf{24}$ divided by 20

Practice Solve each proportion.

a. $\dfrac{a}{12} = \dfrac{6}{8}$ 9

b. $\dfrac{30}{b} = \dfrac{20}{16}$ 24

c. $\dfrac{14}{21} = \dfrac{c}{15}$ 10

d. $\dfrac{30}{25} = \dfrac{24}{d}$ 20

e. $\dfrac{30}{100} = \dfrac{n}{40}$ 12

f. $\dfrac{m}{100} = \dfrac{9}{12}$ 75

Problem set 39 Dan made a line graph to show his height on each birthday. Refer to this graph to answer problems 1 and 2.

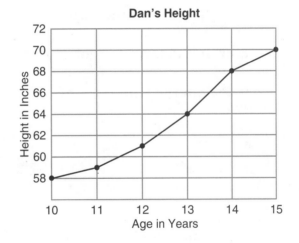

Dan's Height

1. How many inches did Dan grow between his twelfth and
   (38) thirteenth birthdays?   3 inches

2. Between which two birthdays did Dan grow the most?
   (38) between his thirteenth and fourteenth birthdays

3. There were 12 princes and 16 princesses in the palace.
   (36) What was the ratio of princes to princesses in the palace?
   $\frac{3}{4}$

4. On the first 4 days of their trip, the Curtis family drove
   (28) 497 miles, 513 miles, 436 miles, and 410 miles. What was
   the average number of miles they drove on the first 4 days
   of their trip?   464 miles

5. Don receives a weekly allowance of $4.50. How much
   (13) allowance does he receive in a year (52 weeks)? $234

6.

105 adults

$\frac{3}{7}$ were less than 5 feet tall
| 15 adults |
| 15 adults |
| 15 adults |

$\frac{4}{7}$ were 5 feet tall or taller
| 15 adults |
| 15 adults |
| 15 adults |
| 15 adults |

6. Draw a diagram for this statement. Then answer the
(22) questions that follow.

> *Three sevenths of the 105 adults in the Khoikhoi clan were less than 5 feet tall.*

(a) How many of the adults were less than 5 feet tall?
45 adults

(b) How many of the adults were 5 feet tall or taller?
60 adults

Refer to this figure to answer problems 7 and 8. Dimensions are in millimeters. Angles are right angles.

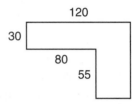

7. What is the area of the figure? 5800 mm²
(37)

8. What is the perimeter of the figure? 410 mm
(19)

9. Name the number of shaded circles
(31)

(a) as a decimal number. 2.5

(b) as a mixed number. $2\frac{1}{2}$

10. Round 0.9166666
(33)

(a) to the nearest hundredth. 0.92

(b) to the nearest hundred thousandth. 0.91667

11. $1.40
    ×   9
    ―――――
    $12.60

11. Sharon pulled into the service station and bought 9.16
(33) gallons of gasoline priced at 1.39\frac{9}{10}$ per gallon. Estimate the total cost.

12. Use digits to write each number.
(31)

(a) One hundred and seventy-five thousandths 100.075

(b) One hundred seventy-five thousandths 0.175

13. Refer to this figure to name
(7)

    (a) an acute angle. ∠RPS

    (b) an obtuse angle. ∠QPR

    (c) a straight angle. ∠QPS

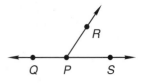

14. Find the next three numbers in this sequence and state
(2,35) the rule of the sequence.

$$100, 10, 1, 0.1, \ldots \quad 0.01, 0.001, 0.0001$$
Divide a term by 10 to find the next term of the sequence.

Solve:

15. $\dfrac{8}{12} = \dfrac{6}{x}$ 9   **16.** $\dfrac{16}{y} = \dfrac{2}{3}$ 24   **17.** $\dfrac{21}{14} = \dfrac{n}{4}$ 6
(39)   (39)   (39)

18. $m + 0.36 = 0.75$ 0.39   **19.** $1.4 - w = 0.8$ 0.6
(35)   (35)

20. $8x = 7.2$ 0.9   **21.** $\dfrac{y}{0.4} = 1.2$ 0.48
(35)   (35)

Simplify:

22. $9.6 + 12 + 8.59$ 30.19   **23.** $3.15 - (2.1 - 0.06)$ 1.11
(35)   (35)

24. $4\dfrac{5}{12} + 6\dfrac{5}{8}$ $11\frac{1}{24}$ **25.** $4\dfrac{1}{4} - 1\dfrac{3}{5}$ $2\frac{13}{20}$
(30)   (23,30)

26. $8\dfrac{1}{3} \cdot 1\dfrac{4}{5}$ 15   **27.** $5\dfrac{5}{6} \div 7$ $\frac{5}{6}$
(26)   (26)

28. Use the triangle below to answer questions (a) and (b).
(37)

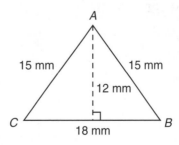

    (a) What is the perimeter of △ABC?   48 mm

    (b) What is the area of △ABC?   108 mm²

29. What is the probability of rolling an odd prime number
(36) on a toss of a single number cube (die)? $\frac{2}{6} = \frac{1}{3}$

30. Use common denominators to arrange these numbers in
(30) order from least to greatest. $\frac{1}{2}, \frac{7}{12}, \frac{2}{3}, \frac{5}{6}$

$$\frac{2}{3}, \frac{1}{2}, \frac{5}{6}, \frac{7}{12}$$

LESSON
40

Sum of the Angle Measures of a Triangle • Angle Pairs

Facts Practice: $+ - \times \div$ Fractions (Test G in Test Masters)

Mental Math:

  a. 0.18×100 **b.** $4 \times \$1.25$ **c.** $\frac{3}{4} = \frac{?}{24}$

  d. Reduce $\frac{12}{32}$ **e.** $\sqrt{144} + \sqrt{121}$ **f.** $\frac{2}{3}$ of 60

  g. Start with $10.00, ÷ 4, add two quarters, × 3, find half of that, subtract two dimes.

Problem Solving:

Copy this problem and fill in the missing digits.

$$\begin{array}{r} 2\_ \\ \_7\overline{)4\_\_} \\ \underline{==} \\ \_8 \\ \underline{==} \\ 0 \end{array}$$

Sum of the angle measures of a triangle

A square has four angles that each measure 90°. If we draw a segment from one vertex of a square to the opposite vertex, we have drawn a diagonal that divides the square into two congruent triangles. We show this in the figure below.

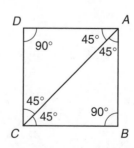

Segment *AC* divides the right angle at *A* into two angles each measuring 45° (90° ÷ 2 = 45°). Segment *AC* also divides the right angle at *C* into two 45° angles. Each triangle has angles that measure 90°, 45°, and 45°. The sum of these angles is 180°.

$$90° + 45° + 45° = 180°$$

The three angles of every triangle have measures that total 180°. We illustrate this fact with the following activity.

Activity: Sum of the Angle Measures of a Triangle

Materials needed:

- Paper
- Ruler or straight edge
- Protractor
- Scissors

With a ruler or straight edge draw two or three triangles of various shapes large enough to easily fold later. Let the longest side of each triangle be the base of that triangle and indicate the height (altitude) of the triangle by drawing a series of dashes perpendicular to the base. The dashes should extend from the base to the opposite vertex. Use the corner of a paper or a protractor if necessary to assure the indicated height is perpendicular to the base.

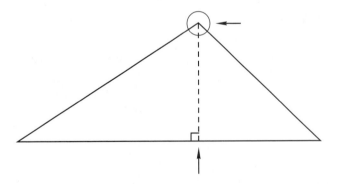

After the drawings are completed, carefully cut out each triangle. Then select a triangle for folding. First fold the vertex with the dash down to the point on the base where the row of dashes intersects the base.

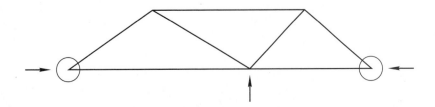

Then fold each of the other two vertices to the same point. When finished, your folded triangle should look like this.

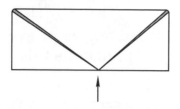

If you sketch a semicircle about the meeting point you will see that the three angles of the triangle together form a half circle. That is, the sum of their measures is 180°.

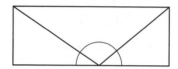

Repeat the folding activity with the other triangle(s) you drew.

Example 1 Find the measure of ∠A in triangle ABC.

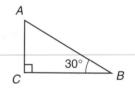

Solution The sum of the measures of the angles is 180°. Angle B measures 30° and angle C is a right angle that measures 90°. So using this information we can write the following equation:

$$m\angle A + 90° + 30° = 180°$$

$$m\angle A = \mathbf{60°}$$

Angle pairs Two intersecting lines form four angles. We have labeled these four angles ∠1, ∠2, ∠3, and ∠4 for easy reference.

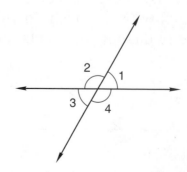

Angle 1 and $\angle2$ are **adjacent angles,** sharing a common side. Notice that together they form a straight angle. A straight angle measures 180°, so the sum of the measures of $\angle1$ and $\angle2$ is 180°. A pair of angles whose sum is 180° are called **supplementary angles.**

Notice that $\angle1$ and $\angle4$ are also supplementary angles. If we know that $\angle1$ measures 60°, then we can calculate that $\angle2$ measures 120° (60 + 120° = 180°) and that $\angle4$ measures 120°. So $\angle2$ and $\angle4$ have the same measure.

Another pair of supplementary angles is $\angle2$ and $\angle3$, and the fourth pair of supplementary angles is $\angle3$ and $\angle4$. Knowing that $\angle2$ or $\angle4$ measures 120°, we can calculate that $\angle3$ measures 60°. So $\angle1$ and $\angle3$ have the same measure.

Angles 1 and 3 are not adjacent angles, they are **vertical angles.** Likewise $\angle2$ and $\angle4$ are vertical angles. Vertical angles are a pair of non-adjacent angles formed by a pair of intersecting lines. Vertical angles have the same measure.

A pair of angles whose measures total 90° are called **complementary angles.** In this triangle, $\angle A$ and $\angle B$ are complementary because the sum of their measures is 90°.

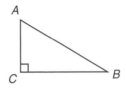

Example 2   Find the measure of $\angle x$, $\angle y$, and $\angle z$.

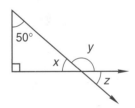

Solution   The measures of the three angles of a triangle total 180°. The right angle of the triangle measures 90°. So the two acute angles total 90°. One of the acute angles is 50°, so $\angle x$ measures **40°.**

Together $\angle x$ and $\angle y$ form a straight angle measuring 180° (so they are supplementary). Since $\angle x$ measures 40°, $\angle y$ measures the rest of 180° which is **140°.**

Angle z and $\angle y$ are supplementary. Also, $\angle z$ and $\angle x$ are vertical angles. Since vertical angles have the same measure, $\angle z$ measures **40°.**

Practice

a. The sides of a regular triangle are equal in length, and the angles are equal in measure. What is the measure of each angle of a regular triangle and why? Each angle measures 60° because they equally share 180°. $\frac{180°}{3} = 60°$

Refer to rectangle *ABCD* to answer questions b–d.

c. ∠*CAB* measures 70° because it is the third angle of a triangle whose other angles measure 90° and 20°: 180° − (90° + 20°) = 70°.

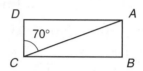

d. They are not vertical angles. Their angles are equal in measure but they are not non-adjacent angles formed by two intersecting lines.

b. What is the measure of ∠*ACB* and why? 20°; Angle *ACB* and ∠*ACD* are complementary: 90° − 70° = 20°

c. What is the measure of ∠*CAB* and why?

d. Are angles *ACD* and *CAB* vertical angles? Why or why not?

e. Find the measure of ∠*x*, ∠*y*, and ∠*z* in this figure. m∠*x* = 60°; m∠*y* = 120°; m∠*z* = 60°

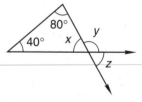

Problem set 40

1. The bag contained only red marbles and white marbles in
(36) the ratio of 3 to 2.

    (a) What fraction of the marbles was white? $\frac{2}{5}$

    (b) What is the probability that a marble drawn from the bag will be white? $\frac{2}{5}$

2. John ran 4 laps of the track in 6 minutes, 20 seconds.
(28)

    (a) How many seconds did it take John to run 4 laps? 380 seconds

    (b) John's average time for running each lap was how many seconds? 95 seconds

3. The Curtises' car traveled an average of 24 miles per
(13) gallon of gas. At that rate, how far could the car travel on a full tank of 18 gallons? 432 miles

4. Normal body temperature is 98.6°F. Allan's temperature
(12,35) was 103.4°F. His temperature was how many degrees
above normal? 4.8°F

5. The length of the rectangle is twice
(19,20) its width.

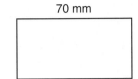
70 mm

(a) What is the perimeter of the
rectangle? 210 mm

(b) What is the area of the rectangle?
2450 mm²

6.

200 sheep

⅝ grazed { 25 sheep / 25 sheep / 25 sheep / 25 sheep / 25 sheep

⅜ drank { 25 sheep / 25 sheep / 25 sheep

6. Draw a diagram for this statement. Then answer the
(22) questions that follow.

*Five eighths of the 200 sheep in the flock grazed
in the meadow. The rest drank from the brook.*

(a) How many of the sheep grazed in the meadow?
125 sheep

(b) How many of the sheep drank from the brook?
75 sheep

7. *AB* is 30 mm. *CD* is 45 mm. *AD* is 100 mm. Find *BC* in
(34) centimeters. 2.5 cm

A   B   C   D

8. Round 0.083333
(33)

(a) to the nearest thousandth. 0.083

(b) to the nearest tenth. 0.1

9. Use words to write each number.
(31)

(a) 12.054 twelve and fifty-
four thousandths

(b) $10\frac{11}{100}$ ten and eleven
hundredths

10. The coordinates of the three vertices of a triangle are
(37) (−2, 5), (4, 0), and (−2, 0). What is the area of the triangle?
15 units²

11. What decimal number names the point marked *B* on this
(34) number line? 0.76

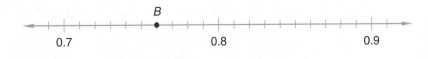

B

0.7   0.8   0.9

Refer to this figure to answer problems 12 and 13.

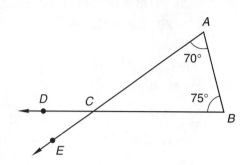

12. Find the measure of each of these angles.
(40)

(a) $\angle ACB$ 35°   (b) $\angle ACD$ 145°   (c) $\angle DCE$ 35°

13. Angle ACD is supplementary to $\angle ACB$. Name another
(40) angle supplementary to $\angle ACB$. $\angle BCE$

14. (a) Which property is illustrated by this equation?
(1,2)
identity property
of multiplication $\dfrac{12}{0.5} \cdot \dfrac{10}{10} = \dfrac{120}{5}$

(b) Find the quotient of $\frac{120}{5}$. 24

Solve:

15. $\dfrac{8}{10} = \dfrac{W}{25}$ 20   **16.** $\dfrac{n}{1.5} = \dfrac{6}{9}$ 1   **17.** $\dfrac{9}{12} = \dfrac{15}{m}$ 20
(39)   (39)   (39)

18. $4 = a + 1.8$ 2.2   **19.** $3.9 = t - 0.39$ 4.29
(35)   (35)

Simplify:

20. 2.7×0.18 0.486   **21.** $(0.15)(0.05)$ 0.0075
(35)   (35)

22. 15×1.5 22.5   **23.** $14.4 \div 12$ 1.2
(35)   (35)

24. $5.6 - (4 - 1.25)$ 2.85   **25.** $5 - (3.14 + 1.2)$ 0.66
(35)   (35)

26. $6\dfrac{1}{4} \cdot 1\dfrac{3}{5}$ 10   **27.** $7 \div 5\dfrac{5}{6}$ $1\frac{1}{5}$
(26)   (26)

28. $\dfrac{8}{15} + \dfrac{12}{25}$ $1\frac{1}{75}$ **29.** $4\dfrac{2}{5} - 1\dfrac{3}{4}$ $2\frac{13}{20}$
(30)   (23,30)

30. Estimate the answer to the following question. What
(33) number is $\frac{1}{4}$ of 31.975? $\frac{1}{4} \times 32 = 8$

INVESTIGATION 4

Stem-and-Leaf Plots, Box-and-Whisker Plots

A high school counselor administered a math test to eighth grade students in local middle schools to help advise students during high school registration. The scores of one group of students are listed below.

40, 30, 43, 48, 26, 50, 55, 40, 34, 42, 47, 47, 52, 25, 32,
38, 41, 36, 32, 21, 35, 43, 51, 58, 26, 30, 41, 45, 23, 36,
41, 51, 53, 39, 28

To organize the scores, the counselor created a **stem-and-leaf plot.** Noticing that the scores ranged from a low of 21 to a high of 58, the counselor chose the initial digits of 20, 30, 40, and 50 to serve as the stem digits.

Stem

2
3
4
5

Then the counselor used the ones' place digits of the scores as the leaves of the stem-and-leaf plot. (The "stem" of a stem-and-leaf plot may have more than one digit. Each "leaf" is only one digit.)

Stem	Leaf
2	1 3 5 6 6 8
3	0 0 2 2 4 5 6 6 8 9
4	0 0 1 1 1 2 3 3 5 7 7 8
5	0 1 1 2 3 5 8

3 | 2 represents
a score of 32

The counselor included a key to the left to help a reader interpret the plot. The top row of leaves indicates the six scores 21, 23, 25, 26, 26, and 28.

1. Looking at this stem-and-leaf plot we see that there is one score of 21, one 23, one 25, and two 26's. Scanning through all of the scores, which score occurs more than twice? 41

The number that occurs most frequently in a set of numbers is the **mode.** The mode of these 35 scores is 41.

2. Looking at the plot we immediately see that the lowest score is 21 and the highest score is 58. What is the difference of these scores? 37

The difference between the least and greatest numbers in a set is the **range** of the numbers. We find the range of this set of scores by subtracting 21 from 58.

3. The **median** of a set of numbers is the middle number of the set when the numbers are arranged in order. The counselor drew a vertical segment through the median on the stem-and-leaf plot. Which score was the median score? 40

Half of the scores are at or below the median score, and half of the scores are at or above the median score. There are 35 scores, and half of 35 is $17\frac{1}{2}$. This means there are 17 whole scores below the median and 17 whole scores above the median. The $\frac{1}{2}$ means that the median is one of the scores on the list. (The median of an even number of scores is the mean—the average—of the two middle scores.) We may count up from the lowest score or down from the highest score 17 scores. The next score is the median. We find that the median score is 40.

	2	1 3 5 6 6 8
3	2 represents	3	0 0 2 2 4 5 6 6 8 9
a score of 32	4	0 0 1 1 1 2 3 3 5 7 7 8
	5	0 1 1 2 3 5 8

median

Next the counselor found the middle number of the lower 17 scores and the middle number of the upper 17 scores. The middle number of the lower half of scores is the **first quartile** or **lower quartile**. The middle number of the upper half of scores is the **third quartile** or **upper quartile**. The second quartile is the median.

4. What are the first and third quartiles of these 35 scores? 32 and 47

There are 17 scores below the median. Half of 17 is $8\frac{1}{2}$. We count up 8 whole scores from the lowest score. The next score is the lower quartile score. Likewise, since there are also 17 scores above the median, we count down 8 whole scores from the highest score. The next score is the upper quartile score. Note that if there is an even number of numbers above and below the median, the quartiles are the mean of the two central numbers in each half.

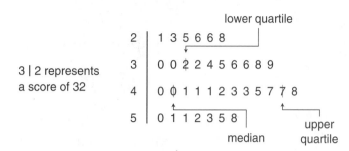

3 | 2 represents a score of 32

Counting the scores on the stem-and-leaf plot we find 8 scores below the first quartile, 8 scores between the first quartile and the median, 8 scores between the median and the third quartile, and 8 scores above the third quartile. The median and quartiles have "quartered" the scores.

After locating the median and quartiles, the counselor created a **box-and-whisker plot** of the scores, which shows the location of certain scores compared to a number line. The five dots on a box-and-whisker plot show the **extremes** of the scores—the lowest score and highest score—as well as the lower quartile, median, and upper quartile. A "box" divided by the median shows the location of the **middle half** of the scores. The "whiskers" show the scores below the first quartile and above the third quartile.

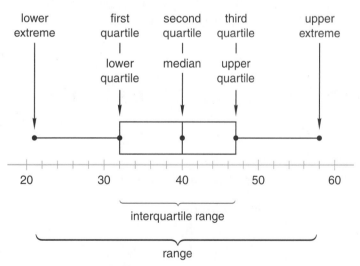

5. Create a stem-and-leaf plot for the following set of scores. Then draw vertical segments on the plot indicating the median and the first and third quartiles.

> *15, 26, 26, 27, 28, 29, 29, 30, 32, 33, 35, 36, 38, 38, 38, 38, 40, 41, 42, 43, 45, 45, 46, 47, 47, 48, 50, 52, 54, 55, 57, 58*

5. 1 | 5
    2 | 6 6 7 8 9 9
    3 | 0 | 2 3 5 6 8 8 8 8 |
    4 | 0 1 2 3 5 5 6 7 | 7 8
    5 | 0 2 4 5 7 8

2 | 9 represents a score of 29

6. What is the lower quartile, median, and upper quartile of this set of scores? 31, 39, 47

7. What is the mode of this set of scores? 38

8. What are the upper and lower extremes of these scores? 15 and 58

9. What is the range of the scores? 43

10. The **interquartile range** is the difference between the upper and lower quartiles. What is the interquartile range of these scores? 16

11. Create a box-and-whisker plot for this set of scores using the calculations you have made for the median and the quartiles.

12. An **outlier** is a number in a set of numbers that is distant from the other numbers in the set. In this set of scores there is an outlier. Which score is the outlier? 15

Extensions

a. Extend this investigation by creating a stem-and-leaf plot and a box-and-whisker plot for scores on a recent class test.

b. Have students measure their heights to the nearest centimeter and display the gathered data in stem-and-leaf and box-and-whisker plots.

LESSON 41

Evaluating Expressions • Distributive Property

Facts Practice: Proportions (Test I in Test Masters)

Mental Math:

   a. 5×140 **b.** 1.54×10 **c.** $\frac{3}{5} = \frac{15}{x}$

   d. $5^2 - 4^2$ **e.** Estimate: 39×29 **f.** $\frac{3}{10}$ of 70

   g. Find the sum, difference, product, and quotient of $\frac{2}{3}$ and $\frac{1}{2}$.

Problem Solving:

Six blocks were used to build this three-step shape. How many blocks would be needed to build a nine-step shape?

Evaluating expressions In Lesson 20 it was stated that the area (A) of a rectangle is related to the length (l) and width (w) of the rectangle by this formula.

$$A = lw$$

This formula means that the area of a rectangle equals the product of its length and width. If we are given measures for l and w, we can replace the letters in the formula with numbers and calculate the area.

Example 1 Find A in $A = lw$ when l is 8 ft and w is 4 ft.

Solution We replace l and w in the formula with 8 ft and 4 ft, respectively. Then we simplify.

$$A = lw$$
$$A = (8 \text{ ft})(4 \text{ ft})$$
$$A = \mathbf{32 \ ft^2}$$

The letters used in a formula or other algebraic expressions are called **variables** because their values can vary. When we replace the variables with numbers we can **evaluate** the expression. We evaluate an expression by finding its numerical value when its variables are replaced by numbers.

Example 2 Evaluate $2(l + w)$ when l is 8 and w is 4.

Solution In place of l and w we substitute 8 and 4. Then we simplify.

$$2(l + w)$$
$$2(8 + 4)$$
$$2(12)$$
$$\mathbf{24}$$

Distributive property There are two formulas commonly used to relate the perimeter (p) of a rectangle to its length and width.

$$p = 2(l + w)$$
$$p = 2l + 2w$$

Both formulas describe how to find the perimeter of a rectangle if we are given its length and width. The first formula means "add the length and width and then double this sum." The second formula means "double the length and double the width and then add."

Example 3   Use the two perimeter formulas to find the perimeter of this rectangle.

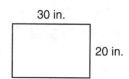

30 in.

20 in.

Solution   In both formulas we replace l with 30 in. and w with 20 in. Then we simplify.

$$p = 2(l + w) \qquad\qquad p = 2l + 2w$$
$$p = 2(30 \text{ in.} + 20 \text{ in.}) \qquad p = 2(30 \text{ in.}) + 2(20 \text{ in.})$$
$$p = 2(50 \text{ in.}) \qquad\qquad p = 60 \text{ in.} + 40 \text{ in.}$$
$$p = \textbf{100 in.} \qquad\qquad\quad p = \textbf{100 in.}$$

Both formulas in Example 3 yield the same result because the two formulas are equivalent.

$$2(l + w) = 2l + 2w$$

These equivalent expressions illustrate the **distributive property of multiplication over addition,** often called simply the **distributive property.** Applying the distributive property we distribute or "spread" the multiplication over the terms that are being added (or subtracted) within the parentheses. In this case we multiply l by 2 giving us $2l$, and we multiply w by 2 giving us $2w$.

$$2(l + w) = 2l + 2w$$

The distributive property is often expressed in equation form using variables like this.

$$a(b + c) = ab + ac$$

The distributive property also applies over subtraction.

$$a(b - c) = ab - ac$$

Example 4   Show two ways to simplify this expression.

$$6(20 + 5)$$

Solution   One way is to add 20 and 5 and then multiply the sum by 6.

$$\textbf{6(20 + 5)}$$
$$\textbf{6(25)}$$
$$\textbf{150}$$

Another way is to multiply 20 by 6 and multiply 5 by 6. Then add the products.

$$6(20 + 5)$$

$$6 \cdot 20 + 6 \cdot 5$$

$$120 + 30$$

$$150$$

Practice   **a.** Find A in $A = bh$ when b is 15 in. and h is 8 in. 120 in.²

b. Evaluate $\dfrac{ab}{2}$ when a is 6 ft and b is 8 ft. 24 ft²

c. Write an equation using the letters x, y, and z, that illustrates the distributive property of multiplication over addition. $x(y + z) = xy + xz$

d. Show two ways to simplify this expression.
$6(15) = 90$; $6 \cdot 20 - 6 \cdot 5 = 120 - 30 = 90$
$$6(20 - 5)$$

e. Write two formulas for finding the perimeter of a rectangle. $p = 2(l + w)$; $p = 2l + 2w$

Problem set 41

1. Two hundred wildebeests and 150 gazelles grazed on the
(36) savannah. What was the ratio of gazelles to wildebeests grazing on the savannah? $\frac{3}{4}$

2. In their first 5 games, the Celtics scored 105 points, 112
(28) points, 98 points, 113 points, and 107 points. What was the average number of points the Celtics scored in their first 5 games? 107 points

3. The crowd watched with anticipation as the pole vault bar
(28) was set to 19 feet, 6 inches. How many inches is 19 feet, 6 inches? 234 inches

4. Which property is illustrated by each of these equations?
(2,41)

4.(a) associative property of addition

(a) $(a + b) + c = a + (b + c)$

(b) $a(bc) = (ab)c$ associative property of multiplication

(c) $a(b + c) = ab + ac$ distributive property

5. Draw a sketch to help with this problem. From Tad's
(35) house to John's house is 2.3 kilometers. From John's
house to school is 0.8 kilometer. Tad rode from his house
to John's house and then to school. Later he rode from
school to John's house to his house. Altogether, how far
did Tad ride? 6.2 kilometers

6. About 70% of the earth's surface is water.
(36)

(a) About what fraction of the earth's surface is land? $\frac{3}{10}$

(b) On the earth's surface, what is the ratio of water area
to land area? $\frac{7}{3}$

7. The stem-and-leaf plot below shows the distribution of
(Inv. 4) test scores for a class of 20 students. For these scores find

```
                              1 | 1
  2 | 4 represents 24         2 | 2 4 5 6 6 7 8 9
  correct answers             3 | 0 0 0 1 3 3 5 6 7 9
                              4 | 0
```

(a) the median. 30 correct answers

(b) the first quartile. 26 correct answers

(c) the third quartile. 34 correct answers

(d) any outliers. 11 correct answers

8. Make a box-and-whisker plot of the test scores in
(Inv. 4) problem 7.

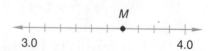

9. Refer to this figure to answer ques-
(37) tions (a) and (b). All angles are right
angles. Dimensions are in feet.

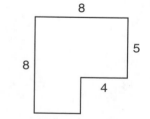

(a) What is the area of the figure?
52 ft²

(b) What is the perimeter of the figure?
32 ft

10. Name the point marked *M* on this number line
(34)

M
3.0   4.0

(a) as a decimal number. 3.6

(b) as a mixed number. $3\frac{3}{5}$

11. What is the sum of the first four prime numbers? 17
(21)

12. Dimensions of this triangle are in
(37) millimeters.

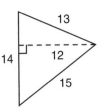

   (a) What is the perimeter of this
      triangle? 42 mm

   (b) What is the area of this triangle?
      84 mm²

13. Use digits to write each number.
(31)
   (a) Sixty-seven hundred thousandths 0.00067

   (b) One hundred and twenty-three thousandths 100.023

14. Evaluate $2\pi r$ when π is 3.14 and r is 10. 62.8
(41)

15. Write $\frac{3}{5}$, $\frac{1}{2}$, and $\frac{5}{7}$ with a common denominator and arrange
(30) the renamed fractions in order from least to greatest.
$\frac{35}{70}$, $\frac{42}{70}$, $\frac{50}{70}$

Solve:

16. $\dfrac{x}{2.4} = \dfrac{10}{16}$ 1.5
(39)

17. $\dfrac{18}{8} = \dfrac{m}{20}$ 45
(39)

18. $3.45 + a = 7.6$ 4.15
(35)

19. $3y = 0.144$ 0.048
(35)

Simplify:

20. $(3.4)(5.6)$ 19.04
(35)

21. $(0.4)(0.6)(0.02)$ 0.0048
(35)

22. $4.315 \div 5$ 0.863
(35)

23. $\dfrac{6.5}{100}$ 0.065
(35)

24. $7.4 \div 8$ 0.925
(35)

25. $4\dfrac{7}{24} - 3\dfrac{9}{32}$ $1\frac{1}{96}$
(30)

26. $3\dfrac{1}{3} + 1\dfrac{5}{6} + \dfrac{7}{12}$ $5\frac{3}{4}$
(30)

27. $4\dfrac{1}{6} - \left(4 - 1\dfrac{1}{4}\right)$ $1\frac{5}{12}$
(23,30)

28. $3\dfrac{1}{5} \cdot 2\dfrac{5}{8} \cdot 1\dfrac{3}{7}$ 12
(26)

29. $4\dfrac{1}{2} \div 6$ $\frac{3}{4}$
(26)

30. Find the measure of $\angle x$, $\angle y$, and $\angle z$ in this figure.
(40) m$\angle x$ = 48°; m$\angle y$ = 132°; m$\angle z$ = 48°

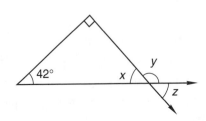

LESSON
42

Repeating Decimals

Facts Practice: Measurement Facts (Test H in Test Masters)

Mental Math:

a. $3 \times 78¢$ **b.** 0.4×100 **c.** $\frac{4}{y} = \frac{20}{25}$
d. $\sqrt{121} - 3^2$ **e.** Estimate: $1\frac{7}{8} \times 3\frac{1}{8}$ **f.** $\frac{4}{5}$ of 35

g. Start with three score and 10, $+ 2$, $\div 8$, $\sqrt{\ }$, $\times 5$, $+ 1$, $\sqrt{\ }$, $+ 1$, square that number.

Problem Solving:

Half of a gallon is a half gallon. Half of a half gallon is a quart. Half of a quart is a pint. Half of a pint is a cup. If milk from a full gallon container is used to fill empty half-gallon, quart, pint, and cup containers, how much milk will be left in the gallon container?

1 gallon

$\frac{1}{2}$ gallon

1 quart

1 pint

1 cup

When a decimal number is divided, the answer is sometimes a decimal number that will not end with a remainder of zero. Instead the answer will have one or more digits in a pattern that repeats indefinitely. Here we show two examples.

$$
\begin{array}{r}
7.1666\ldots \\
6\overline{)43.0000\ldots} \\
\underline{42} \\
1\ 0 \\
\underline{6} \\
40 \\
\underline{36} \\
40 \\
\underline{36} \\
40 \\
\underline{36} \\
4
\end{array}
\qquad
\begin{array}{r}
0.31818\ldots \\
11\overline{)3.50000\ldots} \\
\underline{3\ 3} \\
20 \\
\underline{11} \\
90 \\
\underline{88} \\
20 \\
\underline{11} \\
90 \\
\underline{88} \\
2
\end{array}
$$

The repeating digits of a decimal number are called the **repetend.** In 7.1666..., the repetend is 6. In 0.31818..., the repetend is 18 (not 81). One way to indicate that a decimal number is a repeating decimal number is to write the number with a bar over the repetend where the repetend first appears to the right of the decimal point. We will write each answer as a decimal with a bar over the repetend.

$$7.1666... = 7.1\overline{6} \qquad 0.31818... = 0.3\overline{18}$$

Example 1 Rewrite each of these repeating decimals with a bar over the repetend.

(a) 0.0833333...

(b) 5.14285714285714...

(c) 454.5454545...

Solution (a) The repeating digit is 3.

$$0.08\overline{3}$$

(b) This is a six digit repeating pattern.

$$5.\overline{142857}$$

(c) The repetend is always to the right of the decimal point. We do not write a bar over a whole number.

$$454.\overline{54}$$

Example 2 Round each number to five decimal places.

(a) $5.31\overline{6}$ (b) $25.\overline{405}$

Solution (a) We remove the bar and write the repeating digits to the right of the desired decimal place.

$$5.31\overline{6} = 5.316666...$$

Then we round to five places.

$$5.3166\textcircled{6}6... \longrightarrow \textbf{5.31667}$$

(b) We remove the bar and continue the repeating pattern beyond the fifth decimal place.

$$25.\overline{405} \longrightarrow 25.405405...$$

Then we round to five places.

$$25.4054\textcircled{0}5... \longrightarrow \textbf{25.40541}$$

Example 3   Divide 1.5 by 11 and write the quotient

(a) with a bar over the repetend.

(b) rounded to the nearest hundredth.

Solution   (a) Since place value is fixed by the decimal point, we can write zeros in the places to the right of the decimal point. We continue dividing until the repeating pattern is apparent. The repetend is 36 (not 63). We write the quotient with a bar over 36 where it first appears.

$$0.13636\ldots = \mathbf{0.1\overline{36}}$$

$$
\begin{array}{r}
0.13636\ldots \\
11\overline{)1.50000\ldots} \\
\underline{1\ 1} \\
40 \\
\underline{33} \\
70 \\
\underline{66} \\
40 \\
\underline{33} \\
70 \\
\underline{66} \\
4
\end{array}
$$

(b) The hundredths' place is the second place to the right of the decimal point.

$$0.1\text{③}636\ldots \longrightarrow \mathbf{0.14}$$

 When a division problem is entered into a calculator and the display is filled with a decimal number, it is likely that the quotient is a repeating decimal. However, since a calculator either truncates (cuts off) or rounds the number displayed, the repetend may not be obvious. For example, to convert the fraction $\frac{1}{7}$ to a decimal, we perform the indicated division by dividing 1 by 7. We enter

$$\boxed{1}\ \boxed{÷}\ \boxed{7}\ \boxed{=}$$

An eight-digit display shows

$$\boxed{0.1428571}$$

We might wonder if the final digit, 1, is the beginning of another 142857 pattern. We can get a peek at the next digit by shifting the digits displayed one place to the left. We can do this by multiplying the numerator by 10 and dividing again. This time we divide 10 by 7.

$$\boxed{1}\ \boxed{0}\ \boxed{÷}\ \boxed{7}\ \boxed{=}$$

The display shows

$$\boxed{\texttt{1.4285714}}$$

The only digit we are concerned about in this display is the last digit. Seeing the final digit, 4, following the 1 increases the likelihood that the 142857 pattern is repeating. Why do we see another digit displayed using this technique? Each digit shifts one place to the left which replaces the zero in the original display.

Practice   Write each repeating decimal with a bar over the repetend.

   a. 2.72727... $2.\overline{72}$ **b.** 0.816666... $0.81\overline{6}$

Round each number to the nearest thousandth.

   c. $0.\overline{6}$ 0.667   **d.** $5.3\overline{81}$ 5.382

Divide 1.7 by 12 and write the quotient

   e. with a bar over the repetend. $0.141\overline{6}$

   f. rounded to four decimal places. 0.1417

Problem set 42

1. Two fifths of the children in the nursery were boys. What
(36) was the ratio of boys to girls in the nursery? $\frac{2}{3}$

2. Four hundred thirty-two students were assigned to 16
(13,28) classrooms. What was the average number of students per classroom? 27 students

3. The migrating birds flew for 7 hours at an average rate of
(13) 23 miles per hour. How far did the birds travel in 7 hours?
161 miles

4. Draw a diagram for this statement. Then answer the
(22) questions that follow.

   Seven ninths of the 450 students in the assembly were enthralled by the speaker.

   (a) How many students were enthralled? 350 students

   (b) How many students were not enthralled? 100 students

4.

450 students	
	50 students
	50 students
	50 students
$\frac{7}{9}$ were	50 students
enthralled	50 students
	50 students
	50 students
	50 students
$\frac{2}{9}$ were not	50 students
enthralled	50 students

5. Round each number to four decimal places.
(42)

   (a) $5.1\overline{6}$ 5.1667   (b) $5.\overline{27}$ 5.2727

6. Refer to this pie graph to answer questions (a) and (b).
(38)

Class Test Grades

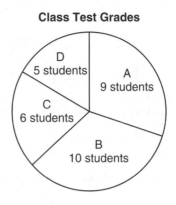

(a) How many more students earned an A or B than earned a C or D? 8 students

(b) What fraction of the students in the class earned an A? $\frac{3}{10}$

7. The coordinates of the vertices of a triangle are (–6, 0),
(37) (0, –6), and (0, 0). What is the area of the triangle? 18 units²

8. All angles in the figure are right angles.
(37) Dimensions are in inches.

(a) Find the perimeter of the figure.
   80 in.

(b) Find the area of the figure. 320 in.²

9. Divide 1.7 by 11 and write the quotient
(42)

(a) with a bar over the repetend. 0.1$\overline{54}$

(b) rounded to three decimal places. 0.155

10. Use digits to write the sum of the decimal numbers
(31,35) twenty-seven thousandths and fifty-eight hundredths.
   0.607

12.(a)

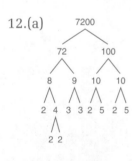

11. What is the probability of rolling a composite number
(36) with one roll of a die (number cube)? $\frac{2}{6} = \frac{1}{3}$

12. (a) Make a factor tree showing the prime factorization of
(21)   7200. (Start with the factors 72 and 100.)

(b) Write the prime factorization of 7200 using exponents.
    $7200 = 2^5 \cdot 3^2 \cdot 5^2$

13.

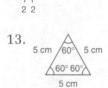

13. Use a protractor and a ruler to help you draw a triangle
(17) with three 60° angles and sides 5 cm long.

14. What is the least common multiple of 12 and 15? 60
(27)

Solve:

15. $\dfrac{21}{24} = \dfrac{w}{40}$ 35
(39)

16. $\dfrac{1.2}{x} = \dfrac{9}{6}$ 0.8
(39)

17. $m + 9.6 = 14$ 4.4
(35)

18. $n - 4.2 = 1.63$ 5.83
(35)

19. Evaluate $\frac{1}{2}bh$ when $b = 12$ and $h = 10$. 60
(41)

20. Show two ways to simplify this expression. 4(11) = 44;
(41) $4 \cdot 5 + 4 \cdot 6 = 20 + 24 = 44$
$$4(5 + 6)$$

21. Instead of dividing 686 by 14, we can find the quotient by
(27) dividing what number by 7? 343

22. Multiply $4.56 by 0.08 and round the product to the
(35) nearest cent. $0.36

23. Estimate the quotient of $23.8 \div 5.975$ by rounding each
(33) number to the nearest whole number before dividing.
$24 \div 6 = 4$

24. What are the missing words in the following sentence?
(Inv. 2)

> *The longest chord of a circle is the __(a)__, which
> is twice the length of the __(b)__.* (a) diameter (b) radius

Simplify:

25. $7.1 \div 4$ 1.775
(35)

26. $6\dfrac{1}{4} + 5\dfrac{5}{12} + \dfrac{2}{3}$ $12\frac{1}{3}$
(30)

27. $4 - \left(4\dfrac{1}{6} - 1\dfrac{1}{4}\right)$ $1\frac{1}{12}$
(23,30)

28. $6\dfrac{2}{5} \cdot 2\dfrac{5}{8} \cdot 2\dfrac{6}{7}$ 48
(26)

29. $6 \div 4\dfrac{1}{2}$ $1\frac{1}{3}$
(26)

30. Find the measure of $\angle a$, $\angle b$, and $\angle c$ in this figure.
(40) m$\angle a$ = 140°; m$\angle b$ = 50°; m$\angle c$ = 130°

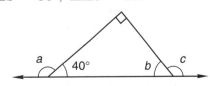

LESSON
43

Converting Decimals to Fractions • Converting Fractions to Decimals • Converting Percents to Decimals

Facts Practice: Proportions (Test I in Test Masters)

Mental Math:

   a. $6 \times 48¢$ **b.** $3.5 \div 100$ **c.** $\frac{n}{4} = \frac{21}{12}$
   d. $7^2 - \sqrt{100}$ **e.** Estimate: 9.95×6 **f.** $\frac{1}{5}$ of 300
   g. Find the sum, difference, product, and quotient of $\frac{2}{3}$ and $\frac{1}{4}$.

Problem Solving:

You can roll six different numbers (1–6) with one number cube. You can roll eleven different numbers (2–12) with two number cubes. If four number cubes are rolled at once, how many different totals are possible?

Converting decimals to fractions

To write a decimal number as a fraction, we write the digits after the decimal point as the numerator of the fraction. For the denominator of the fraction we write the place value of the last digit. Then we reduce.

Example 1 Write 0.125 as a fraction.

Solution The digits 125 form the numerator of the fraction. The denominator of the fraction is 1000 because 5 is in the thousandths' place.

$$0.125 = \frac{125}{1000}$$

Notice that the denominator of the fraction has as many zeros as the decimal number has decimal places. Now we reduce.

$$\frac{125}{1000} = \frac{1}{8}$$

Example 2 Write 11.42 as a mixed number.

Solution The number 11 is the whole number part. The numerator of the fraction is 42, and the denominator is 100 because 2 is in the hundredths' place.

$$11.42 = 11\frac{42}{100}$$

Now we reduce the fraction.

$$11\frac{42}{100} = 11\frac{21}{50}$$

Converting fractions to decimals

To change a fraction to a decimal number, we perform the division indicated by the fraction. The fraction $\frac{1}{4}$ indicates that 1 is divided by 4.

$$4\overline{)1}$$

It may appear that we cannot perform this division. However, if we fix place values with a decimal point and write zeros in the decimal places to the right of the decimal point, we can perform the division. The result is a decimal number that is equal to the fraction $\frac{1}{4}$.

$$\begin{array}{r} 0.25 \\ 4\overline{)1.00} \\ \underline{8} \\ 20 \\ \underline{20} \\ 0 \end{array}$$
Thus, $\frac{1}{4} = 0.25$.

Some fractions convert to repeating decimals. We convert $\frac{1}{3}$ to a decimal by dividing 1 by 3.

$$\begin{array}{r} 0.33... \\ 3\overline{)1.00...} \\ \underline{9} \\ 10 \\ \underline{9} \\ 1 \end{array}$$
Thus, $\frac{1}{3} = 0.\overline{3}$.

Every fraction converts to either a terminating decimal (like 0.25) or a repeating decimal (like $0.\overline{3}$).

Example 3   Write each of these numbers as a decimal number.

(a) $\dfrac{23}{100}$ (b) $\dfrac{7}{4}$ (c) $3\dfrac{4}{5}$ (d) $\dfrac{2}{3}$

Solution   (a) Fractions with denominators of 10, 100, 1000, etc., can be written directly as decimal numbers, without performing the division. The decimal part will have the same number of places as the number of zeros in the denominator.

$$\frac{23}{100} = \mathbf{0.23}$$

(b) An improper fraction is equal to or greater than 1. When we change an improper fraction to a decimal number, the decimal number will be greater than or equal to 1.

$$\frac{7}{4} \longrightarrow 4\overline{)7.00} \qquad \frac{7}{4} = 1.75$$

$$
\begin{array}{r}
1.75 \\
4\overline{)7.00} \\
\underline{4} \\
3\,0 \\
\underline{2\,8} \\
20 \\
\underline{20} \\
0
\end{array}
$$

(c) To change a mixed number to a decimal number, we may change the mixed number to an improper fraction and then divide. Another way is to separate the fraction from the whole number and change the fraction to a decimal number. Then we write the whole number and the decimal number as one number. Here we show both ways.

$$3\frac{4}{5} = \frac{19}{5} \qquad \text{or} \qquad 3\frac{4}{5} = 3 + \frac{4}{5}$$

$$
\begin{array}{r}
3.8 \\
5\overline{)19.0} \\
\underline{15} \\
4\,0 \\
\underline{4\,0} \\
0
\end{array}
\qquad\qquad
\begin{array}{r}
0.8 \\
5\overline{)4.0} \\
\underline{4\,0} \\
0
\end{array}
$$

$$3\frac{4}{5} = 3.8 \qquad\qquad 3\frac{4}{5} = 3.8$$

(d) To change $\frac{2}{3}$ to a decimal number, we divide.

$$\frac{2}{3} \longrightarrow 3\overline{)2.000\ldots} \qquad \frac{2}{3} = 0.\overline{6}$$

$$
\begin{array}{r}
0.666\ldots \\
3\overline{)2.000\ldots} \\
\underline{1\,8} \\
20 \\
\underline{18} \\
20 \\
\underline{18} \\
2
\end{array}
$$

Note: We will write repeating decimal numbers with a bar over the repetend unless directed otherwise.

Converting percents to decimals

Recall that percent means "per hundred" or "hundredths." So 75% means 75 hundredths which can be written as a fraction or as a decimal.

$$75\% = \frac{75}{100} = 0.75$$

Likewise, 5% means 5 hundredths.

$$5\% = \frac{5}{100} = 0.05$$

We see that a percent may be written as a decimal using the same digits but with the decimal point shifted two places to the left.

Examples and *Solutions*

4. 25% = **0.25**   **5.** 125% = **1.25**   **6.** 2.5% = **0.025**

7. 50% = 0.50 = **0.5**   **8.** $7\frac{1}{2}\% = 7.5\% = $ **0.075**

Many scientific calculators do not have a percent key. Designers of these calculators assume that the user will mentally convert percents to decimals before entering the calculation.

If your calculator does have a percent key, you may find the decimal equivalent of the percent by entering 1 × the percent. For example, enter

The calculator displays the decimal equivalent 0.25.

Practice*

Change each decimal number to a reduced fraction or to a mixed number.

a. 0.24 $\frac{6}{25}$ **b.** 45.6 $45\frac{3}{5}$ **c.** 2.375 $2\frac{3}{8}$

Change each fraction or mixed number to a decimal number.

d. $\frac{23}{4}$ 5.75   **e.** $4\frac{3}{5}$ 4.6   **f.** $\frac{5}{8}$ 0.625   **g.** $\frac{5}{6}$ 0.8$\overline{3}$

Convert each percent to a decimal number.

h. 8% 0.08   **i.** 12.5% 0.125   **j.** 150% 1.5   **k.** $6\frac{1}{2}\%$ 0.065

**Problem set
43**

1. The ratio of Celtic soldiers to Roman soldiers was 2 to 5.
$^{(36)}$ What fraction of the soldiers was Celtic? $\frac{2}{7}$

2. Eric ran 8 laps in 11 minutes, 44 seconds.
$^{(28)}$

    (a) How many seconds did it take Eric to run 8 laps?
704 seconds

    (b) What is the average number of seconds it took Eric to run each lap? 88 seconds

3. Some gas was still in the tank. Jan added 13.3 gallons of
$^{(11,35)}$ gas, which filled the tank. If the tank held a total of 21.0 gallons of gas, how much gas was in the tank before Jan added the gas? 7.7 gallons

4. From 1750 to 1850, the estimated population of the world
$^{(5,12)}$ increased from seven hundred twenty-five million to one billion, two hundred thousand. How many more people were living in the world in 1850 than in 1750?
275,200,000 people

5.

15 games

$\frac{2}{3}$ won $\begin{cases} \boxed{5 \text{ games}} \\ \boxed{5 \text{ games}} \end{cases}$
$\frac{1}{3}$ lost $\begin{cases} \boxed{5 \text{ games}} \end{cases}$

5. Draw a diagram from this statement. Then answer the
$^{(22,36)}$ questions that follow.

    The Jets won two thirds of their 15 games and lost the rest.

    (a) How many games did the Jets win? 10 games

    (b) What was the Jets' won-lost ratio? $\frac{2}{1}$

6. This stem-and-leaf plot shows the distribution of finish
$^{(Inv.\,4)}$ times in a 100-meter sprint. For these times find

11	2
12	3 4 8
13	0 3 4 5 6
14	1 4 7 8
15	2 5

12 | 3 represents
12.3 seconds

    (a) the median. 13.5 seconds

    (b) the lower quartile. 12.8 seconds

    (c) the upper quartile. 14.7 seconds

7. Make a box-and-whisker plot of the 100-meter times in
(Inv. 4) problem 6.

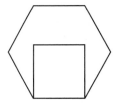

8. A square and a regular hexagon share
(19) a common side, as shown. The
perimeter of the hexagon is 120 mm.
What is the perimeter of the square?
80 mm

9. Write each of these numbers as a reduced fraction or
(43) mixed number.

(a) 0.375 $\frac{3}{8}$ (b) 5.55 $5\frac{11}{20}$

10. Write each of these numbers as a decimal number.
(43)

(a) $2\frac{2}{5}$ 2.4   (b) $\frac{1}{8}$ 0.125

11. Round each number to the nearest thousandth.
(42)

(a) $0.\overline{45}$ 0.455

(b) $3.\overline{142857}$ 3.143

12. Divide 1.9 by 12 and write the quotient
(42)

(a) with a bar over the repetend. $0.158\overline{3}$

(b) rounded to three decimal places. 0.158

13. Four and five hundredths is how much greater than one
(31,35) hundred sixty-seven thousandths? 3.883

14.
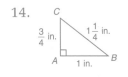

14. Draw segment AB to be 1 inch long. Draw segment AC
(8) perpendicular to $\overline{AB}$. Let segment AC be $\frac{3}{4}$ inch long.
Complete triangle ABC by drawing segment BC. Measure
segment BC with a ruler. How long is segment BC?

15. $\frac{26}{52} = \frac{1}{2}$

15. A normal deck of cards is composed of four suits (red
(36) heart, red diamond, black spade, black club) of 13 cards
(2 through 10, jack, queen, king, ace) for a total of 52
cards. If one card is drawn from a normal deck of cards,
what is the probability that the card will be a red card?

16.(a)

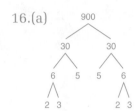

16. (a) Make a factor tree showing the prime factorization of
(21)   900. (Start with the factors 30 and 30.)

(b) Write the prime factorization of 900 using exponents.
   $900 = 2^2 \cdot 3^2 \cdot 5^2$

(c) Write the prime factorization of $\sqrt{900}$.
   $\sqrt{900} = 30 = 2 \cdot 3 \cdot 5$

Solve:

17. $\dfrac{10}{18} = \dfrac{c}{4.5}$ 2.5
(39)

18. $1.9 = w + 0.42$ 1.48
(35)

19. The eyedropper held 2 milliliters of liquid. How many
(32)   eyedroppers of liquid would it take to fill a one-liter
container?   500 eyedroppers

20. (a) Write 8% as a decimal number.   0.08
(43)

(b) Find 8% of $8.90 by multiplying $8.90 by the answer
to part (a). Round the answer to the nearest cent. $0.71

21. (a) What is the perimeter of this
(37)   triangle?   2.4 m

(b) What is the area of this triangle?
   0.24 m²

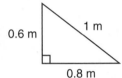

---

22. The division
problems are
equivalent
problems because
the quotients are
equal.

22. Compare and explain the reasons for your answer.
(27)

$$\frac{32}{2} \bigcirc \frac{320}{20}$$

23. Evaluate $a(b + c)$ if $a = 2$, $b = 3$, and $c = 4$.   14
(41)

Simplify:

24. $6.5 \div 4$ 1.625
(35)

25. $3\dfrac{3}{10} - 1\dfrac{11}{15}$ $1\frac{17}{30}$
(23,30)

26. $5\dfrac{1}{2} + 6\dfrac{3}{10} + \dfrac{4}{5}$ $12\frac{3}{5}$
(30)

27. $7\dfrac{1}{2} \cdot 3\dfrac{1}{3} \cdot \dfrac{4}{5} \div 5$ 4
(26)

28. Find the measure of $\angle a$, $\angle b$, and $\angle c$
(40)   in this figure.
   $m\angle a = 70°$; $m\angle b = 60°$; $m\angle c = 120°$

29. Find the next coordinate pair in this
(Inv. 3)   sequence.   (5, 10)

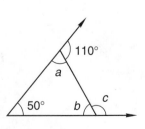

$(1, 2), (2, 4), (3, 6), (4, 8), \ldots$

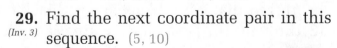

30. Refer to the figure to answer the
(Inv. 2) following questions:

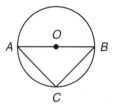

(a) What is the measure of central angle *AOB*? 180°

(b) What appears to be the measure of inscribed angle *ACB*? 90°

(c) Chord *AC* is congruent to chord *BC*. What appears to be the measure of inscribed angle *ABC*? 45°

LESSON
44

Division Answers

Facts Practice: Measurement Facts (Test H in Test Masters)

Mental Math:

a. 5 × 64¢   **b.** 0.5 ÷ 10   **c.** $\frac{3}{m} = \frac{12}{24}$

d. Estimate: 596 ÷ 11   **e.** $\frac{\sqrt{144}}{12}$ **f.** $\frac{3}{4}$ of 200

g. Start with the number of meters in a kilometer, ÷ 10, $\sqrt{}$, × 5, − 1, $\sqrt{}$, × 5, + 1, $\sqrt{}$.

Problem Solving:

The prime number 7 is the average of which two different prime numbers?

We have written answers to division problems with remainders different ways. We can write them with a remainder or as a mixed number.

$$\begin{array}{r} 6\ \text{r}\ 3 \\ 4\overline{)27} \\ \underline{24} \\ 3 \end{array} \qquad \begin{array}{r} 6\frac{3}{4} \\ 4\overline{)27} \\ \underline{24} \\ 3 \end{array}$$

We may also write the answer as a decimal number. We fix place values with a decimal point, affix zeros to the right of the decimal point, and continue dividing.

$$\begin{array}{r} 6.75 \\ 4\overline{)27.00} \\ \underline{24} \\ 3\ 0 \\ \underline{2\ 8} \\ 20 \\ \underline{20} \\ 0 \end{array}$$

Example 1   Divide 54 by 4 and write the answer

(a) with a remainder.

(b) as a mixed number.

(c) as a decimal.

Solution   (a) We divide and find the result is **13 r 2.**

(b) The remainder is the numerator of a fraction and the divisor is the denominator, so this answer can be written as $13\frac{2}{4} = \mathbf{13\frac{1}{2}}.$

$$
\begin{array}{r}
13\ \text{r}\ 2 \\
4\overline{)54} \\
\underline{4} \\
14 \\
\underline{12} \\
2
\end{array}
$$

(c) We fix place values by placing the decimal point to the right of 54. Then we can write zeros in the following places and continue dividing until the remainder is zero. The result is **13.5.**

$$
\begin{array}{r}
13.5 \\
4\overline{)54.0} \\
\underline{4} \\
14 \\
\underline{12} \\
2\ 0 \\
\underline{2\ 0} \\
0
\end{array}
$$

Sometimes a division answer written as a decimal number will be a repeating decimal number or will have more decimal places than the problem requires. In this book we show the complete division of the number unless the problem states that the answer is to be rounded.

Example 2   Divide 37.4 by 9 and round the quotient to the nearest thousandth.

Solution   We continue dividing until the answer has four decimal places. Then we round to the nearest thousandth.

$$4.15\textcircled{5}5\ldots \longrightarrow \mathbf{4.156}$$

$$
\begin{array}{r}
4.1555\ldots \\
9\overline{)37.4000\ldots} \\
\underline{36} \\
1\ 4 \\
\underline{9} \\
50 \\
\underline{45} \\
50 \\
\underline{45} \\
50 \\
\underline{45} \\
5
\end{array}
$$

Often problems involving division require us to interpret the results of the division and express our answer in other ways. Consider the following example.

Example 3 Vans will be used to transport 27 students on a field trip. Each van can carry 6 students.

(a) How many vans can be filled?

(b) How many vans will be needed?

(c) If all but one of the vans is filled, then how many students are in the van that is not full?

Solution Dividing 27 by 6 gives us these forms of the quotient.

$$\begin{array}{r} 4 \text{ r } 3 \\ 6\overline{)27} \end{array} \qquad \begin{array}{r} 4\frac{1}{2} \\ 6\overline{)27} \end{array} \qquad \begin{array}{r} 4.5 \\ 6\overline{)27.0} \end{array}$$

The questions require us to interpret the results of the division.

(a) The whole number 4 in the quotient means that **4 vans** can be filled to capacity.

(b) Four vans will hold 24 students. Since 27 students are going on the field trip another van is needed. So **5 vans** will be needed.

(c) The fifth van is carrying the remaining **3 students.**

Practice Divide 55 by 4 and write the answer

a. with a remainder. 13 r 3

b. as a mixed number. $13\frac{3}{4}$

c. as a decimal number. 13.75

d. Divide 5.5 by 3 and round the answer to three decimal places. 1.833

e. Ninety-three students are assigned to four classrooms as equally as possible. How many students are in each of the four classrooms? 23, 23, 23, and 24 students

Problem set 44

1. The rectangle was 24 inches long and 18 inches wide. What was the ratio of its length to its width? $\frac{4}{3}$
(36)

2. Amber's test scores were 90, 95, 90, 85, 80, 85, 90, 80, 95, and 100. What was her mean (average) test score? 89
(28)

3. The report stated that two out of every five young people
(14) were unable to find a job. What fraction of the young people were able to find a job? $\frac{3}{5}$

4. Rachel bought a sheet of fifty 33-cent stamps from the
(28) post office. She paid for the stamps with a $20 bill. How much money should she get back? $3.50

5. Ninety-seven thousandths is how much less than two and
(31,35) ninety-eight hundredths? Write the answer in words.
two and eight hundred eighty-three thousandths

6.

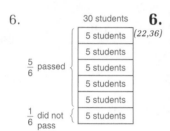

6. Draw a diagram for this statement. Then answer the
(22,36) questions that follow.

Five sixths of the 30 students passed the test.

(a) How many students did not pass the test? 5 students

(b) What was the ratio of students who passed the test to students who did not pass the test? $\frac{5}{1}$

7. Sketch this figure on your paper.
(19) Find the length of each unmarked side and find the perimeter of the polygon. Dimensions are in meters. All angles are right angles. 78 meters

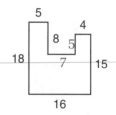

8. (a) Write 0.75 as a reduced fraction. $\frac{3}{4}$
(43)

(b) Write $\frac{5}{8}$ as a decimal number. 0.625

(c) Write 125% as a decimal number. 1.25

9. If a card is drawn from a normal deck of cards, what is
(36) the probability that the card will be a heart? $\frac{1}{4}$

10. 2(3 + 4) equals which of the following? B. (2 · 3) + (2 · 4)
(41)

A. (2 · 3) + 4   B. (2 · 3) + (2 · 4)

C. 2 + 7   D. 23 + 24

11. Find the next three numbers in this sequence.
(2)

1, 3, 6, 10, ...   15, 21, 28

12. Divide 5.4 by 11 and write the answer
(42,44)

(a) with a bar over the repetend. $0.4\overline{90}$

(b) rounded to the nearest thousandth. 0.491

13. What composite number is equal to the product of the
(21) first four prime numbers? 210

14. (a) Arrange these numbers in order from least to greatest:
(4,33)

$$1.2, -12, 0.12, 0, \frac{1}{2} \quad {\scriptstyle -12,\ 0,\ 0.12,\ \frac{1}{2},\ 1.2}$$

(b) Which numbers in (a) are integers? $0, -12$

15. Each math book is $1\frac{1}{2}$ inches thick.
(26)

(a) A stack of 12 math books would stand how many
inches tall? 18 inches

(b) How many math books would make a stack one yard
tall? 24 books

16. What is the sum of the numbers marked M and N on this
(34,35) number line? 5

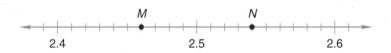

Solve:

17. $\dfrac{25}{15} = \dfrac{n}{1.2}$ $\;2$
(39)

18. $\dfrac{p}{90} = \dfrac{4}{18}$ $\;20$
(39)

19. $4 = 3.14 + x$ $\;0.86$
(35)

20. $0.1 = 1 - z$ $\;0.9$
(35)

21. Estimate the value of πd when π is 3.14159 and d is 9.847
(33,41) meters. 30 meters

22. Draw a square with sides 2.5 cm long. See student work.
(34,35)

(a) What is the area of the square? 6.25 cm^2

(b) What is the perimeter of the square? 10 cm

23. The coordinates of the vertices of a triangle are $(-2, 0)$,
(37) $(4, 0)$, and $(3, 3)$. What is the area of the triangle? 9 sq. units

Simplify:

24. 16.42 ÷ 8   2.0525
(35)

25. 0.153 ÷ 9   0.017
(35)

26. $5\frac{3}{4} + \frac{5}{6} + 2\frac{1}{2}$ $9\frac{1}{12}$
(30)

27. $3\frac{1}{3} - \left(5 - 1\frac{5}{6}\right)$ $\frac{1}{6}$
(23,30)

28. $3\frac{3}{4} \cdot 3\frac{1}{3} \cdot 8$ 100
(26)

29. $7 \div 10\frac{1}{2}$ $\frac{2}{3}$
(26)

30. Figure *ABCD* is a rectangle. The
(40)   measure of ∠*ADB* is 35°. Find the
      measure of

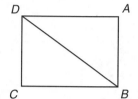

(a) ∠*ABD*.   55°

(b) ∠*CBD*.   35°

(c) ∠*BDC*.   55°

State the reason for each answer.

(a) The other two angles of △*ABD* are 35° and 90°. For the total to be 180°, this angle is 55°.

(b) Since the figure is a rectangle, ∠*ABC* is 90°. We found that ∠*ABD* is 55°; ∠*CBD* is the complement of ∠*ABD*, so the measure is 35°.

(c) ∠*BDC* is the complement of a 35° angle. Also, ∠*BDC* is the third angle of a triangle whose other two angles measure 35° and 90°.

LESSON
45

Dividing by a Decimal Number

Facts Practice: Proportions (Test I in Test Masters)

Mental Math:

  a. 7 × $1.50   **b.** 1.25×10^2 **c.** $\frac{4}{6} = \frac{10}{w}$
  d. $5^2 \cdot \sqrt{16}$ **e.** Estimate: $4\frac{1}{8} \times 2\frac{6}{7}$ **f.** $\frac{2}{3}$ of 75
  g. Find the sum, difference, product, and quotient of $\frac{3}{4}$ and $\frac{2}{3}$.

Problem Solving:

Copy this problem and fill in the missing digits.

$$\begin{array}{r} \_\,8\,\_ \\ \times \qquad \_ \\ \hline 8\,\_\_\,8 \end{array}$$

Dan has $2.00 and wants to buy popsicles for his friends. If popsicles cost $0.25 each, how many can Dan buy?

This is a problem we may be able to solve quickly by mental calculation. Dan can buy 4 popsicles priced at $0.25 for $1.00, so he can buy 8 popsicles for $2.00. However, how do we get an answer of "8 popsicles" from what seems to be this division problem?

$$0.25 \overline{\smash{\big)}\ \$2.00}$$

In this lesson we will consider how to get the "8." In a later lesson we will consider how to get the "popsicles." Notice that dividing $2.00 by $0.25 is dividing by a decimal number ($0.25).

$$\frac{\$2.00}{\$0.25}$$

If we wish to divide by a whole number instead of by a decimal number, we may change to this equivalent division problem.

$$\frac{200¢}{25¢}$$

Changing from dollars to cents shifts the decimal point two places to the right. The units cents over cents reduce to 1, and 200 divided by 25 is 8.

$$\frac{200¢}{25¢} = 8$$

Recall that we can form equivalent division problems by multiplying (or dividing) the dividend and divisor by the same number. We use this method to change division-by-a-decimal problems to division-by-a-whole number problems.

If we want to divide 1.36 by 0.4, we have

$$\frac{1.36}{0.4}$$

We can change the divisor to the whole number 4 by multiplying both the dividend and divisor by 10.

$$\frac{1.36}{0.4} \times \frac{10}{10} = \frac{13.6}{4}$$

The quotient of 13.6 divided by 4 is the same as the quotient of 1.36 divided by 0.4. This means that both of these division problems have the same answer.

$$0.4 \overline{\smash{\big)}\ 1.36} \quad \text{is equivalent to} \quad 4 \overline{\smash{\big)}\ 13.6}$$

To divide by a decimal number, we move the decimal point in the divisor to the right to make the divisor a whole number. Then we move the decimal point in the dividend the same number of places to the right.

Example 1 Divide: 3.36 ÷ 0.06

Solution We use a division box and write

$$0.06\overline{)3.36}$$

First we move the decimal point in 0.06 two places to the right to make it 6.

$$006.\overline{)3.36}$$

Then we move the decimal point in 3.36 the same number of places to the right. By this action we have simply formed an equivalent division problem by multiplying both numbers by 100.

$$006.\overline{)336.}$$

The decimal point in the answer is just above the new location of the decimal point.

$$6\overline{)336.}^{\,\,.}$$

Now we divide.

$$
\begin{array}{r}
56. \\
6\overline{)336.} \\
\underline{30} \\
36 \\
\underline{36} \\
0
\end{array}
$$

Thus, 3.36 ÷ 0.06 = **56.**

Example 2 Divide: 0.144 ÷ 0.8

Solution We want the divisor, 0.8, to be a whole number. By moving the decimal point one place to the right the divisor becomes the whole number 8. Then we move the decimal point in the dividend one place to the right and divide.

$$
\begin{array}{r}
0.18 \\
08.\overline{)1.44} \\
\underline{8} \\
64 \\
\underline{64} \\
0
\end{array}
$$

Example 3 Divide: $15.4 \div 0.07$

Solution We move both decimal points two places. This makes an empty place in the division box, which we fill with a zero. We keep dividing until we reach the decimal point. We find **220** as the answer.

$$
\begin{array}{r}
220. \\
0\underset{\smile}{07}.\overline{)1540}.\underset{\smile}{} \\
\underline{14} \\
14 \\
\underline{14} \\
00 \\
\underline{0} \\
0
\end{array}
$$

Example 4 Divide: $21 \div 0.5$

Solution We move the decimal point in 0.5 one place to the right. The decimal point on 21 is to the right of the 1. We shift this decimal point one place to the right forming the equivalent division problem $210 \div 5$.

$$
\begin{array}{r}
42. \\
0\underset{\smile}{5}.\overline{)210}.\underset{\smile}{} \\
\underline{20} \\
10 \\
\underline{10} \\
0
\end{array}
$$

Example 5 Divide: $1.54 \div 0.8$

Solution We do not write a remainder. We write zeros in the places to the right of the 4. We continue dividing until the remainder is zero, until the digits begin repeating, or until we have divided to the desired number of decimal places.

$$
\begin{array}{r}
1.925 \\
0\underset{\smile}{8}.\overline{)15}.\underset{\smile}{400} \\
\underline{8} \\
7\,4 \\
\underline{7\,2} \\
20 \\
\underline{16} \\
40 \\
\underline{40} \\
0
\end{array}
$$

Example 6 How many $0.35 erasers can be purchased for $7.00?

Solution We record the problem as 7.00 divided by 0.35. We shift both decimal points two places and divide. The quotient is 20, and the answer to the question is **20 erasers.**

$$
\begin{array}{r}
20. \\
0\underset{\smile}{35}.\overline{)700}.\underset{\smile}{} \\
\underline{70} \\
00 \\
\underline{0} \\
0
\end{array}
$$

Practice* Divide:

a. $5.16 \div 0.6$ 8.6   **b.** $0.144 \div 0.09$ 1.6

c. $23.8 \div 0.07$ 340   **d.** $24 \div 0.08$ 300

f. If we multiply $\frac{0.25}{0.5}$ by $\frac{10}{10}$ the result is $\frac{2.5}{5}$. Since $\frac{10}{10}$ equals 1, we have not changed the value by multiplying, we have only changed the form.

e. How many $0.75 pens can be purchased with $12.00?
16 pens

f. Explain why these division problems are equivalent.

$$\frac{0.25}{0.5} = \frac{2.5}{5}$$

Problem set 45

1. Raisins and nuts were mixed in a bowl. If five eighths of the mixture was made up of nuts, what was the ratio of raisins to nuts? $\frac{3}{5}$
(36)

2. The taxi ride cost 1 dollar plus 40¢ more for each quarter mile traveled. What was the total cost for a 2-mile trip?
(28) $4.20

3. Fifty-four and five hundredths is how much greater than fifty and forty thousandths? Use words to write the answer. four and one hundredth
(31,35)

4. Refer to this election tally sheet to answer questions (a) and (b).
(38)

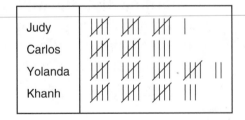

Vote Totals

Judy	ЖҐ ЖҐ ЖҐ I
Carlos	ЖҐ ЖҐ IIII
Yolanda	ЖҐ ЖҐ ЖҐ · ЖҐ II
Khanh	ЖҐ ЖҐ ЖҐ III

(a) The winner of the election received how many more votes than the runner-up? 4 votes

(b) What fraction of the votes did Carlos receive? $\frac{1}{5}$

5. Draw a diagram for this statement. Then answer the questions that follow.
(22,36)

Four sevenths of those who rode the Giant Gyro at the fair were euphoric. All the rest were vertiginous.

(a) What fraction of those who rode the ride were vertiginous? $\frac{3}{7}$

(b) What was the ratio of euphoric to vertiginous riders? $\frac{4}{3}$

5.

Riders on the Giant Gyro

$\frac{4}{7}$ were euphoric	$\frac{1}{7}$ of riders
	$\frac{1}{7}$ of riders
	$\frac{1}{7}$ of riders
	$\frac{1}{7}$ of riders
$\frac{3}{7}$ were vertiginous	$\frac{1}{7}$ of riders
	$\frac{1}{7}$ of riders
	$\frac{1}{7}$ of riders

6. What is the least common multiple of 10 and 16?   80
(27)

7. Find the product of 5^2 and 10^2.   2500
(20)

8. The perimeter of this rectangle is 56 cm.
(19,20)

10 cm

(a) What is the length of the rectangle?   18 cm

(b) What is the area of the rectangle?   180 cm²

9. (a) Write 62.5 as a mixed number. $62\frac{1}{2}$
(43)

(b) Write $\frac{9}{100}$ as a decimal number.   0.09

(c) Write 7.5% as a decimal number.   0.075

10. Round each number to five decimal places.
(42)

(a) $23.\overline{54}$ 23.54545   (b) $0.91\overline{6}$ 0.91667

11. A 2-liter bottle of water has a mass of 2 kilograms. How
(32) many grams is that?   2000 grams

12. Find 6.5% of $5.00 by multiplying $5.00 by 0.065. Round
(35) the answer to cents. $0.33

13. Divide 5.1 by 9 and write the quotient
(42,44)

(a) rounded to the nearest thousandth.   0.567

(b) with a bar over the repetend. $0.5\overline{6}$

14. If a card is drawn from a normal deck of cards, what is
(36) the probability that the card will be an ace? $\frac{1}{13}$

15.
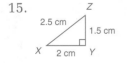

15. Draw segment *XY* to be 2 cm long. Draw segment *YZ*
(34) perpendicular to $\overline{XY}$ and 1.5 cm long. Complete
triangle *XYZ* by drawing segment *XZ*. How long is
segment *XZ*?

16. What is (a) the perimeter and (b) the area of the triangle in
(37) problem 15?   (a) 6 cm   (b) 1.5 cm²

Solve:

17. $\dfrac{3}{w} = \dfrac{25}{100}$ 12
(39)

18. $\dfrac{1.2}{4.4} = \dfrac{3}{a}$ 11
(39)

19. $m + 0.23 = 1.2$ 0.97
(35)

20. $r - 1.97 = 0.65$ 2.62
(35)

Simplify:

21. $(0.15)(0.15)$ 0.0225
(35)

22. $1.2 \times 2.5 \times 4$ 12
(35)

23. $14.14 \div 5$ 2.828
(35)

24. $0.096 \div 0.12$ 0.8
(45)

25. $\dfrac{5}{8} + \dfrac{5}{6} + \dfrac{5}{12}$ $1\frac{7}{8}$
(30)

26. $4\dfrac{1}{2} - \left(2\dfrac{1}{3} - 1\dfrac{1}{4}\right)$ $3\frac{5}{12}$
(30)

27. $\dfrac{7}{15} \cdot 10 \cdot 2\dfrac{1}{7}$ 10
(26)

28. $6\dfrac{3}{5} \div 1\dfrac{1}{10}$ 6
(26)

29. How many $0.21 pencils can be purchased for $7.00?
(45) 33 pencils

30. Amanda drew and cut out a triangle
(40) and wrote the letters *a*, *b*, and *c* in
the corners as shown. Then she tore
off the three corners of the triangle
and fit the pieces together to form
this semicircular shape.

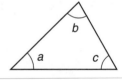

(a) Try the activity described in this
problem and tape or glue the fitted
corners to your paper.
See student work.

(b) Describe the characteristic of triangles demonstrated
by this activity.
The sum of the angle measures of a triangle is 180°.

LESSON
46

Unit Price • Rates • Sales Tax

Facts Practice: $+ - \times \div$ Decimals (Test J in Test Masters)

Mental Math:

a. $9 \times \$0.82$

b. $3.6 \div 10^2$

c. $\frac{4}{8} = \frac{a}{20}$

d. Estimate: 4.97×1.9

e. $\sqrt{16} + 2^3$

f. $\frac{9}{10}$ of 80

g. Start with the number of vertices on a quadrilateral, add the number of years in a decade, and subtract half a dozen. Then multiply by the number of feet in a yard. What is the answer?

Problem Solving:

Each student in the class may think of a three-digit number composed of three different digits and write it down. Create another three-digit number by reversing the order of the digits. Then subtract the smaller number from the larger number. Is the difference divisible by 9?

Unit price As an aid to grocery store customers, the unit price for various products is often posted. The **unit price** is the cost for a single-unit measurement of the product. The unit price can be found by dividing the price by the number of units in the measurement.

Example 1 What is the unit price of a 24-ounce box of cereal that costs $3.60?

Solution The cereal is measured in ounces. The unit price is the cost of 1 ounce. We divide the price by 24 ounces.

$$\frac{\$3.60}{24 \text{ ounces}} = \frac{\$0.15}{1 \text{ ounce}}$$

The unit price is $0.15 for one ounce, which is **15¢ per ounce.**

Example 2 What is the unit price of a 36-ounce box of cereal that costs $4.50?

Solution The unit price for the cereal is the price per ounce. We divide the price by 36 ounces.

$$\frac{\$4.50}{36 \text{ ounces}} = \frac{\$0.125}{1 \text{ ounce}}$$

The unit price is **12.5¢ per ounce.**

Unit pricing helps customers determine which brand or which size package provides the better buy. From the two previous examples, we see that the larger box of cereal was the better buy because it cost less per ounce.

Rates   Unit price is an example of a **rate.** A rate is a ratio of two measurements. The two measurements in the unit price ratio are price divided by quantity. Other examples of rates include speed, which is distance divided by time and mileage which is distance divided by quantity of fuel used.

Example 3   Hans pedaled 84 kilometers in 4 hours. What was his average speed?

Solution   Speed is a ratio of distance to time.

$$\frac{84 \text{ km}}{4 \text{ hr}} = 21\frac{\text{km}}{\text{hr}}$$

Performing the division we find that Hans pedaled at an average speed of **21 km/hr.**

Example 4   Dan rode his motorcycle on an interstate trip. He traveled 243 miles on 4.5 gallons of gas. Dan's motorcycle averaged how many miles per gallon on the trip?

Solution   Miles per gallon means miles divided by gallons.

$$\frac{243 \text{ mi}}{4.5 \text{ gal}} = \mathbf{54}\frac{\textbf{mi}}{\textbf{gal}}$$

We may choose to reverse the terms of a ratio. For instance, if Laura can walk 6 miles in 2 hours, we can write these two rates.

$$\frac{6 \text{ mi}}{2 \text{ hr}} = 3\frac{\text{mi}}{\text{hr}} \quad (3 \text{ miles per hour})$$

$$\frac{2 \text{ hr}}{6 \text{ mi}} = \frac{1}{3}\frac{\text{hr}}{\text{mi}} \quad \left(\frac{1}{3} \text{ hour per mile}\right)$$

Example 5   For a 5% service fee, a merchant agreed to exchange 20 dollars for 2400 yen or 2400 yen for 20 dollars. Disregarding the fee, write two reduced rates for the stated exchange rate.

Solution   We write and reverse the two rates.

$$\frac{2400 \text{ yen}}{20 \text{ dollars}} = \mathbf{120}\frac{\textbf{yen}}{\textbf{dollar}}$$

$$\frac{20 \text{ dollars}}{2400 \text{ yen}} = \frac{\textbf{1}}{\textbf{120}}\frac{\textbf{dollar}}{\textbf{yen}}$$

Notice that the two rates are reciprocals.

Sales tax   To find the amount of **sales tax** on a purchase, we multiply the full price of the purchase by the tax rate.

Example 6   A bicycle is on sale for $119.95. The tax rate is 6 percent.

(a) What is the tax on the bicycle?

(b) What is the total price including tax?

Solution   (a) To find the tax, we change 6 percent to the decimal 0.06 and multiply $119.95 by 0.06. We round the result to the nearest cent.

$$\begin{array}{r} \$119.95 \\ \times \quad 0.06 \\ \hline \$7.1970 \end{array} \longrightarrow \textbf{\$7.20}$$

(b) To find the total price, including tax, we add the tax to the price.

$$\begin{array}{rl} \$119.95 & \text{price} \\ +\quad \$7.20 & \text{tax} \\ \hline \textbf{\$127.15} & \text{total} \end{array}$$

Example 7   Find the total price, including tax, of an $18.95 book, a $1.89 pen, and a $2.29 pad of paper. The tax rate is 5 percent.

Solution   We begin by finding the combined price of the items.

$$\begin{array}{rl} \$18.95 & \text{book} \\ \$1.89 & \text{pen} \\ +\quad \$2.29 & \text{paper} \\ \hline \$23.13 & \end{array}$$

Next we multiply the combined price by 0.05 (5 percent) and round the product to the nearest cent.

$$\begin{array}{r} \$23.13 \\ \times \quad 0.05 \\ \hline \$1.1565 \end{array} \longrightarrow \$1.16 \text{ tax}$$

Then we add the tax to the price to find the total.

$$\begin{array}{rl} \$23.13 & \text{price} \\ +\quad \$1.16 & \text{tax} \\ \hline \textbf{\$24.29} & \text{total} \end{array}$$

Example 8   The restaurant bill was about $20.00. Ginger wants to leave a 15% tip for the server. How much money should Ginger leave for the tip?

Solution   A tip or gratuity is an amount of money paid to acknowledge the service of others. For restaurant service the tip is customarily 15%–20% of the price of the food that is served. To find 15% of $20.00 we multiply $20.00 by 0.15.

$$
\begin{array}{r}
\$20 \\
\times \ \ 0.15 \\
\hline
\$3.00
\end{array}
$$

Ginger should leave a tip of **$3.00.**

Practice   **a.** What is the unit price of a 28-ounce box of cereal that costs $1.12? 4¢ per ounce

b. What is the unit price of an 11-ounce can of soup that costs 55¢? 5¢ per ounce

c. Which is the better buy: an 18-ounce jar of jelly that costs $1.98, or a 24-ounce jar of jelly that costs $2.28?
The 24-ounce jar is the better buy because $\frac{9.5¢}{oz}$ is less than $\frac{11¢}{oz}$.

d. The Smiths drove 416 miles in 8 hours. What was their average speed? 52 mi/hr or 52 mph

e. Their car traveled the first 322 miles of the trip on 14 gallons of gas, which is an average of how many miles per gallon? 23 mi/gal or 23 mpg

f. When Monica landed in Belgium, she exchanged 40 dollars for 1640 francs.

f.(a) $41\frac{\text{francs}}{\text{dollar}}$

(b) $\frac{1}{41}\frac{\text{dollar}}{\text{franc}}$

(a) What was the rate of exchange in francs per dollar?

(b) What was the rate of exchange in dollars per franc?

g. Find the sales tax on a $36.89 radio if the tax rate is 7 percent. $2.58

h. Find the total price of the radio in problem g, including tax. $39.47

i. Find the total price, including 6 percent tax, for a $6.95 dinner, a 95¢ beverage, and a $2.45 dessert. $10.97

j. After paying a restaurant bill of about $15.00, Hector returned to the table and left a tip of 15%. How much money did Hector leave for a tip? $2.25

Problem set 46

1. Brand X costs $2.40 for 16 ounces. Brand Y costs $1.92 for 12 ounces. Find the unit price for each brand. Which brand is the better buy? Brand X = $0.15 per ounce; Brand Y = $0.16 per ounce; Brand X is the better buy.
(46)

2. The new coupe traveled 702 kilometers down the autobahn in 6 hours. The new coupe averaged how many kilometers per hour? 117 kilometers per hour
(46)

3. Forty-eight sheep were on the farm. Thirty-six cows were also on the farm. What was the ratio of sheep to cows? $\frac{4}{3}$
(36)

4. At four different stores the price of one gallon of milk was $2.86, $2.83, $2.98, and $3.09. Find the average price per gallon rounded to the nearest cent. $2.94
(28)

5. Two and three hundredths is how much less than three and two tenths? Write the answer in words.
(31,35)
    one and seventeen hundredths

6. A math book is $1\frac{1}{2}$ inches thick. How many of the math books will fit on a shelf that is 2 feet long? 16 books
(26)

7.

48 roses	
$\frac{3}{8}$ were red	6 roses
	6 roses
	6 roses
$\frac{5}{8}$ were not red	6 roses
	6 roses
	6 roses
	6 roses
	6 roses

7. Draw a diagram for this statement. Then answer the questions that follow.
(22)

   Three eighths of the 48 roses were red.

   (a) How many roses were red? 18 roses

   (b) How many roses were not red? 30 roses

   (c) What fraction of the roses were not red? $\frac{5}{8}$

8. Replace each circle with the proper comparison symbol.
(33)

   (a) 3.0303 $\bigcirc$< 3.303   (b) 0.6 $\bigcirc$= 0.600

9. From goal line to goal line, a football field is 100 yards long. How many feet long is a football field? 300 feet
(16)

10. (a) Write 0.080 as a fraction. $\frac{2}{25}$
(43)

    (b) Write $37\frac{1}{2}\%$ as a decimal. 0.375

    (c) Write $\frac{1}{11}$ as a decimal with a bar over the repetend.
    $0.\overline{09}$

11. The price of a CD is $14.95. The sales tax rate is 7%.
(46)

    (a) What is the tax on the CD? $1.05

    (b) What is the price of the CD including tax? $16.00

12. The coordinates of the three vertices of a triangle are
(37) (4, 0), (5, 3), and (0, 0). What is the area of the triangle?
6 units²

13. If a card is drawn from a normal deck of cards, what is
(36) the probability that the card will be a face card (jack,
queen, king)? $\frac{3}{13}$

14. What is the average of the first five prime numbers? 5.6
(21,28)

Solve:

15. $\frac{10}{12} = \frac{2.5}{a}$ 3
(39)

16. $\frac{6}{8} = \frac{b}{100}$ 75
(39)

17. $4.7 - w = 1.2$ 3.5
(35)

18. $10x = 10^2$ 10
(3,20)

19. 0.3(0.4 + 0.5)

0.3(0.9)

0.27

or

0.3(0.4 + 0.5)

0.12 + 0.15

0.27

19. Evaluate $x(y + z)$ if $x = 0.3$, $y = 0.4$, and $z = 0.5$.
(41) Show two ways.

20. In this figure all angles are right
(37) angles. Dimensions are in inches.

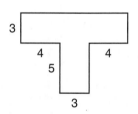

(a) What is the perimeter of the
figure? 38 in.

(b) What is the area of the figure?
48 in.²

21. This circle with center O has been divided into three
(Inv. 2) sectors as shown. Find the measure of each of these
central angles.

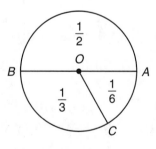

(a) $\angle AOB$ 180°   (b) $\angle BOC$ 120°   (c) $\angle AOC$ 60°

Simplify:

22. $1\frac{11}{18} + 2\frac{11}{24}$ $4\frac{5}{72}$
(30)

23. $5\frac{5}{6} - \left(3 - 1\frac{1}{3}\right)$ $4\frac{1}{6}$
(30)

24. $\frac{2}{3} \times 4 \times 1\frac{1}{8}$ 3
(26)

25. $6\frac{2}{3} \div 4$ $1\frac{2}{3}$
(26)

26. $3.45 + 6 + (5.2 - 0.57)$ **27.** $2.4 \div 0.016$ 150
(35)   14.08   (45)

28. Describe how to estimate the product of $6\frac{7}{8}$ and $5\frac{1}{16}$.
(29)   Round $6\frac{7}{8}$ to 7 and round $5\frac{1}{16}$ to 5. Then multiply 7 and 5.

In this figure $\triangle ABC$ is congruent to $\triangle CDA$. Refer to this figure for problems 29 and 30.

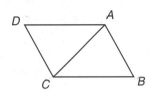

29. Name the angle or side in $\triangle ABC$ that corresponds to the
(18)   following angle and side from $\triangle CDA$.

     (a) $\angle ACD$ $\angle CAB$ (b) $\overline{DC}$ $\overline{BA}$

30. The measure of $\angle ACB$ is 45°, and the measure of $\angle ADC$
(40)   is 60°. Find the measure of

     (a) $\angle B$.   60°   (b) $\angle CAB$.   75°   (c) $\angle CAD$.   45°

LESSON 47

Powers of 10

Facts Practice: Proportions (Test I in Test Masters)

Mental Math:

   a. $5 \times \$8.20$ **b.** 0.015×10^3

   c. $\frac{c}{10} = \frac{9}{15}$ **d.** Estimate: $\$4.95 \times 19$

   e. $2^2 \cdot 2^3$ **f.** $\frac{5}{6}$ of 60

   g. Find the sum, difference, product, and quotient of $\frac{1}{2}$ and $\frac{2}{5}$.

Problem Solving:

   If 2 chickens lay a total of 2 eggs in 2 days, then how many eggs would 4 chickens lay in 4 days?

Place value as powers of 10

The positive powers of 10 are easy to write. The exponent matches the number of zeros in the product.

$$10^2 = 10 \cdot 10 = 100 \qquad \text{(two zeros)}$$
$$10^3 = 10 \cdot 10 \cdot 10 = 1000 \qquad \text{(three zeros)}$$
$$10^4 = 10 \cdot 10 \cdot 10 \cdot 10 = 10,000 \qquad \text{(four zeros)}$$

Notice that when we multiply powers of 10 the exponent of the product equals the sum of the exponents of the factors.

$$10^3 \times 10^3 = 10^6$$

$$1000 \times 1000 = 1{,}000{,}000$$

Also, when we divide powers of 10, the exponent of the quotient equals the difference of the exponents of the dividend and divisor.

$$10^6 \div 10^3 = 10^3$$

$$1{,}000{,}000 \div 1000 = 1000$$

We can use powers of 10 to show place value, as we see in the chart below. Notice that 10^0 equals 1.

Trillions			Billions			Millions			Thousands			Units (Ones)			Decimal point
hundreds	tens	ones	hundreds	tens	ones	hundreds	tens	ones	hundreds	tens	ones	hundreds	tens	ones	
10^{14}	10^{13}	10^{12}	10^{11}	10^{10}	10^9	10^8	10^7	10^6	10^5	10^4	10^3	10^2	10^1	10^0	.

Powers of 10 are sometimes used to write numbers in expanded notation.

Example 1   Write 5206 in expanded notation using powers of 10.

Solution   The number 5206 means $5000 + 200 + 6$. We will write each number as a digit times its place value.

$$5000 \quad + \quad 200 \quad + \quad 6$$
$$\left(5 \times 10^3\right) + \left(2 \times 10^2\right) + \left(6 \times 10^0\right)$$

Multiplying by powers of 10   When we multiply a decimal number by a power of 10, the answer has the same digits in the same order. Only their place values are changed.

Example 2   Multiply: 46.235×10^2

Solution   This time we will write 10^2 as 100 and multiply.

$$
\begin{array}{r}
46.235 \\
\times \quad 100 \\
\hline
4623.500 = \mathbf{4623.5}
\end{array}
$$

We see that the same digits occur in the same order. Only the place values have changed as the decimal point has been shifted two places to the right. **Thus, to multiply a decimal number by a positive power of 10, we need only to shift the decimal point to the right the number of places indicated by the exponent.**

Example 3   Multiply: 3.14×10^4

Solution   The power of 10 shows us the number of places to move the decimal point to the right. We move the decimal point four places to the right.

$$3.14 \times 10^4 = \mathbf{31{,}400}$$

Sometimes powers of 10 are written with words instead of with digits. For example, we might read that 1.5 million spectators lined the parade route. The expression 1.5 million means $1.5 \times 1{,}000{,}000$ which is $1{,}500{,}000$.

Example 4   Write $2\frac{1}{2}$ billion in standard form.

Solution   First we write $2\frac{1}{2}$ as the decimal number 2.5. Then we multiply by one billion (10^9), which shifts the decimal point 9 places.

$$2.5 \text{ billion} = 2.5 \times 10^9 = \mathbf{2{,}500{,}000{,}000}$$

Dividing by powers of 10   When dividing by positive powers of 10, the quotient has the same digits as the dividend only with smaller place values.

$$4.75 \div 10^3 \longrightarrow 1000\overline{)4.75000}^{\,0.00475}$$

To divide a number by a positive power of 10 we may shift the decimal point to the left the number of places indicated by the exponent.

Example 5   Divide: $3.5 \div 10^4$

Solution   The decimal point of the quotient is 4 places to the left of the decimal point in 3.5.

$$3.5 \div 10^4 = \mathbf{0.00035}$$

Practice   Write each number in expanded notation by using powers of 10.

a. 456 $(4 \times 10^2) + (5 \times 10^1) + (6 \times 10^0)$

b. 1760 $(1 \times 10^3) + (7 \times 10^2) + (6 \times 10^1)$

c. 186,000 $(1 \times 10^5) + (8 \times 10^4) + (6 \times 10^3)$

Simplify:

d. 24.25×10^3 24,250   **e.** 25×10^6 25,000,000

f. $12.5 \div 10^3$ 0.0125   **g.** $4.8 \div 10^4$ 0.00048

Find the missing exponent.

h. $10^3 \cdot 10^4 = 10^\square$ 7   **i.** $10^8 \div 10^2 = 10^\square$ 6

Write each of the following numbers in standard form.

j. $2\frac{1}{2}$ million   **k.** 15 billion   **l.** 1.6 trillion
2,500,000   15,000,000,000   1,600,000,000,000

Problem set 47   Refer to the graph to answer problems 1, 2, and 3.

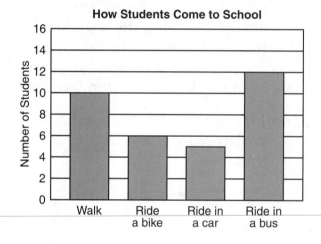

1. Answer true or false.
(38)

(a) Twice as many students walk to school as ride to school in a car. true

(b) The majority of the students ride to school in a bus or car. true

2. What is the ratio of those who walk to school to those who ride the bus? $\frac{5}{6}$
(38)

3. What fraction of the students ride the bus? $\frac{4}{11}$
(38)

4. What is the mean (average) of these numbers? 1.56
(28,35)

$$1.2, \ 1.4, \ 1.5, \ 1.7, \ 2$$

5. (a) The newspaper reported that 134.8 million viewers watched the Super Bowl. Write that number in standard form. 134,800,000 viewers
(47)

(b) Write 5280 in expanded notation using powers of 10.
$(5 \times 10^3) + (2 \times 10^2) + (8 \times 10^1)$

6.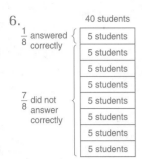

$\frac{1}{8}$ answered correctly

$\frac{7}{8}$ did not answer correctly

6. Draw a diagram of this statement. Then answer the
(22) questions that follow.

> *Only one eighth of the 40 students correctly
> answered question 5.*

(a) How many students correctly answered question 5?
5 students

(b) How many students did not correctly answer
question 5? 35 students

7. A gallon of punch (128 ounces) is poured into 12-ounce
(44) glasses.

(a) How many glasses can be *filled*? 10 glasses

(b) How many glasses are needed to hold all of the punch?
11 glasses

8. A cubit was an ancient unit of measure equal to the
(8) distance from the elbow to the fingertips.

(a) Estimate the number of inches from your elbow to
your fingertips. Answers may vary.

(b) Measure the distance from your elbow to your
fingertips to the nearest inch. Answers may vary.

9. (a) Write 0.375 as a fraction. $\frac{3}{8}$
(43)

(b) Write $62\frac{1}{2}\%$ as a decimal. 0.625

10. Find the tax on a $56.40 purchase if the sales tax rate is 8%.
(46) $4.51

11. Round $53{,}714.\overline{54}$ to the nearest
(42)

(a) thousandth. 53,714.545

(b) thousand. 54,000

12. Find the missing exponent.
(47)

(a) $10^5 \cdot 10^2 = 10^{\square}$ 7   (b) $10^8 \div 10^4 = 10^{\square}$ 4

13. The point marked by the arrow
(34) represents what decimal number?
3.03

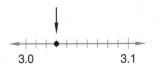

Solve:

14.
(39)
$\dfrac{6}{10} = \dfrac{w}{100}$ 60

15.
(39)
$\dfrac{3.6}{x} = \dfrac{16}{24}$ 5.4

16.
(35)
$\dfrac{a}{1.5} = 1.5$ 2.25

17.
(35)
$9.8 = x + 8.9$ 0.9

18. In figure *ABCDEF*, all angles are right
(19) angles and *AF* = *AB* = *BC*. Segment
BC is twice the length of segment *CD*.
If *CD* is 3 cm, what is the perimeter of
the figure? 42 cm

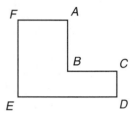

19. Recalling the activities in Investigation 2, use a compass
$(Inv.\ 2)$ to draw a circle with a radius of 1 inch. Then inscribe a
regular hexagon in the circle.

(a) What is the diameter of the circle? 2 inches

(b) What is the perimeter of the regular hexagon? 6 inches

Simplify:

20.
(20)
$\sqrt{16 \cdot 25}$ 20

21.
(47)
3.6×10^3 3600

22.
(30)
$4\dfrac{1}{5} + 5\dfrac{1}{3} + \dfrac{1}{2}$ $10\frac{1}{30}$

23.
$(23,30)$
$6\dfrac{1}{8} - \left(5 - 1\dfrac{2}{3}\right)$ $2\frac{19}{24}$

24.
(26)
$8\dfrac{1}{3} \times 3\dfrac{3}{5} \times \dfrac{1}{3}$ 10

25.
(26)
$3\dfrac{1}{8} \div 6\dfrac{1}{4}$ $\frac{1}{2}$

26. $26.7 + 3.45 + 0.036 + 12 + 8.7$ 50.886
(35)

27. The figures illustrate one triangle rotated into three
(37) different positions. Dimensions are in inches.

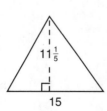
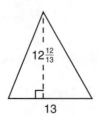
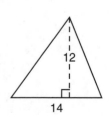

(a) What is the perimeter of the triangle? 42 in.

(b) What is the area of the triangle? 84 in.²

28. Simplify and compare: 1.25 < 12.5
(47)

$$125 \div 10^2 \bigcirc 0.125 \times 10^2$$

29. Arrange these fractions in order from least to greatest.
(30)

$$\frac{2}{3}, \frac{1}{2}, \frac{7}{12}, \frac{5}{6}$$

30. In this figure find the measure of
(40)

(a) $\angle a$.   50°

(b) $\angle b$.   65°

(c) Describe how to find the measure of $\angle c$.

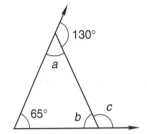

30.(c) Together, $\angle b$ and $\angle c$ form a straight angle that is 180°. To find the measure of $\angle c$ we subtract the measure of $\angle b$ from 180°.

LESSON
48

Fraction-Decimal-Percent Equivalents

Facts Practice: + − × ÷ Decimals (Test J in Test Masters)

Mental Math:

a. 7 × $35.00   **b.** 12.75 ÷ 10   **c.** $\frac{6}{4} = \frac{9}{n}$

d. $\frac{10^2}{5^2}$ **e.** Estimate: $6\frac{1}{6} \times 3\frac{4}{5}$ **f.** $\frac{3}{8}$ of 80

g. 10 × 8, + 1, $\sqrt{}$, + 2, × 4, − 2, ÷ 6, × 9, + 1, $\sqrt{}$, ÷ 2, ÷ 2, ÷ 2

Problem Solving:

If the counting numbers 1 through 9 are arranged in three columns of three numbers with the same sum, then what is the sum of the numbers in each column?

We may describe part of a whole using a fraction, a decimal, or a percent.

The shaded portion is $\frac{1}{2}$ of the circle.

The shaded portion is 0.5 of the circle.

The shaded portion is 50% of the circle.

To convert a fraction or a decimal to a percent, we multiply the number by 100%.

Example 1   Write $\frac{7}{10}$ as a percent.

Solution   To change a number to its percent equivalent, we multiply the number by 100%.

$$\frac{7}{10} \times 100\% = \frac{700\%}{10}$$
$$= 70\%$$

Example 2   Write $\frac{2}{3}$ as a percent.

Solution   We multiply by 100 percent.

$$\frac{2}{3} \times 100\% = \frac{200\%}{3}$$
$$= 66\frac{2}{3}\%$$

Notice the mixed-number form of the percent.

Example 3   Write 0.8 as a percent.

Solution   We multiply 0.8 by 100%.

$$0.8 \times 100\% = 80\%$$

Future problem sets will contain problems that allow us to practice changing from percents to fractions to decimal numbers. The problems will require that we complete a table as we show in the following example.

Example 4   Complete the table.

FRACTION	DECIMAL	PERCENT
$\frac{1}{3}$	(a)	(b)
(c)	1.5	(d)
(e)	(f)	60%

Solution   For (a) and (b) we find the decimal and percent equivalent to $\frac{1}{3}$.

(a) $3\overline{)1.00}$ → $0.\overline{3}$

(b) $\dfrac{1}{3} \times 100\% = \dfrac{100\%}{3} = 33\dfrac{1}{3}\%$

For (c) and (d) we find a fraction (or a mixed number) and a percent equivalent to 1.5.

(c) $1.5 = 1\dfrac{5}{10} = 1\dfrac{1}{2}$

(d) $1.5 \times 100\% = \mathbf{150\%}$

For (e) and (f) we find a fraction and decimal number equivalent to 60%.

(e) $60\% = \dfrac{60}{100} = \dfrac{3}{5}$

(f) $60\% = \dfrac{60}{100} = \mathbf{0.6}$

Practice*   Complete the table.

FRACTION	DECIMAL	PERCENT
$\dfrac{2}{3}$	**a.** $0.\overline{6}$	**b.** $66\frac{2}{3}\%$
c. $1\frac{1}{10}$	1.1	**d.** 110%
e. $\frac{1}{25}$	**f.** 0.04	4%

Problem set 48

1. Sam pedaled hard. He traveled 80 kilometers in 2.5 hours.
$^{(46)}$ What was his average speed in kilometers per hour?
$32 \frac{\text{kilometers}}{\text{hour}}$

2. Write the prime factorization of 1008 and 1323. Then
$^{(24)}$ reduce $\frac{1008}{1323}$. $\frac{2\cdot2\cdot2\cdot2\cdot3\cdot3\cdot7}{3\cdot3\cdot3\cdot7\cdot7} = \frac{16}{21}$

3. In 1803, the United States purchased the Louisiana
$^{(12)}$ Territory from France for \$15 million. In 1867, the United States purchased Alaska from Russia for \$7.2 million. The purchase of Alaska occurred how many years after the purchase of the Louisiana Territory?   64 years

4. Red and blue marbles were in the bag. Five twelfths of
$^{(36)}$ the marbles were red.

    (a) What fraction of the marbles were blue? $\frac{7}{12}$

    (b) What was the ratio of red marbles to blue marbles? $\frac{5}{7}$

5. 6-ounce can is \$0.15 per ounce; 9-ounce can is \$0.14 per ounce; 9-ounce can is a better buy

5. A 6-ounce can of peaches sells for 90¢. A 9-ounce can of
$^{(46)}$ peaches sells for \$1.26. Find the unit price for each size. Which size is the better buy?

6. The average of two numbers is the number halfway
(28) between the two numbers. What number is halfway
between two thousand, five hundred fifty and two
thousand, nine hundred? 2725

7. The graph shows how one family spends their annual
(38) income. Use this graph to answer questions (a)–(c).

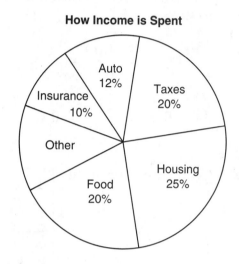

How Income is Spent

(a) What percent of the family's income is spent on
"other"? 13%

(b) What fraction of the family's income is spent on
food? $\frac{1}{5}$

(c) If $3200 is spent on insurance, how much is spent on
taxes? $6400

8.   336 pages

| 42 pages |
| 42 pages |

$\frac{5}{8}$ read

| 42 pages |
| 42 pages |
| 42 pages |
| 42 pages |

$\frac{3}{8}$ not read

| 42 pages |
| 42 pages |
| 42 pages |

8. Draw a diagram of this statement. Then answer the
(22) questions that follow.

Van has read five eighths of the 336-page novel.

(a) How many pages has Van read? 210 pages

(b) How many more pages are left to read? 126 pages

9. Complete the table.
(48)

FRACTION	DECIMAL	PERCENT
$\frac{1}{2}$	(a) 0.5	(b) 50%
(c) $\frac{1}{10}$	0.1	(d) 10%
(e) $\frac{1}{4}$	(f) 0.25	25%

10. 0.545

10. Write $0.5\overline{4}$ as a decimal rounded to three decimal places.
(42)

11. (a) Estimate the length of $\overline{AB}$ in centimeters.
(32)   See student answer.

A   B

(b) Use a centimeter scale to find the length of $\overline{AB}$ to the nearest centimeter. 5 centimeters

12. The exponent
is 3, and the base
is 5.

12. (a) Identify the exponent and the base in the expression 5^3.
(20,47)
(b) Find the missing exponent: $10^4 \cdot 10^4 = 10^{\square}$ 8

13. If the perimeter of a regular hexagon is 1 foot, each side is
(18,19) how many inches long? 2 inches

14. Copy this figure on your paper. Find
(19) the length of the unmarked sides and
find the perimeter of the polygon.
Dimensions are in centimeters. All
angles are right angles. 100 cm

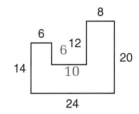

15. The moped traveled 78 miles on 1.2 gallons of gas. The
(46) moped averaged how many miles per gallon? 65 mpg

Solve:

16. $\dfrac{6}{100} = \dfrac{15}{w}$ 250
(39)

17. $\dfrac{20}{x} = \dfrac{15}{12}$ 16
(39)

18. $1.44 = 6m$ 0.24
(35)

19. $\dfrac{1}{2} = \dfrac{1}{3} + f$ $\frac{1}{6}$
(30)

Simplify:

20. $2^5 + 1^4 + 3^3$ 60
(20)

21. $\sqrt{10^2 \cdot 6^2}$ 60
(20)

22. $3\dfrac{5}{6} - \left(1\dfrac{1}{4} + 1\dfrac{1}{6}\right)$ $1\frac{5}{12}$
(30)

23. $8\dfrac{3}{4} + \left(4 - \dfrac{2}{3}\right)$ $12\frac{1}{12}$
(23,30)

24. $\dfrac{15}{16} \cdot \dfrac{24}{25} \cdot 1\dfrac{1}{9}$ 1
(26)

25. $1\dfrac{1}{3} \div \left(2\dfrac{2}{3} \div 4\right)$ 2
(26)

26. Find the value of $\dfrac{a}{b}$ when $a = \$13.93$ and $b = 0.07$.
(41,45) $199.00

27. 9 sq. units
27. The coordinates of three vertices of a triangle are $(-1, -1)$,
(37) $(5, -1)$, and $(5, -4)$. What is the area of the triangle?

28. Students in the class were asked the number of siblings
(36,38) they had, and the answers were tallied. If one student
from the class is selected at random, what is the
probability that the selected student would have more
than one sibling? $\frac{2}{5}$

Number of Siblings	Number of Students
0				
1	⦀⦀ ||||
2	⦀⦀
3			
4 or more		

29. What is the total price of a $50.00 item including 7.5%
(46) sales tax? $53.75

30. Find the measures of ∠a, ∠b, and ∠c
(40) in this figure. m∠a = 40°; m∠b = 50°;
m∠c = 130°

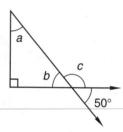

LESSON
49

Adding Mixed Measures

Mental Math:

Mental Math:
a. $52.00
b. 257.5
c. 10
d. 6
e. 20
f. 60
g. $\frac{14}{15}, \frac{4}{15}, \frac{1}{5}, 1\frac{4}{5}$

a. 8 × $6.50

b. 25.75 × 10

c. $\frac{4}{x} = \frac{40}{100}$

d. Estimate: 12.11 ÷ 1.9

e. $\sqrt{400}$

f. $\frac{3}{10}$ of 200

g. Find the sum, difference, product, and quotient of $\frac{3}{5}$ and $\frac{1}{3}$.

Problem Solving:

Problem Solving:
1. 3Q, 2D, 1N
2. 1HD, 1Q, 1D, 3N
3. 1HD, 5D

Jarod has 6 coins that total $1.00. What possible combinations of coins does Jarod have?

A mixed measure is a measurement that includes two or more
units of the same category of units in the description.

Ivan is 5 feet, 8 inches tall.

The movie was 1 hour and 48 minutes long.

To add mixed measures, we align the numbers so that we add the same units. Then we simplify when possible.

Example 1 Add and simplify: 1 yd, 2 ft, 7 in. + 2 yd, 2 ft, 8 in.

Solution We add like units, and then we simplify from right to left.

$$
\begin{array}{r}
1 \text{ yd } 2 \text{ ft } 7 \text{ in.} \\
+ 2 \text{ yd } 2 \text{ ft } 8 \text{ in.} \\
\hline
3 \text{ yd } 4 \text{ ft } 15 \text{ in.}
\end{array}
$$

We change 15 in. to 1 ft, 3 in. and add to 4 ft. Now we have

3 yd, 5 ft, 3 in.

Then we change 5 ft to 1 yd, 2 ft and add to 3 yd. Now we have

4 yd, 2 ft, 3 in.

Example 2 Add and simplify:

$$
\begin{array}{r}
2 \text{ hr } 40 \text{ min } 35 \text{ s} \\
+ 1 \text{ hr } 45 \text{ min } 50 \text{ s} \\
\hline
\end{array}
$$

Solution We add. Then we simplify from right to left.

$$
\begin{array}{r}
2 \text{ hr } 40 \text{ min } 35 \text{ s} \\
+ 1 \text{ hr } 45 \text{ min } 50 \text{ s} \\
\hline
3 \text{ hr } 85 \text{ min } 85 \text{ s}
\end{array}
$$

We change 85 s to 1 min, 25 s and add to 85 min. Now we have

3 hr, 86 min, 25 s

Then we simplify 86 min to 1 hr, 26 min and combine hours.

4 hr, 26 min, 25 s

Practice* **a.** Change 70 inches to feet and inches. 5 feet, 10 inches

b. Change 6 feet, 3 inches to inches. 75 inches

c. Simplify: 5 ft, 20 in. 6 ft, 8 in.

d. Add: 2 yd, 1 ft, 8 in. + 1 yd, 2 ft, 9 in. 4 yd, 1 ft, 5 in.

e. Add: 5 hr, 42 min, 53 s + 6 hr, 17 min, 27 s 12 hr, 20 s

Problem set   **1.** What is the quotient when the sum of 0.2 and 0.05 is
49 (35,45) divided by the product of 0.2 and 0.05?   25

2. Darren carried the football 20 times and gained a total of
(44) 184 yards. What was the average number of yards he
gained on each carry? Write the answer as a decimal
number.   9.2 yards

3. Robin bought two dozen arrows for six dollars. What was
(46) the cost of each arrow?   25¢ per arrow

4. Jeffrey counted the sides on three octagons, two
(18) hexagons, a pentagon, and two quadrilaterals. Altogether,
how many sides did he count?   49 sides

5. What is the mean of these numbers?   6.39
(28,35)

$$6.21, 4.38, 7.5, 6.3, 5.91, 8.04$$

6.

72 billy goats	
$\frac{2}{9}$ were gruff	8 goats
	8 goats
	8 goats
	8 goats
	8 goats
$\frac{7}{9}$ were cordial	8 goats
	8 goats
	8 goats
	8 goats

6. Draw a diagram of this statement. Then answer the
(22,36) questions that follow.

*Only two ninths of the 72 billy goats were gruff.
The rest were cordial.*

(a) How many of the billy goats were cordial?   56 billy goats

(b) What was the ratio of gruff billy goats to cordial billy
goats? $\frac{2}{7}$

7. Arrange these numbers in order from least to greatest.
(42)

$$0.\overline{5}, 0.5, 0.\overline{54} \quad 0.5, 0.\overline{54}, 0.\overline{5}$$

8. (a) Estimate the length of segment *AB* in inches.
(8)   Answers may vary.

A   B

(b) Measure the length of segment *AB* to the nearest
eighth of an inch. $2\frac{5}{8}$ inches

9. Write each of these numbers as a percent.
(48)

(a) 0.9   90%   (b) $1\frac{3}{5}$ 160%   (c) $\frac{5}{6}$ $83\frac{1}{3}\%$

10. Complete the table.
(48)

FRACTION	DECIMAL	PERCENT
(a) $\frac{3}{4}$	(b) 0.75	75%
(c) $\frac{1}{20}$	(d) 0.05	5%

11. Mathea's resting heart rate is 62 beats per minute. While
(13) she is resting, about how many times will her heart beat
in an hour? 3720 times

12. What is the probability of rolling an even prime number
(36) with one roll of a die (number cube)? $\frac{1}{6}$

13. A $\frac{1}{2}$-inch by $\frac{1}{2}$-inch square was cut
(37) from a 1-inch by 1-inch square.

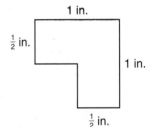

(a) What was the area of the original
square? 1 in.²

(b) What is the area of the square
that was removed? $\frac{1}{4}$ in.²

(c) What is the area of the remaining figure? $\frac{3}{4}$ in.²

14. What is the perimeter of the figure in problem 13? 4 in.
(19)

15. Here we show a triangle with sides 6 cm, 8 cm, and 10 cm
(37) long in three orientations. What is the height of the triangle
when the base is

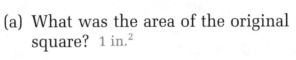

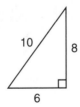   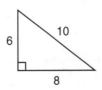   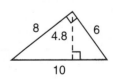

(a) 6 cm? 8 cm   (b) 8 cm? 6 cm   (c) 10 cm? 4.8 cm

Solve:

16. $\dfrac{y}{100} = \dfrac{18}{45}$ 40
(39)

17. $\dfrac{35}{40} = \dfrac{1.4}{m}$ 1.6
(39)

18. $\dfrac{1}{2} - n = \dfrac{1}{6}$ $\frac{1}{3}$
(30)

19. $9d = 2.61$ 0.29
(35)

Simplify:

20. $\sqrt{100} + 4^3$ 74
(20)

21. 3.14×10^4 31,400
(47)

22. $3\frac{3}{4} + \left(4\frac{1}{6} - 2\frac{1}{2}\right)$ $5\frac{5}{12}$
(23,30)

23. $6\frac{2}{3} \cdot \left(3\frac{3}{4} \div 1\frac{1}{2}\right)$ $16\frac{2}{3}$
(26)

24.   3 days   8 hr 15 min
(49)   + 2 days 15 hr 45 min
_____
            6 days

25.   1 yd 2 ft 6 in.
(49)   + 2 yd 1 ft 9 in.
_____
            4 yd 1 ft 3 in.

26. Describe how to estimate the quotient when 35.675 is
(29,33) divided by $2\frac{7}{8}$.
Round 35.675 to 36. Round $2\frac{7}{8}$ to 3. Then divide 36 by 3.

27. The bat cost $18.50. The ball cost $3.50. What was the
(46) total price of the bat and ball including 6% sales tax?
$23.32

28. Evaluate LWH when $L = 0.5$, $W = 0.2$, and $H = 0.1$.
(41) 0.01

29. $18.00 \div 0.06$ $300.00
(45)

30. This quadrilateral is a rectangle. Find
(40) the measure of $\angle a$, $\angle b$, and $\angle c$.
$m\angle a = 32°$; $m\angle b = 58°$; $m\angle c = 122°$

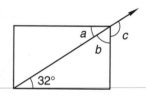

LESSON
50

Unit Multipliers and
Unit Conversion

Facts Practice: Proportions (Test I in Test Masters)

Mental Math:

  a. $5 \times \$48.00$ **b.** 0.0125×10^2 **c.** $\frac{y}{20} = \frac{40}{100}$
  d. $\sqrt{225}$ **e.** Estimate: $4\frac{3}{4} \times 1\frac{7}{8}$ **f.** $\frac{2}{5}$ of 40
  g. Start with half a dozen, + 4, square it, ÷ 2, + 6, ÷ 8, × 7,
     + 1, ÷ 10, − 10.

Problem Solving:

Copy this problem and fill in the missing digits.

```
      _ _ _
    ×     _
    _____
     1 0 0 1
```

Let's take a moment to review the procedure for reducing a fraction. When we reduce a fraction, we replace pairs of numbers that appear as factors in both the numerator and denominator with ones, since each pair simply equals the factor 1.

$$\frac{24}{36} = \frac{\overset{1}{\cancel{2}} \cdot \overset{1}{\cancel{2}} \cdot 2 \cdot \overset{1}{\cancel{3}}}{\underset{1}{\cancel{2}} \cdot \underset{1}{\cancel{2}} \cdot 3 \cdot \underset{1}{\cancel{3}}} = \frac{2}{3}$$

Also recall that we may reduce before we multiply. This is sometimes called **canceling.**

$$\frac{2}{\underset{1}{\cancel{3}}} \cdot \frac{\overset{1}{\cancel{3}}}{5} = \frac{2}{5}$$

We may apply this procedure to units as well. We may cancel units before we multiply.

$$\frac{5 \ \cancel{ft}}{1} \cdot \frac{12 \text{ in.}}{1 \ \cancel{ft}} = 60 \text{ in.}$$

In this instance we performed the division 5 ft ÷ 1 ft, which means, how many feet are in 5 feet? The answer is simply 5. Then we multiplied 5 × 12 in.

We remember that we change the name of a number by multiplying by a fraction whose value equals 1. Here we change the name of 3 to $\frac{12}{4}$ by multiplying by $\frac{4}{4}$.

$$3 \cdot \frac{4}{4} = \frac{12}{4}$$

The fraction $\frac{12}{4}$ is another name for 3 because 12 ÷ 4 equals 3.

Whenever the numerator and denominator of a fraction are equal (and are not zero), the fraction is equal to 1. There is an unlimited number of fractions that are equal to 1. A fraction equal to 1 may have units, such as

$$\frac{12 \text{ inches}}{12 \text{ inches}}$$

Since 12 inches equals 1 foot, we can write two more fractions that equal 1.

$$\frac{12 \text{ inches}}{1 \text{ foot}} \qquad \frac{1 \text{ foot}}{12 \text{ inches}}$$

Because these fractions have units and are equal to 1, we call them **unit multipliers.** Unit multipliers are very useful for converting from one unit of measure to another. For instance, if we want to convert 5 feet to inches, we can multiply 5 feet by a multiplier that has inches on top. The feet units cancel, and the product is 60 inches.

$$5 \, \cancel{ft} \cdot \frac{12 \text{ in.}}{1 \, \cancel{ft}} = 60 \text{ in.}$$

Note that 5 ft and $\frac{5 \text{ ft}}{1}$ are equivalent.

$$5 \text{ ft} = \frac{5 \text{ ft}}{1}$$

You may use either form.

If we want to convert 96 inches to feet, we can multiply 96 inches by a unit multiplier that has a numerator of feet and a denominator of inches. The inch units cancel. The product is 8 feet.

$$96 \, \cancel{\text{in.}} \cdot \frac{1 \text{ ft}}{12 \, \cancel{\text{in.}}} = 8 \text{ ft}$$

Notice that we selected unit multipliers that canceled the unit we wanted to remove and kept the unit we wanted in the answer.

When we set up unit conversion problems, we will write the numbers involved in this order.

$$\boxed{\begin{array}{c}\text{Given} \\ \text{measure}\end{array}} \times \boxed{\begin{array}{c}\text{Unit} \\ \text{multiplier}\end{array}} = \boxed{\begin{array}{c}\text{Converted} \\ \text{measure}\end{array}}$$

Example 1 Write two unit multipliers for these equivalent measures.

$$3 \text{ ft} = 1 \text{ yd}$$

Solution We write one measure as the numerator and its equivalent as the denominator.

$$\frac{3 \text{ ft}}{1 \text{ yd}} \quad \text{and} \quad \frac{1 \text{ yd}}{3 \text{ ft}}$$

Example 2 Use one of the unit multipliers from Example 1 to convert

(a) 240 yards to feet.

(b) 240 feet to yards.

Solution (a) We are given a measure in yards. We want the answer in feet. We write this down.

$$240 \text{ yd} \cdot \boxed{\begin{array}{c}\text{Unit}\\\text{multiplier}\end{array}} = \quad \text{ft}$$

We want to cancel the unit "yd" and keep the unit "ft," so we select the unit multiplier that has a numerator of ft and a denominator of yd. Then we multiply and cancel units.

$$240 \ \cancel{\text{yd}} \cdot \frac{3 \text{ ft}}{1 \ \cancel{\text{yd}}} = \textbf{720 ft}$$

The answer is reasonable because feet are smaller units than yards, so it takes more feet than yards to measure the same distance.

(b) We are given the measure in feet, and we want the answer in yards. We choose the unit multiplier that has a numerator of yd.

$$240 \ \cancel{\text{ft}} \cdot \frac{1 \text{ yd}}{3 \ \cancel{\text{ft}}} = \textbf{80 yd}$$

The answer is reasonable because yards are longer units than feet, so it takes fewer yards than feet to measure the same distance.

Example 3 Convert 350 millimeters to centimeters. (1 cm = 10 mm)

Solution We are given millimeters and are asked to convert to centimeters. We form a unit multiplier from the equivalence that has a numerator of cm.

$$350 \ \cancel{\text{mm}} \cdot \frac{1 \text{ cm}}{10 \ \cancel{\text{mm}}} = \textbf{35 cm}$$

Practice* Write two unit multipliers for each pair of equivalent measures.

a. 1 yd = 36 in. $\frac{1 \text{ yd}}{36 \text{ in.}}$ and $\frac{36 \text{ in.}}{1 \text{ yd}}$

b. 100 cm = 1 m $\frac{100 \text{ cm}}{1 \text{ m}}$ and $\frac{1 \text{ m}}{100 \text{ cm}}$

c. 16 oz = 1 lb $\frac{16 \text{ oz}}{1 \text{ lb}}$ and $\frac{1 \text{ lb}}{16 \text{ oz}}$

Use unit multipliers to perform the following conversions.

d. Convert 10 yards to inches. 360 inches

e. Twenty-four feet is how many yards? (1 yd = 3 ft) 8 yd

f. In old England 12 pence equaled 1 shilling. Merlin had 24 shillings. This was the same as how many pence?
288 pence

Problem set 50

1. When the product of 3.5 and 0.4 is subtracted from the
(35) sum of 3.5 and 0.4, what is the difference? 2.5

2. The face of the spinner is divided
(36) into ten equal parts.

(a) What fraction of this circle is marked with a 1? $\frac{2}{5}$

(b) What percent of this circle is marked with a number greater than 1? 60%

(c) If the arrow is spun, what is the probability that it will stop on a number greater than 2? $\frac{3}{10}$

3. 13-ounce box =
9¢ per ounce;
18-ounce box =
8¢ per ounce;
18-ounce box is
the better buy.

3. The 13-ounce box of cooked cereal costs $1.17, while the
(46) 18-ounce box costs $1.44. Find the unit cost for both sizes. Which size is the better buy?

4. Nelson covered the first 20 miles in $2\frac{1}{2}$ hours. What was
(46) his average speed in miles per hour?
$8 \frac{\text{miles}}{\text{hour}}$

5. The parking lot charges $2 for the first hour plus 50¢ for
(28) each additional half hour or part thereof. What is the total charge for parking in the lot for 3 hours and 20 minutes?
$4.50

6. The train traveled at an average speed of 60 miles per
(13) hour. How long did it take the train to travel 420 miles?
7 hours

7.

30 football players
$\frac{2}{5}$ were endomorphic { 6 players / 6 players / 6 players
$\frac{3}{5}$ were not endomorphic { 6 players / 6 players

7. Draw a diagram of this statement. Then answer the
(22) questions that follow.

Forty percent of the 30 football players were endomorphic.

(a) How many of the football players were endomorphic?
12 football players

(b) What percent of the football players were not endomorphic? 60%

8. Which percent best identifies the
(8) shaded part of this circle? B. 40%

   A. 25%   B. 40%

   C. 50%   D. 60%

9. Write $3\frac{5}{6}$ as a decimal number rounded to four decimal
(43) places. 3.8333

10. Use exponents to write 7.5 million in expanded notation.
(47) $\left(7 \times 10^6\right) + \left(5 \times 10^5\right)$

11. Write each number as a percent.
(48)

   (a) 0.6 60%   (b) $\frac{1}{6}$ $16\frac{2}{3}\%$ (c) $1\frac{1}{2}$ 150%

12. Complete the table.
(48)

FRACTION	DECIMAL	PERCENT
(a) $\frac{3}{10}$	(b) 0.3	30%
(c) $2\frac{1}{2}$	(d) 2.5	250%

13. List the prime numbers between 90 and 100. 97
(21)

14. The dashes divide this figure into a rectangle and a triangle.
(37)

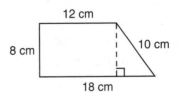

   (a) What is the area of the rectangle? 96 cm²

   (b) What is the area of the triangle? 24 cm²

   (c) What is the combined area of the rectangle and triangle?
      120 cm²

15.

15. Use a compass to draw a circle with a radius of $1\frac{1}{2}$ in.
(Inv. 2) Then use a protractor to draw a central angle in the circle
of 60°. Shade the sector that is formed by the 60° central
angle.

Solve:

16.
(39)
$\dfrac{10}{x} = \dfrac{7}{42}$ 60

17.
(39)
$\dfrac{1.5}{1} = \dfrac{w}{4}$ 6

18. $3.56 = 5.6 - y$ 2.04
(35)

19.
(30)
$\dfrac{3}{20} = w + \dfrac{1}{15}$ $\frac{1}{12}$

20. Which property is illustrated by each of the following
(2,41) equations?

(a) $x(y + z) = xy + xz$ distributive property

(b) $x + y = y + x$ commutative property of addition

(c) $1x = x$ identity property of multiplication

21. Which is equivalent to $\dfrac{10^6}{10^2}$?   B. 10^4
(47)

A. 10^3 B. 10^4 C. 1000   D. 30

22. The coordinates of three vertices of a square are (2, 0),
(Inv. 3) (0, –2), and (–2, 0).

(a) What are the coordinates of the fourth vertex?   (0, 2)

(b) Counting whole square units and half square units,
find the area of the square.   8 sq. units

23. If 10 cookies are shared equally by 4 children, how many
(44) cookies will each child receive? $2\frac{1}{2}$ cookies

24. This is a box-and-whisker plot of test scores. Refer to this
(Inv. 4) plot to answer parts (a), (b), and (c) of this problem:

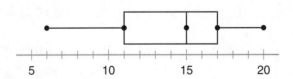

(a) What was the range of scores?   20 – 6 = 14

(b) What was the median score?   15

(c) Write another question that can be answered by referring to this plot and answer the question.
See student work.

25.
(49)

$$\begin{array}{r} 5 \text{ hr } 48 \text{ min } 45 \text{ s} \\ + 6 \text{ hr } 20 \text{ min } 20 \text{ s} \\ \hline 12 \text{ hr } \quad 9 \text{ min } \quad 5 \text{ s} \end{array}$$

26.
(49)

$$\begin{array}{r} 4 \text{ yd } 2 \text{ ft } 7 \text{ in.} \\ + 3 \text{ yd } \qquad 5 \text{ in.} \\ \hline 8 \text{ yd} \end{array}$$

27.
(26,30)
$5\dfrac{1}{6} - \left(1\dfrac{3}{4} \div 2\dfrac{1}{3}\right)$ $4\frac{5}{12}$

28.
(26,30)
$3\dfrac{5}{7} + \left(3\dfrac{1}{8} \cdot 2\dfrac{2}{5}\right)$ $11\frac{3}{14}$

29. In this figure $\triangle ABC$ is congruent to
(40) $\triangle DCB$. Find the measure of

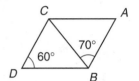

(a) $\angle BAC$. 60°

(b) $\angle BCA$. 50°

(c) $\angle CBD$. 50°

30. Show two ways to evaluate $a(b - c)$ if $a = 4$, $b = 5$,
(41) and $c = 3$.

$$\begin{array}{cc} 4(5 - 3) & \text{or} \quad 4(5 - 3) \\ 4(2) & 20 - 12 \\ 8 & 8 \end{array}$$

INVESTIGATION
5

Creating Graphs

Recall from Investigation 4 that we considered a stem-and-leaf plot that a counselor created to display student test scores. If we were to rotate the plot 90°, the display resembles a vertical bar graph or **histogram.**

2	1 3 5 6 6 8
3	0 0 2 2 4 5 6 6 6 8 9
4	0 0 1 1 2 3 3 5 7 7 8
5	0 1 1 2 3 5 8

A histogram is a special type of bar graph that displays data in equal-sized intervals. There are no spaces between the bars. The height of the bars in this histogram show the number of test scores in each interval.

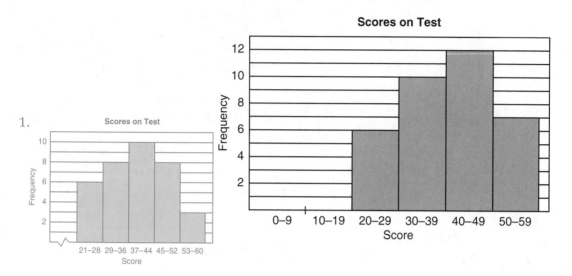

1.

1. Changing the intervals can change the appearance of a histogram. Create a new histogram for the test scores itemized in the stem-and-leaf plot using the following intervals: 21–28, 29–36, 37–44, 45–52, and 53–60. Draw a break in the horizontal scale (∿) between 0 and 20.

Histograms and other bar graphs are useful for showing comparisons, but sometimes the visual effect can be misleading. When viewing a graph it is important to carefully note the scale. Compare these two bar graphs which display the same information.

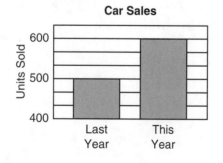

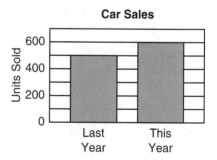

2. The graph on the left creates the visual impression that sales doubled because the vertical scale starts at 400 units instead of being equally divided from 0 units to 600 units.

2. Which of the two graphs visually exaggerates the growth in sales from one year to the next? How was the exaggerated visual effect created?

3. Larry made this bar graph comparing his test score to Moe's test score. Create another bar graph that shows the same information in a less misleading way.

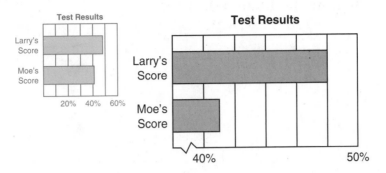

Changes over time are often displayed by line graphs. A **double line graph** may compare two performances over time. The graph below illustrates the differences in the growing value of a $1000 investment compounded at 7% and at 10% annual interest rates.

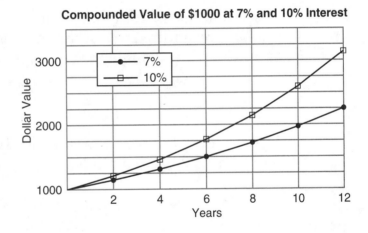

4. Create a double line graph using the information in this table. Label the axes and select and number the scales. Make a legend (or key) so that the reader can distinguish between the two graphed lines.

Stock Values ($)

First Trade Of	XYZ Corp	ZYX Corp
1993	30	30
1994	36	28
1995	34	36
1996	46	40
1997	50	46
1998	50	42

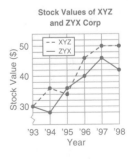

A pie graph (or circle graph) is commonly used to show components of a budget. The entire circle, 100%, may represent monthly income. The sectors of the circle show how the income is allocated.

We see that the sector labeled "food" is 20% of the area of the circle, representing 20% of the income. To make a 20% sector we draw a central angle that measures 20% of 360°.

20% of 360°

$$0.2 \times 360° = 72°$$

With a protractor we draw a central angle of 72° to make a sector that is 20% of a circle.

5. Create a pie graph for the following table to show how Kerry spends a school day. First calculate the number of degrees in the central angle for each sector of the pie graph. Next use a compass to draw a circle with a radius of about $2\frac{1}{2}$ inches. Then, with a protractor and straight edge, divide the circle into sectors of the correct size and label each sector.

How Kerry Spends a Day

Activity	% of Day	Central $\angle$
School	25%	90°
Recreation	10%	36°
Traveling	5%	18°
Homework	10%	36°
Eating	5%	18°
Sleeping	40%	144°
Other	5%	18°

Extensions   **a.** Create a histogram for scores on a recent class test.

b. Create a circle graph showing the portions of students in the class with various eye colors.

c. Explore the graph creating capabilities of database computer programs.

LESSON
51

Scientific Notation for Large Numbers

Mental Math:
a. $14.00
b. 450
c. 12
d. 5000 m
e. 200
f. 25
g. $1\frac{3}{8}$, $\frac{3}{8}$, $\frac{7}{16}$, $1\frac{3}{4}$
Problem Solving:
  1,000,000

Facts Practice: $+ - \times \div$ Decimals (Test J in Test Masters)

Mental Math:

a. $4 \times \$3.50$

b. 4.5×10^2

c. $\frac{5}{20} = \frac{3}{x}$

d. Convert 5 km to m.

e. $15^2 - 5^2$

f. $\frac{5}{9}$ of 45

g. Find the sum, difference, product, and quotient of $\frac{7}{8}$ and $\frac{1}{2}$.

Problem Solving:

The first five perfect squares are 1, 4, 9, 16, and 25. What number is the 1000th perfect square?

The numbers used in scientific measurement are often very large or very small and occupy many places when written in standard form. For example, a light-year is about

$$9{,}461{,}000{,}000{,}000 \text{ km}$$

Scientific notation is a way of expressing numbers as a product of a decimal number and a power of 10. In scientific notation a light-year is

$$9.461 \times 10^{12} \text{ km}$$

The power of 10 indicates where the decimal point is located when the number is written in standard form. Consider this notation.

$$4.62 \times 10^6$$

To write this number in standard form we shift the decimal point in 4.62 six places (for 10^6) to the right. We use zeros as placeholders.

$$4620000. \longrightarrow 4{,}620{,}000$$

To write a number in scientific notation, it is customary to place the decimal point to the right of the first nonzero digit. Then we use a power of 10 to indicate the actual location of the decimal point. To write

$$405,700,000$$

in scientific notation, we begin by placing the decimal point to the right of 4 and counting the places to the original decimal point.

$$4.05700000$$

8 places

We see that the original decimal point is eight places to the right of where we put it. We omit the terminal zeros and write

$$4.057 \times 10^8$$

Example 1 Write 2.46×10^8 in standard form.

Solution We shift the decimal point in 2.46 eight places to the right, using zeros as placeholders.

$$246000000. \longrightarrow \mathbf{246,000,000}$$

Example 2 Write 40,720,000 in scientific notation.

Solution We begin by placing the decimal point after the 4.

$$4.0720000$$

7 places

Now we discard the terminal zeros and write 10^7 to show that the original decimal point really is seven places to the right.

$$\mathbf{4.072 \times 10^7}$$

Example 3 Compare: $1.2 \times 10^4 \bigcirc 2.1 \times 10^3$

Solution Since 1.2×10^4 equals 12,000 and 2.1×10^3 equals 2100, we see that

$$\mathbf{1.2 \times 10^4 > 2.1 \times 10^3}$$

Scientific calculators will display the results of an operation in scientific notation if the number would otherwise exceed the display capabilities of the calculator. For example, if we multiply one million by one million, we would enter

| 1 | 0 | 0 | 0 | 0 | 0 | 0 | × |

| 1 | 0 | 0 | 0 | 0 | 0 | 0 | = |

The answer, one trillion, contains more digits than can be displayed by many calculators. Instead of displaying one trillion in standard form, the calculator displays one trillion in some modified form of scientific notation such as

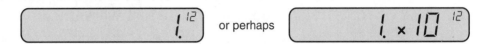

$$1.^{^{12}}$$ or perhaps $$1. \times 10^{^{12}}$$

Practice   Write each number in scientific notation.

   a. 15,000,000 1.5×10^7 **b.** 400,000,000,000 4×10^{11}

   c. 5,090,000 5.09×10^6 **d.** two hundred fifty billion
                                                2.5×10^{11}

Write each number in standard form.

   e. 3.4×10^6 **f.** 5×10^8 **g.** 1×10^5
   3,400,000   500,000,000   100,000

Compare:

   h. 1.5×10^5 ⊘ 1.5×10^6

   i. one million ⊜ 1×10^6

Problem set 51   Refer to this double line graph to answer problems 1 and 2.

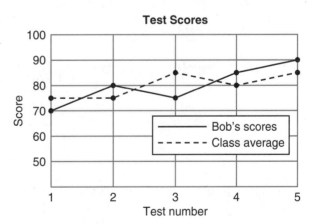

   1. On how many tests was Bob's score better than the class
   (38)   average?   3 tests

   2. What was Bob's average score on these five tests?   80
   (28,38)

   3. In the pattern on a soccer ball, a regular
   (19)   hexagon and a regular pentagon share
   a common side. If the perimeter of
   the hexagon is 9 in., what is the
   perimeter of the pentagon? $7\frac{1}{2}$ in.

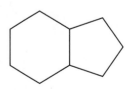

4. The store sold juice for 40¢ per can or 6 cans for $1.98.
(46) How much can be saved per can by buying 6 cans at the
6-can price?   7¢ per can

5. Five sevenths of those people who saw the phenomenon
(14,36) were convinced. The rest were unconvinced.

(a) What fraction of those who saw the phenomenon
were unconvinced? $\frac{2}{7}$

(b) What was the ratio of the convinced to the
unconvinced? $\frac{5}{2}$

6. (a) Write twelve million in scientific notation. 1.2×10^7
(51)
(b) Write 17,600 in scientific notation. 1.76×10^4

7. (a) Write 1.2×10^4 in standard form.   12,000
(51)
(b) Write 5×10^6 in standard form.   5,000,000

8. Write each number as a decimal.
(43)

(a) $\dfrac{1}{8}$ 0.125   (b) $87\dfrac{1}{2}\%$ 0.875

9. Round to the nearest thousand.
(33)
(a) 29,647   30,000   (b) 5280.08   5000

10. Complete the table.
(48)

Fraction	Decimal	Percent
(a) $\frac{2}{5}$	(b) 0.4	40%
(c) $\frac{1}{25}$	(d) 0.04	4%

11. Find the number of degrees in the
(Inv. 5) central angle of each sector of this
circle. (a) 180° (b) 90° (c) 45° (d) 45°

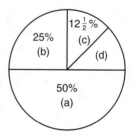

12. What is the total price including 5% sales tax of a $15.80
(46) item? $16.59

13. Bud is thinking of a positive, single-digit, even number.
(36) Lou guesses it is seven. What is the probability that Lou's
guess is correct?   0

14. These two quadrilaterals are congruent. Refer to these
(18) figures to answer questions (a) and (b).

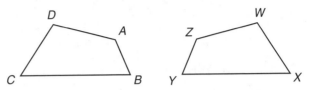

(a) Which angle in *WXYZ* is congruent to ∠*A* in *ABCD*?
∠*Z*

(b) Which segment in *ABCD* is congruent to $\overline{WX}$ in
WXYZ? $\overline{DC}$

Refer to this figure to answer problems 15 and 16. Dimensions
are in meters. All angles are right angles.

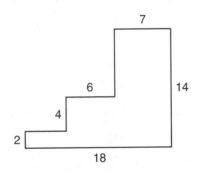

15. What is the perimeter of the figure? 64 m
(19)

16. What is the area of the figure? 144 m²
(37)

Solve:

17. $\dfrac{24}{x} = \dfrac{60}{40}$ 16
(39)

18. $\dfrac{6}{4.2} = \dfrac{n}{7}$ 10
(39)

19. $5m = 8.4$ 1.68
(35)

20. $6.5 - y = 5.06$ 1.44
(35)

Simplify:

21. $5^2 + 3^3 + \sqrt{64}$ 60
(20)

22. 16 cm · $\dfrac{10 \text{ mm}}{1 \text{ cm}}$ 160 mm
(50)

27. 0.5(0.5 + 0.6)
0.5(1.1)
0.55
or
0.5(0.5 + 0.6)
0.25 + 0.3
0.55

23.   5 days 18 hr 50 min
(49) + 2 days   8 hr 25 min
———————————————
  8 days   3 hr 15 min

24.   3 yd 2 ft 5 in.
(49) + 1 yd   9 in.
——————————————
  5 yd   2 in.

25. $6\dfrac{2}{3} + \left(5\dfrac{1}{4} - 3\dfrac{7}{8}\right)$ $8\dfrac{1}{24}$
(23,30)

26. $3\dfrac{1}{3} \cdot \left(2\dfrac{2}{3} \div 1\dfrac{1}{2}\right)$ $5\dfrac{25}{27}$
(26)

27. Show two ways to evaluate $x(x + y)$ when $x = 0.5$
(41) and $y = 0.6$.

The coordinates of three vertices of a triangle are A (−4, 0), B (0, −4), and C (−8, −4). Graph the triangle and refer to it to answer problems 28 and 29.

28. Use a protractor to find the measures of $\angle A$, $\angle B$, and $\angle C$.
(17)   m$\angle A = 90°$; m$\angle B = 45°$; m$\angle C = 45°$

29. What is the area of $\triangle ABC$?   16 sq. units
(37)

30. When the temperature increases from the freezing
(32)   temperature of water to the boiling temperature of water, it is an increase of 100°C on the Celsius scale. The same increase in temperature is how many degrees on the Fahrenheit scale?   180°F

LESSON 52

Order of Operations

Facts Practice: Powers and Roots (Test K in Test Masters)

Mental Math:

a. $6 \times 75¢$
b. $4.5 \div 10^2$
c. $\frac{15}{5} = \frac{m}{6}$
d. Convert 250 cm to m.
e. $10^3 - 20^2$
f. $\frac{9}{10}$ of 200
g. At 80 km per hour, how far will a car travel in $2\frac{1}{2}$ hours?

Problem Solving:

Find x if $3x + 5 = 80$. Explain your thinking.

Recall that the four fundamental operations of arithmetic are addition, subtraction, multiplication, and division. We may also raise numbers to powers or find their roots. When more than one operation occurs in the same expression, we perform the operations in the order listed below.

ORDER OF OPERATIONS

1. Simplify powers and roots.

2. Multiply and divide in order from left to right.

3. Add and subtract in order from left to right.

Note: If there are parentheses (or other enclosures) we simplify within the parentheses in order, before simplifying outside the parentheses.

The sentence, "Please excuse my dear Aunt Sally" with the initial letter of each word representing parentheses, exponents, multiplication and division, addition and subtraction, reminds us of the order of operations.

Example 1   Simplify: $2 + 4 \times 3 - 4 \div 2$

Solution   We multiply and divide in order from left to right before we add or subtract.

$$2 + 4 \times 3 - 4 \div 2 \qquad \text{problem}$$

$$2 + 12 - 2 \qquad \text{multiplied and divided}$$

$$\textbf{12} \qquad \text{added and subtracted}$$

Example 2   Simplify: $\dfrac{3^2 + 3 \cdot 5}{2}$

Solution   A division bar may serve as a symbol of inclusion. We simplify above and below the bar before dividing.

$$\frac{3^2 + 3 \cdot 5}{2} \qquad \text{problem}$$

$$\frac{9 + 3 \cdot 5}{2} \qquad \text{simplified power}$$

$$\frac{9 + 15}{2} \qquad \text{multiplied above}$$

$$\frac{24}{2} \qquad \text{added above}$$

$$\textbf{12} \qquad \text{divided}$$

Example 3   Evaluate: $a + ab$ if $a = 3$ and $b = 4$

Solution   We will begin by writing parentheses in place of each variable. This step may seem unnecessary, but many errors can be avoided if this step is the first step.

$$a + ab$$

$$(\ ) + (\ )(\ ) \qquad \text{parentheses}$$

Then we replace a with 3 and b with 4.

$$a + ab$$

$$(3) + (3)(4) \qquad \text{substituted}$$

We follow the order of operations by multiplying first. Then we add.

$$(3) + (3)(4) \quad \text{problem}$$
$$3 + 12 \quad \text{multiplied}$$
$$\mathbf{15} \quad \text{added}$$

Example 4 Evaluate: $xy - \dfrac{x}{2}$ if $x = 9$ and $y = \dfrac{2}{3}$

Solution First we replace each variable with parentheses.

$$xy - \frac{x}{2}$$

$$(\ )(\ ) - \frac{(\ )}{2} \quad \text{parentheses}$$

Then we write 9 in place of x and $\frac{2}{3}$ in place of y.

$$xy - \frac{x}{2}$$

$$(9)\left(\frac{2}{3}\right) - \frac{(9)}{2} \quad \text{substituted}$$

We follow the order of operations by multiplying and dividing before we subtract.

$$(9)\left(\frac{2}{3}\right) - \frac{(9)}{2} \quad \text{problem}$$

$$6 - 4\frac{1}{2} \quad \text{multiplied and divided}$$

$$1\frac{1}{2} \quad \text{subtracted}$$

 Calculators with *algebraic-logic* circuitry are designed to perform calculations according to the order of operations. Calculators without an algebraic-logic design perform calculations in sequence. If you have a calculator, you can test its design by selecting a problem, such as that in Example 1, and entering the numbers and operations in order from left to right, concluding with an equals sign. If the problem in Example 1 is used, a displayed answer of 12 indicates an algebraic-logic design.

Practice*   Simplify:

     a. $5 + 5 \cdot 5 - 5 \div 5$ 29

     b. $50 - 8 \cdot 5 + 6 \div 3$ 12

     c. $24 - 8 - 6 \cdot 2 \div 4$ 13

     d. $\dfrac{2^3 + 3^2 + 2 \cdot 5}{3}$ 9

Evaluate:

     e. $ab - bc$ if $a = 5$, $b = 3$, and $c = 4$ 3

     f. $ab + \dfrac{a}{c}$ if $a = 6$, $b = 4$, and $c = 2$ 27

     g. $x - xy$ if $x = \dfrac{2}{3}$ and $y = \dfrac{3}{4}$ $\frac{1}{6}$

Problem set 52

1. If the product of the first three prime numbers is divided
$^{(21)}$ by the sum of the first three prime numbers, what is the
quotient?   3

2. Sean counted a total of 100 sides on the heptagons and
$^{(18)}$ nonagons. If there were 4 heptagons, how many nonagons
were there?   8 nonagons

3. Twenty-five and two hundred seventeen thousandths is
$^{(31,35)}$ how much less than two hundred two and two hundredths?
176.803

4. Albert bought a pack of 3 blank tapes for \$5.95.
$^{(46)}$

     (a) What was the price per tape to the nearest cent?   \$1.98

     (b) The sales tax rate was 7%. What was the total cost of
     the three tapes including tax?   \$6.37

5. Ginger is starting a 330-page book. Suppose she reads for
$^{(28)}$ 4 hours and averages 35 pages per hour.

     (a) How many pages will she read in 4 hours?   140 pages

     (b) After four hours, how many pages will she still have
     to read to finish the book?   190 pages

6.

60 passengers

$\frac{3}{4}$ disembarked {
| 15 passengers |
| 15 passengers |
| 15 passengers |
| 15 passengers |

$\frac{1}{4}$ did not
disembark

6. Convert the percent to a fraction. Then draw a diagram of
(22) this statement and answer the questions that follow.

*Seventy-five percent of the sixty passengers
disembarked at the terminal.*

(a) How many passengers disembarked at the terminal?
45 passengers

(b) What percent of the passengers did not disembark at
the terminal?　25%

7. (a) Write 3,750,000 in scientific notation.　3.75×10^6
(51)

(b) Write eighty million in scientific notation.　8×10^7

8. (a) Write 2.05×10^6 in standard form.　2,050,000
(51)

(b) Write 4×10^1 in standard form.　40

9. Write each number as a decimal.
(43)

(a) $\dfrac{3}{8}$　0.375

(b) 6.5%　0.065

10. Write $3.\overline{27}$ as a decimal number rounded to the nearest
(42) thousandth.　3.273

11. Complete the table.
(48)

Fraction	Decimal	Percent
(a) $2\frac{1}{2}$	(b) 2.5	250%
(c) $\frac{1}{4}$	(d) 0.25	25%

12. Divide 70 by 9 and write the answer
(44)

(a) as a mixed number.　$7\frac{7}{9}$

(b) as a decimal number with a bar over the repetend.　$7.\overline{7}$

13. What decimal number names the
(34) point marked by the arrow?　0.99

0.9　　　　1.0

14.

3 cm

2 cm

14. Draw a rectangle that is 3 cm long and 2 cm wide. Then
(32) answer questions (a) and (b).

(a) What is the perimeter of the rectangle in millimeters?
100 mm

(b) What is the area of the rectangle in square
centimeters?　6 cm^2

15. In quadrilateral *ABCD*, $\overline{AD}$ is parallel
(37) to $\overline{BC}$. Units are centimeters.

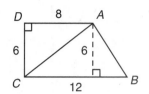

   (a) Find the area of $\triangle ABC$. 36 cm²

   (b) Find the area of $\triangle ACD$. 24 cm²

   (c) What is the combined area of the two triangles?
       60 cm²

Solve:

16. $\dfrac{8}{f} = \dfrac{56}{105}$ 15
(39)

17. $\dfrac{12}{15} = \dfrac{w}{2.5}$ 2
(39)

18. $p + 6.8 = 20$ 13.2
(35)

19. $q - 3.6 = 6.4$ 10
(35)

Simplify:

20. $5^3 - 10^2 - \sqrt{25}$ 20
(20)

21. $4 + 4 \cdot 4 - 4 \div 4$ 19
(52)

22. $\dfrac{4.8 - 0.24}{(0.2)(0.6)}$ 38
(45)

23.
(49)

$$\begin{array}{r} 5 \text{ hr } 45 \text{ min } 30 \text{ s} \\ + 2 \text{ hr } 53 \text{ min } 55 \text{ s} \\ \hline 8 \text{ hr } 39 \text{ min } 25 \text{ s} \end{array}$$

24. $6\dfrac{3}{4} + \left(5\dfrac{1}{3} \cdot 2\dfrac{1}{2}\right)$ $20\frac{1}{12}$
(26,30)

25. $5\dfrac{1}{2} - \left(3\dfrac{3}{4} \div 2\right)$ $3\frac{5}{8}$
(26,30)

26. $8.575 + 12.625 + 8.4 + 70.4$ 100
(35)

27. Evaluate: $ab + \dfrac{a}{b}$ if $a = 4$ and $b = 0.5$ 10
(52)

28. $0.8 \times 1.25 \times 10^6$ 1,000,000
(47)

29. Convert 1.4 meters to centimeters. (1 m = 100 cm)
(50) 140 cm

30. The students in a class of 30 were asked to name their
(36) favorite sport. Twelve said football, 10 said basketball,
     and 8 said baseball. If a student is selected at random,
     what is the probability that the favorite sport of that
     student is basketball? $\frac{1}{3}$

LESSON
53

Multiplying Rates

Facts Practice: Powers and Roots (Test K in Test Masters)

Mental Math:

a. $8 \times \$1.25$

b. 12.75×10

c. $2x + 5 = 75$

d. Convert 35 cm to mm.

e. $\left(\frac{1}{2}\right)^2$

f. $\frac{3}{5}$ of 45

g. 10×6, $+ 4$, $\sqrt{\ }$, $\times 3$, double it, $+ 1$, $\sqrt{\ }$, $\times 8$, $- 1$, $\div 5$, square that number

Problem Solving:

Allen wanted to form a triangle out of straws that were 5 in., 7 in., and 12 in. long. He threaded a piece of string through the three straws, pulled the string tight, and tied it. What was the area of the figure?

If we are traveling in a car at 50 miles per hour (50 mph), we can calculate how far we would travel in 4 hours by multiplying.

$$4 \ \cancel{hr} \times \frac{50 \ mi}{1 \ \cancel{hr}} = 200 \ mi$$

We can find out how long it will take us to travel 300 miles by dividing.

$$300 \ mi \div \frac{50 \ mi}{1 \ hr}$$

$$300 \ \cancel{mi} \times \frac{1 \ hr}{50 \ \cancel{mi}} = \frac{300 \ hr}{50} = 6 \ hr$$

Notice that dividing by a rate is similar to dividing by a fraction. We actually multiply by the reciprocal of the original rate. There are two forms of every rate, and they are reciprocals. Thus we may solve rate problems by multiplying by the correct form of the rate. The following statement expresses a rate:

There were 5 chairs in each row.

We can express this rate in two forms.

(a) $\dfrac{5 \ chairs}{1 \ row}$ (b) $\dfrac{1 \ row}{5 \ chairs}$

Using rate (a) we can find the number of chairs in 6 rows.

$$6 \ \cancel{rows} \times \frac{5 \ chairs}{1 \ \cancel{row}} = 30 \ chairs$$

Using rate (b) we can find the total number of rows needed for 20 chairs.

$$20 \text{ chairs} \times \frac{1 \text{ row}}{5 \text{ chairs}} = 4 \text{ rows}$$

Example 1 Eight ounces of the solution cost 40 cents.

(a) Write the two rates given by this statement.

(b) Find the cost of 32 ounces of the solution.

(c) How many ounces can be purchased for $1.20?

Solution (a) The two rates are

$$\frac{\textbf{8 oz}}{\textbf{40 cents}} \qquad \frac{\textbf{40 cents}}{\textbf{8 oz}}$$

(b) To find the cost, we use the rate that has money on top.

$$32 \text{ oz} \times \frac{40 \text{ cents}}{8 \text{ oz}} \qquad \text{canceled ounces}$$

$$\frac{1280}{8} \text{ cents} \qquad \text{multiplied}$$

$$160 \text{ cents} \qquad \text{simplified}$$

We usually write answers equal to a dollar or more by using a dollar sign. Thus the cost is **$1.60.**

(c) To find the number of ounces, we use the rate that has ounces on top.

$$120 \text{ cents} \times \frac{8 \text{ oz}}{40 \text{ cents}} \qquad \text{canceled cents}$$

$$\frac{960}{40} \text{ oz} \qquad \text{multiplied}$$

$$\textbf{24 oz} \qquad \text{simplified}$$

Note that rates, like fractions, can be reduced. The rates in part (a) of Example 1 can be reduced.

$$\frac{1 \text{ oz}}{5 \text{ cent}} \qquad 5 \frac{\text{cents}}{\text{oz}}$$

However, rates can be used to solve problems without reducing them first as we have seen in parts (b) and (c).

Example 2 Jennifer's speed was 60 miles per hour.

(a) Write the two rates given by this statement.

(b) How far did she drive in 5 hours?

(c) How long would it take her to drive 300 miles?

Solution (a) The two rates are

$$\frac{60 \text{ miles}}{1 \text{ hour}} \qquad \frac{1 \text{ hour}}{60 \text{ miles}}$$

(b) To find how far, we use the rate with miles on top.

$$5 \text{ hours} \times \frac{60 \text{ miles}}{1 \text{ hour}} = \textbf{300 miles}$$

(c) To find how much time, we use the rate with time on top.

$$300 \text{ miles} \times \frac{1 \text{ hour}}{60 \text{ miles}} = \textbf{5 hours}$$

Example 3 If popsicles cost $0.25 each, how many popsicles can Dan buy for $2.00?

Solution We may use rates to solve this problem. The rate of $0.25 per popsicle has two forms.

$$\frac{\$0.25}{1 \text{ popsicle}} \quad \text{and} \quad \frac{1 \text{ popsicle}}{\$0.25}$$

To find how many, we use the rate with popsicles on top.

$$\$2.00 \times \frac{1 \text{ popsicle}}{\$0.25} = \textbf{8 popsicles}$$

Practice In the lecture hall there were 18 rows. Fifteen chairs were in each row.

a. Write the two rates given by this statement. $\frac{15 \text{ chairs}}{1 \text{ row}}; \frac{1 \text{ row}}{15 \text{ chairs}}$

b. Find the total number of chairs in the lecture hall.
270 chairs

A car could travel 24 miles on one gallon of gas.

c. Write the two rates given by this statement. $\frac{24 \text{ miles}}{1 \text{ gallon}}; \frac{1 \text{ gallon}}{24 \text{ miles}}$

d. $6\frac{2}{3}$ gallons   **d.** How many gallons would it take to go 160 miles?

Problem set 53   Refer to this double bar graph to answer problems 1, 2, and 3.

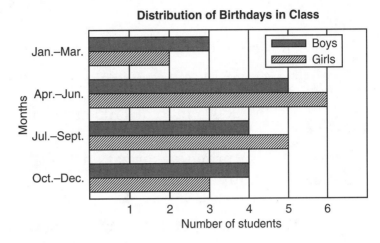

Distribution of Birthdays in Class

Months

Number of students

1. (a) How many boys are in the class? 16 boys
(38)
   (b) How many girls are in the class? 16 girls

2. What percent of the students have birthdays in January
(38) through June? 50%

3. What fraction of the boys have birthdays in April through
(38) June? $\frac{5}{16}$

4. At the book fair Bill bought 4 books. One book cost $3.95.
(28,46) Another book cost $4.47. The other 2 books cost $4.95
   each.

   (a) What was the average price of the books? $4.58

   (b) What was the total price of the books including 8%
   sales tax? $19.79

5.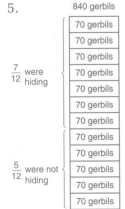

5. Draw a diagram of this statement. Then answer the
(22) questions that follow.

   *Seven twelfths of the 840 gerbils were hiding in
   their burrows.*

   (a) What fraction of the gerbils were not hiding in their
   burrows? $\frac{5}{12}$

   (b) How many gerbils were not hiding in their burrows?
   350 gerbils

6. (a) Write one trillion in scientific notation. 1×10^{12}
(51)
   (b) Write 475,000 in scientific notation. 4.75×10^5

7. (a) Write 7×10^2 in standard form. 700
(51)

   (b) Compare: 2.5×10^6 ⊘ 2.5×10^5

8. Use unit multipliers to perform the following conversions:
(50)

   (a) 35 yards to feet (3 ft = 1 yd) 105 ft

   (b) 2000 cm to m (100 cm = 1 m) 20 m

9. Use prime factorization to help find the least common
(27) multiple of 54 and 36. 108

10. Estimate the difference of 19,827 and 12,092 by rounding
(29) to the nearest thousand before subtracting.
$20,000 - 12,000 = 8,000$

11. Complete the table.
(48)

FRACTION	DECIMAL	PERCENT
(a) $1\frac{1}{2}$	(b) 1.5	150%
(c) $\frac{3}{20}$	(d) 0.15	15%

12. Write each number as a percent.
(48)

   (a) $\dfrac{4}{5}$ 80%
                 (b) 0.06 6%

13. Big Bill is 2 m tall. Stephanie is 165 cm tall. Big Bill is
(32) how many centimeters taller than Stephanie? 35 cm

14. Refer to this figure to answer questions
(37) (a) and (b). Dimensions are in feet.
All angles are right angles.

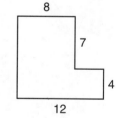

   (a) What is the area of the figure?
      104 ft²

   (b) What is the perimeter of the
      figure? 46 ft

15. The bank would exchange 1.6 Canadian dollars (C$) for 1
(53) U.S. dollar (US$).

   (a) Write two forms of the exchange rate. $\dfrac{1.6\ \text{C\$}}{1\ \text{US\$}}$; $\dfrac{1\ \text{US\$}}{1.6\ \text{C\$}}$

   (b) How many Canadian dollars would the bank
      exchange for 160 U.S. dollars? 256 C$

Solve:

16. $\dfrac{18}{100} = \dfrac{90}{p}$ 500
(39)

17. $\dfrac{6}{9} = \dfrac{t}{1.5}$ 1
(39)

18. $8 = 7.25 + m$ 0.75
(35)

19. $1.5 = 10n$ 0.15
(35)

Simplify:

20. $\sqrt{81} + 9^2 - 2^5$ 58
(20)

21. $16 \div 4 \div 2 + 3 \times 4$ 14
(52)

22. Estimate: $6.85 \times 4\dfrac{1}{16}$
(29,33)   28

23.
(49)
$$3 \text{ yd } 1 \text{ ft } 7\tfrac{1}{2} \text{ in.}$$
$$+ \qquad 2 \text{ ft } 6\tfrac{1}{2} \text{ in.}$$
$$\overline{4 \text{ yd } 1 \text{ ft } 2 \text{ in.}}$$

24. $12\dfrac{2}{3} + \left(5\dfrac{5}{6} \div 2\dfrac{1}{3}\right)$ $15\frac{1}{6}$
(26,30)

25. $8\dfrac{3}{5} - \left(1\dfrac{1}{2} \cdot 3\dfrac{1}{5}\right)$ $3\frac{4}{5}$
(26,30)

26. $10.6 + 4.2 + 16.4 + \left(3.875 \times 10^1\right)$ 69.95
(35,47)

27. Evaluate: $\dfrac{ab}{bc}$ if $a = 6$, $b = 0.9$, and $c = 5$ 1.2
(52)

28. Petersen needed to pack 1000 eggs into flats that held $2\frac{1}{2}$
(44) dozen eggs. How many flats could he fill?   33 flats

29. If there is one chance in five of guessing the correct
(36) answer, then what is the probability of not guessing the
correct answer? $\frac{4}{5}$

30. Find the measure of angles a, b, and c in this figure.
(40)   m$\angle a$ = 50°; m$\angle b$ = 40°; m$\angle c$ = 80°

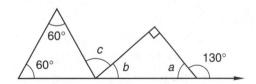

LESSON 54

Ratio Word Problems

Mental Math:
a. $18.00
b. 1.275
c. 8
d. 150 cm
e. 3
f. 27
g. $1\frac{3}{20}, \frac{7}{20}, \frac{3}{10}, 1\frac{7}{8}$
Problem Solving:
   3 girls

Facts Practice: Fraction-Decimal-Percent Equivalents
(Test L in Test Masters)

Mental Math:

a. $4 \times \$4.50$

b. $12.75 \div 10$

c. $\frac{12}{w} = \frac{9}{6}$

d. Convert 1.5 m to cm.

e. $\sqrt{900} - 3^3$

f. $\frac{3}{10}$ of 90

g. Find the sum, difference, product, and quotient of $\frac{3}{4}$ and $\frac{2}{5}$.

Problem Solving:

At first $\frac{1}{3}$ of the students in the room were girls. When 3 boys left, $\frac{1}{2}$ of the remaining students were girls. How many girls were in the room?

In this lesson we will use proportions to solve ratio word problems. Consider the following ratio word problem:

> *The ratio of parrots to macaws was 5 to 7. If there were 750 parrots, how many macaws were there?*

In this problem there are two kinds of numbers, ratio numbers and actual count numbers. The ratio numbers are 5 and 7. The number 750 is an actual count of parrots. We will arrange these numbers into two columns and two rows to form a ratio box. Practicing the use of ratio boxes now will pay dividends in later lessons when we extend the application of ratio boxes to more complex problems.

	Ratio	Actual Count
Parrots	5	750
Macaws	7	M

We were not given the actual count of macaws, so we have used M to stand for the number of macaws. The numbers in this ratio box can be used to write a proportion. By solving the proportion, we find the actual count of macaws.

	Ratio	Actual Count
Parrots	5	750
Macaws	7	M

$$\frac{5}{7} = \frac{750}{M}$$

$$5M = 5250$$

$$M = 1050$$

We find that the actual count of macaws was 1050.

Example   The ratio of boys to girls was 5 to 4. If there were 200 girls in the auditorium, how many boys were there?

Solution   We begin by making a ratio box.

	Ratio	Actual Count
Boys	5	B
Girls	4	200

$$\longrightarrow \quad \frac{5}{4} = \frac{B}{200}$$

$$4B = 1000$$

$$B = 250$$

We use the numbers in the ratio box to write a proportion. Then we solve the proportion and answer the question. There were **250 boys.**

Practice   Solve each of these ratio word problems. Begin by making a ratio box.

a. The girl-boy ratio was 9 to 7. If 63 girls attended, how many boys attended? 49 boys

b. The ratio of sparrows to bluejays in the yard was 5 to 3. If there were 15 bluejays in the yard, how many sparrows were in the yard? 25 sparrows

c. The ratio of tagged fish to untagged fish was 2 to 9. Ninety fish were tagged. How many fish were untagged? 405 untagged fish

Problem set 54

1. Thomas Jefferson died on the fiftieth anniversary of the
(28) signing of the Declaration of Independence. He was born in 1743. The Declaration of Independence was signed in 1776. How many years did Thomas Jefferson live? 83 years

2. The heights of the five basketball players are 190 cm,
(28) 195 cm, 197 cm, 201 cm, and 203 cm. What is the average height of the players to the nearest centimeter? 197 cm

3. Use a ratio box to solve this problem. The ratio of
(54) winners to losers was 5 to 4. If there were 1200 winners, how many losers were there? 960 losers

4. What is the cost of 2.6 pounds of cheese at $1.75 per
(53) pound? $4.55

5. What is the quotient when the least common multiple of 4
(6,27) and 6 is divided by the greatest common factor of 4 and 6?
$\frac{12}{2} = 6$

6.

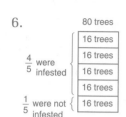

6. Draw a diagram of this statement. Then answer the
(22) questions that follow.

Eighty percent of the 80 trees were infested.

(a) How many trees were infested? 64 trees

(b) How many trees were not infested? 16 trees

7. (a) Write 405,000 in scientific notation. 4.05×10^5
(51)

(b) Write 0.04×10^5 in standard form. 4000

8. Find each missing exponent.
(47)

(a) $10^6 \cdot 10^2 = 10^{\square}$ 8   (b) $10^6 \div 10^2 = 10^{\square}$ 4

9. Use unit multipliers to perform the following conversions:
(50)

(a) 5280 feet to yards (3 ft = 1 yd) 1760 yd

(b) 300 cm to mm (1 cm = 10 mm) 3000 mm

10. Write 3.1415926 as a decimal number rounded to four
(33) decimal places. 3.1416

11. Find the number of degrees in the
(Inv. 5) central angle of each sector of this
circle.
(a) 144° (b) 108° (c) 72° (d) 36°

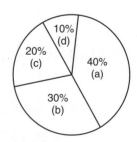

12. A train is traveling at a steady speed of 60 miles per hour.
(53)

(a) How far will the train travel in four hours? 240 miles

(b) How long will it take the train to travel 300 miles?
5 hours

13. Which is equivalent to $\dfrac{2^6}{2^2}$? B. 2^4
(20)

A. 2^3 B. 2^4 C. 1^3 D. 3

Refer to this figure to answer problems 14 and 15. Dimensions are in centimeters. All angles are right angles.

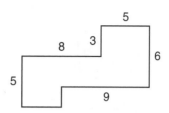

14. What is the perimeter of the figure? 42 cm
(19)

15. What is the area of the figure? 62 cm²
(37)

16. Name each property illustrated.
(2,41)

(a) $\frac{1}{2} + 0 = \frac{1}{2}$ identity property of addition

(b) $5(6 + 7) = 30 + 35$ distributive property

(c) $(5 + 6) + 4 = 5 + (6 + 4)$
associative property of addition

17. On your paper draw a square with sides 0.5 inches long.
(34,35)

(a) What is the perimeter of the square? 2 inches

(b) What is the area of the square? 0.25 square inches

18. The average score is likely to be below the median score. The mean "balances" low scores with high scores. The scores above the median are not far enough above the median to allow the balance point for all the scores to be at or above the median.

18. This box-and-whisker plot was created from student scores on the last math test. Do you think that the mean (average) score on the test is likely to be above, at, or below the median score? Explain your answer.
(Inv. 4)

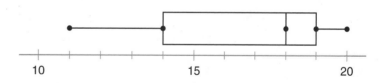

Solve:

19. $6.2 = x + 4.1$ 2.1
(35)

20. $1.2 = y - 0.21$ 1.41
(35)

21. $\frac{24}{r} = \frac{36}{27}$ 18
(39)

22. $\frac{w}{0.16} = 6.25$ 1
(35)

Simplify:

23. $11^2 + 1^3 - \sqrt{121}$ 111
(20)

24. $24 - 4 \times 5 \div 2 + 5$ 19
(52)

25. $\dfrac{(2.5)^2}{2(2.5)}$ 1.25
(35)

26.
(49)
$$
\begin{array}{l}
\quad 1 \text{ week } \; 5 \text{ days } 14 \text{ hr} \\
+ \; 2 \text{ weeks } 6 \text{ days } 10 \text{ hr} \\
\hline
\quad 4 \text{ weeks } \quad 5 \text{ days}
\end{array}
$$

27. $3\dfrac{5}{10} + \left(9\dfrac{1}{2} - 6\dfrac{2}{3}\right)$ $6\frac{1}{3}$
(23,30)

28. $7\dfrac{1}{3} \cdot \left(6 \div 3\dfrac{2}{3}\right)$ 12
(26)

29.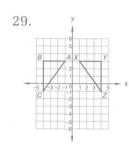

29. The coordinates of the vertices of $\triangle ABC$ are $A\,(-1, 3)$,
(Inv. 3) $B\,(-4, 3)$, and $C\,(-4, -1)$. The coordinates of $\triangle XYZ$ are $X\,(1, 3)$, $Y\,(4, 3)$, and $Z\,(4, -1)$. Graph the triangles and refer to the graph to answer the questions in problem 30.

30. (a) Are $\triangle ABC$ and $\triangle XYZ$ similar? yes
(18)

    (b) Are $\triangle ABC$ and $\triangle XYZ$ congruent? yes

    (c) Which angle in $\triangle ABC$ corresponds to $\angle Z$ in $\triangle XYZ$?
    $\angle C$

LESSON
55

Average, Part 2

Facts Practice: $+ - \times \div$ Decimals (Test J in Test Masters)

Mental Math:

  a. $20 \times \$0.25$

  b. 0.375×10^2

  c. $2x - 5 = 75$

  d. Convert 3000 m to km.

  e. $\left(\dfrac{2}{3}\right)^2$

  f. $\frac{3}{4}$ of 100

  g. At 30 pages an hour, how many pages can Mike read in $2\frac{1}{2}$ hours?

Problem Solving:

Copy this problem and fill in the missing digits.

$$
\begin{array}{r}
\_\,3\,\_ \\
\times \quad \_\,\_ \\
\hline
3\,\_\,\_\,\_ \\
\_\,3\,\_ \quad \\
\hline
9\,\_\,\_\,9
\end{array}
$$

If we know the average of a group of numbers and how many numbers are in the group, we can figure out the sum of the numbers.

Example 1   The average of three numbers is 17. What is their sum?

Solution   We are not told what the numbers are. We are only told their average. Each of these sets of three numbers has an average of 17.

$$\frac{16 + 17 + 18}{3} = \frac{51}{3} = 17$$

$$\frac{10 + 11 + 30}{3} = \frac{51}{3} = 17$$

$$\frac{1 + 1 + 49}{3} = \frac{51}{3} = 17$$

Notice that for each set the sum of the three numbers is 51. Since average means what the numbers would be if they were "equalized," the sum is the same as if each of the three numbers were 17.

$$17 + 17 + 17 = \mathbf{51}$$

Thus, the number of numbers times their average equals the sum of the numbers.

Example 2   The average of four numbers is 25. If three of the numbers are 16, 26, and 30, what is the fourth number?

Solution   If the average of four numbers is 25, their sum is 100.

$$4 \times 25 = 100$$

We are given three of the numbers. The sum of these three numbers plus the fourth number, N, must equal 100.

$$16 + 26 + 30 + N = 100$$

The sum of the first three numbers is 72. Since the sum of the four numbers total 100, the fourth number is **28.**

$$16 + 26 + 30 + (28) = 100$$

Example 3   After 4 tests, Annette's average score was 89. What score does Annette need on her fifth test to bring her average up to 90?

Solution   Although we do not know the specific scores on the first 4 tests, the total is the same as if each of the scores were 89. Thus the total after 4 tests is

$$4 \times 89 = 356$$

The total of her first 4 scores is 356. However, to have an average of 90 after 5 tests, she needs a 5-test total of 450.

$$5 \times 90 = 450$$

Therefore she needs to raise her total from 356 to 450 on the fifth test. To do this, she needs to score **94.**

$$\begin{array}{rl} 356 & \text{4-test total} \\ + 94 & \text{fifth test} \\ \hline 450 & \text{5-test total} \end{array}$$

Practice

a. Ralph scored an average of 18 points in each of his first 5 games. Altogether, how many points did Ralph score in the first 5 games? 90 points

b. The average of four numbers is 45. If three of the numbers are 24, 36, and 52, what is the fourth number? 68

c. After 5 tests, Mike's average score was 91. After 6 tests, his average score was 89. What was his score on the sixth test? 79

Problem set 55

1. Use a ratio box to solve this problem. The ratio of sailboats to rowboats in the bay was 7 to 4. If there were 56 sailboats in the bay, how many rowboats were there?
$^{(54)}$
32 rowboats

2. The average of four numbers is 85. If three of the numbers are 76, 78, and 81, what is the fourth number? 105
$^{(55)}$

3. A one-quart container of oil costs 89¢. A case of 12 one-quart containers costs $8.64. How much is saved per container by buying the oil by the case? $0.17 per container
$^{(46)}$

4. Segment *BC* is how much longer than segment *AB*? $\frac{1}{2}$ in.
$^{(8)}$

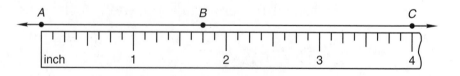

5. Draw a diagram of this statement. Then answer the questions that follow.
$^{(22)}$

Three tenths of the 30 students earned an A.

(a) How many students earned an A? 9 students

(b) What percent of the students earned an A? 30%

5.

30 students	
	3 students
$\frac{3}{10}$ earned an A	3 students
	3 students
	3 students
	3 students
	3 students
$\frac{7}{10}$ did not earn an A	3 students
	3 students
	3 students
	3 students

6. (a) Write 675 million in scientific notation. 6.75×10^8
(51)
   (b) Write 1.86×10^5 in standard form. 186,000

7. Find each missing exponent.
(47)
   (a) $10^8 \cdot 10^2 = 10^{\square}$ 10   (b) $10^8 \div 10^2 = 10^{\square}$ 6

8. Use unit multipliers to perform the following conversions:
(50)
   (a) 24 feet to inches 288 inches

   (b) 500 millimeters to centimeters 50 centimeters

9. Use digits and other symbols to write: "The product of
(31) two hundredths and twenty-five thousandths is five ten
thousandths." $0.02 \cdot 0.025 = 0.0005$

10. What is the total price of a $3.25 sandwich and a $1.10
(46) drink including 7% sales tax? $4.65

11. Complete the table.
(48)

Fraction	Decimal	Percent
$\frac{1}{5}$	(a) 0.2	(b) 20%
(c) $\frac{1}{10}$	0.1	(d) 10%
(e) $\frac{3}{4}$	(f) 0.75	75%

Refer to this figure to answer the
questions in problems 12 and 13.

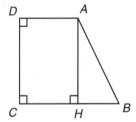

12. (a) Which segment is parallel to $\overline{BC}$?
(7)   AD
   (b) Which two segments are perpen-
       dicular to $\overline{BC}$? $\overline{DC}, \overline{AH}$

   (c) Angle ABC is an acute angle.
       Which angle is an obtuse angle?
       $\angle DAB$

13. If $AD = 6$ cm, $CD = 8$ cm, and $CB = 10$ cm, then
(37)
   (a) what is the area of rectangle $AHCD$? 48 cm^2

   (b) what is the area of $\triangle ABH$? 16 cm^2

   (c) what is the area of figure $ABCD$? 64 cm^2

14. Don is 6 feet, 2 inches tall. Bob is 68 inches tall. Don is
(28) how many inches taller than Bob? 6 inches

15. Monte swam 5 laps in 4 minutes.
(53)

    (a) Write two forms of this rate. $\frac{5\text{ laps}}{4\text{ min}}; \frac{4\text{ min}}{5\text{ laps}}$

    (b) How many laps could Monte swim in 20 minutes at this rate? 25 laps

    (c) How long would it take for Monte to swim 20 laps at this rate? 16 minutes

Solve:

16. $\dfrac{30}{70} = \dfrac{21}{x}$ 49
(39)

17. $\dfrac{1000}{w} = 2.5$ 400
(45)

18. $\frac{1}{2}\left(\frac{1}{4} + \frac{1}{2}\right)$
$\frac{1}{2}\left(\frac{3}{4}\right)$
$\frac{3}{8}$
or
$\frac{1}{2}\left(\frac{1}{4} + \frac{1}{2}\right)$
$\frac{1}{8} + \frac{1}{4}$
$\frac{3}{8}$

18. Show two ways to evaluate $b(a + b)$ when $a = \frac{1}{4}$ and $b = \frac{1}{2}$.
(41)

Simplify:

19. $12^2 - 4^3 - 2^4 - \sqrt{144}$ 52
(20)

20. $50 + 30 \div 5 \cdot 2 - 6$ 56
(52)

21. $10\text{ yd} \cdot \dfrac{36\text{ in.}}{1\text{ yd}}$ 360 in.
(50)

22.
(49)
$$\begin{array}{r} 8\text{ yd }2\text{ ft }7\text{ in.} \\ +\qquad\qquad 5\text{ in.} \\ \hline 9\text{ yd} \end{array}$$

23. $2\dfrac{5}{12} + 6\dfrac{5}{6} + 4\dfrac{7}{8}$ $14\frac{1}{8}$
(30)

24. $6 - \left(7\dfrac{1}{3} - 4\dfrac{4}{5}\right)$ $3\frac{7}{15}$
(23,30)

25. $6\dfrac{2}{3} \cdot 5\dfrac{1}{4} \cdot 2\dfrac{1}{10}$ $73\frac{1}{2}$
(26)

26. $3\dfrac{1}{3} \div 3 \div 2\dfrac{1}{2}$ $\frac{4}{9}$
(26)

27. $3.47 + (6 - 1.359)$ 8.111
(35)

28. $(0.6)(0.28)(0.01)$ 0.00168
(35)

29. $\$1.50 \div 0.075$ $20.00
(45)

30. This quadrilateral is a rectangle. Find the measure of angles a, b, and c.
(40)
m∠a = 38°; m∠b = 52°; m∠c = 38°

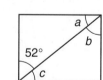

Subtracting Mixed Measures

**LESSON
56**

Mental Math:
a. 75
b. 0.025
c. 12
d. 50 cm
e. 400
f. $35.00
g. −3
Problem Solving:
 9 × 10 = 90

Facts Practice: Fraction-Decimal-Percent Equivalents
(Test L in Test Masters)

Mental Math:

a. 30×2.5 **b.** $0.25 \div 10$
c. $3x + 4 = 40$ **d.** Convert 0.5 m to cm.
e. $25^2 - 15^2$ **f.** $\frac{7}{10}$ of $50.00
g. Square 9, − 1, ÷ 2, − 4, $\sqrt{\ }$, × 3, + 2, ÷ 5, $\sqrt{\ }$, − 5.

Problem Solving:

A palindrome is a word or number that reads the same forwards
and backwards, such as "mom" and "121." How many three-digit
numbers are palindromes?

We have practiced adding mixed measures. In this lesson we
will practice subtracting mixed measures. When subtracting
mixed measures, we may need to convert units in order to
subtract.

Example 1   Subtract: 5 days 10 hr 15 min
                             − 1 day   15 hr 40 min

Solution   Before we can subtract minutes, we must convert 1 hour to
60 minutes. We combine 60 minutes and 15 minutes, making
75 minutes. Then we can subtract.

$$
\begin{array}{r}
\overset{9}{} \nearrow \overset{(60\ min)}{} \\
5\ \text{days}\ \cancel{10}\ \text{hr}\ 15\ \text{min} \\
-\ 1\ \text{day}\ \ 15\ \text{hr}\ 40\ \text{min} \\
\end{array}
\quad \longrightarrow \quad
\begin{array}{r}
\overset{9}{}\ \ \ \overset{75}{} \\
5\ \text{days}\ \cancel{10}\ \text{hr}\ \cancel{15}\ \text{min} \\
-\ 1\ \text{day}\ \ 15\ \text{hr}\ 40\ \text{min} \\
\hline
35\ \text{min}
\end{array}
$$

Next we convert 1 day to 24 hours, and complete the
subtraction.

$$
\begin{array}{r}
\overset{4}{}\ \nearrow \overset{(24\ hr)}{}\ \ \overset{9}{}\ \ \overset{75}{} \\
\cancel{5}\ \text{days}\ \cancel{10}\ \text{hr}\ \cancel{15}\ \text{min} \\
-\ 1\ \text{day}\ \ 15\ \text{hr}\ 40\ \text{min} \\
\hline
35\ \text{min}
\end{array}
\quad \longrightarrow \quad
\begin{array}{r}
\overset{33}{} \\
\overset{4}{}\ \ \overset{\cancel{9}}{}\ \ \overset{75}{} \\
\cancel{5}\ \text{days}\ \cancel{10}\ \text{hr}\ \cancel{15}\ \text{min} \\
-\ 1\ \text{day}\ \ 15\ \text{hr}\ 40\ \text{min} \\
\hline
\mathbf{3\ days\ 18\ hr\ 35\ min}
\end{array}
$$

Example 2   Subtract: 4 yd, 3 in. − 2 yd, 1 ft, 8 in.

Solution   We carefully align the numbers with like units. We convert 1 yd to 3 ft.

$$
\begin{array}{l}
\overset{3 \ \nearrow \ (3\,ft)}{\cancel{4} \ yd} \qquad 3 \ in. \\
- \ 2 \ yd \quad 1 \ ft \quad 8 \ in. \\
\hline
\end{array}
$$

Next we convert 1 ft to 12 in. This combines with 3 in., making 15 in. Then we can subtract.

$$
\begin{array}{l}
\overset{3}{\cancel{4}} \ yd \ \overset{2}{\cancel{3}} \ ft \ \overset{15}{\cancel{3}} \ in. \\
- \ 2 \ yd \ 1 \ ft \ 8 \ in. \\
\hline
\mathbf{1 \ yd \ 1 \ ft \ 7 \ in.}
\end{array}
$$

Practice*   Subtract:

a. $\begin{array}{l} 3\ hr \qquad\qquad 3\ s \\ -\ 1\ hr\ 15\ min\ 55\ s \\ \hline 1\ hr\ \ 44\ min\ \ \ 8\ s \end{array}$

b. $\begin{array}{l} 8\ yd\ 1\ ft\ 5\ in. \\ -\ 3\ yd\ 2\ ft\ 7\ in. \\ \hline 4\ yd\ \ 1\ ft\ 10\ in. \end{array}$

c.   2 days, 3 hr, 30 min − 1 day, 8 hr, 45 min   18 hr, 45 min

Problem set 56   1.   *(31,35)*   Three hundred twenty-nine ten thousandths is how much greater than thirty-two thousandths? Use words to write the answer.   nine ten thousandths

2.   *(54)*   Use a ratio box to solve this problem. The ratio of the length to the width of the rectangle is 4 to 3. If the length of the rectangle is 12 feet,

(a) what is its width?   9 feet

(b) what is its perimeter?   42 feet

3.   *(28)*   The parking lot charges $2 for the first hour and 50¢ for each additional half hour or part thereof. What is the total charge for parking a car in the lot from 11:30 a.m. until 2:15 p.m.? $4

4.   *(55)*   After four tests Trudy's average score was 85. If her score is 90 on the fifth test, what will be her average for all five tests?   86

5. Brand X = 12.5¢ per ounce; Brand Y = 12¢ per ounce; Brand Y is a better buy.

5.   *(46)*   Twelve ounces of Brand X costs $1.50. Sixteen ounces of Brand Y costs $1.92. Find the unit price of each. Which brand is the better buy?

6. Five eighths of the rocks in the box were metamorphic.
(36,48) The rest were igneous.

(a) What fraction of the rocks were igneous? $\frac{3}{8}$

6.(b) $\frac{3}{5}$ (b) What was the ratio of igneous to metamorphic rocks?

(c) What percent of the rocks were metamorphic? $62\frac{1}{2}\%$

7. Refer to this figure to answer questions
(40) (a) and (b).

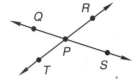

7.(a) $\angle QPR$ and   (a) Name two pairs of vertical angles.
$\angle TPS$, $\angle RPS$ and
$\angle QPT$ (b) Name two angles that are
supplemental to $\angle RPS$. $\angle RPQ$ and $\angle SPT$

8. (a) Write six hundred ten thousand in scientific notation.
(51) 6.1×10^5
(b) Write 1.5×10^4 in standard form. $15{,}000$

9. Use unit multipliers to perform the following conversions:
(50)
(a) 216 hours to days 9 days

(b) 5 minutes to seconds 300 seconds

10. (a) Write $\frac{1}{6}$ as a decimal number rounded to the nearest
(43,48) hundredth. 0.17

(b) Write $\frac{1}{6}$ as a percent. $16\frac{2}{3}\%$

11. How many pennies equal one million dollars? Write the
(51) answer in scientific notation. 1×10^8 pennies

12. Compare: 11 million $\gtrless$ 1.1×10^6
(51)

13. Which even two-digit number is a common multiple of 5
(27) and 7? 70

14. There are 100°C on the Celsius scale from the freezing
(32,54) temperature to the boiling temperature of water. There
are 180°F on the Fahrenheit scale between these
temperatures. So a change in temperature of 10°C on the
Celsius scale is equivalent to a change of how many
degrees on the Fahrenheit scale? $18°F$

Solve:

15. $\dfrac{3}{2.5} = \dfrac{48}{c}$ 40
(39)

16. $k - 0.75 = 0.75$ 1.5
(35)

Refer to the figure below to answer problems 17 and 18. Dimensions are in millimeters. All angles are right angles.

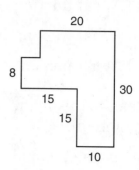

17. What is the perimeter of this figure? 110 mm
(19)

18. What is the area of the figure? 490 mm²
(37)

Simplify:

19. $15^2 - 5^3 - \sqrt{100}$ 90
(20)

20. $6 + 12 \div 3 \cdot 2 - 3 \cdot 4$ 2
(52)

21.
(49)

$\begin{array}{r} 5 \text{ yd } 2 \text{ ft } 3 \text{ in.} \\ + 2 \text{ yd } 2 \text{ ft } 9 \text{ in.} \\ \hline 8 \text{ yd } \quad 2 \text{ ft} \end{array}$

22.
(56)

$\begin{array}{r} 5 \text{ yd } 2 \text{ ft } 3 \text{ in.} \\ - 2 \text{ yd } 2 \text{ ft } 9 \text{ in.} \\ \hline 2 \text{ yd } \quad 2 \text{ ft } 6 \text{ in.} \end{array}$

23. $\dfrac{88 \text{ km}}{1 \text{ hr}} \cdot 4 \text{ hr}$ 352 km
(53)

24. $2\dfrac{3}{4} + \left(5\dfrac{1}{6} - 1\dfrac{1}{4}\right)$ $6\dfrac{2}{3}$
(23,30)

25. $3\dfrac{3}{4} \cdot 2\dfrac{1}{2} \div 3\dfrac{1}{8}$ 3
(26)

26. $3\dfrac{3}{4} \div 2\dfrac{1}{2} \cdot 3\dfrac{1}{8}$ $4\dfrac{11}{16}$
(26)

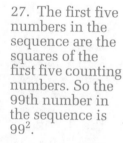

27. The first five numbers in the sequence are the squares of the first five counting numbers. So the 99th number in the sequence is 99^2.

27. Describe how to find the 99th number in this sequence.
(2)

$$1, 4, 9, 16, 25, \dots$$

28. Use a protractor and straight edge to draw a triangle that
(17) has a right angle and a 30° angle. Then measure the shortest and longest sides of the triangle to the nearest millimeter. What is the relationship of the two measurements? See student work. If done accurately, the longest side is twice the length of the shortest side.

29. If the diameter of a wheel is 0.5 meters, then the radius of
(Inv. 2) the wheel is how many centimeters? 25 centimeters

30. Graph the points A (0, 0) and B (4, 2). By inspection, find
(Inv. 3) the point halfway between points A and B. What are the coordinates of this "halfway" point? (2, 1)

LESSON
57

Scientific Notation for Small Numbers

Mental Math:
a. 128
b. 4200
c. 28
d. 0.5 L
e. 100
f. $10.00
g. $2\frac{1}{2}$
Problem Solving:

Facts Practice: Powers and Roots (Test K in Test Masters)

Mental Math:

a. 40×3.2

b. 4.2×10^3

c. $\frac{n}{20} = \frac{7}{5}$

d. Convert 500 mL to L.

e. $15^2 - 5^3$

f. $\frac{2}{5}$ of $25.00

g. Start with the number of pounds in a ton, $\div\ 2$, $-\ 1$, $\div\ 9$, $-\ 11$, $\sqrt{\ }$, $\div\ 2$, $\div\ 2$.

Problem Solving:

Along the road where Jesse lives are telephone poles spaced 100 feet apart. If Jesse runs from the first pole to the seventh pole, how many feet does Jesse run? Draw a picture illustrating the problem.

We have used scientific notation to write large numbers. We may also use scientific notation to write small numbers. When we write a number in scientific notation, the power of 10 indicates the location of the decimal point when the number is written in standard form. If the exponent is a *positive number*, we shift the decimal point *to the right* to express the number in standard form. In the number

$$6.32 \times 10^7$$

the exponent is *positive seven*, so we shift the decimal point seven places *to the right*.

63200000. ⟶ 63,200,000

7 places

If the exponent is a *negative number*, we shift the decimal point *to the left* to write the number in standard form. In the number

$$6.32 \times 10^{-7}$$

the exponent is *negative seven*, so we shift the decimal point seven places *to the left*.

.000000632 ⟶ 0.000000632

7 places

We use zeros as placeholders.

Example 1   Write 4.63×10^{-8} in standard notation.

Solution   The negative exponent indicates that the decimal point is eight places to the left when the number is written in standard form. We shift the decimal point and insert zeros as placeholders.

.0000000463 ⟶ **0.0000000463**

8 places

Example 2   Write 0.0000033 in scientific notation.

Solution   We place the decimal point to the right of the first digit that is not a zero.

0000003.3

6 places

In standard form the decimal point is six places to the left of where we have placed it. So we write

3.3×10^{-6}

Example 3   Compare: zero ◯ 1×10^{-3}

Solution   The expression 1×10^{-3} equals 0.001. Although this number is less than 1, it is still positive, so it is greater than zero.

zero $< 1 \times 10^{-3}$

 Very small numbers may exceed the display capabilities of a calculator. One millionth of one millionth is more than zero, but it is a very small number. On a calculator we enter

| . | 0 | 0 | 0 | 0 | 0 | 1 | × |
| . | 0 | 0 | 0 | 0 | 0 | 1 | = |

The product, one trillionth, contains more digits than can be displayed by many calculators. Instead of displaying one trillionth in standard form, the calculator displays the number in a modified form of scientific notation such as

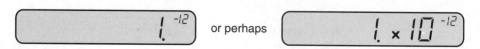

Practice   Write each number in scientific notation.

a. 0.00000025   **b.** 0.000000001   **c.** 0.000105
     2.5 × 10⁻⁷   1 × 10⁻⁹   1.05 × 10⁻⁴

Write each number in standard form.

d. 4.5 × 10⁻⁷   **e.** 1 × 10⁻³   **f.** 1.25 × 10⁻⁵
     0.00000045   0.001   0.0000125

Compare:

g. 1×10^{-3} ⊘ 1×10^{2}

h. 2.5×10^{-2} ⊙ 2.5×10^{-3}

Problem set 57

1. Make a ratio box to solve this problem. The ratio of
(54) walkers to riders was 5 to 3. If 315 were walkers, how
many were riders? 189 riders

2. After five tests Allison's average score was 88. After six
(55) tests her average score had increased to 90. What was her
score on the sixth test? 100

3. When Richard rented a car, he paid $34.95 per day plus
(28) 18¢ per mile. If he rented the car for 2 days and drove 300
miles, how much did he pay? $123.90

4. If lemonade costs $0.52 per quart, then what is the cost
(16) per pint? $0.26 per pint

5.

finished in $\frac{2}{5}$

5. Draw a diagram of this statement. Then answer the
(22) questions that follow.

  Jason finished his math homework in two fifths of
  an hour.

  (a) How many minutes did it take Jason to finish his
  math homework? 24 minutes

  (b) What percent of an hour did it take for Jason to finish
  his math homework? 40%

6. Write each number in scientific notation.
(51,57)
  (a) 186,000 1.86 × 10⁵   (b) 0.00004 4 × 10⁻⁵

7. Write each number in standard form.
(51,57)
  (a) 3.25 × 10¹ 32.5   (b) 1.5 × 10⁻⁶ 0.0000015

8. 2 liters   **8.** Use unit multipliers to convert 2000 milliliters to liters.
(50)

9. Write $\frac{1}{7}$ as a decimal number rounded to five decimal
(43) places.   0.14286

10. What is the probability of rolling a composite number on
(21,36) one toss of a die (number cube)? $\frac{1}{3}$

11. The tickets for two dozen students to enter the
(46) amusement park cost \$330. What was the price per
ticket?   \$13.75

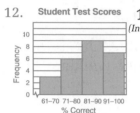

12.

12. This frequency table shows the number of student tests
(Inv. 5) that had scores in four intervals. Sketch a histogram that
illustrates the data in the frequency table.

Student Test Scores

% Correct	Tally	Frequency
91–100	ЖІ ІІ	7
81–90	ЖІ ІІІІ	9
71–80	ЖІ І	6
61–70	ІІІ	3

13. Compare:
(57)

(a) 2.5×10^{-2} ⊜ $2.5 \div 10^2$

(b) one millionth ⊜ 1×10^{-6}

Refer to this figure to answer problems 14 and 15. Dimensions
are in yards. All angles are right angles.

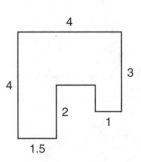

14. What is the perimeter of the figure?   18 yd
(19)

15. What is the area of the figure?   12 yd²
(37)

16. Evaluate $4ac$ if $a = 5$ and $c = 0.5$.   10
(41)

17. Estimate the quotient: $19.89 ÷ 3.987 $5.00
(33)

18. In the following equation, y is 5 more than the product of
(41) 3 and x. Find y when x is 12.   41

$$y = 3x + 5$$

Simplify:

19. $20^2 + 10^3 - \sqrt{36}$ 1394
(20)

20. $48 ÷ 12 ÷ 2 + 2(3)$ 8
(52)

21.   3 yd 2 ft 1 in.
(56) − 1 yd 2 ft 3 in.
   _____
     1 yd   2 ft 10 in.

22.   4 gal 3 qt 1 pt 6 oz
(49) + 1 gal 2 qt 1 pt 5 oz
   _____
     6 gal   2 qt   11 oz

23. $48 \text{ oz} \cdot \dfrac{1 \text{ pt}}{16 \text{ oz}}$ 3 pt
(50)

24. $5\dfrac{1}{3} \cdot \left(7 ÷ 1\dfrac{3}{4}\right)$ $21\dfrac{1}{3}$
(26)

25. $5\dfrac{1}{6} + 3\dfrac{5}{8} + 2\dfrac{7}{12}$ $11\dfrac{3}{8}$
(30)

26. $\dfrac{1}{20} - \dfrac{1}{36}$ $\dfrac{1}{45}$
(30)

27. $\left(4.6 \times 10^{-2}\right) + 0.46$ 0.506
(57)

28. $10 - (2.3 - 0.575)$ 8.275
(35)

29. $0.24 \times 0.15 \times 0.05$ 0.0018
(35)

30. $10 ÷ (0.14 ÷ 70)$ 5000
(45)

LESSON
58

Line Symmetry • Functions, Part 1

Mental Math:
a. 215
b. 0.0042
c. 15
d. 1500 g
e. 10
f. $22.00
g. 1.8, 0.6, 0.72, 2
Problem Solving:

6 handshakes

Facts Practice: Powers and Roots (Test K in Test Masters)

Mental Math:

a. 50×4.3
b. $4.2 ÷ 10^3$
c. $3x - 5 = 40$
d. Convert 1.5 kg to g.
e. $10^3 ÷ 10^2$
f. $\frac{2}{3}$ of $33.00
g. Find the sum, difference, product, and quotient of 1.2 and 0.6.

Problem Solving:

Four friends met at a party and shook one another's hands. How many handshakes were there in all? Draw a diagram to illustrate the problem. (Students may want to act out the story and count the handshakes.)

Line A two dimensional figure has **line symmetry** if it can be
symmetry divided in half so that the halves are mirror images of each
other. Line *r* divides this triangle into two mirror images, so
the triangle is symmetrical, and line *r* is a **line of symmetry.**

Actually, this regular triangle has three lines of symmetry.

Example 1 Sketch a regular quadrilateral and show all lines of
symmetry.

Solution A regular quadrilateral is a square. A square has four lines of
symmetry.

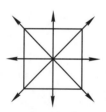

The *y*-axis is a line of symmetry for the figure below.
Notice that corresponding points on the two sides of the
figure are the same distance from the line of symmetry.

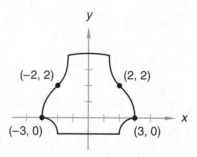

If this figure were folded along the *y*-axis, each point of the
figure on one side of the *y*-axis would be folded against its
corresponding point on the other side of the *y*-axis.

Activity: Line Symmetry

Materials needed:

- Paper and scissors

1. Fold a piece of paper in half.

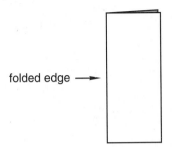

folded edge ⟶

Beginning and ending at the folded edge, cut a pattern out of the folded paper.

Open the cut-out and note its symmetry.

2. Fold a piece of paper twice as shown.

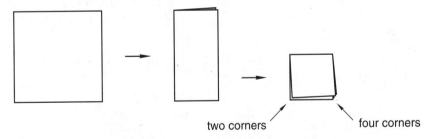

two corners   four corners

Hold the paper on the corner opposite the "four corners" and cut out a pattern that removes the four corners.

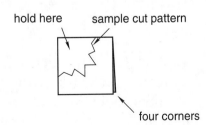

hold here   sample cut pattern

four corners

Unfold the cut-out. How many lines of symmetry do you see?

Functions, part 1 A **function** is a set of number pairs that are related by a certain rule. We will be finding a missing number from a number pair. We study pairs of numbers to determine a rule for the function. Then we use the rule to find the missing number. Note that for a function there is exactly one "out" number for every "in" number.

Example 2 Find the missing number.

```
IN          F          OUT
            U
 3   ───▶   N   ───▶    9
            C
 5   ───▶   T   ───▶   15
            I
 7   ───▶   O   ───▶   □
10   ───▶   N   ───▶   30
```

Solution We study each "in-out" number pair to determine the rule for the function. We see that for each complete pair, if the "in" number is multiplied by 3, it equals the "out" number. Thus the rule of the function is "multiply by 3." We use this rule to find the missing number. We multiply 7 by 3 and find that the missing number is **21.**

Practice **a.** Copy this rectangle on your paper and show its lines of symmetry.

b. The y-axis is a line of symmetry for a triangle. The coordinates of two of its vertices are $(0, 1)$ and $(3, 4)$. What are the coordinates of the third vertex? $(-3, 4)$

Find the missing number in each diagram.

c.
```
IN          F          OUT
            U
 4   ───▶   N   ───▶   20
            C
 3   ───▶   T   ───▶   15
            I
 7   ───▶       ───▶   35
            O
 9   ───▶   N   ───▶   45
```

d.
```
IN          F          OUT
            U
 0   ───▶   N   ───▶    4
            C
 1   ───▶   T   ───▶    5
            I
 3   ───▶       ───▶    7
            O
 5   ───▶   N   ───▶    9
```

Problem set 58 **1.** It is 1.4 kilometers from Jim's house to school. How far
$^{(28,35)}$ does Jim walk going to and from school every day for 5 days? 14 kilometers

2. The parking lot charges 75¢ for each half hour or part of a
$^{(28)}$ half hour. If Edie parks her car in the lot from 10:45 a.m. until 1:05 p.m., how much money will she pay? $3.75

3. If the product of the number N and 17 is 340, what is the
(41) sum of the number N and 17?   37

4. The football team won 3 of their 12 games but lost the rest.
(36)

(a) What was the team's won-lost ratio? $\frac{1}{3}$

(b) What fraction of the games did the team lose? $\frac{3}{4}$

(c) What percent of the games did the team win?   25%

5. Will's bowling average after 5 games was 120. In his next
(55) 3 games Will scored 118, 124, and 142. What was Will's
bowling average after 8 games?   123

6.

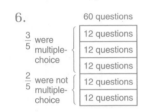

6. Draw a diagram of this statement. Then answer the
(22) questions that follow.

*Three fifths of the 60 questions were multiple-
choice.*

(a) How many of the 60 questions were multiple-choice?
36 questions

(b) What percent of the 60 questions were not multiple-
choice?   40%

7. In this figure, the center of the circle
(Inv. 2) is O and $OB = CB$. Refer to the figure
to answer questions (a)–(d).

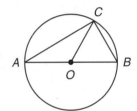

(a) Name three radii. $\overline{OA}, \overline{OB}, \overline{OC}$

(b) Name two chords that are not
diameters. $\overline{AC}, \overline{BC}$

(c) Estimate the measure of central angle BOC.   60°

(d) Estimate the measure of inscribed angle BAC.   30°

8. (a) Write 0.0000001 in scientific notation. 1×10^{-7}
(51,57)

(b) Write 1.5×10^7 in standard form.   15,000,000

9. Compare: 20 qt $\ominus$ 5 gal
(16)

10. Divide 3.45 by 0.18 and write the answer rounded to the
(45) nearest whole number.   19

11. Find the next three numbers in this sequence.
(2)

20, 15, 10, ...   5, 0, −5

12. Complete the table.
(48)

FRACTION	DECIMAL	PERCENT
$\frac{1}{6}$	(a) $0.1\overline{6}$	(b) $16\frac{2}{3}\%$
(c) $\frac{4}{25}$	(d) 0.16	16%

13. Find the missing number.
(58)

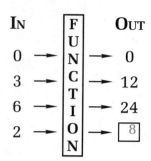

IN → FUNCTION → OUT

0 → 0
3 → 12
6 → 24
2 → 8

14. In this figure, the measure of $\angle D$ is
(40) 35° and the measure of $\angle CAB$ is 35°.
Find the measure of

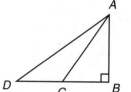

(a) $\angle ACB$. 55°

(b) $\angle ACD$. 125°

(c) $\angle CAD$. 20°

15. The y-axis is a line of symmetry for a triangle. The
(58) coordinates of two of its vertices are (−3, 2) and (0, 5).

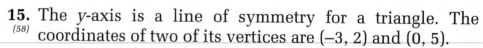

(a) What are the coordinates of the third vertex? (3, 2)

(b) What is the area of the triangle? 9 units²

16. A regular pentagon has how many
(58) lines of symmetry? 5 lines

17. (a) Traveling at 60 miles per hour, how long would it
(53)   take to travel 210 miles? $3\frac{1}{2}$ hours

(b) How long would the same trip take at 70 miles per
     hour? 3 hours

Solve:

18. $\dfrac{1.5}{2} = \dfrac{7.5}{w}$ 10
(39)

19. $1.7 - y = 0.17$ 1.53
(35)

Simplify:

20. $10^3 - 10^2 + 10 - 1$ 909
(20)

21. $6 + 3(2) - 4 - (5 + 3)$ 0
(52)

22.
(49)
$$\begin{array}{r} \text{1 gal 2 qt 1 pt} \\ + \text{ 1 gal 2 qt 1 pt} \\ \hline \text{3 gal   1 qt} \end{array}$$

23.
(56)
$$\begin{array}{r} \text{1 day 3 hr 15 min} \\ - \quad\quad\text{8 hr 30 min} \\ \hline \text{18 hr   45 min} \end{array}$$

24. $2 \text{ mi} \cdot \dfrac{5280 \text{ ft}}{1 \text{ mi}}$ 10,560 ft
(50)

25. $10 - \left(5\dfrac{3}{4} - 1\dfrac{5}{6}\right)$ $6\frac{1}{12}$
(23,30)

26. $\left(2\dfrac{1}{5} + 5\dfrac{1}{2}\right) \div 2\dfrac{1}{5}$ $3\frac{1}{2}$
(26,30)

27. $3\dfrac{3}{4} \cdot \left(6 \div 4\dfrac{1}{2}\right)$ 5
(26)

28. Evaluate: $b^2 - 4ac$ if $a = 3.6$, $b = 6$, and $c = 2.5$ 0
(52)

29. (a) Arrange these numbers in order from **greatest** to **least**.
(4,10)

$$-1, \frac{3}{2}, 2.5, 0, -\frac{1}{2}, 2 \quad 2.5, 2, \tfrac{3}{2}, 0, -\tfrac{1}{2}, -1$$

(b) Which of the numbers in (a) are integers? $-1, 0, 2$

30. Tom could double both numbers before dividing, making the equivalent division problem 70 ÷ 5. He could also double both of these numbers making 140 ÷ 10.

30. Tom had the following division to perform.
(27)

$$35 \div 2\frac{1}{2}$$

Describe how Tom could make an equivalent division problem that would be easier to perform mentally.

LESSON
59

Adding Integers on the Number Line

Facts Practice: Fraction-Decimal-Percent Equivalents
(Test L in Test Masters)

Mental Math:

a. 60×5.4

b. 0.005×10^2

c. $\dfrac{30}{20} = \dfrac{3}{t}$

d. Convert 185 cm to m.

e. $2 \cdot 2^3$

f. $\dfrac{7}{8}$ of $40.00

g. At $7.50 an hour, how much money can Shelly earn in 8 hours?

Problem Solving:

A square and a regular pentagon share a common side. If the perimeter of the pentagon is one meter, what is the area of the square in square centimeters?

Recall that **integers** include all the whole numbers and also the opposites of the positive integers, that is, their negatives. All the numbers in this sequence are integers.

$$..., -3, -2, -1, 0, 1, 2, 3, ...$$

The dots on this number line mark the integers from −5 through +5.

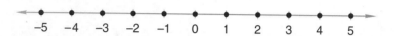

Remember that the numbers between the whole numbers, such as $3\frac{1}{2}$ and 1.3, are not integers.

All numbers on the number line except zero are **signed numbers,** either positive or negative. Zero is neither positive nor negative. Positive and negative numbers have a sign and a value, which is called **absolute value.** The absolute value of a number is its distance from zero.

Numeral	Number	Sign	Absolute Value
+3	Positive three	+	3
−3	Negative three	−	3

The absolute value of both +3 and −3 is 3. Notice on the number line that +3 and −3 are both 3 units from zero. We may use two vertical segments to indicate absolute value.

$$|3| = 3 \qquad\qquad |-3| = 3$$

The absolute value of 3 equals 3.   The absolute value of −3 equals 3.

Example 1 Simplify: $|3 - 5|$

Solution To find the absolute value of 3 − 5, we first subtract 5 from 3 which is −2. Then we find the absolute value of −2 which is **2.**

Absolute value can be represented by distance, whereas the sign can be represented by direction. Thus positive and negative numbers are sometimes called **directed numbers** because the sign of the number (+ or −) can be thought of as indicating direction.

When we add, subtract, multiply, or divide signed numbers we need to pay attention to the signs as well as to the absolute values of the numbers. In this lesson we will practice adding positive and negative numbers.

A number line may be used to illustrate the addition of signed numbers. A positive 3 is indicated by a 3-unit arrow that points to the right. A negative 3 is indicated by a 3-unit arrow that points to the left.

To show the addition of +3 and −3, we begin at zero on the number line and draw the +3 arrow. From this arrowhead we draw the −3 arrow. The sum of +3 and −3 is found at the point on the number line that corresponds to the second arrowhead.

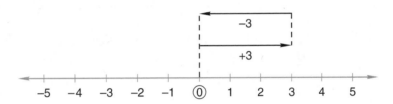

We see that the sum of +3 and −3 is 0. We find the sum of two opposites is always zero.

Example 2 Sketch a number line to show each addition problem.

(a) (−3) + (+5) (b) (−4) + (−2)

Solution (a) We begin at zero and draw an arrow 3 units long that points to the left. From this arrowhead we draw an arrow 5 units long that points to the right. We see that the sum of −3 and +5 is **2.**

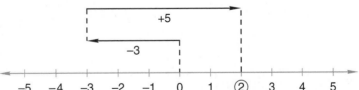

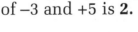

(b) We use arrows to show that the sum of −4 and −2 is **−6.**

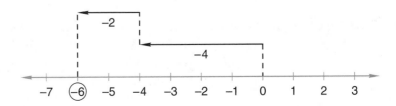

Example 3 Sketch a number line to show this addition problem.

$$(-2) + (+5) + (-4)$$

Solution This time we draw three arrows. We always begin the first arrow at zero. We begin each remaining arrow at the arrowhead of the previous arrow.

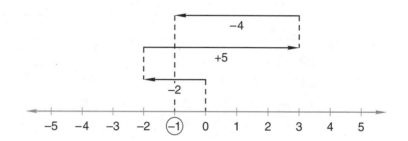

The last arrowhead corresponds to −1 on the number line, so the sum of −2 and +5 and −4 is **−1.**

Practice Sketch a number line to show each addition problem.

a. (−2) + (−3)

b. (+4) + (+2)

c. (−5) + (+2)

d. (+5) + (−2)

e. (−4) + (+4)

f. (−3) + (+6) + (−1)

Simplify:

g. |−3| + |3| 6

h. |3 − 3| 0

i. |5 − 3| 2

Problem set
59

1. School pictures cost $4.25 for an 8 by 10 print. They cost
   (28) $2.35 for a 5 by 7 print, and 60¢ for each wallet-size print.
   What is the total cost of two 5 by 7 prints and six wallet-size prints? $8.30

Refer to this graph to answer problems 2 and 3.

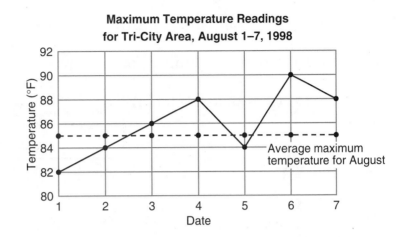

**Maximum Temperature Readings
for Tri-City Area, August 1–7, 1998**

2. The highest temperature reading on August 6, 1998, was
(38) how much greater than the average maximum temperature
for August? 5°F

3. What was the average maximum temperature during the
(28,38) first seven days of August 1998? 86°F

4. The sum of the number n and 12 is 30. What is the
(41) product of n and 12? 216

5. Use a ratio box to solve this problem. The ratio of
(54) sonorous to discordant voices in the crowd was 7 to 4. If
56 voices were discordant, how many voices were
sonorous? 98 sonorous voices

6.

6. Draw a diagram of this statement. Then answer the
(22) questions that follow.

*The Celts won three fourths of their first 20
games.*

(a) How many of their first 20 games did the Celts win?
15 games

(b) What percent of their first 20 games did the Celts fail
to win? 25%

7. Compare: $|-3| \bigcirc |3|$
(59)

8. (a) Write 4,000,000,000,000 in scientific notation. 4×10^{12}
(51)

(b) 3,670,000,000 miles (b) Pluto's average distance from the sun is 3.67×10^9
miles. Write that number in standard form.

9. (a) A micron is 1×10^{-6} meter. Write that number in
(57)   standard form.   0.000001 meter

(b) Compare: 1 millimeter ⊜ 1×10^{-3} meter

10. Use a unit multiplier to convert 300 mm to m.   0.3 m
(50)

11. Complete the table.
(48)

FRACTION	DECIMAL	PERCENT
(a) $\frac{3}{25}$	(b) 0.12	12%
$\frac{1}{3}$	(c) $0.\overline{3}$	(d) $33\frac{1}{3}\%$

12. Sketch a number line to show each addition problem.
(59)

(a)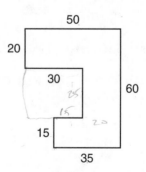

(a) (+2) + (−5)   (b) (−2) + (+5)

(b)

13. Find the missing number.
(58)

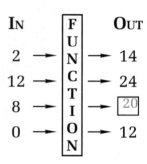

Solve:

14. 4.4 = 8w 0.55
(35)

15. $\dfrac{0.8}{1} = \dfrac{x}{1.5}$ 1.2
(39)

16. $n + \dfrac{11}{20} = \dfrac{17}{30}$ $\frac{1}{60}$
(30)

17. $\dfrac{0.364}{m} = 7$ 0.052
(35)

Refer to this figure to answer problems 18 and 19. Dimensions are in millimeters. All angles are right angles.

18. What is the perimeter of this figure?   250 mm
(19)

19. What is the area of this figure?   2025 mm²
(37)

Simplify:

20. $4 + 5(6) - (7 + 8) - 9$
(52) 10

21. $\sqrt{64} - 2^3 + \sqrt{1}$ 1
(20)

22.
(49)
$$\begin{array}{r} 3 \text{ yd} \quad 2 \text{ ft} \quad 7\frac{1}{2} \text{ in.} \\ + \ 1 \text{ yd} \qquad \quad 5\frac{1}{2} \text{ in.} \\ \hline 5 \text{ yd} \qquad \quad 1 \text{ in.} \end{array}$$

23.
(56)
$$\begin{array}{r} 1 \text{ qt} \quad 1 \text{ pt} \quad 6 \text{ oz} \\ - \qquad \quad 1 \text{ pt} \quad 12 \text{ oz} \\ \hline 1 \text{ pt} \quad 10 \text{ oz} \end{array}$$

24. $2\frac{1}{2} \text{ hr} \cdot \dfrac{50 \text{ mi}}{1 \text{ hr}}$ 125 mi
(53)

25. $\left(\dfrac{5}{9} \cdot 12 \right) \div 6\dfrac{2}{3}$ 1
(26)

26. $3\dfrac{5}{6} - \left(4 - 1\dfrac{1}{9} \right)$ $\frac{17}{18}$
(23,30)

27. $\left(5\dfrac{5}{8} + 6\dfrac{1}{4} \right) \div 6\dfrac{1}{4}$ $1\frac{9}{10}$
(26,30)

28. Evaluate: $a - bc$ if $a = 0.1$, $b = 0.2$, and $c = 0.3$
(52) 0.04

29. Find the tax on an $18.00 purchase when the sales tax
(46) rate is 6.5%. $1.17

30. This table shows the results of a class election. If one
(36) student who voted is selected at random, what is the
probability that the student voted for the candidate who
received the most votes? $\frac{2}{5}$

Vote Tally

Candidate	Votes
Vasquez	||||| ||
Lam	||||| |||||
Enzinwa	||||| |||

**LESSON
60**

Fractional Part of a Number, Part 1 • Percent of a Number

Facts Practice: Metric Conversions (Test M in Test Masters)

Mental Math:

  a. 70×2.3

b. $435 \div 10^2$

  c. $5x - 1 = 49$

d. Convert 75 mm to cm.

  e. $\sqrt{144} - \sqrt{25}$

f. $\frac{4}{5}$ of $1.00

  g. Start with 25¢, double it, double it, double it, × 5, add $20, ÷ 10, ÷ 10.

Problem Solving:

Copy this problem and fill in the missing digits.

$$\begin{array}{r} \_\_\_ \\ \times \qquad \_ \\ \hline 1101 \end{array}$$

Fractional part of a number, part 1   We can solve fractional-part-of-a-number problems by translating the question into an equation. Then we solve the equation. To translate,

we replace **is** with =

we replace **of** with ×

Example 1   What number is 0.6 of 31?

Solution   This problem uses a decimal number to ask the question. We will use W_N to represent *what number*. We will translate *is* by writing an equals sign. We will translate *of* by writing a multiplication symbol.

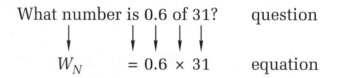

$$W_N = 0.6 \times 31 \qquad \text{equation}$$

To find the answer, we multiply.

$$W_N = \mathbf{18.6} \qquad \text{multiplied}$$

Example 2   Three fifths of 120 is what number?

Solution   This time the question is phrased by using a common fraction. The procedure is the same. We translate directly.

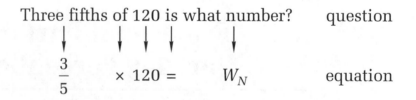

$$\frac{3}{5} \times 120 = W_N \qquad \text{equation}$$

To find the answer, we multiply.

$$W_N = \mathbf{72}$$

Percent of a number   We can translate percent problems into equations the same way we translate fractional-part-of-a-number problems. We convert the percent to either a fraction or a decimal.

Example 3   The jacket sold for $75. Forty percent of the selling price was profit. How much money is 40% of $75?

Solution We translate the question into an equation. We may convert the percent to a fraction or to a decimal. We show both ways.

PERCENT TO FRACTION | PERCENT TO DECIMAL

$$W_N = \frac{40}{100} \times \$75 \qquad\qquad W_N = 0.40 \times \$75$$

$$W_N = \frac{2}{5} \times \$75 \qquad\qquad W_N = 0.4 \times \$75$$

$$W_N = \mathbf{\$30} \qquad\qquad\qquad W_N = \mathbf{\$30}$$

Example 4 A certain used-car salesperson receives a commission of 8% of the selling price of a car. If the salesperson sells a car for $3600, how much is the salesperson's commission?

Solution We want to find 8% of $3600. This time we convert the percent to a decimal.

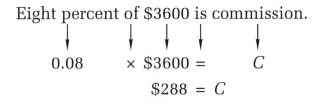

Eight percent of $3600 is commission.

$$0.08 \quad \times \$3600 = \quad C$$

$$\$288 = C$$

The salesperson's commission is **$288.**

Example 5 What number is 25% of 88?

Solution This time we convert the percent to a fraction.

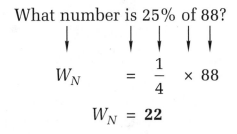

What number is 25% of 88?

$$W_N = \frac{1}{4} \times 88$$

$$W_N = \mathbf{22}$$

Whether a percent should be changed to a fraction or to a decimal is up to the person solving the problem. Often one form makes the problem easier to solve than the other form. With practice the choice of which form to use becomes more apparent.

Practice*   Write equations to solve each problem.

a. What number is $\frac{4}{5}$ of 71? $W_N = \frac{4}{5} \times 71$; $56\frac{4}{5}$

b. Three eighths of $3\frac{3}{7}$ is what number? $\frac{3}{8} \times 3\frac{3}{7} = W_N$; $1\frac{2}{7}$

c. What number is 0.6 of 145? $W_N = 0.6 \times 145$; 87

d. Seventy-five hundredths of 14.4 is what number?
$0.75 \times 14.4 = W_N$; 10.8

e. What number is 50% of 150? $W_N = 0.5 \times 150$; 75

f. Three percent of $39 is how much money?
$0.03 \times \$39 = M$; $1.17

g. What number is 25% of 64? $W_N = 0.25 \times 64$; 16

**Problem set
60**

1. Five and seven hundred eighty-four thousandths is how
$^{(31,35)}$ much less than seven and twenty-one ten thousandths?
1.2181

2. Cynthia was paid 20¢ per board for painting the fence. If
$^{(28)}$ she was paid $10 for painting half the boards, how many
boards were there in all?   100 boards

3. When 72 is divided by n, the quotient is 12. What is the
$^{(41)}$ product when 72 is multiplied by n?   432

4. Four fifths of the students passed the test.
$^{(36)}$

(a) What percent of the students did not pass the test?   20%

(b) What was the ratio of students who passed to students
who did not pass? $\frac{4}{1}$

5. The average height of the five players on the basketball
$^{(55)}$ team was 77 inches. One of the players was 71 inches
tall. Another was 74 inches tall, and two were each 78
inches tall. How tall was the tallest player on the team?
84 inches

6. Write each number in scientific notation.
$^{(51,57)}$

(a) 0.00000008 8×10^{-8} (b) 67.5 billion 6.75×10^{10}

7.

7. Draw a diagram of this statement. Then answer the questions (22,48) that follow.

Two thirds of the 96 members approved of the plan.

(a) How many of the 96 members approved of the plan?
64 members

(b) What percent of the members did not approve of the plan? $33\frac{1}{3}\%$

Write equations to solve problems 8–10.

8. What number is $\frac{3}{4}$ of 17? $W_N = \frac{3}{4} \times 17;\ 12\frac{3}{4}$
(60)

9. What number is 0.7 of 6.5? $W_N = 0.7 \times 6.5;\ 4.55$
(60)

10. If 40% of the selling price of a $65 sweater is profit, then (60) how many dollars profit does the store make when the sweater is sold? $0.4 \times \$65 = P;\ \$26$

11. Compare:
(43,59)

(a) $\dfrac{1}{3}$ $\bigcirc\!\!>$ 0.33

(b) $|5 - 3|$ $\bigcirc\!\!=$ $|3 - 5|$

12. Complete the table.
(48)

Fraction	Decimal	Percent
$\frac{1}{8}$	(a) 0.125	(b) $12\frac{1}{2}\%$
(c) $1\frac{1}{4}$	(d) 1.25	125%

13.(a)
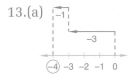

(b)
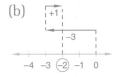

13. Sketch a number line to illustrate the addition of these (59) integers.

(a) $(-3) + (-1)$ (b) $(-3) + (+1)$

14. (a) Write the prime factorization of 3600 using exponents.
(21) $3600 = 2^4 \cdot 3^2 \cdot 5^2$

(b) Write the prime factorization of $\sqrt{3600}$.
$\sqrt{3600} = 60 = 2^2 \cdot 3 \cdot 5$

Solve:

15. $p - \dfrac{1}{30} = \dfrac{1}{20}$ $\frac{1}{12}$
(30)

16. $9m = 0.117$ 0.013
(35)

17. Find the number of degrees in the
(Inv. 5) central angle of each sector of this
circle. (a) 180° (b) 120° (c) 60°

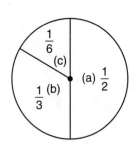

Refer to this figure to answer problems 18–20. Dimensions
between labeled points are in feet. The measure of ∠EDF
equals the measure of ∠ECA.

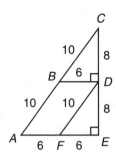

18. (a) Name a triangle congruent to triangle *DEF*. △CDB
(18)

    (b) Name a triangle similar to △*DEF*, but not congruent to
△*DEF*. △CEA

19. (a) Find the area of △*BCD*. 24 ft²
(37)

    (b) Find the area of △*ACE*. 96 ft²

20. By subtracting the areas of the two smaller triangles from
(37) the area of the large triangle, find the area of the
quadrilateral *ABDF*. 48 ft²

Simplify:

21. $3^2 + 4(3 + 2) - 8 \div 4 + \sqrt{36}$ 33
(52)

22.   3 days 16 hr 48 min
(49) + 1 day   15 hr 54 min
      5 days   8 hr   42 min

23. $19\frac{3}{4} + 27\frac{7}{8} + 24\frac{5}{6}$ $72\frac{11}{24}$
(30)

24. $3\frac{3}{5} - \left(\frac{5}{6} \cdot 4\right)$ $\frac{4}{15}$
(30)

25. $\left(1\frac{1}{4} \div \frac{5}{12}\right) \div 24$
(26)
    $\frac{1}{8}$ or 0.125

26. $6.5 - (0.65 - 0.065)$
(35) 5.915

27. $0.3 \div (3 \div 0.03)$ 0.003
(45)

28. Convert 3.5 centimeters to meters using a unit multiplier.
(50) (1 m = 100 cm) 0.035 m

29. The first division problem (27,45) can be multiplied by $\frac{100}{100}$ to form the second division problem. Since $\frac{100}{100}$ equals 1, the quotients are the same.

29. Explain why these two division problems are equivalent. Then give a money example of the two divisions.

$$\frac{1.5}{0.25} = \frac{150}{25} \qquad \frac{\$1.50}{\$0.25} = \frac{150¢}{25¢}$$

30. The x-axis is a line of symmetry for $\triangle ABC$. The (58) coordinates of A are (3, 0), and the coordinates of B are (0, –2). Find the coordinates of point C. (0, 2)

INVESTIGATION 6

Classifying Quadrilaterals

Recall from Lesson 18 that a four-sided polygon is a quadrilateral. Refer to these quadrilaterals to answer the questions that follow.

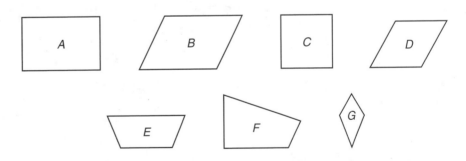

1. Which figures have four right angles? A, C

2. Which figures have four sides of equal length? C, D

3. Which figures have two pairs of parallel sides? A, B, C, D

4. Which figure has just one pair of parallel sides? E

5. Which figures have no pairs of parallel sides? F, G

6. A, B, C, D, G **6.** Which figures have two pairs of equal-length sides?

As we consider the characteristics of various quadrilaterals, we can sort them by their characteristics. One way to sort is by noting the number of parallel sides. A quadrilateral with two pairs of parallel sides is a **parallelogram.** Here we show four parallelograms.

7. Which of the figures *A–G* are parallelograms?   *A, B, C, D*

A quadrilateral with just one pair of parallel sides is a **trapezoid.** These figures are trapezoids. Can you find the parallel sides? (Notice that the parallel sides are not the same length.)

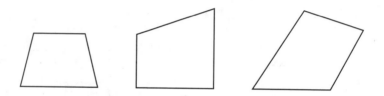

8. Which of the figures *A–G* is a trapezoid?   *E*

A quadrilateral with no pairs of parallel sides is a **trapezium.** Here we show two examples.

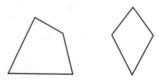

9. Which of the figures *A–G* are trapeziums?   *F, G*

We may sort quadrilaterals by the lengths of their sides. If the four sides are the same length, the quadrilaterals are **equilateral.** An equilateral quadrilateral is a **rhombus.** A rhombus is a type of parallelogram. Here we show two examples.

10. Which of the figures *A–G* are rhombuses?   *C, D*

We may sort quadrilaterals by the measures of their angles. If the four angles are of equal measure, then each angle is a right angle and the quadrilateral is a **rectangle.** A rectangle is a type of parallelogram.

11. Which of the figures *A–G* are rectangles? *A, C*

Notice that a square is both a rectangle and a rhombus. A square is also a parallelogram. We may use a **Venn diagram** to illustrate the relationships.

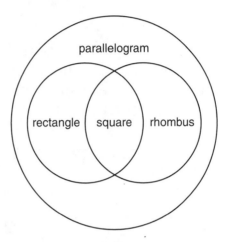

Any figure that is within the circle labeled "rectangle" is a parallelogram as well. Any figure within the circle labeled "rhombus" is also a parallelogram. A figure within both the rectangle and rhombus circles is a square.

12.
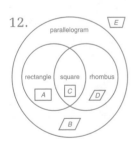

12. Copy the Venn diagram above on your paper. Then refer to quadrilaterals *A*, *B*, *C*, *D*, and *E* at the beginning of this investigation. Draw each of the quadrilaterals in the Venn diagram in the proper location. (One of the figures will be outside of the parallelogram category.)

A student made a model of a rectangle out of straws and pipe cleaners (Figure J). Then the student shifted the sides so that two angles became obtuse and two angles became acute (Figure K).

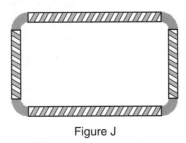

Figure J

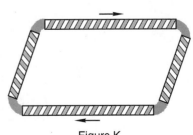

Figure K

Refer to figures J and K to answer questions 13–16.

13. Is Figure K a rectangle? Figure K does not have four right angles so it is not a rectangle.

14. Is Figure K a parallelogram? Figure K has two pairs of parallel sides so it is a parallelogram.

15. Does the perimeter of Figure K equal the perimeter of Figure J? The lengths of the sides were not changed so the perimeters of both figures are the same.

16.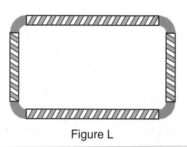
The area of Figure K is less than the area of Figure J. The area becomes less and less the more the sides are shifted.

16. Does the area of Figure K equal the area of Figure J?

Another student made a model of a rectangle out of straws and pipe cleaners (Figure L). Then the student reversed the positions of two of the straws so that the straws that were the same length were adjacent to each other instead of opposite each other (Figure M).

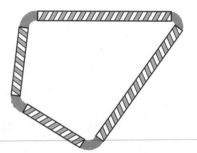

Figure L

Figure M

Figure M does not have a pair of parallel sides so it is a trapezium, but it is a special type of trapezium called a **kite.**

17. Which of the figures *A–G* is a kite? G

18. If two sides of a kite are 2 ft and 3 ft, what is the perimeter of the kite? 10 ft

Notice that a kite has a line of symmetry.

19. Sketch a kite and show its line of symmetry.

20. Sketch a rhombus that is not a square and show its lines of symmetry.

21. Sketch a rectangle that is not a square and show its lines of symmetry.

22. Sketch a rhombus that is a rectangle. Show its lines of symmetry.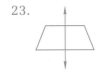

23.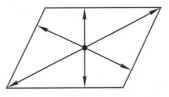

23. Not every trapezoid has a line of symmetry. An **isosceles trapezoid** does have a line of symmetry. The non-parallel sides of an isosceles trapezoid are the same length. Sketch an isosceles trapezoid and show its line of symmetry.

A parallelogram that is not a rhombus or rectangle does not have line symmetry. However, every parallelogram does have **point symmetry.** A figure is symmetrical about a point if every line drawn through the point intersects the figure at points that are equal distances from the point of symmetry.

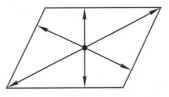

We can locate the point of symmetry of a parallelogram by finding the point where the diagonals of the parallelogram intersect. A **diagonal** of a polygon is a segment between non-consecutive vertices.

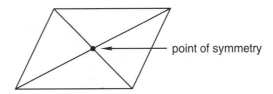

point of symmetry

In the following question we learn a way to test for point symmetry.

24. Draw two or three parallelograms on grid paper. Be sure that one of the parallelograms is a rectangle and one is not a rectangle. Locate and mark the point in each parallelogram where the diagonals intersect. Then carefully cut out the parallelograms. If we rotate a figure with point symmetry a half turn (180°) about its point of symmetry, the figure will appear to be in the same position it was in before it was rotated. Place the point of a pencil on one of the cut-out parallelograms where the diagonals intersect and rotate the parallelogram 180°. Is the point of intersection a point of symmetry? See student work. Yes.

Repeat the rotation with the other parallelogram(s) you cut out.

25. Which of the figures *A–G* have point symmetry? *A, B, C, D*

Here we have named figures illustrated at the beginning of the lesson. You may want to refer to these figures to answer the following problems.

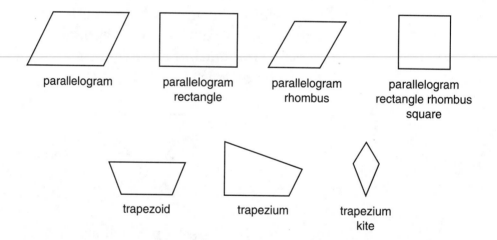

parallelogram

parallelogram
rectangle

parallelogram
rhombus

parallelogram
rectangle rhombus
square

trapezoid

trapezium

trapezium
kite

28. False. All squares have two pairs of parallel sides, and trapezoids have only one pair of parallel sides.

30. True. A quadrilateral is a trapezoid if and only if it has one pair of parallel sides. No quadrilateral is both a trapezoid and a parallelogram.

Answer true or false and state your reason(s) for your answer.

26. A square is a rectangle.
True. A square is a parallelogram with four right angles.

27. All rectangles are parallelograms.
True. All rectangles have two pairs of parallel sides.

28. Some squares are trapezoids.

29. Some parallelograms are rectangles.
True. Some parallelograms have four right angles.

30. No trapezoid is a parallelogram.

LESSON
61

Area of a Parallelogram •
Angles of a Parallelogram

Facts Practice: Fraction-Decimal-Percent Equivalents
(Test L in Test Masters)

Mental Math:

a. 50×4.6

b. 2.4×10^{-1}

c. $\frac{a}{20} = \frac{12}{8}$

d. Convert 1.5 km to m.

e. $3^2 - 2^3$

f. $\frac{7}{10}$ of $3.00

g. What is the total cost of a $20 item plus 6% sales tax?

Problem Solving:

 The first nine perfect squares are less than 100. Altogether, how many perfect squares are less than 1000?

Area of a parallelogram

Recall from Investigation 6 that a parallelogram is a quadrilateral in which both pairs of opposite sides are parallel.

Parallelogram   Parallelogram   Not a
                                                         parallelogram

In this lesson we will practice finding the areas of parallelograms. We may use a paper parallelogram and scissors to help us understand the concept.

Activity 1: Area of a Parallelogram

Cut a piece of paper to form a parallelogram as shown. You may use graph paper if available.

 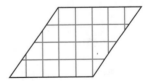

Next, sketch a segment perpendicular to two of the parallel sides of the parallelogram. Cut the parallelogram into two pieces along the segment you drew.

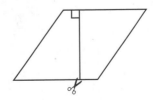

Finally, reverse the positions of the two pieces and fit them together to form a rectangle. The area of the original parallelogram equals the area of this rectangle.

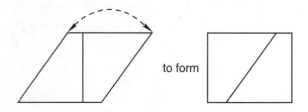

to form

The dimensions of a rectangle are often called the length and the width. When describing a parallelogram we do not use the words "length" and "width." Instead we use the words **base** and **height.**

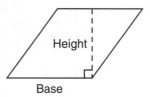

Height

Base

Notice that the height is not one of the sides of the parallelogram (unless the parallelogram is a rectangle). Instead, **the height is perpendicular to the base.** Multiplying the base and height gives us the area of a rectangle. However, as we saw in Activity 1, the area of the rectangle equals the area of the parallelogram we are considering. Thus, we find the area of a parallelogram by multiplying its base and height.

> **Area of a parallelogram = base · height**

Example 1   Find (a) the perimeter and (b) the area of this parallelogram. Dimensions are in inches.

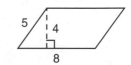

Solution   (a) We find the perimeter by adding the lengths of the sides. The opposite sides of a parallelogram are equal in length. So the perimeter is

5 in. + 8 in. + 5 in. + 8 in. = **26 in.**

(b) We find the area of a parallelogram by multiplying the base and the height. The base is 8 in. and the height is 4 in. So the area is

(8 in.)(4 in.) = **32 in.^{2}**

Angles of a parallelogram Figures J and K of Investigation 6 illustrated a "straw" rectangle shifted to form a parallelogram that was not a rectangle. Two of the angles became obtuse angles, and the other two angles became acute angles.

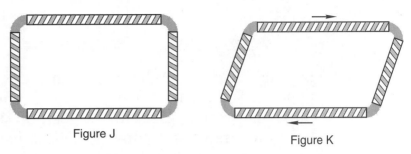

Figure J   Figure K

In other words, two of the angles became more than 90°, and two of the angles became less than 90°. Each angle became greater than or less than 90° *by the same amount*. If, by shifting the sides of the "straw" rectangle, the obtuse angles became 10° greater than 90° (so that they became 100° angles), then the acute angles became 10° *less than* 90° (so that they became 80° angles). The following activity illustrates this relationship.

Activity 2: Angles of a Parallelogram

Materials needed:
- Each pair or small group of students needs a protractor, plain paper, two pairs of plastic straws, thread or lightweight string, and perhaps a paper clip for threading the straws. (The straws within a pair need to be the same length. The two pairs may be different lengths.)

Make a "straw" parallelogram by running a string or thread through two pairs of plastic straws. If the pairs of straws are of different lengths, alternate the lengths as you thread them (long-short-long-short).

Bring the two ends of the string or thread together, loop the string a couple of times, pull until the string is snug but not bowing the straws, and tie a knot.

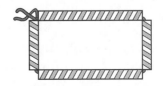

You should be able to shift the sides of the parallelogram to various positions.

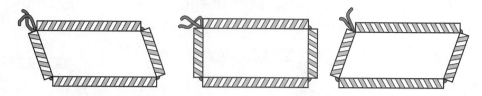

Lay the "straw" parallelogram on a desktop with a piece of paper under it. On the paper you will trace the parallelogram. Shift the parallelogram into a position you want to measure, hold the straws and paper still (this may require more than two hands) and carefully trace with a pencil around the *inside* of the parallelogram.

Set the "straw" parallelogram aside and use a protractor to measure each angle of the traced parallelogram. Write the measure inside each angle. Some groups may wish to trace and measure the angles of a second parallelogram with a different shape before answering the following questions:

1. What were the measures of the two obtuse angles of one parallelogram?

2. What were the measures of the two acute angles of the same parallelogram?

3. What was the sum of the measures of one obtuse angle and one acute angle of the same parallelogram?

(If you traced two parallelograms, answer the three questions again for the second parallelogram.)

Record several groups' answers on the board. Can any general conclusions be formed?

The quality of all types of measurement is affected by the quality of the measuring instrument, the material being measured, and the person performing the measurement. However, even rough measurements can suggest underlying relationships. The rough measurements performed in Activity 2 should suggest these relationships between the angles of a parallelogram.

1. Non-adjacent angles (angles "across" the parallelogram from each other) have equal measures.
2. Adjacent angles (angles that share a common side) are supplementary—that is, their sum is 180°.

Example 2 In parallelogram *ABCD*, m∠*D*† is 110°. Find the measures of angles *A*, *B*, and *C* in the parallelogram.

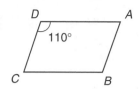

Solution The two obtuse angles have equal measures, so **m∠*B* = 110°**. Adjacent angles are supplementary, so **m∠*A* = 70°** and **m∠*C* = 70°**.

Practice Find the perimeter and area of each parallelogram. Dimensions are in centimeters.

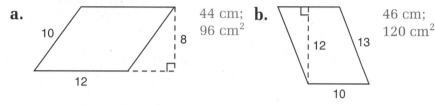

a. 44 cm; 96 cm²

b. 46 cm; 120 cm²

c. 40 cm; 90 cm²

For problems **d.–g.**, find the measures of the angles marked *d*, *e*, *f*, and *g* in this parallelogram. d. 105° e. 75° f. 105° g. 75°

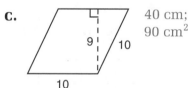

Figure *ABCD* is a parallelogram. Refer to this figure to find the measures of the following angles.

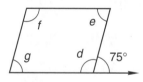

h. ∠*A* 60°   **i.** ∠*ADB* 30°   **j.** ∠*ABC* 120°

Problem set 61

1. If ½ gallon of milk costs $1.12, what is the cost per pint?
(16,46) $0.28 per pint

2. Use a ratio box to solve this problem. The cookie recipe
(54) called for oatmeal and brown sugar in the ratio of 2 to 1. If 3 cups of oatmeal were called for, how many cups of brown sugar were needed? 1½ cups

---

†The abbreviation m∠*D* is read, "the measure of angle *D*."

3. Matt ran the 400-meter race 3 times. His fastest time was
(55) 54.3 seconds. His slowest time was 56.1 seconds. If his
average time was 55.0 seconds, what was his time for the
third race? 54.6 seconds

4. It is $4\frac{1}{2}$ miles to the end of the trail. If Paula runs to the
(46) end of the trail and back in 60 minutes, what is her
average speed in miles per hour? 9 miles per hour

5. Sixty-three million, one hundred thousand is how much
(51) greater than seven million, sixty thousand? Write the
answer in scientific notation. 5.604×10^7

6. Only three tenths of the print area of the newspaper
(36,48) carried news. The rest of the area was filled with
advertisements.

(a) What percent of the print area was filled with
advertisements? 70%

(b) What was the ratio of news area to advertisement
area? $\frac{3}{7}$

(c) If, without looking, Patty opens the newspaper and
places a finger on the page, what is the probability
that her finger will be on an advertisement? $\frac{7}{10}$

7. (a) Write 0.00105 in scientific notation. 1.05×10^{-3}
(51,57)
(b) Write 3.02×10^5 in standard form. 302,000

8. Use prime factorization to reduce $\frac{128}{192}$. $\frac{2}{3}$
(24)

9. Use a unit multiplier to convert 1760 yards to feet.
(50) 5280 feet

Quadrilateral *ABDE* is a rectangle and $\overline{EC} \parallel \overline{FB}$. Refer to this
figure to answer problems 10, 11, and 12.

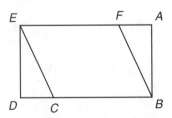

10. Classify each of the following quadrilaterals:
(Inv. 6)
(a) *ECBF* parallelogram

(b) *ECBA* trapezoid

11. In the figure on the previous page, $AB = ED = 4$ cm,
(37,61) $BC = EF = 6$ cm, and $BD = AE = 8$ cm.

(a) What is the area of quadrilateral $BCEF$? 24 cm²

(b) What is the area of triangle ABF? 4 cm²

(c) What is the area of quadrilateral $ECBA$? 28 cm²

12. Classify each of the following angles as acute, right, or
(7) obtuse:

(a) $\angle ECB$ (b) $\angle EDC$ (c) $\angle FBA$
    obtuse angle   right angle   acute angle

13.(a) 8   **13.** Following is an ordered list of the number of correct
(b) 6 (Inv. 4) answers on a ten-question quiz taken by 19 students.
(c) 9   Find (a) the median, (b) the first quartile, and (c) the third
(d) 2   quartile of these scores. (d) Identify any outliers.

2, 5, 5, 6, 6, 6, 7, 7, 7, 8, 8, 8, 8, 9, 9, 10, 10, 10, 10

14. Refer to this parallelogram to answer questions (a)–(c).
(Inv. 6,61)

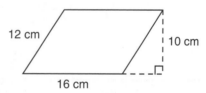

(a) What is the perimeter of this parallelogram? 56 cm

(b) What is the area of this parallelogram? 160 cm²

(c) Trace the parallelogram on your paper and locate its
    point of symmetry.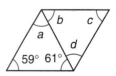

15. This parallelogram is divided by a
(40,61) diagonal into two congruent triangles.
Find the measure of

(a) $\angle a$. 60°   (b) $\angle b$. 61°   (c) $\angle c$. 59°   (d) $\angle d$. 60°

16. Tara noticed that the tape she was using to wrap packages
(50) was 2 cm wide. How many meters wide was the tape?
0.02 m

17. A circle is drawn on rectangular coordinates with its
(Inv. 3) center on the origin. The circle intersects the x-axis at
(5, 0) and (−5, 0).

(a) At what coordinates does the circle intersect the y-axis?
    (0, 5), (0, −5)

(b) What is the diameter of the circle? 10 units

18. The scale is balanced so the 3 items on the left have a total mass of 50 g. The labeled masses total 15 g, so the cube must be 35 g because 35 g + 15 g = 50 g.

18. On one tray of a balanced scale was a (3) 50-g mass. On the other tray was a small cube, a 10-g mass, and a 5-g mass. What was the mass of the small cube? Describe how you found your answer.

Simplify:

19. $10 + 10 \times 10 - 10 \div 10$ 109
(52)

20. $10^4 - \sqrt{9^2} + 2^3$ 9999
$(20,52)$

21.
(49)
$$\begin{array}{r} 3 \text{ gal } 3 \text{ qt } 1 \text{ pt } 9 \text{ oz} \\ + \qquad\qquad\qquad 7 \text{ oz} \\ \hline 4 \text{ gal} \end{array}$$

22.
(56)
$$\begin{array}{r} 3 \text{ yd} \\ - 1 \text{ yd } 2 \text{ ft } 7 \text{ in.} \\ \hline 1 \text{ yd} \qquad 5 \text{ in.} \end{array}$$

23. $2.75 \text{ L} \cdot \dfrac{1000 \text{ mL}}{1 \text{ L}}$
(50) 2750 mL

24. $5\dfrac{7}{8} + \left(3\dfrac{1}{3} - 1\dfrac{1}{2}\right)$ $7\dfrac{17}{24}$
$(23,30)$

25. $4\dfrac{4}{5} \cdot 1\dfrac{1}{9} \cdot 1\dfrac{7}{8}$ 10
(26)

26. $6\dfrac{2}{3} \div \left(3\dfrac{1}{5} \div 8\right)$ $16\dfrac{2}{3}$
(26)

27. $12 - (0.8 + 0.97)$ 10.23
(35)

28. $(2.4)(0.05)(0.005)$ 0.0006
(35)

29. $0.2 \div \left(4 \times 10^2\right)$ 0.0005
(47)

30. $0.36 \div (4 \div 0.25)$ 0.0225
(45)

LESSON 62

Classifying Triangles

Facts Practice: Metric Conversions (Test M in Test Masters)

Mental Math:
a. 43
b. 0.025
c. 3
d. 2.5 kg
e. 1
f. $16.00
g. 0

Problem Solving:
After Alice, 128 m remain. If the pattern continues, the baton will get closer to but will not cross the finish line.

Mental Math:

a. 5×8.6

b. 2.5×10^{-2}

c. $10x + 2 = 32$

d. Convert 2500 g to kg.

e. $10^3 \div 10^3$

f. $\frac{2}{3}$ of $24.00

g. 8^2, $- 4$, $\div 2$, $\times 3$, $+ 10$, $\sqrt{\ }$, $\times 2$, $+ 5$, $\sqrt{\ }$, $- 4$, square that number, $- 1$

Problem Solving:

Marsha started the 1024-m race and ran half the distance to the finish line and handed the baton to Greg. Greg ran half the remaining distance and handed off to Alice, who ran half the remaining distance. How far from the finish line did Alice stop? If the team continues this pattern, how many more runners will they need in order to cross the finish line?

Recall from Lesson 7 that we classify angles as acute angles, right angles, and obtuse angles.

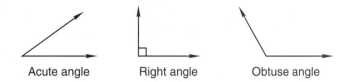

Acute angle   Right angle   Obtuse angle

We use the same words to describe triangles that contain these angles. If every angle of a triangle measures less than 90°, the triangle is an **acute triangle.** If the triangle contains a 90° angle, then the triangle is a **right triangle.** An **obtuse triangle** contains one angle that measures more than 90°.

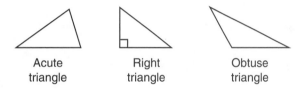

Acute   Right   Obtuse
triangle   triangle   triangle

When describing triangles we may refer to the sides and angles as "opposite" each other. For example, we might say, "The side opposite the right angle is the longest side of a right triangle." The side opposite an angle is the side "on the other side of" the triangle. In this right triangle, $\overline{AB}$ is the side opposite $\angle C$, and $\angle C$ is the angle opposite side AB.

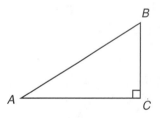

Each angle of a triangle has a side that is opposite that angle. The lengths of the sides of a triangle are in the same order as the measures of their opposite angles. This means that the longest side of a triangle is opposite the largest angle, and the shortest side is opposite the smallest angle.

Example 1 Name the sides of this triangle in order from shortest to longest.

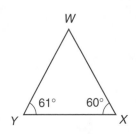

Solution   First we note the measures of all three angles. The sum of their measures is 180°, so the measure of ∠W is 59°. Since ∠W is the smallest of the three angles, the side opposite ∠W, which is $\overline{XY}$, is the shortest side. The next angle in order of size is ∠X, so $\overline{YW}$ is the next longer side. The largest angle is ∠Y, so $\overline{WX}$ is the longest side.

$$\overline{XY}, \overline{YW}, \overline{WX}$$

If two angles of a triangle are the same measure, then their opposite sides are the same length.

Example 2   Which sides of this triangle are the same length?

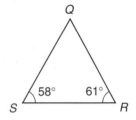

Solution   First we find that the measure of ∠Q is 61°. So angles Q and R have the same measure. This means that their opposite sides are the same length. The side opposite ∠Q is $\overline{SR}$. The side opposite ∠R is $\overline{SQ}$. So the sides that are the same length are $\overline{SR}$ and $\overline{SQ}$.

If all three angles of a triangle are the same measure, then all three sides are the same length.

Example 3   In ΔJKL, JK = KL = LJ. Find the measure of ∠J.

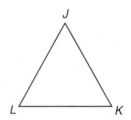

Solution   If two or more sides of a triangle are the same length, then the angles opposite those sides are equal in measure. In ΔJKL, all three sides are the same length, so all three angles are the same measure. The angles equally share 180°. We find the measure of each angle by dividing 180° by 3.

$$180° ÷ 3 = 60°$$

We find that the measure of ∠J is **60°**.

The triangle in Example 3 is a regular triangle. We usually call a regular triangle an **equilateral triangle.** The three angles of an equilateral triangle each measure 60°, and the three sides are the same length.

If a triangle has at least two sides of the same length (and thus two angles of the same measure), the triangle is called an **isosceles triangle.** The triangle in Example 2 is an isosceles triangle as are each of these triangles.

 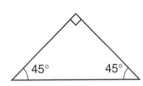 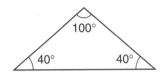

If the three sides of a triangle are all different lengths and the angles are all different measures, then the triangle is called a **scalene triangle.** Here we show a scalene triangle, an isosceles triangle, and an equilateral triangle. The tick marks on the sides indicate sides of equal length, while tick marks on the arcs indicate angles of equal measure.

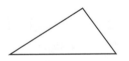 **Scalene** triangles have three sides that are all different lengths.

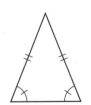 **Isosceles** triangles have at least two sides that are the same length.

 Equilateral triangles have three sides that are the same length. Equilateral triangles are **regular triangles.**

Example 4   The perimeter of an equilateral triangle is 2 feet. How many inches long is each side?

Solution   All three sides of an equilateral triangle are equal in length. Since 2 feet equals 24 inches, we divide 24 inches by 3 and find that the length of each side is **8 inches.**

Example 5   Sketch an isosceles right triangle.

Solution   "Isosceles" means the triangle has at least two sides that are the same length. "Right" means the triangle contains a right angle. We sketch a right angle, making both segments equal in length. Then we complete the triangle.

Practice   Classify each triangle by its angles.

a.

right triangle

b.
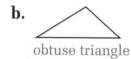
obtuse triangle

c.

acute triangle

Classify each triangle by its sides.

d.

3   4
5
scalene triangle

e.
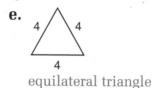
4   4
4
equilateral triangle

f.
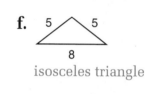
5   5
8
isosceles triangle

g. If we know that two sides of an isosceles triangle are 3 cm and 4 cm and that its perimeter is not 10 cm, then what is its perimeter? 11 cm

h. Name the angles of this triangle in order from the smallest to largest.
$\angle L$, $\angle N$, $\angle M$

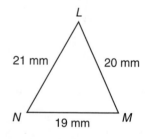

Problem set 62

1. At 1:30 p.m., David found a parking meter that still had
(28) 10 minutes until it expired. He put 2 dimes into the meter and went to his meeting. If 5 cents buys 15 minutes of parking time, at what time will the meter expire? 2:40 p.m.

Use the information in the following paragraph to answer problems 2 and 3.

The Barkers started their trip with a full tank of gas and a total of 39,872 miles on their car. They stopped and filled the gas tank 4 hours later with 8.0 gallons of gas. At that time the car's total mileage was 40,060.

2. How far did they travel in 4 hours? 188 miles
(12)

3. The Barkers' car traveled an average of how many miles
(46) per gallon during the first 4 hours of the trip?
23.5 miles per gallon

4. When 24 is multiplied by w, the product is 288. What is
(41) the quotient when 24 is divided by w? 2

5. Use a ratio box to solve this problem. There were 144
(54) Bolsheviks in the crowd. If the ratio of Bolsheviks to
czarists was 9 to 8, how many czarists were in the crowd?
128 czarists

6.

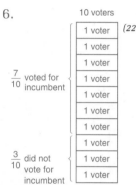

6. Draw a diagram of this statement. Then answer the
(22,48) questions that follow.

> *Exit polls showed that 7 out of 10 voters cast
> their ballot for the incumbent.*

(a) According to the exit polls, what percent of the voters
cast their ballot for the incumbent? 70%

(b) According to the exit polls, what fraction of the voters
did not cast their ballot for the incumbent? $\frac{3}{10}$

7. Write an equation to solve this problem. $W_N = \frac{5}{6} \times 3\frac{1}{3}$; $2\frac{7}{9}$
(60)
What number is $\frac{5}{6}$ of $3\frac{1}{3}$?

8. What is the total price of a $10,000 car plus 8.5% sales tax?
(46) $10,850

9. Write 1.86×10^5 in standard form. Then use words to
(51) write this number. 186,000; one hundred eighty-six thousand

10. Compare: 1 quart $\bigcirc$ 1 liter
(32)

11.

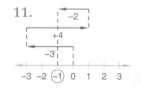

11. Sketch a number line to show $(-3) + (+4) + (-2)$.
(59)

12. Complete the table.
(48)

Fraction	Decimal	Percent
$\frac{5}{8}$	(a) 0.625	(b) $62\frac{1}{2}\%$
(c) $2\frac{3}{4}$	(d) 2.75	275%

13. Evaluate: $x + \dfrac{x}{y} - y$ if $x = 12$ and $y = 3$ 13
(52)

14. Find each missing exponent.
(47)
(a) $2^5 \cdot 2^3 = 2^{\square}$ 8   (b) $2^5 \div 2^3 = 2^{\square}$ 2

15. Angle *ZWX* measures 90°.
(62)

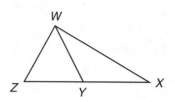

(a) Which triangle is an acute triangle? △*ZWY*

(b) Which triangle is an obtuse triangle? △*WYX*

(c) Which triangle is a right triangle? △*ZWX*

16. In this figure dimensions are in
(37) inches and angles are right angles.

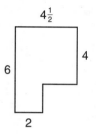

(a) What is the perimeter of the figure?
21 in.

(b) What is the area of the figure?
22 in.²

17. (a) Classify this triangle by its sides.
(37,62)   isosceles triangle

(b) What is the measure of each acute
angle of the triangle? 45°

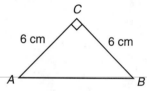

(c) What is the area of the triangle?
18 cm²

(d) The longest side of this triangle is opposite which
angle? ∠*C*

Solve:

18. $7q = 1.428$ 0.204
(35)

19. $\dfrac{30}{70} = \dfrac{w}{\$2.10}$ $0.90
(39)

Simplify:

20. $5^2 + 2^5 - \sqrt{49}$ 50
(20,52)

21. $3(8) - (5)(2) + 10 \div 2$
(52) 19

22.
(49)

$$\begin{array}{r} 1 \text{ yd } 2 \text{ ft } 3\frac{3}{4} \text{ in.} \\ + \quad\quad 2 \text{ ft } 6\frac{1}{2} \text{ in.} \\ \hline 2 \text{ yd } 1 \text{ ft } 10\frac{1}{4} \text{ in.} \end{array}$$

23. $1 \text{ L} - 50 \text{ mL} = ? \text{ mL}$
(32) 950 mL

24. $\dfrac{60 \text{ mi}}{1 \text{ hr}} \cdot \dfrac{1 \text{ hr}}{60 \text{ min}}$ $1\frac{\text{mi}}{\text{min}}$
(50)

25. $2\dfrac{7}{24} + 3\dfrac{9}{32}$ $5\frac{55}{96}$
(30)

26. $2\dfrac{2}{5} \div \left(4\dfrac{1}{5} \div 1\dfrac{3}{4}\right)$ 1
(26)

27. $20 - \left(7\dfrac{1}{2} \div \dfrac{2}{3}\right)$ $8\frac{3}{4}$
(23,26)

28.

28. Sketch an equilateral triangle and show its lines of symmetry.
(58,62)

29. Evaluate: $|x - y|$ if $x = 3$ and $y = 4$ 1
(52,59)

30. On one tray of a balanced scale was a 1-kg mass. On the other tray was a box and a 250-g mass. What was the mass of the box? 750 g
(3,32)

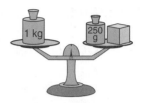

LESSON 63

Symbols of Inclusion

Mental Math:
a. 1230
b. 0.004
c. 6
d. 500 mL
e. 14
f. $9.00
g. 1400
Problem Solving:

$\frac{120 \text{ mi}}{1 \text{ hr} + 2 \text{ hr}}$

$= 40$ mph

Facts Practice: Fraction-Decimal-Percent Equivalents
(Test L in Test Masters)

Mental Math:

a. 5×246 **b.** 4×10^{-3}

c. $\frac{15}{20} = \frac{x}{8}$ **d.** Convert 0.5 L to mL.

e. $\sqrt{196}$ **f.** $\frac{3}{8}$ of $24.00

g. Instead of multiplying 50 and 28, double 50, find half of 28, and multiply those numbers.

Problem Solving:

The Smiths traveled the 60-mile road to town at 60 mph. The traffic was heavy on the return trip, and they averaged just 30 mph. What was their average speed for the round trip?

Parentheses, brackets, and braces

Parentheses are called **symbols of inclusion.** We have used parentheses to show which operation to perform first. To simplify the following expression, we add 5 and 7 before subtracting their sum from 15.

$$15 - (5 + 7)$$

Brackets, [ ], and **braces,** { }, are also symbols of inclusion. When an expression contains multiple symbols of inclusion, we simplify within the innermost symbols first.

To simplify the expression

$$20 - [15 - (5 + 7)]$$

we simplify within the parentheses first.

$$20 - [15 - (12)] \qquad \text{simplified within parentheses}$$

Next we simplify within the brackets.

$$20 - [3] \qquad \text{simplified within brackets}$$
$$17 \qquad \text{subtracted}$$

Example 1 Simplify: $50 - [20 + (10 - 5)]$

Solution First we simplify within the parentheses.

$$50 - [20 + (5)] \qquad \text{simplified within parentheses}$$
$$50 - [25] \qquad \text{simplified within brackets}$$
$$\mathbf{25} \qquad \text{subtracted}$$

Example 2 Simplify: $12 - (8 - |4 - 6| + 2)$

Solution Absolute value symbols may serve as symbols of inclusion. In this problem we first find the absolute value of $4 - 6$ as the first step of simplifying within the parentheses.

$$12 - (8 - 2 + 2) \qquad \text{found absolute value of } 4 - 6$$
$$12 - (8) \qquad \text{simplified within parentheses}$$
$$\mathbf{4} \qquad \text{subtracted}$$

Division bar As we have noted, a division bar also serves as a symbol of inclusion. We simplify above and below the division bar before we divide. We follow the order of operations within the symbol of inclusion.

Example 3 Simplify: $\dfrac{4 + 5 \times 6 - 7}{10 - (9 - 8)}$

Solution We simplify above and below the bar before we divide. Above the bar we multiply first. Below the bar we simplify within the parentheses first. This gives us

$$\frac{4 + 30 - 7}{10 - (1)}$$

We continue by simplifying above and below the division bar.

$$\frac{27}{9}$$

Now we divide and get

$$3$$

Calculators with parenthesis keys are usually capable of dealing with many levels of parentheses (parentheses within parentheses within parentheses). When performing calculations such as the one in Example 1, we press the "open parenthesis" key, (, for each opening parenthesis, bracket, or brace. We press the "close parenthesis" key,) , for each closing parenthesis, bracket, or brace. For the problem in Example 1, the key strokes are

To perform calculations such as the one in Example 3 using a calculator, we follow one of these two procedures.

1. We perform the calculations above the bar and record the result. We perform the calculations below the bar and record the result. Then we perform the division using the two recorded numbers.

2. To perform the calculation with one uninterrupted sequence of keystrokes, we picture the problem like this:

$$\frac{4 + 5 \times 6 - 7 =}{[10 - (9 - 8)]} =$$

We press the equals key after the 7 in this problem to complete the calculations above the bar. Then we press ÷ for the division bar. We place all the operations below the division bar within a set of parentheses so that the denominator is handled by the calculator as though it were one number.

If you have a calculator with parenthesis keys and algebraic logic, perform these calculations and note the display at the indicated location in the sequence of keystrokes.

What number is displayed and what does this number represent? 27; This is the numerator.

What number is displayed and what does this number represent? 9; This is the denominator.

What number is displayed and what does this number represent? 3; This is the quotient.

Practice Simplify:

a. $30 - [40 - (10 - 2)]$ –2   **b.** $100 - 3[2(6 - 2)]$ 76

c. $\dfrac{10 + 9 \cdot 8 - 7}{6 \cdot 5 - 4 - 3 + 2}$ 3   **d.** $\dfrac{1 + 2(3 + 4) - 5}{10 - 9(8 - 7)}$ 10

e. $12 + 3(8 - |{-2}|)$ 30

**Problem set
63**

1. Jennifer and Jason each earn $6 per hour doing yard work. On one job Jennifer worked 3 hours and Jason worked $2\frac{1}{2}$ hours. Altogether, how much money were they paid? $33
(28)

2. When Jim is resting, his heart beats 70 times per minute. When Jim is jogging, his heart beats 150 times per minute. During a half hour of jogging, Jim's heart beats how many more times than it would if he were resting?
2400 more times
(28,53)

3. Use a ratio box to solve this problem. The ratio of brachiopods to trilobites in the fossil find was 2 to 9. If 720 trilobites were found, how many brachiopods were found? 160 brachiopods
(54)

4. During the first 5 days of the journey, the wagon train averaged 18 miles per day. During the next 2 days the wagon train traveled 16 miles and 21 miles, respectively. If the total journey is 1017 miles, how much farther does the wagon train have to travel? 890 miles
(55)

5. Write an equation to solve this problem. What number is 35% of 840? $W_N = 0.35 \times 840$; 294
(60)

6. The average distance from Earth to the Sun is 1.496×10^8 km. Use words to write that number.
one hundred forty-nine million, six hundred thousand kilometers
(51)

7.

40 cars

$\frac{3}{10}$ were tankers	4 cars
	4 cars
	4 cars
$\frac{7}{10}$ were not tankers	4 cars
	4 cars
	4 cars
	4 cars
	4 cars
	4 cars
	4 cars

7. Draw a diagram of this statement. Then answer the questions that follow.
(22,48)

Twelve of the 40 cars pulled by the locomotive were tankers.

(a) What fraction of the cars were tankers? $\frac{3}{10}$

(b) What percent of the cars were not tankers? 70%

8. The top speed of Dan's pet snail is 2×10^{-3} mile per hour.
$^{(57)}$ Use words to write that number.
two-thousandths mile per hour

9. Use a unit multiplier to convert 1.5 km to m.   1500 m
$^{(50)}$

10. Divide 4.36 by 0.012 and write the answer with a bar over
$^{(45)}$ the repetend. $363.\overline{3}$

11.
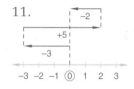

11. Sketch a number line and draw arrows to show
$^{(59)}$ $(-3) + (+5) + (-2)$.

12. Complete the table.
$^{(48)}$

FRACTION	DECIMAL	PERCENT
(a) $\frac{33}{100}$	(b) 0.33	33%
$\frac{1}{3}$	(c) $0.\overline{3}$	(d) $33\frac{1}{3}\%$

13. Describe the rule of this function.
$^{(58)}$ Divide the "in" number by 3 to find the
"out" number.

IN	FUNCTION	OUT
3		1
12		4
6		2
15		5

14. What is the probability of drawing a red face card by
$^{(36)}$ drawing one card from a normal deck? $\frac{3}{26}$

In this figure, $AB = AD = BD = CD = 5$ cm. The measure of
angle ABC is 90°. Refer to this figure for problems 15–17.

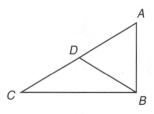

15. (a) Classify $\triangle BCD$ by its sides.   isosceles triangle
$^{(62)}$

    (b) What is the perimeter of the equilateral triangle?   15 cm

    (c) Which triangle is a right triangle? $\triangle ABC$

16. Find the measure of each of the following angles:
(40)

    (a) ∠*BAC* 60°   (b) ∠*ADB* 60°   (c) ∠*BDC* 120°

    (d) ∠*DBA* 60°   (e) ∠*DBC* 30°   (f) ∠*DCB* 30°

17. What is the ratio of the length of the shortest side of △*ABC*
(36) to the length of the longest side? $\frac{1}{2}$

Solve:

18. $\dfrac{5}{18} = x + \dfrac{1}{12}$ $\frac{7}{36}$
(30)

19. $2 = 0.4p$ 5
(45)

Simplify:

20. $3[24 - (8 + 3 \cdot 2)] - \dfrac{6 + 4}{|-2|}$ 25
(63)

21. $3^3 - \sqrt{3^2 + 4^2}$ 22
(52)

22.
(56)

$$\begin{array}{r} 1\ \text{week}\ \ 2\ \text{days}\ \ 7\ \text{hr} \\ -\ \underline{\qquad\qquad 5\ \text{days}\ \ 9\ \text{hr}} \\ 3\ \text{days}\ \ 22\ \text{hr} \end{array}$$

23. $\dfrac{20\ \text{mi}}{1\ \text{gal}} \cdot \dfrac{1\ \text{gal}}{4\ \text{qt}}$ $5\frac{\text{mi}}{\text{qt}}$
(50)

24. $4\dfrac{2}{3} + 3\dfrac{5}{6} + 2\dfrac{5}{9}$ $11\frac{1}{18}$
(30)

25. $12\dfrac{1}{2} \cdot 4\dfrac{4}{5} \cdot 3\dfrac{1}{3}$ 200
(26)

26. $6\dfrac{1}{3} - \left(1\dfrac{2}{3} \div 3\right)$ $5\frac{7}{9}$
(26,30)

27. Evaluate: $x^2 + 2xy + y^2$ if $x = 3$ and $y = 4$ 49
(52)

28.

28. Sketch an isosceles triangle that is not equilateral and
(58,62) show its line of symmetry.

29. The coordinates of the four vertices of a parallelogram are
(61) (0, 0), (4, 0), (1, −3), and (−3, −3).

    (a) Graph the parallelogram. See student work.

    (b) Find the area of the parallelogram. 12 sq. units

    (c) What is the measure of each acute angle of the parallelogram? 45°

30. Three identical boxes are balanced
(3) on one side of a scale by a 750-g mass
on the other side of the scale. What is
the mass of each box? 250 g

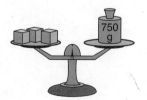

LESSON
64

Facts Practice: + − × ÷ Mixed Numbers (Test N in Test Masters)

Mental Math:

a. 3.6×50

b. 7.5×10^2

c. $4x - 5 = 35$

d. Convert 20 cm to mm.

e. $\sqrt{9 + 16}$

f. $\frac{5}{9}$ of $1.80

g. $1.5 + 1, \times 2, + 3, \div 4, - 1.5$

Problem Solving:

When all the cards from a 52-card deck are dealt to three players, each player receives 17 cards and there is one extra card. Dean invented a new deck of cards so that any number of players up to 6 can play and there will be no extra cards. How many cards are in Dean's deck if the number is less than 100?

Mental Math:
a. 180
b. 750
c. 10
d. 200 mm
e. 5
f. $1.00
g. 0.5
Problem Solving:
    60 cards

From our practice on the number line we have seen that when we add two negative numbers, the sum is a negative number. When we add two positive numbers, the sum is a positive number.

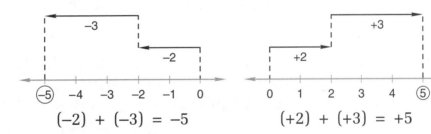

$$(-2) + (-3) = -5 \qquad (+2) + (+3) = +5$$

We have also seen that when we add a positive number and a negative number, the sum is positive, negative, or zero depending upon which, if either, of the numbers has the greater absolute value.

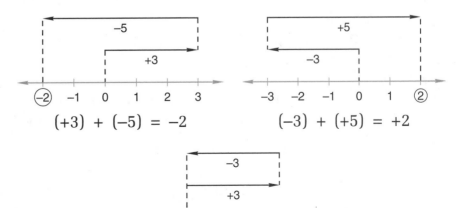

$$(+3) + (-5) = -2 \qquad (-3) + (+5) = +2$$

$$(+3) + (-3) = 0$$

We can summarize these observations with the following statements.

---

1. **The sum of two numbers with the same sign has an absolute value equal to the sum of their absolute values. Its sign is the same as the sign of the numbers.**
2. **The sum of two numbers with opposite signs has an absolute value equal to the difference of their absolute values. Its sign is the same as the sign of the number with the greater absolute value.**
3. **The sum of two opposites is zero.**

We can use these observations to help us add signed numbers without drawing a number line.

Example 1 Find each sum:

(a) $(-54) + (-78)$ (b) $(+45) + (-67)$ (c) $(-92) + (+92)$

Solution (a) Since the signs are the same, we add the absolute values and use the same sign for the sum.

$$(-54) + (-78) = \mathbf{-132}$$

(b) Since the signs are different, we find the difference of the absolute values and keep the sign of −67 because its absolute value, 67, is greater than 45.

$$(+45) + (-67) = \mathbf{-22}$$

(c) The signs of the numbers are different. The difference of the absolute values of −92 and 92 is zero. Zero has no sign. The sum of two opposites is zero.

$$(-92) + (+92) = \mathbf{0}$$

Example 2 Find the sum: $(-3) + (-2) + (+7) + (-4)$

Solution We will show two methods.

Method 1: Adding in order from left to right, add the first two numbers. Then add the third number. Then add the fourth number.

$(-3) + (-2) + (+7) + (-4)$	problem
$(-5) + (+7) + (-4)$	added −3 and −2
$(+2) + (-4)$	added −5 and +7
$\mathbf{-2}$	added +2 and −4

Method 2: Employing the commutative and associative properties, rearrange the terms and add all numbers with the same sign first.

$$(-3) + (-2) + (-4) + (+7) \qquad \text{rearranged}$$
$$(-9) + (+7) \qquad\qquad \text{added}$$
$$-2 \qquad\qquad\qquad\quad \text{added}$$

Example 3 Find each sum:

(a) $\left(-2\dfrac{1}{2}\right) + \left(-3\dfrac{1}{3}\right)$ (b) $(+4.3) + (-7.24)$

Solution These numbers are not integers, but the method for adding these signed numbers is the same as the method for adding integers.

(a) The signs are both negative. We add the absolute values and keep the same sign.

$$\left(-2\dfrac{1}{2}\right) + \left(-3\dfrac{1}{3}\right) = -5\dfrac{5}{6}$$

$$2\dfrac{1}{2} = 2\dfrac{3}{6}$$
$$+\ 3\dfrac{1}{3} = 3\dfrac{2}{6}$$
$$\overline{\qquad\qquad 5\dfrac{5}{6}}$$

(b) The signs are different. We find the difference of the absolute values and keep the sign of -7.24.

$$(+4.3) + (-7.24) = -2.94$$

$$\begin{array}{r} {}^{6}\;{}^{1}\\ \cancel{7}.24 \\ -\ 4.3 \\ \hline 2.94 \end{array}$$

Practice* Find each sum:

   a. $(-56) + (+96)$ +40   **b.** $(-28) + (-145)$ −173

   c. $(-5) + (+7) + (+9) + (-3)$ **d.** $(-3) + (-8) + (+15)$ +4
      +8

   e. $(-12) + (-9) + (+16)$ −5   **f.** $(+12) + (-18) + (+6)$ 0

   g. $\left(-3\dfrac{5}{6}\right) + \left(+5\dfrac{1}{3}\right)$ $+1\frac{1}{2}$ **h.** $(-1.6) + (-11.47)$ −13.07

Problem set 64

1. Two trillion is how much more than seven hundred fifty billion? Write the answer in scientific notation.
$^{(51)}$
   1.25×10^{12}

2. The taxi cost \$2.25 for the first mile and 15¢ for each additional tenth of a mile. For a 5.2-mile trip Eric paid \$10 and told the driver to keep the change. How much was the driver's tip?   \$1.45
$^{(28)}$

3. Gilbert wanted to buy packages of crackers and cheese
(44) from the vending machine. Each package cost 35¢.
Gilbert had 5 quarters, 3 dimes, and 2 nickels. How many
packages of crackers and cheese could he buy? 4 packages

4. The two prime numbers p and m are between 50 and 60.
(21) Their difference is 6. What is their sum? 112

5. What is the mean of 1.74, 2.8, 3.4, 0.96, 2, and 1.22? 2.02
(28)

6.

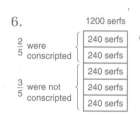

$\frac{2}{5}$ were conscripted

$\frac{3}{5}$ were not conscripted

6. Draw a diagram of this statement. Then answer the
(22,48) questions that follow.

> *The viceroy conscripted two fifths of the 1200
> serfs in the province.*

(a) How many of the serfs in the province were
conscripted? 480 serfs

(b) What percent of the serfs in the province were not
conscripted? 60%

7. Write an equation to solve this problem. What number is
(60) $\frac{5}{9}$ of 100? $W_N = \frac{5}{9} \times 100$; $55\frac{5}{9}$

8. (a) The temperature at the center of the Sun is about
(51,57) 1.6×10^7 degrees Celsius. Use words to write that
number. sixteen million degrees Celsius

(b) A red blood cell is about 7×10^{-6} meter in diameter.
Use words to write that number. seven millionths meter

9. (a) 1.6×10^7 ⧀>⧀ 7×10^{-6}
(57)
(b) 7×10^{-6} ⧀>⧀ 0

10. Divide 456 by 28 and write the answer
(44)
(a) as a mixed number. $16\frac{2}{7}$

(b) as a decimal rounded to two decimal places. 16.29

(c) rounded to the nearest whole number. 16

11. Find each sum:
(64)
(a) $(-63) + (-14)$ –77

(b) $(-16) + (+20) + (-32)$ –28

12. Complete the table.
(48)

Fraction	Decimal	Percent
(a) $2\frac{1}{2}$	2.5	(b) 250%
$\frac{4}{9}$	(c) $0.\overline{4}$	(d) $44\frac{4}{9}\%$

13. The figure shows an equilateral
(Inv. 2,62) triangle inscribed in a circle.

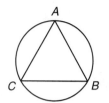

    (a) What is the measure of the inscribed angle *BCA*?   60°

13.(b) The chords are $\overline{AB}$, $\overline{BC}$, and $\overline{CA}$. Each chord is shorter than the diameter, which is the longest chord of a circle.

    (b) Select a chord of this circle and state whether the chord is longer or shorter than the diameter of the circle and why.

14. Evaluate: $x + xy$ if $x = \dfrac{2}{3}$ and $y = \dfrac{3}{4}$ $1\frac{1}{6}$
(52)

Refer to this hexagon to answer problems 15 and 16. Dimensions are in meters. All angles are right angles.

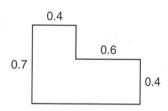

15. What is the perimeter of the hexagon?   3.4 m
(19)

16. What is the area of the hexagon?   0.52 m²
(37)

Solve:

17. $\dfrac{4}{9} = y - \dfrac{2}{9}$ $\frac{2}{3}$ **18.** $25x = 10$ 0.4 or $\frac{2}{5}$
(15)   (44)

19. The product of *x* and 12 is 84. The product of *y* and 12 is
(41) 48. What is the product of *x* and *y*?   28

20. The center of a circle with a radius of three units is (1, 1).
(Inv. 3) Which of these points is on the circle?   B. (−2, 1)

     A. (4, 4)   B. (−2, 1)   C. (−4, 1)   D. (3, 0)

Simplify:

21. $\dfrac{3^2 + 4^2}{\sqrt{3^2 + 4^2}}$ 5
(63)

22. $2\dfrac{4}{5} \div \left(6 \div 2\dfrac{1}{2}\right)$ $1\dfrac{1}{6}$
(26)

23. $100 - [20 + 5(4) + 3(2 + 1)]$ 51
(63)

24.   5 gal 2 qt 1 pt 7 oz
(49) + 1 gal 1 qt 1 pt 9 oz
————————————————
      7 gal   1 pt

25. $\left(1\dfrac{1}{2}\right)^2 - \left(4 - 2\dfrac{1}{3}\right)$ $\dfrac{7}{12}$
(26,30)

26. $0.1 - (0.01 - 0.001)$
(35) 0.091

27. $5.1 \div (5.1 \div 1.5)$ 1.5
(45)

28. Write $3\dfrac{1}{5}$ as a decimal number and subtract it from 4.375.
(43) 1.175

29. What is the probability of rolling an even prime number
(36) with one toss of a single die? $\dfrac{1}{6}$

30. Figure $ABCD$ is a parallelogram. Find the measure of
(61)

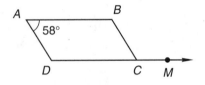

(a) $\angle B$. 122°   (b) $\angle BCD$. 58°   (c) $\angle BCM$. 122°

**LESSON
65**

Ratio Problems Involving Totals

Facts Practice: Metric Conversions (Test M in Test Masters)

Mental Math:

a. 0.42×50

b. 1.25×10^{-1}

c. $\dfrac{9}{w} = \dfrac{15}{10}$

d. Convert 0.75 m to mm.

e. $5^3 - 10^2$

f. $\dfrac{9}{10}$ of $4.00

g. What is the total cost of a $20.00 item plus 7% sales tax?

Problem Solving:

Copy this problem and fill in the missing digits.

$$
\begin{array}{r}
91\frac{1}{2} \\
\underline{)} \\
== \\
-- \\
== \\
-
\end{array}
$$

Some ratio problems require that we use the total to solve the problem. Consider the following problem:

The ratio of boys to girls was 5 to 4. If there were 180 students in the assembly, how many girls were there?

We begin by making a ratio box. This time we add a third row for the total number of students.

	Ratio	Actual Count
Boys	5	B
Girls	4	G
Total	9	180

In the ratio column we wrote 5 for boys and 4 for girls, then *added these to get 9 for the total ratio number.* We were given 180 as the actual count of students. This is a total. We can use two rows from this table to write a proportion. Since we were asked to find the number of girls, we will use the "girls" row. Since we know both total numbers, we will also use the "total" row. Then we solve the proportion.

	Ratio	Actual Count
Boys	5	B
Girls	4	G
Total	9	180

$$\frac{4}{9} = \frac{G}{180}$$
$$9G = 720$$
$$G = 80$$

We find that there were 80 girls. We can use this answer to complete the ratio box.

	Ratio	Actual Count
Boys	5	100
Girls	4	80
Total	9	180

Example   The ratio of football players to soccer players in the room was 5 to 7. If 48 players were in the room, how many were football players?

Solution We use the information in the problem to form a table. We include a row for the total number of players. The total ratio number is 12.

	Ratio	Actual Count
Football players	5	F
Soccer players	7	S
Total players	12	48

$$\frac{5}{12} = \frac{F}{48}$$

$$12F = 240$$

$$F = 20$$

To find the number of football players, we wrote a proportion from the "football players" row and the "total players" row. We solved the proportion to find that there were **20 football players** in the room. From this information we can complete the ratio box.

	Ratio	Actual Count
Football players	5	20
Soccer players	7	28
Total players	12	48

Practice Solve these problems. Begin by drawing a ratio box.

a. Acrobats and clowns converged on the center ring in the ratio of 3 to 5. If a total of 72 acrobats and clowns performed in the center ring, how many were clowns? 45 clowns

b. The ratio of young men to young women at the prom was 8 to 9. If 240 young men were in attendance, how many young people attended in all? 510 young people

Problem set 65

1. If 5 pounds of apples cost $2.40, then
(46)

(a) what is the price per pound? $0.48 per pound

(b) what is the cost for 8 pounds of apples? $3.84

2. (a) Simplify and compare: 0.27 = 0.27
(41)

$$(0.3)(0.4) + (0.3)(0.5) \bigcirc 0.3(0.4 + 0.5)$$

(b) What property is illustrated by this comparison?
distributive property

3. Use a ratio box to solve this problem. The ratio of big fish
(65) to little fish in the pond was 4 to 11. If there were 1320 fish in the pond, how many big fish were there? 352 big fish

4. The car traveled 350 miles on 15 gallons of gasoline. The
(44,46) car averaged how many miles per gallon? Round the
answer to the nearest tenth. $23.3\frac{\text{miles}}{\text{gallon}}$

5. The average of 2 and 4 is 3. What is the average of the
(28) reciprocals of 2 and 4? $\frac{3}{8}$

6. Write 12 billion in scientific notation. 1.2×10^{10}
(51)

7.

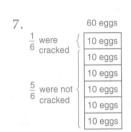

7. Draw a diagram of this statement. Then answer the
(22,36) questions that follow.

One sixth of the five dozen eggs were cracked.

(a) How many eggs were not cracked? 50 eggs

(b) What was the ratio of eggs that were cracked to eggs
that were not cracked? $\frac{1}{5}$

(c) What percent of the eggs were cracked? $16\frac{2}{3}\%$

8.(a)

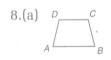

8. (a) Draw segment *AB*. Draw segment *DC* parallel to
(Inv. 6) segment *AB* but not the same length. Draw segments
between the endpoints of segments *AB* and *DC* to
form a quadrilateral.

(b) What type of quadrilateral was formed in part (a)?
trapezoid

9. Find the area of each triangle. Dimensions are in
(37) centimeters.

(a)

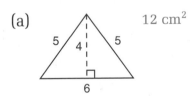

12 cm²

(b)

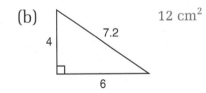

12 cm²

(c)

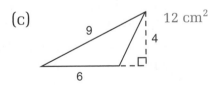

12 cm²

10. What is the average of the two numbers indicated by
(28,34) arrows on this number line? 0.82

Write equations to solve problems 11 and 12.

11. What number is 75 percent of 64? $W_N = 0.75 \times 64;\ 48$
(60)

12. What is the tax on a $7.40 item if the sales tax rate is 8%?
(46) $T = 0.08 \times \$7.40;\ \$0.59$

13. Find each sum:
(64)

(a) $(-3) + (-8)$ -11

(b) $(+3) + (-8)$ -5

(c) $(-3) + (+8) + (-5)$ 0

14. A circle is drawn on a coordinate plane with its center at
(Inv. 3) the origin. One point on the circle is (3, 4). Use a compass and graph paper to graph the circle. Then answer questions (a) and (b).

(a) What are the coordinates of the points where the circle intersects the *x*-axis? (5, 0), (−5, 0)

(b) What is the diameter of the circle? 10 units

15. Use a unit multiplier to convert 0.95 liters to milliliters.
(50)   950 milliliters

16. Evaluate: $ab + a + \dfrac{a}{b}$ if $a = 5$ and $b = 0.2$ 31
(52)

17. How many small blocks were used to
(13) build this cube? 27 blocks

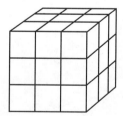

18. Recall that one angle is the complement of another angle
(40) if their sum is 90°, and that one angle is the supplement of another if their sum is 180°. In this figure, (a) which angle is a complement of ∠*BOC*? (b) which angle is a supplement of ∠*BOC*? (a) ∠*COD* (b) ∠*AOB*

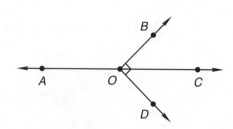

19. Round each number to the nearest whole number to
(29,33) estimate the product of 19.875 and $4\frac{7}{8}$. 100

20. Refer to $\triangle ABC$ to answer the following
(58,62) questions:

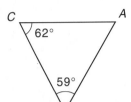

(a) What is the measure of $\angle A$? 59°

(b) Which side of the triangle is the longest side? $\overline{AB}$

(c) Triangle ABC is an acute triangle. It is also what other type of triangle? isosceles triangle

(d) Triangle ABC's line of symmetry passes through which vertex? C

21.(a) We arrange the numbers in order and look for the middle number. Since there is an even number of scores there is no one middle number. So the median is the mean of the two middle numbers.

21. (a) Describe how to find the median of this set of 12
(Inv. 4) scores.

18, 17, 15, 20, 16, 14, 15, 16, 17, 18, 16, 19

(b) What is the median of the set of scores? 16.5

22. For (a) and (b) answer true or false.
(62)

(a) All equilateral triangles are congruent. false

(b) All equilateral triangles are similar. true

Simplify:

23. $\dfrac{10^3 \cdot 10^3}{10^2}$ 10^4 or 10,000
(47)

24. $\begin{array}{r} 1 \text{ yd } 2 \text{ ft } 7 \text{ in.} \\ + \quad\quad 1 \text{ ft } 9 \text{ in.} \\ \hline 2 \text{ yd} \quad 1 \text{ ft} \quad 4 \text{ in.} \end{array}$
(49)

25. $\begin{array}{r} 4 \text{ days } 5 \text{ hr } 15 \text{ min} \\ - 1 \text{ days } 7 \text{ hr } 50 \text{ min} \\ \hline 2 \text{ days} \quad 21 \text{ hr} \quad 25 \text{ min} \end{array}$
(56)

26. $4.5 \div (0.4 + 0.5)$ 5
(45)

27. $\dfrac{3 + 0.6}{3 - 0.6}$ 1.5
(52)

28. $4\frac{1}{5} \div \left(1\frac{1}{6} \cdot 3\right)$ $1\frac{1}{5}$
(26)

29. $3^2 + \sqrt{4 \cdot 7 - 3}$ 14
(52)

30. $|-3| + 4[(5 - 2)(3 + 1)]$
(63) 51

LESSON 66

Circumference and Pi

Facts Practice: $+ - \times \div$ Mixed Numbers (Test N in Test Masters)

Mental Math:

a. $3.65 + 1.2 + 2$ **b.** 1.2×10^{-3}

c. $9y + 3 = 75$ **d.** Convert 20 decimeters (dm) to meters.

e. $\sqrt{144} + 2^3$ **f.** 25% of 24

g. Estimate the product of 3.14 and 25.

Problem Solving:

The product of $10 \times 10 \times 10$ is 1000. Find three prime numbers whose product is 1001.

Recall from Investigation 2 that a **circle** is a smooth curve, every point of which is the same distance from the **center.** The distance from the center to the circle is the **radius.** The plural of radius is **radii.** The distance across a circle through the center is the **diameter.** The distance around a circle is the **circumference.**

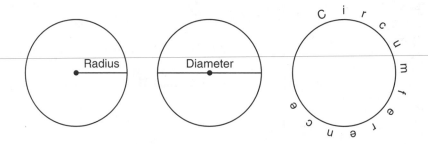

We see that the diameter of a circle is twice the radius of the circle. In the following activity we will investigate the relationship between the diameter and the circumference.

Activity: Circumference and Pi

This activity requires a tape measure (preferably metric) and a number of circular objects. A calculator may also be useful.

Select a circular object and measure its circumference and its diameter as precisely as you can. To calculate the number of diameters that equal the circumference, divide the circumference by the diameter. Round the quotient to two decimal places. Then repeat the activity with another circular object of a different size. Record the results in a table similar to the one shown below. Compare your results with the results of other students in the class. The circumference of each circular object is about how many times its diameter?

Sample Table

Object	Circumference	Diameter	$\dfrac{\text{Circumference}}{\text{Diameter}}$
Waste basket	94 cm	30 cm	3.13
Plastic cup	22 cm	7 cm	3.14

How many diameters equal a circumference? This question has been asked by people for thousands of years. They found that the answer did not depend on the size of the circle. The circumference of a circle is slightly more than three diameters.

Another way to illustrate this fact is to cut a length of string equal to the diameter of a particular circle and find how many of these lengths are needed to reach around the circle. No matter what the size of the circle, it takes three diameters plus a little extra to equal the circumference.

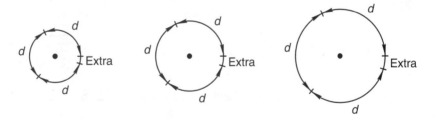

The extra amount needed is about, but not exactly, one seventh of a diameter. Thus the number of diameters needed to equal the circumference of a circle is about

$$3\frac{1}{7} \quad \text{or} \quad \frac{22}{7} \quad \text{or} \quad 3.14$$

Neither $3\frac{1}{7}$ nor 3.14 is exact. They are approximations. There is no fraction or decimal number that exactly states the number of diameters in a circumference. (Some computers have calculated the number to more than 1 million decimal places.) We use the symbol π, which is the Greek letter **pi** (pronounced like "pie"), to stand for this number. Note that π is not a variable. Rather, π is a **constant** because its value does not vary, although various approximations may be used for π in calculations.

The circumference of a circle is π times the diameter of the circle. This idea is expressed by the formula

$$C = \pi d$$

In this formula, C stands for circumference and d for diameter. To perform calculations with π, we can use an approximation. The commonly used approximations for π are

$$3.14 \quad \text{and} \quad \frac{22}{7}$$

For calculations that require great accuracy, more accurate approximations for π may be used, such as

$$3.14159265359$$

Sometimes the calculation is performed leaving π as π. Unless directed to use another approximation, we will use 3.14 for π to perform the calculations in this book.

Example 1   The radius of a circle is 10 cm. What is the circumference?

Solution   If the radius is 10 cm, the diameter is 20 cm.

$$\text{Circumference} = \pi \cdot \text{diameter}$$
$$\approx 3.14 \cdot 20 \text{ cm}$$
$$\approx 62.8 \text{ cm}$$

The circumference is about **62.8 cm.**

Example 2   Find the circumference of each circle.

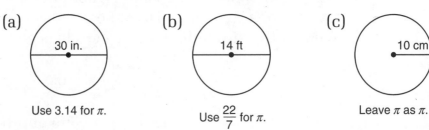

(a) 30 in. — Use 3.14 for π.

(b) 14 ft — Use $\frac{22}{7}$ for π.

(c) 10 cm — Leave π as π.

Solution

(a) $C = \pi d$
$C \approx 3.14(30 \text{ in.})$
$C \approx \textbf{94.2 in.}$

(b) $C = \pi d$
$C \approx \frac{22}{7}(14 \text{ ft})$
$C \approx \textbf{44 ft}$

(c) $C = \pi d$
$C = \pi(20 \text{ cm})$
$C = \textbf{20}\boldsymbol{\pi}\textbf{ cm}$

Note the form of answer (c): first 20 times π, then the unit of measure.

Practice* Find the circumference of each circle.

a.

Use 3.14 for π.
25.12 in.

b.

Use $\frac{22}{7}$ for π.

132 mm

c.

Leave π as π.
4π ft

d. Sylvia used a compass to draw a circle. If the point of the compass was 3 inches from the point of the pencil, what was the circumference of the circle? (Use 3.14 for π.) 18.84 inches

Problem set 66 *(38,60)*

1. According to this graph, what percent of Dan's income was spent on items other than food and housing? If his income was $25,000, how much did he spend on food? 33%; $6250

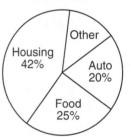

How Dan Spent His Income

Housing 42%
Other
Auto 20%
Food 25%

2. *(28)* It is $1\frac{1}{4}$ miles from Tim's house to school. How far does Tim travel in 5 days walking to school and back?
$12\frac{1}{2}$ miles

3. *(35)* When the sum of 1.9 and 2.2 is subtracted from the product of 1.9 and 2.2, what is the difference? 0.08

4. *(65)* Use a ratio box to solve this problem. There was a total of 520 dimes and quarters in the soda machine. If the ratio of dimes to quarters was 5 to 8, how many dimes were there?
200 dimes

5. *(51)* Saturn's average distance from the Sun is about 900 million miles. Write that number in scientific notation.
9×10^8 miles

6.

400 acres

| 40 acres |
| 40 acres |
| 40 acres |
| 40 acres |
| 40 acres |
| 40 acres |
| 40 acres |
| 40 acres |
| 40 acres |
| 40 acres |

$\frac{3}{10}$ were planted with alfalfa

$\frac{7}{10}$ were not planted with alfalfa

6. *(22,48)* Draw a diagram of this statement. Then answer the questions that follow.

Three tenths of the 400 acres were planted with alfalfa.

(a) What percent of the land was planted with alfalfa?
30%

(b) How many of the 400 acres were not planted with alfalfa? 280 acres

7. Twelve of the 30 students earned an A on the test.
(36,48)

(a) What fraction of the students earned an A? $\frac{2}{5}$

(b) What percent of the students earned an A? 40%

7.(c) A randomly
selected test is
more likely not
to be an A test
because less than
half the tests are
A's.

(c) If one of the tests is selected at random, which is more likely: that it is an A test or not an A test? Why?

8. Find the circumference of each circle.
(66)

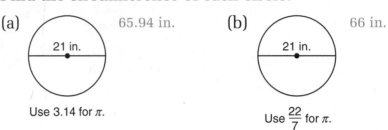

(a) 65.94 in.

21 in.

Use 3.14 for π.

(b) 66 in.

21 in.

Use $\frac{22}{7}$ for π.

9. Refer to the figure to answer questions
(37,61) (a)–(c). Dimensions are in centimeters.

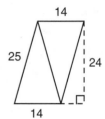

(a) What is the area of the parallelogram? 336 cm^2

(b) The two triangles are congruent. What is the area of one of the triangles? 168 cm^2

(c) Each triangle is isosceles. What is the perimeter of one of the triangles? 64 cm

10. Write 32.5 billion in scientific notation. 3.25×10^{10}
(51)

Write equations to solve problems 11 and 12.

11. What number is 90 percent of 3500?
(60) $W_N = 0.9 \times 3500;\ 3150$

12. What number is $\frac{5}{6}$ of $2\frac{2}{5}$? $W_N = \frac{5}{6} \times 2\frac{2}{5};\ 2$
(60)

13. Complete the table.
(48)

FRACTION	DECIMAL	PERCENT
(a) $\frac{9}{20}$	0.45	(b) 45%
(c) $\frac{3}{40}$	(d) 0.075	7.5% or $7\frac{1}{2}$%

14. Find each sum:
(64)

(a) $(5) + (-4) + (6) + (-1)$ 6

(b) $3 + (-5) + (+4) + (-2)$ 0

15. Use a unit multiplier to convert 1.4 kilograms to grams.
(50) 1400 grams

16. In this figure, two sides of a
(40,61) parallelogram are extended to form
two sides of a right triangle. The
measure of ∠M is 35°. Find the
measure of

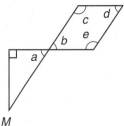

(a) ∠a. 55°   (b) ∠b. 55°

(c) ∠c. 125°   (d) ∠d. 55°   (e) ∠e. 125°

17. Estimate this product by rounding each number to one
(29) nonzero digit before multiplying. 30,000,000

$$(2876)(513)(18)$$

18. Compare: $\dfrac{1.2}{0.3}$ ⊜ $\dfrac{120}{30}$
(27)

19.

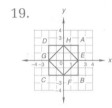

19. The coordinates of the vertices of square $ABCD$ are $(2, 2)$,
(Inv. 3) $(2, -2)$, $(-2, -2)$, and $(-2, 2)$. The coordinates of the vertices
of square $EFGH$ are $(2, 0)$, $(0, -2)$, $(-2, 0)$, and $(0, 2)$. Draw
both squares on the same coordinate plane and answer
these questions.

(a) What is the area of square $ABCD$? 16 units²

(b) What is the length of one side of square $ABCD$? 4 units

(c) Counting two half squares on the grid as one square
unit, what is the area of square $EFGH$? 8 units²

(d) Remembering that the length of the side of a square is
the square root of its area, what is the length of one
side of square $EFGH$? √8 units (How to simplify √8 will be
taught in a later course.)

Solve:

20. $\dfrac{0.9}{1.5} = \dfrac{12}{n}$ 20
(39)

21. $\dfrac{11}{24} + w = \dfrac{11}{12}$ $\frac{11}{24}$
(30)

Simplify:

22.
(49)

    4 lb 12 oz
+ 1 lb   7 oz
————————
  6 lb   3 oz

23. $\dfrac{3 \text{ ft}}{1 \text{ yd}} \cdot \dfrac{12 \text{ in.}}{1 \text{ ft}}$ $36\frac{\text{in.}}{\text{yd}}$
(50)

24. $16 \div (0.8 \div 0.04)$ 0.8
(45)

25. $0.4[0.5 - (0.6)(0.7)]$
(63) 0.032

26. $\dfrac{3}{8} \cdot 1\dfrac{2}{3} \cdot 4 \div 1\dfrac{2}{3}$ $1\frac{1}{2}$
(26)

27. $30 - 5[4 + (3)(2) - 5]$ 5
(63)

28. Example: If a dozen popsicles cost $2.88, what is the price of each popsicle?

28. Write a word problem for this division: $2.88 ÷ 12.
(13)

29. Two identical boxes balance a 9-ounce weight. What is the weight of each box?
(3) $4\frac{1}{2}$ ounces

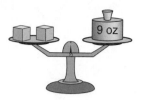

30. Refer to the circle with center at M to answer (a)–(c).
(Inv. 2,62)

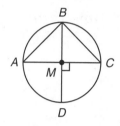

(a) Name two chords that are not diameters. $\overline{AB}, \overline{BC}$

(b) Classify $\triangle AMB$ by sides.   isosceles triangle

(c) What is the measure of inscribed angle ABC?   90°

LESSON 67

Geometric Solids

Facts Practice: Metric Conversions (Test M in Test Masters)

Mental Math:

Mental Math:
a. 33.6
b. 3850
c. 5
d. 200 dm
e. 100
f. 18
g. 720
Problem Solving:
   90 minutes

a. 43.6 − 10

b. 3.85 × 10^3

c. $\frac{5}{10} = \frac{2.5}{m}$

d. Convert 20 m to decimeters (dm).

e. $10^3 ÷ 10$

f. 75% of 24

g. A mental calculation technique for multiplying is to double one factor and halve the other factor. The product is the same. Use this technique to multiply 45 and 16.

$$35 \xrightarrow{×2} 70$$
$$\underline{× 14} \xrightarrow{÷2} \underline{× 7}$$
$$490 \qquad 490$$

Problem Solving:

If Tom reads 5 pages in 4 minutes and Jerry reads 4 pages in 5 minutes, and if they both begin reading 200-page books at the same time, then Tom will finish how many minutes before Jerry?

Geometric solids are shapes that take up space. Below we show a few geometric solids.

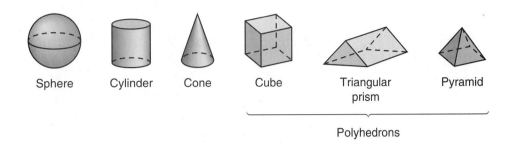

Sphere   Cylinder   Cone   Cube   Triangular prism   Pyramid

Polyhedrons

Some geometric solids, such as spheres, cylinders, and cones, have one or more curved surfaces. If a solid has only flat surfaces that are polygons, the solid is called a **polyhedron.** Cubes, triangular prisms, and pyramids are examples of polyhedrons.

When describing a polyhedron, we may refer to its faces, edges, or vertices. A **face** is one of the flat surfaces. An **edge** is formed where two faces meet. A **vertex** (plural, **vertices**) is formed where three or more edges meet.

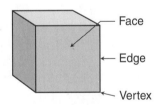

— Face

← Edge

← Vertex

A **prism** is a special kind of polyhedron. A prism has a polygon of a constant size "running through" the prism that appears at opposite faces of the prism and determines the name of the prism. For example, the opposite faces of this prism are congruent triangles. So this prism is called a **triangular prism.**

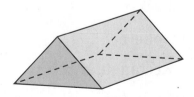

Notice that if we made a perpendicular cut through this triangular prism, we would see the same size triangle appear at the cut.

To draw a prism, we draw two identical, parallel polygons, as shown below. Then we draw segments connecting corresponding vertices. We may use dashes to indicate edges hidden from view.

Rectangular prism: We draw two congruent rectangles.

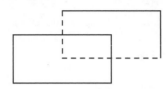

Then we connect the corresponding vertices (using dashes for hidden edges).

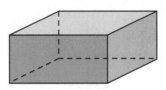

Triangular prism: We draw two congruent triangles.

We connect corresponding vertices.

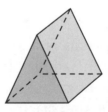

Example 1   Use the name of a geometric solid to describe the shape of each object.

(a) Basketball   (b) Shoe box   (c) Can of beans

Solution   (a) **Sphere**

(b) **Rectangular prism**

(c) **Cylinder**

Example 2   A cube has how many (a) faces, (b) edges, and (c) vertices?

Solution   (a) **6 faces**   (b) **12 edges**   (c) **8 vertices**

Example 3   Draw a cube.

Solution   A cube is a special kind of rectangular prism. All faces are squares.

Workers involved in the manufacturing of packaging materials make boxes and other containers out of flat sheets of cardboard or sheet metal. If we cut apart a box of cereal and unfold it, we see the six rectangles that form the faces of the box.

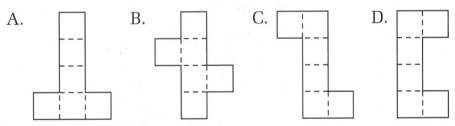

If we find the area of each rectangle and add those areas together, we can calculate the **surface area** of the box of cereal.

Example 4   Which of these patterns cannot be folded to form a cube?

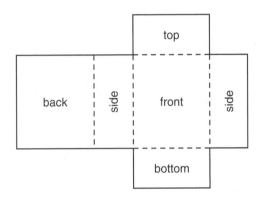

A.   B.   C.   D.

Solution   **Pattern D** will not fold into a cube.

Example 5   If each edge of a cube is 5 cm, what is the surface area (the combined area of all of the faces) of the cube?

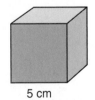

5 cm

Solution   A cube has six congruent square faces. Each face of this cube is 5 cm by 5 cm. So the area of one face is 25 cm², and the area of all six faces is

$$6 \times 25 \text{ cm}^2 = \textbf{150 cm}^2$$

Practice   Use the name of a geometric solid to describe each shape.

a.
Tent
triangular prism

b.
Funnel
cone

c.
Box
rectangular prism

A triangular prism has how many of each?

d. Faces   5 faces   **e.** Edges   9 edges   **f.** Vertices
6 vertices

Draw a representation of each shape.

g. Sphere   **h.** Rectangular prism

i. Cylinder

j. What three-dimensional figure would
be formed by folding this pattern?
triangular prism

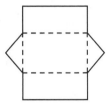

k. Calculate the surface area of a cube whose edges are 3 cm
long.   54 cm²

**Problem set
67**

1. The bag contains 20 red marbles, 30 white marbles, and
(36)   40 blue marbles.

(a) What is the ratio of red to blue marbles? $\frac{1}{2}$

(b) What is the ratio of white to red marbles? $\frac{3}{2}$

(c) If one marble is drawn from the bag, what is the
probability that the marble will not be white? $\frac{2}{3}$

2. When the product of $\frac{1}{3}$ and $\frac{1}{2}$ is subtracted from the sum
(30)   of $\frac{1}{3}$ and $\frac{1}{2}$, what is the difference? $\frac{2}{3}$

3. With the baby in his arms, Papa weighed 180 pounds.
(12,23)   Without the baby in his arms, Papa weighed $165\frac{1}{2}$ pounds.
How much did the baby weigh? $14\frac{1}{2}$ pounds

4. On his first 5 tests Cliff averaged 92 points. On his next 3
(28,55)   tests Cliff scored 94 points, 85 points, and 85 points,
respectively.

(a) What was his average for his last 3 tests?   88 points

(b) What was his average for all 8 tests?   90.5 points

5. Use a ratio box to solve this problem. The jeweler's tray
(65) was filled with diamonds and rubies in the ratio of 5 to 2.
If 210 gems filled the tray, how many were diamonds?
150 diamonds

6.

360 dolls

72 dolls
72 dolls
72 dolls
72 dolls
72 dolls

$\frac{4}{5}$ were sold

$\frac{1}{5}$ were not sold

6. Draw a diagram of this statement. Then answer the
(22,48) questions that follow.

> *Four fifths of the 360 dolls were sold during
> November.*

(a) How many of the dolls were sold during November?
288 dolls

(b) What percent of the dolls were not sold during
November? 20%

7. The three-dimensional figure that
(67) can be formed by folding this pattern
has how many

(a) edges? 12 edges

(b) faces? 6 faces

(c) vertices? 8 vertices

8. Refer to these triangles to answer the questions.
(58,62) Dimensions are in meters.

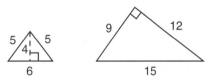

(a) What is the area of the scalene triangle? 54 m²

(b) What is the perimeter of the isosceles triangle? 16 m

(c) If one acute angle of the right triangle measures 37°,
then the other acute angle measures how many degrees?
53°

(d) Which of the two triangles is not symmetrical?
The right triangle is not symmetrical.

9. What is the average of the two numbers marked by arrows
(28,34) on this number line? 7.74

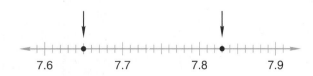

10. Write twenty-five ten thousandths in scientific notation.
⁽⁵⁷⁾ 2.5×10^{-3}

Write equations to solve problems 11 and 12.

11. What number is 24 percent of 75? $W_N = 0.24 \times 75$; 18
⁽⁶⁰⁾

12. What number is 120% of 12? $W_N = 1.2 \times 12$; 14.4
⁽⁶⁰⁾

13. Find each sum:
⁽⁶⁴⁾

(a) $(-2) + (-3) + (-4)$ −9   (b) $(+2) + (-3) + (+4)$ 3

14. Complete the table.
⁽⁴⁸⁾

Fraction	Decimal	Percent
(a) $\frac{1}{25}$	(b) 0.04	4%
$\frac{7}{8}$	(c) 0.875	(d) 87.5%

or $87\frac{1}{2}\%$

15. Use a unit multiplier to convert 700 mm to cm. 70 cm
⁽⁵⁰⁾

16. Find the product of M and its reciprocal if M is $11\frac{1}{9}$. 1
⁽⁹⁾

17. Describe the rule of the function and find the missing number.
⁽⁵⁸⁾

Multiply the "in" number by 7 to find the "out" number.

In	Function	Out
7	→	49
0	→	0
11	→	77
1	→	7

18. Round 7856.427
⁽³³⁾

(a) to the nearest hundredth. 7856.43

(b) to the nearest hundred. 7900

19. The diameter of Debbie's bicycle tire is 24 inches. What is the circumference of the tire to the nearest inch? 75 inches
⁽⁶⁶⁾

20. Consider angles A, B, C, and D below.
⁽⁴⁰⁾

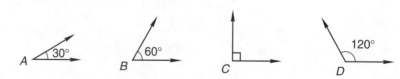

(a) Which two angles are complementary? $\angle A$ and $\angle B$

(b) Which two angles are supplementary? $\angle B$ and $\angle D$

21.(a) 2(5 ft + 3 ft)
      2(8 ft)
      16 ft
     or
2(5 ft + 3 ft)
10 ft + 6 ft
     16 ft

21. (a) Show two ways to simplify 2(5 ft + 3 ft).
₍₄₁₎
    (b) Which property is illustrated in part (a)?
       distributive property

22. Solve: $\dfrac{2.5}{w} = \dfrac{15}{12}$ 2
₍₃₉₎

Simplify:

23. $9 + 8\{7 \cdot 6 - 5[4 + (3 - 2 \cdot 1)]\}$ 145
₍₆₃₎

24. 1 yd − 1 ft, 3 in.   1 ft, 9 in.
₍₅₆₎

25. $6.4 - (0.6 - 0.04)$ 5.84   **26.** $\dfrac{3 + 0.6}{(3)(0.6)}$ 2
₍₃₅₎   ₍₅₂₎

27. $1\dfrac{2}{3} + 3\dfrac{1}{4} - 1\dfrac{5}{6}$ $3\dfrac{1}{12}$ **28.** $\dfrac{3}{5} \div 3\dfrac{1}{5} \cdot 5\dfrac{1}{3} \cdot |{-1}|$ 1
₍₃₀₎   _(26,59)

29. $3\dfrac{3}{4} \div \left(3 \div 1\dfrac{2}{3}\right)$ $2\dfrac{1}{12}$ **30.** $5^2 - \sqrt{4^2} + 2^3$ 29
₍₂₆₎   ₍₅₂₎

LESSON
68

Mental Math:
a. 1.25
b. $\frac{3}{4}$
c. 9
d. 30
e. 200 cm
f. 8
g. 7 m; 3 m²
Problem Solving:
  6 triangles

Algebraic Addition

Facts Practice: + − × ÷ Mixed Numbers (Test N in Test Masters)

Mental Math:
  a. 0.75 + 0.5   **b.** $\sqrt{1} - \left(\frac{1}{2}\right)^2$
  c. $4w - 1 = 35$ **d.** 12 × 2.5 (halve, double)
  e. 20 dm to cm   **f.** $33\frac{1}{3}\%$ of 24
  g. Find the perimeter and area of a rectangle that is 2 m long and
      1.5 m wide.

Problem Solving:
  How many different triangles are in this figure?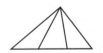

Recall that the graphs of −3 and 3 are the same distance from zero on the number line. The graphs are on the opposite sides of zero.

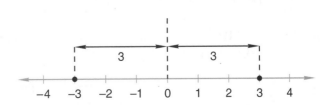

This is why we say that 3 and −3 are the opposites of each other.

3 is the opposite of −3

−3 is the opposite of 3

We can read −3 as *the opposite of 3*. Then −(−3) can be read as *the opposite of the opposite of 3*. This means that −(−3) is another way to write 3.

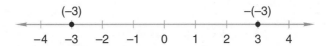

There are two ways to simplify the expression 7 − 3. The first way is to let the minus sign mean to subtract. If we subtract 3 from 7, the answer is 4.

$$7 - 3 = 4$$

The second way is to use the thought process of **algebraic addition.** To use algebraic addition, we let the minus sign mean that −3 is a negative number and treat the problem as an addition problem. This is what we think.

$$7 + (-3) = 4$$

We get the same answer both ways. The only difference is in the way we think about the problem.

We can also use algebraic addition to simplify this expression.

$$7 - (-3)$$

We use an addition thought and think that 7 is added to −(−3). This is what we think.

$$7 + [-(-3)]$$

But the opposite of −3 is 3, so we can write

$$7 + [3] = 10$$

We will practice using the thought process of algebraic addition because algebraic addition can be used to simplify expressions that would be very difficult to simplify if we used the thought process of subtraction.

Example 1   Simplify: −3 − (−2)

Solution   We think addition. We think we are to *add* −3 and −(−2). This is what we think.

$$(-3) + [-(-2)]$$

The opposite of −2 is 2 itself. So we have

$$(−3) + [2] = −1$$

Example 2 Simplify: −(−2) − 5 − (+6)

Solution We see three numbers. *We think addition.* We think

$$[−(−2)] + (−5) + [−(+6)]$$

We simplify the first and third numbers and get

$$[+2] + (−5) + [−6] = −9$$

Note that this time we write 2 as +2. Either 2 or +2 may be used.

Practice* Use algebraic addition to find these sums.

   a. (−3) − (+2) −5   **b.** (−3) − (−2) −1

   c. (+3) − (2) 1   **d.** (−3) − (+2) − (−4) −1

   e. (−8) + (−3) − (+2) −13   **f.** (−8) − (+3) + (−2) −13

Problem set 68

1. The mass of the beaker and the liquid was 1037 g. The mass of the empty beaker was 350 g. What was the mass of the liquid? 687 g
(12)

2. Use a ratio box to solve this problem. Jenny's soccer ball is covered with a pattern of pentagons and hexagons in the ratio of 3 to 5. If there are 12 pentagons, how many hexagons are in the pattern? 20 hexagons
(54)

3. When the sum of $\frac{1}{4}$ and $\frac{1}{2}$ is divided by the product of $\frac{1}{4}$ and $\frac{1}{2}$, what is the quotient? 6
(25,30)

4. Pens were on sale 4 for $1.24.
(46)

   (a) What was the price per pen? $0.31 per pen

   (b) How much would 100 pens cost? $31.00

5. Christy rode her bike 60 miles in 5 hours.
(46)

   (a) What was her average speed in miles per hour? 12 miles per hour

   (b) What was the average number of minutes it took to ride each mile? 5 minutes per mile

6. Sound travels about 331 meters per second in air. About
(32) how many seconds does it take sound to travel a
kilometer? 3 seconds

7. The following scores were made on a test:
(Inv. 4)

$$72, 80, 84, 88, 100, 88, 76$$

(a) Which score was made most often? 88

(b) What was the median of the scores? 84

(c) What is the mean of the scores? 84

8. What is the average of the two numbers marked by arrows
(28,34) on this number line? 9.1

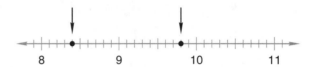

9. This rectangular shape is two cubes
(67) high and two cubes deep.

(a) How many cubes were used to
build this shape? 12 cubes

(b) What is the name of this shape?
rectangular prism

10. Find the circumference of each circle.
(66)

(a) 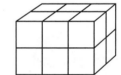 125.6 cm   (b) 40π cm

40 cm   20 cm

Use 3.14 for π.   Leave π as π.

11.

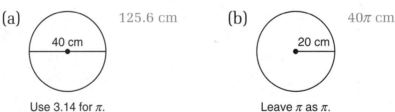

(a) right triangle
(b) isosceles
    triangle

11. The coordinates of the vertices of △ABC are A (1, −1),
(58,62) B (−3, −1), and C (1, 3). Draw the triangle and answer
these questions.

(a) What type of triangle is △ABC classified by angles?

(b) What type of triangle is △ABC classified by sides?

(c) Triangle ABC's one line of symmetry passes through
which vertex? A

(d) What is the measure of ∠B? 45°

(e) What is the area of △ABC? 8 sq. units

12. Multiply twenty thousand and thirty thousand, and write
(51) the product in scientific notation. 6×10^8

Write equations to solve problems 13 and 14.

13. What number is 75 percent of 400? $W_N = 0.75 \times 400; \; 300$
(60)

14. What number is 150% of $1\frac{1}{2}$?
(60) $W_N = 1.5 \times 1.5; \; 2.25$ or $W_N = 1\frac{1}{2} \times 1\frac{1}{2}; \; 2\frac{1}{4}$.

15. Simplify:
(68)

(a) $(-4) - (-6)$ 2

(b) $(-4) - (+6)$ –10

(c) $(-6) - (-4)$ –2

(d) $(+6) - (-4)$ 10

16. Find the surface area of a cube that
(67) has edges 4 inches long. 96 in.^{2}

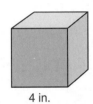

4 in.

17. Complete the table.
(48)

Fraction	Decimal	Percent
$\frac{3}{25}$	(a) 0.12	(b) 12%
(c) $1\frac{1}{5}$	(d) 1.2	120%

18. Evaluate: $x^2 + 2xy + y^2$ if $x = 4$ and $y = 5$ 81
(52)

19. Use the name of a geometric solid to describe each object.
(67)

(a)
rectangular prism

(b)
cone

(c)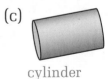
cylinder

20. In this figure, parallelogram *ABCD* is
(40,61) divided by a diagonal into two
congruent triangles. Angle *DCA* and
∠*BAC* have equal measures and are
complementary. Find the measure of

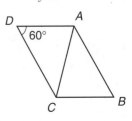

(a) ∠*DCA*. 45°

(b) ∠*DAC*. 75°

(c) ∠*CAB*. 45°

(d) ∠*ABC*. 60°

(e) ∠*BCA*. 75°

(f) ∠*BCD*. 120°

21. Example:
How many $0.25
pens can you buy
with $3.00?

21. Write a word problem for this division: $3.00 ÷ $0.25
(13)

Solve:

22. $\frac{4}{c} = \frac{3}{7\frac{1}{2}}$ 10
(39)

23. $(1.5)^2 = 15w$ 0.15
(35)

Simplify:

24. 1 gal − 1 qt, 1 pt, 1 oz 2 qt, 15 oz
(56)

25. 16 ÷ (0.04 ÷ 0.8) 320
(45)

26. $10 - [0.1 - (0.01)(0.1)]$
(63)   9.901

27. $\frac{5}{8} + \frac{2}{3} \cdot \frac{3}{4} - \frac{3}{4}$ $\frac{3}{8}$
(30,52)

28. $4\frac{1}{2} \cdot 3\frac{3}{4} \div 1\frac{2}{3}$ $10\frac{1}{8}$
(26)

29. $\sqrt{5^2 - 2^4}$ 3
(52)

30. $3 + 6[10 - (3 \cdot 4 - 5)]$
(63)   21

LESSON 69

More on Scientific Notation

Mental Math:
a. 2.5
b. 0.075
c. 2
d. 630
e. 2 dm
f. 16
g. $3\frac{1}{2}$

Problem Solving:
6 oz

Facts Practice: Metric Conversions (Test M in Test Masters)

Mental Math:

a. 4 − 1.5

b. 75×10^{-3}

c. $\frac{x}{4} = \frac{1.5}{3}$

d. 18 × 35 (halve, double)

e. 20 cm to dm

f. $66\frac{2}{3}\%$ of 24

g. 5^2, × 3, − 3, ÷ 8, $\sqrt{}$, × 7, − 1, ÷ 4, × 10, − 1, $\sqrt{}$, ÷ 2

Problem Solving:

On a balanced scale are four identical cubes and a 12-ounce weight distributed as shown. What is the weight of each cube?

When we write a number in scientific notation, we usually put the decimal point just to the right of the first digit that is not zero. To write

$$4600 \times 10^5$$

in scientific notation, we will use two steps. First we will write 4600 in scientific notation. In place of 4600 we will write 4.6×10^3. Now we have

$$4.6 \times 10^3 \times 10^5$$

For the second step we change the two powers of 10 into one power of 10. We recall that 10^3 means the decimal point is 3 places to the right and 10^5 means the decimal point is 5 places to the right. Since 3 places to the right and 5 places to the right is 8 places to the right, the power of 10 is 8.

$$4.6 \times 10^8$$

To perform the exercises in this lesson, first change the decimal number to scientific notation. Then change the two powers of 10 to one power of 10.

Example 1 Write 25×10^{-5} in scientific notation.

Solution First we write 25 in scientific notation.

$$2.5 \times 10^1 \times 10^{-5}$$

Then we combine the powers of 10 by remembering that 1 place to the right and 5 places to the left equals 4 places to the left.

$$\mathbf{2.5 \times 10^{-4}}$$

Example 2 Write 0.25×10^4 in scientific notation.

Solution First we write 0.25 in scientific notation.

$$2.5 \times 10^{-1} \times 10^4$$

Since 1 place to the left and 4 places to the right equals 3 places to the right we can write

$$\mathbf{2.5 \times 10^3}$$

With practice you will soon be able to perform these exercises mentally.

Practice* Write each number in the proper form of scientific notation.

a. 0.16×10^6 $\quad$ 1.6×10^5 $\qquad$ b. 24×10^{-7} $\quad$ 2.4×10^{-6}

c. 30×10^5 $\quad$ 3×10^6 $\qquad$ d. 0.75×10^{-8} $\quad$ 7.5×10^{-9}

e. 14.4×10^8 $\quad$ 1.44×10^9 $\qquad$ f. 12.4×10^{-5} $\quad$ 1.24×10^{-4}

Problem set 69 $^{(Inv. 4)}$ **1.** The following is a list of scores Jan received in a diving competition:

| 7.0 | 6.5 | 6.5 | 7.4 | 7.0 | 6.5 | 6.0 |

(a) Which score was received the most often? $\quad$ 6.5

(b) What is the median of the scores? $\quad$ 6.5

(c) What is the mean of the scores? $\quad$ 6.7

(d) What is the range of the scores? $\quad$ 1.4

2. Use a ratio box to solve this problem. The team won 15
(65) games and lost the rest. If the team's won-lost ratio was
5 to 3, how many games were played? 24 games

3. Brian swam 4 laps in 6 minutes. At that rate, how many
(53) minutes will it take Brian to swim 10 laps? 15 minutes

4. Write each number in the proper form of scientific
(69) notation.

(a) 15×10^5 1.5×10^6 (b) 0.15×10^5 1.5×10^4

5. Refer to the following sentence to answer questions (a)–(c).
(36,60)

> *The survey found that only 2 out of 5 Lilliputians
> believe in giants.*

(a) According to the survey, what fraction of the
Lilliputians do not believe in giants? $\frac{3}{5}$

(b) If 60 Lilliputians were selected for the survey, how
many of them would believe in giants? 24 Lilliputians

(c) What is the probability that a randomly selected
Lilliputian who participated in the survey would
believe in giants? $\frac{2}{5}$

6. The diameter of the tree stump was 40 cm. Find the
(66) circumference of the tree stump to the nearest centimeter.
126 cm

7. Use the name of a geometric solid to describe the shape of
(67) these objects.

(a) A volleyball   (b) A water pipe   (c) A tepee
sphere   cylinder   cone

8. (a) What is the perimeter of this
(58,62)   equilateral triangle? $1\frac{7}{8}$ in.

(b) What is the measure of each of its
angles? 60°

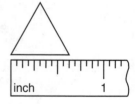

8.(c)

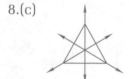

(c) Trace the triangle on your paper
and show its lines of symmetry.

9. Simplify:
(68)

(a) $(-4) + (-5) - (-6)$ -3

(b) $(-2) + (-3) - (-4) - (+5)$ -6

10. Find the circumference of each circle.
(66)

(a) 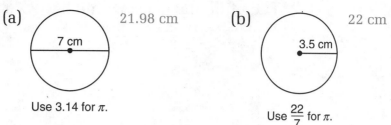 21.98 cm

(b) 22 cm

Use 3.14 for π.

Use $\frac{22}{7}$ for π.

11. Refer to the figure to answer questions
(37) (a)–(c). Dimensions are in millimeters.
Corners that look square are square.

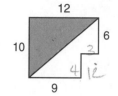

(a) What is the area of the hexagon?
108 mm^2

(b) What is the area of the shaded
triangle? 60 mm^2

(c) What fraction of the hexagon is shaded? $\frac{5}{9}$

Write equations to solve problems 12 and 13.

12. What number is 50 percent of 200? $W_N = \frac{1}{2} \times 200$; 100
(60)

13. What number is 250% of 4.2? $W_N = 2.5 \times 4.2$; 10.5
(60)

14. Complete the table.
(48)

FRACTION	DECIMAL	PERCENT
$\frac{3}{20}$	(a) 0.15	(b) 15%
(c) $1\frac{1}{2}$	(d) 1.5	150%

15. Refer to this figure to answer the following questions.
(40)

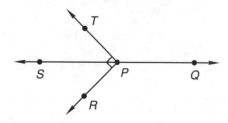

(a) Which angle is supplementary to $\angle SPT$? $\angle TPQ$

(b) Which angle is complementary to $\angle SPT$? $\angle SPR$

(c) If $\angle QPR$ measures 125°, then what is the measure
of $\angle QPT$? 145°

16. Evaluate: $a^2 - \sqrt{a} + ab$ if $a = 4$ and $b = 0.5$ 16
(52)

17. Describe the rule of this function.
(58) Then find the missing number.
Multiply the "in" number by 2, then subtract 1 to find the "out" number.

IN	FUNCTION	OUT
8 →		→ 15
6 →		→ 11
10 →		→ 19
4 →		→ $\boxed{7}$

18. Divide 144 by 11 and write the answer
(44)

(a) as a decimal with a bar over the repetend. $13.\overline{09}$

(b) rounded to the nearest whole number. 13

19. Anders used this formula to convert from degrees Celsius
(41) to degrees Fahrenheit.

$$°F = 1.8°C + 32$$

If the Celsius temperature (°C) is 20°C, what is the Fahrenheit temperature (°F)? 68°F

20. The prime number 19 is the average of which two different
(21,28) prime numbers? 7 and 31

Solve:

21. $t + \dfrac{5}{8} = \dfrac{15}{16}$ $\frac{5}{16}$
(30)

22. $\dfrac{a}{8} = \dfrac{3\frac{1}{2}}{2}$ 14
(39)

Simplify:

23.
(49)
$$\begin{array}{r} 5 \text{ ft} \ 7 \text{ in.} \\ + \ 6 \text{ ft} \ 8 \text{ in.} \\ \hline 12 \text{ ft} \ \ 3 \text{ in.} \end{array}$$

24. $\dfrac{350 \text{ m}}{1 \text{ s}} \cdot \dfrac{60 \text{ s}}{1 \text{ min}} \cdot \dfrac{1 \text{ km}}{1000 \text{ m}}$ $21\frac{\text{km}}{\text{min}}$
(50)

25. $6 - (0.5 \div 4)$ 5.875
(35)

26. $\$7.50 \div 0.075$ $100.00
(45)

27. $\left(3\dfrac{3}{4} \div 1\dfrac{2}{3}\right) \cdot 3$ $6\frac{3}{4}$
(26)

28. $4\dfrac{1}{2} + \left(5\dfrac{1}{6} \div 1\dfrac{1}{3}\right)$ $8\frac{3}{8}$
(26,30)

29. Use prime factorization to reduce $\frac{432}{675}$. $\frac{16}{25}$
(24)

30. (a) Convert $2\frac{1}{4}$ to a decimal and add it to 0.15.   2.4
(43)

(b) Convert 6.5 to a mixed number and add it to $\frac{5}{6}$. $7\frac{1}{3}$

LESSON
70

Mental Math:
a. 8.1
b. 625
c. 6
d. $240.00
e. 2000 mm
f. 15
g. 2 m; 0.25 m²
Problem Solving:

$$\begin{array}{r} 97 \\ \times\ 7 \\ \hline 679 \end{array}$$

Facts Practice: $+ - \times \div$ Mixed Numbers (Test N in Test Masters)

Mental Math:

   a. $4.8 + 3 + 0.3$ **b.** 25^2

   c. $5m - 3 = 27$ **d.** $\$4.80 \times 50$ (halve, double)

   e. 20 dm to mm   **f.** 60% of 25

   g. Find the perimeter and area of a square that has sides 0.5 m long.

Problem Solving:

   Copy this problem and fill in the missing digits.

$$\begin{array}{r} \_\,\_ \\ \times\ \_ \\ \hline 679 \end{array}$$

Recall from Lesson 67 that geometric solids are shapes that take up space. We use the word **volume** to describe the space occupied by a shape. To measure volume, we use units that occupy space. The units that we use to measure volume are cubes of certain sizes. We can use sugar cubes to help us think of volume.

Example 1   This rectangular prism was constructed of sugar cubes. Its volume is how many cubes?

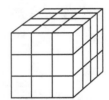

Solution   To find the volume of the prism, we calculate the number of cubes it contains. We see that there are 3 layers of cubes. Each layer contains 3 rows of cubes with 4 cubes in each row, or 12 cubes. Three layers with 12 cubes in each layer means that the volume of the prism is **36 cubes.**

    Volumes are measured by using cubes of a standard size. A cube whose edges are 1 centimeter long has a volume of 1 cubic centimeter, which we abbreviate by writing 1 cm³.

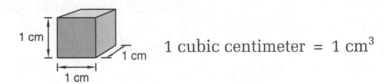

1 cubic centimeter = 1 cm³

Similarly, if each of the edges is 1 foot long, the volume is 1 cubic foot. If each of the edges is 1 meter long, the volume is 1 cubic meter.

$$1 \text{ cubic foot} = 1 \text{ ft}^3 \qquad 1 \text{ cubic meter} = 1 \text{ m}^3$$

To calculate the volume of a solid, we can imagine constructing the solid out of sugar cubes of the same size. We would begin by constructing the base and then building up the layers to the specified height.

Example 2 Find the number of 1-cm cubes that can be placed inside a rectangular box with the dimensions shown.

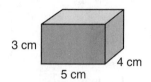

Solution The base of the box is 5 cm by 4 cm. So we can place 5 rows of 4 cubes on the base. Thus there are 20 cubes on the first layer.

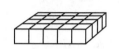

Since the box is 3 cm high, we can fit 3 layers of cubes in the box.

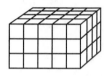

$$\frac{20 \text{ cubes}}{1 \text{ layer}} \times 3 \text{ layers} = 60 \text{ cubes}$$

We find that **60 1-cm cubes** can be placed in the box.

Example 3 What is the volume of this cube? Dimensions are in inches.

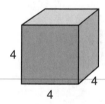

Solution The base is 4 in. by 4 in. Thus, 16 cubes can be placed on the base.

Since the big cube is 4 in. high, there are 4 layers of small cubes.

$$\frac{16 \text{ cubes}}{1 \text{ layer}} \times 4 \text{ layers} = 64 \text{ cubes}$$

Each small cube has a volume of 1 cubic inch. Thus, the volume of the big cube is **64 cubic inches** (64 in.^3).

Practice **a.** This rectangular prism was constructed of sugar cubes. Its volume is how many sugar cubes? 72 cubes

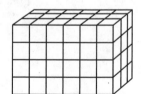

b. Find the number of 1-cm cubes that can be placed inside a box with dimensions as illustrated.
1000 1-cm cubes

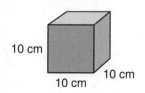

c. What is the volume of this rectangular prism? Dimensions are in feet. 240 ft³

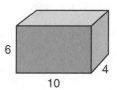

Problem set
70

1. It was 38 kilometers from the encampment to the castle. Milton galloped to the castle and cantered back. If the round trip took 4 hours, what was his average speed in kilometers per hour? 19 kilometers per hour
(53)

2. The vertices of two angles of a triangle are (3, 1) and (0, −4). The y-axis is a line of symmetry of the triangle.
(37,58)

(a) What are the coordinates of the third vertex of the triangle? (−3, 1)

(b) What is the area of the triangle? 15 sq. units

3. A little too large, because the diameter equals the circumference divided by π, which is more than 3. Therefore, the diameter must be less than 200 cm.

3. Using a tape measure, Gretchen found that the circumference of the great oak was 600 cm. Using 3 in place of π, she estimated that the tree's diameter was 200 cm. Was her estimate for the diameter a little too large or a little too small? Why?
(66)

4. Grapes were priced at 3 pounds for $1.29.
(46)

(a) What was the price per pound? $0.43 per pound

(b) How much would 10 pounds of grapes cost? $4.30

5. If the product of nine tenths and eight tenths is subtracted from the sum of seven tenths and six tenths, what is the difference? 0.58
(35)

6. Three fourths of the batter's 188 hits were singles.
(22,48)

(a) How many of the batter's hits were singles? 141 hits

(b) What percent of the batter's hits were not singles? 25%

7. On an inch ruler, which mark is halfway between the $1\frac{1}{2}$-inch mark and the 3-inch mark? $2\frac{1}{4}$-inch mark
(8)

8. Find the number of 1-cm cubes that can be placed in this box.
75 1-cm cubes
(70)

9. Find the circumference of each circle.
(66)

(a) 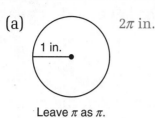 2π in.

Leave π as π.

(b) 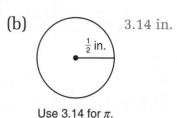 3.14 in.

Use 3.14 for π.

10. Write each number in scientific notation.
(69)

(a) 12×10^{-6} 1.2×10^{-5}

(b) 0.12×10^{-6} 1.2×10^{-7}

11. What is the average of the three numbers marked by arrows on the number line? 0.85
(28,34)

12. Use a unit multiplier to convert 1.25 kilograms to grams.
(50) 1250 grams

13. Find each missing exponent.
(47)

(a) $2^6 \cdot 2^3 = 2^{\square}$ 9

(b) $2^6 \div 2^3 = 2^{\square}$ 3

14. Write an equation to solve this problem. What number is $\frac{1}{6}$ of 100? $W_N = \frac{1}{6} \times 100$; $16\frac{2}{3}$
(60)

15. Complete the table.
(48)

Fraction	Decimal	Percent
(a) $\frac{7}{50}$	(b) 0.14	14%
$\frac{5}{6}$	(c) $0.8\overline{3}$	(d) $83\frac{1}{3}\%$

16. Simplify:
(68)

(a) $(-6) - (-4) + (+2)$ 0

(b) $(-5) + (-2) - (-7) - (+9)$ -9

17. Evaluate: $ab - (a - b)$ if $a = 0.4$ and $b = 0.3$ 0.02
(52)

18. Round $29,374.\overline{65}$ to the nearest whole number. 29,375
(42)

19. Estimate the product of 6.085 and $7\frac{15}{16}$. 48
(29,33)

20. What three-dimensional figure can be
⁽⁶⁷⁾ formed by folding this pattern? Sketch
the three-dimensional figure.

pyramid;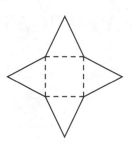

21. What is the surface area of a cube with edges 2 ft long?
⁽⁶⁷⁾ 24 ft²

Solve:

22. $4.3 = x - 0.8$ 5.1
⁽³⁵⁾

23. $\dfrac{2}{d} = \dfrac{1.2}{1.5}$ 2.5
⁽³⁹⁾

Simplify:

24.   10 lb
⁽⁵⁶⁾ − 6 lb 7 oz
    ——————————
    3 lb 9 oz

25. $\dfrac{\$5.25}{1\ hr} \cdot \dfrac{8\ hr}{1\ day} \cdot \dfrac{5\ days}{1\ week}$
⁽⁵³⁾ $\frac{\$210.00}{week}$

26. $3\dfrac{3}{4} \div \left(1\dfrac{2}{3} \cdot 3\right)$ $\frac{3}{4}$
⁽²⁶⁾

27. $4\dfrac{1}{2} + 5\dfrac{1}{6} - 1\dfrac{1}{3}$ $8\frac{1}{3}$
⁽³⁰⁾

28. $(0.06 \div 5) \div 0.004$ 3
⁽⁴⁵⁾

29. Write $9\frac{1}{2}$ as a decimal number and multiply it by 9.2. 87.4
⁽⁴³⁾

30. (a) What is the total price of a $15 meal including 6%
⁽⁴⁶⁾   sales tax? $15.90

   (b) A 15% tip on a $15 meal would be how much money?
       $2.25

INVESTIGATION 7

Balanced Equations

Since Lesson 3 we have solved equations informally by using various strategies for finding the missing number. In this investigation we will practice a more formal, algebraic method for solving equations. To help us see equations from this new perspective we will use a balance scale as a visual aid.

Equations are sometimes called **balanced equations** because the two sides of the equation "balance" each other. A balance scale can be used as a model of an equation. We replace the equals sign with a balanced scale. The left and right sides of the equation are placed on the left and right trays of the balance. For example, $x + 12 = 33$ becomes

Using a balance-scale model we think of how to get the unknown number, in this case x, alone on one side of the scale. Using our example, we could remove 12 (subtract 12) from the left side of the scale. However, if we did that the scale would no longer be balanced. So we make this rule for ourselves.

> **Whatever operation we perform on one side of an equation, we also perform on the other side of the equation to maintain a balanced equation.**

We see that there are two steps to the process.

Step 1: Select the operation that will isolate the variable.

Step 2: Perform the selected operation on both sides of the equation.

In our example we select "subtract 12" as the operation required to isolate x (to "get x by itself"). Then we perform this operation on both sides of the equation.

Select operation:

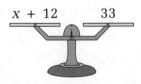

To isolate x, *subtract 12*.

Perform operation:

To keep the scale balanced, subtract 12 *from both sides of the equation.*

After subtracting 12 from both sides of the equation, x is isolated on one side of the scale, and 21 balances x on the other side of the scale. This shows that $x = 21$. We check our solution by replacing x with 21 in the original equation.

$$x + 12 = 33 \qquad \text{original equation}$$
$$21 + 12 = 33 \qquad \text{replaced } x \text{ with 21}$$
$$33 = 33 \qquad \text{simplified left side}$$

Both sides of the equation equal 33. This shows that the solution, $x = 21$, is correct.

Now we will illustrate a second equation, $45 = x + 18$, with a balance-scale model.

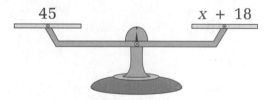

This time the unknown number is on the right side of the balance scale, added to 18.

1. Select the operation that will isolate the variable and write that operation on your paper. subtract 18

2. Describe the operation to be performed that will keep the scale balanced. Subtract 18 from both sides of the equation.

3. Describe what will remain on the left and right side of the balance scale after the operation is performed.
On the left side will be 27, and on the right side will be x.

We show the line-by-line solution of this equation below.

$$45 = x + 18 \qquad \text{original equation}$$
$$45 - 18 = x + 18 - 18 \qquad \text{subtracted 18 from both sides}$$
$$27 = x + 0 \qquad \text{both sides simplified}$$
$$27 = x \qquad x + 0 = x$$

We check the solution by replacing x with 27 in the original equation.

$$45 = x + 18 \qquad \text{original equation}$$
$$45 = 27 + 18 \qquad \text{replaced } x \text{ with } 27$$
$$45 = 45 \qquad \text{simplified right side}$$

By checking the solution in the original equation we see that the solution is correct. Now we will revisit this equation to illustrate one more idea.

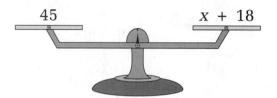

4. Suppose the contents of the two trays of the balance scale were reversed. That is, $x + 18$ was moved to the left side, and 45 was moved to the right side. Would the scale still be balanced? Write what the equation would be.
Yes, the equation would still be balanced.; $x + 18 = 45$

Now we will consider an equation that involves multiplication rather than addition.

$$2x = 132$$

Since $2x$ means two x's $(x + x)$, we may show this equation on a balance scale two ways.

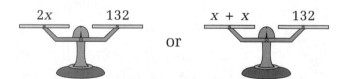

Our goal is to isolate x. That is, to perform the operations necessary to get one x alone on one side of the scale. We do not subtract 2 because 2 is not added to x. We do not subtract x because there is no x to subtract from the other side of the equation. To isolate x in this equation we *divide by 2*. To keep the equation balanced we *divide both sides by 2*.

Select operation:

To isolate x, *divide by 2*.

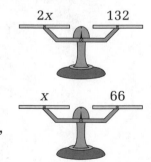

Perform operation:

To keep the equation balanced, divide *both sides by 2*.

Here we show the line-by-line solution of this equation.

$$2x = 132 \qquad \text{original equation}$$

$$\frac{2x}{2} = \frac{132}{2} \qquad \text{divided both sides by 2}$$

$$1x = 66 \qquad \text{simplified both sides}$$

$$x = 66 \qquad 1x = x$$

Next we show the check of the solution.

$$2x = 132 \qquad \text{original equation}$$

$$2(66) = 132 \qquad \text{replaced } x \text{ with 66}$$

$$132 = 132 \qquad \text{simplified left side}$$

This check shows that the solution, $x = 66$, is correct.

5.

5. Sketch a balance-scale model for the equation, $3x = 132$.

6. Select the operation that will isolate the variable and write that operation on your paper. divide by 3

7. Describe the operations to be performed that will keep the scale balanced. Divide both sides of the equation by 3.

8.

8. Sketch a balance scale and show what is on both sides of the scale after the operations are performed.

9. Write the line-by-line solution of this equation. $3x = 132$
$\frac{3x}{3} = \frac{132}{3}$
$x = 44$

10. $3x = 132$
  $3(44) = 132$
   $132 = 132$ ✓

10. Show the check of the solution.

Most students choose to solve the equation $3x = 132$ by dividing both sides of the equation by 3. There is another operation that could be selected that is often useful, which we will describe next. First note that the number multiplying the variable, in this case 3, is called the **coefficient** of x. Instead of dividing by the coefficient of x, we could choose to **multiply by the reciprocal** of the coefficient. In this case we could multiply by $\frac{1}{3}$.

$$3x = 132$$

$$\frac{1}{3} \cdot 3x = \frac{1}{3} \cdot 132$$

$$1x = \frac{132}{3}$$

$$x = 44$$

13. $\frac{3}{4}x = \frac{9}{10}$

$\frac{4}{3} \cdot \frac{3}{4}x = \frac{9}{10} \cdot \frac{4}{3}$

$1x = \frac{36}{30}$

$x = \frac{6}{5} \left(\text{or } 1\frac{1}{5}\right)$

14. $\frac{3}{4}x = \frac{9}{10}$

$\frac{3}{4} \cdot 1\frac{1}{5} = \frac{9}{10}$

$\frac{3}{4} \cdot \frac{6}{5} = \frac{9}{10}$

$\frac{18}{20} = \frac{9}{10}$

$\frac{9}{10} = \frac{9}{10} \checkmark$

15.(c) $x + 2.5 = 7$

$x + 2.5 - 2.5 = 7 - 2.5$

$x + 0 = 4.5$

$x = 4.5$

(d) $x + 2.5 = 7$

$4.5 + 2.5 = 7$

$7 = 7 \checkmark$

16.(c) $3.6 = y + 2$

$3.6 - 2 = y + 2 - 2$

$1.6 = y + 0$

$1.6 = y$

(d) $3.6 = y + 2$

$3.6 = 1.6 + 2$

$3.6 = 3.6 \checkmark$

17.(c) $4w = 132$

$\frac{4w}{4} = \frac{132}{4}$

$w = 33$

(d) $4w = 132$

$4(33) = 132$

$132 = 132 \checkmark$

18.(c) $1.2m = 1.32$

$\frac{1.2m}{1.2} = \frac{1.32}{1.2}$

$m = 1.1$

(d) $1.2m = 1.32$

$1.2(1.1) = 1.32$

$1.32 = 1.32 \checkmark$

19.(c) $x + \frac{3}{4} = \frac{5}{6}$

$x + \frac{3}{4} - \frac{3}{4} = \frac{5}{6} - \frac{3}{4}$

$x + 0 = \frac{10}{12} - \frac{9}{12}$

$x = \frac{1}{12}$

(d) $x + \frac{3}{4} = \frac{5}{6}$

$\frac{1}{12} + \frac{3}{4} = \frac{5}{6}$

$\frac{1}{12} + \frac{9}{12} = \frac{5}{6}$

$\frac{10}{12} = \frac{5}{6}$

$\frac{5}{6} = \frac{5}{6} \checkmark$

When solving equations with whole number or decimal number coefficients, it is usually easier to think about dividing by the coefficient. However, when solving equations with fractional coefficients it is usually easier to multiply by the reciprocal of the coefficient. Refer to the following equation for questions 11–14.

$$\frac{3}{4}x = \frac{9}{10}$$

11. Select the operation that will result in $\frac{3}{4}x$ becoming $1x$ in the equation.   multiply by $\frac{4}{3}$

12. Describe the operations to be performed to keep the equation balanced.   Multiply both sides of the equation by $\frac{4}{3}$.

13. Write a line-by-line solution of the equation.

14. Show the check of the solution.

We find that the solution to the equation is $\frac{6}{5}$ $\left(\text{or } 1\frac{1}{5}\right)$. In arithmetic we usually convert improper fractions to mixed numbers. In algebra we usually leave improper fractions in improper form unless the problem states or implies that a mixed number answer is preferable.

For each of the following equations, (a) state the operation selected to isolate the variable, (b) describe the operations to be performed to keep the equation balanced, (c) write a line-by-line solution of the equation, and (d) show the check of the solution.

15. $x + 2.5 = 7$ (a) subtract 2.5   (b) Subtract 2.5 from both sides of the equation.

16. $3.6 = y + 2$ (a) subtract 2   (b) Subtract 2 from both sides of the equation.

17. $4w = 132$ (a) divide by 4   (b) Divide both sides of the equation by 4.

18. $1.2m = 1.32$ (a) divide by 1.2   (b) Divide both sides of the equation by 1.2.

19. $x + \dfrac{3}{4} = \dfrac{5}{6}$ (a) subtract $\frac{3}{4}$ (b) Subtract $\frac{3}{4}$ from both sides of the equation.

20.(c) $\frac{3}{4}x = \frac{5}{6}$

$\frac{4}{3} \cdot \frac{3}{4}x = \frac{5}{6} \cdot \frac{4}{3}$

$1x = \frac{20}{18}$

$x = \frac{10}{9}$

(d) $\frac{3}{4}x = \frac{5}{6}$

$\frac{3}{4} \cdot \frac{10}{9} = \frac{5}{6}$

$\frac{30}{36} = \frac{5}{6}$

$\frac{5}{6} = \frac{5}{6}$ ✓

20. $\dfrac{3}{4}x = \dfrac{5}{6}$ (a) multiply by $\frac{4}{3}$ (b) Multiply both sides of the equation by $\frac{4}{3}$.

21. Make up an addition equation with decimal numbers. Solve and check it. See student work.

22. Make up a multiplication equation with a fractional coefficient. Solve and check it. See student work.

LESSON 71

Finding the Whole Group When a Fraction is Known

Facts Practice: Classifying Quadrilaterals and Triangles (Test O in Test Masters)

Mental Math:

a. $(-3) + (-12)$

b. 4.5×10^{-3}

c. $\frac{w}{100} = \frac{24}{30}$

d. $12 \times 2\frac{1}{2}$ (halve, double)

e. 50 cm to m

f. 75% of $36

g. What is the total cost of a $30 item plus 8% sales tax?

Problem Solving:

Bry has three different shirts and three different ties he can wear with each shirt. How many different shirt-tie combinations can Bry wear? Designating the shirts A, B, and C, and the ties 1, 2, and 3, one combination is A1. List all the possible combinations.

Drawing diagrams of fraction problems can help us understand problems such as the following:

Three fifths of the fish in the pond were bluegill. If there were 45 bluegill in the pond, how many fish were in the pond?

The 45 bluegill are 3 of the 5 parts. We divide 45 by 3 and find there are 15 fish in each part. Since each of the 5 parts is 15 fish, there were 75 fish in all.

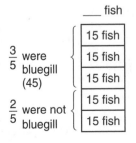

Example 1 When Sean finished page 51, he was $\frac{3}{8}$ of the way through his book. His book had how many pages?

Solution Sean read 51 pages. This is 3 of 8 parts of the book. Since $51 \div 3$ is 17, each part is 17 pages. Thus the whole book, all 8 parts, totals 8×17, which is **136 pages.**

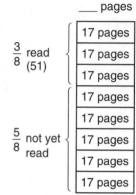

Example 2 As Sandra went from room to room she found that $\frac{3}{5}$ of the lights were on and that 30 lights were off. How many lights were on?

Solution Since $\frac{3}{5}$ of the lights were on, $\frac{2}{5}$ of the lights were off. Because $\frac{2}{5}$ of the lights was 30 lights, each fifth was 15 lights. Thus **45 lights** were on.

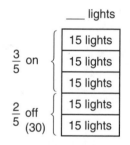

a.
25 students
$\frac{3}{5}$ were boys (15) { 5 students / 5 students / 5 students
$\frac{2}{5}$ were girls { 5 students / 5 students

Practice Draw a diagram to solve each problem.

a. Three fifths of the students in the class are boys. If there are 15 boys in the class, how many students are there in all? 25 students

b.
40 clowns
$\frac{5}{8}$ had happy faces { 5 clowns / 5 clowns / 5 clowns / 5 clowns / 5 clowns
$\frac{3}{8}$ did not have happy faces (15) { 5 clowns / 5 clowns / 5 clowns

b. Five eighths of the clowns had happy faces. If 15 clowns did not have happy faces, how many clowns were there in all? 40 clowns

c. Vincent was chagrined when he looked at the clock, for in $\frac{3}{4}$ of an hour he had only answered 12 homework questions. At that rate, how many questions would Vincent answer in an hour? 16 questions

Problem set 71 (32,53)

c.
16 questions
$\frac{3}{4}$ had been answered (12) { 4 questions / 4 questions / 4 questions
$\frac{1}{4}$ will be answered { 4 questions

1. Nine seconds elapsed from the time Mark saw the lightning until he heard the thunder. The lightning was about how many kilometers from Mark? (Sound travels about 331 meters per second in air.) 3 kilometers

2. What is the average of the three numbers marked by (28,34) arrows on this number line? 3.43

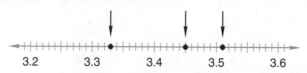

3. On his first 2 tests Nate's average score was 80 percent. On
(55) his next 3 tests Nate's average score was 90 percent. What
was his average score for all 5 tests? 86 percent

4. Twenty billion is how much more than nine billion?
(51) Write the answer in scientific notation. 1.1×10^{10}

5. What is the sum of the first five prime numbers? 28
(21)

6. Use a ratio box to solve this problem. The ratio of new
(65) ones to used ones in the box was 4 to 7. In all there were
242 new ones and used ones in the box. How many new
ones were in the box? 88 new ones

7.

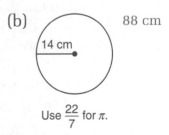

7. Draw a diagram of this statement. Then answer the
(71) questions that follow.

> When Debbie finished page 78, she was $\frac{3}{5}$ of the
> way through her book.

(a) How many pages are in her book? 130 pages

(b) How many pages does she have left to read? 52 pages

8. Find the number of 1-inch cubes that
(70) can be placed in this box. Dimensions
are in inches. 64 1-inch cubes

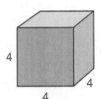

9. What is the surface area of the cube
(67) in problem 8? 96 in.²

10. Find the circumference of each circle.
(66)

(a) 87.92 cm

28 cm

Use 3.14 for π.

(b) 88 cm

14 cm

Use $\frac{22}{7}$ for π.

11. Write each number in scientific notation.
(69)

(a) 25×10^6 2.5×10^7 (b) 25×10^{-6} 2.5×10^{-5}

12. Complete the table.
(48)

FRACTION	DECIMAL	PERCENT
(a) $\frac{1}{10}$	0.1	(b) 10%
(c) $\frac{1}{200}$	(d) 0.005	0.5%

13. Write an equation to solve each problem.
(60)

     (a) What number is 35% of 80? $W_N = 0.35 \times 80$; 28

     (b) Three fourths of 24 is what number? $\frac{3}{4} \times 24 = W_N$; 18

14. Describe the rule of this function.
(58) Then find the missing number. Add 7
to the "in" number to find the "out" number.

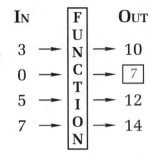

15. Sketch a rectangular prism. A rectangular prism has how
(67) many vertices? ; 8 vertices

16. Figure *ABCD* is a trapezoid. Dimen-
(37,62) sions are in centimeters.

     (a) Find the perimeter of the trapezoid.
        36 cm

     (b) Find the area of the right triangle.
        24 cm^2

     (c) Find the area of the isosceles triangle. 48 cm^2

     (d) Combine the areas of the triangles to find the area of
        the trapezoid. 72 cm^2

17. The restaurant bill was $16.50. Marcia planned to leave a
(46) tip of about 15%. She has a few dollar bills and quarters
in her purse. About how much money should she leave
for the tip? about $2.50

18. The principal tallied the number of
(Inv. 4) middle-grade classrooms in the
school that had a certain number of
students in the classroom. Make a
box-and-whisker plot from this
information.

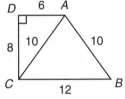

Distribution of Students in Middle-Grade Classrooms

Number of Students	Tally of Classes
26	II
27	III
28	IIII
29	III
30	II
31	I

19.

19. The coordinates of three vertices of triangle *ABC* are
(Inv. 3) *A* (0, 6), *B* (8, −2), and *C* (−9, −3). Graph the triangle. Then
use a protractor to find the measure of $\angle A$, $\angle B$, and $\angle C$ to
the nearest degree. $m\angle A = 90°$; $m\angle B = 48°$; $m\angle C = 42°$

20. Evaluate: $y - xy$ if $x = 0.1$ and $y = 0.01$ 0.009
(52)

Solve each equation. Show each step. Check the solution.

21. $m + 5.75 = 26.4$ 20.65   **22.** $\dfrac{3}{4}x = 48$ 64
(Inv. 7)   (Inv. 7)

23. What is the name of a parallelogram whose sides are
(Inv. 6) equal in length but whose angles are not necessarily right
angles? rhombus

Simplify:

24. $\dfrac{4^2 + \{20 - 2[6 - (5 - 2)]\}}{\sqrt{36}}$ 5
(63)

25.   1 yd
(56) $-$ 1 ft 1 in.
              _____
              1 ft 11 in.

26. $3.5 \text{ hr} \cdot \dfrac{60 \text{ min}}{1 \text{ hr}} \cdot \dfrac{60 \text{ s}}{1 \text{ min}}$
(50)
12,600 s

27. $6\dfrac{2}{3} \div \left(4\dfrac{1}{2} \cdot 2\dfrac{2}{3}\right)$ $\frac{5}{9}$
(26)

28. $7\dfrac{1}{2} - 5\dfrac{1}{6} + 1\dfrac{1}{3}$ $3\frac{2}{3}$
(30)

29. (a) $(-5) + (-6) - |-7|$ (b) $(-15) - (-24) - (+8)$ 1
(68) -18

30. Write 1.5 as a mixed number and subtract it from $2\frac{2}{3}$. $1\frac{1}{6}$
(30,43)

LESSON
72

Implied Ratios

Facts Practice: $+ - \times \div$ Mixed Numbers (Test N in Test Masters)

Mental Math:

a. $(-10) + (+17)$ **b.** $\left(\frac{2}{3}\right)^2$
c. $6x + 2 = 32$ **d.** What decimal is 10% of 36?
e. 500 g to kg   **f.** $33\frac{1}{3}\%$ of $36
g. Find 15% of $30 by finding 10% of $30 plus half of 10% of $30.

Problem Solving:

On a balanced scale are four identical
blocks marked X along with a 6-oz and an
18-oz weight distributed as shown. What is
the weight of each block marked X? Write
an equation that is illustrated by this
balanced scale.

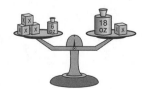

Many rate problems can be solved by completing a proportion. Consider the following problem:

If 12 books weigh 20 pounds, how much would 30 books weigh?

We will illustrate two methods for solving this problem. First we will use the rate method. If 12 books weigh 20 pounds, we can write two rates.

(a) $\dfrac{12 \text{ books}}{20 \text{ pounds}}$ 　　　　　　(b) $\dfrac{20 \text{ pounds}}{12 \text{ books}}$

To find the weight of 30 books, we could multiply 30 books by rate (b).

$$30 \text{ books} \times \frac{20 \text{ pounds}}{12 \text{ books}} = 50 \text{ pounds}$$

We find that 30 books would weigh 50 pounds.

Now we will solve the same problem by completing a proportion. We will record the information in a ratio box. Instead of using the words "ratio" and "actual count," we will write "Case 1" and "Case 2." We will use p to stand for pounds.

	Case 1	Case 2
Books	12	30
Pounds	20	p

From the table we write a proportion and solve it.

$$\frac{12}{20} = \frac{30}{p} \qquad \text{proportion}$$

$$12p = 20 \cdot 30 \qquad \text{cross multiplied}$$

$$\frac{\overset{1}{\cancel{12}}p}{\underset{1}{\cancel{12}}} = \frac{20 \cdot 30}{12} \qquad \text{divided by 12}$$

$$p = 50 \qquad \text{simplified}$$

We find that 30 books would weigh 50 pounds.

Example 1　If 5 pounds of grapes cost $1.20, how much would 12 pounds of grapes cost? Use a ratio box to solve the problem.

Solution   First we draw the ratio box. We use d for dollars.

	Case 1	Case 2
Pounds	5	12
Dollars	1.2	d

Now we write the proportion and solve for d.

$$\frac{5}{1.2} = \frac{12}{d} \qquad \text{proportion}$$

$$5d = 12(1.2) \qquad \text{cross multiplied}$$

$$\frac{\overset{1}{\cancel{5}}d}{\underset{1}{\cancel{5}}} = \frac{12(1.2)}{5} \qquad \text{divided by 5}$$

$$d = 2.88 \qquad \text{simplified}$$

We find that 12 pounds of grapes cost **$2.88**.

Example 2   Mrs. C can tie 25 bows in 3 minutes. How many bows can she tie in 1 hour at that rate? Work the problem (a) using rates and (b) using a ratio box.

Solution   We can use either minutes or hours but not both. *The units must be the same in both cases.* Since there are 60 minutes in 1 hour, we will use 60 minutes instead of 1 hour.

(a) $60 \, \cancel{\text{min}} \times \dfrac{25 \text{ bows}}{3 \, \cancel{\text{min}}} = 500 \text{ bows}$

Mrs. C can tie **500 bows** in one hour.

(b)

	Case 1	Case 2
Bows	25	b
Minutes	3	60

Next we write the proportion, cross multiply, and solve by dividing by 3.

$$\frac{25}{3} = \frac{b}{60} \qquad \text{proportion}$$

$$25 \cdot 60 = 3b \qquad \text{cross multiplied}$$

$$\frac{25 \cdot 60}{3} = \frac{\overset{1}{\cancel{3}}b}{\underset{1}{\cancel{3}}} \qquad \text{divided by 3}$$

$$b = \textbf{500} \qquad \text{simplified}$$

Example 3   Six is to 15 as 9 is to what number?

Solution   We can sort the numbers in this question using a case 1-case 2 ratio box.

	Case 1	Case 2
First number	6	9
Second number	15	n

Now we write and solve a proportion.

$$\frac{6}{15} = \frac{9}{n}$$

$$6n = 9 \cdot 15$$

$$\frac{\cancel{6}n}{\cancel{6}} = \frac{9 \cdot 15}{6}$$

$$n = 22\frac{1}{2}$$

Practice   **a.** Use a case 1-case 2 ratio box to solve this problem. Kevin rode 30 km in 2 hours. At that rate, how long would it take him to ride 75 km?   5 hours

b. If 6 bales are needed to feed 40 head of cattle, how many bales are needed to feed 50 head of cattle? Use the rate method and then use a ratio box to solve this problem. $7\frac{1}{2}$ bales

c. Five is to 15 as 9 is to what number?   27

Problem set 72

1. Napoleon Bonaparte was born in 1769 and died in 1821. For how many years did he live?   52 years
(12)

2. In her first 4 games Jill averaged 4 points per game. In her next 6 games Jill averaged 9 points per game. What was her average number of points per game after 10 games? 7 points
(55)

3. Use a unit multiplier to convert 2.5 liters to milliliters. 2500 milliliters
(50)

4. If the product of $\frac{1}{2}$ and $\frac{2}{5}$ is subtracted from the sum of $\frac{1}{2}$ and $\frac{2}{5}$, what is the difference? $\frac{7}{10}$
(30)

5. Use a ratio box to solve this problem. The ratio of
(54) carnivores to herbivores in the jungle was 2 to 7. If there
were 126 carnivores in the jungle, how many herbivores
were there? 441 herbivores

6. Use a ratio box to solve this problem. If 4 books weigh 9
(72) pounds, how many pounds would 14 books weigh?
$31\frac{1}{2}$ pounds

7. Write an equation to solve each problem.
(60)

(a) Two fifths of 60 is what number? $\frac{2}{5} \times 60 = W_N$; 24

(b) How much money is 75% of $24? $M = 0.75 \times \$24$; $18

8. The diameter of a bicycle tire is 20 in. Find the distance
(66) around the tire to the nearest inch. 63 in.

9.
225 votes

$\frac{2}{3}$ for Edmund (150) — 75 votes / 75 votes

$\frac{1}{3}$ not for Edmund — 75 votes

9. Draw a diagram of this statement. Then answer the
(71) questions that follow.

*Edmund received 150 votes. This was two thirds
of the votes cast.*

(a) How many votes were cast? 225 votes

(b) How many votes were not for Edmund? 75 votes

10. The volume of a block of ice with the
(70) dimensions shown is equal to how
many 1 in. by 1 in. by 1 in. ice cubes?
480 ice cubes

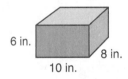

6 in. 8 in. 10 in.

11. Find the area of each of the six surfaces of the block of ice
(67) shown in problem 10. Then add the areas to find the total
surface area of the block of ice. 376 in.²

12. Write each number in scientific notation.
(69)

(a) 0.6×10^6 6×10^5

(b) 0.6×10^{-6} 6×10^{-7}

13. What is the average of the three numbers marked by
(28,34) arrows on this number line? 1.46

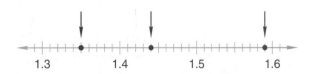

1.3   1.4   1.5   1.6

14. Complete the table.
₍₄₈₎

FRACTION	DECIMAL	PERCENT
$\frac{3}{5}$	(a) 0.6	(b) 60%
(c) $\frac{1}{40}$	(d) 0.025	2.5%

15.(a) 8100 =
$2^2 \cdot 3^4 \cdot 5^2$

15. (a) Write the prime factorization of 8100 using exponents.
₍₂₁₎

(b) Find $\sqrt{8100}$. 90

16. (a) Find the area of the parallelogram.
_(37,61) 48 in.^{2}

(b) Find the area of the shaded triangle. 24 in.^{2}

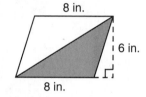

8 in.

6 in.

8 in.

(c) If each acute angle of the parallelogram measures 72°, then what is the measure of each obtuse angle of the parallelogram?
108°

17. Only the triangular prism is a polyhedron because it is the only figure whose faces are polygons.

17. Name each geometric solid and describe why only one of
₍₆₇₎ the figures is a polyhedron.

(a) sphere   (b)   (c) 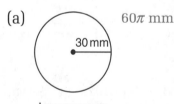 cylinder

triangular prism

18. Find the circumference of each circle.
₍₆₆₎

(a) 60π mm

30 mm

Leave π as π.

(b)   188.4 mm

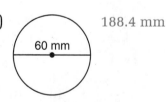

60 mm

Use 3.14 for π.

19. Compare: $\dfrac{2}{3}$ $\boxed{<}$ 0.667
₍₄₃₎

20. The dots on this number line represent all integers greater
₍₄₎ than or equal to −3 that are also less than or equal to +3.

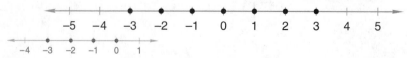

Sketch a number line on your paper and graph all integers greater than −4 that are not positive.

21. Evaluate: $x^2 - y^2$ if $x = 5$ and $y = 4$ 9
(52)

Write a line-by-line solution of each equation and show a check of the solution.

22. $m - \dfrac{2}{3} = 1\dfrac{3}{4}$ $2\frac{5}{12}$ **23.** $\dfrac{2}{3}w = 24$ 36
(Inv. 7)   (Inv. 7)

Simplify:

24. $\dfrac{[30 - 4(5 - 2)] + 5\left(3^3 - 5^2\right)}{\sqrt{9} + \sqrt{16}}$ 4
(63)

25. $\begin{array}{r} 2 \text{ gal } 1 \text{ qt} \\ -\ 1 \text{ gal } 1 \text{ qt } 1 \text{ pt} \\ \hline 3 \text{ qt } 1 \text{ pt} \end{array}$ **26.** $\dfrac{1}{2}$ mi $\cdot \dfrac{5280 \text{ ft}}{1 \text{ mi}} \cdot \dfrac{1 \text{ yd}}{3 \text{ ft}}$
(56)   (50)   880 yd

27. $\left(2\dfrac{1}{2}\right)^2 \div \left(4\dfrac{1}{2} \cdot 6\dfrac{2}{3}\right)$ $\frac{5}{24}$ **28.** $7\dfrac{1}{2} - \left(5\dfrac{1}{6} + 1\dfrac{1}{3}\right)$ 1
(26)   (30)

29. (a) $(-7) + |+5| + (-9)$ (b) $(16) + (-24) - (-18)$
(68) -11 10

30. Write the sum of $5\frac{1}{4}$ and 1.9 as a decimal. 7.15
(43)

LESSON

73

Multiplying and Dividing Signed Numbers

Facts Practice: Classifying Quadrilaterals and Triangles
(Test O in Test Masters)

Mental Math:

a. $(+15) + (-25)$ b. 8.75×10^3
c. $\dfrac{12}{x} = \dfrac{2.5}{7.5}$ d. $3\dfrac{1}{2} \times 18$ (double, halve)
e. 500 mL to L   f. $66\dfrac{2}{3}\%$ of $36
g. Estimate 15% of 39 by finding 10% of 40 plus half of 10% of 40.

Problem Solving:

Floor tiles which are one-foot square and come 20 in a box will be used to cover the floor of a rectangular workroom that is 20 ft, 6 in. long and 14 ft, 6 in. wide. (a) If cut-off portions of tiles may be used, how many boxes of tile are needed? (b) If cut-off tiles may not be used, how many boxes are needed?

We can develop the rules for the multiplication and division of signed numbers if we remember that multiplication is a shorthand notation for repeated addition. We remember that 2 times 3 means $3 + 3$ and that 2 times -3 means $(-3) + (-3)$, so

$$2(3) = 6 \quad \text{and} \quad 2(-3) = -6$$

We remember that division undoes multiplication, so the following must be true:

$$\text{If} \quad 2(3) = 6 \quad \text{then} \quad \frac{6}{2} = 3 \quad \text{and} \quad \frac{6}{3} = 2$$

Likewise,

$$\text{if} \quad 2(-3) = -6 \quad \text{then} \quad \frac{-6}{2} = -3 \quad \text{and} \quad \frac{-6}{-3} = +2$$

We use these examples to illustrate the fact that when we multiply or divide two positive numbers the answer is a positive number. Also, when we multiply or divide two numbers whose signs are different, the answer is a negative number. But what happens if we multiply two negative numbers? Since 2 times -3 equals -6

$$2(-3) = -6$$

then the *opposite of* 2 times -3 should equal the *opposite of* -6, which is 6.

$$(-2)(-3) = +6$$

And since division undoes multiplication, these division examples must also be true.

$$\frac{+6}{-2} = -3 \quad \text{and} \quad \frac{+6}{-3} = -2$$

These conclusions give us the rules for the multiplication and division of signed numbers.

RULES FOR MULTIPLICATION AND DIVISION

1. If the two numbers that are multiplied or divided have the same sign, the answer is a positive number.

2. If the two numbers that are multiplied or divided have different signs, the answer is a negative number.

Here are some examples.

	MULTIPLICATION	DIVISION

$$(+6)(+2) = +12 \qquad \frac{+6}{+2} = +3$$

$$(-6)(-2) = +12 \qquad \frac{-6}{-2} = +3$$

$$(-6)(+2) = -12 \qquad \frac{-6}{+2} = -3$$

$$(+6)(-2) = -12 \qquad \frac{+6}{-2} = -3$$

Example Divide or multiply:

(a) $\dfrac{-12}{+4}$ (b) $\dfrac{-12}{-3}$ (c) $(6)(-3)$ (d) $(-6)(-4)$

Solution We divide or multiply as indicated. If both signs are the same, the answer is positive. If one sign is positive and the other is negative, the answer is negative. Showing the positive sign is permitted but is not necessary.

(a) **–3** (b) **+4** (c) **–18** (d) **+24**

Practice Divide or multiply:

a. $(-7)(3)$ –21 b. $(+4)(-8)$ –32 c. $(8)(+5)$ 40

d. $(-8)(-3)$ 24 e. $\dfrac{25}{-5}$ –5 f. $\dfrac{-27}{-3}$ 9

g. $\dfrac{-28}{4}$ –7 h. $\dfrac{+30}{6}$ 5 i. $\dfrac{+45}{-3}$ –15

Problem set 73

1. (72) Use a ratio box to solve this problem. If Mrs. C can wrap 12 packages in 5 minutes, how many packages can she wrap in 1 hour? 144 packages

2. (55) Lydia walked for 30 minutes a day for 5 days. The next 3 days she walked for an average of 46 minutes per day. What was the average amount of time she spent walking during those 8 days? 36 minutes

3. (45) If the sum of 0.2 and 0.5 is divided by the product of 0.2 and 0.5, what is the quotient? 7

4. Use a unit multiplier to convert 23 cm to mm. 230 mm
(50)

5. Use a ratio box to solve this problem. The ratio of
(65) paperback books to hardbound books in the school library
was 3 to 11. If there were 9240 hardbound books in the
library, how many books were there in all? 11,760 books

6. Write each number in scientific notation.
(69)

(a) 24×10^{-5} 2.4×10^{-4} (b) 24×10^7 2.4×10^8

7.
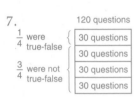
120 questions

$\frac{1}{4}$ were true-false { 30 questions / 30 questions

$\frac{3}{4}$ were not true-false { 30 questions / 30 questions

7. Draw a diagram of this statement. Then answer the
(71) questions that follow.

The 30 true-false questions amounted to $\frac{1}{4}$ of the test's questions.

(a) How many questions were on the test? 120 questions

(b) How many of the questions were not true-false?
90 questions

8. Write an equation to solve each of these problems.
(60)

(a) Five ninths of 45 is what number? $\frac{5}{9} \times 45 = W_N$; 25

(b) What number is 80% of 760? $W_N = 0.8 \times 760$; 608

9. Divide or multiply:
(73)

(a) $\dfrac{-36}{9}$ -4

(b) $\dfrac{-36}{-6}$ 6

(c) $9(-3)$ -27

(d) $(+8)(+7)$ 56

10. The face of the spinner is divided
(21,36) into eighths. If the arrow is spun
once, what is the probability that it
will stop on a composite number? $\frac{3}{8}$

11. The x-axis is a line of symmetry for $\triangle RST$. The coordinates
(58,62) of R and S are (6, 0) and (−2, −2), respectively.

(a) What are the coordinates of T? (−2, 2)

(b) What type of triangle is $\triangle RST$ classified by sides?
isosceles triangle

(c) If the measure of $\angle R$ is approximately 28°, then what
is the approximate measure of $\angle S$? 76°

12. If the signs of the two factors are the same—both positive or both negative—then the product is positive. If the signs of the two factors are different, the product is negative.

12. Describe how to determine whether the product of two
(73) signed numbers is positive or negative.

13. Find the number of 1-ft cubes that will
(70) fit inside a closet with dimensions as
shown. 96 1-ft cubes

8 ft
3 ft
4 ft

14. Find the circumference of each circle.
(66)

(a) 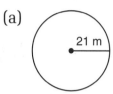   131.88 m   (b) 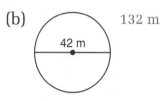   132 m

21 m   42 m

Use 3.14 for π.   Use $\frac{22}{7}$ for π.

15. Complete the table.
(48)

FRACTION	DECIMAL	PERCENT
(a) $2\frac{1}{2}$	2.5	(b) 250%
(c) $\frac{1}{500}$	(d) 0.002	0.2%

Classify each triangle in problems 16–18 as acute, right, or obtuse. Also classify each triangle as equilateral, isosceles, or scalene. Then find the area of each triangle. Dimensions are in centimeters.

16.
(37,62)

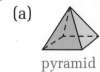

8
10
6

right; scalene;
24 cm²

17.
(37,62)

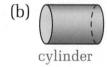

4
8
4.44
5

obtuse; scalene;
10 cm²

18.
(37,62)

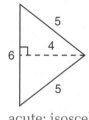

5
4
6
5

acute; isosceles;
12 cm²

19. Name each three-dimensional figure.
(67)

(a) 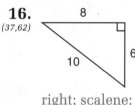   (b)   (c)

pyramid   cylinder   cone

20. Compare: $\frac{2}{3}$ of 96 $\;\boxed{<}\;$ $\frac{5}{6}$ of 84
(60)

21. Evaluate: $ab - (a - b)$ if $a = \frac{5}{6}$ and $b = \frac{3}{4}$ $\frac{13}{24}$
(52)

Solve and check. Show your work.

22.
(Inv. 7)
$\frac{3}{5}w = 15$　25

23.
(Inv. 7)
$b - 1.6 = (0.4)^2$　1.76

24.
(Inv. 7)
$20w = 5.6$　0.28

Simplify:

25.
(49)
　2 yd　1 ft　7 in.
+ 1 yd　2 ft　8 in.
_____
　4 yd　1 ft　3 in.

26.
(50)
$0.5 \text{ m} \cdot \dfrac{100 \text{ cm}}{1 \text{ m}} \cdot \dfrac{10 \text{ mm}}{1 \text{ cm}}$

500 mm

27.
(26)
$12\frac{1}{2} \cdot 4\frac{1}{5} \cdot 2\frac{2}{3}$　140

28.
(26)
$7\frac{1}{2} \div \left(6\frac{2}{3} \cdot 1\frac{1}{5}\right)$　$\frac{15}{16}$

29.
(68)
(a) $(-8) + (-7) - (-15)$　0

(b) $(-15) + (+11) - |+24|$

−28

30.
(26,43)
Find the product of 2.25 and $1\frac{1}{3}$.　3

LESSON
74

Fractional Part of a Number, Part 2

Facts Practice: + − × ÷ Mixed Numbers (Test N in Test Masters)

Mental Math:

a. $(-8) - (-12)$

b. 45×10^{-3}

c. $7w + 1 = 50$

d. Estimate 15% tip on a $19.81 bill.

e. 400 m to km

f. 80% of $25

g. 10% of 80, × 2, $\sqrt{}$, × 7, − 1, ÷ 3, $\sqrt{}$, × 12, $\sqrt{}$, ÷ 6

Problem Solving:

Gil rode the Whirling Dervish at the fair. The cylindrical chamber spins, forcing riders against the outer wall while the floor drops away. If the chamber is 30 feet in diameter and if it spins around 30 times during a ride, how far do the riders travel? Do riders travel more or less than half of a mile?

Whirling Dervish
|←——30 ft——→|

Mental Math:
a. 4
b. 0.045
c. 7
d. $3.00
e. 0.4 km
f. $20
g. 1
Problem Solving:
2826 ft, which is more than $\frac{1}{2}$ mile

In some fractional-part-of-a-number problems the fraction is unknown. In some fractional-part-of-a-number problems the total is unknown. As we discussed in Lesson 60 we can translate these problems to equations by replacing the word **of** with a multiplication sign and by replacing the word **is** with an equals sign.

Example 1   What fraction of 56 is 42?

Solution   We translate this statement directly into an equation by replacing **what fraction** with W_F, replacing **of** with a multiplication symbol, and replacing **is** with an equals sign.

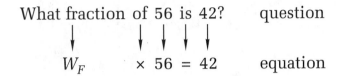

$$
\begin{array}{ll}
\text{What fraction of 56 is 42?} & \text{question}\\[4pt]
W_F \qquad \times\ 56\ =\ 42 & \text{equation}
\end{array}
$$

To solve, we divide both sides by 56.

$$\frac{W_F \times 56}{56} = \frac{42}{56} \qquad \text{divided by 56}$$

$$W_F = \frac{3}{4} \qquad \text{simplified}$$

If the question had been, "What decimal part of 56 is 42?" the procedure would have been the same. As the last step we would have written $\frac{3}{4}$ as the decimal number 0.75.

$$W_D = 0.75$$

Example 2   Seventy-five is what decimal part of 20?

Solution   We make a direct translation.

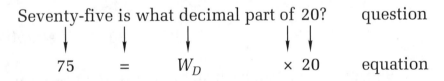

$$
\begin{array}{ll}
\text{Seventy-five is what decimal part of 20?} & \text{question}\\[4pt]
75 \qquad = \qquad W_D \qquad\quad \times\ 20 & \text{equation}
\end{array}
$$

To solve, we divide both sides by 20.

$$\frac{75}{20} = \frac{W_D \times 20}{20} \qquad \text{divided by 20}$$

$$W_D = \mathbf{3.75} \qquad \text{simplified}$$

If the question had asked "What fractional part," we would have written the answer as a fraction or as a mixed number.

$$\frac{75}{20} = W_F \qquad \text{fraction}$$

$$\frac{15}{4} = W_F \qquad \text{reduced}$$

$$3\frac{3}{4} = W_F \qquad \text{mixed number}$$

Example 3   Three fourths of what number is 60?

Solution   In this problem the total is the unknown. We can still do a direct translation from the question to the equation.

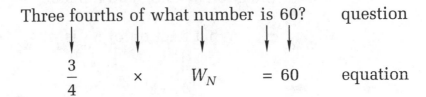

$$\frac{3}{4} \times W_N = 60 \qquad \text{equation}$$

To solve, we multiply both sides by $\frac{4}{3}$.

$$\frac{4}{3} \times \frac{3}{4} \times W_N = 60 \times \frac{4}{3} \qquad \text{multiplied by } \frac{4}{3}$$

$$W_N = \mathbf{80} \qquad \text{simplified}$$

Had the question been phrased by using 0.75 instead of $\frac{3}{4}$, the procedure would have been the same.

Seventy-five hundredths of what number is 60?   question

$$0.75 \times W_N = 60 \qquad \text{equation}$$

To solve, we can divide both sides by 0.75.

$$\frac{0.75 \times W_N}{0.75} = \frac{60}{0.75} \qquad \text{divided by 0.75}$$

$$W_N = 80 \qquad \text{simplified}$$

Practice   Translate each statement into an equation and solve.

a. What fraction of 130 is 80? $W_F \times 130 = 80$; $\frac{8}{13}$

b. Seventy-five is what decimal part of 300?
$75 = W_D \times 300$; 0.25

c. Eighty is 0.4 of what number? $80 = 0.4 \times W_N$; 200

d. Sixty is $\frac{5}{6}$ of what number? $60 = \frac{5}{6} \times W_N$; 72

e. Sixty is what fraction of 90? $60 = W_F \times 90$; $\frac{2}{3}$

f. What decimal part of 80 is 60? $W_D \times 80 = 60$; 0.75

g. Forty is 0.08 of what number? $40 = 0.08 \times W_N$; 500

h. Six fifths of what number is 60? $\frac{6}{5} \times W_N = 60$; 50

Problem set
74

1. During the first 3 days of the week, Mike read an average
(55) of 28 pages per day. During the next 4 days, Mike
averaged 42 pages per day. For the whole week, Mike
read an average of how many pages per day? 36 pages

2. Twelve ounces of Brand X costs $1.14. Sixteen ounces of
(46) Brand Y costs $1.28. Brand X costs how much more per
ounce than Brand Y? 1.5¢ per ounce

3. Use a unit multiplier to convert $4\frac{1}{2}$ feet to inches. 54 inches
(50)

4. Use a ratio box to solve this problem. The ratio of left-
(65) handed students to right-handed students in the math
class was 2 to 3. If 18 of the students were right-handed,
how many students were there in the math class?
30 students

5. Use a ratio box to solve this problem. If 5 pounds of
(72) apples cost $1.40, how much would 8 pounds of apples
cost? $2.24

6.

300 triathletes
50 triathletes
50 triathletes

$\frac{5}{6}$ completed
the course

50 triathletes
50 triathletes
50 triathletes
50 triathletes

$\frac{1}{6}$ did not
complete
the course

50 triathletes

6. Draw a diagram of this statement. Then answer the
(22,36) questions that follow.

*Five sixths of the 300 triathletes completed the
course.*

(a) How many triathletes completed the course?
250 triathletes
(b) What was the ratio of triathletes who completed the
course to those who did not complete the course? $\frac{5}{1}$

Write equations to solve problems 7–10.

7. Fifteen is $\frac{3}{8}$ of what number? $15 = \frac{3}{8} \times W_N$; 40
(74)

8. Seventy is what decimal part of 200? $70 = W_D \times 200$; 0.35
(74)

9. Two fifths of what number is 120? $\frac{2}{5} \times W_N = 120$; 300
(74)

10. The store made a 60% profit on the $180.00 selling price
(60) of the coat. What was the store's profit?
$P = 0.6 \times 180.00; $108.00

11. (a) What is the volume of this cube?
(67,70)   27 in.^{3}
(b) What is its surface area? 54 in.^{2}

3 in.

12. Find the circumference of each circle.
(66)

(a) 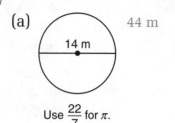 44 m

14 m

Use $\frac{22}{7}$ for π.

(b) 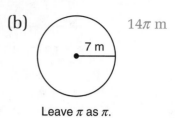 14π m

7 m

Leave π as π.

13. Complete the table.
(48)

FRACTION	DECIMAL	PERCENT
$3\frac{1}{2}$	(a) 3.5	(b) 350%
(c) $\frac{7}{20}$	(d) 0.35	35%

14. The shoe salesperson received a 20% commission on the
(60) sale of a $35.00 pair of shoes. What was the salesperson's
commission? $W_N = 0.2 \times \$35.00;\ \$7.00$

15.(a) Multiply the "in" number by 3 then add 1 to find the "out" number.

15. (a) Describe the rule of this function.
(58)

(b) Find the missing numbers in the function.

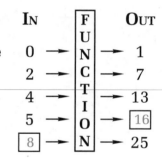

IN

0 → 1
2 → 7
4 → 13
5 → 16
8 → 25

OUT

FUNCTION

16. Write 425 million in scientific notation. 4.25×10^8
(51)

Refer to the figure to answer problems 17 and 18. $\overline{AE} \parallel \overline{BD}$,
$\overline{AB} \parallel \overline{EC}$, and $EC = ED$.

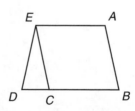

17. (a) What type of quadrilateral is figure *ABCE*? parallelogram
(Inv. 6,62)

(b) What type of quadrilateral is figure *ABDE*? trapezoid

17. (c) isosceles

(c) What type of triangle is $\triangle ECD$ classified by sides?

18. If the measure of $\angle A$ is 100°, then what is the measure of
(40,61)
     (a) $\angle ABC$? 80°   (b) $\angle BCE$? 100°   (c) $\angle ECD$? 80°

     (d) $\angle EDC$? 80°   (e) $\angle DEC$? 20°   (f) $\angle DEA$? 100°

19. Arrange these numbers in order from least to greatest:
(33)   0.0103, 0.013, 0.021, 0.1023
$$0.013, \ 0.1023, \ 0.0103, \ 0.021$$

20. Evaluate: $(m + n) - mn$ if $m = 1\frac{1}{2}$ and $n = 2\frac{2}{3}$ $\frac{1}{6}$
(52)

Show a line-by-line solution of each of these equations. Then show a check of the solution.

21. $p + 3\frac{1}{5} = 7\frac{1}{2}$ $4\frac{3}{10}$ **22.** $3n = 0.138$ 0.046
(Inv. 7)   (Inv. 7)

23. $n - 0.36 = 4.8$ 5.16   **24.** $\frac{2}{3}x = \frac{8}{9}$ $\frac{4}{3}$
(Inv. 7)   (Inv. 7)

Simplify:

25. $\sqrt{49} + \left\{ 5\left[3^2 - \left(2^3 - \sqrt{25} \right) \right] - 5^2 \right\}$ 12
(63)

26.   4 hr   5 min   15 s
(56)   − 1 hr   15 min   30 s
          2 hr   49 min   45 s

27. (a) $(-9) + (-11) - (+14)$ (b) $(26) + (-43) - |-36|$
(68)   −34   −53

28. (a) $(-3)(12)$ −36   (b) $(-3)(-12)$ 36
(73)

     (c) $\dfrac{-12}{3}$ −4   (d) $\dfrac{-12}{-3}$ 4

29. Write the sum of $8\frac{1}{3}$ and 7.5 as a mixed number. $15\frac{5}{6}$
(30,43)

30. Florence was facing north. If she turns 180°, which
(17)   direction will she be facing?   south

LESSON 75

Area of a Complex Figure • Area of a Trapezoid

Facts Practice: Classifying Quadrilaterals and Triangles
(Test O in Test Masters)

Mental Math:

   a. $(-15) - (+20)$ **b.** 15^2

   c. $\frac{30}{40} = \frac{g}{12}$ **d.** $25 \times \$2.40$ (double, halve)(twice)

   e. 250 mg to g   **f.** 10% of $35

   g. What decimal is half of 10% of 36?

Problem Solving:

   Find the missing fraction: $\frac{5}{6} \times \frac{3}{10} \times \frac{16}{3} \times \frac{?}{?} = 1$

Area of a complex figure

We have practiced finding the areas of figures that can be divided into two or more rectangles. In this lesson we will begin finding the areas of figures that include triangular regions as well.

Example 1

Find the area of this figure. Corners that look square are square. Dimensions are in millimeters.

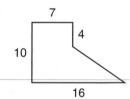

Solution

We divide the figure into smaller polygons, the measurements of which we can be certain. In this case we draw dashes that divide the figure into a rectangle and a triangle.

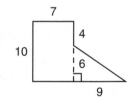

$$\text{Area of rectangle} = 7 \times 10 = 70 \text{ mm}^2$$

$$+ \text{ Area of triangle} = \frac{6 \times 9}{2} = 27 \text{ mm}^2$$

$$\overline{\text{Total area} \hspace{4.5cm} = \mathbf{97 \text{ mm}^2}}$$

When dividing figures we use only the information provided or calculated, and we avoid assumptions. For this figure it may *appear* that extending the slanted segment would divide the figure into two triangles. However, that is an incorrect assumption that leads to an incorrect answer.

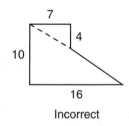

Incorrect

Example 2   Find the area of this figure. Corners that look square are square. Dimensions are in centimeters.

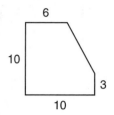

Solution   There are many ways to divide this figure.

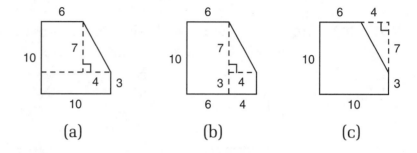

(a)   (b)   (c)

We decide to use (c). We will find the area of the big rectangle and subtract from it the area of the triangle.

$$\text{Area of rectangle} = 10 \times 10 = 100 \text{ cm}^2$$

$$- \text{ Area of triangle} = \frac{4 \times 7}{2} = 14 \text{ cm}^2$$

$$\text{Area of figure} = \textbf{86 cm}^2$$

Area of a trapezoid   Recall that a quadrilateral with just one pair of parallel sides is a trapezoid. One way to find the area of a trapezoid is to divide the trapezoid into two triangular regions and find the combined area of the triangles.

Example 3   Find the area of this trapezoid. Dimensions are in centimeters.

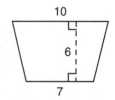

Solution   We can divide the trapezoid into two triangles by drawing either diagonal. We show both ways.

Both figures have two triangles which we have labeled A and B. The height of each triangle is 6 cm.

$$\text{Area of triangle } A = \frac{10 \times 6}{2} = 30 \text{ cm}^2$$

$$+ \text{ Area of triangle } B = \frac{7 \times 6}{2} = 21 \text{ cm}^2$$

$$\text{Total area} \qquad\qquad\qquad = \textbf{51 cm}^2$$

Practice*   Find the area of each figure. Dimensions are in centimeters. Corners that look square are square.

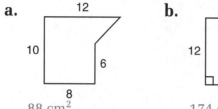

a.

12

10

6

8

88 cm^2

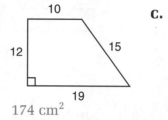

b.

10

12

15

19

174 cm^2

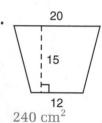

c.

20

15

12

240 cm^2

Problem set 75

1. Pablo ran an 8-lap race. For the first 5 laps he averaged 72
(55) seconds per lap. For the rest of the race he averaged 80 seconds per lap. What was his average lap time for the whole race?   75 seconds

2. If 30 ounces of cereal costs $2.49, what is the cost per
(46) ounce?   8.3¢ per ounce

3. One thousand, five hundred meters is how many
(32) kilometers?   1.5 kilometers

4. The sum of $\frac{1}{2}$ and $\frac{3}{5}$ is how much greater than the product
(30) of $\frac{1}{2}$ and $\frac{3}{5}$? $\frac{4}{5}$

5. The ratio of Marci's age to Chelsea's age is 3 to 2. If Marci
(54) is 60 years old, she is how many years older than Chelsea?
20 years

6. Compare: 12.5×10^{-4} $\bigcirc$$=$ 1.25×10^{-3}
(57,69)

7. Use a ratio box to solve this problem. Martha rode 40 miles
(72) in 3 hours. At this rate, how long would it take Martha to ride 100 miles? $7\frac{1}{2}$ hours

8.

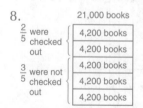

21,000 books

$\frac{2}{5}$ were checked out { 4,200 books / 4,200 books

$\frac{3}{5}$ were not checked out { 4,200 books / 4,200 books / 4,200 books

8. Draw a diagram of this statement. Then answer the
(22) questions that follow.

     Two fifths of the library's 21,000 books were checked out during the school year.

(a) How many books were checked out?   8,400 books

(b) How many books were not checked out?   12,600 books

Write equations to solve problems 9–12.

9. Sixty is $\frac{5}{12}$ of what number? $60 = \frac{5}{12} \times W_N$; 144
(74)

10. Seventy percent of $35.00 is how much money?
(60) $0.7 \times \$35.00 = M$; $24.50

11. Thirty-five is what fraction of 80? $35 = W_F \times 80$; $\frac{7}{16}$
(74)

12. Fifty-six is what decimal part of 70? $56 = W_D \times 70$; 0.8
(74)

13. Simplify:
(73)

(a) $\frac{-120}{4}$ −30

(b) (−12)(11) −132

(c) $\frac{-120}{-5}$ 24

(d) 12(+20) 240

14. Find the volume of this rectangular
(70) prism. Dimensions are in centimeters.
3000 cm³

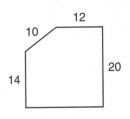

15. The diameter of the plate was 11 inches. Find its circum-
(66) ference to the nearest half inch. $34\frac{1}{2}$ inches

16. Find the area of this trapezoid.
(75) Dimensions are in inches. 112 in.²

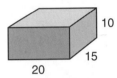

17. A corner was trimmed from a square
(75) sheet of paper to leave the paper in this
shape. Dimensions are in centimeters.

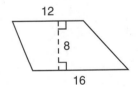

(a) What was the length of each side
of the square paper before the
corner was trimmed? 20 cm

(b) Find the perimeter of the figure. 76 cm

(c) Find the area of the figure. 376 cm²

18. Complete the table.
(48)

FRACTION	DECIMAL	PERCENT
(a) $1\frac{1}{4}$	(b) 1.25	125%
$\frac{1}{8}$	(c) 0.125	(d) $12\frac{1}{2}$%

19. The taxi cab bill was $12.50. Sandra tipped the driver
(46) 20%. Altogether, how much money did Sandra pay the
driver? $15.00

20. Evaluate: $x^3 - xy - \dfrac{x}{y}$ if $x = 2$ and $y = 0.5$ 3
(52)

Solve and check. Show each step.

21. $\dfrac{5}{8}x = 40$ 64
(Inv. 7)

22. $1.2w = 26.4$ 22
(Inv. 7)

23. $y + 3.6 = 8.47$ 4.87
(Inv. 7)

Simplify:

24. $9^2 - \left[3^3 - \left(9 \cdot 3 - \sqrt{9}\right)\right]$ 78
(63)

25.
(56)
$$\begin{array}{r} 2 \text{ hr } 48 \text{ min } 20 \text{ s} \\ - 1 \text{ hr } 23 \text{ min } 48 \text{ s} \\ \hline 1 \text{ hr } 24 \text{ min } 32 \text{ s} \end{array}$$

26. $100 \text{ yd} \cdot \dfrac{3 \text{ ft}}{1 \text{ yd}} \cdot \dfrac{12 \text{ in.}}{1 \text{ ft}}$
(50)
     3600 in.

27. $5\dfrac{1}{3} \cdot \left(3 \div 1\dfrac{1}{3}\right)$ 12
(26)

28. $3\dfrac{1}{5} + 2\dfrac{1}{2} - 1\dfrac{1}{4}$ $4\frac{9}{20}$
(30)

29. (a) $(-26) + (-15) - (-40)$ −1
(68)
   (b) $(-5) + (-4) - (-3) - (+2)$ −8

30. Find each missing exponent.
(47)
   (a) $5^5 \cdot 5^2 = 5^{\square}$ 7   (b) $5^5 \div 5^2 = 5^{\square}$ 3

LESSON
76

Complex Fractions

Mental Math:
a. −12
b. 0.0625
c. 4
d. 18
e. 0.5 cm
f. 8
g. $26.50
Problem Solving:
Kim: 7, 7, 3, 1, 1, 1
7, 3, 3, 3, 3, 1
Shell: 7, 7, 3, 3
4 attempts

Facts Practice: + − × ÷ Integers (Test P in Test Masters)

Mental Math:

a. (+6) + (−18)

b. 6.25×10^{-2}

c. $9a - 4 = 32$

d. 12 is $\frac{2}{3}$ of what number?

e. 5 mm to cm

f. What is $\frac{2}{3}$ of 12?

g. What is the total cost of a $25 video game plus 6% sales tax?

Problem Solving:

Kim hit a target like the one shown 6 times, earning a total score of 20. Find two sets of scores Kim could have earned. Shell earned a total score of exactly 20 in the fewest possible number of attempts. How many attempts did Shell make?

A **complex fraction** is a fraction that has one or more fractions as the numerator or denominator—a fraction that contains a fraction. Each of the following is a complex fraction:

$$\frac{\frac{3}{5}}{\frac{2}{3}} \qquad \frac{25\frac{2}{3}}{100} \qquad \frac{15}{7\frac{1}{3}} \qquad \frac{\frac{a}{b}}{\frac{b}{c}}$$

To simplify these fractions, we multiply the fraction by a fraction name for 1 that makes the denominator 1.

Example 1   Simplify: $\dfrac{\frac{3}{5}}{\frac{2}{3}}$

Solution   We focus our attention on the denominator of the complex fraction, which is $\frac{2}{3}$. We will multiply the denominator by the reciprocal of $\frac{2}{3}$, which is $\frac{3}{2}$, so that the new denominator is 1. We will also multiply the numerator by $\frac{3}{2}$.

$$\frac{\frac{3}{5}}{\frac{2}{3}} \times \frac{\frac{3}{2}}{\frac{3}{2}} = \frac{\frac{9}{10}}{1} = \frac{9}{10}$$

We multiplied the complex fraction by a complex name for 1 that made the denominator 1. Since $\frac{9}{10}$ divided by 1 is $\frac{9}{10}$, the complex fraction simplifies to $\frac{9}{10}$.

An alternative method for simplifying some complex fractions is to treat the fraction as a division problem. We may change the format of the division problem to a more familiar form.

$$\text{dividend} \quad \dfrac{\dfrac{3}{5}}{\dfrac{2}{3}} \quad \longrightarrow \quad \dfrac{3}{5} \div \dfrac{2}{3}$$
$$\text{divisor}$$

Then we simplify the division using the method described in Lesson 25.

$$\frac{3}{5} \div \frac{2}{3}$$

$$\frac{3}{5} \cdot \frac{3}{2} = \frac{9}{10}$$

Example 2 Simplify: $\dfrac{25\dfrac{2}{3}}{100}$

Solution First we write both numerator and denominator as fractions.

$$\dfrac{\dfrac{77}{3}}{\dfrac{100}{1}}$$

Now we multiply above and below by $\frac{1}{100}$.

$$\dfrac{\dfrac{77}{3}}{\dfrac{100}{1}} \cdot \dfrac{\dfrac{1}{100}}{\dfrac{1}{100}} = \dfrac{\dfrac{77}{300}}{\dfrac{1}{1}} = \mathbf{\dfrac{77}{300}}$$

Example 3 Simplify: $\dfrac{15}{7\dfrac{1}{3}}$

Solution We begin by writing both numerator and denominator as improper fractions.

$$\dfrac{\dfrac{15}{1}}{\dfrac{22}{3}}$$

Now we multiply above and below by $\frac{3}{22}$.

$$\frac{\dfrac{15}{1}}{\dfrac{22}{3}} \cdot \frac{\dfrac{3}{22}}{\dfrac{3}{22}} = \frac{\dfrac{45}{22}}{1} = 2\frac{1}{22}$$

Example 4   Change $83\frac{1}{3}$ percent to a fraction.

Solution   A percent is a fraction that has a denominator of 100. Thus $83\frac{1}{3}\%$ is

$$\frac{83\dfrac{1}{3}}{100}$$

Next we write both numerator and denominator as fractions.

$$\frac{\dfrac{250}{3}}{\dfrac{100}{1}}$$

Now we multiply above and below by $\frac{1}{100}$.

$$\frac{\dfrac{250}{3}}{\dfrac{100}{1}} \cdot \frac{\dfrac{1}{100}}{\dfrac{1}{100}} = \frac{\dfrac{250}{300}}{1} = \frac{5}{6}$$

Practice   Simplify:

a. $\dfrac{37\dfrac{1}{2}}{100}$ $\frac{3}{8}$ **b.** $\dfrac{12}{\dfrac{5}{6}}$ $14\frac{2}{5}$ **c.** $\dfrac{\dfrac{2}{5}}{\dfrac{2}{3}}$ $\frac{3}{5}$

Change each percent to a fraction.

d. $66\frac{2}{3}\%$ $\frac{2}{3}$ **e.** $8\frac{1}{3}\%$ $\frac{1}{12}$ **f.** $4\frac{1}{6}\%$ $\frac{1}{24}$

Problem set 76

1. Nestor finished a 42-kilometer bicycle race in 1 hour and 45 minutes $\left(1\frac{3}{4}\,\text{hr}\right)$. What was his average speed in kilometers per hour?   24 kilometers per hour
⁽⁴⁶⁾

2. Kim's scores in the diving competition were 7.9, 8.3, 8.1, 7.8, 8.4, 8.1, and 8.2. The highest and lowest scores were not counted. What was the average of the remaining scores?   8.12
⁽²⁸⁾

3. Use a ratio box to solve this problem. The ratio of good
(65) guys to bad guys in the movie was 2 to 5. If there were 35
guys in the movie, how many of them were good?
10 good guys

4. Use a unit multiplier to convert 3.5 grams to milligrams.
(50) 3500 milligrams

5. Change $16\frac{2}{3}$ percent to a fraction. $\frac{1}{6}$
(76)

6. Davie was facing north. If he turns 90° in a clockwise
(17) direction, what direction will he be facing? east

7. One sixth of the rock's mass was quartz. If the mass of the
(60) rock was 144 grams, what was the mass of the quartz in
the rock? 24 grams

8. If $a = 8$, what does $\sqrt{2a}$ equal? 4
(41)

9. Simplify:
(73)

(a) $\dfrac{-60}{-12}$ 5

(b) $(-8)(6)$ −48

(c) $\dfrac{40}{-8}$ −5

(d) $(-5)(-15)$ 75

---

10. What is the circumference of this
(66) circle? 30π cm

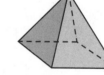

30 cm

Leave π as π.

11. The figure shows a pyramid with a
(67) square base. Copy the figure and find
the number of its (a) faces, (b) edges,
and (c) vertices.
(a) 5 faces   (b) 8 edges   (c) 5 vertices

Write equations to solve problems 12–15.

12. What number is 10 percent of $37.50?
(60) $W_N = 0.1 \times \$37.50$; $3.75

13. What number is $\frac{5}{8}$ of 72? $W_N = \frac{5}{8} \times 72$; 45
(60)

14. Twenty-five is what fraction of 60? $25 = W_F \times 60$; $\frac{5}{12}$
(74)

15. Sixty is what decimal part of 80? $60 = W_D \times 80$; 0.75
(74)

16. In this figure $AC = AB$. Angles DCA
(62) and ACB are supplementary. Find
the measure of

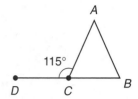

(a) $\angle ACB$. 65°

(b) $\angle ABC$. 65°

(c) $\angle CAB$. 50°

17. Complete the table.
(48)

Fraction	Decimal	Percent
$\frac{5}{6}$	(a) $0.8\overline{3}$	(b) $83\frac{1}{3}\%$
(c) $\frac{1}{1000}$	(d) 0.001	0.1%

18. A square sheet of paper with an area
(75) of 81 in.² has a corner cut off,
forming a pentagon as shown.

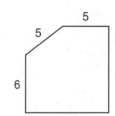

(a) What is the perimeter of the
pentagon? 34 in.

(b) What is the area of the pentagon? 75 in.²

19. What type of parallelogram has four congruent angles but
(Inv. 6) not necessarily four congruent sides? rectangle

20. When water increases in temperature from freezing to
(28) boiling, the reading on a thermometer increases from 0°C
to 100°C on the Celsius scale and from 32°F to 212°F on
the Fahrenheit scale. The temperature halfway between
0°C and 100°C is 50°C. What temperature is halfway
between 32°F and 212°F? 122°F

Solve each equation. Show each step. Check the solution.

21. $x - 25 = 96$ 121
(Inv. 7)

22. $\frac{2}{3}m = 12$ 18
(Inv. 7)

23. $2.5p = 6.25$ 2.5
(Inv. 7)

24. $10 = f + 3\frac{1}{3}$ $6\frac{2}{3}$
(Inv. 7)

Simplify:

25. $\sqrt{13^2 - 5^2}$ 12
(20)

26. 1 ton − 400 lb 1600 lb
(16)

27. $3\dfrac{3}{4} \times 4\dfrac{1}{6} \times (0.4)^2$ (fraction answer) $2\frac{1}{2}$
(26,43)

28. $3\dfrac{1}{8} + 6.7 + 8\dfrac{1}{4}$ (decimal answer)   18.075
(43)

29. (a) $(-3) + (-5) - (-3) - |+5|$ −10
(68)

  (b) $(-73) + (-24) - (-50)$ −47

30. $\dfrac{\dfrac{5}{6}}{\dfrac{2}{3}}$ $1\frac{1}{4}$
(76)

LESSON
77

More on Percent

Facts Practice: $+ - \times \div$ Integers (Test P in Test Masters)

Mental Math:

  a. $(+12) - (-18)$ **b.** 4×10^6

  c. $\dfrac{100}{150} = \dfrac{30}{a}$ **d.** Estimate 15% of $61.

  e. 25 cm to m   **f.** 12 is $\frac{3}{4}$ of n

  g. 10% of 50, × 6, + 2, ÷ 4, × 2, $\sqrt{\ }$, × 9, $\sqrt{\ }$, × 7, ÷ 2

Problem Solving:

On a balanced scale are five identical blocks marked X, a 25-g mass, and a 100-g mass as shown. What is the mass of each block marked X? Write an equation illustrated by this balanced scale.

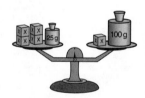

In Lesson 74 we practiced fractional part problems involving fractions and decimals. In this lesson we will practice similar problems involving percents. We translate the problem to an equation. Then we solve the equation.

Example 1   What percent of 40 is 25?

Solution   We can translate the question to an equation and solve.

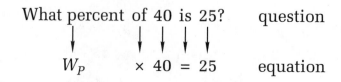

What percent of 40 is 25?   question

$W_P \qquad\quad \times\ 40\ =\ 25$ equation

To solve we divide both sides of the equation by 40.

$$\frac{W_P \times \overset{1}{\cancel{40}}}{\underset{1}{\cancel{40}}} = \frac{25}{40} \qquad \text{divided by 40}$$

$$W_P = \frac{5}{8} \qquad \text{simplified}$$

Since the question asked "what percent" and not "what fraction," we convert the fraction $\frac{5}{8}$ to a percent.

$$\frac{5}{8} \times 100\% = \mathbf{62\frac{1}{2}\%} \qquad \text{converted to a percent}$$

So $62\frac{1}{2}\%$ (or 62.5%) of 40 is 25.

Example 2 What percent of $3.50 is $0.28?

Solution We translate and solve.

What percent of $3.50 is $0.28?   question

$$W_P \qquad \times \ \$3.50 = \$0.28 \qquad \text{equation}$$

$$\frac{W_P \times \overset{1}{\cancel{\$3.50}}}{\underset{1}{\cancel{\$3.50}}} = \frac{\$0.28}{\$3.50} \qquad \text{divided by \$3.50}$$

$$W_P = \frac{0.28}{3.5} \qquad \text{simplified}$$

We perform the decimal division.

$$W_P = \frac{0.28}{3.5} = \frac{2.8}{35} = 0.08 \qquad \text{divided}$$

This is a decimal answer. The question asked for a percent answer. We convert the decimal 0.08 to 8%.

$$W_P = \mathbf{8\%} \qquad \text{converted to a percent}$$

Example 3 Seventy-five percent of what number is 600?

Solution We translate the question to an equation and solve. We may translate 75% to a fraction or to a decimal. We choose a fraction for this example.

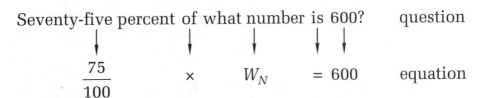

Seventy-five percent of what number is 600?   question

$$\frac{75}{100} \qquad \times \qquad W_N \qquad = 600 \qquad \text{equation}$$

To solve, we multiply both sides by 100 over 75.

$$\frac{\overset{1}{\cancel{100}}}{\underset{1}{\cancel{75}}} \cdot \frac{\overset{1}{\cancel{75}}}{\underset{1}{\cancel{100}}} \times W_N = 600 \cdot \frac{100}{75} \qquad \text{multiplied by } \frac{100}{75}$$

$$W_N = \mathbf{800} \qquad \text{simplified}$$

We could have used the fraction $\frac{3}{4}$ for $\frac{75}{100}$ with the same result.

Example 4   Fifty is what percent of 40?

Solution   Since 50 is more than 40, the answer will be greater than 100%. We translate directly to an equation and solve.

$$\begin{array}{ccccc} \text{Fifty} & \text{is} & \text{what percent} & \text{of} & \text{40?} \qquad \text{question} \\ \downarrow & \downarrow & \downarrow & \downarrow & \downarrow \\ 50 & = & W_P & \times & 40 \qquad \text{equation} \end{array}$$

We divide both sides by 40.

$$\frac{50}{40} = \frac{W_P \times \overset{1}{\cancel{40}}}{\underset{1}{\cancel{40}}} \qquad \text{divided by 40}$$

$$\frac{5}{4} = W_P \qquad \text{simplified}$$

We convert $\frac{5}{4}$ to a percent.

$$W_P = \frac{5}{4} \times 100\% = \mathbf{125\%} \qquad \text{converted to a percent}$$

Example 5   Sixty is 150 percent of what number?

Solution   We translate directly, writing 150% either as a decimal or as a fraction. We will use the decimal form here.

$$\begin{array}{ccccc} \text{Sixty} & \text{is} & \text{150\%} & \text{of} & \text{what number?} \qquad \text{question} \\ \downarrow & \downarrow & \downarrow & \downarrow & \downarrow \\ 60 & = & 1.5 & \times & W_N \qquad \text{equation} \end{array}$$

We divide both sides of the equation by 1.5.

$$\frac{60}{1.5} = \frac{\overset{1}{\cancel{1.5}} \times W_N}{\underset{1}{\cancel{1.5}}} \qquad \text{divided by 1.5}$$

$$\mathbf{40} = W_N \qquad \text{simplified}$$

Practice*   **a.** Twenty-four is what percent of 40? 60%

b. What percent of 6 is 2? $33\frac{1}{3}\%$

c. Fifteen percent of what number is 45? 300

d. What percent of 4 is 6? 150%

e. Twenty-four is 120% of what number? 20

f. Rework Example 5 writing 150% as a fraction instead of as a decimal. Fraction is $\frac{3}{2}$; answer is 40.

g. What percent of $5.00 is $0.35? 7%

Problem set 77   **1.** Use a ratio box to solve this problem. Tammy saved $^{(65)}$ nickels and pennies in a jar. The ratio of nickels to pennies was 2 to 5. If there were 70 nickels in the jar, how many coins were there in all? 245 coins

Refer to the line graph to answer problems 2–4.

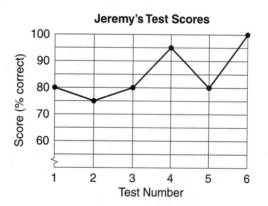

2. If there were 50 questions on Test 1, how many questions $^{(38,60)}$ did Jeremy answer correctly? 40 questions

3. What was Jeremy's average score? (What was the mean of $^{(28,38)}$ his scores?) 85%

4. (a) Which score did Jeremy make most often? (What was $^{(38,Inv.\,4)}$ the mode of the scores?) 80%

(b) What was the difference between his highest score and his lowest score? (What was the range of the scores?) 25%

5. Name the shape of each object.
(67)

    (a) A marble sphere

    (b) A length of pipe cylinder

    (c) A box of tissue rectangular prism

6. Use a case 1-case 2 ratio box to solve this problem. One
(72) hundred inches equals 254 centimeters. How many centimeters equals 250 inches? 635 centimeters

7.

30 people	
$\frac{3}{5}$ agreed	6 people
	6 people
	6 people
$\frac{2}{5}$ disagreed (12)	6 people
	6 people

7. Draw a diagram of this statement. Then answer the
(36,71) questions that follow.

    Three fifths of those present agreed, but the remaining 12 disagreed.

    (a) What fraction of those present disagreed? $\frac{2}{5}$

    (b) How many were present? 30

    (c) How many of those present agreed? 18

    (d) What was the ratio of those who agreed to those who disagreed? $\frac{3}{2}$

Write equations to solve problems 8–11.

8. Forty is $\frac{4}{25}$ of what number? $40 = \frac{4}{25} \times W_N$; 250
(74)

9. Twenty-four percent of 10,000 is what number?
(60) $0.24 \times 10,000 = W_N$; 2400

10. Twelve percent of what number is 240?
(77) $0.12 \times W_N = 240$; 2000

11. Twenty is what percent of 25? $20 = W_P \times 25$; 80%
(77)

12. Simplify:
(73)

    (a) 25(–5) –125   (b) –15(–5) 75

    (c) $\dfrac{-250}{-5}$ 50   (d) $\dfrac{-225}{15}$ –15

13. Complete the table.
(48)

FRACTION	DECIMAL	PERCENT
(a) $\frac{1}{5}$	0.2	(b) 20%
(c) $\frac{1}{50}$	(d) 0.02	2%

14. What is the total price of a $21.00 item including 7.5%
(46) sales tax? $22.58

15. Simplify:
(76)

(a) $\dfrac{14\frac{2}{7}}{100}$ $\frac{1}{7}$

(b) $\dfrac{60}{\frac{2}{3}}$ 90

16. Find the area of this symmetrical
(75) figure. Dimensions are in feet. Corners
that look square are square. 96 ft²

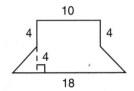

17. Sketch a picture of a cube with edges 2 cm long.
(67,70)

(a) What is the volume of the cube? 8 cm³

(b) Describe how to find the surface area of a cube.

(b) One way to
find the surface
area of a cube is to
find the area of
one square face of
the cube then
multiply that area
by 6.

18. Write 12 billion in scientific notation. 1.2×10^{10}
(51)

19. Find the circumference of each circle.
(66)

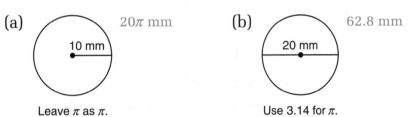

(a) 10 mm 20π mm

(b) 20 mm   62.8 mm

Leave π as π.   Use 3.14 for π.

Solve each equation. Show each step. Check the solution.

20. $3x = 26.7$ 8.9
(Inv. 7)

21. $y - 3\frac{1}{3} = 7$ $10\frac{1}{3}$
(Inv. 7)

22. $\frac{2}{3}x = 48$ 72
(Inv. 7)

23. The rule of this function has two steps.
(58) Describe the rule of this function and
find the missing numbers.
Multiply the "in" number by 4 and add 1 to
find the "out" number.

In	FUNCTION	Out
3		13
1		5
2		9
4		17
0		1

Simplify:

24. $5^2 - \left\{ 2^3 + 3\left[4^2 - (4)(\sqrt{9}) \right] \right\}$ 5
(63)

25. $\begin{array}{r} 4 \text{ gal } 3 \text{ qt } 1 \text{ pt} \\ + 1 \text{ gal } 2 \text{ qt } 1 \text{ pt} \\ \hline 6 \text{ gal } 2 \text{ qt} \end{array}$
(49)

26. $1 \text{ ft}^2 \cdot \dfrac{12 \text{ in.}}{1 \text{ ft}} \cdot \dfrac{12 \text{ in.}}{1 \text{ ft}}$
(50) 144 in.^{2}

27. $5\dfrac{1}{3} \div \left(1\dfrac{1}{3} \div 3 \right)$ 12
(26)

28. $3\dfrac{1}{5} - 2\dfrac{1}{2} + 1\dfrac{1}{4}$ $1\frac{19}{20}$
(30)

29. $3\dfrac{1}{3} \div 2.5$ (Write the answer as a mixed number.) $1\frac{1}{3}$
(43)

30. (a) $(-3) + (-4) - (+5)$ (b) $(-6) - (-16) - (+30)$
(68)   −12   −20

LESSON 78

Facts Practice: Classifying Quadrilaterals and Triangles (Test O in Test Masters)

Mental Math:

a. $(-8) - (-16)$

b. $\left(\frac{3}{4} \right)^2$

c. $10p + 3 = 63$

d. 5% of $640.00 (double, halve)

e. 750 g to kg

f. 12 is $\frac{1}{6}$ of m

g. Estimate a 15% tip on a $31.49 bill.

Problem Solving:

When you point a vertex of a die toward you, the dots on three faces are visible. A cube has 8 vertices, so 8 combinations of three faces can be seen by turning a die. List the total number of dots that can be seen in each of the eight positions.

Mental Math:
a. 8
b. $\frac{9}{16}$
c. 6
d. $32.00
e. 0.75 kg
f. 72
g. $4.50 to $4.80
Problem Solving:
6, 7, 9, 10, 11, 12, 14, 15

The symbols ≥ and ≤ We have used the symbols >, <, and = to compare two numbers. In this lesson we will introduce the symbols ≥ and ≤. We will also practice graphing on the number line.

The symbols ≥ and ≤ combine the greater than/less than sign with the equals sign. Thus, reading from left to right, the symbol

$$\geq$$

is read, "greater than or equal to," and, reading from left to right, the symbol

$$\leq$$

is read, "less than or equal to."

Graphing on the number line   To graph a number on the number line, we draw a dot at the point that represents the number. Thus, when we graph 4 on the number line, it looks like this:

This time we will graph *all the numbers that are greater than or equal to 4*. We might think the graph should look like this:

It is true that all the dots mark points that represent numbers that are greater than or equal to 4. However, we did not graph *all* the numbers that are greater than 4. For instance, we did not graph 10, 11, 12, and so on. Also, we did not graph $4\frac{1}{2}$, $5\frac{1}{3}$, $6\frac{3}{4}$, and so on. If we graph all of these numbers, the dots are so close together that we end up with a ray that goes on and on. Thus a graph of all the numbers greater than or equal to 4 looks like this:

The large dot marks the 4. The shaded line marks the numbers greater than 4. The arrowhead shows that this shaded line goes on without end.

Graphing inequalities   Expressions such as the following are called **inequalities:**

$$\text{(a) } x \leq 4 \qquad \text{(b) } x > 4$$

We read (a) as "x is less than or equal to 4." We read (b) as "x is greater than 4."

We can graph inequalities on the number line by graphing all the numbers that make the inequality a true statement.

Example 1   Graph on a number line: $x \leq 4$

Solution   We are told to graph all numbers that are less than or equal to 4. We draw a dot at the point that represents 4, and then we shade all the points to the left of the dot. The arrowhead shows that the shading continues without end.

Example 2   Graph on a number line: $x > 4$

Solution   We are told to graph all numbers greater than 4 *but not including 4*. We do not start the graph at 5 because we also need to graph numbers like $4\frac{1}{2}$ and 4.001. To show that the graph does not include 4, *we draw an empty circle at 4* and then shade the number line to the right of the circle.

Practice   **a.** On a number line, graph all the numbers less than 2.

b. On a number line, graph all the numbers greater than or equal to 1.

Graph each inequality on a number line.

c. $x \leq -1$ **d.** $x > -1$

Problem set 78

1. Use a ratio box to solve this problem. If 4 cartons are needed to feed 30 hungry children, how many cartons are needed to feed 75 hungry children? 10 cartons
(72)

2. Gabriel's average score after 4 tests was 88. What score must Gabriel average on the next 2 tests to have a 6-test average of 90? 94
(55)

3. If the sum of $\frac{2}{3}$ and $\frac{3}{4}$ is divided by the product of $\frac{2}{3}$ and $\frac{3}{4}$, what is the quotient? $2\frac{5}{6}$
(30)

4. Use a ratio box to solve this problem. The ratio of monocotyledons to dicotyledons in the nursery was 3 to 4. If there were 84 dicotyledons in the nursery, how many monocotyledons were there? 63 monocotyledons
(54)

5. The diameter of a nickel is 21 millimeters. Find the circumference of a nickel to the nearest millimeter.
(66)
66 millimeters

6. Graph each inequality on a separate number line.
(78)

    (a) $x > 2$ (b) $x \leq 1$

7. Use a unit multiplier to convert 1.5 kg to g. 1500 g
(50)

8. Five sixths of 30 people who participated in the taste test
(65) preferred the taste of Brand X. The rest preferred Brand Y.

(a) How many more people preferred Brand X than
preferred Brand Y? 20 more people

(b) What was the ratio of the number of people who
preferred Brand Y to the number who preferred
Brand X? $\frac{1}{5}$

Write equations to solve problems 9–12.

9. Forty-two is seven tenths of what number?
(74) $42 = \frac{7}{10} \times W_N$; 60

10. One hundred fifty percent of what number is 600?
(77) $1.5 \times W_N = 600$; 400

11. Forty percent of 50 is what number? $0.4 \times 50 = W_N$; 20
(60)

12. Forty is what percent of 50? $40 = W_P \times 50$; 80%
(77)

13. (a) Write 1.5×10^{-3} in standard form. 0.0015
(57,69)

(b) Write 25×10^6 in scientific notation. 2.5×10^7

14. Simplify:
(73)

(a) $\frac{-45}{9}$ -5 (b) $\frac{-450}{15}$ -30

(c) 15(−20) −300   (d) −15(−12) 180

15. Complete the table.
(48)

FRACTION	DECIMAL	PERCENT
(a) $\frac{1}{2}$	(b) 0.5	50%
$\frac{1}{12}$	(c) $0.08\overline{3}$	(d) $8\frac{1}{3}\%$

16. Simplify: $\dfrac{83\frac{1}{3}}{100}$ $\frac{5}{6}$
(76)

17. Find the area of this trapezoid.
(75) Dimensions are in millimeters.
640 mm²

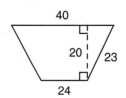

18.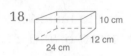

18. A box of tissues is 24 cm long, 12 cm wide, and 10 cm
(70) high. Sketch a picture of the box and find its volume.
2880 cm³

19. one possible
pattern:

19. Sketch a picture of the box described in problem 18 cut
(67) open and unfolded so that the six faces are lying flat.

20. Describe the rule of this function.
(58) Then find the missing numbers.
Multiply the "in" number by 5 and subtract 1
to find the "out" number.

In	FUNCTION	Out
2 →		→ 9
3 →		→ 14
4 →		→ 19
5 →		→ 24
1 →		→ 4

21. A merchant sold an item for $18.50. If 30% of the selling
(60) price was profit, how much profit did the merchant make
on the sale? $5.55

Solve each equation. Show each step. Check the solution.

22. $m + 8.7 = 10.25$ 1.55
(Inv. 7)

23. $\frac{4}{3}w = 36$ 27
(Inv. 7)

24. $0.7y = 48.3$ 69
(Inv. 7)

Simplify:

25. $\left\{4^2 + 10\left[2^3 - (3)(\sqrt{4})\right]\right\} - \sqrt{36}$ 30
(63)

26. $|5 - 3| - |3 - 5|$ 0
(59)

27. $1 \text{ m}^2 \cdot \frac{100 \text{ cm}}{1 \text{ m}} \cdot \frac{100 \text{ cm}}{1 \text{ m}}$ 10,000 cm²
(50)

28. $7\frac{1}{2} \cdot 3 \cdot \left(\frac{2}{3}\right)^2$ 10
(26)

29. $3\frac{1}{5} - \left(2\frac{1}{2} - 1\frac{1}{4}\right)$ $1\frac{19}{20}$
(30)

30. (a) $(-10) - (-8) - (+6)$ −8
(68)

(b) $(+10) + (-20) - (-30)$ 20

LESSON 79

Insufficient Information • Quantitative Comparisons

Mental Math:
a. −40
b. 3750
c. 250
d. $1.80
e. 1.2 L
f. 25
g. 25
Problem Solving:

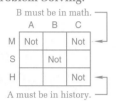

B must be in math.

A must be in history.

So C must be in science.

Facts Practice: + − × ÷ Integers (Test P in Test Masters)

Mental Math:

   a. (−25) + (−15)   **b.** 3.75 × 10³

   c. $\frac{c}{100} = \frac{25}{10}$ **d.** Estimate 15% of $11.95.

   e. 1200 mL to L   **f.** 20 is $\frac{4}{5}$ of n

   g. Square 5, × 2, − 1, $\sqrt{}$, × 8, − 1, ÷ 5, × 3, − 1, ÷ 4, × 9, + 3, ÷ 3.

Problem Solving:

Chad earned an A, a B, and a C on tests in math, science, and history, although the A was not in math, the B was not in science, and the C was not in history. If the lowest grade was not in math, what test grades did Chad earn in which subjects? Make a table to show your work.

Insufficient information

Sometimes we encounter problems for which there is **insufficient** (not enough) **information** to determine the answer. The following problem provides insufficient information to answer the question:

> *A 10-pound bag of potatoes costs $1.49. What is the average price of each potato?*

Since we do not know the number of potatoes in the bag, we do not have enough information to find the average price of each potato.

We will practice recognizing problems with insufficient information as we answer quantitative comparison problems like the examples in this lesson.

Quantitative comparisons

We have practiced comparing numbers using the symbols >, <, and =. In this lesson we will begin considering comparison problems in which insufficient information has been provided to determine the comparison.

Example 1 The numbers x and y are whole numbers. Compare:

$$x \bigcirc y$$

Solution We are told that x and y are whole numbers, but we are not given information that will let us determine which is greater, or if x and y are equal. Since we do not have enough information to determine the comparison, as our answer we write **insufficient information.**

Example 2   The number x is positive and y is negative. Compare:

$$x \bigcirc y$$

Solution   We are not given enough information to determine what each number is. However, we are given enough information to determine the comparison. Any positive number is greater than any negative number. Thus, the answer is

$$x > y$$

Example 3   If $a - b = 0$, compare: $a \bigcirc b$

Solution   The equation does not provide enough information to determine the value of either number. However, since their difference is zero, the two numbers must be equal.

$$a = b$$

Practice   Answer each comparison by writing >, <, =, or insufficient information.

   a. If $x - y = 1$, compare: $x \ (>) \ y$

   b. If $\dfrac{m}{n} = 1$, compare: $m \ (=) \ n$

   c. If $a \cdot b = 1$, compare: $a \bigcirc b$ insufficient information

   d. The number x is not positive and y is not negative.
   insufficient information
   Compare: $x \bigcirc y$
   (*y* could be greater, or both *x* and *y* could be zero.)

Problem set 79

1. The average number of students in 4 classrooms was
   (55) 33.5. If the students were regrouped into 5 classrooms, what would be the average number of students in each room?   26.8 students

2. Nelda drove 315 kilometers and used 35 liters of
   (46) gasoline. Her car averaged how many kilometers per liter of gas? $9 \frac{\text{kilometers}}{\text{liter}}$

3. The ratio of winners to losers was 7 to 5. If the total
   (65) number of winners and losers was 1260, how many more winners were there than losers?   210 more winners

4. Write each number in scientific notation.
(69)

(a) 37.5×10^{-6} 3.75×10^{-5} (b) 37.5×10^{6} 3.75×10^{7}

5. Compare: $x \bigcirc y$ if $\dfrac{y}{x} = 2$ insufficient information
(79)

$(x < y$ if both are positive; $x > y$ if both are negative$)$

6. Graph each inequality on a separate number line.
(78)

(a) $x < 1$ [number line: -2 -1 0 1 2] (b) $x \geq -1$ [number line: -2 -1 0 1 2]

7. Use a case 1-case 2 ratio box to solve this problem.
(72) Four inches of snow fell in 3 hours. At that rate, how long would it take for 1 foot of snow to fall? 9 hours

8.

	32 students
	4 students
$\frac{3}{8}$ earned A's (12)	4 students
	4 students
	4 students
	4 students
$\frac{5}{8}$ did not earn A's	4 students
	4 students
	4 students

8. Draw a diagram of this statement. Then answer the
(71) questions that follow.

Twelve students earned A's. This was $\frac{3}{8}$ of the students in the class.

(a) How many students did not earn A's? 20 students

(b) What percent of the students did not earn A's? $62\frac{1}{2}\%$

Write equations to solve problems 9–12.

9. Thirty-five is 70% of what number? $35 = 0.7 \times W_N$; 50
(77)

10. What percent of 20 is 17? $W_P \times 20 = 17$; 85%
(77)

11. What percent of 20 is 25? $W_P \times 20 = 25$; 125%
(77)

12. Three hundred sixty is 75 percent of what number?
(77) $360 = \frac{3}{4} \times W_N$; 480

13. Simplify:
(73)

(a) $\dfrac{144}{-8}$ -18 (b) $\dfrac{-144}{+6}$ -24

(c) $-12(12)$ -144 (d) $-16(-9)$ 144

14. Complete the table.
(48)

Fraction	Decimal	Percent
$\frac{1}{25}$	(a) 0.04	(b) 4%
(c) $\frac{2}{25}$	(d) 0.08	8%

15. At the Citrus used car lot a salesperson is paid a commission
(60) of 5% of the sale price for every car he or she sells. How much commission is a salesperson paid who sells a car for $4500? $225

16. Simplify: $\dfrac{62\frac{1}{2}}{100}$ $\frac{5}{8}$
(76)

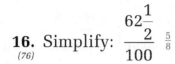

17. A square sheet of paper with an area of 100 in.² has a
(75) corner cut off as shown in the figure.

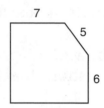

7

5

6

(a) What is the perimeter of the shape?
   38 in.

(b) What is the area of the shape? 94 in.²

18. In the figure, each small cube is
(67,70) 1 cubic centimeter.

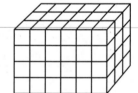

(a) What is the volume of this rectangular prism? 72 cm³

(b) What is the total surface area of the rectangular solid? 108 cm²

19. Find the circumference of each circle.
(66)

(a)   3.14 m   (b)   π m

1 m   0.5 m

Use 3.14 for π.   Leave π as π.

20. Identify each triangle as acute, right, or obtuse. Then
(62) identify each triangle as equilateral, isosceles, or scalene.

20. (a) right; scalene
(b) obtuse; isosceles
(c) acute; equilateral

(a)   (b)   (c)

Solve each equation. Show every step. Check the solution.

21. $1.2x = 2.88$ 2.4
(Inv. 7)

22. $3\frac{1}{3} = x + \frac{5}{6}$ $2\frac{1}{2}$
(Inv. 7)

23. $\frac{3}{2}w = \frac{9}{10}$ $\frac{3}{5}$
(Inv. 7)

Simplify:

24. $\dfrac{\sqrt{100} + 5\left[3^3 - 2(3^2 + 3)\right]}{5}$ 5
(63)

25.
(56)

$$\begin{array}{r} 3 \text{ hr } 15 \text{ min } 24 \text{ s} \\ - 2 \text{ hr } 45 \text{ min } 30 \text{ s} \\ \hline 29 \text{ min } \quad 54 \text{ s} \end{array}$$

26. $1 \text{ yd}^2 \cdot \dfrac{3 \text{ ft}}{1 \text{ yd}} \cdot \dfrac{3 \text{ ft}}{1 \text{ yd}}$ 9 ft²
(50)

27. $7\frac{1}{2} \cdot \left(3 \div \frac{5}{9}\right)$ $40\frac{1}{2}$
(26)

28. $4\frac{5}{6} + 3\frac{1}{3} + 7\frac{1}{4}$ $15\frac{5}{12}$
(30)

29. $3\frac{3}{4} \div 1.5$ (decimal answer) 2.5
(43)

30. (a) $(-10) - (+20) - (-30)$ 0
(68)
  (b) $(-10) - |(-20) - (+30)|$ −60

LESSON

80

Transformations

Mental Math:
a. −75
b. 1600
c. 8
d. 25
e. 1.5 km
f. 9
g. 6 m; 2.25 m²
Problem Solving:
  1, 3, 6, 10, 15

Facts Practice: Classifying Quadrilaterals and Triangles
  (Test O in Test Masters)

Mental Math:

  a. $(-30) - (+45)$
  b. 40^2
  c. $5q - 4 = 36$
  d. 15 is $\frac{3}{5}$ of n
  e. 1500 m to km
  f. What is $\frac{3}{5}$ of 15?
  g. Find the perimeter and area of a square with sides 1.5 m long.

Problem Solving:

  Here are the first three terms of a sequence:

$$\sqrt{1^3}, \ \sqrt{1^3 + 2^3}, \ \sqrt{1^3 + 2^3 + 3^3}, \ ...$$

  Simplify these three terms. Then write and simplify the next two terms of the sequence.

Recall that two figures are congruent if they are the same shape and size. These two triangles are congruent, but they are not in the same position.

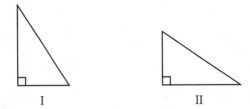

We can move triangle I to the position of triangle II through three types of position change. One change of position is to "flip" triangle I over as though flipping a coin from heads to tails.

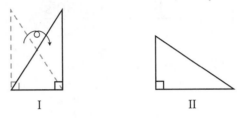

A second change of position is to "slide" triangle I to the right.

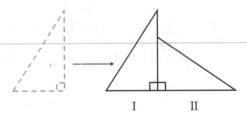

The third change of position is to "turn" triangle I 90° clockwise.

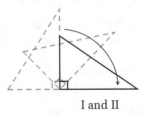

I and II

These "flips, slides, and turns" are called **transformations** and have special names listed in this table.

Transformations

Movement	Name
flip	reflection
slide	translation
turn	rotation

A **reflection** of a figure in a line (a "flip") produces a mirror image of the figure that is reflected.

If we reflect $\triangle ABC$ in the y-axis, the reflection of every point of $\triangle ABC$ appears on the opposite side of the y-axis the same distance from the y-axis as the original point. We may refer to the reflected triangle as $\triangle A'B'C'$ which we read as "triangle A prime, B prime, C prime."

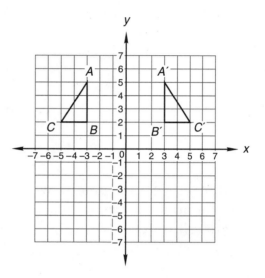

If we then reflect $\triangle A'B'C'$ in the x-axis we see $\triangle A''B''C''$ (triangle A double prime, B double prime, C double prime) in the fourth quadrant.

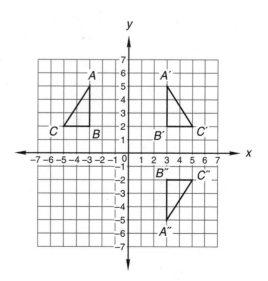

Example 1 The coordinates of the vertices of $\triangle RST$ are $R\,(4, 3)$, $S\,(4, 1)$, and $T\,(1, 1)$. Draw $\triangle RST$ and its reflection in the x-axis, $\triangle R'S'T'$. What are the coordinates of the vertices of $\triangle R'S'T'$?

Solution   We graph the vertices of $\triangle RST$ and draw the triangle. The reflection of every point of $\triangle RST$ in the x-axis appears on the opposite side of the x-axis the same distance from the x-axis as the original point. We locate the reflected vertices and draw $\triangle R'S'T'$.

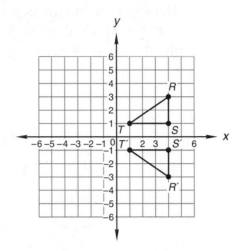

Note that if a segment were drawn between a point and its reflection, the segment would be perpendicular to the line of reflection, which in this case is the x-axis. The coordinates of the vertices of $\triangle R'S'T'$ are **R' (4, –3), S' (4, –1),** and **T' (1, –1).**

A **translation** "slides" a figure to a new position without turning or flipping the figure. If we translate quadrilateral *JKLM* 6 units to the right and 2 units down, quadrilateral *J'K'L'M'* appears in the position shown. To perform the transformation we translate each vertex 6 units to the right and 2 units down. Then we draw the sides of the quadrilateral.

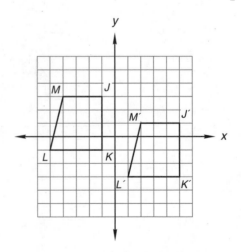

Example 2   The coordinates of the vertices of rectangle *ABCD* are *A* (4, 3), *B* (4, 1), *C* (1, 1), and *D* (1, 3). Draw □*ABCD* and its image, □*A'B'C'D'*, translated to the left 5 units and down 4 units. What are the coordinates of the vertices of □*A'B'C'D'*?

Solution We graph the vertices of ▱*ABCD* and draw the rectangle. Then we graph its image by translating each vertex 5 units to the left and 4 units down.

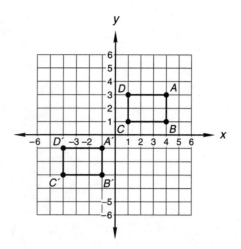

We find that the coordinates of the vertices of ▱*A′B′C′D′* are *A′* (–1, –1), *B′* (–1, –3), *C′* (–4, –3), and *D′* (–4, –1).

A **rotation** of a figure "turns" the figure about a specified point called the *center of rotation*. At the beginning of this lesson we rotated triangle I 90° clockwise. The center of rotation was the vertex of the right angle. In the illustration below, triangle *ABC* is rotated 180° about the origin.

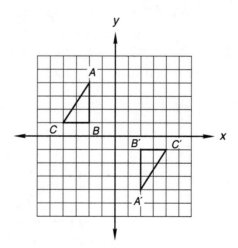

Note that rotating this book 180° moves the original figure into the position of the rotated figure. One way to view the effect of a rotation of a figure is to trace the figure on a piece of transparency film. Then place the point of a pencil on the center of rotation and turn the transparency film through the described rotation.

Example 3   The coordinates of the vertices of $\triangle PQR$ are P (3, 4), Q (3, 1), and R (1, 1). Draw $\triangle PQR$ and also draw its image, $\triangle P'Q'R'$, after a counterclockwise rotation of 90° about the origin. What are the coordinates of the vertices of $\triangle P'Q'R'$?

Solution   We graph the vertices of $\triangle PQR$ and draw the triangle.

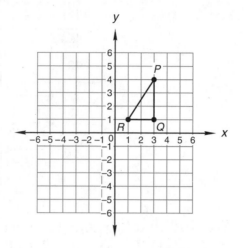

Then we place a piece of transparency film over the coordinate plane and trace the triangle. We also place a mark on the transparency aligned with either the x-axis or the y-axis. This mark will align with the other axis after the transparency is rotated 90°. After tracing the triangle on the transparency, we place the point of a pencil on the film over the origin, which is the center of rotation in this example. While keeping the graph paper still, we rotate the film 90° (one quarter turn) counterclockwise. The image of the triangle rotates to the position shown while the original triangle remains in place.

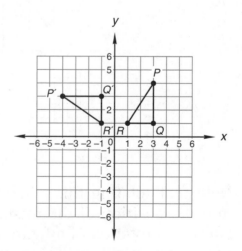

We name the rotated image $\triangle P'Q'R'$ and through the transparency see that the coordinates of the vertices are

P′ (–4, 3), Q′ (–1, 3), and **R′ (–1, 1).** If transparency film is not available, another method can be used to determine the rotated position. First, we must physically or mentally rotate the coordinate plane.

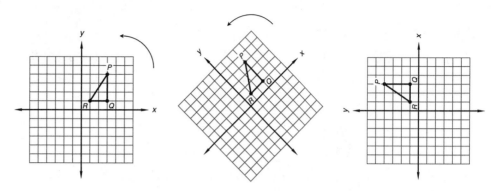

Note that without using transparency film the image moves to the proper position by rotating the graph paper. Using this method, imagine that the *x*-axis and *y*-axis have not rotated. We can find the coordinates of △*P′Q′R′* by leaving the axes in their normal orientation.

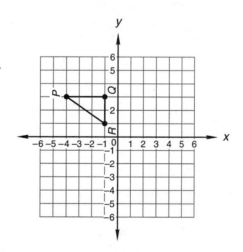

Practice

a. Perform each of the examples in this lesson if you have not already done so.

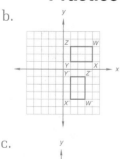

b.

b. The vertices of rectangle *WXYZ* are *W* (4, 3), *X* (4, 1), *Y* (1, 1), and *Z* (1, 3). Draw the rectangle and draw its image □*W′X′Y′Z′* after a 90° clockwise rotation about the origin. What are the coordinates of the vertices of □*W′X′Y′Z′*? *W′* (3, −4), *X′* (1, −4), *Y′* (1, −1), *Z′* (3, −1)

c.

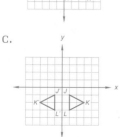

c. The vertices of △*JKL* are *J* (1, −1), *K* (3, −2), and *L* (1, −3). Draw the triangle and its image in the *y*-axis, △*J′K′L′*. What are the coordinates of the vertices of △*J′K′L′*? *J′* (−1, −1), *K′* (−3, −2), *L′* (−1, −3)

d.

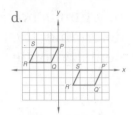

d. Translate $\square PQRS$ 6 units to the right and 3 units down to $\square P'Q'R'S'$. The coordinates of the vertices of $\square PQRS$ are $P\,(0, 3)$, $Q\,(-1, 1)$, $R\,(-4, 1)$, and $S\,(-3, 3)$. What are the coordinates of the vertices of $\square P'Q'R'S'$?
$P'\,(6, 0)$, $Q'\,(5, -2)$, $R'\,(2, -2)$, $S'\,(3, 0)$

Problem set
80

1. Tina mowed lawns for 4 hours and earned $7.00 per
(55) hour. Then she washed windows for 3 hours and earned $6.30 per hour. What was Tina's average hourly pay for the 7-hour period? $6.70

2. Evaluate: $x + \left(x^2 - xy\right) - y$ if $x = 4$ and $y = 3$ 5
(52)

3. Compare: $a \bigcirc b$ if $ab = 2$ insufficient information
(79)

4. Use a ratio box to solve this problem. When Nelson
(65) cleaned his room, he found that the ratio of clean clothes to dirty clothes was 2 to 3. If 30 articles of clothing were discovered, how many were clean?   12 articles of clothing

5. The diameter of a half dollar is 3 centimeters. Find the
(66) circumference of a half dollar to the nearest millimeter.
94 millimeters

6. Use a unit multiplier to convert $1\frac{1}{2}$ quarts to pints.   3 pints
(50)

7. Graph each inequality on a separate number line.
(78)
     (a) $x > -2$ -3 -2 -1 0 1   (b) $x \le 0$ -3 -2 -1 0 1

8. Use a ratio box to solve this problem. In 25 minutes, 400
(72) customers entered the attraction. At this rate, how many customers would enter the attraction in 1 hour?
960 customers

9.

	72 inches
$\frac{1}{4}$ of total height	18 inches
	18 inches
$\frac{3}{4}$ of total height	18 inches
	18 inches

9. Draw a diagram of this statement. Then answer the
(71) questions that follow.

> *Nathan found that it was 18 inches from his knee joint to his hip joint. This was $\frac{1}{4}$ of his total height.*

(a) What was Nathan's total height in inches?   72 inches

(b) What was Nathan's total height in feet?   6 feet

Write equations to solve problems 10–13.

10. Six hundred is $\frac{5}{9}$ of what number? $600 = \frac{5}{9} \times W_N$; 1080
(74)

11. Two hundred eighty is what percent of 400?
(77) $280 = W_P \times 400$; 70%

12. What number is 4 percent of 400? $W_N = 0.04 \times 400$; 16
(60)

13. Sixty is 60 percent of what number? $60 = 0.6 \times W_N$; 100
(77)

14. Simplify:
(73)

(a) $\dfrac{600}{-15}$ -40

(b) $\dfrac{-600}{-12}$ 50

(c) 20(–30) -600

(d) +15(40) 600

15. Bill is paid a commission equal to 6% of the price of the
(60) appliance he sells. If Bill sells a refrigerator for $850, what is Bill's commission on the sale? $51

16. Complete the table.
(48)

FRACTION	DECIMAL	PERCENT
(a) $\frac{3}{10}$	0.3	(b) 30%
$\frac{5}{12}$	(c) $0.41\overline{6}$	(d) $41\frac{2}{3}\%$

17. Express in scientific notation.
(69)

(a) 30×10^6 3×10^7

(b) 30×10^{-6} 3×10^{-5}

18. Find the area of this trapezoid.
(75) Dimensions are in meters. $25\ \text{m}^2$

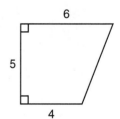

19. Each edge of a cube is 5 inches.
(67,70)

(a) What is the volume of the cube? 125 in.^{3}

(b) What is the surface area of the cube? 150 in.^{2}

20. In a bag are 100 marbles: 10 red, 20 white, 30 blue, and
(36) 40 green. If one marble is drawn from the bag, what is the probability that the marble will not be red, white, or blue? $\frac{2}{5}$

Solve each equation. Show each step. Check the solution.

21. $17a = 408$ 24
(Inv. 7)

22. $\dfrac{3}{8}m = 48$ 128
(Inv. 7)

23. $1.4 = x - 0.41$ 1.81
(Inv. 7)

Simplify:

24.
(52)
$$\frac{2^3 + 4 \cdot 5 - 2 \cdot 3^2}{\sqrt{25} \cdot \sqrt{4}} \quad 1$$

25.
(43)
$7\frac{1}{7} \times 1.4$ 10

26.
(56)
$$\begin{array}{r} 10 \text{ lb} \quad 6 \text{ oz} \\ - \quad 7 \text{ lb} \quad 11 \text{ oz} \\ \hline 2 \text{ lb} \quad 11 \text{ oz} \end{array}$$

27. $1 \text{ cm}^2 \cdot \dfrac{10 \text{ mm}}{1 \text{ cm}} \cdot \dfrac{10 \text{ mm}}{1 \text{ cm}}$
(50)
100 mm^2

28.
(26)
$7\frac{1}{2} \div \left(3 \cdot \frac{5}{9} \right)$ $4\frac{1}{2}$

29.
(30)
$4\frac{5}{6} + 3\frac{1}{3} - 7\frac{1}{4}$ $\frac{11}{12}$

30.

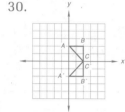

30. Triangle ABC with its vertices at $A\,(0, 2)$, $B\,(2, 2)$, and
(80) $C\,(2, 0)$ is reflected in the x-axis. Draw triangle ABC and
its image $\triangle A'B'C'$.

INVESTIGATION
8

Using a Compass and Straight Edge, Part 2

In Investigation 2 we used a compass to draw circles, and we used a compass and straight edge to inscribe a regular hexagon and a regular triangle in a circle. In this investigation we will use a compass and straight edge to **bisect** (divide in half) a line segment and bisect an angle. We will also inscribe a square and a regular octagon in a circle.

Materials needed:

- Compass
- Ruler/Straight edge
- Protractor

Bisecting a line segment Use a metric ruler to draw a segment 6 cm long. Label the endpoints A and C.

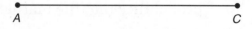

Next open a compass so that the distance between the pivot point and pencil point is more than half the length of the segment to be bisected (in this case, more than 3 cm). You will be swinging arcs from both endpoints of the segment, so once you have set the compass, do not change the setting. Place the pivot point of the compass on one endpoint of the segment and make a faint curve by lightly swinging an arc on both sides of the segment as shown.

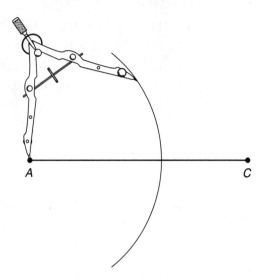

Then move the pivot point of the compass to the other endpoint of the segment and, without resetting the compass, swing an arc that intersects the other arc on both sides of the segment. Draw a line through the two points where the arcs intersect to divide the original segment into two parts. Label the point where the line intersects the segment point *B*.

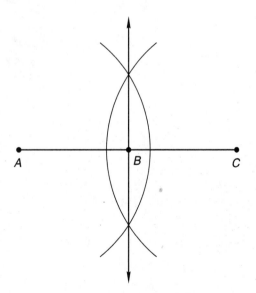

1. Use a metric ruler to find *AB* and *BC*. 3 cm; 3 cm

2. Where the line and segment intersect, four angles are formed. What is the measure of each angle? 90°

Using a compass and straight edge to create geometric figures is called **construction.** In this investigation you constructed the **perpendicular bisector** of the segment.

3. Why is the line you constructed called the perpendicular bisector? The line is perpendicular to the segment and divides the segment in half.

Inscribing a square in a circle We can use a perpendicular bisector to help us inscribe a square in a circle. Draw a dot on your paper to be the center of a circle. Set the distance between the points of your compass to 2 cm. Then place the pivot point of the compass on the dot and draw a circle. Use a straight edge to faintly draw a diameter of the circle.

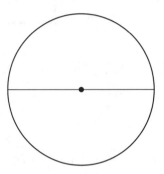

The two points where the diameter intersects the circle are the endpoints of the diameter. Open the compass a little more than the radius of the circle and construct the perpendicular bisector of the diameter you drew.

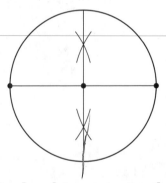

Make the perpendicular bisector another diameter of the circle. The two diameters divide the circle into quarters. Draw chords between the points on the circle that are the endpoints of the two diameters.

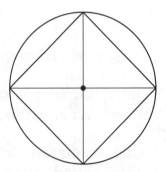

You have inscribed a square in a circle.

4. Each angle of the square is an inscribed angle of the circle. What is the measure of each angle of the square?
90°

5. Within the square inscribed in the circle above are four small right triangles. Two sides of each small triangle are radii of the circle. If the radius of the circle is 2 cm, then

5.(b) We add the areas of the four triangles. So the area of the square is 8 cm².

(a) what is the area of each of the small triangles? 2 cm²

(b) how can we find the area of the inscribed square?

Bisecting an angle Use a protractor and straight edge to draw an angle. We will use a 60° angle for illustration, but a larger or smaller angle may be drawn. With the pivot point of the compass on the vertex of the angle, draw an arc that intersects the sides of the angle. For reference we will call these points R and S. The vertex we have labeled V.

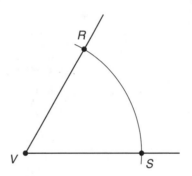

Set the compass so that it is open more than half the distance between R and S. With the pivot point on R swing an arc. Then with the pivot point on S swing an arc so that the two arcs intersect as shown. We have labeled the point of intersection T.

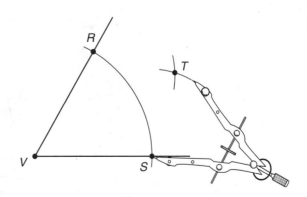

Using a straight edge, draw a ray from the vertex (V) through point T. Ray VT divides ∠RVS into two congruent angles.

6. Use your protractor to measure the original angle you drew and the two smaller angles formed when you constructed the ray. Record all three angle measures for **your answer.** Each of the smaller angles should be half the measure of the larger angle.

7. The ray divided the original angle into two congruent angles. That is, the ray divided the angle in half.

7. In this activity you constructed an **angle bisector.** Why is the ray called an angle bisector?

Inscribing a regular octagon in a circle

Draw a circle and a diameter of the circle. Then construct a diameter that is a perpendicular bisector of the first diameter. Your work should look like the following circle. For reference, we have labeled points X, Y, and Z on the circle, and have labeled the center of the circle M.

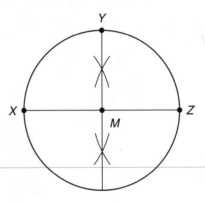

Swing intersecting arcs from points Y and Z to locate the angle bisector of $\angle YMZ$. Also swing intersecting arcs from points X and Y to locate the angle bisector of $\angle XMY$ as shown.

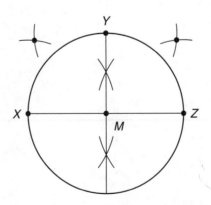

Draw two lines through the center of the circle that pass through the points where the arcs intersect. These two lines together with the first two diameters you drew divide the circle into eighths.

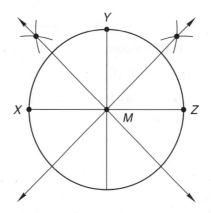

8. What is the measure of each small central angle that is formed? 45°

There are 8 points of intersection around the circle. Draw chords from point to point around the circle to draw a regular octagon inscribed in the circle.

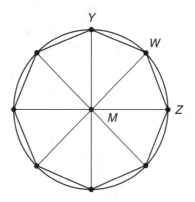

Refer to the inscribed octagon to answer the following questions:

9. Segments *MY*, *MW*, and *MZ* are radii of the same circle. Classify △*YMW* by sides and classify △*WMZ* by sides.
  Both triangles are isosceles.

10. What is the measure of the following angles?

   (a) ∠*YMW* 45°   (b) ∠*WMZ* 45°

11. What is the measure of each of the following angles?

   (a) ∠*MYW* $67\frac{1}{2}°$ (b) ∠*MWY* $67\frac{1}{2}°$

   (c) ∠*MWZ* $67\frac{1}{2}°$ (d) ∠*MZW* $67\frac{1}{2}°$

12. (a) What is the measure of ∠*YWZ*? 135°

   (b) What is the measure of each inscribed angle formed by the sides of the octagon? 135°

Using Proportions to Solve Percent Problems

Mental Math:
a. +100
b. 0.0012
c. 60
d. $3.60
e. 2.5 cm
f. 36
g. $27
Problem Solving:
21, 34, 55

Facts Practice: $+ - \times \div$ Integers (Test P in Test Masters)

Mental Math:

  a. $(-10)(-10)$ **b.** 12×10^{-4} **c.** $\frac{40}{t} = \frac{6}{9}$

  d. 15% of $24.00   **e.** 25 mm to cm   **f.** 24 is $\frac{2}{3}$ of n

  g. What is the total cost of a $25 item plus 8% sales tax?

Problem Solving:

  Find the next three numbers in this sequence.

$$1, 1, 2, 3, 5, 8, 13, \ldots$$

A percent is a ratio in which 100 represents the total number in the group. Thus, percent problems can be solved using the same method we use to solve ratio problems. Consider the following problem and explanation:

> *Thirty percent of the class passed the test. If 21 students did not pass the test, how many students were in the class?*

The problem is about 2 parts of a whole class. We recognize this as a "part-part-whole" problem. One part of the class passed the test; the other part of the class did not pass the test. The whole class is 100 percent. The part that passed was 30 percent. Thus, the part that did not pass must have been 70 percent. We will record these numbers in a ratio box just as we do with ratio problems.

	Percent	Actual Count
Passed	30	
Did not pass	70	
Whole class	100	

As we read the problem, we find an actual count as well. There were 21 students who did not pass the test. We record 21 in the appropriate place of the table and use letters in the remaining places of the table.

	Percent	Actual Count
Passed	30	P
Did not pass	70	21
Whole class	100	W

We will use a table to help write a proportion so that we can solve the problem. **We will use the numbers in two of three rows to write a proportion. This time we will use the numbers in the second row because we know both numbers. Since the problem asks for the total number of students in the class, we will also use the third row.** Then we solve the proportion.

	Percent	Actual Count
Passed	30	P
Did not pass	70	21
Whole class	100	W

$$\frac{70}{100} = \frac{21}{W}$$

$$70W = 2100$$

$$W = 30$$

By solving the proportion, we find that there were 30 students in the whole class.

Example 1 Forty percent of the leprechauns had never seen the pot of gold. If 480 leprechauns had seen the pot of gold, how many of the leprechauns had not seen it?

Solution We may solve this problem just as we solve a ratio problem. We use the percents to fill the ratio column of the table. All the leprechauns were 100 percent. The part that had never seen the pot of gold was 40 percent. Therefore, the part that had seen the pot of gold was 60 percent. The number 480 was the actual count of the leprechauns who had seen the gold. We write these numbers in the table.

	Percent	Actual Count
Had not seen	40	N
Had seen	60	480
Total	100	T

Now we use the table to write a proportion. Since we know both numbers in the second row, we will use that row in the proportion. Since the problem asks us to find the actual count of leprechauns who had not seen the pot of gold, we will also use the first row in the proportion.

	Percent	Actual Count
Had not seen	40	N
Had seen	60	480
Total	100	T

$$\frac{40}{60} = \frac{N}{480}$$

$$60N = 19{,}200$$

$$N = 320$$

We find that **320 leprechauns** had not seen the pot of gold.

Example 2   Twenty-seven of the 45 elves who worked in the toy factory had to work the night shift. What percent of the elves had to work the night shift?

Solution   We make a ratio box and write in the numbers. The total number of elves was 45, so 18 elves worked the day shift.

	Percent	Actual Count
Night shift	P_N	27
Day shift	P_D	18
Total	100	45

We use P_N to stand for the percent who worked the night shift. We use this row and the total row to write the proportion.

	Percent	Actual Count
Night shift	P_N	27
Day shift	P_D	18
Total	100	45

$$\frac{P_N}{100} = \frac{27}{45}$$

$$45P_N = 2700$$

$$P_N = 60$$

We find that **60 percent** of the elves had to work the night shift.

Practice   Use a ratio box to solve each problem.

a. Twenty-one of the 70 acres were planted in alfalfa. What percent of the acres was not planted in alfalfa? 70%

b. Lori figures she still has 60 percent of the book to read. If she has read 120 pages, how many pages does she still have to read? 180 pages

Problem set 81

1. The coordinates of the vertices of $\triangle ABC$ are $A\,(2, -1)$, $B\,(5, -1)$, and $C\,(5, -3)$. Draw the triangle and its image $\triangle A'B'C'$ reflected in the x-axis. What are the coordinates of the vertices of $\triangle A'B'C'$? $A'\,(2, 1)$, $B'\,(5, 1)$, $C'\,(5, 3)$
(80)

1.
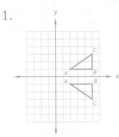

Use the information given to answer problems 2 and 3.

On his first 15 tests, Paul earned: 70, 85, 80, 85, 90, 80, 85, 80, 90, 95, 85, 90, 100, 85, 90.

2. (a) What was Paul's average (mean) test score? 86
(Inv. 4)

(b) If Paul's scores were arranged in order from lowest to highest, which would be the middle score? (What is the median of the scores?) 85

3. (a) Which score did Paul earn most often? (What is the
(Inv. 4)   mode of the scores?) 85

    (b) What was the difference between Paul's highest score
and his lowest score? (What is the range of the scores?)
30

4. Danny is 6'1" (6 ft, 1 in.) tall. His sister is 5'6½" tall. Danny
(56)   is how many inches taller than his sister? $6\frac{1}{2}$ inches

5. Use a ratio box to solve this problem. Michelle bought 5
(72)   pencils for 75¢. At this rate, how much would she pay for
a dozen pencils? $1.80

6. Graph each inequality on a separate number line.
(78)

    (a) $x < 4$![number line 1 2 3 4 5 with open circle at 4]   (b) $x \geq -2$![number line -3 -2 -1 0 1 with closed circle at -2]

7.

60 questions	
12 questions	
12 questions	
12 questions	
12 questions	
12 questions	

$\frac{4}{5}$ answered correctly (48)

$\frac{1}{5}$ answered incorrectly

7. Draw a diagram of this statement. Then answer the
(36,71)   questions that follow.

    *Gilbert answered 48 questions correctly. This was
$\frac{4}{5}$ of the questions on the test.*

    (a) How many questions were on the test? 60 questions

    (b) What was the ratio of Gilbert's correct answers to his
incorrect answers? $\frac{4}{1}$

8. If point B is located halfway between points A and C,
(8)   what is the length of segment AB? $1\frac{7}{8}$ inches

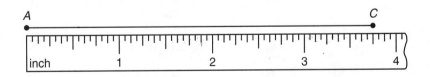

9. Use a ratio box to solve this problem. The ratio of gleeps
(65)   to bobbles was 9 to 5. If the total number of gleeps and
bobbles was 2800, then how many gleeps were there?
1800 gleeps

10. If $x = 9$, what does $x^2 + \sqrt{x}$ equal? 84
(41)

11. insufficient
information
($m < n$ if both
are positive;
$m > n$ if both
are negative)

11. Compare: $m \bigcirc n$ if $\dfrac{m}{n} = 0.5$
(79)

12. Complete the table.
(48)

Fraction	Decimal	Percent
$2\frac{1}{4}$	(a) 2.25	(b) 225%
(c) $\frac{9}{400}$	(d) 0.0225	$2\frac{1}{4}\%$

Write equations to solve problems 13 and 14.

13. The store owner makes a profit of 40% of the selling price
(60) of an item. If an item sells for $12, how much profit does
the store owner make? $p = 0.4 \times \$12$; $4.80

14. Fifty percent of what number is 0.4? $0.5 \times W_N = 0.4$; 0.8
(77)

15. Simplify: $\dfrac{16\frac{2}{3}}{100}$ $\frac{1}{6}$
(76)

Use ratio boxes to solve problems 16 and 17.

16. Nathan correctly answered 21 of the 25 questions. What
(81) percent of the questions did he answer correctly? 84%

17. Twenty percent of the 4000 acres were left fallow. How
(81) many acres were not left fallow? 3200 acres

18. (a) Angles
ABC and *CBD* are
supplementary
(total 180°) so
m∠*CBD* = 40°.

  (b) Angles
CBD and *DBE* are
complementary
(total 90°) so
m∠*DBE* = 50°.

  (c) Angles
DBE and *EBA* are
supplementary
(total 180°) so
m∠*EBA* = 130°.

18. Given that the measure of ∠*ABC* is 140°,
(40)

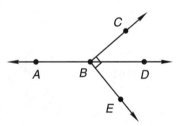

(a) what is the measure of ∠*CBD* and how do you know?

(b) what is the measure of ∠*DBE* and how do you know?

(c) what is the measure of ∠*EBA* and how do you know?

(d) what is the sum of the measures of ∠*ABC*, ∠*CBD*,
∠*DBE*, and ∠*EBA*? 360°

19. Write the prime factorization of the two terms of this
(24) fraction and then reduce the fraction.

$$\frac{3000}{6300} \quad \frac{2 \cdot 2 \cdot 2 \cdot 3 \cdot 5 \cdot 5 \cdot 5}{2 \cdot 2 \cdot 3 \cdot 3 \cdot 5 \cdot 5 \cdot 7} = \frac{10}{21}$$

20. (a) What is the area of this isosceles
(58,75)   trapezoid? Dimensions are in
           inches. 180 in.²

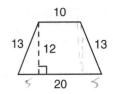

20.(b)   (b) Trace this trapezoid on your
           paper. Then draw its line of
           symmetry.

21. Describe the rule of this function and
(58) find the missing numbers.
      Double the "in" number then subtract 1 to
      find the "out" number.

In	FUNCTION	Out
4 →		→ 7
−1 →		→ −3
6 →		→ 11
3 →		→ 5
0 →		→ −1

22. Write each number in scientific notation.
(69)

   (a) 56×10^7 5.6×10^8 (b) 56×10^{-7} 5.6×10^{-6}

Solve each equation. Show each step. Check the solution.

23. $5x = 16.5$ 3.3   **24.** $3\frac{1}{2} + a = 5\frac{3}{8}$ $1\frac{7}{8}$
(Inv. 7)   (Inv. 7)

Simplify:

25. $3^2 + 5\left[6 - \left(10 - 2^3\right)\right]$ 29
(63)

26. $\sqrt{2^2 \cdot 3^4 \cdot 5^2}$ 90
(52)

27. $2\frac{2}{3} \times 4.5 \div 6$ (fraction answer) 2
(43)

28. $\left(3\frac{1}{2}\right)^2 - (5 - 3.4)$ (decimal answer) 10.65
(26,43)

29. (a) $(-12)(-9)$ 108   (b) $(-3)(25)$ −75
(73)

   (c) $\dfrac{-100}{5}$ −20   (d) $\dfrac{25}{-5}$ −5

30. (a) $(-3) + |-4| - (-5)$ 6   (b) $(-18) - (+20) + (-7)$
(68)   −45

LESSON
82

Area of a Circle

Facts Practice: Percent-Decimal-Fraction Equivalents
(Test U in Test Masters)

Mental Math:
a. 18
b. 0.01
c. 9
d. 31.4 ft
e. 1.5 m
f. 32
g. 60
Problem Solving:
18 ounces;
60 + 2W
= 4W + 24

Mental Math:

a. $(-6) - (-24)$ **b.** $(0.1)^2$ **c.** $8n + 6 = 78$

d. 3.14×10 ft   **e.** 150 cm to m   **f.** 24 is $\frac{3}{4}$ of n

g. 25% of 24, × 5, − 2, ÷ 2, + 1, ÷ 3, × 7, + 1, $\sqrt{}$, × 10

Problem Solving:

Six identical blocks marked W, a 24-oz weight, and a 60-oz weight are distributed on a balanced scale as shown. What is the weight of each block marked W? Write an equation illustrated by this balanced scale.

We can find the areas of some polygons by multiplying the two perpendicular dimensions.

- We find the area of a rectangle by multiplying the length times the width.

$$A = lw$$

- We find the area of a parallelogram by multiplying the base times the height.

$$A = bh$$

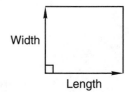

- We find the area of a triangle by multiplying the base times the height (which gives us the area of a parallelogram), then dividing by 2.

$$A = \frac{bh}{2} \quad \text{or} \quad A = \frac{1}{2}bh$$

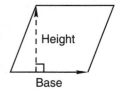

To find the area of a circle, we again begin by multiplying two perpendicular dimensions. We multiply the radius times the radius. This gives us the area of a square built on the radius.

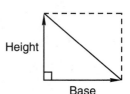

If the radius of the circle is 3, the area of the square is 3^2, which is 9. If the radius of the circle is r, the area of the square is r^2. We see that the area of the circle is less than the area of four of these squares.

However, the area of the circle is more than the area of three squares.

The number of squares whose area exactly equals the area of the circle is a number between 3 and 4. The exact number is π. Thus, to find the area of the circle, we first find the area of the square built on the radius. Then we multiply that area by π. This is summarized by the equation

$$A = \pi r^2$$

Example Find the area of each circle.

(a)

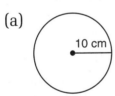

Use 3.14 for π.

(b)

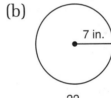

Use $\frac{22}{7}$ for π.

(c)

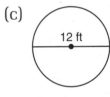

Leave π as π.

Solution (a) The area of a square built on the radius is 100 cm². We multiply this by π.

$$A = \pi r^2$$
$$A \approx (3.14)(100 \text{ cm}^2)$$
$$A \approx \textbf{314 cm}^2$$

(b) The area of a square built on the radius is 49 in.². We multiply this by π.

$$A = \pi r^2$$
$$A \approx \frac{22}{\overset{1}{\cancel{7}}} \cdot \overset{7}{\cancel{49}} \text{ in.}^2$$
$$A \approx \textbf{154 in.}^2$$

(c) Since the diameter is 12 ft, the radius is 6 ft. The area of a square built on the radius is 36 ft². We multiply this by π.

$$A = \pi r^2$$

$$A = \pi \cdot 36 \text{ ft}^2$$

$$A = 36\pi \text{ ft}^2$$

Practice*   **a.** Using 3.14 for π, calculate the area to the nearest square foot of circle (c) in the Example problem in this lesson.
113 ft²

Find the area of each of these circles.

b.

Use 3.14 for π.
50.24 cm²

c.

Leave π as π.
16π cm²

d.

Use $\frac{22}{7}$ for π.
50$\frac{2}{7}$ cm²

Problem set 82

1. Find the volume of this rectangular
(70) prism. Dimensions are in feet. 20 ft³

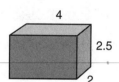

2. The heights of the 5 basketball starters were 6'3", 6'5",
(28) 5'11", 6'2", and 6'1". Find the average height of the 5 starters. (*Hint:* Change all measures to inches before dividing.) 6'2"

3. Use a ratio box to solve this problem. The student-teacher
(54) ratio at the high school was 20 to 1. If there were 48 high school teachers, then how many students were there?
960 students

4. An inch is 2.54 centimeters. Use a unit multiplier to
(50) convert 2.54 centimeters to meters. 0.0254 meter

5. Graph each inequality on a separate number line.
(78)

(a) $x < -2$

(b) $x \geq 0$

6. Use a case 1-case 2 ratio box to solve this problem. Don's
(72) heart beats 225 times in 3 minutes. At that rate, how many times will his heart beat in 5 minutes? 375 times

7.

25 students

$\frac{2}{5}$ were boys
| 5 students |
| 5 students |

$\frac{3}{5}$ were girls (15)
| 5 students |
| 5 students |
| 5 students |

7. Draw a diagram of this statement. Then answer the questions that follow.

(36,71)

> *Two fifths of the students in the class were boys. There were 15 girls in the class.*

(a) How many students were in the class? 25 students

(b) What was the ratio of girls to boys in the class? $\frac{3}{2}$

8. If $x = 5$ and $y = 3$, compare: $x^2 - y^2 \; \textcircled{=} \; (x + y)(x - y)$

(79)

9. What percent of this circle is shaded? 52%

(Inv. 1)

25%
23%

10. Compare: $a \; \textcircled{<} \; b$ if $a - b$ is negative

(79)

11. Find the circumference of each circle.

(66)

(a)   43.96 cm

7 cm

Use 3.14 for π.

(b)   44 cm

14 cm

Use $\frac{22}{7}$ for π.

12. Find the area of each circle in problem 11.

(82) (a) 153.86 cm^2 (b) 154 cm^2

13. Complete the table.

(48)

FRACTION	DECIMAL	PERCENT
(a) $1\frac{3}{5}$	1.6	(b) 160%
(c) $\frac{2}{125}$	(d) 0.016	1.6%

14. Write an equation to solve this problem. How much money is 6.4% of $25? $M = 0.064 \times \$25$; $1.60

(60)

15. Express in scientific notation.

(69)

(a) 12×10^5 1.2×10^6

(b) 12×10^{-5} 1.2×10^{-4}

16. Use a ratio box to solve this problem. Sixty-four percent of the students correctly described the process of photosynthesis. If 63 students did not correctly describe the process of photosynthesis, then how many students correctly described this process? 112 students

(81)

17. Use a ratio box to solve this problem. Ginger still has 40
(81) percent of her book to read. If she has read 180 pages,
how many pages does she still have to read? 120 pages

18. Find the area of this figure.
(75) Dimensions are in inches. Corners
that look square are square. 59 in.²

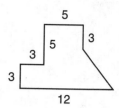

19.

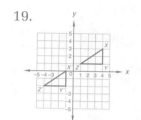

19. The coordinates of the vertices of △XYZ are X (4, 3), Y (4, 1),
(80) and Z (1, 1). Draw △XYZ and its image △X'Y'Z' translated
5 units to the left and 3 units down. What are the coordinates
of the vertices of △X'Y'Z'? X' (–1, 0), Y' (–1, –2), Z' (–4, –2)

20. Write the prime factorization of the two terms of this
(24) fraction and then reduce the fraction.

$$\frac{240}{816}$$ $\frac{2 \cdot 2 \cdot 2 \cdot 2 \cdot 3 \cdot 5}{2 \cdot 2 \cdot 2 \cdot 2 \cdot 3 \cdot 17} = \frac{5}{17}$

21. The figure illustrates regular hexagon
(Inv. 2) ABCDEF inscribed in a circle with
center M.

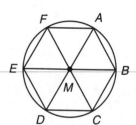

(a) How many illustrated chords are
diameters? 3 chords

(b) How many illustrated chords are
not diameters? 6 chords

(c) What is the measure of central angle AMB? 60°

(d) What is the measure of inscribed angle ABC? 120°

22. Write 100 million in scientific notation. 1×10^8
(51)

Solve each equation. Show each step. Check the solution.

23. $\frac{3}{4}x = 36$ 48
(Inv. 7)

24. $3.2 + a = 3.46$ 0.26
(Inv. 7)

Simplify:

25. $\frac{\sqrt{3^2 + 4^2}}{5}$ 1
(52)

26. $(8 - 3)^2 - (3 - 8)^2$ 0
(52)

27. $3\frac{1}{2} \div (7 \div 0.2)$ (decimal answer)   0.1
(43,45)

28. $4.5 + 2\frac{2}{3} - 3$ (mixed-number answer) $4\frac{1}{6}$
(43)

29. (a) $\dfrac{(-3)(-4)}{(-2)}$ -6 (b) $(-2)(+3)(-4)$ 24
(73)

30. (a) $(-3) + (-4) - (-2)$ -5 (b) $(-20) + (+30) - |-40|$
(68) -30

LESSON 83

Multiplying Powers of 10 • Multiplying Numbers in Scientific Notation

Mental Math:
a. -20
b. $6,750,000$
c. 20
d. $\$18$
e. 0.5 g
f. 64
g. 150 mi
Problem Solving:
  10

Facts Practice: Area (Test Q in Test Masters)

Mental Math:

  a. $(-60) \div (+3)$ **b.** 6.75×10^6 **c.** $\frac{100}{150} = \frac{m}{30}$

  d. 15% of $120   **e.** 500 mg to g   **f.** 24 is $\frac{3}{8}$ of n

  g. At 60 mph how far will a car travel in $2\frac{1}{2}$ hours?

Problem Solving:

  How many different triangles of any size are in this figure?

Multiplying powers of 10

Here we show two powers of 10.

$$10^3 \text{ and } 10^4$$

We remember that

$$10^3 \text{ means } 10 \cdot 10 \cdot 10$$

and

$$10^4 \text{ means } 10 \cdot 10 \cdot 10 \cdot 10$$

We can multiply powers of 10.

$$\underbrace{10^3}_{10 \cdot 10 \cdot 10} \cdot \underbrace{10^4}_{10 \cdot 10 \cdot 10 \cdot 10}$$

We see that 10^3 times 10^4 means that 7 tens are multiplied. We can write this as 10^7.

$$10^3 \cdot 10^4 = 10^7$$

As we focus our attention on the exponents, we see that

$$3 + 4 = 7$$

This example illustrates an important rule of mathematics.

When we multiply powers of 10, we add the exponents.

Multiplying numbers in scientific notation

To multiply numbers that are written in scientific notation, we multiply the decimal numbers to find the decimal number part of the product. Then we multiply the powers of 10 to find the power-of-10 part of the product. We remember that when we multiply powers of 10, we add the exponents.

Example 1 Multiply: $(1.2 \times 10^5)(3 \times 10^7)$

Solution We multiply 1.2 by 3 and get 3.6. Then we multiply 10^5 by 10^7 and get 10^{12}. The product is

$$3.6 \times 10^{12}$$

Example 2 Multiply: $(4 \times 10^6)(3 \times 10^5)$

Solution We multiply 4 by 3 and get 12. Then we multiply 10^6 by 10^5 and get 10^{11}. The product is

$$12 \times 10^{11}$$

We rewrite this expression in the proper form of scientific notation.

$$(1.2 \times 10^1) \times 10^{11} = 1.2 \times 10^{12}$$

Example 3 Multiply: $(2 \times 10^{-5})(3 \times 10^{-7})$

Solution We multiply 2 by 3 and get 6. To multiply 10^{-5} by 10^{-7} we add the exponents and get 10^{-12}. Thus, the product is

$$6 \times 10^{-12}$$

Example 4 Multiply: $(5 \times 10^3)(7 \times 10^{-8})$

Solution We multiply 5 by 7 and get 35. We multiply 10^3 by 10^{-8} and get 10^{-5}. The product is

$$35 \times 10^{-5} \qquad \text{product}$$
$$(3.5 \times 10^1) \times 10^{-5}$$
$$3.5 \times 10^{-4} \qquad \text{simplified}$$

Practice*　Multiply and write each product in scientific notation.

　　a. $\left(4.2 \times 10^6\right)\left(1.4 \times 10^3\right)$　5.88×10^9

　　b. $\left(5 \times 10^5\right)\left(3 \times 10^7\right)$　1.5×10^{13}

　　c. $\left(4 \times 10^{-3}\right)\left(2.1 \times 10^{-7}\right)$　8.4×10^{-10}

　　d. $\left(6 \times 10^{-2}\right)\left(7 \times 10^{-5}\right)$　4.2×10^{-6}

Problem set 83

1. The 16-ounce box cost \$1.12. The 24-ounce box cost
(46) \$1.32. The smaller box cost how much more per ounce than the larger box?　$1\frac{1}{2}\ \frac{\text{cents}}{\text{ounce}}$ more

2. Use a ratio box to solve this problem. The ratio of good
(65) apples to bad apples in the basket was 5 to 2. If there were 70 apples in the basket, how many of them were good?
50 apples

3. Jan's average score after 15 tests was 82. Her average
(55) score on the next 5 tests was 90. What was her average score for all 20 tests?　84

4. Jackson earns \$6 per hour at a part-time job. How much
(53) does he earn if he works for 2 hours and 30 minutes?　\$15

5. Use a unit multiplier to convert 24 shillings to pence.
(50) (1 shilling = 12 pence)　288 pence

6. Graph $x \leq -1$ on a number line.
(78)

7. Use a case 1-case 2 ratio box to solve this problem. Five is
(72) to 12 as 20 is to what number?　48

8. If $a = 1.5$, then what does $4a + 5$ equal?　11
(41)

9. Four fifths of the football team's 30 points were scored on
(22) pass plays. How many points did the team score on pass plays?　24 points

10. If x and y are integers, compare: $x(x + y) \bigcirc x^2 + xy$
(79)

11. Find the circumference of each circle.
(66)

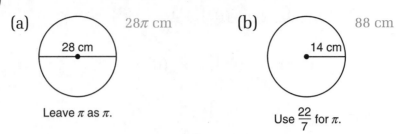

(a)   28π cm

28 cm

Leave π as π.

(b)   88 cm

14 cm

Use $\frac{22}{7}$ for π.

12. Find the area of each circle in problem 11.
(82)   (a) 196π cm²   (b) 616 cm²

13. The edges of a cube are 10 cm long.
(67,70)

(a) What is the volume of the cube? 1000 cm³

(b) What is the surface area of the cube? 600 cm²

14. Complete the table.
(48)

FRACTION	DECIMAL	PERCENT
(a) $2\frac{1}{2}$	(b) 2.5	250%
$\frac{7}{12}$	(c) $0.58\overline{3}$	(d) $58\frac{1}{3}\%$

15. What is the sales tax on an $8.50 purchase if the tax rate
(46)   is $6\frac{1}{2}\%$? $0.55

Use ratio boxes to solve problems 16 and 17.

16. Judy found that there were 12 minutes of commercials
(81)   during every hour of prime time programming. Commercials were shown for what percent of each hour?
20%

17. Thirty percent of the boats that traveled up the river on
(81)   Monday were steam powered. If 42 of the boats that traveled up the river were not steam powered, then how many boats were there in all? 60 boats

18. Write the prime factorization of the numerator and
(24)   denominator of this fraction. Then reduce the fraction.

$$\frac{420}{630} \qquad \frac{2 \cdot 2 \cdot 3 \cdot 5 \cdot 7}{2 \cdot 3 \cdot 3 \cdot 5 \cdot 7} = \frac{2}{3}$$

19. Find the area of this trapezoid.
(75)   900 m²

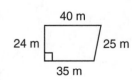

40 m

24 m   25 m

35 m

20. In this figure ∠A and ∠B of △ABC are
(40) congruent. The measure of ∠E = 54°.
Find the measure of

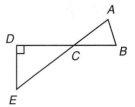

(a) ∠ECD. 36°   (b) ∠ECB. 144°

(c) ∠ACB. 36°   (d) ∠BAC. 72°

21. Describe the rule of this function and
(58) find the missing numbers.
Multiply the "in" number by 2 and then add
1 to find the "out" number.

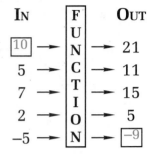

IN	FUNCTION	OUT
10		21
5		11
7		15
2		5
−5		−9

22. Multiply and write each product in scientific notation.
(83)
(a) $(3 \times 10^4)(6 \times 10^5)$ (b) $(1.2 \times 10^{-3})(4 \times 10^{-6})$
    1.8×10^{10} 4.8×10^{-9}

Solve each equation. Show every step. Check the solution.

23. $b - 1\frac{2}{3} = 4\frac{1}{2}$ $6\frac{1}{6}$ **24.** $0.4y = 1.44$ 3.6
(Inv. 7)   (Inv. 7)

Simplify:

25. $1 + 2 + 2^2 + 2^3 + 2^4$ **26.** $0.6 \times 3\frac{1}{3} \div 2$ 1
(52) 31   (43)

27. $\dfrac{5}{24} - \dfrac{7}{60}$ $\frac{11}{120}$
(30)

28. (a) $\dfrac{(-4)(-6)}{(-2)(-3)}$ 4   (b) $(-3)(-4)(-5)$ −60
(73)

29. (a) $(-3) + (-4) - (-5)$ (b) $(-15) - (+14) + (+10)$
(68)   −2   −19

30.

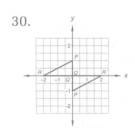

30. The coordinates of the vertices of △PQR are P (0, 1), Q (0, 0),
(80) and R (−2, 0). Draw the triangle and its image △P′Q′R′ after a
180° clockwise rotation about the origin. What are the
coordinates of the vertices of △P′Q′R′?
P′ (0, −1), Q′ (0, 0), R′ (2, 0)

LESSON
84

Facts Practice: Area (Test Q in Test Masters)

Mental Math:

  a. $(-12) - (-12)$ **b.** 25^2 **c.** $6m - 10 = 32$
  d. $3.14 \times 30 \text{ cm}$ **e.** 1.5 cm to mm   **f.** 30 is $\frac{5}{6}$ of n
  g. $12 \times 12, -4, \div 10, +1, \times 2, +3, \div 3, \times 5, -1, \div 6, \sqrt{\ }$

Problem Solving:

A rectangular tablecloth was draped over a rectangular table. Eight inches of cloth hung over the left edge of the table, 3 inches over the back, 4 inches over the right edge, and 7 inches over the front. In which directions (L, B, R, and F) and how many inches should the tablecloth be shifted so that the amount of cloth hanging over opposite edges is equal?

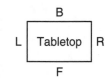

We have used the word "term" in arithmetic to refer to the numerator or denominator of a fraction. For example, we reduce a fraction to its lowest *terms*. In algebra we use the word **term** to refer to a part of an algebraic expression or equation. An algebraic expression may contain one, two, three, or more terms.

Some Algebraic Expressions

Type of Expression	Number of Terms	Example
monomial	1	$-2x$
binomial	2	$a^2 - 4b^2$
trinomial	3	$3x^2 - x - 4$

Terms are separated from other terms in an expression by plus or minus signs that are not enclosed by parentheses or other symbols of inclusion. Here we have separated the terms of the binomial and trinomial examples with slashes.

$$a^2 \ / \ - 4b^2 \qquad 3x^2 \ / \ - x \ / \ - 4$$

Each term contains a signed number and may contain one or more variables (letters). Sometimes the signed number part is *understood* and not written. For instance, the signed number part of a^2 is +1. So a^2 actually means $+1a^2$. Likewise, the term

$-x$ is understood to mean $-1x$. **When a term is written without a number, it is understood that the number is 1. When a term is written without a sign, it is understood that the sign is positive.** It is not necessary for a term to have a factor that is a variable. The third term of the trinomial above is -4. A term that does not contain a variable is often called a **constant term,** because its value does not change as the value of a variable term can change.

Constant terms can be combined by algebraic addition.

$$3x + 3 - 1 = 3x + 2 \qquad \text{added } +3 \text{ and } -1$$

Variable terms can also be combined by algebraic addition if they are **like terms.** Like terms have identical letter parts. That is, the same variables appear in the terms with the same exponents. The terms $-3xy$ and $+xy$ are both xy terms. They are like terms and can be combined by algebraically adding the signed number part of the terms.

$$-3xy + xy = -2xy$$

The signed number part of $+xy$ is $+1$. We get $-2xy$ from adding $-3xy$ and $+1xy$.

Example 1 Collect like terms.

$$3x + y + x - y$$

Solution There are four terms in this expression. There are two x terms and two y terms. We may use the commutative property to rearrange the terms.

$$3x + x + y - y$$

Adding $+3x$ and $+1x$ we get $+4x$. Then adding $+1y$ and $-1y$ we get $0y$ which is 0.

$$3x + x + y - y$$
$$4x + 0$$
$$\mathbf{4x}$$

Example 2 Collect like terms.

$$3x + 2x^2 + 4 + x^2 - x - 1$$

Solution In this expression there are three kinds of terms: x^2 terms, x terms, and constant terms. Using the commutative property we arrange the terms so that like terms are together.

$$2x^2 + x^2 + 3x - x + 4 - 1$$

Now we collect like terms.

$$2x^2 + x^2 + 3x - x + 4 - 1$$

$$\mathbf{3x^2 + 2x + 3}$$

Notice that x^2 terms and x terms are not like terms and cannot be combined by addition. There are other possible arrangements of the collected terms such as:

$$2x + 3x^2 + 3$$

However, we customarily arrange terms in descending order of exponents so that the term with the largest exponent is on the left and the constant term is on the right.

Practice   Describe each of these expressions as a monomial, a binomial, or a trinomial.

    a. $x^2 - y^2$ binomial   **b.** $3x^2 - 2x - 1$ trinomial

    c. $-2x^3yz^2$ monomial   **d.** $-2x^2y - 4xy^2$ binomial

Collect like terms.

    e. $3a + 2a^2 - a + a^2$ **f.** $5xy - x + xy - 2x$
       $3a^2 + 2a$ $6xy - 3x$

    g. $3 + x^2 + x - 5 + 2x^2$ **h.** $3\pi + 1.4 - \pi + 2.8$
       $3x^2 + x - 2$ $2\pi + 4.2$

Problem set
84 *(Inv. 4)*

1. Refer to this graph to answer questions (a)–(c).

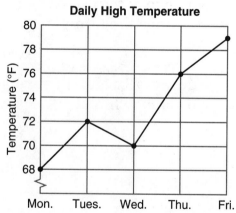

Daily High Temperature

(a) What was the range in the daily high temperature from Monday to Friday? 11°F

(b) Which day had the greatest increase in temperature from the previous day? Thursday

(c) Wednesday's high temperature was how much lower than the average high temperature for these 5 days? 3°F

2. An increase in temperature of 10°C on the Celsius scale
$^{(32)}$ corresponds to an increase of how many degrees on the
Fahrenheit scale? 18°F

3. Collect like terms. $2xy + xy - 3x + x$ $3xy - 2x$
$^{(84)}$

4. Frank's scores on 10 tests were as follows:
$^{(Inv.\ 4)}$

$$90, 90, 100, 95, 95, 85, 100, 100, 80, 100$$

For this set of scores find the (a) mean, (b) median,
(c) mode, and (d) range. (a) 93.5   (b) 95   (c) 100   (d) 20

5. Use a ratio box to solve this problem. The ratio of
$^{(65)}$ rowboats to sailboats in the bay was 3 to 7. If the total
number of rowboats and sailboats in the bay was 210,
how many sailboats were in the bay? 147 sailboats

6. Recall that the four quadrants of a coordinate plane are
$^{(Inv.\ 3)}$ numbered 1st, 2nd, 3rd, and 4th in a counterclockwise
direction with the upper right quadrant being the 1st
quadrant. In which quadrant are the x-numbers negative
and the y-numbers positive? 2nd

7. Write a proportion to solve this problem. If 4 cost $1.40,
$^{(72)}$ how much would 10 cost? $3.50

8. Five eighths of the members supported the treaty,
$^{(71)}$ whereas 36 opposed the treaty. How many members
supported the treaty? 60 members

9. Evaluate each expression for $x = 5$.
$^{(52)}$

(a) $x^2 - 2x + 1$ 16   (b) $(x - 1)^2$ 16

10. Compare: $f \ominus g$ if $\dfrac{f}{g} = 1$
$^{(79)}$

11. (a) Find the circumference of this
$^{(66,82)}$ circle. 18.84 in.

(b) Find the area of this circle.
28.26 in.²

6 in.

Use 3.14 for π.

12. 480 centimeters **12.** Use a unit multiplier to convert 4.8 meters to centimeters.
$^{(50)}$

13. Sketch a rectangular prism. A rectangular prism has how
(67) many faces? 6 faces

14. Complete the table.
(48)

Fraction	Decimal	Percent
$1\frac{4}{5}$	(a) 1.8	(b) 180%
(c) $\frac{9}{500}$	(d) 0.018	1.8%

15. A merchant priced a product so that 30% of the selling
(60) price is profit. If a product sells for $18.00, then how much
money is profit for the merchant? Write an equation to
solve the problem. $p = 0.3 \times \$18.00$; $5.40

16. Simplify: $\dfrac{12\frac{1}{2}}{100}$ $\frac{1}{8}$
(76)

Use ratio boxes to solve problems 17 and 18.

17. When the door was left open, 36 pigeons flew the coop. If
(81) this was 40 percent of all pigeons, how many pigeons were
there originally? 90 pigeons

18. Sixty percent of the gnomes were 3 feet tall or less. If
(81) there were 300 gnomes in all, how many were more than
3 feet tall? 120 gnomes

19. A square sheet of paper with a peri-
(75) meter of 48 in. has a corner cut off,
forming a pentagon as shown.

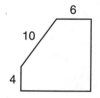

(a) What is the perimeter of the
pentagon? 44 in.

(b) What is the area of the pentagon? 120 in.²

20. The face of this spinner has been divided into seven
(36,Inv. 5) sectors, the central angles of which have the following
measures:

A 60°   *B* 90°   *C* 45°   *D* 30°

E 75°   *F* 40°   *G* 20°

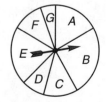

If the arrow is spun once, what is the probability that it
will stop in sector

(a) *A*? $\frac{1}{6}$ (b) *C*? $\frac{1}{8}$ (c) *E*? $\frac{5}{24}$

21. **Rule:** To find a term in the sequence, double the preceding term and add 1.

Note: Other rule descriptions are possible including "The value of the nth term is $2^n - 1$." Discuss various rules proposed by students.

21. Describe the rule of this sequence. Then find the next
(2) three numbers of the sequence.

$$1, 3, 7, 15, 31, \ldots \quad 63, 127, 255$$

22. Multiply and write the product in scientific notation.
(83)

(a) $(1.5 \times 10^{-3})(3 \times 10^6)$ 4.5×10^3

(b) $(3 \times 10^4)(5 \times 10^5)$ 1.5×10^{10}

Solve each question. Show each step. Check the solution.

23. $b - 4.75 = 5.2$ 9.95
(Inv. 7)

24. $\dfrac{2}{3}y = 36$ 54
(Inv. 7)

Simplify:

25. $\sqrt{5^2 - 4^2} + 2^3$ 11
(52)

26. $1 \text{ m} - 45 \text{ mm}$ 955 mm
(32)

27. $\dfrac{9}{10} \div 2\dfrac{1}{4} \cdot 24$ (decimal answer)   9.6
(43)

28. $(10^2)(10^2)(10^2)$ 10^6 or 1,000,000
(83)

29. (a) $\dfrac{(-8)(+6)}{(-3)(+4)}$ 4
(73)

(b) $(+3)(-5)(+2)$ -30

30. (a) $(+30) - (-50) - (+20)$ 60
(68)

(b) $(-3) - (-4) - (5)$ -4

Order of Operations with Signed Numbers • Functions, Part 2

Facts Practice: $+ - \times \div$ Integers (Test P in Test Masters)

Mental Math:

    a. $(+12)(-6)$ **b.** $(4 \times 10^3)(2 \times 10^6)$

    c. $\frac{1}{1.5} = \frac{80}{n}$ **d.** $12 is $\frac{1}{4}$ of how much money (m)?

    e. 0.8 km to m   **f.** What is $\frac{1}{4}$ of $12?

    g. Find the perimeter and area of a square with sides 2.5 m long.

Problem Solving:

There are three numbers whose sum is 180. The second number is twice the first number, and the third number is three times the first number (n, $2n$, and $3n$). Find the three numbers. (Try guess and check, and try writing an equation.)

```
__
__
+ __
===
180
```

Order of operations with signed numbers

To simplify expressions that involve several operations, we perform the operations in a prescribed order. We have practiced simplifying expressions with whole numbers. In this lesson we will begin simplifying expressions that contain both whole numbers and negative numbers.

Example 1 Simplify: $(-2) + (-2)(-2) - \dfrac{(-2)}{(+2)}$

Solution First we multiply and divide in order from left to right.

$$(-2) + (-2)(-2) - \dfrac{(-2)}{(+2)}$$

$$(-2) + \underbrace{(+4)} \quad - \underbrace{(-1)}$$

Then we add and subtract in order from left to right.

$$\underbrace{(-2) + (+4)} - (-1)$$

$$\underbrace{(+2) \quad - (-1)}$$

$$\mathbf{+3}$$

Mentally separating an expression into its terms can make an expression easier to simplify.

$$(-2) \;/\; + (-2)(-2) \;\Big/ - \dfrac{(-2)}{(+2)}$$

First we simplify each term. Then we combine the terms.

$$(-2) \; / \; + \; (-2)(-2) \; \Big/ \; - \; \frac{(-2)}{(+2)}$$

$$-2 \; / \quad + \; 4 \quad / \; + \; 1$$

$$\mathbf{3}$$

Example 2 Simplify each term of this expression and then combine the terms.

$$-3(2 - 4) - 4(-2)(-3) + \frac{(-3)(-4)}{2}$$

Solution We will emphasize the three separate terms with slashes before each plus or minus sign not enclosed by parentheses or other symbols of inclusion.

$$-3(2 - 4) \; / \; - \; 4(-2)(-3) \; \Big/ \; + \; \frac{(-3)(-4)}{2}$$

Next we simplify each term.

$$-3(2 - 4) \; / \; - \; 4(-2)(-3) \; \Big/ \; + \; \frac{(-3)(-4)}{2}$$

$$-3(-2) \quad / \quad + \; 8(-3) \quad \Big/ \quad + \; \frac{12}{2}$$

$$+6 \quad / \quad - \; 24 \quad / \quad + \; 6$$

Now we combine the simplified terms.

$$+6 - 24 + 6$$

$$-18 + 6$$

$$\mathbf{-12}$$

Example 3 Simplify: $(-2) - [(-3) - (-4)(-5)]$

Solution There are only two terms, −2 and the quantity in brackets. We simplify within brackets first. Within the brackets we follow the order of operations, multiplying and dividing before adding and subtracting.

$$(-2) \; / \; - \; [(-3) - (-4)(-5)]$$

$$(-2) \; / \quad - \; [(-3) - (+20)]$$

$$(-2) \; / \qquad - \; (-23)$$

$$(-2) \; / \qquad + \; 23$$

$$\mathbf{+21}$$

Functions, part 2   We remember that a function is a relationship between two sets of numbers. We have practiced finding missing numbers in functions when some number pairs have been given. For instance, the missing numbers in the functions on the left and the right below are 14 and 7, respectively.

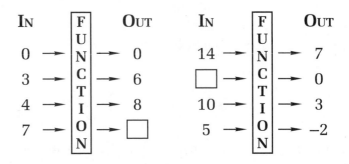

We have found the missing numbers by first finding the rule of the function. The rule of the function on the left is "Multiply the 'in' number by 2 to find the 'out' number." The rule of the function on the right is "Subtract 7 from the 'in' number to find the 'out' number."

Often the rule of a function is expressed as an equation with an x standing for the "in" number and y standing for the "out" number. If we write the rule of the function on the left as an equation, we get

$$y = 2x$$

If we write the rule of the function on the right as an equation, we get

$$y = x - 7$$

Beginning with this lesson we will practice finding missing numbers in functions when the rule is given as an equation.

Example 4   Find the missing numbers in the function.

$$y = 2x + 1$$

x	y
4	☐
7	☐
0	☐

Solution   The letter y stands for the "out" number. The letter x stands for the "in" number. We are given three "in" numbers and are asked to find the "out" number for each using the rule of the function. The expression $2x + 1$ shows us what to do to find y, the "out" number. It shows us we should multiply the x number by 2 and then add 1. The first x number is 4. We multiply by 2 and add 1.

$$y = 2x + 1$$
$$y = 2(4) + 1 \qquad \text{substituted}$$
$$y = 8 + 1 \qquad \text{multiplied}$$
$$y = 9 \qquad \text{added}$$

We find that the y number is 9 when x is 4. The next x number is 7. We multiply by 2 and add 1.

$$y = 2x + 1$$
$$y = 2(7) + 1 \qquad \text{substituted}$$
$$y = 14 + 1 \qquad \text{multiplied}$$
$$y = 15 \qquad \text{added}$$

The third x number is 0. We multiply by 2 and add 1.

$$y = 2x + 1$$
$$y = 2(0) + 1 \qquad \text{substituted}$$
$$y = 0 + 1 \qquad \text{multiplied}$$
$$y = 1 \qquad \text{added}$$

The missing numbers are **9, 15,** and **1.**

Practice Simplify:

a. $(-3) + (-3)(-3) - \dfrac{(-3)}{(+3)}$ 7

b. $(-3) - [(-4) - (-5)(-6)]$ 31

c. $(-2)[(-3) - (-4)(-5)]$ 46

d. $(-5) - (-5)(-5) + |-5|$ -25

Find the missing numbers in each function.

e. $y = 3x - 1$

x	y
3	8
1	2
0	-1

f. $y = \dfrac{1}{2}x$

x	y
6	3
0	0
8	4

g. $y = 8 - x$

x	y
7	1
1	7
4	4

h. $y = x^2$

x	y
1	1
2	4
3	9

h. Roberta studied a function and found that when x was 1, y was 1; when x was 2, y was 4; when x was 3, y was 9. Make a table of x, y pairs for this function, and above the table write an equation that expresses the rule of the function.

Problem set 85

1. Use a ratio box to solve this problem. The team's ratio of
(65) games won to games played was 3 to 4. If the team played
24 games, how many games did the team fail to win?
6 games

2. Find the (a) mean, (b) median, (c) mode, and (d) range of
(Inv. 4) the following group of scores: (a) 84   (b) 85   (c) 90   (d) 30

70, 80, 90, 80, 70, 90, 75, 95, 100, 90

3. Use a ratio box to solve this problem. Mary was chagrined
(54) to find that the ratio of dandelions to marigolds in the
garden was 11 to 4. If there were 44 marigolds in the
garden, how many dandelions were there? 121 dandelions

4. Use a unit multiplier to convert 0.98 liter to milliliters.
(50) 980 milliliters

5. Graph $x > 0$ on a number line. $\xrightarrow{\quad -1 \quad 0 \quad 1 \quad 2 \quad 3 \quad}$
(78)

6. Use a ratio box to solve this problem. If sound travels 2
(72) miles in 10 seconds, how far does sound travel in 1
minute? 12 miles

7.

$50,000
| $5,000 |
| $5,000 |
| $5,000 |
$\frac{7}{10}$ of the goal ($35,000) | $5,000 |
| $5,000 |
| $5,000 |
| $5,000 |
| $5,000 |
$\frac{3}{10}$ of the goal | $5,000 |
| $5,000 |

7. Draw a diagram of this statement. Then answer the
(71) questions that follow.

*Thirty-five thousand dollars was raised in the
charity drive. This was seven tenths of the goal.*

(a) The goal of the charity drive was to raise how much
money? $50,000

(b) The drive fell short of the goal by what percent? 30%

8. Compare: $2a \bigcirc a^2$ if a is a whole number
(79) insufficient information

9. The radius of a circle is 4 meters.
(66,82)

(a) What is the circumference of the circle? 25.12 m

(b) What is the area of the circle? 50.24 m²

10. What fraction of this circle is shaded?
(Inv. 1) $\frac{7}{20}$

11. A certain rectangular box is 5 in. long, 4 in. wide, and 3 in.
(70) high. Sketch the box and find its volume. 60 in.³

11.
3 in.
5 in.   4 in.

12. one possible pattern:

12. Imagine the box described in problem 11 is cut open and unfolded. Sketch the unfolded pattern and find the surface area. 94 in.²
(67)

13. Complete the table.
(48)

Fraction	Decimal	Percent
$\frac{1}{40}$	(a) 0.025	(b) $2\frac{1}{2}\%$
(c) $\frac{1}{400}$	(d) 0.0025	0.25%

14. When the Nelsons sold their house they paid the realtor a fee of 6% of the selling price. If the house sold for $180,000, how much was the realtor's fee? $10,800
(60)

15. (a) Write the prime factorization of 17,640 using exponents.
(21) 17,640 = $2^3 \cdot 3^2 \cdot 5 \cdot 7^2$

(b) How can you tell by looking at the answer to (a) that $\sqrt{17,640}$ is not a whole number? The exponents of the prime factors of 17,640 are not all even numbers.

16. Simplify: $\dfrac{8\frac{1}{3}}{100}$ $\frac{1}{12}$
(76)

Use ratio boxes to solve problems 17 and 18.

17. Max was delighted when he found that he had correctly answered 38 of the 40 questions. What percent of the questions had he answered correctly? 95%
(81)

18. Before the clowns arrived, only 35 percent of the children wore happy faces. If 91 children did not wear happy faces, how many children were there in all? 140 children
(81)

19. (a) Name this shape. parallelogram
(Inv. 6,61)

(b) Find its perimeter. 57 cm

(c) Find its area. 192 cm²

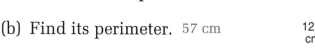

19.(d)

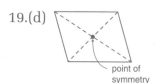

point of symmetry

(d) This figure does not have line symmetry but it does have point symmetry. Trace this figure on your paper and locate its point of symmetry.

20. Refer to this figure to answer questions (a)–(d).
(40)

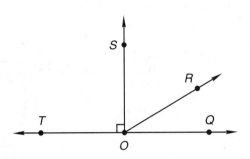

(a) Find m∠*TOS*. 90°

(b) Find m∠*QOT*. 180°

(c) Angle *QOR* is one third of a right angle. Find m∠*QOR*.
30°

(d) Find m∠*TOR*. 150°

21. Find the missing numbers in this
(85) function.

$y = 2x - 1$

x	y
5	9
3	5
1	1

22. Compare: $(5 \times 10^{-3})(6 \times 10^{8})$ ⊜ $(5 \times 10^{8})(6 \times 10^{-3})$
(51,83)

Solve each equation. Show each step. Check the solution.

23. $13.2 = 1.2w$ 11
(Inv. 7)

24. $c + \dfrac{5}{6} = 1\dfrac{1}{4}$ $\frac{5}{12}$
(Inv. 7)

Simplify:

25. $3\{20 - [6^2 - 3(10 - 4)]\}$ 6
(63)

26. 3 hr 15 min 25 s
(56) − 2 hr 45 min 30 s
        ‾‾‾‾‾‾‾‾‾‾‾‾‾‾‾‾
         29 min   55 s

27. $6\dfrac{3}{5} + 4.9 + 12.25$ (decimal answer) 23.75
(43)

28. (a) $(-2) + (-2)(+2) - \dfrac{(-2)}{(-2)}$ −7
(85)

(b) $(-3) - [(-2) - (+4)(-5)]$ −21

29. Collect like terms. $x^2 + 6x - 2x - 12$ $x^2 + 4x - 12$
(84)

30.

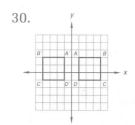

30. The coordinates of three vertices of square $ABCD$ are
(80) A (1, 2), B (4, 2), and C (4, –1).

(a) Find the coordinates of D and draw the square. D (1, –1)

(b) Reflect square $ABCD$ in the y-axis and draw its image, square $A'B'C'D'$. What are the coordinates of the vertices of this reflection?
A' (–1, 2), B' (–4, 2), C' (–4, –1), D' (–1, –1)

LESSON
86

Mental Math:
a. –58
b. 9×10^{-6}
c. 8
d. $2.70
e. 200 mL
f. $90
g. $214

Problem Solving:

Number Families

Facts Practice: Scientific Notation (Test R in Test Masters)

Mental Math:

a. $(-18) + (-40)$ b. $(3 \times 10^{-3})(3 \times 10^{-3})$

c. $7x + 4 = 60$ d. Estimate 15% of $17.90.

e. 0.2 L to mL   f. $30 is $\frac{1}{3}$ of m

g. What is the total cost of a $200 item plus 7% sales tax?

Problem Solving:

Here are the front, top, and side views of an object. Sketch a three-dimensional view of the object from the perspective of the upper right front.

Front   Right Side

Top

In mathematics we give special names to certain sets of numbers. Some of these sets or families of numbers are the counting numbers, the whole numbers, the integers, and the rational numbers. In this lesson we will review each of these number families and discuss how they are related.

- **The Counting Numbers.** Counting numbers are the numbers we say when we count. The first counting number is 1, the next is 2, then 3, and so on.

    Counting numbers: 1, 2, 3, 4, 5, …

- **The Whole Numbers.** The whole number family includes all of the counting number family and has one more member, which is zero.

    Whole numbers: 0, 1, 2, 3, 4, 5, …

If we use a dot to mark each of the whole numbers on the number line, the graph looks like this.

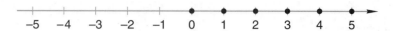

Notice that there are no dots on the negative side of the number line, because no whole number is a negative number. Also notice that there are no dots between the whole numbers because numbers between whole numbers are not "whole." We put an arrowhead on the right end of the number line to indicate that the whole numbers continue without end.

- **The Integers.** The integer family includes all of the whole numbers. The integer family also includes the opposites (negatives) of the positive whole numbers. The list of integers goes on and on in both directions as indicated by the ellipses.

    Integers: ..., −4, −3, −2, −1, 0, 1, 2, 3, 4, ...

A graph of the integers looks like this.

The set of integers does not include $\frac{1}{2}$, $\frac{5}{3}$, and other fractions. Note the arrowheads on both ends of the number line to indicate that the integers continue without end in both directions.

- **The Rational Numbers.** The rational number family includes all numbers that can be written as a fraction (or *ratio*) of two integers. Here are some examples of rational numbers.

$$\frac{1}{2} \qquad \frac{5}{3} \qquad \frac{-3}{2} \qquad \frac{-4}{1} \qquad \frac{0}{2} \qquad \frac{3}{1}$$

Notice that the family of rational numbers includes all the integers, because every integer can be written as a fraction whose denominator is the number 1. For example, we can write −4 as a fraction by writing

$$\frac{-4}{1}$$

The set of rational numbers also includes all the positive and negative mixed numbers, because these numbers can be written as fractions. For example, we can write $4\frac{1}{5}$ as

$$\frac{21}{5}$$

Sometimes rational numbers are written in decimal form, in which case the decimal number will either terminate

$$\frac{1}{8} = 0.125$$

or it will repeat.

$$\frac{5}{6} = 0.8\overline{3}$$

The following diagram may be helpful in visualizing the relationships between these families of numbers. The diagram shows that the set of rational numbers includes all the other number families described in this lesson.

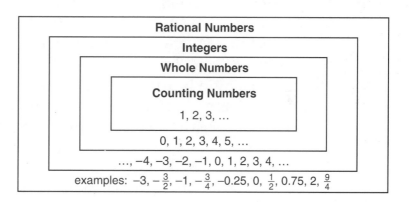

Rational Numbers

Integers

Whole Numbers

Counting Numbers

1, 2, 3, ...

0, 1, 2, 3, 4, 5, ...

..., −4, −3, −2, −1, 0, 1, 2, 3, 4, ...

examples: $-3, -\frac{3}{2}, -1, -\frac{3}{4}, -0.25, 0, \frac{1}{2}, 0.75, 2, \frac{9}{4}$

Example 1 Graph the integers that are less than 4.

Solution We sketch a number line and draw a dot at every integer that is less than 4. Since the set of integers includes whole numbers, we draw dots at 3, 2, 1, and 0. Since the set of integers also includes the negatives of the positive whole numbers, we continue to draw dots at −1, −2, −3, and so on. We draw an arrowhead to indicate that the graph of integers which are less than 4 continues without end.

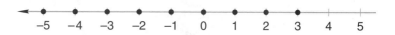

Example 2   Answer true or false.

(a) All whole numbers are integers.

(b) All rational numbers are integers.

Solution   (a) **True.** Every whole number is included in the family of integers.

(b) **False.** Although every integer is a rational number, it is not true that every rational number is an integer. Rational numbers such as $\frac{1}{2}$ and $\frac{5}{3}$ are not integers.

Practice   a. Graph the integers that are greater than −4.

b. Graph the whole numbers that are less than 4.

Answer true or false.

c. Every integer is a whole number. false

d. Every integer is a rational number. true

Problem set 86

1. *Heavenly Scent* was priced at $28.50 for 3 ounces, while *Eau de Rue* cost only $4.96 for 8 ounces. *Heavenly Scent* cost how much more per ounce than *Eau de Rue*?
   (46)
   $8.88 per ounce

2. Use a ratio box to solve this problem. The ratio of rookies to veterans in the camp was 2 to 7. Altogether there were 252 rookies and veterans in the camp. How many of them were rookies? 56 rookies
   (65)

3. The seven linemen weighed 197 lb, 213 lb, 246 lb, 205 lb, 238 lb, 213 lb, and 207 lb. Find the (a) mode, (b) median, (c) mean, and (d) range of this group of measures.
   (Inv. 4)
   (a) 213 lb   (b) 213 lb   (c) 217 lb   (d) 49 lb

4. Convert 12 bushels to pecks. (1 bushel = 4 pecks)
   (50)   48 pecks

5. The Martins drove the car from 7 a.m. to 4 p.m. and traveled 468 miles. Their average speed was how many miles per hour? 52 miles per hour
   (46)

6. Graph the integers that are less than or equal to 3.
   (86)

7. Use a ratio box to solve this problem. Nine is to 6 as what number is to 30? 45
   (72)

8. Nine tenths of the school's 1800 students attended the
(22) homecoming game.

    (a) How many of the school's students attended the
        homecoming game? 1620 students

    (b) What percent of the school's students did not attend
        the homecoming game? 10%

9. Evaluate: $\sqrt{b^2 - 4ac}$ if $a = 1$, $b = 5$, and $c = 4$ 3
(52)

10. Compare: $a^2 \bigcirc a$ if a is positive
(79) insufficient information

11. (a) Find the circumference of this
(66,82)   circle. 24π in.

12 in.

    (b) Find the area of this circle.
        144π in.²

Leave π as π.

12. Find each missing exponent.
(47)

    (a) $10^8 \cdot 10^{-3} = 10^{\square}$ 5   (b) $10^5 \div 10^8 = 10^{\square}$ −3

13. The figure shown is a triangular
(67) prism. Copy the shape on your paper
and find the number of its (a) faces,
(b) edges, and (c) vertices.

    (a) 5 faces (b) 9 edges (c) 6 vertices

14. Complete the table.
(48)

Fraction	Decimal	Percent
(a) $\frac{9}{10}$	0.9	(b) 90%
$\frac{11}{12}$	(c) $0.91\overline{6}$	(d) $91\frac{2}{3}\%$

15. Milton was facing north. If he turns 360° clockwise, what
(17) direction will he be facing? north

Use ratio boxes to solve problems 16 and 17.

16. The sale price of $24 was 60 percent of the regular price.
(81) What was the regular price? $40

17. Forty-eight corn seeds sprouted. This was 75 percent of
(81) the seeds that were planted. How many of the planted
seeds did not sprout? 16 seeds

18. Thirty is what percent of 20? 150%
(77)

19.(a) trapezoid **19.** (a) Classify this quadrilateral.
(Inv. 6,75)

(b) Find its perimeter. 90 mm

(c) Find its area. 450 mm²

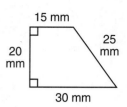

20.
(17)

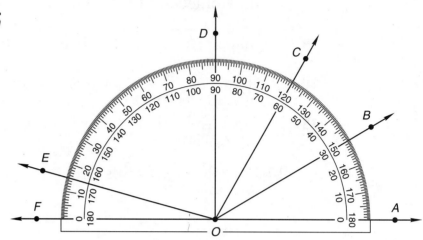

Find the measure of each angle.

(a) ∠COF 120°   (b) ∠AOE 165°   (c) ∠BOE 135°

21. Find the missing numbers in this
(85) function.

$y = 3x + 1$

x	y
4	13
7	22
0	1

22. Multiply and write the product in scientific notation.
(83)

(a) $(1.2 \times 10^5)(1.2 \times 10^{-8})$ 1.44×10^{-3}

(b) $(6 \times 10^{-3})(7 \times 10^{-4})$ 4.2×10^{-6}

Solve each equation. Show each step. Check the solution.

23. $56 = \dfrac{7}{8}w$ 64
(Inv. 7)

24. $4.8 + c = 7.34$ 2.54
(Inv. 7)

Simplify:

25. $\sqrt{10^2 - 6^2} - \sqrt{10^2 - 8^2}$ 2
(52)

26. 5 lb 9 oz 10 lb
(49) + 4 lb 7 oz

27. $1.4 \div 3\frac{1}{2} \times 10^3$ (decimal answer) 400
(43,45)

28. (a) $(-4)(-5) - (-4)(+3)$ (b) $(-2)[(-3) - (-4)(+5)]$
(85)   32   −34

29. Collect like terms. $x^2 + 3xy + 2x^2 - xy$ $3x^2 + 2xy$
(84)

30. The factorization of $6x^2y$ is $2 \cdot 3 \cdot x \cdot x \cdot y$. Write the
(21) factorization of $9xy^2$. $3 \cdot 3 \cdot x \cdot y \cdot y$

LESSON
87

Multiplying Algebraic Terms

Facts Practice: Area (Test Q in Test Masters)

Mental Math:

   a. $(-60) - (-30)$ **b.** $\left(2 \times 10^5\right)\left(4 \times 10^{-3}\right)$
   c. $\frac{f}{100} = \frac{10}{25}$ **d.** 3.14 × 20 ft
   e. 750 g to kg   **f.** $50 is $\frac{2}{5}$ of m
   g. $33\frac{1}{3}$% of 12, × 9, $\sqrt{}$, × 8, + 1, $\sqrt{}$, × 3, − 1, ÷ 2, ÷ 2, ÷ 2

Problem Solving:

On this scale, three identical blocks marked
M and a 250-g mass balance another block
marked M and a 1000-g mass. Find the mass
of each block marked M. Write an equation
illustrated by this balanced scale.

Recall from Lesson 84 that like terms can be added, and that
adding like terms does not change the variable part of the
term.

$$3x + 2x = 5x$$

When we multiply terms, all of the factors in the terms that
are multiplied appear in the product.

$$(3x)(2x) = 3 \cdot 2 \cdot x \cdot x$$
$$= 6x^2$$

We multiply the numerical parts of the terms and gather
variable factors with exponents. Terms may be multiplied
even if they are not like terms.

$$(-2x)(-3y) = 6xy$$

Example 1   Simplify: $(-3x^2y)(2x)(-4xy)$

Solution   The minus signs of these terms indicate negative numbers and not subtraction. These three terms are multiplied to make one term. Here we list all the factors.

$$(-3) \cdot x \cdot x \cdot y \cdot (+2) \cdot x \cdot (-4) \cdot x \cdot y$$

Using the commutative property we rearrange these factors as shown.

$$(-3)(+2)(-4) \cdot x \cdot x \cdot x \cdot x \cdot y \cdot y$$

Using the associative property we group the factors by multiplying the numerical factors and gathering the variable factors with exponents.

$$\mathbf{24x^4y^2}$$

Example 2   Simplify: $(-2ab)(a^2b)(3b^3)$

Solution   The numerical factors are –2, 1, and 3, and their product is –6. The product of a and a^2 is a^3. The product of b, b, and b^3 is b^5.

$$(-2ab)(a^2b)(3b^3) = \mathbf{-6a^3b^5}$$

Practice   Find the following products:

   a. $(-3x)(-2xy)$ $6x^2y$

   b. $3x^2(xy^3)$ $3x^3y^3$

   c. $(2a^2b)(-3ab^2)$ $-6a^3b^3$

   d. $(-5x^2y)(-4x)$ $20x^3y$

   e. $(-xy^2)(xy)(2y)$ $-2x^2y^4$

   f. $(-3m)(-2mn)(m^2n)$ $6m^4n^2$

   g. $(4wy)(3wx)(-w^2)(x^2y)$ $-12w^4x^3y^2$

   h. $5d(-2df)(-3d^2fg)$ $30d^4f^2g$

**Problem set
87**

   1. How far will a jet travel in 2 hours and 30 minutes if its
   (53) average speed is 450 miles per hour?   1125 miles

2. 0.125 meter   **2.** Use a unit multiplier to convert 12.5 centimeters to meters.
   (50)

3. Use a ratio box to solve this problem. If 240 of the 420
(54) students in the auditorium were girls, what was the ratio
of boys to girls in the auditorium? $\frac{3}{4}$

4. Geoff and his two brothers are very tall. Geoff's height is
(28) 18'3". The heights of his two brothers are 17'10" and
17'11". What is the average height of Geoff and his
brother giraffes? 18'

5. The Martins' car traveled 468 miles on 18 gallons of gas.
(46) Their car averaged how many miles per gallon?
26 miles per gallon

6. On a number line, graph the whole numbers that are less
(86) than or equal to 5.
-1 0 1 2 3 4 5 6

7. Use a ratio box to solve this problem. The road was steep.
(72) Every 100 yards the elevation increased 36 feet. How many
feet did the elevation increase in 1500 yards? 540 feet

8. The quadrilateral in this figure is a
(61) parallelogram. Find the measure of

(a) $\angle a$. 75°   (b) $\angle b$. 105°

(c) $\angle c$. 75°   (d) $\angle d$. 75°

(e) $\angle e$. 105°

9. If $x = -4$ and $y = 3x - 1$, then y equals what number?
(41) −13

10. (a) Find the circumference of this
(66,82)   circle. 440 mm

(b) Find the area of this circle.
15,400 mm^2

70 mm

Use $\frac{22}{7}$ for π.

11. The coordinates of the vertices of parallelogram $ABCD$
(Inv. 3,61) are A (5, 5), B (10, 5), C (5, 0), and D (0, 0).

(a) Find the area of the parallelogram. 25 units^2

(b) Find the measure of each angle of the parallelogram.
m$\angle A$ = 135°; m$\angle B$ = 45°; m$\angle C$ = 135°; m$\angle D$ = 45°

12. The shape shown was built of 1-inch
(70) cubes. What is the volume of the
shape? 48 in.^{3}

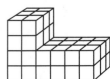

13. Complete the table.
(48)

FRACTION	DECIMAL	PERCENT
(a) $\frac{1}{8}$	(b) 0.125	$12\frac{1}{2}\%$
$\frac{7}{8}$	(c) 0.875	(d) $87\frac{1}{2}\%$

14. Write an equation to solve this problem. What number is
(60) 25 percent of 4? $W_N = \frac{1}{4} \times 4$; 1

Use ratio boxes to solve problems 15 and 16.

15. The sale price of $24 was 80 percent of the regular price.
(81) What was the regular price? $30

16. David had finished 60 percent of the race, but he still had
(81) 2000 meters to run. How long was his race? 5000 meters

17. One hundred is what percent of 80? 125%
(77)

18. Find the area of this figure. Dimen-
(75) sions are in centimeters. 94 cm²

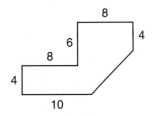

19. In the figure, angle *AOE* is a straight angle and
(40) m∠*AOB* = m∠*BOC* = m∠*COD*.

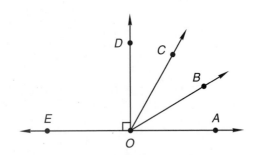

(a) Find m∠*AOB*. 30°

(b) Find m∠*AOC*. 60°

(c) Find m∠*EOC*. 120°

(d) Which angle is the supplement of ∠*EOC*? ∠*COA*

20. Simplify: $\dfrac{66\frac{2}{3}}{100}$ $\frac{2}{3}$
(76)

21. Find the missing numbers in this function.
(85)

$$y = \frac{24}{x}$$

x	y
3	8
4	6
12	2

22. Multiply and write the product in scientific notation.
(83)

(a) $(4 \times 10^{-5})(2.1 \times 10^{-7})$ 8.4 × 10⁻¹²

(b) $(4 \times 10^5)(6 \times 10^7)$ 2.4 × 10¹³

Solve each equation. Show each step. Check each solution.

23. $d - 8.47 = 9.1$ 17.57
(Inv. 7)

24. $0.25m = 3.6$ 14.4
(Inv. 7)

Simplify:

25. $\dfrac{3 + 5.2 - 1}{4 - 3 + 2}$ 2.4
(52)

26. 1 kg − 75 g 925 g
(32)

27. $3.7 + 2\dfrac{5}{8} + 15$ (decimal answer) 21.325
(43)

28. (a) $(-5) - (-2)[(-3) - (+4)]$ −19
(85)

(b) $\dfrac{(-3) + (-3)(+4)}{(+3) + (-4)}$ 15

29. (a) $(3x)(4y)$ 12xy
(87)

(b) $(6m)(-4m^2n)(-mnp)$ 24m⁴n²p

30. Collect like terms. $3ab + a - ab - 2ab + a$ 2a
(84)

LESSON 88

Multiple Unit Multipliers • Converting Units of Area

Mental Math:
a. −75
b. 3 × 10⁹
c. 12
d. $15
e. 25.4 mm
f. $2.50
g. 1250 mi
Problem Solving:
  1 skilling, 2 ore

Facts Practice: Scientific Notation (Test R in Test Masters)

Mental Math:

  a. $(-15)(+5)$ **b.** $(1.5 \times 10^4)(2 \times 10^5)$

  c. $3t + 4 = 40$ **d.** $7\frac{1}{2}\% \times \$200$ (double, halve)

  e. 2.54 cm to mm **f.** $1.50 is $\frac{3}{5}$ of m

  g. At 500 mph, how far will an airliner fly in $2\frac{1}{2}$ hours?

Problem Solving:

In the land of Florin, a gilder is worth 6 skillings and a skilling is worth 4 ore. Vicini offered to pay André 10 skillings and 2 ore for the job, but André wanted 2 gilders. André wanted how much more than Vicini's offer?

Multiple unit multipliers

We may multiply a number by 1 repeatedly without changing the number.

$$5 \cdot 1 = 5$$

$$5 \cdot 1 \cdot 1 = 5$$

$$5 \cdot 1 \cdot 1 \cdot 1 = 5$$

Since unit multipliers are forms of 1, we may also multiply a measure by several unit multipliers without changing the measure.

$$10 \,\cancel{yd} \cdot \frac{3 \,\cancel{ft}}{1 \,\cancel{yd}} \cdot \frac{12 \text{ in.}}{1 \,\cancel{ft}} = 360 \text{ in.}$$

Ten yards is the same distance as 360 inches. We used one unit multiplier to change from yards to feet and a second unit multiplier to change from feet to inches. Of course, we did not need to use two unit multipliers. Instead we could have changed from yards to inches using the unit multiplier

$$\frac{36 \text{ in.}}{1 \text{ yd}}$$

However, sometimes it prevents mistakes if we use more than one unit multiplier to perform some conversions.

Example 1 Use two unit multipliers to convert 5 hours to seconds.

Solution We are changing units from hours to seconds. This is our plan.

$$\text{hours} \longrightarrow \text{seconds}$$

We will perform the conversion in two steps. We will change from hours to minutes with one unit multiplier and from minutes to seconds with a second unit multiplier. For each arrow in our plan we write a unit multiplier.

hours ⟶ minutes ⟶ seconds

$$5 \cancel{hr} \cdot \frac{60 \cancel{min}}{1 \cancel{hr}} \cdot \frac{60 \text{ s}}{1 \cancel{min}} = \textbf{18,000 s}$$

Converting units of area To convert from one unit of area to another, it is helpful to use two unit multipliers.

Consider this rectangle, which has an area of 6 ft².

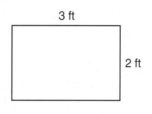

$$3 \text{ ft} \cdot 2 \text{ ft} = 6 \text{ ft}^2$$

Recall that the expression 6 ft² means 6 ft · ft. Thus, to convert 6 ft² to in.², we convert from

ft · ft   to   in. · in.

To perform the conversion, we use two unit multipliers.

$$6 \text{ ft}^2 = 6 \cancel{ft} \cdot \cancel{ft} \cdot \frac{12 \text{ in.}}{1 \cancel{ft}} \cdot \frac{12 \text{ in.}}{1 \cancel{ft}} = 864 \text{ in.} \cdot \text{in.} = 864 \text{ in.}^2$$

Example 2 Convert 5 yd² to square feet.

Solution Since 5 yd² means 5 yd · yd, we use two unit multipliers to convert to ft².

$$5 \cancel{yd} \cdot \cancel{yd} \cdot \frac{3 \text{ ft}}{1 \cancel{yd}} \cdot \frac{3 \text{ ft}}{1 \cancel{yd}} = 45 \text{ ft} \cdot \text{ft} = \textbf{45 ft}^2$$

Example 3 Convert 1.2 m² to square centimeters.

Solution This time, instead of writing 1.2 m² as 1.2 m · m, we will simply keep it in mind.

$$1.2 \cancel{m^2} \cdot \frac{100 \text{ cm}}{1 \cancel{m}} \cdot \frac{100 \text{ cm}}{1 \cancel{m}} = \textbf{12,000 cm}^2$$

Practice   Use two unit multipliers to perform each conversion.

a. 5 yards to inches   180 inches

b. $1\frac{1}{2}$ hours to seconds   5400 seconds

c. 15 yd² to square feet   135 ft²

d. 20 cm² to square millimeters   2000 mm²

Problem set 88

1. Jackson earns $6 per hour at a part-time job. How much does he earn working 3 hours and 15 minutes? $19.50
(53)

2. Mikki was not happy with her test average after 6 tests. On the next 4 tests, Mikki's average score was 93, which raised her average score for all 10 tests to 84. What was Mikki's average score on the first 6 tests?   78
(55)

3. Use two unit multipliers to convert 6 ft² to square inches.   864 in.²
(88)

4. Use a ratio box to solve this problem. The ratio of woodwinds to brass instruments in the orchestra was 3 to 2. If there were 15 woodwinds, how many brass instruments were there?   10 brass instruments
(54)

5. Graph the counting numbers that are less than 4.
(86)

0 1 2 3 4

6. Use a ratio box to solve this problem. Artichokes were on sale 8 for $2. At that price, how much would 3 dozen artichokes cost? $9
(72)

7.

27 lights	
$\frac{2}{3}$ were on (18)	9 lights
	9 lights
$\frac{1}{3}$ were off	9 lights

7. Draw a diagram of this statement. Then answer the questions that follow.
(71)

When Sandra walked through the house, she saw that 18 lights were on and only $\frac{1}{3}$ of the lights were off.

(a) How many lights were off?   9 lights

(b) What percent of the lights were on? $66\frac{2}{3}\%$

8. Evaluate: $a - [b - (a - b)]$ if $a = 5$ and $b = 3$ 4
(63)

9. Compare: $x \bigcirc< y$ if x and y are negative and $\dfrac{x}{y} = 2$
(79)

10. A horse was tied to a stake by a rope that was 30 feet long
(66,82) so that the horse could move about in a circle.

(a) What is the circumference of the circle? 188.4 ft

(b) What is the area of the circle? 2826 ft²

11. What percent of this circle is shaded?
(Inv. 1) 25%

12.

3 cm

3 cm   3 cm

12. Sketch a cube with edges 3 cm long.
(67,70)

(a) What is the volume of the cube? 27 cm³

(b) What is the surface area of the cube? 54 cm²

13. Collect like terms. $2x + 3y - 5 + x - y - 1$
(84) $3x + 2y - 6$

14. Complete the table.
(48)

FRACTION	DECIMAL	PERCENT
(a) $\frac{1}{8}$	0.125	(b) $12\frac{1}{2}\%$
$\frac{3}{8}$	(c) 0.375	(d) $37\frac{1}{2}\%$

15. Simplify: $\dfrac{60}{1\frac{1}{4}}$ 48
(76)

Use ratio boxes to solve problems 16 and 17.

16. The regular price was $24. The sale price was $18. The
(81) sale price was what percent of the regular price? 75%

17. The auditorium seated 375, but this was enough for only
(81) 30 percent of those who wanted a seat. How many
wanted a seat but could not get one? 875

18. Write an equation to solve this problem. Twenty-four is
(77) 25 percent of what number? $24 = \frac{1}{4} \times W_N$; 96

19.(a) trapezoid   **19.** (a) Classify this quadrilateral.
(Inv. 6,75)

(b) Find its perimeter. 140 mm

(c) Find its area. 900 mm²

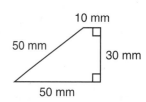

20. Find the missing numbers in this function.
(85)

$y = x - 5$

x	y
10	5
7	2
5	0

21. Multiply and write the product in scientific notation.
(83)

(a) $(9 \times 10^{-6})(4 \times 10^{-8})$ 3.6×10^{-13}

(b) $(9 \times 10^6)(4 \times 10^8)$ 3.6×10^{15}

Solve each equation. Show each step. Check each solution.

22. $8\frac{5}{6} = d - 5\frac{1}{2}$ $14\frac{1}{3}$
(Inv. 7)

23. $\frac{5}{6}m = 90$ 108
(Inv. 7)

24.

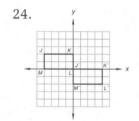

24. Three vertices of rectangle $JKLM$ are at $J(-4, 2)$, $K(0, 2)$, and $L(0, 0)$.
(80)

(a) Find the coordinates of M and draw the rectangle. $M(-4, 0)$

(b) Translate $\square JKLM$ 4 units right, 2 down to $\square J'K'L'M'$. Draw the translated image and write the coordinates of its vertices. $J'(0, 0)$, $K'(4, 0)$, $L'(4, -2)$, $M'(0, -2)$

25. Collect like terms. $x^2 + 2x - x - 2$ $x^2 + x - 2$
(84)

26. Which of the following does not equal 4^3? D. $4^2 + 4$
(20,52)

A. 2^6 B. $4 \cdot 4^2$ C. $\dfrac{4^4}{4}$ D. $4^2 + 4$

27. Find 50% of $\frac{2}{3}$ of 0.12 and write the answer as a decimal.
(43) 0.04

Simplify:

28. $6\{5 \cdot 4 - 3[6 - (3 - 1)]\}$ 48
(63)

29. (a) $\dfrac{(-3)(-4) - (-3)}{(-3) - (+4)(+3)}$ −1
(85)

(b) $(+5) + (-2)[(+3) - (-4)]$ −9

30. (a) $(-2x)(-3x)$ $6x^2$ (b) $(ab)(2a^2b)(-3a)$ $-6a^4b^2$
(87)

Diagonals • Exterior Angles

Mental Math:
a. +20
b. 7.5 × 10⁴
c. 10
d. $0.64
e. 187 cm
f. $2.50
g. 8
Problem Solving:
    4:00; 8:00

Facts Practice: Area (Test Q in Test Masters)

Mental Math:

 a. $(-80) \div (-4)$ **b.** $\left(2.5 \times 10^{-4}\right)\left(3 \times 10^{8}\right)$

 c. $\frac{8}{g} = \frac{2}{2.5}$ **d.** Estimate $7\frac{3}{4}\%$ of $8.29.

 e. 1.87 m to cm   **f.** $1.00 is $\frac{2}{5}$ of m

 g. 10% of 80, × 3, + 1, $\sqrt{\ }$, × 7, + 1, ÷ 2, ÷ 2, $\sqrt{\ }$, × 10,
    + 2, ÷ 4

Problem Solving:

 At three o'clock and at nine o'clock the hands of a clock form
 angles equal to $\frac{1}{4}$ of a circle. At what hours do the hands of a
 clock form angles equal to $\frac{1}{3}$ of a circle?

Diagonals A **diagonal** of a polygon is a line segment passing through the
polygon between two vertices. In the figure below, segment AC
is a diagonal of quadrilateral $ABCD$.

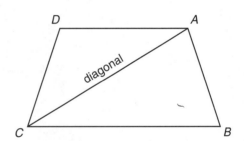

Example 1 From one vertex of regular hexagon
$ABCDEF$, how many diagonals can be
drawn? (Trace the hexagon and illustrate
your answer.)

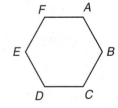

Solution We may select any vertex from which to draw the diagonals.
We choose vertex A. Segments AB and AF are sides of the
hexagon and are not diagonals. Segments drawn from A to C,
D, and E are diagonals. So **three diagonals** can be drawn.

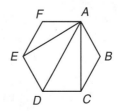

Notice in Example 1 that the three diagonals from vertex *A* divide the hexagon into four triangles. We will draw arcs to emphasize each angle of the four triangles.

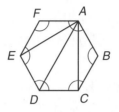

We see that ∠*B* of the hexagon is also ∠*B* of △*ABC*. Angle *C* of the hexagon includes ∠*BCA* of △*ABC* and ∠*ACD* of △*ACD*. Are there any angles of any of the four triangles that are not included in the angles of the hexagon?

No. All the angles of the triangles can be accounted for in the angles of the hexagon.

Although we may not know the measure of each angle of each triangle, we nevertheless can conclude that the measures of the six angles of the hexagon have the same total as the measures of the angles of four triangles, which is 4 × 180°, or 720°.

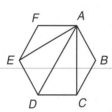

The sum of the measures of the six angles of the hexagon is 720°.

$$4 \times 180° = 720°$$

Since hexagon *ABCDEF* is a regular hexagon, we can calculate the measure of each angle of the hexagon.

Example 2   Nelda inscribed a regular hexagon in a circle. Find the measure of each angle of the regular hexagon *ABCDEF*.

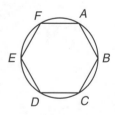

Solution   From the explanation above we know that the hexagon can be divided into four triangles. So the sum of the measures of the angles of the hexagon is 4 × 180°, which is 720°. Since the hexagon is regular, the six angles equally share the available 720°. So we divide 720° by 6 to find the measure of each angle.

$$720° \div 6 = 120°$$

We find that each angle of the hexagon measures **120°**.

Exterior angles

Angles that open to the interior of a polygon are called **interior angles.** In Example 2 we found that each interior angle of a regular hexagon measures 120°. Performing the following activity we experience another perspective of the angles of a polygon.

Activity: Exterior Angles

An experience that corresponds to this activity is creating a regular polygon in the Logo programing language available at some schools.

Before performing this activity the teacher and/or students should lay out and mark a regular hexagon in the classroom or on the playground. The hexagon should have sides at least five feet long. Two or three students with a length of string (for the radius) and a piece of chalk can do this by following the directions for inscribing a hexagon in Investigation 2.

When the hexagon has been prepared, each student should walk the perimeter of the hexagon focusing on these two observations.

1. Notice the direction you were facing when you started around the hexagon and the direction you were facing when you finished going around the hexagon after making six turns.

2. Notice how much you turned at each "corner" of the hexagon. Did you turn more than, less than, or the same as you would at the corner of a square?

Going around the hexagon, we made a turn at every corner. If we did not turn we would continue going straight.

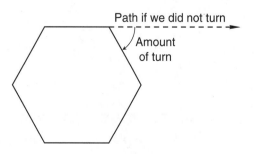

The amount of turn we made at the corner in order to stay on the hexagon instead of going straight is an **exterior angle** of the hexagon at that vertex.

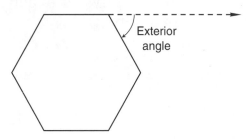

We can calculate the measure of each exterior angle of a regular hexagon by remembering how many turns we made and the direction we were facing when we started and when we finished. We made six small turns. After the sixth turn we were facing in the same direction we were facing when we started, for the first time since we started. In other words, after the sixth small turn we had completed one full turn of 360°.

Example 3 What is the measure of each exterior angle of a regular hexagon?

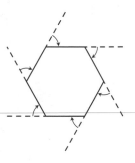

Solution Traveling all the way around the hexagon completes one full turn of 360°. Each exterior angle of a regular hexagon is the same measure, so we can find the measure by dividing 360° by 6.

$$360° \div 6 = 60°$$

We find that each exterior angle measures **60°**.

Notice that an interior angle of a polygon and its exterior angle are supplementary, so their measures total 180°.

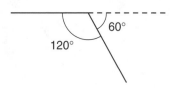

If all the turns are in the same direction, the sum of the exterior angles of any polygon is 360°.

Practice

a. Perform Examples 1, 2, and 3 from this lesson if you have not already done so.
For answers, see *Solutions* to Examples 1, 2, and 3.

b. one possibility

b. Trace this regular pentagon. How many diagonals can be drawn from one vertex? Show your work.
2 diagonals

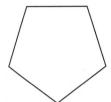

c. The diagonals drawn in problem b divide the pentagon into how many triangles? 3 triangles

d. What is the sum of the measures of the five interior angles of a pentagon? 3 × 180° = 540°

e. What is the measure of each interior angle of a regular pentagon? $\frac{540°}{5}$ = 108°

f. What is the measure of each exterior angle of a regular pentagon? $\frac{360°}{5}$ = 72°

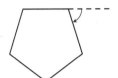

g. What is the sum of the measures of an interior and exterior angle of a regular pentagon? 108° + 72° = 180°

Problem set 89

1. Use a ratio box to solve this problem. Jason's remote control car traveled 440 feet in 10 seconds. At that rate, how long would it take the car to travel a mile?
(72)
120 seconds or 2 minutes

2. In the forest there were lions, tigers, and bears. The ratio of lions to tigers was 3 to 2. The ratio of tigers to bears was 3 to 4. If there were 18 lions, how many bears were there? Use a ratio box to find how many tigers there were. Then use another ratio box to find the number of bears.
(54)
16 bears

3. Bill measured the shoe box and found that it was 30 cm long, 15 cm wide, and 12 cm high. What was the volume of the shoe box? 5400 cm³
(70)

4. A baseball player's batting average is a ratio found by dividing the number of hits by the number of at-bats and writing the result as a decimal number rounded to the nearest thousandth. If Erika had 24 hits in 61 at-bats, what was her batting average? 0.393
(44)

5. Use two unit multipliers to convert 18 square feet to
(88) square yards. 2 square yards

6. Graph the integers greater than –4.
(86)

7.

16 dollars

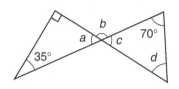

$\frac{3}{4}$ of regular price ($12)

$\frac{1}{4}$ of regular price

7. Draw a diagram of this statement. Then answer the
(71) questions that follow.

> *Jimmy bought the shirt for $12. This was $\frac{3}{4}$ of the
> regular price.*

(a) What was the regular price of the shirt? $16

(b) Jimmy bought the shirt for what percent of the regular price? 75%

8. Use this figure to find the measure of each angle.
(40)

(a) $\angle a$ 55° (b) $\angle b$ 125° (c) $\angle c$ 55° (d) $\angle d$ 55°

9. (a) What is the circumference of this
(66,82) circle? 132 in.

(b) What is the area of this circle?
1386 in.²

21 in.

Use $\frac{22}{7}$ for π.

10. Simplify: $\dfrac{91\frac{2}{3}}{100}$ $\frac{11}{12}$
(76)

11. Evaluate: $\dfrac{ab + a}{a + b}$ if $a = 10$ and $b = 5$ 4
(52)

12. Compare: $a^2 \;\textcircled{<}\; a$ if $a = 0.5$
(79)

13. Complete the table.
(48)

FRACTION	DECIMAL	PERCENT
$\frac{7}{8}$	(a) 0.875	(b) $87\frac{1}{2}$%
(c) $8\frac{3}{4}$	(d) 8.75	875%

14.

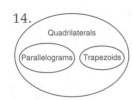

14. Draw a Venn diagram illustrating the relationship of
(Inv. 6) quadrilaterals, parallelograms, and trapezoids.

Use ratio boxes to solve problems 15 and 16.

15. Forty-five percent of the 3000 fast-food customers ordered
(81) a hamburger. How many of the customers ordered a
hamburger? 1350 customers

16. The sale price of $24 was 75 percent of the regular price.
(81) The sale price was how many dollars less than the regular
price? $8

17. Write an equation to solve this problem. Twenty is what
(77) percent of 200? $20 = W_P \times 200$; 10%

18.(a)

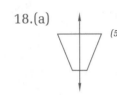

18. (a) Trace this isosceles trapezoid and
(58,75) draw its line of symmetry.

(b) Find the area of this trapezoid.
480 mm²

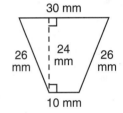

30 mm

26
mm

24
mm

26
mm

10 mm

19. What is the measure of each exterior
(89) angle of a regular triangle? 120°

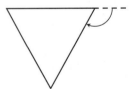

20. Find the missing numbers in this
(85) function.

$$y = \frac{1}{3}x$$

x	y
12	4
9	3
18	6

22.(a)

10 cm   10 cm

4 cm

(b) There can
only be one
answer because
a 4 cm, 4 cm,
10 cm triangle
cannot exist.

21. Multiply and write the product in scientific notation.
(83)

$$\left(1.25 \times 10^{-3}\right)\left(8 \times 10^{-5}\right) \quad 1 \times 10^{-7}$$

22. The lengths of two sides of an isosceles triangle are 4 cm
(62) and 10 cm.

(a) Sketch the triangle and find its perimeter. 24 cm

(b) Can there be more than one answer? Why or why not?

Solve each equation. Show each step. Check each solution.

23. $\frac{4}{9}p = 72$ 162
(Inv. 7)

24. $12.3 = 4.56 + f$ 7.74
(Inv. 7)

25. Collect like terms. $2x + 3y - 4 + x - 3y - 1$ $3x - 5$
(84)

Simplify:

26. $\dfrac{9 \cdot 8 - 7 \cdot 6}{6 \cdot 5}$ 1
(63)

27. $3.2 \times \left(\dfrac{1}{4}\right)^2 \times 10^2$ 20
(26,43)

28. $13\dfrac{1}{3} - \left(4.75 + \dfrac{3}{4}\right)$ (fraction answer) $7\frac{5}{6}$
(43)

29. (a) $\dfrac{(+3) + (-4)(-6)}{(-3) + (-4) - (-6)}$ -27
(85)

   (b) $(-5) - (+6)(-2) + (-2)(-3)(-1)$ 1

30. (a) $(3x^2)(2x)$ $6x^3$
(87)

   (b) $(-2ab)(-3b^2)(-a)$ $-6a^2b^3$

LESSON
90

Mixed-Number Coefficients •
Negative Coefficients

Facts Practice: Percent-Decimal-Fraction Equivalents
(Test U in Test Masters)

Mental Math:

   a. $(-50) - (-30)$

   b. $(4.2 \times 10^{-6})(2 \times 10^{-4})$

   c. $4w - 8 = 36$

   d. Estimate 15% of $23.89.

   e. 800 g to kg

   f. $1.00 is $\frac{4}{5}$ of m

   g. A cube with edges 10 in. long has a volume of how many cubic inches?

Problem Solving:

If four people meet and shake hands, we can picture the number of handshakes by drawing a pattern of 4 dots (for people) and drawing segments (for handshakes) between the dots. Then we count the segments (6). Use this method to count the number of handshakes if 5 people meet and shake hands.

Mixed-number coefficients

We have been solving equations like this one

$$\frac{4}{5}x = 7$$

by multiplying both sides of the equation by the reciprocal of the coefficient of x. Here the coefficient of x is $\frac{4}{5}$, so we multiply both sides by the reciprocal of $\frac{4}{5}$, which is $\frac{5}{4}$.

$$\frac{\overset{1}{\cancel{5}}}{\underset{1}{\cancel{4}}} \cdot \frac{\overset{1}{\cancel{4}}}{\underset{1}{\cancel{5}}}x = \frac{5}{4} \cdot 7 \qquad \text{multiplied by } \frac{5}{4}$$

$$x = \frac{35}{4} \qquad \text{simplified}$$

When solving an equation that has a mixed-number coefficient, we convert the mixed number to an improper fraction as the first step. Then we multiply both sides by the reciprocal of the improper fraction.

Example 1 Solve: $3\frac{1}{3}x = 5$

Solution First we write $3\frac{1}{3}$ as an improper fraction.

$$\frac{10}{3}x = 5 \qquad \text{fraction form}$$

Then we multiply both sides of the equation by $\frac{3}{10}$, which is the reciprocal of $\frac{10}{3}$.

$$\frac{\overset{1}{\cancel{3}}}{\underset{1}{\cancel{10}}} \cdot \frac{\overset{1}{\cancel{10}}}{\underset{1}{\cancel{3}}}x = \frac{3}{\underset{2}{\cancel{10}}} \cdot \overset{1}{\cancel{5}} \qquad \text{multiplied by } \frac{3}{10}$$

$$x = \frac{3}{2} \qquad \text{simplified}$$

In arithmetic, we usually convert an improper fraction such as $\frac{3}{2}$ to a mixed number. Recall that in algebra, we usually leave improper fractions in fraction form.

Example 2   Solve: $2\dfrac{1}{2}y = 1\dfrac{7}{8}$

Solution   Since we will be multiplying both sides of the equation by a fraction, we first convert both mixed numbers to improper fractions.

$$\frac{5}{2}y = \frac{15}{8} \qquad \text{fraction form}$$

Then we multiply both sides by $\frac{2}{5}$, which is the reciprocal of $\frac{5}{2}$.

$$\frac{\overset{1}{\cancel{2}}}{\underset{1}{\cancel{5}}} \cdot \frac{\overset{1}{\cancel{5}}}{\underset{1}{\cancel{2}}}y = \frac{\overset{1}{\cancel{2}}}{\underset{1}{\cancel{5}}} \cdot \frac{\overset{3}{\cancel{15}}}{\underset{4}{\cancel{8}}} \qquad \text{multiplied by } \frac{2}{5}$$

$$y = \frac{3}{4} \qquad \text{simplified}$$

Negative coefficients   To solve an equation with a negative coefficient we multiply (or divide) both sides of the equation by a negative number. The coefficient of x in this equation is negative.

$$-3x = 126$$

To solve this equation we may either divide both sides of the equation by -3 or multiply both sides by $-\frac{1}{3}$ to make the coefficient of x a positive 1. We show both ways.

$$-3x = 126 \qquad\qquad\qquad -3x = 126$$

$$\frac{-3x}{-3} = \frac{126}{-3} \qquad\qquad \left(-\frac{1}{3}\right)(-3x) = \left(-\frac{1}{3}\right)(126)$$

$$x = -42 \qquad\qquad\qquad\quad x = -42$$

Example 3   Solve: $-\dfrac{2}{3}x = \dfrac{4}{5}$

Solution   We multiply both sides of the equation by the reciprocal of $-\frac{2}{3}$, which is $-\frac{3}{2}$.

$$-\frac{2}{3}x = \frac{4}{5} \qquad \text{equation}$$

$$\left(-\frac{3}{2}\right)\left(-\frac{2}{3}x\right) = \left(-\frac{3}{2}\right)\left(\frac{4}{5}\right) \qquad \text{multiplied by } -\frac{3}{2}$$

$$x = -\frac{6}{5} \qquad \text{simplified}$$

Example 4   Solve: $-5x = 0.24$

Solution   We may either multiply both sides by $-\frac{1}{5}$ or divide both sides by -5. Since the right side of the equation is a decimal number it looks like dividing by -5 will be easier.

$$-5x = 0.24 \qquad \text{equation}$$

$$\frac{-5x}{-5} = \frac{0.24}{-5} \qquad \text{divided by } -5$$

$$x = -\mathbf{0.048} \qquad \text{simplified}$$

Practice   Solve:

a. $1\frac{1}{8}x = 36$ 32

b. $3\frac{1}{2}a = 490$ 140

c. $2\frac{3}{4}w = 6\frac{3}{5}$ $\frac{12}{5}$

d. $2\frac{2}{3}y = 1\frac{4}{5}$ $\frac{27}{40}$

e. $-3x = 0.45$ -0.15

f. $-\frac{3}{4}m = \frac{2}{3}$ $-\frac{8}{9}$

g. $-10y = -1.6$ 0.16

h. $-2\frac{1}{2}w = 3\frac{1}{3}$ $-\frac{4}{3}$

Problem set 90

1. *(31,35)* The sum of 0.8 and 0.9 is how much greater than the product of 0.8 and 0.9? Use words to write the answer.
ninety-eight hundredths

2. *(Inv. 4)* For this set of scores find the (a) mean, (b) median, (c) mode, and (d) range.   (a) 8.5   (b) 8.5   (c) 8   (d) 4

$$8, 6, 9, 10, 8, 7, 9, 10, 8, 10, 9, 8$$

3. *(46)* The 24-ounce container was priced at $1.20. This container costs how much more per ounce than the 32-ounce container priced at $1.44?   0.5¢ per ounce

4. *(89)* The figure illustrated is a regular decagon. One of the exterior angles is labeled a and one of the interior angles is labeled b.

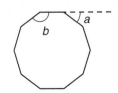

(a) What is the measure of each exterior angle of the decagon?   36°

(b) What is the measure of each interior angle?   144°

5. Collect like terms. $x^2 + 2xy + y^2 + x^2 - y^2$ $2x^2 + 2xy$
(84)

Use ratio boxes to solve problems 6 and 7.

6. The sale price of $36 was 90 percent of the regular price.
(81) What was the regular price? $40

7. Seventy-five percent of the citizens voted for Graham. If
(81) there were 800 citizens, how many of them did not vote
for Graham?   200 citizens

8. Write equations to solve (a) and (b).
(77)

(a) Twenty-four is what percent of 30? $24 = W_P \times 30$; 80%

(b) Thirty is what percent of 24? $30 = W_P \times 24$; 125%

9. Use two unit multipliers to convert 2 square feet to
(88) square inches.   288 square inches

10.

10.	750 doctors
$\frac{2}{5}$ of doctors (300) did	150 doctors
	150 doctors
	150 doctors
$\frac{3}{5}$ of doctors did not	150 doctors
	150 doctors
	150 doctors

10. Draw a diagram of this statement. Then answer the
(71) questions that follow.

*Three hundred doctors recommended Brand X.
This was $\frac{2}{5}$ of the doctors surveyed.*

(a) How many doctors were surveyed?   750 doctors

(b) How many doctors surveyed did not recommend
Brand X?   450 doctors

11. If $x = 4.5$ and $y = 2x + 1$, then y equals what number?
(41) 10

12. Compare: $a \bigcirc{>} ab$ if $a < 0$ and $b > 1$
(79)

13. If the perimeter of a square is 1 foot, what is the area of
(20) the square in square inches?   9 square inches

14. Complete the table.
(48)

Fraction	Decimal	Percent
(a) $1\frac{3}{4}$	1.75	(b) 175%

15. If the sales tax rate is 6%, what is the total price of a $325
(46) printer including sales tax? $344.50

16. Multiply and write the product in scientific notation.
(83)

$$\left(6 \times 10^4\right)\left(8 \times 10^{-7}\right) \quad 4.8 \times 10^{-2}$$

17. A cereal box 8 inches long, 3 inches
(67,70) wide, and 12 inches tall is shown.

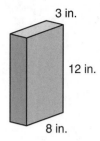

3 in.

12 in.

8 in.

(a) What is the volume of the cereal box? 288 in.³

(b) What is the surface area of the box? 312 in.²

18. (a) Find the circumference of this
(66,82) circle. 314 mm

(b) Find the area of this circle.
7850 mm²

50 mm

Use 3.14 for π.

19. List the whole numbers that are not counting numbers. 0
(86)

20.

20. The coordinates of three vertices of rectangle *WXYZ* are
(80) *W* (0, 3), *X* (5, 3), and *Y* (5, 0).

(a) Find the coordinates of *Z* and draw the rectangle.
Z (0, 0)

(b) Draw the image of □*WXYZ* rotated 90° counter-clockwise about the origin to *W′X′Y′Z′*. Write the coordinates of the vertices.
W′ (–3, 0), *X′* (–3, 5), *Y′* (0, 5), *Z′* (0, 0)

21. What mixed number is $\frac{2}{3}$ of 20? $13\frac{1}{3}$
(60)

22. On a number line graph $x \le 4$.
(78)

-1 0 1 2 3 4 5

Solve:

23. $x + 3.5 = 4.28$ **24.** $2\frac{2}{3}w = 24$ 9 **25.** $-4y = 1.4$
(Inv. 7) 0.78 (90) (90) –0.35

Simplify:

26. $10^4(10^3 \div 10^2)$ **27.** $(-2x^2)(-3xy)(-y)$ $-6x^3y^2$
(47) 10^5 or 100,000 (87)

28. $\dfrac{8}{75} - \dfrac{9}{100}$ $\frac{1}{60}$
(30)

29. (a) $(-3) + (-4)(-5) - (-6)$ 23
(85)

(b) $\dfrac{(-2)(-4)}{(-4) - (-2)}$ –4

30. Compare for $x = 10$ and $y = 5$:
(79)

$$x^2 - y^2 \;\ominus\; (x + y)(x - y)$$

INVESTIGATION 9

Graphing Functions

Functions may be displayed in graphic form on a coordinate plane. To graph a function we let each (x, y) pair of numbers serve as coordinates of a point on the plane.

$$y = x + 1$$

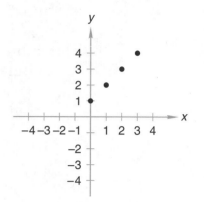

x	y	coordinates
0	1	(0, 1)
1	2	(1, 2)
2	3	(2, 3)
3	4	(3, 4)

On the coordinate plane above we graphed four pairs of numbers that satisfy the function. Although the table lists only four pairs of numbers for the function, the graph of the function is capable of displaying additional pairs of numbers that satisfy the function. By extending a line through and beyond the graphed points we graph all possible pairs of numbers that satisfy the equation. Each point on the graphed line below represents a pair of numbers that satisfy the function $y = x + 1$.

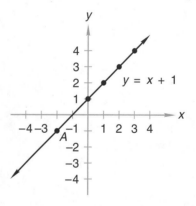

For instance, the (x, y) coordinates of point A are $(-2, -1)$. So $x = -2$ and $y = -1$ should satisfy the function of $y = x + 1$. We substitute -2 for x and -1 for y in the equation to demonstrate that this pair of numbers satisfies the function.

$$y = x + 1 \qquad \text{equation}$$
$$(-1) = (-2) + 1 \qquad \text{substituted}$$
$$-1 = -1 \qquad \text{simplified}$$

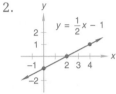
1. Select another point on the graph of y = x + 1 and determine the coordinates of the point. Then replace x and y in the function y = x + 1 with the x and y coordinates of the point selected to determine if the numbers satisfy the function. Show the substitution.

2. This table lists three pairs of numbers that satisfy the function $y = \frac{1}{2}x - 1$. On a coordinate plane graph all the pairs of numbers that satisfy this function. Then answer the following questions:

$$y = \frac{1}{2}x - 1$$

x	y
0	−1
2	0
4	1

(a) Besides the three (x, y) pairs listed in the table, what is another pair of numbers that satisfies the function?

(b) Can we find a pair of numbers that satisfies the function in which the x-number is negative and the y-number is positive? Why or why not?

The relationship between the length of a side of a square and the perimeter of the square is a function that may be graphed. In the equation we use s for the length of the side and p for the perimeter. We are graphing the numerical relationship of the measures so we will not designate units. It is assumed that whatever unit is used to measure the length of the side is also used to measure the perimeter.

Perimeter (p) of a Square with Side of Length s

p = 4s

s	p
1	4
2	8
3	12

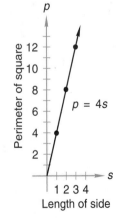

Notice that the x- and y-axes are renamed s and p for this function.

3. The graph of this function is a ray. What are the coordinates of the endpoint of the ray? Why is the graph of this function a ray and not a line?

4. $p = 3s$

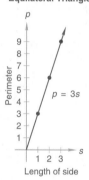

s	p
1	3
2	6
3	9

p = perimeter
of triangle
s = length of side

**Perimeter of an
Equilateral Triangle**

$p = 3s$

4. The relationship between the length of a side of an equilateral triangle and the perimeter of the triangle is a function that may be graphed. Write an equation for the function using s for the length of a side and p for the perimeter of an equilateral triangle. Next make a table of (s, p) pairs for the sides of length 1, 2, and 3. Then draw an s-axis and p-axis on rectangular coordinates and graph the function.

Rates are functions that can be graphed. Many rates involve time as one of the variables, with units of time marked on the horizontal axis. Speed, for example, is a function of distance and time. Suppose Sam enters a walk-a-thon and walks at a steady rate of 3 miles per hour. The distance (d) Sam travels in miles is a function of the number of hours (h) Sam walks at that rate. This relationship is expressed in the following equation.

$$d = 3h$$

We can construct a table that shows how far Sam would walk in 1, 2, or 3 hours.

$$d = 3h$$

h	d
1	3
2	6
3	9

d = distance in miles
h = time in hours

A graph of the function shows how far Sam would walk in any number of hours including fractions of hours.

Distance Sam Walked at 3 mph

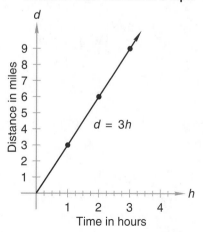

$d = 3h$

Notice that we have labeled each axis of the graph. Also notice that we have adjusted the scale of the graph so that each tick mark on the horizontal scale represents one fourth of an hour (15 minutes).

5.

$d = 6h$

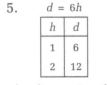

h	d
1	6
2	12

d = distance in miles
h = time in hours

Distance Sam Jogged at 6 Miles Per Hour

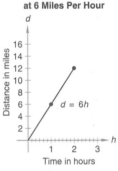

5. Suppose Sam entered a jog-a-thon and was able to jog at a steady pace of 6 miles per hour for 2 hours. Following the pattern described for the walk-a-thon, write an equation for a 6-mile-per-hour rate and make a table that shows how far Sam would jog in 1 hour and in 2 hours. Then draw a graph of the function labeling each axis. Let every tick mark on the time axis represent 10 minutes.

6. Refer to the graph for question 5 to find the distance Sam would jog in 40 minutes. 4 miles

7. Refer to the graph in question 5 to find how long it would take Sam to jog 9 miles. $1\frac{1}{2}$ hours

8. Why is the graph of the distance Sam jogged a segment and not a ray? Sam did not continue jogging forever. He stopped after 2 hours.

The graph of a function may be a curve. The relationship between the length of a side of a square and the area of the square is the function graphed below. We use the letters A and s to represent the area in square units and length of the side of the square, respectively.

$A = s^2$

s	A
$\frac{1}{2}$	$\frac{1}{4}$
1	1
2	4
3	9

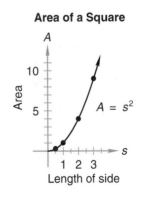

The dots on the graph of the function show the (s, A) pairs from the table. Other (s, A) pairs of numbers are represented by other points on the curve. Notice that the graph of the function becomes steeper as the side of the square becomes longer.

9. Half of the area of a square is shaded. As the square becomes larger the area of the shaded region becomes greater as indicated by this function in which *A* represents the area of half a square and *s* represents the length of the side of the square. Copy this table and find the missing numbers.

$$A = \frac{1}{2}s^2$$

s	A
1	$\frac{1}{2}$
2	2
3	$4\frac{1}{2}$
4	8

10. **Area of Half of a Square**

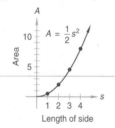

10. Plot the coordinates from the table in question 9 on a graph entitled "Area of Half of a Square." Then draw a smooth curve from the origin through the graphed points. Be sure to label the axes of the graph.

LESSON 91

Evaluations with Signed Numbers • Signed Numbers without Parentheses

Mental Math:
a. −134
b. 1.44 × 10⁶
c. 60
d. 15
e. 1500 mL
f. $200
g. 15
Problem Solving:
  5 yd × 4 yd
  = 20 yd²

Facts Practice: Scientific Notation (Test R in Test Masters)

Mental Math:

  a. (−84) + (−50)   **b.** $(1.2 \times 10^3)(1.2 \times 10^3)$

  c. $\frac{w}{90} = \frac{80}{120}$ **d.** $6 \times 2\frac{1}{2}$ (*Think: 6 × 2 + 6 × $\frac{1}{2}$*)

  e. 1.5 L to mL   **f.** $20 is $\frac{1}{10}$ of *m*

  g. 50% of 40, + 1, ÷ 3, × 7, + 1, × 2, $\sqrt{\ }$, × 5, − 1, $\sqrt{\ }$, × 4, + 2, ÷ 2

Problem Solving:

  Carpeting is sold by the square yard. A room that is 15 feet long and 12 feet wide requires how many square yards of carpeting to cover the floor?

Evaluations with signed numbers   We have practiced evaluating expressions such as

$$x - xy - y$$

by using positive numbers in place of x and y. In this lesson we will practice evaluating such expressions by using negative numbers as well. When evaluating expressions that contain signed numbers, it is helpful to replace each letter with parentheses as the first step. Doing this will help prevent making mistakes in signs.

Example 1   Evaluate: $x - xy - y$ if $x = -2$ and $y = -3$

Solution   We write parentheses for each variable.

$$(\ ) - (\ )(\ ) - (\ )   \quad \text{parentheses}$$

Now we write the proper numbers within the parentheses.

$$(-2) - (-2)(-3) - (-3)   \quad \text{insert numbers}$$

We multiply first.

$$(-2) - (+6) - (-3)   \quad \text{multiplied}$$

Then we add algebraically from left to right.

$$(-8) - (-3)   \quad \text{added } -2 \text{ and } -6$$

$$-5   \quad \text{added } -8 \text{ and } +3$$

Signed numbers without parentheses   Signed numbers are often written without parentheses. To simplify an expression such as

$$-3 + 4 - 5 - 2$$

we simply add algebraically from left to right.

$$-3 \quad +4 \quad -5 \quad -2 \ = \ -6$$

Another way to simplify this expression is to use the commutative and associative properties to rearrange and regroup the terms by their signs.

$$\begin{array}{c} -3 + 4 - 5 - 2 \\ +4 \underbrace{- 3 - 5 - 2} \\ +4 \qquad -10 \end{array}$$

Then we algebraically add the remaining terms.

$$+4 - 10 = -6$$

Using slashes to visually distinguish the terms of an expression can also make the simplification task easier to see as we show in the next example.

Example 2   Simplify: $-2 + 3(-2) - 2(+4)$

Solution   We draw a slash before each plus or minus sign that is not enclosed to emphasize the separate terms.

$$-2 \: / \: +3(-2) \: / \: -2(+4)$$

Next we simplify each term.

$$-2 \: / \: +3(-2) \: / \: -2(+4)$$
$$-2 \qquad -6 \qquad\quad -8$$

Then we algebraically add the terms.

$$-2 - 6 - 8 = \mathbf{-16}$$

Practice   Evaluate each expression. Write parentheses as the first step.

a. $x + xy - y$ if $x = 3$ and $y = -2$ -1

b. $-m + n - mn$ if $m = -2$ and $n = -5$ -13

Simplify:

c. $-3 + 4 - 5 - 2$ -6 **d.** $-2 + 3(-4) - 5(-2)$ -4

e. $-3(-2) - 5(2) + 3(-4)$ -16 **f.** $-4(-3)(-2) - 6(-4)$ 0

Problem set 91

1. For his first 6 tests, Ted's average score was 86. For his
$^{(55)}$ next 4 tests, his average score was 94. What was his average score for his first 10 tests?   89.2

2. The mean of these numbers is how much greater than the
$^{(Inv.\ 4)}$ median?   3

$$3, \: 12, \: 7, \: 5, \: 18, \: 6, \: 9, \: 28$$

3. The Martins completed the 130-mile trip in $2\frac{1}{2}$ hours. What
$^{(46)}$ was their average speed in miles per hour?   52 miles per hour

Use ratio boxes to solve problems 4–7.

4. The ratio of laborers to supervisors at the job site was 3
$^{(65)}$ to 5. Of the 120 laborers and supervisors at the job site, how many were laborers?   45 laborers

5. Vera bought 3 notebooks for $8.55. At this rate, how
(72) much would 5 notebooks cost? $14.25

6. The sale price was 90 percent of the regular price. If the
(60) regular price was $36, what was the sale price? $32.40

7. Forty people came to the party. This was 80 percent of
(81) those who were invited. How many were invited? 50 people

8. Write equations to solve these problems.
(77)

8.(a)
$20 = 0.4 \times W_N$; 50

(a) Twenty is 40 percent of what number?

(b) Twenty is what percent of 40? $20 = W_P \times 40$; 50%

9. Use two unit multipliers to convert 3600 in.^{2} to square feet.
(88) 25 square feet

10.
80 questions

$\frac{3}{4}$ were
multiple
choice (60)

20 questions
20 questions
20 questions
20 questions

$\frac{1}{4}$ were not
multiple
choice

20 questions

10. Draw a diagram of this statement. Then answer the
(71) questions that follow.

*Three fourths of the questions on the test were
multiple-choice. There were 60 multiple-choice
questions.*

(a) How many questions were on the test? 80 questions

(b) What percent of the questions on the test were not
multiple-choice? 25%

11. Evaluate: $x - y - xy$ if $x = -3$ and $y = -2$ −7
(91)

12. Compare: $m \bigcirc n$ if m is an integer and n is a whole
(79)   number insufficient information

13. (a) trapezoid
(Inv. 6,75)

13. (a) Classify this quadrilateral.

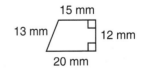

(b) Find the perimeter of this figure.
60 mm

(c) Find the area of this figure.
210 mm^2

(d) If the acute interior angle of this figure measures 75°,
what does the obtuse interior angle measure? 105°

14. Which property is illustrated by each equation?
(2,41)

14.(a) associative
property of
addition

(a) $a + (b + c) = (a + b) + c$

(b) $ab = ba$ commutative property of multiplication

(c) $a(b + c) = ab + ac$ distributive property

15.
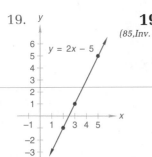
12 in. 12 in.

5 in.

15. The lengths of two sides of an isosceles triangle are 5 in.
(62) and 1 ft. Sketch the triangle and find its perimeter in inches. 29 inches

16. Multiply and write the product in scientific notation.
(83)

$$(2.4 \times 10^{-4})(5 \times 10^{-7})\ \ 1.2 \times 10^{-10}$$

17. A pyramid with a square base has
(67) how many

(a) faces? 5 faces   (b) edges? 8 edges   (c) vertices?
5 vertices

18. (a) Find the circumference of this
(66,82)   circle. 25.12 cm

(b) Find the area of this circle.
50.24 cm^2

8 cm

Use 3.14 for π.

19. y

6
5 y = 2x − 5
4
3
2
1
       x
−1 1 3 4 5
−2
−3

19. Find the missing numbers in this
(85,Inv. 9) function. Then plot the (x, y) number pairs on a coordinate plane and draw a line showing all (x, y) pairs that satisfy the function.

$y = 2x - 5$

x	y
2	−1
3	1
5	5

20. Use the information in the figure to answer these
(40) questions.

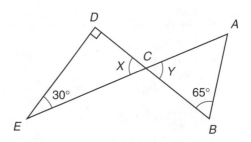

D

A

C

X Y

30° 65°

E B

20.(d) No. The triangles are not the same shape. The triangles do not have matching angles.

(a) What is m∠X? 60°

(b) What is m∠Y? 60°

(c) What is m∠A? 55°

(d) Are the two triangles similar? Why or why not?

21. (a) Add algebraically: $-3x - 3 - x - 1$ $-4x - 4$
(84,87)

   (b) Multiply: $(-3x)(-3)(-x)(-1)$ $9x^2$

22. Graph all integers greater than or equal to -3.
(86)

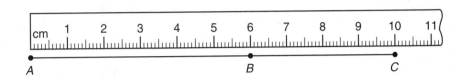

23. Segment AB is how many millimeters longer than
(34) segment BC? 20 mm

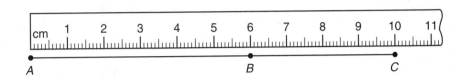

Solve each equation showing all steps.

24. $5 = y - 4.75$ **25.** $3\frac{1}{3}y = 7\frac{1}{2}$ $\frac{9}{4}$ **26.** $-9x = 414$ -46
(Inv. 7) 9.75   (90)   (90)

Simplify:

27. $\dfrac{32 \text{ ft}}{1 \text{ s}} \cdot \dfrac{60 \text{ s}}{1 \text{ min}}$ $1920 \frac{\text{ft}}{\text{min}}$
(50)

28. $5\dfrac{1}{3} + 2.5 + \dfrac{1}{6}$ (mixed number answer) 8
(43)

29. $\dfrac{2\dfrac{3}{4} + 3.5}{2\dfrac{1}{2}}$ (decimal answer) 2.5
(43,45)

30. (a) $\dfrac{(-3) - (-4)(+5)}{(-2)}$ $-8\frac{1}{2}$ (b) $-3(+4) - 5(+6) - 7$ -49
(85,91)

LESSON 92

Percent of Change

Mental Math:
a. −25
b. 2.25 × 10⁻¹⁰
c. 16
d. 20
e. 30 cm
f. $60
g. $36.00
Problem Solving:
10 triangles;
1800°

Facts Practice: Order of Operations (Test S in Test Masters)

Mental Math:

a. $(-75) - (-50)$

b. $(1.5 \times 10^{-5})(1.5 \times 10^{-5})$

c. $50 = 3m + 2$

d. $6 \times 3\frac{1}{3}$ (*Think: 6 × 3 + 6 × $\frac{1}{3}$*)

e. 0.3 m to cm

f. $6 is 10% of m

g. At $8.00 per hour how much money will Kim earn working $4\frac{1}{2}$ hours?

Problem Solving:

A hexagon can be divided into four triangles by three diagonals drawn from a single vertex. Into how many triangles can a dodecagon be divided by diagonals drawn from one vertex? What is the sum of the measures of the interior angles of a dodecagon?

The percent problems that we have considered until now have used a percent to describe part of a whole. In this lesson we will consider percent problems that use a percent to describe an amount of change. The change may be an increase or a decrease. Adding sales tax to a purchase is an example of an increase. Marking down the price of an item for a sale is an example of a decrease.

INCREASE

$$\text{Original number} + \text{amount of change} = \text{new number}$$

DECREASE

$$\text{Original number} - \text{amount of change} = \text{new number}$$

We may use a ratio box to help us with "increase-decrease" problems just as we have with ratio problems and "part-part-whole" problems. However, there are some differences in the way we set up the ratio box. When we make a table for a "part-part-whole" problem, the bottom number in the percent column is 100 percent.

	Percent	Actual Count
Part		
Part		
Whole	100	

When we set up a ratio box for an "increase-decrease" problem, we also have three rows. The three rows represent the original number, the amount of change, and the new number. We will use the words **"original," "change,"** and **"new"** on the left side of the ratio box. Most "increase-decrease" problems consider the original amount to be 100 percent. So the top number in the percent column will be 100 percent.

	Percent	Actual Count
Original	100	
Change		
New		

If the change is an **increase,** we **add** it to the original amount to get the new amount. If the change is a **decrease,** we **subtract** it from the original amount to get the new amount.

Example 1   The county's population increased 15 percent from 1980 to 1990. If the population in 1980 was 120,000, what was the population in 1990?

Solution   First we identify the type of problem. The percent describes an amount of change. This is an increase problem. We make a ratio box and write the words "original," "change," and "new" down the side. Since the change was an increase, we write a plus sign in front of "change." In the percent column we write 100 percent for the original (1980 population), 15 percent for the change, and add to get 115 percent for the new (1990 population).

	Percent	Actual Count
Original	100	120,000
+ Change	15	C
New	115	N

$$\frac{100}{115} = \frac{120,000}{N}$$

In the actual count column we write 120,000 for "original," and use letters for "change" and "new." We are asked for the "new" number. Since we know both numbers in the first row, we use the first and third rows to write the proportion.

$$\frac{100}{115} = \frac{120,000}{N}$$

$$100N = 13,800,000$$

$$N = 138,000$$

The county's population in 1990 was **138,000.**

Example 2   The price was reduced 30 percent. If the sale price was $24.50, what was the original price?

Solution   First we identify the problem. This is a decrease problem. We make a ratio box and write "original," "change," and "new" down the side with a minus sign in front of "change." In the percent column we write 100 percent for original, 30 percent for change, and 70 percent for new. The sale price is the new actual count. We are asked to find the original price.

	Percent	Actual Count
Original	100	R
− Change	30	C
New	70	24.50

$$\frac{100}{70} = \frac{R}{24.50}$$
$$70R = 2450$$
$$R = 35$$

The original price before it was reduced was **$35.00.**

Example 3   A merchant bought an item at wholesale for $20, and marked the price up 75% to sell the item at retail. What was the merchant's retail price for the item?

Solution   This is an increase problem. We make a table and record the given information.

	Percent	Actual Count
Original (Wholesale)	100	20
+ Change (Markup)	75	M
New (Retail)	175	R

$$\frac{100}{175} = \frac{20}{R}$$
$$100R = 3500$$
$$R = 35$$

The merchant's retail price for the item was **$35.**

Practice   Use a ratio box to solve each problem.

a. The regular price was $24.50, but the item was on sale for 30 percent off. What was the sale price? $17.15

b. The number of students taking algebra increased 20 percent in one year. If 60 students are taking algebra this year, how many took algebra last year? 50 students

c. Bikes were on sale for 20 percent off. Tom bought one for $120. How much money did he save by buying the bike at the sale price instead of at the regular price? $30

d. The clothing store bought shirts for $15 each and marked up the price 80% to sell the shirts at retail. What was the retail price of each shirt? $27

Problem set 92

1. The product of the first three prime numbers is how much less than the sum of the next three prime numbers? 1
(21)

2. After 5 tests Amanda's average score was 88. What score must she average on the next 2 tests to have a 7-test average of 90? 95
(55)

3. Jenna finished a 2-mile race in 15 minutes. What was her average speed in miles per hour? 8 miles per hour
(46)

Use ratio boxes to solve problems 4–7.

4. Forty-five of the 80 students in the club were girls. What was the ratio of boys to girls in the club? $\frac{7}{9}$
(65)

5. Two dozen sparklers cost $3.60. At that rate, how much would 60 sparklers cost? $9.00
(72)

6. The county's population increased 20 percent from 1980 to 1990. If the county's population in 1980 was 340,000, what was the county's population in 1990? 408,000
(92)

7. Because of unexpected cold weather, the cost of tomatoes increased 50 percent in one month. If the cost after the increase was 96¢ per pound, what was the cost before the increase? 64¢ per pound
(92)

8. Write equations to solve these problems.
(77)

(a) Sixty is what percent of 75? $60 = W_P \times 75$; 80%

(b) Seventy-five is what percent of 60?
$75 = W_P \times 60$; 125%

9. Use two unit multipliers to convert 100 cm² to square millimeters. 10,000 square millimeters
(88)

10.

256 trees

| 32 trees |
| 32 trees |
| 32 trees |
| 32 trees |
| 32 trees |
| 32 trees |
| 32 trees |
| 32 trees |

$\frac{5}{8}$ were deciduous (160)

$\frac{3}{8}$ were not deciduous

10. Draw a diagram of this statement. Then answer the questions that follow.
(71)

Five eighths of the trees in the grove were deciduous. There were 160 deciduous trees in the grove.

(a) How many trees were in the grove? 256 trees

(b) How many of the trees in the grove were not deciduous? 96 trees

11. If $x = -5$ and $y = 3x - 1$, then y equals what number?
(91) -16

12. Compare: 30% of 20 $\,\textcircled{=}\,$ 20% of 30
(60)

13. (a) Find the area of this isosceles
(58,75)   trapezoid. 45 cm^2

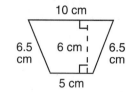

13.(b) (b) Trace the figure and draw its line
of symmetry.

14. A merchant bought a stereo wholesale for $90.00 and
(46,92) marked up the price 75% to sell the stereo at retail.

(a) What was the retail price of the stereo? $157.50

(b) If the stereo sells at the retail price, and the sales tax
rate is 6%, then what is the total price, including
sales tax? $166.95

15. Multiply and write the product in scientific notation.
(83)

$$\left(8 \times 10^{-5}\right)\left(3 \times 10^{12}\right) \quad 2.4 \times 10^8$$

16. Complete the table.
(48)

FRACTION	DECIMAL	PERCENT
$2\frac{1}{3}$	(a) $2.\overline{3}$	(b) $233\frac{1}{3}\%$
(c) $\frac{1}{30}$	(d) $0.0\overline{3}$	$3\frac{1}{3}\%$

17. One ace is missing from an otherwise normal deck of
(36) cards. If a card is selected at random, what is the
probability that the selected card will be an ace? $\frac{3}{51} = \frac{1}{17}$

18. What number is 250 percent of 60? 150
(60)

19. A triangular prism has how many
(67)

(a) triangular faces? 2

(b) rectangular faces? 3

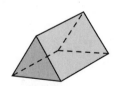

20. John measured the diameter of his bicycle tire and found
(66) that it was 24 inches. What is the distance around the tire
to the nearest inch? (Use 3.14 for π.) 75 inches

21.

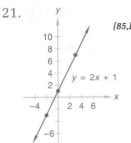

21. Find the missing numbers in this
(85,Inv. 9) function. Then plot the (x, y) pairs on
a coordinate plane and draw a line
showing all (x, y) pairs that satisfy the
function.

$y = 2x + 1$

x	y
0	$\boxed{1}$
3	$\boxed{7}$
−2	$\boxed{-3}$

22. The ratio of the measures of two angles was 4 to 5. If the
(65) sum of their measures was 180°, what was the measure of
the smaller angle? 80°

23. Simplify:
(84,87)

(a) $x + y + 3 + x − y − 1$ 2x + 2

(b) $(3x)(2x) + (3x)(2)$ $6x^2 + 6x$

24.

24. Draw a pair of parallel lines. Draw a second pair of parallel
(Inv. 6) lines that intersect but are not perpendicular to the first
pair. What kind of quadrilateral is formed? parallelogram

Solve each equation. Show all steps.

25. $3\frac{1}{7}x = 66$ 21
(90)

26. $w − 0.15 = 4.9$ 5.05
(Inv. 7)

27. $−8y = 600$ −75
(90)

Simplify:

28. $(2 \cdot 3)^2 − 2(3^2)$ 18
(52)

29. $5 − \left(3\frac{1}{3} − 1.5\right)$ $3\frac{1}{6}$
(43)

30. (a) $\dfrac{(−8)(−6)(−5)}{(−4)(−3)(−2)}$ 10
(85,91)

(b) $−6 − 5(−4) − 3(−2)(−1)$
8

LESSON 93

Two-Step Equations and Inequalities

Mental Math:
a. 200
b. 7.5×10^4
c. 250
d. 288 in.^{2}
e. 18
f. 54
g. 15 cm
Problem Solving:
68°F

Facts Practice: Order of Operations (Test S in Test Masters)

Mental Math:

a. $(-25)(-8)$

b. $(2.5 \times 10^8)(3 \times 10^{-4})$

c. $\frac{100}{x} = \frac{22}{55}$

d. 2 ft^2 equals how many square inches?

e. $8 \times 2\frac{1}{4}$

f. 10% less than 60

g. Estimate the product of 3.14 and 4.9 cm.

Problem Solving:

Michelle's grandfather taught her how to convert from degrees Celsius to degrees Fahrenheit, "Double the Celsius number, subtract 10%, then add 32°." Use this method to convert 20° Celsius to degrees Fahrenheit.

Since Investigation 7 we have practiced solving balanced equations, showing step-by-step solutions. The equations we have solved have been one-step equations. In this lesson we will practice solving two-step equations.

This balance scale illustrates a two-step equation.

$$2x + 5 = 35$$

On the left side of the equation are two terms, $2x$ and 5. We first isolate the variable term by subtracting 5 from (or adding a -5 to) both sides of the equation.

$$2x + 5 - 5 = 35 - 5 \quad \text{subtracted 5 from both sides}$$

$$2x = 30 \quad \text{simplified}$$

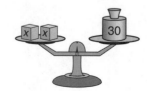

We see that $2x$ equals 30, so we divide by 2 $\left(\text{or multiply by } \frac{1}{2}\right)$ to find $1x$.

$$\frac{2x}{2} = \frac{30}{2} \quad \text{divided both sides by 2}$$

$$x = 15 \quad \text{simplified}$$

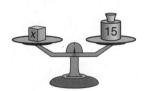

Example 1 Solve this equation and show all steps.

$$0.4x + 1.2 = 6$$

Solution First we isolate the variable term by subtracting 1.2 from both sides of the equation. Then we divide both sides by 0.4.

$$0.4x + 1.2 = 6 \qquad \text{equation}$$

$$0.4x + 1.2 - 1.2 = 6 - 1.2 \quad \text{subtracted 1.2 from both sides}$$

$$0.4x = 4.8 \qquad \text{simplified}$$

$$\frac{0.4x}{0.4} = \frac{4.8}{0.4} \qquad \text{divided both sides by 0.4}$$

$$x = \mathbf{12} \qquad \text{simplified}$$

Example 2 Solve this equation and show all steps.

$$-\frac{2}{3}x - \frac{1}{2} = \frac{1}{3}$$

Solution We isolate the variable term by adding $\frac{1}{2}$ to both sides of the equation. Then we find $1x$ by multiplying both sides of the equation by $-\frac{3}{2}$.

$$-\frac{2}{3}x - \frac{1}{2} = \frac{1}{3} \qquad \text{equation}$$

$$-\frac{2}{3}x - \frac{1}{2} + \frac{1}{2} = \frac{1}{3} + \frac{1}{2} \qquad \text{added } \tfrac{1}{2} \text{ to both sides}$$

$$-\frac{2}{3}x = \frac{5}{6} \qquad \text{simplified}$$

$$\left(-\frac{3}{2}\right)\left(-\frac{2}{3}x\right) = \left(-\frac{3}{2}\right)\left(\frac{5}{6}\right) \qquad \text{multiplied both sides by } -\tfrac{3}{2}$$

$$x = -\frac{\mathbf{5}}{\mathbf{4}} \qquad \text{simplified}$$

Example 3   Solve: $-15 = 3x + 6$

Solution   The variable term is on the right side of the equals sign. We may exchange the entire right side of the equation with the entire left side if we wish (just as we may exchange the entire contents of one pan of a balance scale with the contents of the other pan). However, we will solve this equation without exchanging the sides of the equation.

$$-15 = 3x + 6 \qquad \text{equation}$$
$$-15 - 6 = 3x + 6 - 6 \qquad \text{subtracted 6 from both sides}$$
$$-21 = 3x \qquad \text{simplified}$$
$$\frac{-21}{3} = \frac{3x}{3} \qquad \text{divided both sides by 3}$$
$$-7 = x \qquad \text{simplified}$$

In this lesson we have practiced procedures for solving equations. We may follow similar procedures for solving inequalities in which the variable term is positive.[†] To solve an inequality we isolate the variable while maintaining the inequality.

Example 4   Solve then graph this inequality. $2x - 5 \geq 1$

Solution   We see that the variable term ($2x$) is positive. We begin by adding 5 to both sides of the inequality. Then we divide both sides of the inequality by 2.

$$2x - 5 \geq 1 \qquad \text{inequality}$$
$$2x - 5 + 5 \geq 1 + 5 \qquad \text{added 5 to both sides}$$
$$2x \geq 6 \qquad \text{simplified}$$
$$\frac{2x}{2} \geq \frac{6}{2} \qquad \text{divided both sides by 2}$$
$$\mathbf{x \geq 3} \qquad \text{simplified}$$

We check the solution by replacing x in the original inequality with numbers equal to and greater than 3. We try 3 and 4 below.

$$2x - 5 \geq 1 \qquad \text{original inequality}$$
$$2(3) - 5 \geq 1 \qquad \text{replaced } x \text{ with 3}$$
$$1 \geq 1 \qquad \text{simplified and checked}$$
$$2(4) - 5 \geq 1 \qquad \text{replaced } x \text{ with 4}$$
$$3 \geq 1 \qquad \text{simplified and checked}$$

[†]Other procedures are used to solve inequalities in which the variable term is negative and will be taught in a later course.

Now we graph the solution $x \geq 3$.

This graph indicates that all numbers greater than or equal to 3 satisfy the original inequality.

Practice*   Solve each equation. Show all steps.

a. $8x - 15 = 185$ 25   **b.** $0.2y + 1.5 = 3.7$ 11

c. $\dfrac{3}{4}m - \dfrac{1}{3} = \dfrac{1}{2}$ $\frac{10}{9}$ **d.** $1\dfrac{1}{2}n + 3\dfrac{1}{2} = 14$ 7

e. $-6p + 36 = 12$ 4   **f.** $38 = 4w - 26$ 16

g. $-\dfrac{5}{3}m + 15 = 60$ –27   **h.** $4.5 = 0.6d - 6.3$ 18

Solve and graph these inequalities.

i. $2x + 5 \geq 1$ **j.** $2x - 5 < 1$

Problem set 93

1. From Don's house to the lake is 30 kilometers. If he
(46) completed the round trip on his bike in 2 hours and 30 minutes, what was his average speed in kilometers per hour?   24 kilometers per hour

2. Find (a) the mean and (b) the range for this set of
(Inv. 4) numbers.   (a) 9   (b) 37

$$3, 9, 7, 5, 10, 4, 5, 8, 5, 4, 8, 40$$

Use ratio boxes to solve problems 3–5.

3. The ratio of red marbles to blue marbles in a bag of 600
(36,65) red and blue marbles was 7 to 5.

(a) How many marbles were blue?   250 blue marbles

(b) If one marble is drawn from the bag, what is the probability that the marble will be blue? $\frac{5}{12}$

4. The machine could punch out 500 plastic pterodactyls in
(72) 20 minutes. At that rate, how many could it punch out in $1\frac{1}{2}$ hours?   2250 plastic pterodactyls

5. (a) The price was reduced by 25 percent. If the regular
(92)   price was $24, what was the sale price? $18

(b) The price was reduced by 25 percent. If the sale price was $24, what was the regular price? $32

6. Multiply: $(-3x^2)(2xy)(-x)(3y^2)$ $18x^4y^3$
(87)

7. Two aces are missing from an otherwise normal deck of
(36) cards. If one card is selected from the deck at random, what is the probability that the selected card will be an ace? $\frac{2}{50} = \frac{1}{25}$

8. Use two unit multipliers to convert 7 days to minutes.
(88) 10,080 minutes

9.

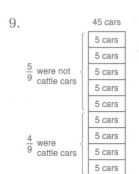

45 cars

$\frac{5}{9}$ were not cattle cars

$\frac{4}{9}$ were cattle cars

9. Draw a diagram of this statement. Then answer the
(22) questions that follow.

> Five ninths of the 45 cars pulled by the locomotive were not cattle cars.

(a) How many cattle cars were pulled by the locomotive?
20 cattle cars
(b) What percent of the cars pulled by the locomotive were not cattle cars? $55\frac{5}{9}\%$

10. Compare: $\dfrac{1}{3}$ ⟶ $\boxed{>}$ ⟵ 33%
(33,48)

11. Evaluate: $ab - a - b$ if $a = -3$ and $b = -1$ 7
(91)

12. Find the total price, including 5 percent tax, for a meal
(46) that includes a $7.95 dish, a 90¢ beverage, and a $2.35 dessert. $11.76

13. A corner was cut from a square sheet
(75) of paper, resulting in this pentagon. Dimensions are in inches.

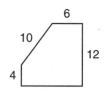

(a) What is the perimeter of this pentagon? 44 in.

(b) What is the area of this pentagon? 120 in.²

14. Complete the table.
(48)

FRACTION	DECIMAL	PERCENT
(a) $\frac{2}{25}$	0.08	(b) 8%
(c) $\frac{1}{12}$	(d) $0.08\overline{3}$	$8\frac{1}{3}\%$

15. A retailer buys a toy for $3.60 and marks up the price
(92) 120%. What is the retail price of the toy? $7.92

16. Multiply and write the product in scientific notation.
(83)
$$\left(8 \times 10^{-3}\right)\left(6 \times 10^{7}\right) \quad 4.8 \times 10^{5}$$

17. Each edge of a cube is 10 cm.
(67,70)

(a) What is the volume of the cube? 1000 cm^3

(b) What is the surface area of the cube? 600 cm^2

18. (a) What is the area of this circle?
(66,82) 314 cm^2

(b) What is the circumference of this circle? 62.8 cm

Use 3.14 for π.

19. Collect like terms. $-x + 2x^2 - 1 + x - x^2$ $x^2 - 1$
(84)

20.

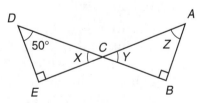

20. Find the missing numbers in the table for this function. Then graph the function. (Plot the points and draw a line.)
(85,Inv. 9)

$y = 2x + 3$

x	y
1	5
0	3
-2	-1

21. Write an equation to solve this problem. Sixty is $\frac{3}{8}$ of what number? $60 = \frac{3}{8} \times W_N$; 160
(74)

22.

$x > 2$

$\begin{array}{ccccc} 0 & 1 & 2 & 3 & 4 \end{array}$

22. Solve and graph this inequality. $2x - 5 > -1$
(93)

23. Use the information in the figure to answer these questions.
(40)

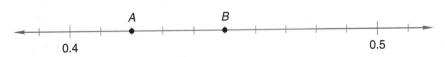

(a) Find the measure of $\angle X$, $\angle Y$, and $\angle Z$.
    $m\angle X = 40°$; $m\angle Y = 40°$; $m\angle Z = 50°$

(b) Are the two triangles similar? Why or why not?

23.(b) Yes. The triangles are the same shape. Their corresponding angles are congruent.

24. What is the sum of the numbers labeled A and B on this number line? 0.87
(34)

Solve and show each step.

25. $3x + 2 = 9$ $\frac{7}{3}$
(93)

26. $\frac{2}{3}w + 4 = 14$ 15
(93)

27. $0.2y - 1 = 7$ 40
(93)

28. $-\frac{2}{3}m = -6$ 9
(90)

Simplify:

29. $3\left(2^3 + \sqrt{16}\right) - \sqrt{36}$ 30
(63)

30. (a) $\dfrac{(-9)(+6)(-5)}{(-4) - (-1)}$ -90
(85,91)

(b) $-3(4) + 2(3) - 1$ -7

LESSON
94

Compound Probability

Mental Math:
a. 24
b. 6×10^{-5}
c. 0.6
d. 86°F
e. 16
f. 55
g. 5

Problem Solving:

2X + 4.3
= 4X + 1.7;
X = 1.3 lb

Facts Practice: Scientific Notation (Test R in Test Masters)

Mental Math:

a. $(-144) \div (-6)$

b. $\left(1.5 \times 10^{-8}\right)\left(4 \times 10^3\right)$

c. $5w + 1.5 = 4.5$

d. Convert 30°C to degrees Fahrenheit.

e. $6 \times 2\frac{2}{3}$

f. 10% more than 50

g. 25% of 40, × 4, + 2, ÷ 6, × 9, + 1, $\sqrt{}$, × 3, + 1, $\sqrt{}$

Problem Solving:

Six identical blocks marked X, a 1.7-lb weight, and a 4.3-lb weight were balanced on a scale as shown. Write an equation to represent this balanced scale and find the weight of each block marked X.

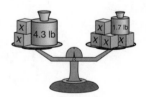

We know that the probability of getting heads on one toss of a coin is $\frac{1}{2}$. We can state this fact with the following notation in which $P(H)$ stands for "the probability of heads."

$$P(H) = \frac{1}{2}$$

The probability of getting heads on the second toss of a coin is also $\frac{1}{2}$. So the probability of getting two heads in a row is $\frac{1}{2}$ times $\frac{1}{2}$, or $\frac{1}{4}$. We can illustrate this probability with a tree diagram. If we toss a coin one time, we can get heads or tails.

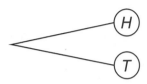

If the first toss came up heads, the second toss could come up either heads or tails.

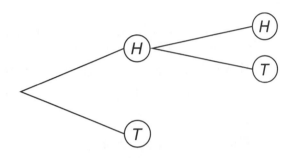

If the first toss came up tails, the second toss could come up either heads or tails.

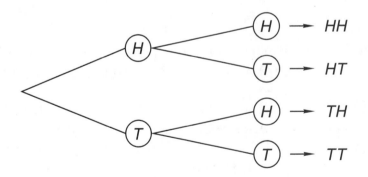

We see that there are these 4 possible outcomes:

$$HH \quad HT \quad TH \quad TT$$

Since any one of the four outcomes is equally likely, the probability of each outcome is one fourth.

Thus, the probability of getting HH is $\frac{1}{4}$, which we can express this way.

$$P(H, H) = \frac{1}{4}$$

> **The probability of independent events occurring in a specified order is the product of the probabilities of each event.**

Thus $P(H, H, T)$ is $\dfrac{1}{2} \cdot \dfrac{1}{2} \cdot \dfrac{1}{2} = \dfrac{1}{8}$

so $P(H, T, T, H)$ is $\dfrac{1}{2} \cdot \dfrac{1}{2} \cdot \dfrac{1}{2} \cdot \dfrac{1}{2} = \dfrac{1}{16}$

and $P(T, H, T, H, T)$ is $\left(\dfrac{1}{2}\right)^5 = \dfrac{1}{32}$

Example 1   The face of this spinner is divided into 4 congruent sectors. What is the probability of getting a 2 on the first spin and a 1 on the second spin?

Solution   The probability of getting a 2 is $\frac{1}{4}$. The probability of getting a 1 is $\frac{1}{4}$. The probability of independent events occurring in a specified order is the product of the individual probabilities.

$$P(2, 1) = \frac{1}{4} \cdot \frac{1}{4} = \frac{1}{16}$$

Example 2   Jim tossed a coin once and it turned up heads. What is the probability that he will get heads on the next toss of the coin?

Solution   Past events do not affect the probability of future events. There are only 2 possible outcomes. The next toss of the coin will turn up either heads or tails. The probability that it will turn up heads is $\frac{1}{2}$.

Example 3   What is the probability of rolling a 12 with one roll of a pair of dice?

Solution   There is only one combination of two die faces that total 12, and that is 6 and 6. The probability of one die stopping its roll with 6 on top is $\frac{1}{6}$. So the probability of two dice stopping with 6 on top is $\frac{1}{6}$ times $\frac{1}{6}$ which is $\frac{1}{36}$.

$$P(6, 6) = \left(\frac{1}{6}\right)^2 = \frac{1}{36}$$

The following table shows the 36 possible face combinations of two dice. Since only one combination results in a total of 12, the probability of rolling 12 is $\frac{1}{36}$. We see that the probability of rolling 11 is $\frac{2}{36}$, which is $\frac{1}{18}$, and the probability of rolling 10 is $\frac{3}{36}$, which is $\frac{1}{12}$.

Outcome of First Die

	$\bullet$	$\because$	$\therefore$	$\because\because$	$\vdots\cdot$	$\vdots\vdots$
$\bullet$	2	3	4	5	6	7
$\because$	3	4	5	6	7	8
$\therefore$	4	5	6	7	8	9
$\because\because$	5	6	7	8	9	10
$\vdots\cdot$	6	7	8	9	10	11
$\vdots\vdots$	7	8	9	10	11	12

(Outcome of Second Die)

Example 4 With one roll of a pair of dice, what is the probability of rolling a number greater than 9?

Solution Method 1: From the table we see that there are 36 possible combinations. So 36 is the bottom term of the probability ratio. Also from the table we see that 6 of the combinations total more than 9 (3 total 10, 2 total 11, 1 totals 12). So 6 is the top term of the probability ratio.

$$P(> 9) = \frac{6}{36} = \frac{1}{6}$$

Method 2: We regard each rolled die as an independent event. We think about the combinations that total more than 9. If the first die stops on 1, 2, or 3, there is no way for the total to reach 10, 11, or 12. If the first die stops on 4, the second die must stop on 6. We calculate this probability.

$$P(4, 6) = \frac{1}{6} \cdot \frac{1}{6} = \frac{1}{36}$$

If the first die stops on 5, the second die may stop on 5 or 6 (2 favorable outcomes).

$$P(5, 5 \text{ or } 6) = \frac{1}{6} \cdot \frac{2}{6} = \frac{2}{36}$$

If the first die stops on 6, the second die may stop on 4, 5, or 6 (3 favorable outcomes).

$$P(6, 4 \text{ or } 5 \text{ or } 6) = \frac{1}{6} \cdot \frac{3}{6} = \frac{3}{36}$$

We add these probabilities to find the total probability of rolling a number greater than 9.

$$\frac{1}{36} + \frac{2}{36} + \frac{3}{36} = \frac{6}{36}$$

$$\text{So } P(> 9) = \frac{6}{36} = \frac{1}{6}$$

Example 5   From a well-mixed deck of cards, Sam selected and held one card, then a second card, then a third card, and finally a fourth card. What is the probability that the four cards Sam selected are aces?

Solution   Each card Sam draws needs to be an ace. There are 4 chances out of 52 that the first card is an ace. That leaves 3 aces in 51 cards for the second draw, which leaves 2 aces in 50 cards for the third draw, and 1 ace in 49 cards for the fourth draw.

$$P(A, A, A, A) = \frac{4}{52} \cdot \frac{3}{51} \cdot \frac{2}{50} \cdot \frac{1}{49}$$

We show the calculation.

$$P(A, A, A, A) = \frac{\overset{1}{\cancel{4}}}{\underset{13}{\cancel{52}}} \cdot \frac{\overset{1}{\cancel{3}}}{\underset{17}{\cancel{51}}} \cdot \frac{\overset{1}{\cancel{2}}}{\underset{25}{\cancel{50}}} \cdot \frac{1}{49} = \frac{1}{270{,}725}$$

 A calculator with an **exponent key** such as y^x (or x^y) can be used to calculate probabilities.

Suppose you were going to take a 10-question true-false test. Instead of reading the questions, you decide to guess every answer. What is the probability of guessing the correct answer to all 10 questions?

The probability of correctly guessing the first answer is $\frac{1}{2}$. The probability of correctly guessing the first two answers is $\frac{1}{2} \cdot \frac{1}{2}$ or $\left(\frac{1}{2}\right)^2$. $\left[\text{Since } \frac{1}{2} \cdot \frac{1}{2} = \frac{1}{4}, \text{ we may also write } \left(\frac{1}{2}\right)^2 \text{ as } \frac{1}{2^2}.\right]$ The probability of correctly guessing the first three answers is $\left(\frac{1}{2}\right)^3$ or $\frac{1}{2^3}$. Thus, to find the probability of guessing the correct answer to all ten questions is $\left(\frac{1}{2}\right)^{10}$ or $\frac{1}{2^{10}}$. To find 2^{10} on a calculator with a $\boxed{y^x}$ (or $\boxed{x^y}$) key we use these key strokes:

$$\boxed{2} \;\; \boxed{y^x} \;\; \boxed{1} \;\; \boxed{0} \;\; \boxed{=}$$

The number displayed is 1024. Thus the probability of correctly guessing all ten true-false answers is

$$\frac{1}{1024}$$

This outcome is just as likely as tossing heads with a coin 10 times in a row.

$\frac{1}{4^{20}} \approx \frac{1}{1 \times 10^{12}}$; This is less than one chance in a trillion.

Probabilities that are extremely unlikely may be displayed by a calculator in scientific notation. Find the probability of correctly guessing the correct answer to every question on a 20-question, 4-option multiple-choice test.

Practice

a. To win the game, Victor needs to roll a 9 with a pair of dice. What is the probability that he will do that on the first try? $\frac{1}{9}$

b.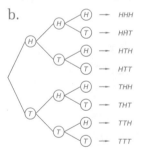

b. Draw a tree diagram like the one at the beginning of the lesson that shows the eight possible outcomes of 3 coin tosses.

c. Jasmine is taking a four-option multiple-choice test. There are two answers she does not know. If she can correctly rule out one option on one question but no options on the other question, what is the probability she will correctly guess both answers? $\frac{1}{3} \cdot \frac{1}{4} = \frac{1}{12}$

Problem set 94

1. Twenty-one billion is how much more than 9.8 billion? Write the answer in scientific notation. 1.12×10^{10}
(51)

2. The train traveled at an average speed of 48 miles per hour for the first 2 hours and at 60 miles an hour for the next 4 hours. What was the train's average speed for the 6-hour trip? (Average speed equals total miles divided by total time.) 56 miles per hour
(53,55)

3. A 10-pound box of detergent costs $8.40. A 15-pound box
(46) costs $10.50. Which box costs the most per pound? How
much more per pound does it cost?
10-pound box; $0.14 per pound more

4. In a rectangular prism, what is the ratio of faces to edges?
(36,67) $\frac{1}{2}$

Use ratio boxes to solve problems 5–8.

5. The team's won-lost ratio was 3 to 2. If the team won 12
(65) games and did not tie any games, then how many games
did the team play? 20 games

6. Twenty-four is to 36 as 42 is to what number? 63
(72)

7. The number that is 20% less than 360 is what percent of
(92) 360? 80%

8. During his slump, Matt's batting average dropped by 20
(92) percent to 0.260. What was Matt's batting average before
his slump? 0.325

9. Use two unit multipliers to perform each conversion.
(88)

(a) 12 ft^2 to square inches 1728 square inches

(b) 1 kilometer to millimeters 1,000,000 millimeters

10.

300 male serfs	
$\frac{2}{5}$ were conscripted (120)	60 male serfs
	60 male serfs
	60 male serfs
$\frac{3}{5}$ were not conscripted	60 male serfs
	60 male serfs

10. Draw a diagram of this statement. Then answer the
(71) questions that follow.

*The duke conscripted two fifths of the male serfs
in his dominion. He conscripted 120 serfs in all.*

(a) How many male serfs were in the duke's dominion?
300 serfs
(b) How many male serfs in his dominion were not
conscripted? 180 serfs

11. If a pair of dice is tossed once, what is the probability that
(94) the total number rolled will be

(a) 1? 0   (b) 2? $\frac{1}{36}$ (c) 3? $\frac{1}{18}$

12. If $y = 4x - 3$ and $x = -2$, then y equals what number?
(91) -11

13. The perimeter of a certain square is 4 yards. Find the area
(20) of the square in square feet. 9 square feet

14. The sale price of the new car was $14,500. The tax rate was
(46,60) 6.5 percent.

    (a) What was the sales tax on the car? $942.50

    (b) What was the total price including tax? $15,442.50

    (c) If the commission paid to a salesperson is 2% of the sale price, how much is the commission on a $14,500 sale? $290

15. Complete the table.
(48)

Fraction	Decimal	Percent
(a) $\frac{2}{3}$	(b) $0.\overline{6}$	$66\frac{2}{3}\%$
$1\frac{3}{4}$	(c) 1.75	(d) 175%

16. (a) What is 200 percent of $7.50? $15.00
(60,92)

    (b) What is 200 percent more than $7.50? $22.50

17. Multiply and write the product in scientific notation.
(83)
$$(2 \times 10^8)(8 \times 10^2) \quad 1.6 \times 10^{11}$$

18. Robbie stores 1-inch cubes in a box
(70) with inside dimensions as shown. How many cubes will fit in this box?
96 cubes

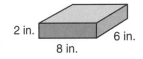
2 in.   6 in.
8 in.

19. The length of each side of the square
(82) equals the diameter of the circle. The area of the square is how much greater than the area of the circle? 42 in.²

14 in.

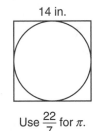

Use $\frac{22}{7}$ for π.

20. Divide 7.2 by 0.11 and write the quotient with a bar over
(42,45) the repetend. $65.\overline{45}$

21.
(85,Inv. 9)
Find the missing numbers in the table for this function. Then graph the function.

$y = 3x - 2$

x	y
3	7
0	-2
-1	-5

21.
$y = 3x - 2$
(graph showing line through points with axis marks −4 −2 2 4 6, y-axis marks 2 4 6 8)

22.
$x < 2$
−1 0 1 2 3

22. Solve and graph this inequality. $2x - 5 < -1$
(93)

23. In the figure, the measure of ∠*AOC* is
⁽⁴⁰⁾ half the measure of ∠*AOD*. The measure of ∠*AOB* is one third the measure of ∠*AOD*.

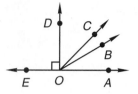

(a) Find m∠*AOB*. 30°

(b) Find m∠*EOC*. 135°

24. The length of segment *BC* is how much less than the
⁽⁸⁾ length of segment *AB*? $\frac{1}{4}$ in.

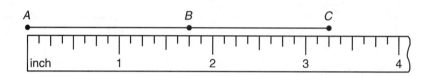

Solve:

25. $3x - 2 = 9$ $\frac{11}{3}$
⁽⁹³⁾

26. $-6\frac{2}{3}m = 1\frac{1}{9}$ $-\frac{1}{6}$
⁽⁹⁰⁾

27. $1.2p + 4 = 28$ 20
⁽⁹³⁾

Simplify:

28. (a) $6x^2 + 3x - 2x - 1$ $6x^2 + x - 1$
^(84,87)

(b) $(5x)(3x) - (5x)(-4)$ $15x^2 + 20x$

29. (a) $\dfrac{(-8) - (-6) - (4)}{-3}$ 2   (b) $-5(-4) - 3(-2) - 1$ 25
^(85,91)

30. Evaluate: $b^2 - 4ac$ if $a = -1$, $b = -2$, and $c = 3$ 16
⁽⁹¹⁾

LESSON
95

Volume of a Right Solid

Facts Practice: Order of Operations (Test S in Test Masters)

Mental Math:

a. $(72) + (-100)$

b. $(2.5 \times 10^6)(2.5 \times 10^6)$

c. $\frac{60}{100} = \frac{y}{1.5}$

d. Convert 25°C to degrees Fahrenheit.

e. $8 \times 2\frac{3}{4}$

f. 50% more than 60

g. 10% of 300 is how much more than 20% of 100?

Problem Solving:

Copy this problem on your paper and fill in the missing digits.

$$\begin{array}{r} \_3 \\ \times\ \_\_ \\ \hline \_\_\_ \\ \_\_\_ \\ \hline 9\_\_1 \end{array}$$

A **right solid** is a geometric solid whose sides are perpendicular to the base. **The volume of a right solid equals the product of the area of the base and the height.** This rectangular solid is a right solid. It is 5 m long and 2 m deep, so the area of the base is 10 m^2.

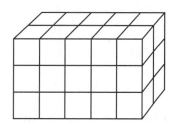

One cube will fit on each square meter of the base and the cubes are stacked 3 m high, so

$$\text{Volume} = \text{area of the base} \times \text{height}$$
$$= 10\text{ m}^2 \times 3\text{ m}$$
$$= 30\text{ m}^3$$

The volume of any solid equals the area of the base times the height. If the base of a right solid is a circle, the solid is called a right circular cylinder. If the base of the solid is a polygon, the solid is called a prism.

Right square
prism

Right triangular
prism

Right circular
cylinder

Example 1 Find the volume of this right triangular prism. Dimensions are in centimeters. We show two views of the prism.

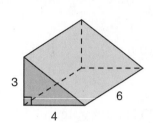

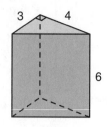

Solution The area of the base is the area of the triangle.

$$\text{Area of base} = \frac{(4 \text{ cm})(3 \text{ cm})}{2} = 6 \text{ cm}^2$$

The volume equals the area of the base times the height.

$$\text{Volume} = (6 \text{ cm}^2)(6 \text{ cm}) = \textbf{36 cm}^3$$

Example 2 The diameter of this right circular cylinder is 20 cm. Its height is 25 cm. What is its volume? Leave π as π.

Solution First we find the area of the base. The diameter of the circular base is 20 cm, so the radius is 10 cm.

$$\text{Area of base} = \pi r^2 = \pi(10 \text{ cm})^2 = 100\pi \text{ cm}^2$$

The volume equals the area of the base times the height.

$$\text{Volume} = (100\pi \text{ cm}^2)(25 \text{ cm}) = \textbf{2500}\pi \textbf{ cm}^3$$

Practice Find the volume of each right solid shown. Dimensions are in centimeters.

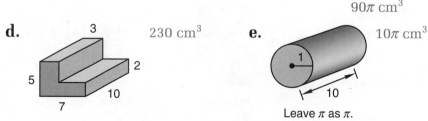

a.

8
12
6
288 cm³

b.

6
12
10
360 cm³

c.

10
6
Leave π as π.
90π cm³

d.
3
2
5
10
7
230 cm³

e.
1
10
10π cm³
Leave π as π.

Problem set 95

1. The taxi ride cost $1.40 plus 35¢ for each tenth of a mile.
(55) What was the average cost per mile for a 4-mile taxi ride?
$3.85 per mile

2. The table shows how many students
(Inv. 4) earned certain scores on the last test.
Create a box-and-whisker plot for
these scores.

70 75 80 85 90 95 100

Class Test Scores

Score	Number of Students
100	||||
95	||||| |
90	||||| |||
85	||||| ||
80	|||
75	|
70	|

3. The coordinates of the vertices of $\triangle ABC$ are $A(-1, -1)$,
(80) $B(-1, -4)$, and $C(-3, -2)$. The reflection of $\triangle ABC$ in the
y-axis is its image $\triangle A'B'C'$. Draw both triangles and state
the coordinates of the vertices of $\triangle A'B'C'$.
$A'(1, -1)$, $B'(1, -4)$, $C'(3, -2)$

4. If Jackson is paid $6 per hour, how much will he earn in
(53) 4 hours and 20 minutes? $26

5. What is the ratio of the shaded area to
(36,75) the unshaded area of this rectangle? $\frac{1}{3}$

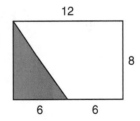

6. If 600 pounds of sand costs $7.20, what would be the cost
(72) of 1 ton of sand at the same price per pound? $24.00

7. The cost of production rose 30 percent. If the new cost is
(92) $3.90 per unit, what was the old cost per unit? $3.00

8. If a grocery store marks up cereal 30%, then what is the
(92) retail price of a large box of cereal that costs the store
$3.90? $5.07

9. Use two unit multipliers to convert 1000 mm² to square
(88) centimeters. 10 cm²

10.

150 Lilliputians	
$\frac{3}{5}$ believed	30 Lilliputians
	30 Lilliputians
	30 Lilliputians
$\frac{2}{5}$ did not believe (60)	30 Lilliputians
	30 Lilliputians

10. Draw a diagram of this statement. Then answer the
(71) questions that follow.

> *Three fifths of the Lilliputians believed in giants.*
> *The other 60 Lilliputians did not believe in giants.*

(a) How many Lilliputians were there? 150 Lilliputians

(b) How many Lilliputians believed in giants?
90 Lilliputians

11. Compare: $a \bigcirc b$ if a is a counting number and b is
(79) an integer insufficient information

12. Evaluate: $m(m + n)$ if $m = -2$ and $n = -3$ 10
(91)

13. If a pair of dice is tossed once, what is the probability that
(94) the number rolled is

(a) 7? $\frac{1}{6}$ (b) a number less than 7?
$\frac{15}{36} = \frac{5}{12}$

14. Find the volume of this triangular
(95) prism. Dimensions are in millimeters.
30,000 mm^3

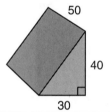

15. The diameter of a soup can was 6 cm. Its height was 10 cm.
(95) What was the volume of the soup can? (Use 3.14 for π.)
282.6 cm^3

16. Find the total cost, including 6 percent tax, of 3 tacos at
(46) $1.25 each, 2 soft drinks at 95¢ each, and a shake at $1.30.
$7.37

17. Complete the table.
(48)

FRACTION	DECIMAL	PERCENT
$2\frac{3}{4}$	(a) 2.75	(b) 275%
(c) $\frac{7}{80}$	(d) 0.0875	$8\frac{3}{4}\%$

18. Simplify:
(84,87)

(a) $(-2xy)(-2x)(x^2y)$ $4x^4y^2$

(b) $6x - 4y + 3 - 6x - 5y - 8$ $-9y - 5$

19. Multiply and write the product in scientific notation.
(83)

$(8 \times 10^{-6})(4 \times 10^4)$ 3.2×10^{-1}

20. (a) Find the missing numbers in the table of this function. Then graph the function.

$$y = \frac{1}{2}x + 1$$

(b) At what point on the *y*-axis does the graph of the function intersect the *y*-axis? (0, 1)

x	*y*
6	4
4	3
−2	0

20.(a)
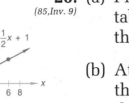
$y = \frac{1}{2}x + 1$

21. Divide 1000 by 48 and write the quotient as a mixed number. $20\frac{5}{6}$

22. Find the measures of the following angles:

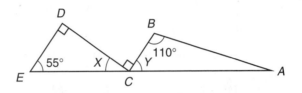

(a) $\angle X$ 35°   (b) $\angle Y$ 55°   (c) $\angle A$ 15°

23. Graph all the negative numbers that are greater than −2.

23.

24. What is the average of the numbers labeled *A* and *B* on this number line? 1.54

Solve:

25. $-5w + 11 = 51$ −8   **26.** $\frac{4}{3}x - 2 = 14$ 12

27. Solve and graph: $0.9x + 1.2 \le 3$ $x \le 2$

Simplify:

28. $\sqrt{1^3 + 2^3} + (1 + 2)^3$ 30   **29.** $5 - 2\frac{2}{3}\left(1\frac{3}{4}\right)$ $\frac{1}{3}$

30. (a) $\dfrac{(-10) + (-8) - (-6)}{(-2)(+3)}$ 2   (b) $-8 + 3(-2) - 6$ −20

LESSON 96

Estimating Angle Measures • Distributive Property with Algebraic Terms

Facts Practice: Two-Step Equations (Test T in Test Masters)

Mental Math:

  a. $(-27) - (-50)$ **b.** $(5 \times 10^5)(2 \times 10^7)$

  c. $160 = 80 + 4y$ **d.** Convert 15°C to degrees Fahrenheit.

  e. $9 \times 1\frac{2}{3}$ **f.** 25% more than $80

  g. Estimate 15% of $49.75.

Problem Solving:

  What is the average of these fractions?

$$\frac{1}{4}, \frac{1}{6}, \frac{1}{12}$$

Estimating angle measures

We have practiced reading the measure of an angle from a protractor scale. The ability to measure an angle with a protractor is an important skill. The ability to **estimate** the measure of an angle is also a valuable skill. In this lesson we will learn a technique to help us estimate the measure of an angle. We will also practice using a protractor as we check our estimates.

To estimate a measurement, we need a mental image of the units to be used in the measurement. To estimate angle measure, we need a mental image of a degree scale—a mental protractor. We can "build" a mental image of a protractor from a mental image we already have—the face of a clock.

This clock face is a full circle. A full circle is 360°. A clock face is divided into 12 numbered divisions. From one numbered division to the next is $\frac{1}{12}$ of a full circle. One twelfth of 360° is 30°. Thus, the measure of the angle formed by the hands of the clock at 1 o'clock is 30°, at 2 o'clock is 60°, and at 3 o'clock is 90°. A clock face is further divided into 60 smaller divisions. From one small division to the next is $\frac{1}{60}$ of a circle. One sixtieth of 360° is 6°.

$$60 \overline{)360°}^{\,6°}$$

Thus, **from one minute mark to the next on the face of a clock is 6°.**

Here we have drawn an angle on the face of a clock. The vertex of the angle is at the center of the clock. One side of the angle is set at 12.

The other side of the angle is at "8 minutes after." Since each minute of separation represents 6°, the measure of this angle is 8 × 6°, which is 48°. With some practice we can usually estimate the measure of an angle within 5° of its actual measure.

Example 1 (a) Record your estimate of the measure of ∠BOC.

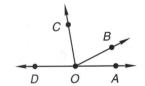

(b) Use a protractor to find the measure of ∠BOC.

(c) By how many degrees did your estimate miss your measurement?

Solution (a) We use a mental image of a clock face on ∠BOC with one side of the angle set at 12. Mentally we may see that the other side is more than 10 minutes after. Perhaps it is 12 minutes after. Since 12 × 6° is 72°, we estimate that m∠BOC is **72°**.

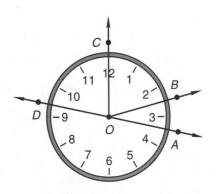

(b) We trace angle *BOC* on our paper and extend the sides so that we can use a protractor. We find that m∠*BOC* is **75°**.

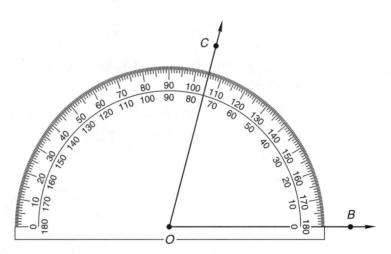

(c) Our estimate, 72°, misses our measurement, 75°, by **3°**.

Distributive property with algebraic terms Recall from Lesson 41 that the distributive property "spreads" multiplication over terms that are algebraically added. We illustrated the distributive property with this equation.

$$a(b + c) = ab + ac$$

The distributive property is frequently used in algebra to simplify expressions and solve equations.

Example 2 Simplify:

 (a) $2(x - 3)$ (b) $-2(x + 3)$

 (c) $-2(x - 3)$ (d) $x(x - 3)$

Solution (a) We multiply 2 and x, and we multiply 2 and -3.

$$2(x - 3) = \mathbf{2x - 6}$$

(b) We multiply -2 and x, and we multiply -2 and 3.

$$-2(x + 3) = \mathbf{-2x - 6}$$

(c) We multiply -2 and x, and we multiply -2 and -3.

$$-2(x - 3) = \mathbf{-2x + 6}$$

(d) We multiply x and x, and we multiply x and -3.

$$x(x - 3) = \mathbf{x^2 - 3x}$$

Example 3 Simplify: $x^2 + 2x + 3(x - 2)$

Solution   We first use the distributive property to clear parentheses. Then we add like terms.

$$x^2 + 2x + 3(x - 2) \qquad \text{expression}$$
$$x^2 + 2x + 3x - 6 \qquad \text{distributive property}$$
$$\mathbf{x^2 + 5x - 6} \qquad \text{added } 2x \text{ and } 3x$$

Practice   Counting minute marks, find the measure of each angle shown on the clock face.

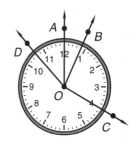

   a. $\angle AOB$ 24°

   b. $\angle AOC$ 120°

   c. $\angle AOD$ 42°

In practice problems d–g, estimate the measure of each angle. Then use a protractor and measure each angle. By how many degrees did your estimate miss your measurement?

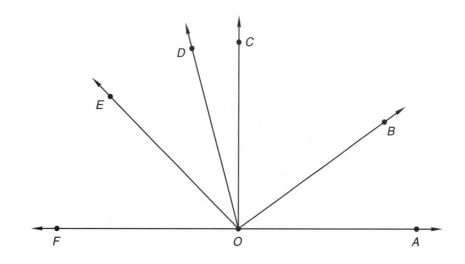

   d. $\angle BOC$ See student work.; 55°   **e.** $\angle DOC$
                                                 See student work.; 15°

   f. $\angle FOE$ See student work.; 45°   **g.** $\angle FOB$
                                                 See student work.; 145°

Simplify:

   h. $x(x - y)$ $x^2 - xy$ **i.** $-3(2x - 1)$ $-6x + 3$

   j. $-x(x - 2)$ $-x^2 + 2x$ **k.** $-2(4 - 3x)$ $-8 + 6x$

   l. $x^2 + 2x - 3(x + 2)$ **m.** $x^2 - 2x - 3(x - 2)$
     $x^2 - x - 6$ $x^2 - 5x + 6$

Problem set 96

1. In May the merchant bought 3 tons of beans at an average price of $280 per ton. In June the merchant bought 5 tons of beans at an average price of $240 per ton. What was the average price of all the beans bought by the merchant in May and June? $255 per ton
(55)

2. What is the quotient when 9 squared is divided by the square root of 9? 27
(20)

3. The Adams' car has a 16-gallon gas tank. How many tanks of gas will the car use on a 2000-mile trip if the car averages 25 miles per gallon? 5 tanks
(28)

4. In a triangular prism, what is the ratio of the number of vertices to the number of edges? $\frac{2}{3}$
(36,67)

Use ratio boxes to solve problems 5–7.

5. If 58 dollars can be exchanged for 100 mark, what is the cost in dollars of an item that sells for 250 mark?
(72)
145 dollars

6. Sixty is 20 percent less than what number? 75
(92)

7. The average number of customers per day increased 25 percent during the sale. If the average number of customers before the sale was 120 per day, what was the average number of customers per day during the sale?
(92)
150 customers per day

8. Write equations to solve these problems.
(77)

(a) Sixty is what percent of 50? $60 = W_P \times 50$; 120%

(b) Fifty is what percent of 60? $50 = W_P \times 60$; $83\frac{1}{3}\%$

9. Use two unit multipliers to convert 1.2 m² to square centimeters. 12,000 square centimeters
(88)

10. Triangle *ABC* is similar to triangle *EDC*.
(18,40)

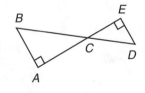

(a) List three pairs of corresponding angles and three pairs of corresponding sides.

10.(a)
∠A and ∠E,
∠B and ∠D,
∠ACB and ∠ECD;
$\overline{AB}$ and $\overline{ED}$,
$\overline{BC}$ and $\overline{DC}$,
$\overline{AC}$ and $\overline{EC}$.

(b) If m∠ABC = 53°, then what is m∠ECD? 37°

11. Compare: $x + y \; \bigcirc \; x - y$ if $y > 0$
(79)

12. Evaluate: $c(a + b)$ if $a = -4$, $b = -3$, and $c = -2$
(91) 14

13. The perimeter of a certain square is 1 yard. Find the area
(20) of the square in square inches. 81 square inches

14. The face of this spinner is divided
(94) into one half and two fourths. What
is the probability of this spinner

(a) stopping on 3 twice in a row? $\frac{1}{16}$

(b) stopping on 1 four times in a row?
$\frac{1}{16}$

15. Find the volume of each solid. Dimensions are in
(95) centimeters.

(a) 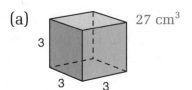 27 cm³

(b) 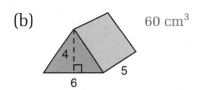 60 cm³

16. Find the total price, including 7 percent tax, of 20 square
(46) yards of carpeting priced at $14.50 per square yard.
$310.30

17. Complete the table.
(48)

FRACTION	DECIMAL	PERCENT
(a) $\frac{3}{80}$	(b) 0.0375	$3\frac{3}{4}$%

18. Raincoats regularly priced at $24 were on sale for $33\frac{1}{3}$% off.
(60,92)

(a) What is $33\frac{1}{3}$% of $24? $8

(b) What is $33\frac{1}{3}$% less than $24? $16

19. Multiply and write the product in scientific notation.
(83)

$$(3 \times 10^3)(8 \times 10^{-8}) \quad 2.4 \times 10^{-4}$$

20. (a) Find the circumference of this
(66,82)   circle. 12π m

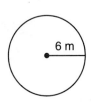

(b) Find the area of this circle.
36π m²

Leave π as π.

21. Use the clock face to estimate the measure of each angle.
(96)

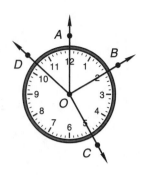

   (a) $\angle BOC$ 90°

   (b) $\angle COA$ 150°

   (c) $\angle DOA$ 48°

22. (a) What is the measure of each exterior angle of a regular octagon?
(89)
    45°

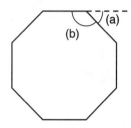

   (b) What is the measure of each interior angle of a regular octagon?
    135°

23. Find the coordinates of the vertices of $\square Q'R'S'T'$ which is the image of $\square QRST$ translated 4 units right and 4 units down. $Q'\,(8, -4)$, $R'\,(4, 0)$, $S'\,(0, -4)$, $T'\,(4, -8)$
(80)

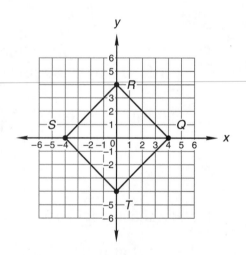

24. Solve and graph: $0.8x + 1.5 < 4.7$
(93)

    $x < 4$

Solve each equation. Show all steps.

25. $2\frac{1}{2}x - 7 = 13$ 8   **26.** $-3x + 8 = -10$ 6
(93)   (93)

Simplify:

27. $3^3 - \sqrt{49} + 3 \cdot 2^4$ 68
(52)

28. (a) $-3(x - 4)$ $-3x + 12$ (b) $x(x + y)$ $x^2 + xy$
(96)

29. (a) $\dfrac{(-4) - (-8)(-3)(-2)}{-2}$ -22 (b) $(-3)^2 + 3^2$ 18
(85)

30. (a) $\left(-4ab^2\right)\left(-3b^2c\right)(5a)$ (b) $a^2 + ab - ab - b^2$
(84,87) $60a^2b^4c$ $a^2 - b^2$

LESSON 97

Similar Triangles • Indirect Measure

Facts Practice: Order of Operations (Test S in Test Masters)

Mental Math:

a. $(-5)(-5)(-5)$ **b.** $\left(5 \times 10^6\right)\left(6 \times 10^5\right)$

c. $\dfrac{m}{4.5} = \dfrac{0.6}{3}$ **d.** Convert 5°C to degrees Fahrenheit.

e. $10 \times 6\frac{1}{2}$ **f.** 25% less than $80

g. $\sqrt{100}$, × 7, + 2, ÷ 8, × 4, $\sqrt{}$, × 5, − 2, ÷ 2, ÷ 2, ÷ 2

Problem Solving:

Find the numbers that complete this table for a hexagon and for an n-gon. (An n-gon is a polygon with "n" sides.)

Type of Polygon	Number of Diagonals from One Vertex	Sum of Interior ∠'s
quadrilateral	1	2 × 180°
pentagon	2	3 × 180°
hexagon		
n-gon		

Similar triangles

We often use "tick marks" to indicate that the measures of angles are equal (or that the angles are congruent).

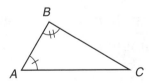
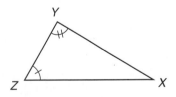

Yes, since the sum of the angle measures of each triangle is 180°, the remaining angles must have the same measure.

In these figures the single tick marks indicate that angles A and Z have equal measures. The double tick marks indicate that angles B and Y have equal measures. May we conclude that angles C and X also have equal measures?

Recall from Lesson 18 that if three angles in one triangle have the same measures as three angles in another triangle, the triangles are *similar triangles*. So triangles *ABC* and *ZYX* are similar. Also recall that similar triangles have 3 pairs of corresponding angles and 3 pairs of corresponding sides. Here we show the corresponding angles and sides for the triangles above.

Corresponding Angles	Corresponding Sides
∠*A* and ∠*Z*	$\overline{AB}$ and $\overline{ZY}$
∠*B* and ∠*Y*	$\overline{BC}$ and $\overline{YX}$
∠*C* and ∠*X*	$\overline{CA}$ and $\overline{XZ}$

In this lesson we will focus our attention on the following characteristic of similar triangles:

> **The lengths of corresponding sides of similar triangles are proportional.**

This means that ratios formed by corresponding sides are equal, as we illustrate with the two triangles below.

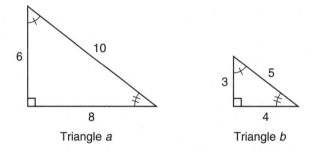

Triangle *a*   Triangle *b*

The lengths of the corresponding sides of triangles *a* and *b* are 6 and 3, 8 and 4, and 10 and 5. These pairs of lengths may be written as equal ratios.

$$\frac{\text{triangle } a}{\text{triangle } b} \qquad \frac{6}{3} = \frac{8}{4} = \frac{10}{5}$$

Notice that each of these ratios equals 2. If we choose to put the lengths of the sides of triangle *b* on top we get three ratios equal to $\frac{1}{2}$.

$$\frac{\text{triangle } b}{\text{triangle } a} \qquad \frac{3}{6} = \frac{4}{8} = \frac{5}{10}$$

We may write proportions using equal ratios in order to find the lengths of unknown sides of similar triangles.

Example 1 Find the length of side a.

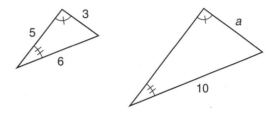

Solution The triangles are similar so the lengths of the corresponding sides are proportional. We will write a proportion and solve for a. We decide to write the ratios so that the sides from the left triangle are on top.

$$\frac{6}{10} = \frac{3}{a} \qquad \text{equal ratios}$$

$$6a = 30 \qquad \text{cross multiplied}$$

$$a = \mathbf{5} \qquad \text{solved}$$

Indirect measure Sarah looked up and said, "I wonder how tall that tree is." Beth looked down and said, "It's about 25 feet tall." Beth did not *directly* measure the height of the tree. Instead she used her knowledge of proportions to *indirectly* estimate the height of the tree.

The lengths of the shadows cast by two objects are proportional to the heights of the two objects.

We may separate the objects and their shadows into two similar figures.

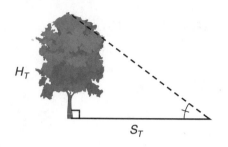

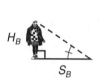

Assuming the ground is flat and level, the tree and Beth are perpendicular to the ground. The angle of the sun's light is the same for both objects at the same moment. The height of Beth (H_B) and the length of the shadow of Beth (S_B) are proportional to the height of the tree (H_T) and the length of the shadow of the tree (S_T). We may record the relationship in a ratio box.

	Beth	Tree
Height of object	H_B	H_T
Length of shadow	S_B	S_T

How did Beth perform the calculation? We suggest two ways. First, knowing her own height (5 ft), perhaps she estimated the length of her shadow (6 ft) and the length of the shadow of the tree (30 ft). She could then solve this proportion in which all numbers represent numbers of feet.

$$\frac{5}{6} = \frac{H_T}{30}$$

$$6H_T = 5 \cdot 30$$

$$H_T = 25$$

Another way Beth might have estimated the height of the tree is by estimating that the shadow of the tree was five times as long as her own shadow. If the tree's shadow was five times as long as her shadow, then the tree's height would be five times her height.

$$5 \text{ ft} \times 5 = 25 \text{ ft}$$

Example 2   To indirectly measure the height of a light pole on the playground, a class of students measured the length of the shadow (24 ft) cast by the pole while also measuring the length of the shadow (40 cm) cast by a vertical meter stick. About how tall was the light pole?

Solution We sketch the objects and their shadows using the given information.

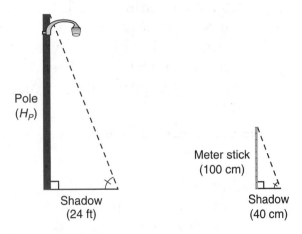

Note: Figures not drawn to scale.

We use a ratio box to record the given information. Then we write and solve a proportion.

	Meter Stick	**Pole**
Height of object	100 cm	H_P
Length of shadow	40 cm	24 ft

$$\frac{100}{40} = \frac{H_P}{24}$$

$$40H_P = 24 \cdot 100$$

$$H_P = 60$$

We find that the height of the light pole was about **60 feet.** Note that the two objects were measured using different units. Exercise caution in mixing units in proportions to be sure that the solution is expressed in the desired units. You may choose to perform the calculation using units as we show below.

$$\frac{100 \text{ cm}}{40 \text{ cm}} = \frac{H_P}{24 \text{ ft}}$$

$$40 \text{ cm} \cdot H_P = 24 \text{ ft} \cdot 100 \text{ cm}$$

$$H_P = \frac{\overset{6}{\cancel{24}} \text{ ft} \cdot \overset{10}{\cancel{100}} \cancel{\text{cm}}}{\underset{\underset{1}{\cancel{4}}}{\cancel{40}} \cancel{\text{cm}}}$$

$$H_P = 60 \text{ ft}$$

Activity: Indirect Measure

Are meter sticks held vertically? Does the landscape vary? How are measurements rounded?

Using meter sticks (100 cm), rulers, and/or tape measures, have small groups of students perform an activity like the one described in Example 2 by selecting a tree, building, pole, or other tall object to indirectly measure. If different groups measure the same object, discuss how and why answers differ.

Practice

a. Identify each pair of corresponding angles and each pair of corresponding sides in these two triangles.

corresponding angles: ∠W and ∠R; ∠Y and ∠Q; ∠X and ∠P

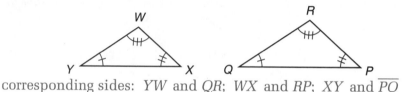

corresponding sides: YW and QR; WX and RP; XY and $\overline{PQ}$

Refer to the figures shown to answer problems b and c.

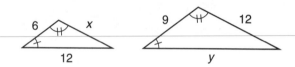

b. Find the length of side x.   8

c. Find the length of side y.   18

d. A tree casts a shadow 18 ft long while a 6 ft pole casts a shadow 9 ft long. How tall is the tree?   12 ft

Problem set 97

1. Ginger gave the clerk $10 for a CD that cost $8.95 plus 6 percent tax. How much money should she get back? $0.51
(46)

2. Three hundred billion is how much less than two trillion? Write the answer in scientific notation. 1.7×10^{12}
(51)

3. During the second semester Joe's test scores were:
(Inv. 4)

95, 90, 80, 85, 90, 100, 85, 90, 95, 80

Find the (a) median, (b) mode, and (c) range of these scores.   (a) 90   (b) 90   (c) 20

Use ratio boxes to solve problems 4 and 5.

4. Coming down the long hill, Nelson averaged 24 miles per
(72) hour. If it took him 5 minutes to come down the hill, how
long was the hill? 2 miles

5. If Nelson traveled 3520 yards in 5 minutes, how far could
(72) he travel in 8 minutes at the same rate? 5632 yards

6. Describe the transformation that moves
(80) $\triangle ABC$ to its image $\triangle A'B'C'$.
translation 5 units to the right

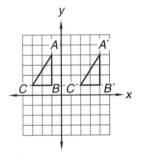

7. Three fourths of a yard is how many inches? 27 inches
(60)

8. Use a ratio box to solve this problem. The ratio of leeks to
(54) radishes growing in the garden was 5 to 7. If 420 radishes
were growing in the garden, how many leeks were there?
300 leeks

Write equations to solve problems 9–11.

9. Forty is 250 percent of what number? $40 = 2.5 \times W_N$; 16
(77)

10. Forty is what percent of 60? $40 = W_P \times 60$; $66\frac{2}{3}\%$
(77)

11. What decimal number is 40 percent of 6? $W_D = 0.4 \times 6$; 2.4
(60)

12. Use a ratio box to solve this problem. The tuition
(92) increased 10 percent this year. If the tuition this year is
$17,600, what was the tuition last year? $16,000

13. What is the average of the two numbers marked by arrows
(28,34) on this number line? 1.91

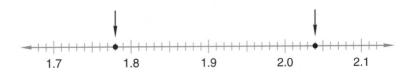

14. Complete the table.
(48)

	FRACTION	DECIMAL	PERCENT
(a)	$3\frac{1}{4}$	3.25	(b) 325%
	$\frac{1}{6}$	(c) $0.1\overline{6}$	(d) $16\frac{2}{3}\%$

15. Compare: $x + y \;\circled{<}\; x - y$ if x is positive and y is
(79)   negative

16. Multiply and write the product in scientific notation.
(83)

$$(5.4 \times 10^8)(6 \times 10^{-4}) \quad 3.24 \times 10^5$$

17. Find (a) the circumference and (b) the area of a circle
(66,82) with a radius of 10 millimeters. (a) 62.8 mm   (b) 314 mm^2

18. Find the area of this trapezoid.
(75) Dimensions are in feet. 80 ft^2

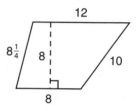

19. Find the volume of each of these solids. Dimensions are
(95) in meters. (Leave π as π.)

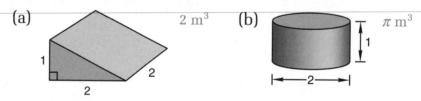

(a) 2 m^3 (b) π m^3

20. Refer to the figure shown. What are the measures of the
(40) following angles?

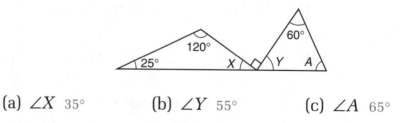

(a) $\angle X$ 35°   (b) $\angle Y$ 55°   (c) $\angle A$ 65°

21. The triangles are similar. Find x. Dimensions are in
(97) centimeters. 8 cm

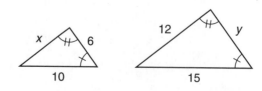

22. How tall is a power pole that casts a 72 foot shadow
$_{(97)}$ while a vertical yard stick casts a 48 inch shadow? (Make
a diagram to illustrate the problem.)
54 feet; See student diagrams.

23. Estimate: $\dfrac{(38,470)(607)}{79}$ 300,000
$_{(29)}$

Solve each equation showing all steps.

24. $1.2m + 0.12 = 12$ 9.9 **25.** $1\dfrac{3}{4}y - 2 = 12$ 8
$_{(93)}$ $\qquad\qquad\qquad$ $_{(93)}$

Simplify:

26. $3x - y + 8 + x + y - 2$ $4x + 6$
$_{(84)}$

27. $\dfrac{15 \text{ mi}}{1 \text{ hr}} \cdot \dfrac{1 \text{ hr}}{60 \text{ min}} \cdot \dfrac{1760 \text{ yd}}{1 \text{ mi}}$ $440 \frac{yd}{min}$
$_{(88)}$

28. (a) $3(x - y)$ $3x - 3y$ $\qquad\qquad$ (b) $x(y - 3)$ $xy - 3x$
$_{(96)}$

29. $3\dfrac{1}{3} \div \left(4.5 \div 1\dfrac{1}{8}\right)$ $\frac{5}{6}$ $\qquad$ **30.** $\dfrac{(-2) - (+3) + (-4)(-3)}{(-2) + (+3) - (+4)}$
$_{(43)}$ $\qquad\qquad\qquad\qquad\qquad$ $_{(85)}$ $\qquad$ $-2\frac{1}{3}$

LESSON
98

Scale • Scale Factor

Facts Practice: Two-Step Equations (Test T in Test Masters)

Mental Math:

a. $(-360) \div (8)$ $\qquad\qquad$ **b.** $(2.5 \times 10^7)(4 \times 10^{-2})$

c. $2c + 1\frac{1}{2} = 6\frac{1}{2}$ $\qquad\qquad$ **d.** Convert 0.02 kg to g.

e. $4 \times 3\frac{3}{4}$ $\qquad\qquad\qquad$ **f.** $33\frac{1}{3}\%$ more than $60

g. At 12 mph, how far can Toby ride a bike in 1 hour and 45
minutes?

Problem Solving:

To convert from degrees Celsius to degrees Fahrenheit, Michelle's
grandfather said, "Double the Celsius number, subtract 10%,
then add 32°." We exercise caution when converting from a
Celsius temperature less than 0°C. Record the steps for
converting from −10°C to degrees Fahrenheit.

Scale   In the preceding lesson we discussed similar triangles. Scale models and scale drawings are other examples of similar shapes. Scale models and scale drawings are reduced (or enlarged) renderings of actual objects. As is true of similar triangles, the lengths of corresponding parts of scale models and the objects they represent are proportional.

The **scale** of the model is stated as a ratio. For instance, if a model airplane is $\frac{1}{24}$ the size of the actual airplane, the scale is stated as $\frac{1}{24}$ or 1:24. We may use the given scale to write a proportion to find a measurement either on the model or on the actual object. A ratio box helps us put the numbers in the proper places.

Example 1   A model airplane is built on a scale of 1:24. If the wingspan of the model is 18 inches, the wingspan of the actual airplane is how many feet?

Solution   We will construct a ratio box as we do with other ratio problems. In one column we write the ratio numbers which are the scale numbers. In the other column we write the measures. The first number of the scale refers to the model. The second number refers to the object. We can use the entries in the ratio box to write a proportion.

	Scale	Measure
Model	1	18
Object	24	w

$$\frac{1}{24} = \frac{18}{w}$$

$$w = 432$$

The wingspan of the model was given in inches. Solving the proportion, we find that the full-size wingspan is 432 inches. We are asked for the wingspan in feet, so we convert units from inches to feet.

$$432 \text{ in.} \cdot \frac{1 \text{ ft}}{12 \text{ in.}} = 36 \text{ ft}$$

We find that the wingspan of the airplane is **36 feet.**

Example 2   Sarah is molding a model of a car from clay. The scale of the model is 1:36. If the height of the car is 4 feet and 6 inches, what should be the height of the model in inches?

Solution   First we convert 4 feet and 6 inches to inches.

$$4 \text{ feet and } 6 \text{ inches} = 54 \text{ inches}$$

Then we construct a ratio box using 1 and 36 as the ratio numbers, write the proportion, and solve.

	Scale	Measure
Model	1	m
Object	36	54

$\longrightarrow$ $\dfrac{1}{36} = \dfrac{m}{54}$

$$36m = 54$$

$$m = \frac{54}{36}$$

$$m = 1\frac{1}{2}$$

The height of the model car should be $1\frac{1}{2}$ **inches.**

Scale factor   We have solved proportions by using cross products. Sometimes a proportion can be solved more quickly by noting the **scale factor.** The scale factor is the number of times larger (or smaller) the terms of one ratio are when compared with the terms of the other ratio. The scale factor in the proportion below is 6 because the terms of the second ratio are 6 times the terms of the first ratio.

$$\frac{3}{4} \times \frac{6}{6} = \frac{18}{24}$$

Example 3   Solve: $\dfrac{3}{7} = \dfrac{15}{n}$

Solution   Instead of finding cross products, we note that 3 times 5 equals 15. Thus the scale factor is 5. We use this scale factor to find n.

$$\frac{3}{7} \times \frac{5}{5} = \frac{15}{35}$$

We find that n is **35.**

Example 4 These two triangles are similar. Calculate the scale factor from the smaller triangle to the larger triangle.

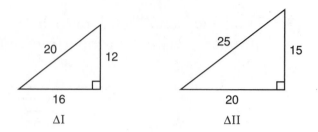

ΔI   ΔII

Solution If we multiply the length of one side of the smaller triangle by the scale factor we get the length of the corresponding side of the larger triangle.

Dimension of ΔI × scale factor = dimension of ΔII

We may select any pair of corresponding sides to calculate the scale factor. We decide to choose the longest sides. We write an equation using f for the scale factor and then solve for f.

$$20f = 25$$

$$f = \frac{25}{20}$$

$$f = \frac{5}{4} \text{ or } \mathbf{1.25}$$

In this book we will express the scale factor in decimal form unless otherwise directed.

Note that the scale factor refers to the *linear measures* of two similar figures and not to the area or volume measures of the figures. The scale factor from Cube A to Cube B below is 2 because the linear measures of Cube B are twice the corresponding measures of Cube A.

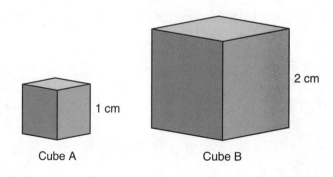

Cube A   Cube B

However, the surface area of Cube B is 4 times the surface area of Cube A, and the volume of Cube B is 8 times the volume of Cube A. Since we multiply two dimensions of a figure to calculate the area of the figure, the relationship between the areas of the two figures is the scale factor times the scale factor, in other words, the scale factor squared. Likewise, the relationship between the volumes of two similar figures is the scale factor cubed.

Example 5 The dimensions of the smaller of two similar rectangular prisms are 2 cm by 3 cm by 4 cm. The dimensions of the larger rectangular prism are 6 cm by 9 cm by 12 cm.

(a) What is the scale factor from the smaller to the larger rectangular prism?

(b) The area of any face of the larger prism is how many times the area of the corresponding face of the smaller prism?

(c) The volume of the larger solid is how many times the volume of the smaller solid?

Solution Before answering the questions we sketch the two figures.

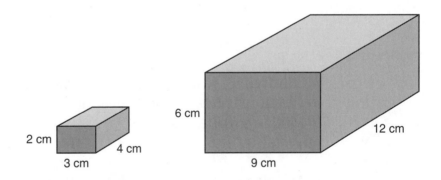

(a) We select any two corresponding linear measures to calculate the scale factor. We will choose the 2 cm and the 6 cm measures.

Dimension of smaller × scale factor = dimension of larger

$$2f = 6$$

$$f = 3$$

We find that the scale factor is **3.**

(b) Since the scale factor from the smaller to the larger figure is 3, the area of any surface of the larger figure should be 3^2 (which is 9) times the area of the corresponding surface of the smaller figure. We will confirm this relationship by comparing the area of a 6 cm by 9 cm face of the larger prism with a 2 cm by 3 cm face of the smaller prism.

$$\text{Area of 6 cm by 9 cm face} = 54 \text{ cm}^2$$

$$\text{Area of 2 cm by 3 cm face} = 6 \text{ cm}^2$$

We see that the area of the selected face of the larger prism is indeed **9 times** the area of the corresponding face of the smaller prism.

(c) Since the scale factor of the linear dimensions of the two figures is 3 the volume of the larger prism should be 3^3 (which is 27) times the volume of the smaller prism. We will confirm this relationship by performing the calculations.

$$\text{Volume of 6 cm by 9 cm by 12 cm prism} = 648 \text{ cm}^3$$

$$\text{Volume of 2 cm by 3 cm by 4 cm prism} = 24 \text{ cm}^3$$

Dividing 648 cm³ by 24 cm³ we find that the larger volume is indeed **27 times** the smaller volume.

$$\frac{648 \text{ cm}^3}{24 \text{ cm}^3} = 27$$

Showing this calculation another way more clearly demonstrates why the larger volume is 3^3 times the smaller volume.

$$\frac{\text{Volume of larger prism}}{\text{Volume of smaller prism}} = \frac{\overset{3}{\cancel{6 \text{ cm}}} \cdot \overset{3}{\cancel{9 \text{ cm}}} \cdot \overset{3}{\cancel{12 \text{ cm}}}}{\underset{1}{\cancel{2 \text{ cm}}} \cdot \underset{1}{\cancel{3 \text{ cm}}} \cdot \underset{1}{\cancel{4 \text{ cm}}}} = 27$$

Practice **a.** The blueprints were drawn to a scale of 1:24. If a length of a wall on the blueprint was 6 in., what was the length in feet of the wall in the house? 12 feet

b. Bret is carving a model ship from balsa wood on a scale of 1:36. If the ship is 54 feet long, the model ship should be how many inches long? 18 inches

Solve by using the scale factor.

c. $\dfrac{5}{7} = \dfrac{15}{w}$ 21

d. $\dfrac{x}{3} = \dfrac{42}{21}$ 6

e. These two rectangles are similar. Calculate the scale factor from the smaller rectangle to the larger rectangle. 2.5

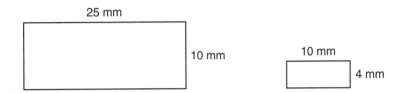

25 mm

10 mm

10 mm

4 mm

f. The area of the larger rectangle above is how many times the area of the smaller rectangle? 6.25 times

Problem set 98

1. Use a ratio box to solve this problem. The regular price of
(92) the item was $45, but the item was on sale for 20 percent off. What was the sale price? $36

2. With one toss of a pair of dice, what is the probability of
(94) rolling

(a) a number greater than 7? $\frac{5}{12}$

(b) a number less than 2? 0

3. Simplify: $(3x)(x) - (x)(2x)$ x^2
(84,87)

4. In her first 6 games, Ann averaged 10 points per game. In
(55) her next 9 games, Ann averaged 15 points per game. How many points per game did Ann average during her first 15 games? 13 points per game

5. Ingrid started her trip at 8:30 a.m. with a full tank of gas
(46) and an odometer reading of 43,764 miles. When she stopped for gas at 1:30 p.m., the odometer read 44,010 miles.

(a) If it took 12 gallons to fill the tank, her car averaged how many miles per gallon? 20.5 miles per gallon

(b) Ingrid traveled at an average speed of how many miles per hour? 49.2 miles per hour

6. Use a ratio box to solve this problem. If 5 dollars equals
(72) 30 kronor, what is the cost in dollars of an item priced at
75 kronor? $12.50

7. Write an equation to solve this problem. Three fifths of
(74) Tom's favorite number is 60. What is Tom's favorite
number? $\frac{3}{5} \times W_N = 60$; 100

8.

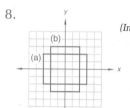

8. On a coordinate plane graph the points (–3, 2), (3, 2), and
(Inv. 3,80) (–3, –2).

   (a) If these points designate three of the vertices of a
rectangle, what are the coordinates of the fourth
vertex of the rectangle? Draw the rectangle. (3, –2)

   (b) Draw the image of the rectangle in (a) after a 90°
clockwise rotation about the origin. What are the
coordinates of the vertices of the rotated image?
(2, 3), (2, –3), (–2, –3), (–2, 3)

9. What is the ratio of counting numbers to integers in this
(36,86) set of numbers? $\frac{1}{3}$

$$\{-3, -2, -1, 0, 1, 2\}$$

10. Find a^2 if $\sqrt{a} = 3$. 81
(20,41)

Write equations to solve problems 11–12.

11. Forty is what percent of 250? $40 = W_P \times 250$; 16%
(77)

12. Forty percent of what number is 60? $0.4 \times W_N = 60$; 150
(77)

13. An antique dealer bought a chair for $40 and sold the
(92) chair for 60% more. What was the selling price? $64

14. Use a ratio box to solve this problem. The number of
(92) students in chorus increased 25 percent this year. If there
are 20 more students in chorus this year than there were
last year, how many students are in chorus this year?
100 students

15. Segment *BC* is how much longer than segment *AB*? $\frac{3}{4}$ inch
(8)

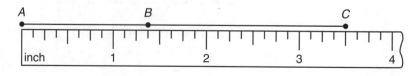

16. Graph on a number line: $x \leq 3$
(78)

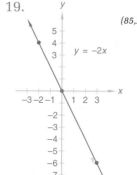

17. Complete the table.
(48)

FRACTION	DECIMAL	PERCENT
(a) $\frac{7}{500}$	(b) 0.014	1.4%

18. Multiply and write the product in scientific notation.
(83)

$$\left(1.4 \times 10^{-6}\right)\left(5 \times 10^{4}\right) \quad 7 \times 10^{-2}$$

19.

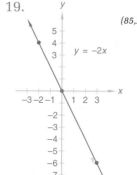

19. Find the missing numbers in the table
(85,Inv. 9) for this function. Then graph the function. Where does the graph of the function intersect the y-axis? (0, 0)

$y = -2x$

x	y
3	-6
0	0
-2	4

20. Find (a) the circumference and (b) the area of a circle that
(66,82) has a diameter of 2 feet. (Use 3.14 for π.)
(a) 6.28 ft (b) 3.14 ft^2

21. Estimate the measure of $\angle ABC$. Then
(96) trace the angle, extend the sides, and measure the angle with a protractor.
See student work.; 40°

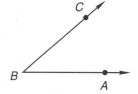

22. Find x and y. Then find the area of the smaller triangle.
(97) Dimensions are in inches.
$x = 12$ in.; $y = 40$ in.; area = 96 in.^{2}

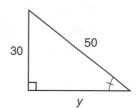

23. Calculate the scale factor from the smaller triangle to the
(98) larger triangle in problem 22. 2.5

Solve:

24. $-\dfrac{3}{5}m + 8 = 20$ -20
(93)

25. $0.3x - 2.7 = 9$ 39
(93)

Simplify:

26. $\sqrt{5^3 - 5^2}$ 10
(52)

27.
(56)

$$\begin{array}{r} 1 \text{ gal } 1 \text{ qt} \\ - 1 \text{ qt } 1 \text{ pt} \\ \hline 3 \text{ qt } 1 \text{ pt} \end{array}$$

28. $(0.25)\left(1\dfrac{1}{4} - 1.2\right)$ 0.0125
(43)

29. $7\dfrac{1}{3} - \left(1\dfrac{3}{4} \div 3.5\right)$ $6\frac{5}{6}$
(43)

30. $\dfrac{(-2)(3) - (3)(-4)}{(-2)(-3) - (4)}$ 3
(85)

LESSON 99

Mental Math:
a. 3
b. 3.2×10^{11}
c. 1
d. 5°F
e. 28
f. $40
g. 10
Problem Solving:
150°

Pythagorean Theorem

Facts Practice: Order of Operations (Test S in Test Masters)

Mental Math:

a. $(-1.5) + (4.5)$
b. $(8 \times 10^6)(4 \times 10^4)$
c. $\frac{0.15}{30} = \frac{0.005}{n}$
d. Convert $-15°C$ to degrees Fahrenheit.
e. $12 \times 2\frac{1}{3}$
f. $33\frac{1}{3}\%$ less than $60
g. What is the square root of the sum of 6^2 and 8^2?

Problem Solving:

At three o'clock the hands of a clock form a 90° angle. What angle is formed by the hands of a clock two hours after three o'clock?

The longest side of a right triangle is called the **hypotenuse.** The other two sides are called **legs.** Every right triangle has a property that makes the right triangle a very important triangle in mathematics. **The area of the square drawn on the hypotenuse of a right triangle equals the sum of the areas of the squares drawn on the legs.**

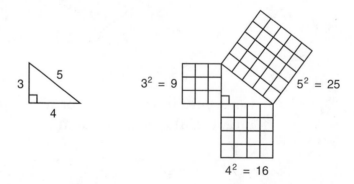

The triangle on the left is a right triangle. On the right we have drawn squares on the sides of the triangle. The areas of the squares drawn on the three sides are 9, 16, and 25. Notice that the area of the largest square equals the sum of the areas of the other two squares.

$$25 = 16 + 9$$

This property of right triangles was known to the Egyptians as early as 2000 B.C., but it is named for a Greek who lived about 650 B.C. The Greek's name was Pythagoras, and the property is called the **Pythagorean theorem.** The Greeks are so proud of this mathematician that they have issued a postage stamp that illustrates the theorem. Here we show a reproduction of this stamp.

To solve problems that require the use of the Pythagorean theorem, we will sketch the right triangle and draw the squares on each side.

Example 1   Copy this triangle. Draw a square on each side. Find the area of each square. Then find c.

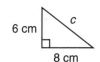

Solution   We copy the triangle and sketch a square on each side of the triangle, using a side of the triangle for one side of each square.

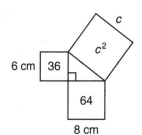

We were given the lengths of the two shorter sides. The areas of the squares on these sides are **36 cm^2** and **64 cm^2**. The sum of the areas of the smaller squares equals the area of the largest square.

$$36 \text{ cm}^2 + 64 \text{ cm}^2 = 100 \text{ cm}^2$$

The area of the largest square is **100 cm^2**. This means that a side of the largest square must be 10 cm because $(10 \text{ cm})^2$ equals 100 cm^2. Thus

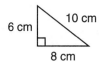

$$c = \textbf{10 cm}$$

Example 2   In this triangle find a. Dimensions are in inches.

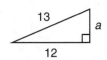

Solution   We copy the triangle and draw a square on each side. The area of the largest square is 169 in.^{2}. The area of one of the smaller squares is 144 in.^{2}. So a^2 plus 144 in.^{2} must equal 169 in.^{2}.

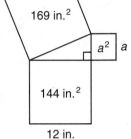

$$a^2 + 144 \text{ in.}^2 = 169 \text{ in.}^2$$

Subtracting 144 in.^{2} from both sides, we find that a^2 equals 25 in.^{2}.

$$a^2 = 25 \text{ in.}^2$$

If a^2 equals 25 in.^{2}, then a equals 5 in. because 5 in. squared is 25 in.^{2}. Dimensions are in inches so we label our answer.

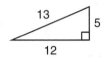

$$a = \textbf{5 in.}$$

Example 3   Find the perimeter of this triangle. Dimensions are in centimeters.

Solution   We can use the Pythagorean theorem to find side c. The areas of the two smaller squares are 16 cm^2 and 9 cm^2. The sum of these areas is 25 cm^2, so the area of the largest square is 25 cm^2. Thus the length of side c is 5 cm. Now we add the lengths of the sides to find the perimeter.

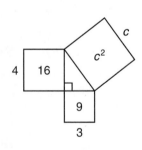

$$\text{Perimeter} = 4 \text{ cm} + 3 \text{ cm} + 5 \text{ cm}$$

$$= \textbf{12 cm}$$

Example 4   Sketch this right triangle and draw squares on the sides. Then write an equation that shows the relationship between the areas of the squares.

Solution   We sketch the triangle and squares. Squaring the lengths of the sides of the triangle gives us the areas of the squares: a^2, b^2, and c^2. The sum of the squares of the legs equals the square of the hypotenuse. This relationship is shown by the following equation:

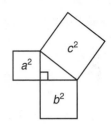

$$a^2 + b^2 = c^2$$

This equation is commonly used to algebraically express the Pythagorean theorem.

Practice   Sketch the triangles and draw the squares on the sides of the triangles as you work problems a–c.

a. Use the Pythagorean theorem to find side *a*.   10

b. Use the Pythagorean theorem to find side *b*.   15

c. Find the perimeter of this triangle. Dimensions are in feet.   24 feet

Problem set 99

1. The meal cost $15. Christie left a tip that was 15 percent of the cost of the meal. How much money did Christie leave for a tip? $2.25
(46)

2. Twenty-five ten thousandths is how much greater than twenty millionths? Write the answer in scientific notation. 2.48×10^{-3}
(57)

3. Find the (a) mean, (b) median, (c) mode, and (d) range of the number of days in the months of a leap year.
(Inv. 4)   (a) 30.5 days   (b) 31 days   (c) 31 days   (d) 2 days

4. The 2-pound box cost $2.72. The 48-ounce box cost $3.60. The smaller box cost how much more per ounce than the larger box?   1¢ more per ounce
(46)

5. Use a ratio box to solve this problem. If 80 pounds of seed cost $96, what would be the cost of 300 pounds of seed? $360
(72)

6. Five eighths of a pound is how many ounces?   10 ounces
(16,60)

7. Use a ratio box to solve this problem. The ratio of
⁽⁶⁵⁾ stalactites to stalagmites in the cavern was 9 to 5. If the
total number of stalactites and stalagmites was 1260, how
many stalagmites were in the cavern? 450 stalagmites

8. Write equations to solve (a) and (b).
⁽⁷⁷⁾

(a) Ten percent of what number is 20? $0.1 \times W_N = 20$; 200

(b) Twenty is what percent of 60? $20 = W_P \times 60$; $33\frac{1}{3}\%$

9. In this figure central angle BDC
⁽⁶²⁾ measures 60° and inscribed angle
BAC measures 30°. Angles ACD and
BCD are complementary.

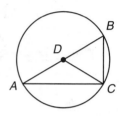

(a) Classify $\triangle ABC$ by angles.
right triangle

(b) Classify $\triangle BCD$ by sides. equilateral triangle

(c) Classify $\triangle ADC$ by sides. isosceles triangle

10. The cost of a 10-minute call to Boise decreased by 20
⁽⁹²⁾ percent. If the cost before the decrease was $3.40, what
was the cost after the decrease? Use a ratio box to solve
the problem. $2.72

11. If an item is on sale for 20% off the regular price, then the
⁽⁹²⁾ sale price is what percent of the regular price? 80%

12. What is the area of the shaded region of this rectangle?
⁽³⁷⁾ 9 units²

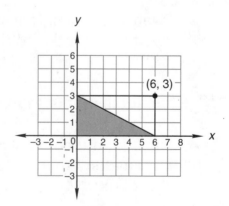

13. Use a ratio box to solve this problem. On a 1:60 scale
⁽⁹⁸⁾ model airplane, the wingspan is 8 inches. The wingspan
of the actual airplane is how many inches? How many
feet is this? 480 inches; 40 feet

14. Complete the table.
(48)

FRACTION	DECIMAL	PERCENT
$1\frac{1}{3}$	(a) $1.\overline{3}$	(b) $133\frac{1}{3}\%$
(c) $\frac{1}{75}$	(d) $0.01\overline{3}$	$1\frac{1}{3}\%$

15. Simplify:
(84,87)

(a) $\left(ax^2\right)(-2ax)\left(-a^2\right)$ $2a^4x^3$ (b) $\frac{1}{2}\pi + \frac{2}{3}\pi - \pi$ $\frac{1}{6}\pi$

16. Multiply and write the product in scientific notation.
(83)
$$\left(8.1 \times 10^{-6}\right)\left(9 \times 10^{10}\right)$$ 7.29×10^5

17. Evaluate: $\sqrt{c^2 - b^2}$ if $c = 15$ and $b = 12$ 9
(20,52)

18. Use the Pythagorean theorem to find c.
(99) 12

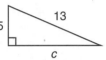

19. Find the volume of this solid. Dimensions are in centimeters. (Use 3.14 for π.) $3140\ cm^3$
(95)

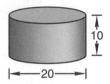

20. Refer to the figure shown. Find the measures of the following angles.
(40)

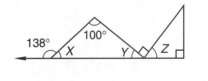

(a) $\angle X$ 42°   (b) $\angle Y$ 38°   (c) $\angle Z$ 52°

21. These triangles are similar. Dimensions are in inches.
(97,98)

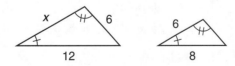

(a) Find x. 9 inches

(b) What is the scale factor from the smaller triangle to the larger triangle? 1.5

(c) The area of the larger triangle is how many times the area of the smaller triangle? (*Hint*: Use the scale factor found in part (b).) 2.25 times

22. Estimate: $\dfrac{(41{,}392)(395)}{81}$ 200,000
₍₂₉₎

Solve:

23. $4n + 1.64 = 2$ 0.09
₍₉₃₎

24. $3\frac{1}{3}x - 1 = 49$ 15
₍₉₃₎

25. $\dfrac{17}{25} = \dfrac{m}{75}$ 51
₍₉₈₎

Simplify:

26. $3^3 + 4^2 - \sqrt{225}$ 28
_(20,52)

27. $\left(1\frac{1}{2}\right)^2 + 6.25 + 2\frac{1}{2}$ 11
_(26,43)

28. $\left(3\frac{1}{3}\right)(0.75)(40)$ 100
₍₄₃₎

29. $\dfrac{-12 - (6)(-3)}{(-12) - (-6) + (3)}$ -2
_(85,91)

30. Using the distributive property, $2(x - 4)$ equals $2x - 8$.
₍₉₆₎ Use the distributive property to multiply $3(x - 2)$. $3x - 6$

LESSON
100

Estimating Square Roots •
Irrational Numbers

Mental Math:
a. 6
b. 2.5×10^{-9}
c. 24
d. $-4°F$
e. 75
f. $16
g. 3
Problem Solving:
  15 handshakes

Facts Practice: Two-Step Equations (Test T in Test Masters)

Mental Math:

  a. $(-1.5) - (-7.5)$ **b.** $\left(5 \times 10^{-5}\right)\left(5 \times 10^{-5}\right)$

  c. $100 = 5w - 20$ **d.** Convert $-20°C$ to degrees Fahrenheit.

  e. $20 \times 3\frac{3}{4}$ **f.** $33\frac{1}{3}\%$ less than $24

  g. 25% of 44, × 3, − 1, ÷ 4, × 7, − 1, ÷ 5, × 9, + 1, $\sqrt{\ }$, − 1, $\sqrt{\ }$

Problem Solving:

If two people shake hands there is one handshake. If three people shake hands there are three handshakes. From this table can you predict the number of handshakes with 6 people? Draw a diagram or act it out to confirm your prediction.

Number in group	2	3	4	5	6
Number of handshakes	1	3	6	10	?

Estimating square roots

These counting numbers are perfect squares.

$$1, 4, 9, 16, 25, 36, 49, 64, \ldots$$

Recall that the square root of a perfect square is an integer.

$$\sqrt{25} = 5 \qquad \sqrt{36} = 6$$

The square root of a number that is between two perfect squares is not an integer but can be estimated.

$$\sqrt{29} = ?$$

Since 29 is between the perfect squares 25 and 36, we may conclude that $\sqrt{29}$ is between $\sqrt{25}$ and $\sqrt{36}$.

$$\sqrt{25} = 5 \qquad \sqrt{29} = ? \qquad \sqrt{36} = 6$$

We see that $\sqrt{29}$ is between 5 and 6. On a number line we find that $\sqrt{29}$ is between 5 and 6 but not exactly halfway between.

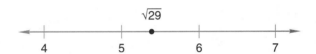

Example 1 Between which two consecutive whole numbers is $\sqrt{200}$?

Solution We remember that $\sqrt{100}$ is 10, so $\sqrt{200}$ is more than 10. We might guess that $\sqrt{200}$ is 20. We check our guess.

$$20 \times 20 = 400 \qquad \text{too large}$$

Our guess is much too large. Next we guess 15.

$$15 \times 15 = 225 \qquad \text{too large}$$

Since 15 is still too large we try 14.

$$14 \times 14 = 196 \qquad \text{too small}$$

We see that 14 is less than $\sqrt{200}$ and 15 is more than $\sqrt{200}$. So $\sqrt{200}$ is between the consecutive whole numbers **14** and **15.**

Irrational numbers

At the beginning of this lesson we found that $\sqrt{29}$ is between 5 and 6. We can refine our estimate by finding a decimal (or fraction) that is closer to $\sqrt{29}$. We try 5.4.

$$5.4 \times 5.4 = 29.16 \qquad \text{too large}$$

Since 5.4 is too large we try 5.3.

$$5.3 \times 5.3 = 28.09 \qquad \text{too small}$$

We see that $\sqrt{29}$ is between 5.3 and 5.4. We may continue refining our estimate by finding numbers closer to $\sqrt{29}$. However, no matter how many numbers we try, we will not find a decimal (or fraction) that equals $\sqrt{29}$.

If we use a calculator we can quickly find a number close to $\sqrt{29}$. If we enter these key strokes

(Depending on the type of calculator.)

the number displayed on an 8-digit calculator is

$$5.3851648$$

This is close to $\sqrt{29}$ but does not equal $\sqrt{29}$, as we see in the first step of checking the answer.

$$
\begin{array}{r}
5.3851648 \\
\times\ 5.3851648 \\
\hline
4
\end{array}
$$

The product of the two factors has as many decimal places as are in both factors combined.

The answer to this multiplication has 14 decimal places (Why?), but we see immediately that the product is not 29.00000000000000 because the digit in the 14th decimal place is 4.

Actually $\sqrt{29}$ is a number that cannot be exactly expressed as a decimal or fraction and therefore is *not a rational* number. Rather $\sqrt{29}$ is an **irrational number**—a number that cannot be expressed as a ratio of two integers. Nevertheless, $\sqrt{29}$ is a number that can express lengths.

For instance, if the legs of this right triangle are exactly 2 cm and 5 cm, then using the Pythagorean theorem we find that the length of the hypotenuse is $\sqrt{29}$ cm.

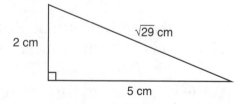

If we measure the hypotenuse with a centimeter ruler, we find that the length is about 5.4 cm, which is an approximation of $\sqrt{29}$ cm.

Other examples of irrational numbers include π (the circumference of a circle with a diameter of 1), $\sqrt{2}$ (the length of the diagonal of a square with sides of 1), and the square roots of counting numbers that are not perfect squares. The irrational numbers, together with the rational numbers, make up the set of **real numbers.**

Real Numbers

Rational Numbers	Irrational Numbers

All of the numbers represented by points on the number line are real numbers and are either rational or irrational.

Example 2 Sketch a number line and show the approximate location of the points representing the following real numbers. Then describe each number as rational or irrational.

$$\pi \qquad \sqrt{2} \qquad 2.\overline{3} \qquad -\frac{1}{2}$$

Solution We sketch a number line marking the location of the integers from −1 through 4. We position π (≈ 3.14) between 3 and 4 but closer to 3. Since $\sqrt{2}$ is between $\sqrt{1}$ (= 1) and $\sqrt{4}$ (= 2), we position $\sqrt{2}$ between 1 and 2 but closer to 1. The repeating decimal $2.\overline{3}$ ($= 2\frac{1}{3}$) is closer to 2 than to 3. The negative fraction $-\frac{1}{2}$ is halfway between 0 and −1.

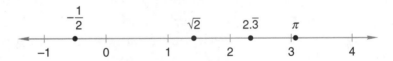

Repeating decimal numbers are rational so both $-\frac{1}{2}$ and $2.\overline{3}$ **are rational, while $\sqrt{2}$ and π are irrational.**

Practice Each square root below is between which two consecutive whole numbers?

   a. $\sqrt{7}$ 2 and 3   **b.** $\sqrt{70}$ 8 and 9   **c.** $\sqrt{700}$ 26 and 27

   d. Find x.   **e.** Find y.

   f. Sketch a number line and show the approximate location of the points representing these real numbers. Which of them are irrational? 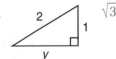 ; $\sqrt{3}, \pi$

Problem set 100

1. ⁽²⁸⁾ Gabriel paid $20 for $2\frac{1}{2}$ pounds of cheese that cost $2.60 per pound and 2 boxes of crackers that cost $1.49 each. How much money should he get back? $10.52

2. ^(21,94) The face of this spinner is divided into fifths.

(a) What is the probability that the spinner will not stop on a prime number on one spin? $\frac{2}{5}$

(b) What is the probability that the spinner will stop on a prime number twice in a row? $\frac{9}{25}$

3. ^(28,86) What is the average of the first 10 counting numbers? 5.5

4. ⁽⁵³⁾ At an average speed of 50 miles per hour, how long would it take to complete a 375-mile trip? $7\frac{1}{2}$ hours

5. ⁽⁷²⁾ Use a ratio box to solve this problem. The Johnsons traveled 300 kilometers in 4 hours. At that rate, how long will it take them to travel 500 kilometers? Write the answer in hours and minutes. 6 hours and 40 minutes

6. ^(60,74) Three fourths of Bill's favorite number is 36. What number is one half of Bill's favorite number? 24

7. ⁽⁶⁵⁾ Use a ratio box to solve this problem. The ratio of winners to losers in the contest was 1 to 15. If there were 800 contestants, how many winners were there? 50 winners

8. ⁽⁷⁷⁾ Write equations to solve questions (a) and (b).

(a) Three hundred is 6 percent of what number?
$300 = 0.06 \times W_N$; 5000

(b) Twenty is what percent of 10? $20 = W_P \times 10$; 200%

9. ⁽⁴⁶⁾ What is the total price of a $40 item including 6.5% tax? $42.60

10. ⁽⁹⁶⁾ Using the distributive property to multiply, $3(x + 3)$ equals $3x + 9$. Use the distributive property to multiply $x(x + 3)$. $x^2 + 3x$

11.

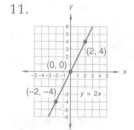

Another point from the 3rd quadrant could be $(-1, -2)$ or $(-3, -6)$.

11. ^(Inv. 9) The ordered pairs $(0, 0)$, $(-2, -4)$, and $(2, 4)$ designate points that lie on the graph of the equation $y = 2x$. Graph the equation on a coordinate plane and name another (x, y) pair from the 3rd quadrant that satisfies the equation.

12. Use a ratio box to solve this problem. The population of
(92) the colony decreased by 30 percent after the first winter.
If the population after the first winter was 350, what was
the population before the first winter? 500

13. Nathan used this graph to mold a scale model of a car
(Inv. 9,98) from clay. The car is 4 feet high, and he used the graph to
see that the model should be 2 inches high.

(a) If the length of the car's bumper is 5 feet, use the
graph to find the proper length of the model's
bumper. $2\frac{1}{2}$ inches

(b) What is the scale factor from the car to the model?
(Write the scale factor as a fraction.) $\frac{1}{24}$

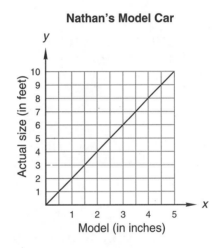

Nathan's Model Car

14. The edge of one cube measures 2 cm. The edge of a larger
(98) cube measures 6 cm.

(a) What is the scale factor from the smaller cube to the
larger cube? 3

(b) The area of each face of the larger cube is how many
times the area of a face of the smaller cube? 9 times

(c) The volume of the larger cube is how many times the
volume of the smaller cube? 27 times

15. Compare: $xy \bigcirc \dfrac{x}{y}$ if x is positive and y is negative
(79)
insufficient information

16. Complete the table.
(48)

Fraction	Decimal	Percent
(a) $\frac{18}{25}$	(b) 0.72	72%

17. Multiply and write the product in scientific notation.
(83)

$$\left(4.5 \times 10^6\right)\left(6 \times 10^3\right) \quad 2.7 \times 10^{10}$$

18. Each square root is between which two consecutive
(100) whole numbers?

(a) $\sqrt{40}$ 6 and 7

(b) $\sqrt{20}$ 4 and 5

19. Find (a) the circumference and (b) the area of a circle that
(66,82) has a radius of 7 inches. $\left(\text{Use } \frac{22}{7} \text{ for } \pi.\right)$
(a) 44 in. (b) 154 in.²

20. Use the Pythagorean theorem to find a.
(99) Dimensions are in centimeters. 8 cm

Find the volume of each solid. Dimensions are in centimeters.
(Use 3.14 for π.)

21.
(95)

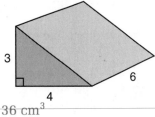

36 cm³

22.
(95)

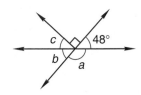

125.6 cm³

10

4

23. In this figure, find the measures of
(40) angles a, b, and c. m$\angle a$ = 132°;
m$\angle b$ = 48°; m$\angle c$ = 42°

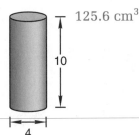

Solve:

24. $-4\frac{1}{2}x + 7 = 70$ -14
(93)

25. $\dfrac{15}{w} = \dfrac{45}{3.3}$ 1.1
(98)

Simplify:

26. $\sqrt{6^2 + 8^2}$ 10
(52)

27. $3\frac{1}{3}\left(7.2 \div \frac{3}{5}\right)$ 40
(43)

28. $8\frac{5}{6} - 2.5 - 1\frac{1}{3}$ 5
(43)

29. $\dfrac{|-18| - (2)(-3)}{(-3) + (-2) - (-4)}$ -24
(85)

30. Sketch a number line and show the approximate location
(100) of $\sqrt{5}$, -0.5, and 1.5.

INVESTIGATION 10

Probability, Chance, and Odds

Probability, chance, and odds are different ways of expressing the likelihood that an event will occur. Recall that probability is the ratio of the number of ways a particular event can happen to the total number of equally likely possible outcomes.

$$\text{Probability} = \frac{\text{number of favorable outcomes}}{\text{number of possible outcomes}}$$

Thus, the probability that this spinner will end up in region A is $\frac{1}{4}$.

Probability may be expressed in decimal form. Since the fraction $\frac{1}{4}$ is equivalent to the decimal 0.25, the probability that the spinner will stop in region A may be expressed as 0.25. Recall that probabilities range from 0 (certain not to occur) to 1 (certain to occur.) It is often easier to compare probabilities when they are expressed as decimals than when they are expressed as fractions.

Example 1 Which is more likely: rolling a 7 with one roll of a pair of dice, or drawing a "face card" with one draw from a normal deck of cards?

Solution The probability of rolling a 7 with a pair of dice is $\frac{6}{36}$, which reduces to $\frac{1}{6}$. The probability of drawing a "face card" is $\frac{12}{52}$, which reduces to $\frac{3}{13}$. We will convert $\frac{1}{6}$ and $\frac{3}{13}$ to decimal form (rounded to two places) to make the comparison.

$$\text{Probability of rolling a } 7 = \frac{1}{6} \quad \text{or about } 0.17$$

$$\text{Probability of drawing a face card} = \frac{3}{13} \quad \text{or about } 0.23$$

The greater the probability number, the greater the likelihood, so **drawing a face card is more likely than rolling a 7.**

1. Express the probability that a flipped coin will land heads up as a decimal. 0.5

2. The probability of rolling a 12 with one roll of a pair of dice is $\frac{1}{36}$. Express this probability as a decimal rounded to two decimal places. 0.03

3. Jim figures that the probability of drawing an ace from a normal deck of cards is $\frac{1}{13}$ or 0.08. Which number is more precise and why? The ratio $\frac{1}{13}$ is more precise than 0.08 because the decimal form is rounded.

Besides expressing probability as a fraction or as a decimal, we may also express probability as a percent. We often use the word **chance** when expressing a probability in percent form, such as, the *chance* of rain is 20%. Referring to the spinner at the beginning of this lesson, we could say that the spinner has a 25% chance of stopping on A, and a 75% chance of not stopping on A. Chance ranges from 0%, describing an event that cannot occur, to 100% for an event that is certain to occur.

4. The weather forecast stated that the chance of rain was 40%. What is the chance that it will not rain? 60%

5. What is the chance that a flipped coin will land heads up? 50%

6. The probability of selecting a "heart" drawing one card from a normal deck of cards is 0.25. What is the chance that a card drawn from a normal deck of cards will not be a heart? 75%

Probability and chance describe the likelihood that a given event will or will not occur. Another way to describe the likelihood of an event is with **odds.** While probability is the ratio of the number of favorable outcomes to the number of possible outcomes, odds means the *ratio of the number of favorable outcomes to the number of unfavorable outcomes.*

Odds = favorable to unfavorable

Using the spinner example, one outcome is A, and three outcomes are not A. Thus, the odds of the spinner ending up in region A are

1 to 3

or

1:3

Note that odds are usually expressed by using the word "to," or with a colon, and not by using a division bar. However, odds are reduced as are other ratios.

Example 2   A 20-percent chance of rain was forecast.

(a) What is the probability that it will rain?

(b) What are the odds that it will rain?

Solution   (a) To express chance as probability, we simply write the percent as a fraction and reduce.

$$20\% = \frac{20}{100} = \frac{1}{5}$$

The probability that it will rain is $\frac{1}{5}$.

(b) Since the probability of rain is $\frac{1}{5}$, the probability that it will not rain is $\frac{4}{5}$. Thus, for every favorable outcome there are 4 unfavorable outcomes. Therefore, the odds that it will rain are **1 to 4.**

Example 3   The odds that a marble drawn from a bag will be red are 3 to 2.

(a) What is the probability that a red marble will be drawn?

(b) What is the chance of drawing a red marble?

Solution   If the odds are 3 to 2, we mean

$$\begin{array}{rl} 3 & \text{favorable outcomes} \\ +\ 2 & \text{unfavorable outcomes} \\ \hline 5 & \text{possible outcomes} \end{array}$$

(a) The probability of drawing a red marble is

$$\frac{\text{favorable}}{\text{possible}} = \frac{3}{5}$$

(b) The chance of drawing a red marble is

$$\frac{3}{5} = 60\%$$

Refer to the following sentence to answer questions 7–9:

> *One marble will be drawn from a bag containing 3 red marbles, 4 white marbles, and 5 blue marbles.*

7. What is the chance of drawing a red marble? 25%

8. What is the probability of drawing a white marble? $\frac{1}{3}$

9. What are the odds of drawing a blue marble? 5 to 7

We can distinguish between **theoretical probability** and **statistical probability.** Theoretical probability can be calculated when the number of favorable outcomes and the number of possible outcomes can be counted without testing. Games of chance are based upon theoretical probability involving actions with cards, dice, spinners, and similar objects with countable outcomes.

Statistical probability is used to determine the likelihood of an event based upon a *record of past experience.* For example, a baseball manager may select a pinch hitter by comparing the batting average of several players against right-handed pitchers. Suppose a baseball player has had 125 hits in 375 at-bats against right-handed pitchers. The manager can calculate the probability that the player will get a hit by dividing the player's previous number of hits by the previous number of at-bats.

$$\text{Probability of a hit} = \frac{125 \text{ hits}}{375 \text{ at-bats}} = \frac{1}{3} \approx 0.333$$

Using a statistical probability we assume that the number of times an event happens out of the number of times the event could have happened is the probability of the event. Statistical probability is used by the insurance industry, which assesses risk and calculates insurance premiums on the basis of statistical records.

10. During the last three basketball seasons Darcy has made 64 free throws and has missed 32 free throws. What is the statistical probability that Darcy will make her next free throw? $\frac{2}{3}$

11. $\frac{3}{200}$ or 0.015

11. During clinical trials of the new medication, 15 of the 1000 participants developed unfavorable side effects. If Roger is treated with the new medication, what is the statistical probability that he will develop unfavorable side effects?

12. The insurance rates (premiums) for younger drivers are much higher than the rates for older drivers.

12. If unmarried drivers under the age of 25 are far more likely to be involved in an auto accident than drivers over the age of 25, then what is probably true about the insurance rates for younger drivers versus older drivers?

Knowing the probability of an event helps us *predict* the outcome of repeated activity. For instance, knowing that the theoretical probability of rolling a 7 with one roll of a pair of dice is $\frac{1}{6}$, we may predict that over a large number of rolls, about $\frac{1}{6}$ of the rolls would result in a sum of 7. If we graph the results of an activity subject to the laws of probability, patterns may emerge that help us visualize the effects of these laws.

Activity: Experimental Probability

Materials needed by each group of 2 to 4 students:

- "Activity Master 5" from the *Math 87 Test Masters*
- One or more pairs of dice

Section A of "Activity Master 5" displays the 36 equally likely outcomes of rolling a pair of dice. Section B is the outline of a bar graph. On the graph draw bars to indicate the theoretical outcome of rolling a pair of dice 36 times.

After completing Section B take turns rolling dice and recording the results for 36 rolls of a pair of dice. Record and graph the results of the tosses in Section C.

If the results of the experiment differ from the theoretical outcome, discuss why you think the results differ and write your reasons in Section D.

Extension Create two classroom bar graphs to represent all of the rolls of all of the groups. First create a Theoretical Outcomes graph and then create an Actual Results graph by combining the actual results from all of the groups. Does increasing the number of rolls (by counting all the rolls in the class) produce actual results closer to theoretical outcomes than were usually attained with just 36 rolls?

LESSON
101

Translating Expressions into Equations

Facts Practice: Percent-Decimal-Fraction Equivalents
(Test U in Test Masters)

Mental Math:

a. $(-2)(-2)(-2)(-2)$ **b.** $\left(5 \times 10^{-5}\right)\left(6 \times 10^{-6}\right)$

c. $\frac{0.2}{w} = \frac{0.4}{0.12}$ **d.** Convert −25°C to degrees Fahrenheit.

e. $\frac{3}{4}$ of $80   **f.** 25% less than $80

g. Estimate a 15% tip on $29.78.

Problem Solving:

Here is a front, top, and side view of an object. Sketch a three-dimensional view of the object from the perspective of the upper right front.

Front   Top   Right Side

An essential skill of mathematics is the ability to translate language, situations, and relationships into mathematical form. Since the earliest lessons of this book we have practiced translating stories into equations which we then solved. In this lesson we will practice translating other common patterns of language into algebraic form. We will also use our knowledge of geometric relationships to write equations to solve geometry problems.

Consider the following examples of mathematical phrases and how they are translated into algebraic form.

Examples of Translations

Phrase	Translation
twice a number	$2n$
five more than a number	$x + 5$
three less than a number	$a - 3$
half of a number	$\frac{1}{2}h$ or $\frac{h}{2}$
the product of a number and seven	$7b$
seventeen is five more than twice a number	$17 = 2n + 5$

The last translation in the examples above resulted in an equation that can be solved to find the unstated number. We will solve a similar equation in the following example.

Example 1   If five less than twice a number is 17, what is the number?

Solution   We will use the letter x to represent the unknown as we translate the sentence into an equation.

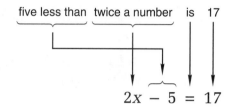

$$2x - 5 = 17$$

Now we solve the equation.

$2x - 5 = 17$	equation
$2x - 5 + 5 = 17 + 5$	added 5 to both sides
$2x = 22$	simplified
$\dfrac{2x}{2} = \dfrac{22}{2}$	divided both sides by 2
$x = 11$	simplified

We find that the number described is **11.**

Five less than twice 11 is 17.

We may also translate geometric relationships into algebraic expressions.

Example 2   The angles marked x and $2x$ in this figure are supplementary. What is the measure of the larger angle?

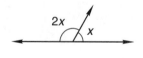

Solution   The sum of the angle measures is 180°. We write this relationship as an equation.

$$2x + x = 180°$$

Since $2x + x = 3x$, we may simplify then solve the equation.

$2x + x = 180°$	equation
$3x = 180°$	simplified
$\dfrac{3x}{3} = \dfrac{180°}{3}$	divided both sides by 3
$x = 60°$	simplified

The solution of the equation is 60°, but 60° is not the answer to the question. We were asked to find the measure of the larger angle which is designated in the diagram as $2x$. Since x is 60°, we find $2x$ by multiplying 2(60°). We find that the larger angle is **120°.**

Practice* Write and solve an equation for each of these problems.

a. Six more than the product of a number and three is 30. What is the number? $3x + 6 = 30$; 8

b. Ten less than half of what number is 30? $\frac{1}{2}x - 10 = 30$; 80

c. What is the measure of the smallest angle in this figure? $3x + 2x = 90°$; 36°

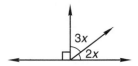

d. Find the measure of each angle of this triangle. $x + 2x + 3x = 180°$; $x = 30°$; $2x = 60°$; $3x = 90°$

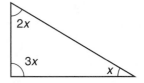

Problem set **1.** The following marks are Darren's 100-meter dash times, in seconds, during track season. Find the (a) median, (b) mode, and (c) range of these times.
101 (Inv. 4)
(a) 11.9   (b) 11.8 and 11.9   (c) 0.7

12.3, 11.8, 11.9, 11.7, 12.0, 11.9, 12.1, 11.6, 11.8

2. How much money does Jackson earn working for 3 hours and 45 minutes at $6 per hour? $22.50
(53)

Use ratio boxes to solve problems 3–6.

3. The recipe called for 3 cups of flour and 2 eggs to make 6 servings. If 15 cups of flour were used to make more servings, how many eggs should be used? 10 eggs
(72)

4. Lester can type 48 words per minute. At that rate, how many words can he type in 90 seconds? 72 words
(72)

5. Ten students scored 100 percent. This was 40 percent of the class. How many students were in the class?
(81)
25 students

6. The dress was on sale for 40 percent off the regular price. If the regular price was $24, what was the sale price?
(92)
$14.40

7. Use the distributive property to clear parentheses. Then simplify by adding like terms. $2x - 12$
(96)

$$3(x - 4) - x$$

8. 24 pints   **8.** Use two unit multipliers to convert 3 gallons to pints.
(88)

9.

24 games

$\frac{5}{6}$ won $\left\{ \begin{array}{c} \text{4 games} \\ \text{4 games} \\ \text{4 games} \\ \text{4 games} \\ \text{4 games} \end{array} \right.$

$\frac{1}{6}$ lost $\left\{ \begin{array}{c} \text{4 games} \end{array} \right.$

9. Draw a diagram of this statement. Then answer the
(36,71) questions that follow.

*The Trotters won $\frac{5}{6}$ of their games. They won
20 games and lost the rest.*

(a) How many games did they play? 24 games

(b) What was the Trotters' ratio of games won to games
lost? $\frac{5}{1}$

10. Between which two consecutive whole numbers is $\sqrt{200}$?
(100) 14 and 15

11. If w is 0.5 and m is the reciprocal of w, compare: $w \enspace \textcircled{<} \enspace m$
(79)

12. The figure at right is a hexagon with
(75) dimensions given in centimeters.
Corners that look square are square.
Find the area of the hexagon. 84 cm²

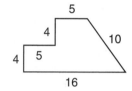

13. Write an equation to solve this problem. Three less than
(101) the product of six and what number is 45? $6n - 3 = 45$; 8

14. Multiply and write the product in scientific notation.
(83)

$$\left(8 \times 10^8\right)\left(4 \times 10^{-2}\right) \quad 3.2 \times 10^7$$

15. Complete the table.
(48)

FRACTION	DECIMAL	PERCENT
(a) $\frac{1}{50}$	0.02	(b) 2%
(c) $\frac{1}{500}$	(d) 0.002	0.2%

16.

<image: graph of y = 2x + 1>

16. Copy and complete this table of
(85,Inv. 9) ordered pairs for the function
$y = 2x + 1$. Then graph the function
on a coordinate plane.

$y = 2x + 1$

x	y
-1	-1
0	1
1	3
2	5

17. (a) 64 in.³
(b) 96 in.²

17. Sketch this cube. Then find its
(67,70) (a) volume and (b) surface area.
Dimensions are in inches.

18. (a) Find the circumference of this
(66,82)   circle. 18π cm

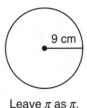
9 cm

(b) Find the area of this circle.
81π cm^2

Leave π as π.

19. What are the odds that a tossed coin will land heads up?
(Inv. 10)   1 to 1

20. The two acute angles in this figure
(101)   are complementary. What are the
measures of the two angles?
$x = 30°$; $2x = 60°$

2x
x

21. Divide 1.23 by 9 and write the quotient
(44)

(a) with a bar over the repetend. $0.13\overline{6}$

(b) rounded to three decimal places. 0.137

22. If BC is 9 cm and AC is 12 cm, then
(99)   what is AB? 15 cm

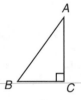
A

B   C

23. If the scale factor from $\triangle ABC$ in problem 22 to $\triangle DEF$ is 2,
(98)   then

(a) what is the perimeter of $\triangle DEF$? 72 cm

(b) what is the area of $\triangle DEF$? 216 cm^2

24. In a bag were 6 red marbles and 4 blue marbles. If Kurt
(94)   pulls a marble out of the bag with his left hand and then
pulls a marble out with his right hand, what is the
probability that the marble in each hand will be blue?
$\frac{4}{10} \cdot \frac{3}{9} = \frac{2}{15}$

Solve:

25. $3\frac{1}{7}d = 88$ 28
(90)

26. Solve and graph: $3x + 20 \geq 14$
(93)

$x \geq -2$

−3 −2 −1 0 1 2 3

Simplify:

27. $5^2 + \left(3^3 - \sqrt{81}\right)$ 43
(52)

28. $3x + 2(x - 1)$ 5x − 2
(96)

29. $\left(4\frac{4}{9}\right)(2.7)\left(1\frac{1}{3}\right)$ 16
(43)

30. $(-2)(-3) - (-4)(-5)$ −14
(85)

LESSON 102

Transversals • Simplifying Equations

Facts Practice: Two-Step Equations (Test T in Test Masters)

Mental Math:

a. $(-0.25) + (-0.75)$
b. $\left(3 \times 10^{10}\right)\left(2 \times 10^{-2}\right)$
c. $3x + 2\frac{1}{2} = 10$
d. Convert 500 mL to L.
e. 150% of $40
f. 150% more than $40
g. Start with a score, − 5, × 2, + 2, ÷ 4, + 1, $\sqrt{\ }$, × 7, − 1, ÷ 10.

Problem Solving:

An octagon can be divided into six triangles by five diagonals drawn from a single vertex. Into how many triangles can a 22-gon be divided by diagonals drawn from a single vertex? What is the sum of the measures of the interior angles of a 22-gon?

Transversals A **transversal** is a line that intersects one or more other lines in a plane. In this lesson we will pay particular attention to the angles that are formed when a transversal intersects a pair of parallel lines. Notice the eight angles that are formed.

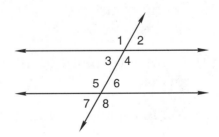

In this figure there are four acute angles numbered 2, 3, 6, and 7, and there are four obtuse angles numbered 1, 4, 5, and 8. All of the acute angles have the same measure, and all of the obtuse angles have the same measure.

Example 1 Transversal *t* intersects parallel lines *l* and *m* so that the measure of ∠*a* is 105°. Find the measure of angles *b*–*h*.

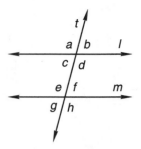

Solution All the obtuse angles have the same measure so ∠***d*, ∠*e*,** and **∠*h* each measure 105°.** Each of the acute angles is a supplement of an obtuse angle, so each acute angle measures

$$180° - 105° = 75°$$

Thus **∠*b*, ∠*c*, ∠*f*,** and **∠*g* each measure 75°.**

When transversals intersect pairs of lines, special pairs of angles are formed. In Example 1 ∠*a* and ∠*e* are **corresponding angles** because the position of ∠*e* (to the left of the transversal and above line *m*) corresponds to the position of ∠*a* (to the left of the transversal and above line *l*). Name three more pairs of corresponding angles in Example 1.

∠*b* and ∠*f*, ∠*c* and ∠*g*, ∠*d* and ∠*h*

Angle *a* and ∠*h* in Example 1 also form a special pair of angles. They are on alternate sides of the transversal and are outside of (not between) the parallel lines. So ∠*a* and ∠*h* are called **alternate exterior angles.** Name another pair of alternate exterior angles in Example 1. ∠*b* and ∠*g*

Angles *d* and *e* in Example 1 are **alternate interior angles** because they are on alternate sides of the transversal and in the interior of (between) the parallel lines. Name another pair of alternate interior angles in Example 1. ∠*c* and ∠*f*

Example 2 Transversal *r* intersects parallel lines *p* and *q* forming angles 1–8.

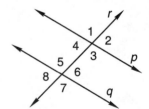

(a) Name four pairs of corresponding angles.

(b) Name two pairs of alternate exterior angles.

(c) Name two pairs of alternate interior angles.

Solution (a) **∠1 and ∠5, ∠2 and ∠6, ∠3 and ∠7, ∠4 and ∠8**

(b) **∠1 and ∠7, ∠2 and ∠8**

(c) **∠4 and ∠6, ∠3 and ∠5**

Simplifying equations   One step to solving some equations is to collect like terms. In this equation we can collect variable terms and constant terms as the first step of the solution.

$$\underbrace{3x - x}_{2x} \underbrace{- 5 + 8}_{+ 3} = 17$$
$$2x \qquad + 3 \quad = 17$$

Example 3   Simplify then solve this equation.

$$3x + 5 - x = 17 + x - x$$

Solution   We collect like terms on each side of the equals sign. On the left side $3x$ and $-x$ equal $2x$. On the right side $+x$ and $-x$ equal zero.

$$3x + 5 - x = 17 + x - x \qquad \text{equation}$$
$$2x + 5 = 17 \qquad \text{simplified}$$

Now we solve the simplified equation.

$$2x + 5 = 17 \qquad \text{equation}$$
$$2x + 5 - 5 = 17 - 5 \qquad \text{subtracted 5 from both sides}$$
$$2x = 12 \qquad \text{simplified}$$
$$\frac{2x}{2} = \frac{12}{2} \qquad \text{divided both sides by 2}$$
$$x = \mathbf{6} \qquad \text{simplified}$$

Example 4   Simplify this equation by removing the variable term from one side of the equation. Then solve the equation.

$$5x - 17 = 2x - 5$$

Solution   We see an x term on both sides of the equals sign. We may remove the x term from either side. We choose to remove the variable term from the right side. We do this by subtracting $2x$ from both sides of the equation.

$$5x - 17 = 2x - 5 \qquad \text{equation}$$
$$5x - 17 - 2x = 2x - 5 - 2x \qquad \text{2x from both sides}$$
$$3x - 17 = -5 \qquad \text{simplified}$$

Now we solve the simplified equation.

$$3x - 17 = -5 \qquad \text{equation}$$
$$3x - 17 + 17 = -5 + 17 \qquad \text{added 17 to both sides}$$
$$3x = 12 \qquad \text{simplified}$$
$$\frac{3x}{3} = \frac{12}{3} \qquad \text{divided both sides by 3}$$
$$x = \mathbf{4} \qquad \text{simplified}$$

Example 5 Solve: $3x + 2(x - 4) = 32$

Solution First we apply the distributive property to clear parentheses.

$$3x + 2(x - 4) = 32 \qquad \text{equation}$$
$$3x + 2x - 8 = 32 \qquad \text{distributive property}$$
$$5x - 8 = 32 \qquad \text{added } 3x \text{ and } 2x$$
$$5x = 40 \qquad \text{added 8 to both sides}$$
$$x = \mathbf{8} \qquad \text{divided both sides by 5}$$

Practice* Refer to this figure to answer problems a, b, c, and d.

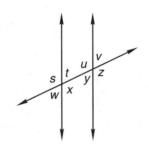

a. Name four pairs of corresponding angles.
   $\angle s$ and $\angle u$, $\angle t$ and $\angle v$, $\angle w$ and $\angle y$, $\angle x$ and $\angle z$
b. Name two pairs of alternate interior angles.
   $\angle t$ and $\angle y$, $\angle x$ and $\angle u$
c. Name two pairs of alternate exterior angles.
   $\angle s$ and $\angle z$, $\angle w$ and $\angle v$
d. If the measure of $\angle w$ is 80°, what is the measure of each of the other angles? $m\angle t, v, y = 80°$; $m\angle s, u, x, z = 100°$

Simplify and solve the following equations:

e. $3w - 10 + w = 90$ 25

f. $x + x + 10 + 2x - 10 = 180$ 45

g. $3y + 5 = y - 25$ –15   h. $4n - 5 = 2n + 3$ 4

i. $3x - 2(x - 4) = 32$ 24   j. $3x = 2(x - 4)$ –8

Problem set   **1.** Boardwalk was 5 spaces away. Alex nervously tossed the
102 [(Inv. 10)]   pair of dice.

(a) What is the probability that the dots on the rolled dice will total 5? $\frac{1}{9}$

(b) What are the odds of Alex avoiding Boardwalk on this turn? 8 to 1

2. Write an equation to solve this problem. Twelve less than
(101) the product of what number and three is 36?
$3x - 12 = 36$; 16

3. The figure shows three sides of a
(89) regular decagon.

(a) What is the measure of each exterior angle? 36°

(b) What is the measure of each interior angle? 144°

Use ratio boxes to solve problems 4–7.

4. The ratio of youths to adults at the convocation was 3 to 7.
(65) If 4500 attended the convocation, how many adults were
present? 3150 adults

5. Every time the knight went over 2, he went up 1. If the
(72) knight went over 8, how far did he go up? 4

6. Eighty percent of those who were invited came to the
(81) party. If 40 people were invited to the party, how many
did not come? 8 people

7. The dress was on sale for 60 percent of the regular price.
(81) If the sale price was $24, what was the regular price? $40

8. Write an equation to solve this problem. Three more than
(101) twice a number is −13. What is the number?
$2n + 3 = -13$; −8

9. The obtuse and acute angles in this
(101) figure are supplementary. What is the
measure of each angle?
$x + 5 = 55°$; $3x - 25 = 125°$

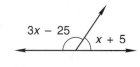

10. Draw a diagram of this statement. Then answer the
(71) questions that follow.

> *Exit polls showed that 7 out of 10 voters cast
> their ballots for the incumbent. The incumbent
> received 1400 votes.*

(a) How many voters cast their ballots? 2000 voters

(b) What percent of the voters did not vote for the
incumbent? 30%

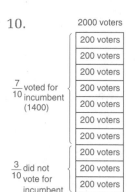

11. Evaluate: $x + xy - xy$ if $x = 3$ and $y = -2$ 3
(91)

12. Compare: $a \, \text{\textcircled{<}} \, a - a$ if $a < 0$
(79)

13. If the perimeter of a square is 1 meter, what is the area of
(32) the square in square centimeters?   625 cm²

14. Find the total price, including tax, of a $12.95 bat, a $7.85
(46) baseball, and a $49.50 glove. The tax rate is 7 percent.
$75.22

15. Multiply and write the product in scientific notation.
(83)

$$\left(3.5 \times 10^5\right)\left(3 \times 10^6\right)$$ 1.05×10^{12}

16. Lines l and m are parallel and are
(102) intersected by transversal q.

(a) Which angle corresponds to $\angle c$?
$\angle g$

(b) Which angle is the alternate
interior angle of $\angle e$? $\angle d$

(c) Which angle is the alternate
exterior angle of $\angle h$? $\angle a$

(d) If $m\angle a$ is 110°, then what is $m\angle f$?   70°

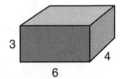

17. (a) What number is 125 percent of 84?   105
(60,92)
(b) What number is 25% more than 84?   105

18. If the chance of rain is 40%, what are the odds that it will
(Inv. 10) not rain?   3 to 2

19. What is the volume of this rectangular
(70) prism? Dimensions are in feet.   72 ft³

20. (a) Find the circumference of this
(66,82)   circle.   44 m

(b) Find the area of this circle.   154 m²

7 m

Use $\frac{22}{7}$ for π.

21.

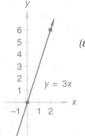

21. Find the missing numbers in this
(85,Inv. 9) table of ordered pairs for the function
$y = 3x$. Then graph the function on a
coordinate plane.

$y = 3x$

x	y
2	6
−1	−3
0	0

Hi David

22. Polygon *ZWXY* is a rectangle. What is the measure of each angle?
(40)

(a) ∠*a* 56°   (b) ∠*b* 34°   (c) ∠*c* 56°

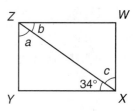

23. On a number line graph $x \geq -2$.
(78)

24. Sketch a number line and show the location of these numbers. Which are rational?
(100)

$\frac{1}{4}$, 0.4 $\sqrt{4}$; All three numbers are rational.

$$0.4, \frac{1}{4}, \sqrt{4}$$

Solve:

25. $3x + x + 1 = 49$ 12
(102)

26. $3y + 2 = y + 32$ 15
(102)

27. $x + 2(x + 3) = 36$ 10
(102)

Simplify:

28. (a) $(3x^2y)(-2x)(xy^2)$
(84,87) $-6x^4y^3$

(b) $-3x + 2y - x - y$
      $-4x + y$

29. $\left(4\frac{1}{2}\right)(0.2)(10^2)$ 90
(43)

30. $\frac{(-4)(+3)}{(-2)} - (-1)$ 7
(85)

**LESSON
103**

Powers of Negative Numbers •
Dividing Terms

Mental Math:
a. 0.5
b. 1.2×10^{-6}
c. 15
d. $-22°F$
e. $200
f. $400
g. 9×10^6
Problem Solving:
  4; 5

Facts Practice: Two-Step Equations (Test T in Test Masters)

Mental Math:

a. $(-2.5) \div (-5)$
b. $(3 \times 10^{-4})(4 \times 10^{-3})$
c. $2y + y = 45$
d. Convert $-30°C$ to degrees Fahrenheit.
e. $33\frac{1}{3}\%$ of $600
f. $33\frac{1}{3}\%$ less than $600
g. The expression $(3 \times 10^3)^2$ means $(3 \times 10^3)(3 \times 10^3)$. Write the product in scientific notation.

Problem Solving:

The expression $\sqrt[3]{8}$ means "the cube root of 8." The cube root of 8 is 2 because $2 \cdot 2 \cdot 2 = 8$. Find $\sqrt[3]{64}$. Find $\sqrt[3]{125}$.

Powers of negative numbers

One way to multiply three or more signed numbers is to multiply the factors in order from left to right, keeping track of the signs with each step, as we show here.

$$
\begin{array}{ll}
(-3)(-4)(+5)(-2)(+3) & \text{problem} \\
(+12)(+5)(-2)(+3) & \text{multiplied } (-3)(-4) \\
(+60)(-2)(+3) & \text{multiplied } (+12)(+5) \\
(-120)(+3) & \text{multiplied } (+60)(-2) \\
-360 & \text{multiplied } (-120)(+3)
\end{array}
$$

Another way to keep track of the signs when multiplying signed numbers is to count the number of negative factors. Notice the pattern in the multiplications below.

$$
\begin{array}{ll}
-1 = -1 & \text{odd} \\
(-1)(-1) = +1 & \text{even} \\
(-1)(-1)(-1) = -1 & \text{odd} \\
(-1)(-1)(-1)(-1) = +1 & \text{even} \\
(-1)(-1)(-1)(-1)(-1) = -1 & \text{odd}
\end{array}
$$

> **When there is an even number of negative factors, the product is positive. When there is an odd number of negative factors, the product is negative.**

Example 1   Find the product: $(+3)(+4)(-5)(-2)(-3)$

Solution   There are three negative factors (an odd number), so the product will be a negative number. We multiply and get

$$(+3)(+4)(-5)(-2)(-3) = \mathbf{-360}$$

We did not consider the signs of the positive factors because positive factors do not affect the sign of the product.

We remember that the exponent of a power indicates how many times the base is used as a factor.

$$(-3)^4 \text{ means } (-3)(-3)(-3)(-3)$$

Example 2   Simplify: (a) $(-2)^4$ (b) $(-2)^5$

Solution   (a) The expression $(-2)^4$ means $(-2)(-2)(-2)(-2)$. Since there is an even number of negative factors, the product is a positive number. Since 2^4 is 16, we find that $(-2)^4$ is **+16.**

(b) The expression $(-2)^5$ means $(-2)(-2)(-2)(-2)(-2)$. This time there is an odd number of negative factors, so the product is a negative number. Since 2^5 equals 32, we find that $(-2)^5$ equals **−32.**

Dividing terms We have multiplied terms by grouping like factors with exponents.

$$(4a^2b)(ab) = 4a^3b^2$$

We divide terms by removing pairs of factors that equal 1.

$$\frac{4a^3b^2}{ab} = \frac{2 \cdot 2 \cdot \overset{1}{\cancel{a}} \cdot a \cdot a \cdot \overset{1}{\cancel{b}} \cdot b}{\underset{1}{\cancel{a}} \cdot \underset{1}{\cancel{b}}}$$

$$= 4a^2b$$

Example 3 Simplify: $\dfrac{12x^3yz^2}{3x^2y}$

Solution We factor the two terms and remove pairs of factors that equal 1. Then we regroup the remaining factors.

$$\frac{12x^3yz^2}{3x^2y} = \frac{2 \cdot 2 \cdot \overset{1}{\cancel{3}} \cdot \overset{1}{\cancel{x}} \cdot \overset{1}{\cancel{x}} \cdot x \cdot \overset{1}{\cancel{y}} \cdot z \cdot z}{\underset{1}{\cancel{3}} \cdot \underset{1}{\cancel{x}} \cdot \underset{1}{\cancel{x}} \cdot \underset{1}{\cancel{y}}}$$

$$= 4xz^2$$

Example 4 Simplify: $\dfrac{10a^3bc^2}{8ab^2c}$

Solution We factor the terms and remove common factors. Then we regroup the remaining factors.

$$\frac{10a^3bc^2}{8ab^2c} = \frac{\overset{1}{\cancel{2}} \cdot 5 \cdot \overset{1}{\cancel{a}} \cdot a \cdot a \cdot \overset{1}{\cancel{b}} \cdot \overset{1}{\cancel{c}} \cdot c}{\underset{1}{\cancel{2}} \cdot 2 \cdot 2 \cdot \underset{1}{\cancel{a}} \cdot \underset{1}{\cancel{b}} \cdot b \cdot \underset{1}{\cancel{c}}}$$

$$= \frac{5a^2c}{4b}$$

Practice Simplify:

    a. $(-5)(-4)(-3)(-2)(-1)$ -120 **b.** $(+5)(-4)(+3)(-2)(+1)$ 120

    c. $(-2)^3$ -8 **d.** $(-3)^4$ 81 **e.** $(-9)^2$ 81 **f.** $(-1)^5$ -1

    g. $\dfrac{6a^2b^3c}{3ab}$ $2ab^2c$ **h.** $\dfrac{8xy^3z^2}{6x^2y}$ $\dfrac{4y^2z^2}{3x}$ **i.** $\dfrac{15mn^2p}{25m^2n^2}$ $\dfrac{3p}{5m}$

Problem set 103

1. The dinner bill totaled $25. Mike left a 15% tip. How
(46) much money did Mike leave for a tip? $3.75

2. The table shows a tally of the scores earned by students
(Inv. 4) on a class test. Find (a) the mode and (b) the median of
the 29 scores in the class. (a) 85 (b) 90

Class Test Scores

Score	Number of Students
100				
95							
90							
85										
80					
70		

3.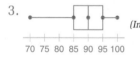

3. Draw a box-and-whisker plot for the data presented in
(Inv. 4) problem 2.

4. The plane completed the flight in $2\frac{1}{2}$ hours. If the flight
(46) covered 1280 kilometers, what was the plane's average
speed in kilometers per hour? 512 kilometers per hour

5. Use a ratio box to solve this problem. Jeremy earned $25
(72) for 4 hours of work. How much would he earn for 7 hours
of work at the same rate? $43.75

6. A mile is about eight fifths kilometers. Eight fifths
(60) kilometers is how many meters? 1600 meters

7. Use a ratio box to solve this problem. If 40 percent of
(54) the lights were on, what was the ratio of lights on to
lights off? $\frac{2}{3}$

8. Use the Pythagorean theorem to find the length of the
(99) longest side of a right triangle whose vertices are (3, 1),
(3, −2), and (−1, −2). 5 units

9. Use a ratio box to solve this problem. Sam saved $25
(92) buying the suit at a sale that offered 20 percent off. What
was the regular price of the suit? $125

10. Darren has made 35 out of 50 free throws. What is the
(Inv. 10) statistical chance that Darren will make his next free
throw? 70%

11. What percent of 25 is 20? 80%
(77)

12. Use a ratio box to solve this problem. The merchant
(92) bought the item for $30 and sold it for 60 percent more.
How much profit did the merchant make on the item? $18

13. (a) The shaded sector is what fraction
(Inv. 8)   of the whole circle? $\frac{1}{3}$

(b) The unshaded sector is what
percent of the circle? $66\frac{2}{3}\%$

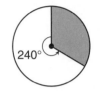

240°

14. (a) Use a ratio box to solve this problem. The $\frac{1}{20}$ scale
(50,98)   model of the rocket stood 54 inches high. What was the
height of the actual rocket? 1080 inches

(b) Find the height of the rocket in part (a) in feet. 90 feet

15. The volume of the rocket in problem 14 is how many
(98) times the volume of the model? 20^3 = 8000

16.

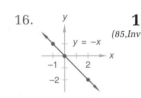

16. Copy this table of ordered pairs for
(85,Inv. 9) the function $y = -x$ and fill in the
blanks. Then graph the function.

$y = -x$

x	y
2	-2
0	0
-1	1

17. Answer this question by writing and solving an equation.
(101) Three less than twice what number is −7? $2x - 3 = -7$; −2

18. Quadrilateral *ABCD* is a rectangle. The measure of ∠*ACB*
(40) is 36°. Find the measure of each of these angles.

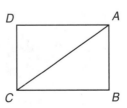

(a) ∠*CAB* 54°   (b) ∠*CAD* 36°   (c) ∠*ACD* 54°

19. These two triangles are similar.
(97,98)

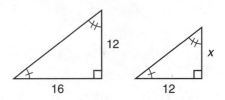

(a) Find x.   9

(b) Find the scale factor from the larger triangle to the smaller triangle.   0.75

20. Estimate the measure of $\angle AOB$. Then use a protractor to
(96)   measure the angle.   50°

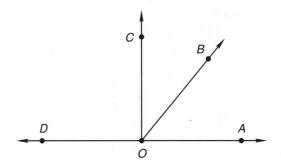

21. Find (a) the circumference and (b) the area of a circle
(66,82)   with a diameter of 2 feet.   (a) 6.28 ft   (b) 3.14 ft^2

22. Which of these numbers is between 12 and 14?   C. $\sqrt{150}$
(100)

   A. $\sqrt{13}$ B. $\sqrt{130}$ C. $\sqrt{150}$

23. Find the volume of this right prism.
(95)   54 units^3

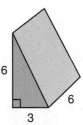

24. Find the volume of this right circular
(95)   cylinder.   84.78 units^3

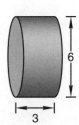

Solve:

25. $3x + x - 5 = 2(x - 2)$ $\frac{1}{2}$
(102)

26. $6\frac{2}{3}f - 5 = 5$ $\frac{3}{2}$
(90,93)

Simplify:

27. $10\frac{1}{2} \cdot 1\frac{3}{7} \div 25$ $\frac{3}{5}$
(26)

28. $12.5 - 8\frac{1}{3} + 1\frac{1}{6}$ $5\frac{1}{3}$
(43)

29. (a) $\dfrac{(-3)(-2)(-1)}{-\left|(-3)(+2)\right|}$ 1
(85,103)

(b) $3^2 - (-3)^2$ 0

30. (a) $\dfrac{6a^3b^2c}{2abc}$ $3a^2b$
(103)

(b) $\dfrac{8x^2yz^3}{12xy^2z}$ $\dfrac{2xz^2}{3y}$

LESSON 104

Semicircles, Arcs, and Sectors

Facts Practice: + − × ÷ Algebraic Terms (Test V in Test Masters)

Mental Math:

a. $(-0.25) - (-0.75)$

b. $\left(5 \times 10^5\right)^2$

c. $80 = 4m - 20$

d. Convert 1 sq. yd to sq. ft.

e. 200% of $25

f. 200% more than $25

g. At 12 mph, how far can Sherry skate in 45 minutes?

Problem Solving:

Five identical blocks marked X and a 60-oz weight were balanced on a scale as shown. Write an equation to represent this balanced scale and find the weight of each block marked X.

A **semicircle** is half of a circle. Thus, the length of a semicircle is half the circumference of a whole circle. The area enclosed by a semicircle and its diameter is half the area of the full circle.

We will practice finding the lengths of semicircles and the areas they enclose by calculating the perimeters and areas of figures that contain semicircles. We will also find the lengths of arcs and areas of sectors that are not semicircles.

Example 1 Find the perimeter of this figure. Dimensions are in meters.

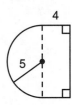

Solution The perimeter of the semicircle is half the perimeter of a circle whose diameter is 10.

$$\text{Perimeter of semicircle} = \frac{\pi d}{2}$$

$$\approx \frac{(3.14)(10 \text{ m})}{2}$$

$$\approx 15.7 \text{ m}$$

Now we can write all the dimensions.

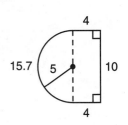

$$\text{Perimeter} \approx 10 \text{ m} + 4 \text{ m} + 15.7 \text{ m} + 4 \text{ m}$$

$$\approx \mathbf{33.7 \text{ m}}$$

Example 2 Find the area of this figure. Dimensions are in meters.

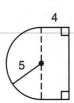

Solution We divide the figure into two parts, and then we find the area of each part.

$$A_1 = \frac{\pi r^2}{2} \qquad\qquad A_2 = l \times w$$

$$\qquad\qquad\qquad\qquad = 4 \text{ m} \times 10 \text{ m}$$

$$\approx \frac{3.14(25 \text{ m}^2)}{2} \qquad\qquad = 40 \text{ m}^2$$

$$\approx 39.25 \text{ m}^2$$

The area of the figure equals $A_1 + A_2$.

$$\text{Total area} = A_1 + A_2$$

$$\approx 39.25 \text{ m}^2 + 40 \text{ m}^2$$

$$\approx \mathbf{79.25 \text{ m}^2}$$

We can calculate the lengths of arcs and the areas of sectors by determining the fraction of a circle represented by the arc or sector.

Example 3 Find the area of the shaded sector of this circle.

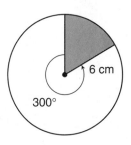

Solution The central angle of the sector is the rest of the circle which is 60°. Since 60° is $\frac{1}{6}$ of a circle $\left(\frac{60}{360} = \frac{1}{6}\right)$, the area of the sector is $\frac{1}{6}$ of the area of the circle.

$$\text{Area of } 60° \text{ sector} = \frac{\pi r^2}{6}$$

$$\approx \frac{3.14(\overset{1}{\cancel{6}} \text{ cm})(6 \text{ cm})}{\underset{1}{\cancel{6}}}$$

$$\approx \textbf{18.84 cm}^2$$

As we discussed in Investigation 2, an arc is part of the circumference of a circle. In the following figure we could refer to arc AB (abbreviated $\overset{\frown}{AB}$):

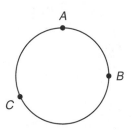

Actually there are two arcs named AB in this figure. Can you find both of them? The arc from A clockwise to B is called a **minor arc** because it is less than a semicircle. The arc from A counterclockwise to B is called a **major arc** because it is greater than a semicircle. Major arcs are sometimes named with three letters. Major arc AB may be named arc ACB.

We can measure the amount of curve in an arc in degrees. The number of degrees in an arc is equal to the measure of the central angle of the arc. If minor $\overset{\frown}{AB}$ in the figure above measures 120°, then the measure of major $\overset{\frown}{AB}$ is 240° because the sum of the measures of the major arc and minor arc is 360°.

Example 4 In this figure, central angle *AOC* measures 70°. How many degrees is the measure of major arc *AC*?

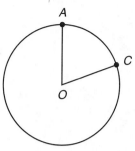

Solution An arc may be described by the measure of its central angle. The arc in the interior of the 70° angle *AOC* is a 70° arc. However, there is a larger arc from point *A* counterclockwise to point *C*. This arc measures 360° minus 70°, which is 290°. The smaller arc *AC* is the minor arc. The larger arc *AC*, which is the rest of the circle, is the major arc. So the measure of major arc *AC* is **290°**.

Example 5 A minor arc with a radius of 2 and centered at the origin is drawn from the positive *x*-axis to the positive *y*-axis. What is the length of the arc?

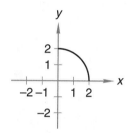

Solution A minor arc is less than 180°. We see that the arc is $\frac{1}{4}$ of a circle, which is 90°. The length of the arc is $\frac{1}{4}$ of the circumference of a circle with a radius of 2 (and a diameter of 4).

$$\text{Length of } 90° \text{ arc} = \frac{\pi d}{4}$$

$$\approx \frac{3.14(\overset{1}{\cancel{4}} \text{ units})}{\underset{1}{\cancel{4}}}$$

$$\approx \textbf{3.14 units}$$

Practice Find **a.** the perimeter and **b.** the area of this figure. Dimensions are in centimeters. (Use 3.14 for π.) a. 29.42 cm b. 44.13 cm²

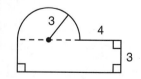

c. Find the area of this 45° sector. (Leave π as π.) 2π cm²

d. Find the perimeter of the figure in problem **c.** (Include the arc and two segments. Use 3.14 for π.) 11.14 cm

Problem set 104

1. The merchant sold the item for $12.50. If 40 percent of the selling price was profit, how much money did the merchant earn in profit? $5.00
   (60)

2. With one toss of a pair of dice, what is the probability of rolling a prime number? (Add the probabilities for each prime number.) $\frac{5}{12}$
   (94)

3. Bill's average score for 10 tests is 88. If his lowest score, 70, is not counted, what is his average for the remaining 9 tests? 90
   (55)

4. The 36-ounce container cost $3.42. The 3-pound container cost $3.84. The smaller container cost how much more per ounce than the larger container? 1.5¢ more per ounce
   (46)

5. Sean read 18 pages in 30 minutes. If he has finished page 128, how many hours will it take him to finish his 308-page book if he continues reading at the same rate? 5 hours
   (72)

6. Matthew was thinking of a certain number. If $\frac{5}{6}$ of the number was 75, what was $\frac{3}{5}$ of the number? 54
   (74)

7. Use a ratio box to solve this problem. The ratio of crawfish to tadpoles in the creek was 2 to 21. If there were 1932 tadpoles in the creek, how many crawfish were there? 184 crawfish
   (54)

8. Write equations to solve (a) and (b).
   (60,77)

   (a) What percent of $60 is $45? $W_P \times \$60 = \$45$; 75%

   (b) How much money is 45 percent of $60?
       $M = 0.45 \times \$60$; $27

In this figure, $\overline{AD}$ is a diameter and $\overline{CB}$ is a radius of 12 units. Central angle ACB measures 60°. Refer to this figure to answer problems 9–11.

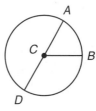

Leave π as π.

9. (a) What is the area of the circle? 144π units^2
   (66,82)

   (b) What is the circumference of the circle? 24π units

10. What is the area of sector *BCD*? 48π units^2
(104)

11. (a) How many degrees is the major arc from *B* through *A*
(104)   to *D* (arc *BAD*)? 240°

(b) How long is arc *BAD*? 16π units

12. $y = 2x - 1$

x	y
−1	−3
0	−1
1	1

12. Make a table of ordered pairs for the function $y = 2x - 1$.
(Inv. 9)   Use −1, 0, and 1 as *x* values in the table. Then graph the
function on a coordinate plane.

13. Complete the table.
(48)

FRACTION	DECIMAL	PERCENT
(a) $\frac{11}{500}$	(b) 0.022	2.2%

14. This graph shows the distance a car would travel at a
(Inv. 9)   certain constant speed in a given number of hours.
According to this graph, how far would a car travel in
1 hour and 15 minutes? 75 miles

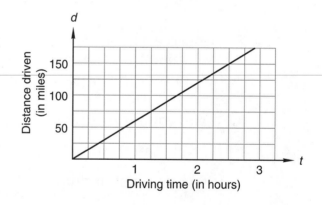

15. Compare: $ab \; \textcircled{<} \; a - b$ if *a* is positive and *b* is negative
(79)

16. Multiply and write the product in scientific notation.
(83)

$$\left(3.6 \times 10^{-4}\right)\left(9 \times 10^{8}\right) \quad 3.24 \times 10^{5}$$

17. Find the area of this figure. Dimen-
(104)   sions are in centimeters.
32.13 cm^2

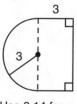

Use 3.14 for π.

18. Find the perimeter of the figure in problem 17. 21.42 cm
(104)

19. (a) Find the volume of this solid
_(67,70) in cubic inches. Dimensions are in feet. 1728 in.³

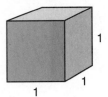

(b) Find the surface area of this cube in square feet. 6 ft²

20. What angle is formed by the hands of a clock at 5:00? 150°
₍₉₆₎

21. Find m∠x. 49°
₍₄₀₎

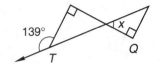

22. The triangles are similar.
_(97,98)

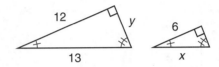

(a) Find x. $6\frac{1}{2}$

(b) Find the scale factor from the smaller triangle to the larger triangle. 2

(c) The area of the larger triangle is how many times the area of the smaller triangle? 4 times

23. Use the Pythagorean theorem to find y in the triangle in
₍₉₉₎ problem 22. 5

Solve:

24. $2\frac{3}{4}w + 4 = 48$ 16
_(90,93)

25. $2.4n + 1.2n - 0.12 = 7.08$ 2
₍₁₀₂₎

Simplify:

26. $\sqrt{(3^2)(10^2)}$ 30
₍₂₀₎

27. (a) $\dfrac{24x^2y}{8x^3y^2}$ $\frac{3}{xy}$
_(102,103)

(b) $3x^2 + 2x(x - 1)$ $5x^2 - 2x$

28. 12.5 − $\left(8\frac{1}{3} + 1\frac{1}{6}\right)$ 3
(43)

29. $4\frac{1}{6} \div 3\frac{3}{4} \div 2.5$ $\frac{4}{9}$
(43)

30. (a) $\dfrac{(-3)(4)}{-2} - \dfrac{(-3)(-4)}{-2}$ 12   (b) $\dfrac{(-2)^3}{(-2)^2}$ −2
(85,103)

LESSON 105

Surface Area of a Right Solid • Surface Area of a Sphere • More on Roots

Facts Practice: Percent-Decimal-Fraction Equivalents
   (Test U in Test Masters)

Mental Math:

   a. $(-2)^4$ **b.** $\left(4 \times 10^{-4}\right)^2$

   c. $2w + 3w = 60$ **d.** Convert −35°C to degrees Fahrenheit.

   e. 200% of $50   **f.** 100% more than $50

   g. Square 10, − 1, ÷ 9, × 4, + 1, ÷ 9, × 10, − 1, $\sqrt{\ }$, × 5, + 1, $\sqrt{\ }$, ÷ 3.

Problem Solving:

   At three o'clock the hands of a clock form a 90° angle. What angle is formed by the hands of a clock $1\frac{1}{2}$ hours after three o'clock?

Surface area of a right solid

Recall that the total area of the outside surfaces of a geometric solid is called the **surface area** of the solid.

This block has six rectangular faces. The areas of the top and bottom are equal. The areas of the front and back are equal, and the areas of the left and right sides are equal. We add the areas of these six faces to find the total surface area.

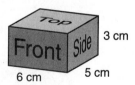

3 cm
6 cm   5 cm

Area of top	= 5 cm × 6 cm =	30 cm²
Area of bottom	= 5 cm × 6 cm =	30 cm²
Area of front	= 3 cm × 6 cm =	18 cm²
Area of back	= 3 cm × 6 cm =	18 cm²
Area of side	= 3 cm × 5 cm =	15 cm²
+ Area of side	= 3 cm × 5 cm =	15 cm²
Total surface area		= 126 cm²

Example 1 Find the surface area of this triangular prism. Units are centimeters.

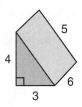

Solution There are two triangular faces and three rectangular faces.

$$\text{Area of triangle} = \frac{3 \text{ cm} \cdot 4 \text{ cm}}{2} = 6 \text{ cm}^2$$

$$\text{Area of triangle} = \frac{3 \text{ cm} \cdot 4 \text{ cm}}{2} = 6 \text{ cm}^2$$

$$\text{Area of rectangle} = 3 \text{ cm} \cdot 6 \text{ cm} = 18 \text{ cm}^2$$
$$\text{Area of rectangle} = 4 \text{ cm} \cdot 6 \text{ cm} = 24 \text{ cm}^2$$
$$+ \;\text{Area of rectangle} = 5 \text{ cm} \cdot 6 \text{ cm} = 30 \text{ cm}^2$$
$$\overline{\text{Total surface area} \qquad\qquad\qquad = \mathbf{84 \text{ cm}^2}}$$

Example 2 What is the area of the label on a soup can with dimensions as shown?

Use $\frac{22}{7}$ for π.

Solution If we remove the label from a soup can we see that it is a rectangle. One dimension of the rectangle is the circumference of the can, and the other dimension is the height of the can.

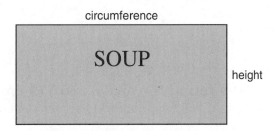

To find the area of the label we multiply these two dimensions.

$$\text{Area} = \text{circumference} \cdot \text{height}$$
$$= \pi d \cdot \text{height}$$
$$\approx \frac{22}{\underset{1}{7}} \cdot \overset{1}{7} \text{ cm} \cdot 10 \text{ cm}$$
$$\approx \mathbf{220 \text{ cm}^2}$$

Surface area of a sphere   To calculate the surface area of a sphere we may first calculate the area of the largest cross section of the sphere. Slicing an orange in half provides a visual representation of a cross section of a sphere.

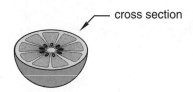

cross section

The circle formed by cutting the orange in half is the cross section of the spherical orange. The surface area of the entire sphere is four times the area of this circle. **To find the surface area of the sphere we calculate the area of its largest cross section $(A = \pi r^2)$, then we multiply the cross sectional area by four.**

$$\boxed{\textbf{Surface area of a sphere} = 4\pi r^2}$$

Example 3   A tennis ball has a diameter of about 6 cm. Find the surface area of the tennis ball to the nearest square centimeter.

Use 3.14 for π.

Solution   A tennis ball is spherical. If its diameter is 6 cm, then its radius is 3 cm.

$$\begin{aligned}
\text{Surface area} &= 4\pi r^2 \\
&\approx 4(3.14)(3 \text{ cm})^2 \\
&\approx 4(3.14)\left(9 \text{ cm}^2\right) \\
&\approx 113.04 \text{ cm}^2
\end{aligned}$$

We round the answer to **113 cm².**

More on roots   The perfect square 25 has two square roots, 5 and −5.

$$5 \cdot 5 = 25 \qquad (-5)(-5) = 25$$

Thus, the equation $x^2 = 25$ has two solutions, 5 and −5.

The positive square root of a number is sometimes called the *principal* square root. So the principal square root of 25 is 5. The radical symbol $\sqrt{}$ implies the principal root. So $\sqrt{25}$ is 5 only and does not include −5.

Example 4 What are the two square roots of 5?

Solution The two square roots of 5 are $\sqrt{5}$ and the opposite of $\sqrt{5}$ which is $-\sqrt{5}$.

A radical symbol may be used to indicate other roots besides square roots. The expression

$$\sqrt[3]{64}$$

means **cube root** of 64. The small 3 is called the **index** of the root. We find the cube root of 64 by finding the number which, when used as a factor three times, yields a product of 64.

$$(?)(?)(?) = 64$$

We find that the cube root of 64 is 4 because

$$4 \cdot 4 \cdot 4 = 64$$

Example 5 Simplify: (a) $\sqrt[3]{1000}$ (b) $\sqrt[3]{-27}$

Solution (a) The cube root of 1000 is **10** because $10 \cdot 10 \cdot 10 = 1000$. Notice that -10 is not a cube root of 1000 because $(-10)(-10)(-10) = -1000$.

(b) The cube root of -27 is **-3** because $(-3)(-3)(-3) = -27$.

Practice **a.** Find the surface area of this rectangular solid. Dimensions are in meters. 192 m²

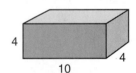

b. Find the surface area of this triangular prism. Dimensions are in inches. 288 in.²

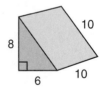

c. Find the area of the label on this can of tuna. 125.6 cm²

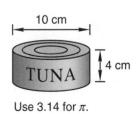

Use 3.14 for π.

d. The diameter of a golf ball is about 4 cm. Find the surface area of a golf ball to the nearest square centimeter. (Use 3.14 for π.) 50 cm²

e. What are the two square roots of 16? 4, −4

Simplify:

f. $\sqrt[3]{125}$ 5

g. $\sqrt[3]{-8}$ −2

Problem set 105

1. Use a ratio box to solve this problem. The regular price of the dress was $30. The dress was on sale for 25% off.
(92)

(a) What was the sale price? $22.50

(b) What percent of the regular price was the sale price?
75%

2. Twenty billion is how much greater than nine hundred million? Write the answer in scientific notation.
(51)
1.91×10^{10}

3. The mean of the following numbers is how much less than the median? 0.51
(Inv. 4)

3.2, 4.28, 1.2, 3.1, 1.17

4. Evaluate: $\sqrt{a^2 - b^2}$ if $a = 10$ and $b = 8$ 6
(52)

5. If Glenda is paid at a rate of $8.50 per hour, how much will she earn if she works $6\frac{1}{2}$ hours? $55.25
(53)

6. Use a ratio box to solve this problem. If 6 kilograms of flour costs $2.48, what is the cost of 45 kilograms of flour? $18.60
(72)

7. Transversal r intersects parallel lines s and t. If the measure of each acute angle is $4x$ and the measure of each obtuse angle is $5x$, then how many degrees is x? 20°
(102)

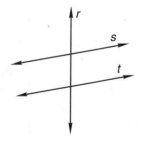

8. Use a ratio box to solve this problem. The ratio of Whigs to Tories at the assembly was 7 to 3. If the total number of Whigs and Tories assembled was 210, how many were Tories? 63 Tories
(65)

Write equations to solve problems 9–11.

9. What percent of $60 is $3? $W_p \times \$60 = \$3$; 5%
(77)

10. What fraction is 10 percent of 4? $W_F = \frac{1}{10} \times 4$; $\frac{2}{5}$
(60)

11. Twelve less than twice what number is 86?
(101) $2x - 12 = 86;$ 49

12. Use a ratio box to solve this problem. The merchant sold
(92)   the item at a 30 percent discount from the regular price. If
the regular price was $60, what was the sale price? $42

13. The coordinates $(-2, -2)$, $(-2, 2)$, and $(1, -2)$ are the
(99)   coordinates of the vertices of a right triangle. Find the
length of the hypotenuse of this triangle.   5 units

14. Compare: $a^3 \enclose{circle}{<} a^2$ if a is negative
(79,103)

15. Use a ratio box to solve this problem. Begin by converting
(98)   60 feet to inches. Brandon is making a model plane at a
1:36 scale. If the length of the actual plane is 60 feet, how
many inches long should he make his model?   20 inches

16. If Carla draws one card from a normal deck of cards,
(94)   keeps the card, then draws another card, what is the
probability that both cards will be hearts? $\frac{13}{52} \cdot \frac{12}{51} = \frac{1}{17}$

17. Bigler bounced a big ball with a diameter of 20 inches.
(105)   Using 3.14 for π, find the surface area of the ball.   1256 in.^{2}

18. Multiply and write the product in scientific notation.
(83)

$$\left(8 \times 10^{-4}\right)\left(3.2 \times 10^{-10}\right) \quad 2.56 \times 10^{-13}$$

19. Find the perimeter of this figure.
(104)   Dimensions are in meters. (Use 3.14
for π.)   81.4 m

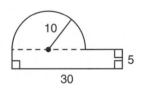

20. Copy this table of ordered pairs for the $y = -2x - 1$
(85,Inv. 9)   function $y = -2x - 1$ and supply the
missing numbers. Then graph the
function.

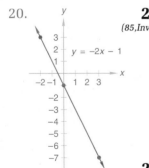

20.

x	y
3	-7
-2	3
0	-1

21. Find (a) the volume and (b) the sur-
(67,70)   face area of this cube. Dimensions
are in millimeters.
(a) 125 mm^3 (b) 150 mm^2

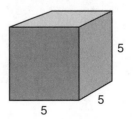

22. Find the volume of this right circular
(95) cylinder. Dimensions are in centimeters. 3140 cm³

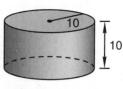

Use 3.14 for π.

23. The total surface area of the cylinder in problem 22
(105) includes the area of two circles and the curved side. What
is the total surface area of the cylinder? 1256 cm²

24. Find m∠b. 30°
(40)

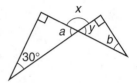

25. The triangles are similar.
(97,98)

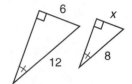

(a) Find x. 4

(b) Find the scale factor from the
smaller triangle to the larger
triangle. 1.5

(c) The area of the larger triangle is how many times the
area of the smaller triangle? 2.25 times

Solve:

26. $4\frac{1}{2}x + 4 = 48 - x$ 8
(102)

27. $\frac{3.9}{75} = \frac{c}{25}$ 1.3
(98)

Simplify:

28. $3.2 \div \left(2\frac{1}{2} \div \frac{5}{8} \right)$ $\frac{4}{5}$ or 0.8
(43)

29. (a) $\frac{(2xy)(4x^2y)}{8x^2y}$ xy
(96,103)

(b) $3(x - 3) - 3$ 3x − 12

30. (a) $\frac{(-10)(-4) - (3)(-2)(-1)}{(-4) - (-2)}$ −17
(85,105)

(b) $(-2)^4 - (-2)^2 + \sqrt[3]{-1}$ 11

Solving Literal Equations • Transforming Formulas

Facts Practice: + − × ÷ Algebraic Terms (Test V in Test Masters)

Mental Math:

a. $(-5)^3$

b. $\left(8 \times 10^3\right)\left(5 \times 10^{-5}\right)$

c. $\frac{a}{3.6} = \frac{0.9}{1.8}$

d. Convert 2 sq. yd to sq. ft.

e. $66\frac{2}{3}\%$ of $45

f. $33\frac{1}{3}\%$ less than $45

g. Estimate a 15% tip on a bill of $39.67.

Problem Solving:

What is the average of these fractions?

$$\frac{1}{12}, \frac{1}{6}, \frac{1}{4}, \frac{1}{3}, \frac{5}{12}$$

Solving literal equations

A **literal equation** is an equation that contains letters instead of numbers. We can rearrange (transform) literal equations by using the rules we have learned.

Example 1 Solve for x: $x + a = b$

Solution We solve for x by isolating x on one side of the equation. We do this by adding $-a$ to both sides of the equation.

$$x + a = b \qquad \text{equation}$$
$$x + a - a = b - a \qquad \text{added } -a \text{ to both sides}$$
$$x = \mathbf{b - a} \qquad \text{simplified}$$

Example 2 Solve for x: $ax = b$

Solution To solve for x, we divide both sides of the equation by a.

$$ax = b \qquad \text{equation}$$

$$\frac{\overset{1}{\cancel{a}}x}{\underset{1}{\cancel{a}}} = \frac{b}{a} \qquad \text{divided by } a$$

$$x = \frac{\boldsymbol{b}}{\boldsymbol{a}} \qquad \text{simplified}$$

Transforming formulas

Formulas are literal equations that we can use to solve certain kinds of problems. Often it is necessary to change the way a formula is written.

Example 3   Solve for w: $A = lw$

Solution   This is a formula for finding the area of a rectangle. We see that w is to the right of the equals sign and is multiplied by l. To undo the multiplication by l, we can divide both sides of the equation by l.

$$A = lw \qquad \text{equation}$$

$$\frac{A}{l} = \frac{\overset{1}{\cancel{l}}w}{\underset{1}{\cancel{l}}} \qquad \text{divided by } l$$

$$w = \frac{A}{l} \qquad \text{simplified}$$

Practice   **a.** Solve for a: $a + b = c$ $a = c - b$

b. Solve for w: $wx = y$ $w = \frac{y}{x}$

c. Solve for y: $y - b = mx$ $y = mx + b$

d. The formula for the area of a parallelogram is

$$A = bh$$

Solve this equation for b. $b = \frac{A}{h}$

Problem set
106

1. Max paid $20.00 for 3 pairs of socks priced at $1.85 per pair
(46) and a T-shirt priced at $8.95. The sales tax was 6 percent. How much money should he get back? $4.63

2. The face of this spinner is divided
(Inv. 10) into twelfths.

(a) If the spinner is spun once, what are the odds that the spinner will end up pointing to a one-digit prime number?   1 to 2

(b) If the spinner is spun twice, what is the chance that it will land on an even number twice?   25%

3. At $2.80 per pound, the cheddar cheese costs how many
(46) cents per ounce?   17.5¢ per ounce

4. Brenda's average score after 6 tests was 90. If her lowest
(55) score, 75, is not counted, what was her average score on the remaining 5 tests?   93

5. The ordered pairs (2, 4), (2, –1), and (0, –1) designate the
(99) vertices of a right triangle. What is the length of the
hypotenuse of the triangle? $\sqrt{29}$ units

6. Use a ratio box to solve this problem. Justin finished 3
(72) problems in 4 minutes. At that rate, how long will it take
him to finish the remaining 27 problems? 36 minutes

7. (a) What are the two square roots of 64? 8 and –8
(105)

(b) What is the cube root of –64? –4

8. Write an equation to solve this problem. What number is
(60) 225 percent of 40? $W_N = 2.25 \times 40$; 90

9.(a)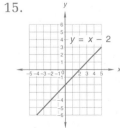

9. (a) Sketch a number line and show the location of these
(100) numbers.

$$|-2|, \frac{2}{2}, \sqrt{2}, 2^2$$

(b) Which of these numbers are rational numbers?
$|-2|, \frac{2}{2}, 2^2$

10. Use a ratio box to solve this problem. The ratio of
(65) residents to visitors in the community pool was 2 to 3. If
there were 60 people in the pool, how many were visitors?
36 visitors

Write equations to solve problems 11 and 12.

11. Sixty-six is $66\frac{2}{3}$ percent of what number? $66 = \frac{2}{3} \times W_N$; 99
(77)

12. Seventy-five percent of what number is 2.4?
(77) $0.75 \times W_N = 2.4$; 3.2

13. Use a ratio box to solve this problem. The number of
(92) students enrolled in chemistry increased 25 percent this
year. If there are 80 students enrolled in chemistry this
year, how many were enrolled in chemistry last year?
64 students

14. Complete the table.
(48)

Fraction	Decimal	Percent
(a) $1\frac{1}{20}$	(b) 1.05	105%

15.

15. Make a table of ordered pairs for the function $y = x - 2$.
(Inv. 9) Then graph the function on a coordinate plane.
See student work.

16. Divide 6.75 by 81 and write the quotient rounded to three
(42) decimal places. 0.083

17. Multiply and write the product in scientific notation.
(83)

$$\left(4.8 \times 10^{-10}\right)\left(6 \times 10^{-6}\right) \quad 2.88 \times 10^{-15}$$

18. Evaluate: $x^2 + bx + c$ if $x = -3$, $b = -5$, and $c = 6$
(91) 30

19. Find the area of this figure. Dimen-
(104) sions are in millimeters. Corners that
look square are square. 269 mm²

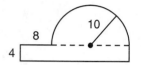

20. Find the surface area of this right
(105) triangular prism. Dimensions are in
centimeters. 132 cm²

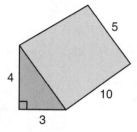

21. Find the volume of this cylinder. Dimensions are in
(95) inches. 31.4 in.³

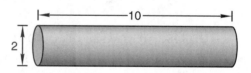

22. Find m∠b. 40°
(40)

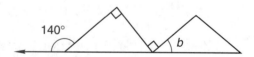

23. (a) Solve for x: $x + c = d$ $x = d - c$
(106)

(b) Solve for n: $an = b$ $n = \frac{b}{a}$

24. Solve: $6w - 2(4 + w) = w + 7$ 5
(102)

25. Solve and graph: $6x + 8 < 14$ $x < 1$
(93)
  -2 -1 0 1 2

26. Thirty-seven is five less than the product of what number
(101) and three? 14

Simplify:

27. $25 - \left[3^2 + 2(5 - 3)\right]$ 12
(63)

28. $\dfrac{6x^2 + (5x)(2x)}{4x}$ $4x$
(103)

29. $3\dfrac{3}{4} - \left[\left(1\dfrac{1}{2}\right)\left(2\dfrac{2}{3}\right) - \dfrac{5}{6}\right]$ $\dfrac{7}{12}$
(63)

30. $(-3)(-2)(+4)(-1) + (-3)^2 + \sqrt[3]{-64} - (-2)^3$ -11
(103,105)

LESSON
107

Slope

Mental Math:
a. 10
b. 6.25×10^{12}
c. 3
d. $-58°F$
e. $45
f. $105
g. 6

Problem Solving:

sixteen	1-by-1
nine	2-by-2
four	3-by-3
+ one	4-by-4
thirty	total

Facts Practice: Percent-Decimal-Fraction Equivalents
(Test U in Test Masters)

Mental Math:

a. $(-2.5)(-4)$

b. $\left(2.5 \times 10^6\right)^2$

c. $2x - 1\dfrac{1}{2} = 4\dfrac{1}{2}$

d. Convert $-50°C$ to degrees Fahrenheit.

e. 75% of $60

f. 75% more than $60

g. $7 \times 8, - 1, \div 5, \times 3, + 2, \div 5, \times 7, + 1, \times 2, - 1, \div 3, + 3, \sqrt{}$

Problem Solving:

In this 3-by-3 square we find nine 1-by-1 squares, four 2-by-2 squares, and one 3-by-3 square. Find the total number of squares of any size in this 4-by-4 square.

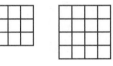

Following are the graphs of two functions. The graph on the left indicates the number of feet that equals the length of a given number of yards. The graph on the right shows the inverse relationship, the number of yards that equals the length of a given number of feet.

Yards to Feet

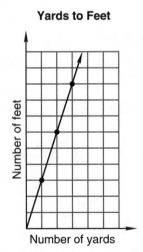

Number of feet

Number of yards

Feet to Yards

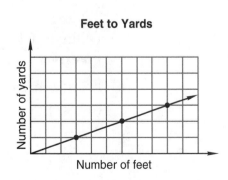

Number of yards

Number of feet

Notice that the graph of the function on the left has a steep upward slant, while the graph of the function on the right also has an upward slant but is not as steep. The "slant" of the graph of a function is called its **slope.** We assign numbers to slopes that indicate how steep the slope is and also whether the slope is upward or downward. If the slope is upward, the number is positive. If the slope is downward, the number is negative. If the graph is horizontal, the slope is neither positive nor negative, it is zero.

Example 1 State whether the slope of each line is positive, negative, zero, or cannot be determined.

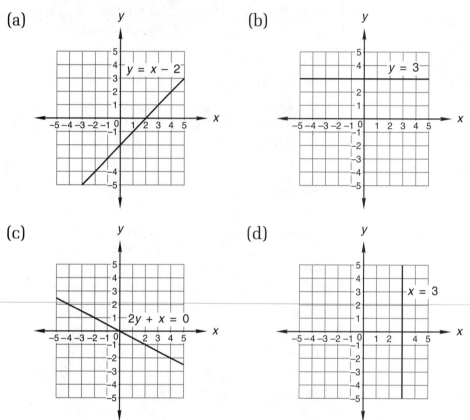

(a)

$y = x - 2$

(b)

$y = 3$

(c)

$2y + x = 0$

(d)

$x = 3$

Solution To determine the sign of the slope, follow the graph of the function with your eyes *from left to right* as though you were reading.

(a) From left to right the graphed line rises so the slope is **positive.**

(b) From left to right the graphed line does not rise or fall so the slope is **zero.**

(c) From left to right the graphed line slopes downward so the slope is **negative.**

(d) There is no left to right component of the graphed line so we cannot determine if the line is rising or falling. The slope is not positive, not negative, and not zero. The slope of a vertical line **cannot be determined.**

To determine the number of the slope of a line it is helpful to sketch a right triangle using the background grid of the coordinate plane and a portion of the graphed line. First we look for points where the graphed line crosses the background grid at intersections of the grid. We have circled some of these points on the graphs below.

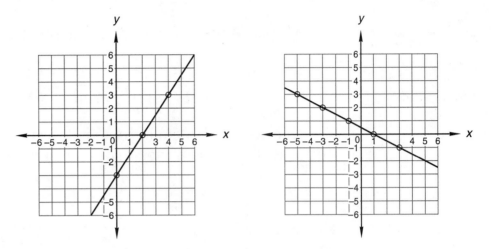

Next we select two points from the graphed line and, following the background grid, sketch the legs of a right triangle that intersect the chosen points. (It is a helpful practice to first select the point to the left and draw the horizontal leg to the right. Then draw the vertical leg.)

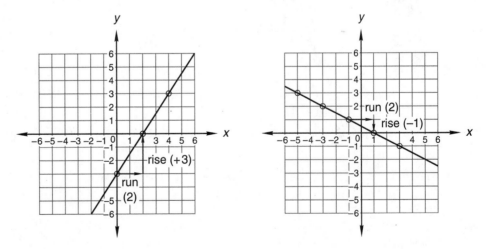

We use the words "run" and "rise" to describe the two legs of the right triangle that is formed. The "run" is the length of the horizontal leg drawn from left to right. The "rise" is the length of the vertical leg. We assign a positive sign to the rise if it goes up to meet the graphed line and a negative sign if it goes down to meet the graphed line. In the graph on the left, the run is 2 and the rise is +3. In the graph on the right, the run is 2 and the rise is −1. We use these numbers to write the slope of each graphed line.

> **The slope of a line is the ratio of its rise to its run ("rise over run").**
>
> $$\text{slope} = \frac{\text{rise}}{\text{run}}$$

So the slopes of the graphed lines are these ratios.

$$\frac{\text{rise}}{\text{run}} = \frac{+3}{2} = \frac{3}{2} \qquad \frac{\text{rise}}{\text{run}} = \frac{-1}{2} = -\frac{1}{2}$$

A line with a rise equal to its run has a slope of 1. A line with a rise that is the opposite of its run has slope of –1.

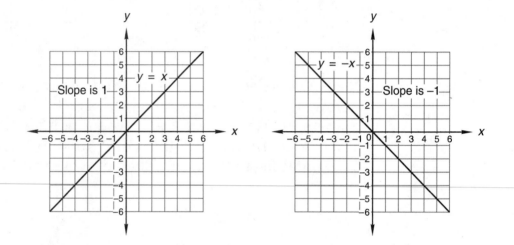

A line that is steeper than the lines above has a slope greater than 1 or less than –1. A line that is less steep than the lines above has a slope that is between –1 and 1.

Example 2   Find the slope of the graphed line.

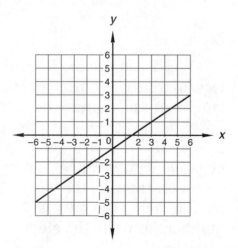

Solution We note that the slope is positive. We locate and select two points where the graphed line passes through intersections of the grid. We choose the points (0, –1) and (3, 1). Starting from the point to the left, (0, –1), we draw a horizontal leg to the right. Then we draw the vertical leg up to (3, 1).

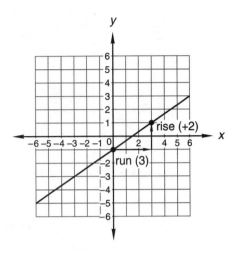

We see that the run is 3 and the rise is positive 2. We write the slope as "rise over run."

$$\text{Slope} = \frac{2}{3}$$

Note that we could have chosen the points (–3, –3) and (3, 1). Had we done so the run would be 6 and the rise 4. However, the slope would be the same because $\frac{4}{6}$ reduces to $\frac{2}{3}$.

Activity: Slope

Materials needed:

- Each student needs a copy of "Activity Master 6" available in the *Math 87 Test Masters.*

Calculate the slope ("rise over run") of each graphed line on the activity master by drawing right triangles.

Practice **a.** Find the slopes of the "Yards to Feet" and the "Feet to Yards" graphs at the beginning of this lesson.
"Yards to Feet," 3; "Feet to Yards," $\frac{1}{3}$

b. Find the slopes of graphs (a) and (c) in Example 1. 1; $-\frac{1}{2}$

c. Mentally calculate the slope of each graphed line below by counting the run and rise rather than by drawing right triangles. $\frac{1}{3}$; $-\frac{2}{3}$; 0; −2

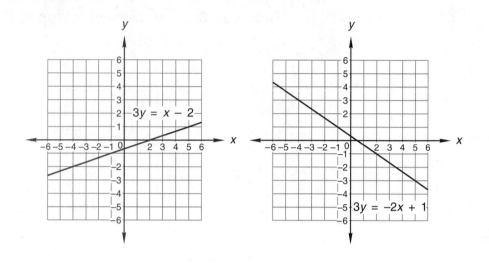

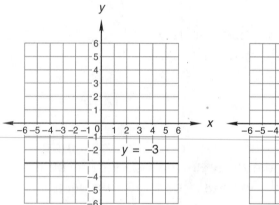

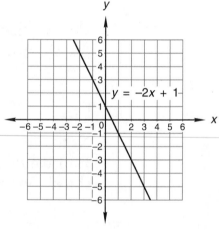

Problem set 107

1. The shirt regularly priced at $21 was on sale for $\frac{1}{3}$ off.
$^{(92)}$ What was the sale price? $14

2. Nine hundred seventy-five billion is how much less than
$^{(51)}$ one trillion? Write the answer in scientific notation.
2.5×10^{10}

3. What is the (a) range and (b) mode of this set of numbers?
$^{(Inv. 4)}$ (a) 11   (b) 16

$$16, 6, 8, 17, 14, 16, 12$$

4. Use a ratio box to solve this problem. Riding her bike
$^{(72)}$ from home to the lake, Sonia averaged 18 miles per hour
(per 60 minutes). If it took her 40 minutes to reach the
lake, how far did she ride? 12 miles

5. The points (3, –2), (–3, –2), and (–3, 6) are the vertices of
(99) a right triangle. Find the perimeter of the triangle. 24 units

6. Use a ratio box to solve this problem. The ratio of
(65) earthworms to cutworms in the garden was 5 to 2. If there
were 140 worms in the garden, how many earthworms
were there? 100 earthworms

7. In this figure ∠ABC is a right angle.
(40) Find the measure of each of these
angles:

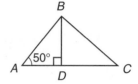

(a) ∠ABD. 40°

(b) ∠DBC. 50°

(c) ∠BCD. 40°

(d) Which triangles in this figure are similar?
All three triangles are similar.

Write equations to solve problems 8–10.

8. Sixty is 125 percent of what number? $60 = 1.25 \times W_N$; 48
(77)

9. Sixty is what percent of 25? $60 = W_P \times 25$; 240%
(77)

10. Sixty is four more than twice what number?
(101) $60 = 2n + 4$; 28

11. Use a ratio box to solve this problem. The average cost of
(92) a new car increased 8 percent in one year. Before the
increase, the average cost of a new car was $16,550. What
was the average cost of a new car after the increase?
$17,874

12. In a can there are 10 yellow marbles, 20 red marbles, 30
(94,Inv. 10) green marbles, and 40 blue marbles.

(a) If a marble is drawn from the can, what is the chance
that the marble will not be red? $\frac{80}{100} = 80\%$

(b) If the first marble is not replaced and a second marble
is drawn from the can, what is the probability that
both marbles will be yellow? $\frac{10}{100} \cdot \frac{9}{99} = \frac{1}{110}$

13. Complete the table.
(48)

FRACTION	DECIMAL	PERCENT
$\frac{5}{6}$	(a) $0.8\overline{3}$	(b) $83\frac{1}{3}\%$

14. When $x > y$ compare: $(x - y)^2 \; \boxed{=} \; (y - x)^2$
(79)

15. Multiply and write the product in scientific notation.
(83)

$$(1.8 \times 10^{10})(9 \times 10^{-6}) \quad 1.62 \times 10^5$$

16. (a) Between which two consecutive whole numbers on a
(100,105)   number line does $\sqrt{600}$ lie?   24 and 25

    (b) What are the two square roots of 10? $\sqrt{10}$ and $-\sqrt{10}$

17.(a)

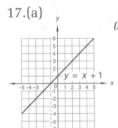

17. Find three pairs of x and y for the function $y = x + 1$.
(Inv. 9,107)   See student work.

    (a) Graph these number pairs on a coordinate plane and draw a line through these points.

    (b) What is the slope of the graphed line?   1

18. If the radius of this circle is 6 cm, then
(104)   what is the area of the shaded region?
24π cm^2

Leave π as π.

19. Find the surface area of this rec-
(105)   tangular solid. Dimensions are in inches.   160 in.^{2}

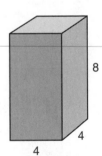

20. Find the volume of this right circular
(95)   cylinder. Dimensions are in centimeters.   502.4 cm^3

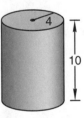

21. If the cylinder in problem 20 is a can,
(105)   and there is a label around the can, then what is the area of the label?
251.2 cm^2

Use 3.14 for π.

22. The polygon $ABCD$ is a rectangle. Find m$\angle x$.   30°
(40)

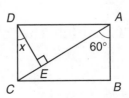

23. Find the slope of this graphed line. 2
(107)

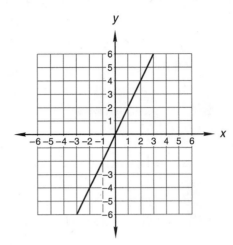

24. Solve for x in each literal equation.
(106)

(a) $x - y = z$ $x = z + y$ (b) $w = xy$ $x = \frac{w}{y}$

Solve:

25. $\frac{a}{21} = \frac{1.5}{7}$ 4.5   **26.** $6x + 5 = 7 + 2x$ $\frac{1}{2}$
(98)   (102)

Simplify:

27. $62 + 5\{20 - [4\frac{2}{3} + 3(2 - 1)]\}$ 67   **28.** $\frac{(6x^2 y)(2xy)}{4xy^2}$ $3x^2$
(63)   (103)

29. $5\frac{1}{6} + 3.5 - \frac{1}{3}$ $8\frac{1}{3}$ **30.** $\frac{(5)(-3)(2)(-4) + (-2)(-3)}{|-6|}$
(43)   (85)

                                                                                           21

LESSON
108

Mental Math:
a. 0
b. 1×10^{-7}
c. 8
d. 27 sq. ft
e. $180
f. $180
g. 210 mi
Problem Solving:
  100

Formulas and Substitution

Facts Practice: $+ - \times \div$ Algebraic Terms (Test V in Test Masters)

Mental Math:

  a. $(-1)^5 + (-1)^6$ **b.** $(2.5 \times 10^{-5})(4 \times 10^{-3})$

  c. $5y - 2y = 24$ **d.** Convert 3 sq. yd to sq. ft.

  e. 150% of $120   **f.** $120 increased 50%

  g. At 60 mph, how far can Freddy drive in $3\frac{1}{2}$ hours?

Problem Solving:

  Recall that $\sqrt[3]{8}$ means "the cube root of 8" and that $\sqrt[3]{8}$ equals 2. Find $\sqrt[3]{1,000,000}$.

A formula is a literal equation that describes a relationship between two or more variables. Formulas are used in mathematics, science, economics, the construction industry, food preparation, and wherever else measurement is used.

To use a formula, we replace the letters in the formula with measures that are known. Then we solve the equation for the measure we wish to find.

Example 1   Use the formula $d = rt$ to find t when d is 36 and r is 9.

Solution   This formula describes the relationship between distance (d), rate (r), and time (t). We replace d with 36 and r with 9 and then solve the equation for t.

$$d = rt \qquad \text{formula}$$
$$36 = 9t \qquad \text{substituted}$$
$$t = \mathbf{4} \qquad \text{divided by 9}$$

Another way to find t is to first solve the formula for t.

$$d = rt \qquad \text{formula}$$
$$t = \frac{d}{r} \qquad \text{divided by } r$$

Then replace d and r with 36 and 9, respectively, and simplify.

$$t = \frac{36}{9} \qquad \text{substituted}$$
$$t = \mathbf{4} \qquad \text{divided}$$

Example 2   Use the formula $F = 1.8C + 32$ to find F when C is 37.

Solution   This formula is used to convert measurements of temperature from degrees Celsius to degrees Fahrenheit. We replace C with 37 and simplify.

$$F = 1.8C + 32 \qquad \text{formula}$$
$$F = 1.8(37) + 32 \qquad \text{substituted}$$
$$F = 66.6 + 32 \qquad \text{multiplied}$$
$$F = \mathbf{98.6} \qquad \text{added}$$

Thus 37 degrees Celsius equals 98.6 degrees Fahrenheit.

Practice   **a.** Use the formula $A = bh$ to find b when A is 20 and h is 4.
5

b. Use the formula $A = \frac{1}{2}bh$ to find b when A is 20 and h is 4.
10

c. Use the formula $F = 1.8C + 32$ to find F when C is −40.
−40

**Problem set
108**

1. The main course cost $8.35. The beverage cost $1.25.
(46) Dessert cost $2.40. Jason left a tip that was 15 percent of the total price of the meal. How much money did Jason leave for a tip? $1.80

2. Twelve hundred thousandths is how much greater than
(57) twenty millionths? Write the answer in scientific notation.
1×10^{-4}

3. Arrange the following numbers in order. Then find the
(Inv. 4) median and the mode of the set of numbers.
4, 7, 8, 8, 8, 9, 9, 10, 12, 15; median = 8.5; mode = 8
8, 12, 9, 15, 8, 10, 9, 8, 7, 4

4. Two cards will be drawn from a normal deck of 52 cards.
(94) The first card will not be replaced before the second card is drawn. What is the probability that both cards will be 5's?
$\frac{4}{52} \cdot \frac{3}{51} = \frac{1}{221}$

5. Use a ratio box to solve this problem. Milton can
(72) exchange $200 for 300 Swiss francs. At that rate, how many dollars would a 240-franc Swiss watch cost? $160

6. Three eighths of a ton is how many pounds? 750 pounds
(60)

7. Use a ratio box to solve this problem. The jar was filled
(65) with red beans and brown beans in the ratio of 5 to 7. If there were 175 red beans in the jar, what was the total number of beans in the jar? 420 beans

Write equations to solve problems 8–10.

8. What number is 2.5 percent of 800? $W_N = 0.025 \times 800$; 20
(60)

9. Ten percent of what number is $2500?
(77) $0.1 \times W_N = \$2500$; $25,000

10. Fifty-six is eight less than twice what number?
(101) $56 = 2x - 8$; 32

11. Use a ratio box to solve this problem. During the off-
(92) season, the room rates at the resort were reduced by 35 percent. If the usual rates were $90 per day, what would be the cost of a 2-day stay during the off-season? $117

12. Find the slope of the graphed line on this coordinate plane.
(107) $-\frac{2}{3}$

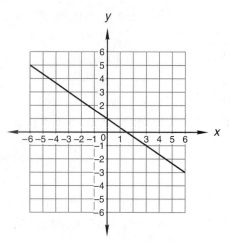

13. Use a ratio box to solve this problem. Liz is drawing a
(98) floor plan of her house. On the plan, 1 inch equals 2 feet.
What is the floor area of a room that measures 6 inches by
$7\frac{1}{2}$ inches on the plan?   180 ft^2

14. Find the measure of each angle of this
(101) triangle by writing and solving an
equation for this figure.
$x = 45°$; $2x = 90°$

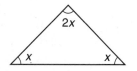

15. Multiply and write the product in scientific notation.
(83)

$$\left(2.8 \times 10^5\right)\left(8 \times 10^{-8}\right) \quad 2.24 \times 10^{-2}$$

16. Use the formula $c = 2.54n$ for converting inches (n) to
(108) centimeters (c) to find c when n is 12.   30.48 cm

17.

$y = 2x$

17. Make a table that shows three pairs of numbers that satisfy
(Inv. 9) the function $y = 2x$. Then graph the number pairs on a
coordinate plane and draw a line through the points.
See student work.

18. Find the perimeter of this figure.
(104) Dimensions are in inches. (Use 3.14
for π.) 20.28 in.

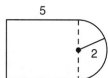

19. Find the surface area of this cube.
(105) Dimensions are in inches.   600 in.^{2}

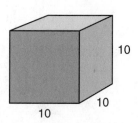

20. Find the volume of this right circular
cylinder. Dimensions are in centimeters. (Use 3.14 for π.) 392.5 cm³

⁽⁹⁵⁾

21. Find m∠x. 30°

⁽⁴⁰⁾

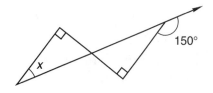

22. The triangles are similar. Dimensions are in centimeters.

^(97,98)

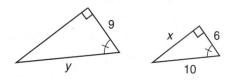

(a) Find y. 15 cm

(b) Find the scale factor from the smaller to the larger
triangle. 1.5

(c) The area of the larger triangle is how many times the
area of the smaller triangle? 2.25 times

23. Use the Pythagorean theorem to find x in the triangle
above. 8 cm

⁽⁹⁹⁾

24. A globe the shape of a sphere has a diameter of 10 inches.
Using 3.14 for π, find the surface area of the globe.
314 in.²

⁽¹⁰⁵⁾

25. Solve: $1\frac{2}{3}x = 32 - x$ 12

⁽¹⁰²⁾

Simplify:

26. $x^2 + x(x + 2)$ $2x^2 + 2x$

⁽⁹⁶⁾

27. $\dfrac{(-4ax)(3xy)}{-6x^2}$ $2ay$

⁽¹⁰³⁾

28. $1.1\{1.1[1.1(1000)]\}$ 1331

⁽⁶³⁾

29. $3\frac{3}{4} \cdot 2\frac{2}{3} \div 10$ 1

⁽²⁶⁾

30. (a) $(-6) - (7)(-4) + \sqrt[3]{125} + \dfrac{(-8)(-9)}{(-3)(-2)}$ 39

^(103,105)

(b) $(-1) + (-1)^2 + (-1)^3 + (-1)^4$ 0

LESSON 109

Equations with Exponents

Facts Practice: $+ - \times \div$ Algebraic Terms (Test V in Test Masters)

Mental Math:

a. $\left(-\frac{1}{2}\right)\left(-\frac{1}{2}\right)$ **b.** $\left(1.2 \times 10^{12}\right)^2$

c. $\frac{2.4}{0.6} = \frac{c}{0.25}$ **d.** Convert 150 cm to m.

e. $12\frac{1}{2}\%$ of \$80   **f.** $12\frac{1}{2}\%$ less than \$80

g. Find $\frac{1}{3}$ of 60, + 5, × 2, − 1, $\sqrt{}$, × 4, − 1, ÷ 3, square that number, − 1, ÷ 2.

Problem Solving:

Here is a front, top, and side view of an object. Sketch a view of the object from the perspective of the upper right front.

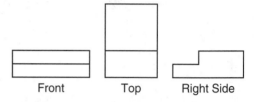

In the equations we have solved in this book so far, the variables have had an exponent of 1. You haven't seen the exponent because we usually do not write an exponent when it is 1. In this lesson we will consider equations that have variables with exponents of 2, such as the following equation:

$$3x^2 + 1 = 28$$

To isolate the variable in this equation takes three steps: first subtract 1 from both sides, next divide both sides by 3, and then find the square root of both sides. We show the results of each step below.

$3x^2 + 1 = 28$	equation
$3x^2 = 27$	subtracted 1 from both sides
$x^2 = 9$	divided both sides by 3
$x = 3, -3$	found the square root of both sides

Notice that there are two solutions, 3 and −3. Both solutions satisfy the equation as we show below.

$$3(3)^2 + 1 = 28 \qquad 3(-3)^2 + 1 = 28$$
$$3(9) + 1 = 28 \qquad 3(9) + 1 = 28$$
$$27 + 1 = 28 \qquad 27 + 1 = 28$$
$$28 = 28 \qquad 28 = 28$$

When the variable of an equation has an exponent of 2, the equation has 2 solutions.

Example 1   Solve: $3x^2 - 1 = 47$

Solution   There are three steps. We show the results of each step.

$$3x^2 - 1 = 47 \qquad \text{equation}$$
$$3x^2 = 48 \qquad \text{added 1 to both sides}$$
$$x^2 = 16 \qquad \text{divided both sides by 3}$$
$$x = \mathbf{4, -4} \qquad \text{found the square root of both sides}$$

Example 2   Solve: $2x^2 = 10$

Solution   We divide both sides by 2. Then we find the square root of both sides.

$$2x^2 = 10 \qquad \text{equation}$$
$$x^2 = 5 \qquad \text{divided both sides by 2}$$
$$x = \mathbf{\sqrt{5}, -\sqrt{5}} \qquad \text{found the square root of both sides}$$

Since $\sqrt{5}$ is an irrational number, we leave it in radical form. The negative of $\sqrt{5}$ is $-\sqrt{5}$ and not $\sqrt{-5}$.

Example 3   Five less than what number squared is 20?

Solution   We translate the question into an equation.

$$n^2 - 5 = 20$$

We solve the equation in two steps.

$$n^2 - 5 = 20 \qquad \text{equation}$$
$$n^2 = 25 \qquad \text{added 5 to both sides}$$
$$n = 5, -5 \qquad \text{found the square root of both sides}$$

There are two numbers that satisfy the conditions of the question, **5** and **–5**.

Example 4   In this figure the area of the larger square is 4 square units, which is twice the area of the smaller square. What is the length of each side of the smaller square?

Solution   We will use s to stand for the length of each side of the smaller square. So s^2 is the area of the small square. Since the area of the large square is twice the area of the small square, we may write this equation.

$$2s^2 = 4$$

We solve the equation in two steps.

$$2s^2 = 4 \qquad \text{equation}$$
$$s^2 = 2 \qquad \text{divided both sides by 2}$$
$$s = \sqrt{2}, -\sqrt{2} \qquad \text{found the square root of both sides}$$

Although there are two solutions to the equation, there is only one answer to the question because lengths are positive and not negative. Each side of the smaller square is $\sqrt{2}$ **units.**

Example 5   Solve: $\dfrac{x}{3} = \dfrac{12}{x}$

Solution   First we cross multiply.

$$\frac{x}{3} = \frac{12}{x} \qquad \text{proportion}$$
$$x^2 = 36 \qquad \text{cross multiplied}$$

Then we find the square root of both sides.

$$x^2 = 36 \qquad \text{equation}$$
$$x = 6, -6 \qquad \text{found the square root of both sides}$$

There are two solutions to the proportion, **6** and **–6.**

Practice   Solve each equation.

a. $3x^2 - 8 = 100$ 6, –6   **b.** $x^2 + x^2 = 12$ $\sqrt{6}, -\sqrt{6}$

c. Five less than twice what negative number squared is 157?
–9

d. If the product of the square of a positive number and 7 is 21, then what is the number? $\sqrt{3}$

e. $\dfrac{w}{4} = \dfrac{9}{w}$ 6, –6

Problem set 109

1. What is the quotient when the product of 0.2 and 0.05 is
(45)   divided by the sum of 0.2 and 0.05?   0.04

2. In this figure, a transversal intersects
(102)   two parallel lines.

(a) Which angle corresponds to $\angle d$?
$\angle z$

(b) Which angle is the alternate interior angle to $\angle d$? $\angle w$

(c) Which angle is the alternate exterior angle to ∠b? ∠y

(d) If the measure of ∠a is *m*, and the measure of ∠b is 3*m*, then how many degrees is the measure of each obtuse angle in this figure? 135°

3. Twenty is five more than the product of ten and what
(101) decimal number? 1.5

4. Use two unit multipliers to convert 1 km² to square meters.
(88) 1,000,000 m²

5. Tim has $5 in quarters and $5 in dimes. What is the ratio
(36) of the number of quarters to the number of dimes? $\frac{2}{5}$

Use a ratio box to solve problems 6–8.

6. Jaime ran the first 3000 meters in 9 minutes. At that rate,
(72) how long will it take Jaime to run 5000 meters? 15 minutes

7. Sixty is 20 percent more than what number? 50
(92)

8. To attract customers, the merchant reduced all prices by
(92) 25 percent. What was the reduced price of an item that cost $36 before the price reduction? $27

9. Write an equation to solve this problem. Sixty is 150
(77) percent of what number? $60 = 1.5 \times W_N$; 40

10. Draw a diagram of this statement. Then answer the
(71) questions that follow.

> *Diane kept $\frac{2}{3}$ of her baseball cards and gave the remaining 234 cards to her brother.*

(a) How many cards did Diane have before she gave some to her brother? 702 cards

(b) How many baseball cards did Diane keep? 468 cards

10.

702 cards

$\frac{2}{3}$ kept { 234 cards
234 cards

$\frac{1}{3}$ gave away { 234 cards
(234)

11. Compare: $a - b \;\bigcirc\!\!>\; b - a$ if $a > b$
(79)

12. Warner knew the correct answer to 15 of the 20 true-false
(94) questions but guessed on the rest. What is the probability of Warner correctly guessing the answers to the remaining true-false questions? $\left(\frac{1}{2}\right)^5 = \frac{1}{32}$

13. Find the area of this trapezoid. Dimen-
(75) sions are in centimeters. 36 cm²

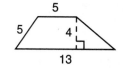

14. Find the volume of this triangular
(95) prism. Dimensions are in inches.
54 in.³

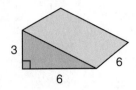

15. A rectangular label wrapped around a
(105) can with these dimensions has an area
of how many square inches? 56.52 in.²

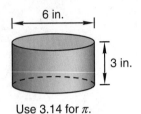

Use 3.14 for π.

16. The skateboard costs $36. The tax rate is 6.5 percent.
(46)

(a) What is the tax on the skateboard? $2.34

(b) What is the total price, including tax? $38.34

17. Complete the table.
(48)

Fraction	Decimal	Percent
(a) $\frac{1}{200}$	(b) 0.005	$\frac{1}{2}\%$

18. What number is $66\frac{2}{3}$ percent more than 48? 80
(92)

19. Multiply and write the product in scientific notation.
(83)

$$\left(6 \times 10^{-8}\right)\left(8 \times 10^4\right)$$ 4.8 × 10⁻³

20.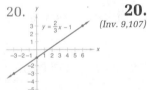

20. Copy and complete the blanks in this
(Inv. 9,107) table of ordered pairs for the function.
Then graph the function. What is the
slope of the graphed line? $\frac{2}{3}$

$$y = \frac{2}{3}x - 1$$

x	y
6	3
0	−1
−3	−3

21. Use a ratio box to solve this problem.
(65) The ratio of the measures of the two
acute angles of the right triangle is 7
to 8. What is the measure of the
smallest angle of the triangle? 42°

22. The relationship between the measures
(101) of four central angles of a circle is
shown in this figure. What is the
measure of the smallest central angle
shown? 36°

23. We can use the Pythagorean theorem
(99) to find the distance between two
points on a coordinate plane. To find
the distance from M to P we sketch a
right triangle and use the lengths of
the legs to find the hypotenuse. What
is the distance from M to P? $\sqrt{29}$ units

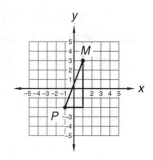

Solve:

24. $3m^2 + 2 = 50$ 4, −4
(109)

25. $7(y - 2) = 4 - 2y$ 2
(102)

Simplify:

26. $\sqrt{144} - (\sqrt{36})(\sqrt{4})$ 0
(20)

27. $x^2y + xy^2 + x(xy - y^2)$
(96) $2x^2y$

28. $\left(1\dfrac{5}{9}\right)(1.5) \div 2\dfrac{2}{3}$ $\dfrac{7}{8}$
(43)

29. $9.5 - \left(4\dfrac{1}{5} - 3.4\right)$ 8.7
(43)

30. (a) $\dfrac{(-18) + (-12) - (-6)(3)}{-3}$ 4
(91,105)

  (b) $\sqrt[3]{1000} - \sqrt[3]{125}$ 5

**LESSON
110**

Simple Interest and Compound Interest • Successive Discounts

Mental Math:
a. $\frac{1}{4}$
b. 5.4×10^{16}
c. $\frac{5}{2}$
d. 1500 mL
e. $90
f. $90
g. 10
Problem Solving:
   135°

Facts Practice: Percent-Decimal-Fraction Equivalents
          (Test U in Test Masters)

Mental Math:

  a. $\left(-\frac{1}{2}\right)^2$
  b. $(9 \times 10^6)(6 \times 10^9)$
  c. $4w - 1 = 9$
  d. Convert 1.5 L to mL.
  e. 150% of $60
  f. $60 increased 50%
  g. Start with the number of minutes in half an hour, multiply by
    the number of feet in a yard, add the number of years in a
    decade, $\sqrt{}$.

Problem Solving:

  At nine o'clock the hands of a clock form a 90° angle. What angle
  is formed by the hands of a clock $1\frac{1}{2}$ hours after nine o'clock?

Simple interest and compound interest

When you put your money in a bank, the bank uses your money to make more money. The bank pays you to let them use your money. The amount of money you deposit is called the **principal**. The amount of money they pay you is called **interest**. The interest is a percentage of the money deposited.

There is a difference between **simple interest** and **compound interest**. Simple interest is interest paid on the principal only and not paid on any accumulated interest. For instance, if you deposited $100 in an account that paid 6% simple interest, you would be paid 6% of $100 ($6.00) each year your $100 was on deposit. If you take your money out after 3 years, you would be paid a total of $118.

Simple Interest

$100.00   principal
  $6.00   first year interest
  $6.00   second year interest
+ $6.00   third year interest
—————————
$118.00   total

Most interest-bearing accounts are compound-interest accounts and not simple-interest accounts. In a compound-interest account, interest is paid on accumulated interest as well as on the principal. If you deposited $100 in an account with 6% annual percentage rate, the amount of interest you would be paid each year increases if the earned interest is left in the account. If you take your money out after three years you would be paid a total of $119.10.

Compound Interest

$100.00   principal
  $6.00   first year interest (6% of $100.00)
—————————
$106.00   total after one year
  $6.36   second year interest (6% of $106.00)
—————————
$112.36   total after two years
  $6.74   third year interest (6% of $112.36)
—————————
$119.10   total after three years

Notice that at 6% simple interest, $100.00 grows to $118.00 in three years, while $100.00 grows to $119.10 when 6% interest is compounded. The difference is not very large in three years, but the difference does become large over time as this table shows.

Total Value of $100 at 6% Interest

Number of Years	Simple Interest	Compound Interest
3	$118.00	$119.10
10	$160.00	$179.08
20	$220.00	$320.71
30	$280.00	$574.35
40	$340.00	$1028.57
50	$400.00	$1842.02

Example 1 Make a table that shows the value of a $1000 investment growing at 10% compounded annually after 1, 2, 3, 4, and 5 years.

Solution After one year, $1000 has grown 10% to $1100. The second year the value increases 10% of $1100, which is $110 to $1210. We continue the pattern for five years.

Total Value of $1000 at 10% Interest

Number of Years	Compound Interest
1	$1100.00
2	$1210.00
3	$1331.00
4	$1464.10
5	$1610.51

Notice that the amount of money in the account after 1 year is 110% of the original deposit of $1000. This 110% is composed of 100%, which is the starting amount, plus 10%, which is the interest earned in a year. Likewise, the amount of money in the account the second year is 110% of the amount in the account after 1 year. To find the amount of money in the account each year, we multiply the previous year's balance by 110% (or the decimal equivalent which is 1.1).

Even with a simple calculator we can calculate compound interest. To perform the calculation in Example 1 we could use 1.1 for 110% and follow this plan.

$$1000 \times 1.1 \times 1.1 \times 1.1 \times 1.1 \times 1.1 =$$

The circuitry of some calculators permits repeating a calculation by pressing the ▦ key repeatedly.[†] To make the calculations in Example 1 we try this keystroke sequence:

This keystroke sequence first enters 1.1 which is the decimal form of 110% (100% principal plus 10% interest), then the times sign, then 1000 for the $1000 investment. Pressing the ▦ key once displays

which is the value ($1100) after one year. Pressing the ▦ key a second time multiplies the displayed number by 1.1, the first number entered. The new number displayed is

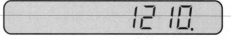

representing $1210, the value after two years. Each time the ▦ key is pressed the calculator displays the account value after another year. Using this method, find the value of the account after 10 years, and after 20 years.

10 yr, $2593.74;
20 yr, $6727.50

Try entering the factors in the reverse order.

$$1 \; 0 \; 0 \; 0 \; \times \; 1 \; . \; 1 \; =$$

No. This keystroke sequence multiplies the displayed number by 1000, the first number entered, and not by 1.1.

Are the same amounts displayed as were displayed with the prior entry when the ▦ key is repeatedly pressed? Why or why not?

Example 2   Use a calculator to find the value of a $2000 investment that earns $7\frac{1}{2}\%$ interest compounded annually after 12 years.

[†]This calculator function varies with make and model of calculator. See instructions for your calculator if the keystroke sequence described in this lesson does not work for you.

Solution   The interest rate is $7\frac{1}{2}\%$ which, in decimal form, is 0.075. We want to find the total value including the principal so we multiply the $2000 investment by $107\frac{1}{2}\%$, which we enter as 1.075. The keystroke sequence is

[1] [.] [0] [7] [5] [×] [2] [0] [0] [0] [=]

We press the [=] key 12 times to find the value after 12 years. We round the final display to the nearest cent, **$4763.56.**

Example 3   Calculate the interest earned on an $8000 deposit in 9 months if the annual interest rate is 6%.

Solution   The deposit earns 6% interest in one year which is

$$0.06 \times \$8000 = \$480$$

In 9 months the deposit earns just $\frac{9}{12}$ of this amount.

$$\frac{9}{12} \times \$480 = \$360$$

Successive discounts   Related to compound interest is **successive discount**. To calculate successive discount we find a percent of a percent. We show two methods for finding successive discounts in the following example.

Example 4   An appliance store reduced the price of a $400 washing machine 25%. When the washing machine did not sell at the sale price, the store reduced the sale price 20% to its clearance price. What was the clearance price of the washing machine?

Solution   One way to find the answer is to first find the sale price and then find the clearance price. We will use a ratio box to find the sale price.

	Percent	Actual Count
Original	100	400
− Change	25	D
New (Sale)	75	S

$$\frac{100}{75} = \frac{400}{S}$$

$$100S = 30,000$$

$$S = 300$$

We find that the sale price was $300. The second discount, 20%, was applied to the sale price, not to the original price. So for the next calculation we consider the sale price to be

100% and the clearance price to be what remains after the discount.

	Percent	Actual Count
Original (Sale)	100	300
– Change	20	D
New (Clearance)	80	C

$$\longrightarrow \quad \frac{100}{80} = \frac{300}{C}$$

$$100C = 24{,}000$$

$$C = 240$$

We find that the clearance price of the washing machine was **$240.**

Another way to look at this problem is to consider what percent of the original price is represented by the sale price. Since the original price was discounted 25%, the sale price represents 75% of the original price.

$$\text{Sale price} = 75\% \text{ of the original price}$$

Furthermore, since the sale price was discounted 20%, the clearance price was 80% of the sale price.

$$\text{Clearance price} = 80\% \text{ of the sale price}$$

So the clearance price was 80% of the sale price which was 75% of the original price.

$$\text{Clearance price} = 80\% \text{ of } 75\% \text{ of } \$400$$

$$= 0.8 \times 0.75 \times \$400$$

$$= 0.6 \times \$400$$

$$= \mathbf{\$240}$$

Practice **a.** When Sarah turned 21 she invested $2000 in an Individual Retirement Account (IRA) that has grown at a rate of 10% compounded annually. If the account continues to grow at that rate, what will be its value when Sarah turns 65? (Use the calculator method taught in this lesson.) $132,528.15

b. Sam deposited $6000 in an account paying 8% interest annually. After 8 months Sam withdrew the $6000 plus interest. Altogether, how much money did Sam withdraw? What fraction of a year's interest was earned? $6320; $\frac{8}{12}$ or $\frac{2}{3}$

c. A television regularly priced at $300 was placed on sale for 20% off. When the television still did not sell, the sale price was reduced 20% for clearance. What was the clearance price of the television? $192

Problem set 110

1. Bill bought 3 paperback books for $5.95 each. The tax rate
(46) was 6 percent. If he paid for the purchase with a $20 bill, how much money did he get back? $1.08

2. Hector has a coupon for 10% off the price of any item in
(110) the store. He decides to buy a shirt regularly priced at $24 that is on sale for 25% off. If he uses his coupon, how much will Hector pay for the shirt before sales tax is applied? $16.20

3.

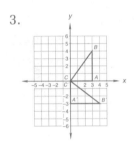

3. Triangle ABC with vertices at A (3, 0), B (3, 4), and C (0, 0)
(80) is rotated 90° clockwise about the origin to its image $\triangle A'B'C'$. Graph both triangles. What are the coordinates of the vertices of $\triangle A'B'C'$? A' (0, –3), B' (4, –3), C' (0, 0)

4. George burned 100 calories running 1 mile. At that rate,
(72) how many miles would he need to run to burn 350 calories? 3.5 miles

5. If a dozen roses cost $4.90, what is the cost of 30 roses?
(72) $12.25

6. A semicircle was cut out of a square
(104) as shown. What is the perimeter of the resulting figure? 32 in.

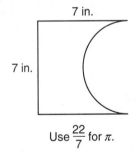

7 in.

7 in.

Use $\frac{22}{7}$ for π.

7. The average of four numbers was 8. Three of the numbers
(55) were 2, 4, and 6. What was the fourth number? 20

Write equations to solve problems 8–10.

8. One hundred fifty is what percent of 60?
(77) $150 = W_P \times 60$; 250%

9. Sixty percent of what number is 150? $0.6 \times W_N = 150$; 250
(77)

10. Six more than the square of what negative number is 150?
(109) $(-x)^2 + 6 = 150$; –12

11.

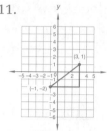

11. Graph the points (3, 1) and (−1, −2) on a coordinate plane.
(99) Then sketch a right triangle and use the Pythagorean theorem to find the distance between the points. 5 units

Use ratio boxes to solve problems 12 and 13.

12. The price of the dress was reduced by 40 percent. If the
(92) sale price was $48, what was the regular price? $80

13. The car model was built on a 1:36 scale. If the length of
(98) the car is 180 inches, how many inches long is the model?
5 inches

14. The positive square root of 80 is between which two
(100) consecutive whole numbers? 8 and 9

15. Make a table of ordered pairs for the function $y = -x + 1$.
(Inv. 9,107) Then graph the function. What is the slope of the graphed line? See student work.; −1

15.

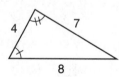

16. Solve and graph: $5x + 12 \geq 2$ $x \geq -2$
(93)

17. Multiply and write the product in scientific notation.
(83)

$$\left(6.3 \times 10^7\right)\left(9 \times 10^{-3}\right)\ 5.67 \times 10^5$$

18. Solve this equation for y. $y = 2x + 4$
(96,106)

$$\frac{1}{2}y = x + 2$$

19. What is the total account value after 3 years on a deposit
(110) of $4000 at 9 percent interest compounded annually?
$5180.12

20. These triangles are similar. Dimensions are in inches.
(97,98)

(a) Find x. 6 in.

(b) Find the scale factor from the larger to the smaller triangle. 0.75

21. Find the volume of this right triangular
(95) prism. Dimensions are in inches.
960 in.³

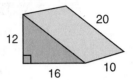

22. Find the total surface area of the right
(105) triangular prism in problem 21.
672 in.²

23. Find m∠x. 110°
(40)

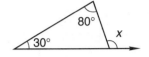

Solve:

24. $\dfrac{w}{2} = \dfrac{18}{w}$ 6, –6
(109)

25. $3\dfrac{1}{3}w^2 - 4 = 26$ 3, –3
(109)

Simplify:

26. $16 - \left\{27 - 3\left[8 - \left(3^2 - 2^3\right)\right]\right\}$ 10
(63)

27. $\dfrac{\left(6ab^2\right)(8ab)}{12a^2b^2}$ 4b
(103)

28. $3\dfrac{1}{3} + 1.5 + 4\dfrac{5}{6}$ $9\frac{2}{3}$
(43)

29. $20 \div \left(3\dfrac{1}{3} \div 1\dfrac{1}{5}\right)$ $7\frac{1}{5}$
(26)

30. $(-3)^2 + (-2)^3$ 1
(103)

INVESTIGATION 11

Scale Factor in Surface Area and Volume

In this investigation we will study the relationship between length, surface area, and volume of three-dimensional shapes. We begin by comparing the measures of cubes of different sizes.

Activity: Scale Factor in Surface Area and Volume

Materials needed:

- Each group of students needs 3 sheets of 1 cm grid paper (See "Activity Master 7" in the *Math 87 Test Masters*), scissors, and tape.

This problem-solving activity asks students to design their own patterns for cubes. The activity is time consuming and may be assigned as out-of-class work prior to addressing the questions in this investigation.

Each group should use the materials to build models of four cubes with edges 1 cm, 2 cm, 3 cm, and 4 cm long. Each group needs to mark, cut, fold, and tape the grid paper so that the *grid is visible* when each model is finished.

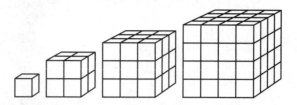

One pattern that folds to form a model of a cube is shown below. Several other patterns also work.

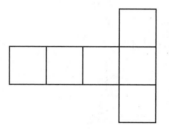

Copy this table on your paper and record the measures for each cube.

Measures of Four Cubes

	1-cm cube	2-cm cube	3-cm cube	4-cm cube
Edge length (cm)	1	2	3	4
Surface area (cm^2)	6	24	54	96
Volume (cm^3)	1	8	27	64

Refer to the table to answer the following questions comparing the cubes.

Compare the 2-cm cube to the 1-cm cube.

1. The edge length of the 2-cm cube is how many times the edge length of the 1-cm cube? 2 times

2. The surface area of the 2-cm cube is how many times the surface area of the 1-cm cube? 4 times

3. The volume of the 2-cm cube is how many times the volume of the 1-cm cube? 8 times

Compare the 4-cm cube to the 2-cm cube.

4. The edge length of the 4-cm cube is how many times the edge length of the 2-cm cube? 2 times

5. The surface area of the 4-cm cube is how many times the surface area of the 2-cm cube? 4 times

6. The volume of the 4-cm cube is how many times the volume of the 2-cm cube? 8 times

Compare the 3-cm cube to the 1-cm cube.

7. The edge length of the 3-cm cube is how many times the edge length of the 1-cm cube? 3 times

8. The surface area of the 3-cm cube is how many times the surface area of the 1-cm cube? 9 times

9. The volume of the 3-cm cube is how many times the volume of the 1-cm cube? 27 times

Use the patterns that can be found in answers 1–9 to predict the comparison of a 6-cm cube to a 2-cm cube.

10. The edge length of a 6-cm cube is how many times the edge length of a 2-cm cube? 3 times

11. The surface area of a 6-cm cube is how many times the surface area of a 2-cm cube? 9 times

12. The volume of a 6-cm cube is how many times the volume of a 2-cm cube? 27 times

13. Calculate (a) the surface area and (b) the volume of a 6-cm cube. (a) 216 cm^2 (b) 216 cm^3

14. The calculated surface area of a 6-cm cube is how many times the surface area of a 2-cm cube? 9 times

15. The calculated volume of a 6-cm cube is how many times the volume of a 2-cm cube? 27 times

In questions 1 through 6 we compared the measures of a 2-cm cube to a 1-cm cube, and we compared the measures of a 4-cm cube to a 2-cm cube. In both sets of comparisons the scale factors from the smaller cube to the larger cube were calculated.

Scale Factors from Smaller Cube to Larger Cube

Measurement	Scale Factor
Edge length	2
Surface area	$2^2 = 4$
Volume	$2^3 = 8$

Likewise, in questions 7–15 we compared the measures of a 3-cm cube to a 1-cm cube and a 6-cm cube to a 2-cm cube. We calculated the following scale factors.

Scale Factors from Smaller Cube to Larger Cube

Measurement	Scale Factor
Edge length	3
Surface area	$3^2 = 9$
Volume	$3^3 = 27$

Refer to the above description of scale factors to answer questions 16–20.

16. Sal calculated the scale factors from a 6-cm cube to a 24-cm cube. From the smaller cube to the larger cube, what are the scale factors for (a) edge length, (b) surface area, and (c) volume? (a) 4 (b) $4^2 = 16$ (c) $4^3 = 64$

17. Brenda noticed that the scale factor relationships for cubes also applies to spheres. She found the approximate diameters of a table tennis ball $\left(1\frac{1}{2} \text{ in.}\right)$, a baseball (3 in.), and a playground ball (9 in.). Find the scale factor for (a) the volume of the table tennis ball to the volume of the baseball and (b) the surface area of the baseball to the surface area of the playground ball. (a) $2^3 = 8$ (b) $3^2 = 9$

18. The photo lab makes 5 in. by 7 in. enlargements from $2\frac{1}{2}$ in. by $3\frac{1}{2}$ in. wallet-sized photos. Find the scale factor from the smaller photo to the enlargement for (a) side length and (b) picture area. (a) 2 (b) $2^2 = 4$

19. Scale factor:
$1.5^2 = 2.25$;

Price:
$$\begin{array}{r} \$10.00 \\ \times \quad 2.25 \\ \hline \$22.50 \end{array}$$

19. Rommy wanted to charge the same price per square inch of cheese pizza regardless of the size of the pizza. Since all of Rommy's pizzas were the same thickness, he based his prices on scale factor for area. If he sells a 10-inch diameter cheese pizza for $10.00, how much should he charge for a 15-inch diameter cheese pizza?

20.
(a) 100
(b) $100^2 = 10,000$
(c) $100^3 = 1,000,000$

20. The Egyptian archeologist knew that the scale factor relationships for cubes also applies to similar pyramids. The archeologist built a $\frac{1}{100}$ scale model of the Great Pyramid. Each edge of the base of the model was 2.3 meters, while each edge of the base of the Great Pyramid measured 230 meters. From the smaller model to the Great Pyramid, what was the scale factor for (a) the length of corresponding edges, (b) the area of corresponding faces, and (c) the volume of the pyramids?

Notice from the chart that you completed near the beginning of this investigation that as the size of the cube became greater, the surface area and volume became much greater. Also notice that the volume increased at a faster rate than the surface area. The ratio of surface area to volume changes as the size of an object changes.

Ratio of Surface Area to Volume of Four Cubes

	1-cm cube	2-cm cube	3-cm cube	4-cm cube
Surface Area to Volume	6 to 1	3 to 1	2 to 1	1.5 to 1

The ratio of surface area to volume affects the size and shape of containers used to package products. The ratio of surface area to volume also affects the world of nature. Consider the relationship between surface area and volume as you answer questions 21–25.

21. Sixty-four 1-cm cubes were arranged to form one large cube. Austin wrapped the large cube with paper and sent the package to Bernard. The volume of the package was 64 cm³. What was the surface area of the exposed wrapping paper? 96 cm²

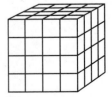

22. When Bernard received the package he divided the contents into eight smaller cubes composed of eight 2-cm cubes. Bernard wrapped the eight packages and sent them on to Charlie. The total volume of the eight packages was still 64 cm³. What was the total surface area of the exposed wrapping paper of the eight packages? 8 × 24 cm² = 192 cm²

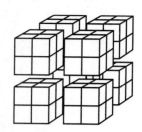

23. Charlie opened each of the eight packages and wrapped each 1-cm cube. Since there were 64 cubes, the total volume was still 64 cm³. What was the total surface area of exposed wrapping paper for all 64 packages? 64 × 6 cm² = 384 cm²

24. After a summer picnic the ice in two large thermos containers was emptied on the ground to melt. A large block of ice in the form of a 6-inch cube fell out of one container. An equal quantity of ice, but in the form of 1-inch cubes, fell scattered out of the other container. Which, if either, do you think will melt sooner, the large block of ice or the small scattered cubes? Explain your answer.

24. Although the volumes are the same, the small cubes will melt sooner than the large block because a much greater surface area is exposed to the warmer surroundings.

25. Because the surface area of a smaller animal is greater for its volume than it is for a larger animal, smaller animals work harder to regulate body temperature than larger animals in the same environment. So smaller animals, like sparrows, need to eat a greater percentage of their weight in food than do larger animals, like hawks.

25. If someone does not eat very much we might say that he or she "eats like a bird." However, birds must eat large amounts, relative to their body weights, in order to maintain their body temperature. Since mammals and birds regulate their own body temperature, there is a limit to how small a mammal or bird may be. Comparing a hawk and a sparrow in the same environment, which of the two might eat a greater percentage of its weight in food every day? Explain your answer.

Extensions

a. Investigate how the weight of a bird and its wingspan are related.

b. Investigate reasons why the largest sea mammals are so much larger than the largest land mammals.

c. Brad's dad is 25% taller than Brad and weighs twice as much. Explain why you think this height-weight relationship may or may not be reasonable.

LESSON
111

Mental Math:
a. 0.05
b. 6.4 × 10⁻⁷
c. 60
d. 144 in.²
e. $50
f. $100
g. $16.00
Problem Solving:
    $3600

Dividing in Scientific Notation

Facts Practice: + − × ÷ Algebraic Terms (Test V in Test Masters)

Mental Math:

   a. $(-0.25) \div (-5)$ **b.** $\left(8 \times 10^{-4}\right)^2$

   c. $3m + 7m = 600$ **d.** Convert 1 ft² to square inches.

   e. $33\frac{1}{3}\%$ of $150   **f.** $150 reduced by $33\frac{1}{3}\%$

   g. Estimate 8% tax on a $198.75 purchase.

Problem Solving:

   Carpeting is sold by the square yard. How much would it cost to carpet a classroom that is 36 ft long and 36 ft wide, if the carpet is priced at $25 per square yard, including tax and installation?

One unit of distance astronomers use to measure distances within our solar system is the **astronomical unit** (AU). An astronomical unit is the average distance between Earth and the Sun, which is roughly 150,000,000 km (or 93,000,000 mi).

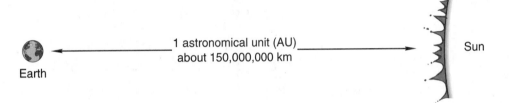

Earth   1 astronomical unit (AU)   Sun
about 150,000,000 km

For instance, at a point in Saturn's orbit when it is 1.5 billion kilometers from the Sun, its distance from the Sun is 10 AU.

$$1{,}500{,}000{,}000 \text{ km} \cdot \frac{1 \text{ AU}}{150{,}000{,}000 \text{ km}} = 10 \text{ AU}$$

This means that the distance from Saturn to the Sun is about 10 times the average distance between Earth and the Sun. When dividing very large or very small numbers it is helpful to use scientific notation. Here we show the same calculation in scientific notation.

$$\frac{1.5 \times 10^9 \text{ km}}{1.5 \times 10^8 \text{ km/AU}} = 10 \text{ AU}$$

In this lesson we will practice dividing numbers in scientific notation.

    Recall that when we multiply numbers in scientific notation we multiply the powers of 10 by adding their exponents.

$$\left(6 \times 10^6\right)\left(1.5 \times 10^2\right) = 9 \times 10^8$$

> **When we divide numbers in scientific notation we divide the powers of 10 by subtracting their exponents.**

$$\frac{6 \times 10^6}{1.5 \times 10^2} = 4 \times 10^4 \quad \longleftarrow \quad (6 - 2 = 4)$$

Example 1 Write each quotient in scientific notation.

(a) $\dfrac{6 \times 10^8}{1.2 \times 10^6}$ (b) $\dfrac{3 \times 10^3}{6 \times 10^6}$ (c) $\dfrac{2 \times 10^{-2}}{8 \times 10^{-8}}$

Solution (a) To find the quotient, we divide 6 by 1.2 and 10^8 by 10^6.

$$1.2\overline{)6.0}^{\ 5.} \qquad 10^8 \div 10^6 = 10^2 \quad \longleftarrow \quad (8 - 6 = 2)$$

The quotient is **5 × 10^2**.

(b) We divide 3 by 6 and 10^3 by 10^6.

$$6\overline{)3.0}^{\ 0.5} \qquad 10^3 \div 10^6 = 10^{-3} \quad \longleftarrow \quad (3 - 6 = -3)$$

The quotient, 0.5×10^{-3}, is not in proper form. We write the quotient in scientific notation.

$$5 \times 10^{-4}$$

(c) We divide 2 by 8 and 10^{-2} by 10^{-8}.

$$8\overline{)2.00}^{\ 0.25} \qquad 10^{-2} \div 10^{-8} = 10^6 \quad \longleftarrow \quad [-2 - (-8) = 6]$$

The quotient, 0.25×10^6, is not in proper form. We write the quotient in scientific notation.

$$2.5 \times 10^5$$

Example 2 The distance from the Sun to Earth is about 1.5×10^8 km. Light travels at a speed of about 3×10^5 km per second. About how many seconds does it take light to travel from the Sun to Earth?

Solution We divide 1.5×10^8 km by 3×10^5 km/s.

$$\frac{1.5 \times 10^8 \text{ km}}{3 \times 10^5 \text{ km/s}} = 0.5 \times 10^3 \text{ s}$$

We may write the quotient so that it is in the proper form of scientific notation, **5 × 10^2 s**. We may also write the answer in standard form, **500 s**. It takes about 500 seconds for light from the Sun to reach Earth.

Practice*   Write each quotient in scientific notation.

a. $\dfrac{3.6 \times 10^9}{2 \times 10^3}$ 1.8×10^6 b. $\dfrac{7.5 \times 10^3}{2.5 \times 10^9}$ 3×10^{-6}

c. $\dfrac{4.5 \times 10^{-8}}{3 \times 10^{-4}}$ 1.5×10^{-4} d. $\dfrac{6 \times 10^{-4}}{1.5 \times 10^{-8}}$ 4×10^4

e. $\dfrac{4 \times 10^{12}}{8 \times 10^4}$ 5×10^7 f. $\dfrac{1.5 \times 10^4}{3 \times 10^{12}}$ 5×10^{-9}

g. $\dfrac{3.6 \times 10^{-8}}{6 \times 10^{-2}}$ 6×10^{-7} h. $\dfrac{1.8 \times 10^{-2}}{9 \times 10^{-8}}$ 2×10^5

Problem set 111

1. (12) The earliest Indian head penny was minted in 1859. The latest Indian head penny was minted in 1909. How many years were the Indian head pennies minted?
51 years (1859 should be counted.)

2. (28) The product of y and 15 is 600. What is the sum of y and 15?   55

3. (36,54) Thirty percent of those gathered agreed that the king should abdicate his throne. All the rest disagreed.

(a) What fraction of those gathered disagreed? $\frac{7}{10}$

(b) What was the ratio of those who agreed to those who disagreed? $\frac{3}{7}$

4. (80) Triangle ABC with vertices at $A\,(0, 3)$, $B\,(0, 0)$, and $C\,(4, 0)$ is translated one unit to the left and one unit down to $\triangle A'B'C'$. What are the coordinates of the vertices of $\triangle A'B'C'$? $A'\,(-1, 2)$, $B'\,(-1, -1)$, $C'\,(3, -1)$

5. (21) (a) Write the prime factorization of 1024 using exponents. 2^{10}
(b) Find $\sqrt{1024}$.   32

6. (89) A portion of a regular polygon is illustrated. Each interior angle measures 150°.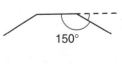

(a) What is the measure of each exterior angle?   30°

(b) The polygon has how many sides?   12 sides

(c) What is the name for a polygon with this number of sides?   dodecagon

7. The sale price of an item on sale for 40% off is $48. What
(92) was the regular price? $80

8. In a bag are 3 red marbles, 4 white marbles, and 5 blue
(94) marbles. One marble is drawn from the bag and not
replaced. A second marble is drawn and not replaced.
Then a third marble is drawn.

(a) What is the probability of drawing a red, a white, and
a blue marble in that order? $\frac{1}{22}$

(b) What is the probability of drawing a blue, a white,
and a red marble in that order? $\frac{1}{22}$

9. Write and solve an equation for the following sentence:
(101) $2x + 6 = 36$; 15

Six more than twice what number is 36?

10. What is the measure of each acute
(101) angle of this triangle? 45°

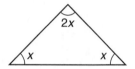

11. Solve for c^2: $c^2 - b^2 = a^2$ $c^2 = a^2 + b^2$
(106)

12. In the figure, if $l \parallel q$ and $m\angle h = 105°$, then what is the
(102) measure of

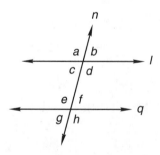

(a) $\angle a$? 105°   (b) $\angle b$? 75°   (c) $\angle c$? 75°   (d) $\angle d$? 105°

13. This formula may be used to convert temperature
(108) measurements from degrees Celsius (C) to degrees
Fahrenheit (F). Find F to the nearest degree when C is 17.
63

$$F = 1.8C + 32$$

14. What is the area of a 45° sector of a
(104) circle with a radius of 12 in.? Use
3.14 for π and round the answer to
the nearest square inch. 57 in.^{2}

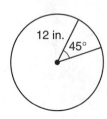

15.
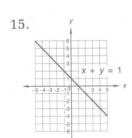

15. Make a table of ordered pairs showing three or four
(Inv. 9) solutions for the equation $x + y = 1$. Then graph all
possible solutions. See student work.

16. Refer to the graph in the previous problem to answer (a)
(107) and (b).

(a) What is the slope of the graph of $x + y = 1$? –1

(b) Where does the graph of $x + y = 1$ intersect the y-axis?
(0, 1)

17. The students in Room 8 decided to
(105) make posters to wrap around school
trash cans to encourage students to
properly dispose of litter. The
illustration shows the dimensions of
the trash can. Converting the
dimensions to feet and using 3.14 for
π, find the number of square feet of
paper needed to wrap around each
trash can. 18.84 ft^2

18. The trash can illustrated in problem 17 has the capacity
(95) to contain how many cubic feet of trash? 9.42 ft^3

19. Find two solutions to each of these equations.
(109)

(a) $2x^2 + 1 = 19$ 3, –3   (b) $2x^2 - 1 = 19$ $\sqrt{10}, -\sqrt{10}$

20. What is the perimeter of a triangle with vertices located at
(99) (–1, 2), (–1, –1), and (3, –1)? 12 units

21. Sal deposited $5000 in an account that paid 5% interest
(110) compounded annually. What was the total value of the
account after 5 years? $6381.41

22. The figure illustrates three similar
(97,99) triangles. If AC is 15 cm and BC is
20 cm,

(a) what is AB? 25 cm

(b) what is CD? 12 cm

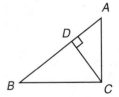

23. Express each quotient in scientific notation.
(111)

(a) $\dfrac{3.6 \times 10^8}{6 \times 10^6}$ 6×10^1 (b) $\dfrac{3.6 \times 10^{-8}}{1.2 \times 10^{-6}}$ 3×10^{-2}

24. In the figure, if the measure of $\angle x$ is 140°, what is the
(40) measure of $\angle y$? 130°

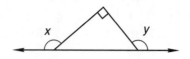

Solve:

25. $5x + 3x = 18 + 2x$ 3   **26.** $\dfrac{3.6}{x} = \dfrac{4.5}{0.06}$ 0.048
(102)   (98)

Simplify:

27. (a) $(-1)^6 + (-1)^5$ 0   (b) $(-10)^6 \div (-10)^5$ −10
(103)

28. (a) $\dfrac{(4a^2b)(9ab^2c)}{6abc}$ $6a^2b^2$ (b) $x(x - c) + cx$ x^2
(96,103)

29. $(-3) + (+2)(-4) - (-6)(-2) - (-8)$ −15
(85)

30. $\dfrac{3\frac{1}{3} \cdot 1\frac{4}{5} + 1.5}{0.03}$ 250
(43,45)

LESSON 112

Applications of the Pythagorean Theorem

Facts Practice: Multiplying and Dividing in Scientific Notation
(Test W in Test Masters)

Mental Math:

a. $(-10)^2 + (-10)^3$ b. $(8 \times 10^6) \div (4 \times 10^3)$

c. $m^2 = 100$ d. Convert 50°C to degrees Fahrenheit.

e. 25% of $2000   f. $2000 increased 25%

g. Start with 2 dozen, + 1, × 4, + 20, ÷ 3, + 2, ÷ 6, × 4, − 3,
   $\sqrt{}$, ÷ 2.

Problem Solving:

Chad was $\frac{1}{4}$ of the way through his book. Twenty pages later he
was $\frac{1}{3}$ of the way through his book. When he is $\frac{3}{4}$ of the way
through the book, how many pages will he have to read until he
finishes the book?

Workers who construct buildings need to be sure that the structures have square corners. If the corner of a 40 foot long building is 89° or 91° instead of 90°, the other end of the building will be about 8 inches out of position.

One way construction workers check to be sure a building under construction is square is by using the Pythagorean theorem. Remember that a 3-4-5 triangle is a right triangle.

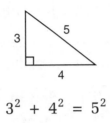

$$3^2 + 4^2 = 5^2$$

Any triangle with sides in the ratio of 3 to 4 to 5 is a right triangle. Because the numbers 3, 4, and 5 satisfy the Pythagorean theorem, they are sometimes called a **Pythagorean triplet.** Multiples of 3-4-5 are also Pythagorean triplets.

3-4-5

6-8-10

9-12-15

12-16-20

Before pouring concrete for the foundation of a building, a construction worker will build wooden forms to hold the concrete. Then the worker or building inspector may use a Pythagorean triplet to check the forms to be sure that they make a right angle. First the perpendicular sides are marked at selected lengths.

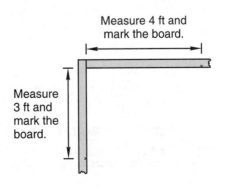

Measure 4 ft and mark the board.

Measure 3 ft and mark the board.

Then the distance between the marks is checked to be sure the three measures are a Pythagorean triplet.

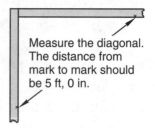

Measure the diagonal. The distance from mark to mark should be 5 ft, 0 in.

If the three measures are a Pythagorean triplet, the worker can be confident that the corner is a 90° angle.

Activity: Application of the Pythagorean Theorem

Materials needed by each group of 2 or 3 students:

- Two new unsharpened pencils (or two rulers)
- A ruler for measuring the pencils (or rulers)
- A protractor

Position two pencils (or two rulers) so that they appear to form a right angle. Mark one pencil at 3 inches from the vertex of the angle and the other pencil at 4 inches from the vertex. Then measure from mark to mark to see if the distance between the marks is 5 inches. Adjust the pencils if necessary.

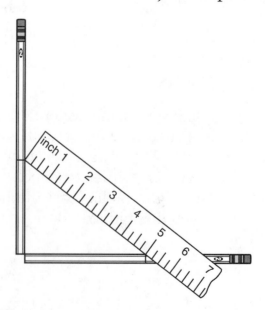

Use a protractor to confirm that the angle formed by the pencils measures 90°.

Repeat the activity, marking the pencils at 6 cm and 8 cm with the distance between marks 10 cm.

Example 1   The numbers 5, 12, and 13 are a Pythagorean triplet because $5^2 + 12^2 = 13^2$. What are the next three multiples of this Pythagorean triplet?

Solution   To find the next three multiples of 5-12-13, we multiply each number by 2, by 3, and by 4.

10-24-26

15-36-39

20-48-52

Example 2   A roof is being built over a 24 ft wide room. The slope of the roof is 4 in 12. Calculate the length of the rafters needed for the roof. (Include 2 ft for the rafter tail.)

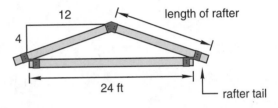

Solution   We consider a rafter to be the hypotenuse of a right triangle. The width of the room is 24 ft, but a rafter spans only half the width of the room. So the base of the right triangle is 12 ft. The slope of the roof, 4 in 12, means that for every 12 horizontal units the roof rises (or falls) 4 vertical units. Thus, since the base of the triangle is 12 ft, its height is 4 ft.

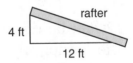

We use the Pythagorean theorem to calculate the hypotenuse.

$$a^2 + b^2 = c^2$$
$$(4 \text{ ft})^2 + (12 \text{ ft})^2 = c^2$$
$$16 \text{ ft}^2 + 144 \text{ ft}^2 = c^2$$
$$160 \text{ ft}^2 = c^2$$
$$\sqrt{160} \text{ ft} = c$$
$$12.65 \text{ ft} \approx c$$

Using a calculator we find that the rafter needs to be about 12.65 feet plus 2 feet for the rafter tail.

$$12.65 \text{ ft} + 2 \text{ ft} = \textbf{14.65 ft}$$

To change 0.65 ft to inches we multiply 0.65×12 in. which equals 7.8 inches. We round this up to 8 inches. So the length of each rafter is about **14 ft, 8 in.**

Example 3   Serena went to a level field to fly a kite. She let out all 200 ft of string and tied it to a stake. Then she walked out on the field until she was directly under the kite, 150 feet from the stake. About how high was the kite?

Solution   We begin by drawing a sketch of the problem. The length of the kite string is the hypotenuse of a right triangle while the distance between Serena and the stake is one leg of the triangle. We use the Pythagorean theorem to find the remaining leg which is the height of the kite.

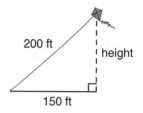

200 ft
height
150 ft

$$a^2 + b^2 = c^2$$

$$a^2 + (150 \text{ ft})^2 = (200 \text{ ft})^2$$

$$a^2 + 22{,}500 \text{ ft}^2 = 40{,}000 \text{ ft}^2$$

$$a^2 = 17{,}500 \text{ ft}^2$$

$$a = \sqrt{17{,}500} \text{ ft}$$

$$a \approx 132 \text{ ft}$$

Using a calculator we find that the height of the kite was about **132 ft.**

Practice   **a.** A 12-foot ladder was leaning against a building. The base of the ladder was 5 feet from the building. How high up the side of the building did the ladder reach? Write the answer in feet and inches rounded to the nearest inch.
10 feet, 11 inches

b. Figure *ABCD* illustrates a rectangular field 400 feet long and 300 feet wide. The path from *A* to *C* is how much shorter than the path from *A* to *B* to *C*? 200 feet

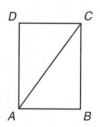

D   C
A   B

Problem set 112   **1.** Sherman deposited $3000 in an account paying 8 percent interest compounded annually. He withdrew his money and interest 3 years later. How much did he withdraw?
(110)
$3779.14

2. What is the square root of the sum of 3 squared and 4 squared? 5
(20,28)

3. Find (a) the median and (b) the mode of the following
(Inv. 4) quiz scores. (a) 90 (b) 95

Class Quiz Scores

Score	Number of Students
100	2
95	7
90	6
85	6
80	3
70	3

4. The trucker completed the 840-kilometer haul in 10 hours
(46) and 30 minutes. What was the trucker's average speed in
kilometers per hour? 80 kilometers per hour

5. Use a ratio box to solve this problem. Barbara earned $28
(72) for 6 hours of work. At that rate, how much would she
earn for 9 hours of work? $42

6. At a yard sale an item marked $1.00 was reduced 50%.
(110) When the item still did not sell, the sale price was
reduced 50%. What was the price of the item after the
second discount? $0.25

7. If 60 percent of the students were boys, what was the
(36) ratio of boys to girls? $\frac{3}{2}$

8. The points (3, 11), (–2, –1), and (–2, 11) are the vertices of
(99) a right triangle. Use the Pythagorean theorem to find the
length of the hypotenuse of this triangle. 13 units

9. Use a ratio box to solve this problem. Mike paid $48 for a
(92) jacket at 25 percent off of the regular price. What was the
regular price of the jacket? $64

10. The frame of this kite is formed by
(112) two perpendicular pieces of wood
whose lengths are shown in inches.
Connecting the four ends of the
sticks is a loop of string. How long is
the string? 70 inches

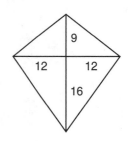

11. What percent of 2.5 is 2? 80%
(77)

12. Use a ratio box to solve this problem. Troy bought a
(92) baseball card for $6 and sold it for 25 percent more than
he paid for it. How much profit did he make on the sale?
$1.50

13. What are the odds of having a coin turn up tails on 4
(Inv. 10) consecutive tosses of a coin? 1 to 15

14. How much interest is earned in 6 months on $4000
(110) deposited at 9 percent simple interest? $180

15. Complete the table.
(48)

Fraction	Decimal	Percent
$\frac{5}{8}$	(a) 0.625	(b) 62.5%

16. Divide and write each quotient in scientific notation.
(111)

(a) $\dfrac{5 \times 10^8}{2 \times 10^4}$ 2.5×10^4 (b) $\dfrac{1.2 \times 10^4}{4 \times 10^8}$ 3×10^{-5}

17. Convert 300 kilograms to grams. 300,000 grams
(50)

18. Solve for t: $d = rt$ $t = \frac{d}{r}$
(106)

19.
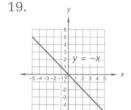

19. Make a table that shows three pairs of numbers for the
(Inv. 9) function $y = -x$. Then graph the number pairs on a
coordinate plane and draw a line through the points.
See student work.

20. Find the perimeter of this figure.
(104) Dimensions are in centimeters. (Use
3.14 for π.) 91.4 cm

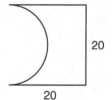

20

20

21. Find the surface area of this right
(105) triangular prism. Dimensions are
in feet. 468 ft²

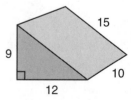

15

9

10

12

22. (a) Write the prime factorization of 1 trillion using
(21) exponents. $2^{12} \cdot 5^{12}$

(b) Find the positive square root of 1 trillion. 1,000,000

23. These triangles are similar. Dimensions are in centimeters.
(97,98)

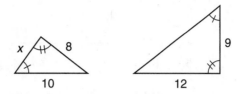

(a) Find x. 6 cm

(b) Find the scale factor from the smaller to the larger triangle. 1.5

Solve:

24. $\dfrac{16}{2.5} = \dfrac{48}{f}$ 7.5
(98)

25. $2\dfrac{2}{3}x - 3 = 21$ 9
(93)

Simplify:

26. $5^2 - \left[40 - 2\left(10 + 3^2\right)\right]$ 23
(63)

27. $2\dfrac{3}{4} - \left(1.5 - \dfrac{1}{6}\right)$ $1\frac{5}{12}$
(43)

28. $3.5 \div 1\dfrac{2}{5} \div 3$ $\frac{5}{6}$
(43)

29. $|-4| - (-3)(-2)(-1) + \dfrac{(-5)(4)(-3)(2)}{-1}$ -110
(85)

30. The large grapefruit was nearly spherical and had a diameter of 14 cm. Using $\frac{22}{7}$ for π, find the approximate surface area of the grapefruit to the nearest hundred square centimeters. 600 square centimeters
(105)

LESSON 113

Volume of Pyramids, Cones, and Spheres

Mental Math:
a. −0.25
b. 2 × 10⁻⁴
c. 0.6
d. 288 in.²
e. $1600
f. $800
g. 2½ hr
Problem Solving:
  5 and 12

Facts Practice: + − × ÷ Algebraic Terms (Test V in Test Masters)

Mental Math:

  a. $0.75 \div (-3)$
  b. $\left(6 \times 10^6\right) \div \left(3 \times 10^{10}\right)$
  c. $10m + 1.5 = 7.5$
  d. Convert 2 ft² to square inches.
  e. $66\frac{2}{3}\%$ of $2400
  f. $2400 reduced by $66\frac{2}{3}\%$
  g. At 500 mph how long will it take a plane to travel 1250 miles?

Problem Solving:

The sum of two numbers is 17, and their product is 60. Use guess and check to find the two numbers.

Volume of pyramids

A **pyramid** is a geometric solid that has three or more triangular faces and a base that is a polygon. Each of these figures is a pyramid.

The volume of a pyramid is $\frac{1}{3}$ the volume of a prism that has the same base and height. Recall that the volume of a prism is equal to the area of its base times its height.

$$\text{Volume of a prism} = \text{area of base} \cdot \text{height}$$

To find the volume of a pyramid, we will first find the volume of a prism that has the same base and height. Then we will divide the result by 3 (or multiply by $\frac{1}{3}$).

Volume of a pyramid $= \dfrac{1}{3} \cdot$ **area of base** $\cdot$ **height**

Example 1

The cube just contains the pyramid. Each edge of the cube is 6 centimeters.

(a) Find the volume of the cube.

(b) Find the volume of the pyramid.

6 cm

Solution (a) The volume of the cube equals the area of the base times the height.

$$\text{Area of base} = 6 \text{ cm} \times 6 \text{ cm} = 36 \text{ cm}^2$$

$$\text{Volume of cube} = \text{area of base} \cdot \text{height}$$
$$= \left(36 \text{ cm}^2\right)\left(6 \text{ cm}\right)$$
$$= \mathbf{216 \text{ cm}^3}$$

(b) The volume of the pyramid is $\frac{1}{3}$ the volume of the cube, so we divide the volume of the cube by 3 $\left(\text{or multiply by } \frac{1}{3}\right)$.

$$\text{Volume of pyramid} = \frac{1}{3}(\text{volume of prism})$$

$$= \frac{1}{3}\left(216 \text{ cm}^3\right)$$

$$= \mathbf{72 \text{ cm}^3}$$

Volume of cones The volume of a cone is $\frac{1}{3}$ the volume of a cylinder with the same base and height.

Volume of a cone $= \dfrac{1}{3} \cdot$ area of base $\cdot$ height

---

Example 2 Find the volume of this circular cone. Dimensions are in centimeters. (Use 3.14 for π.)

30

|← 20 →|

Solution We first find the volume of a cylinder with the same base and height as the cone.

$$\text{Volume of cylinder} = \text{area of circle} \cdot \text{height}$$
$$\approx (3.14)(10 \text{ cm})^2 \cdot 30 \text{ cm}$$
$$\approx 9420 \text{ cm}^3$$

Then we find $\frac{1}{3}$ of this volume.

$$\text{Volume of cone} = \frac{1}{3}(\text{volume of cylinder})$$

$$\approx \frac{1}{3} \cdot 9420 \text{ cm}^3$$

$$\approx \mathbf{3140 \text{ cm}^3}$$

Volume of spheres

There is a special relationship between the volume of a cylinder, the volume of a cone, and the volume of a sphere. Picture two identical cylindrical boxes whose heights are equal to their diameters. In one box is a cone with the same diameter and height as the cylinder. In the other box is a sphere with the same diameter as the cylinder.

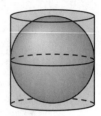

We have learned that the volume of the cone is $\frac{1}{3}$ the volume of the cylinder. Remarkably, the volume of the sphere is twice the volume of the cone, that is, $\frac{2}{3}$ of the volume of the cylinder. Here we use a balance scale to provide another view of this relationship.

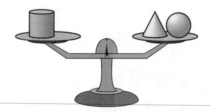

Imagine that each object on the balance scale is a solid, composed of identical materials. The diameters of all three solids are equal. The heights of the cylinder and cone equal their diameters. The balance scale shows that the combined masses of the cone and sphere equal the mass of the cylinder. The cone's mass is $\frac{1}{3}$ of the cylinder's mass, and the sphere's mass is $\frac{2}{3}$ of the cylinder's mass.

The formula for the volume of a sphere can be derived from our knowledge of cylinders and of the relationship between spheres and cylinders. First consider the volume of any cylinder whose height is equal to its diameter. In this diagram we have labeled the diameter, d, the radius, r, and the height, h.

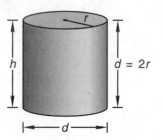

Since the height of this cylinder is equal to its diameter, we may also refer to the height as d or as $2r$, since two radii equal the diameter.

Recall that we can calculate the volume of a cylinder by multiplying the area of its circular base times its height.

$$\text{Volume of cylinder} = \text{area of circle} \cdot \text{height}$$
$$V = \pi r^2 \cdot h$$

For a cylinder whose height is equal to its diameter, we can replace h in the formula with d. Moreover, since the diameter equals 2 radii ($2r$), we can also replace h with $2r$ as we show here.

$V = \pi r^2 \cdot h$ formula for volume of a cylinder

$V = \pi r^2 \cdot 2r$ replaced h with $2r$ which equals the height of the cylinder

$V = 2\pi r^3$ rearranged factors

This formula, $V = 2\pi r^3$, gives the volume of a cylinder whose height is equal to its diameter. The volume of a sphere is $\frac{2}{3}$ of the volume of a cylinder with the same diameter and height.

$$\text{Volume of sphere} = \frac{2}{3} \cdot \text{volume of cylinder}$$

$$= \frac{2}{3} \cdot 2\pi r^3 \qquad \text{substituted}$$

$$= \frac{4}{3}\pi r^3 \qquad \text{multiplied } \frac{2}{3} \text{ and } 2$$

We have found the formula for the volume of a sphere.

$$\boxed{\textbf{Volume of a sphere} = \frac{4}{3}\pi r^3}$$

Example 3   A ball with a diameter of 20 cm has a volume of how many cubic centimeters? (Round the answer to the nearest hundred cubic centimeters.)

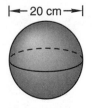

Use 3.14 for π.

Solution   The diameter of the sphere is 20 cm, so its radius is 10 cm. We use the formula for the volume of a sphere and replace π with 3.14 and r with 10 cm.

$$V = \frac{4}{3}\pi r^3 \qquad \text{formula}$$

$$\approx \frac{4}{3}(3.14)(10 \text{ cm})^3 \qquad \begin{array}{l}\text{substituted 3.14 for } \pi \text{ and}\\ \text{10 cm for } r\end{array}$$

$$\approx \frac{4}{3}(3.14)(1000 \text{ cm}^3) \qquad \text{cubed 10 cm}$$

$$\approx \frac{4}{3}(3140 \text{ cm}^3) \qquad \text{multiplied 3.14 and 1000 cm}^3$$

$$\approx 4186\frac{2}{3} \text{ cm}^3 \qquad \text{multiplied } \frac{4}{3} \text{ and 3140 cm}^3$$

$$\approx \mathbf{4200 \text{ cm}^3} \qquad \begin{array}{l}\text{rounded to nearest hundred}\\ \text{cubic centimeters}\end{array}$$

Practice   Pictured are two identical cylindrical boxes whose heights are equal to their diameters. In one box is the largest cone it can contain. In the other box is the largest sphere it can contain. Packing material is used to fill all the voids in the boxes not occupied by the cone or sphere. Use this information to answer questions a–e.

a. What fraction of the box is occupied by the cone? $\frac{1}{3}$

b. What fraction of the box with the cone is occupied by the packing material? $\frac{2}{3}$

c. What fraction of the box is occupied by the sphere? $\frac{2}{3}$

d. What fraction of the box with the sphere is occupied by the packing material? $\frac{1}{3}$

e. If the cone and sphere were removed from their boxes and all the packing material from both boxes was put into one box, what portion of the box would be filled with packing material?   All of the box would be filled. $\left(\frac{1}{3} + \frac{2}{3} = 1\right)$

f. A pyramid with a height of 12 inches and a base 12 inches square is packed in the smallest cubical box that can contain it. What is the volume of the box, and what is the volume of the pyramid? 1728 in.³; 576 in.³

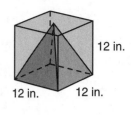

Find the volume of each figure below. For both calculations leave π as π.

g. |←—6 in.—→| 18π in.³

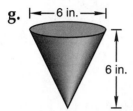

6 in.

h. |←—6 in.—→| 36π in.³

Problem set 113

1. Find the sale price of a $24 item after successive discounts
(110) of 25% and 25%. $13.50

2. Ten billion is how much greater than nine hundred
(51) eighty million? Write the answer in scientific notation.
9.02×10^9

3. The median of the following numbers is how much less
(Inv. 4) than the mean? 0.94

1.4, 0.5, 0.6, 0.75, 5.2

4. Nelda worked for 5 hours and earned $24. How much did
(46) Nelda earn per hour? Christy worked for 6 hours and earned $33. How much did Christy earn per hour? Christy earned how much more per hour than Nelda?
$4.80 per hour; $5.50 per hour; $0.70 more per hour

5. If 24 kilograms of seed costs $31, what is the cost of
(72) 42 kilograms of seed at the same rate? Use a ratio box to solve the problem. $54.25

6. A kilometer is about $\frac{5}{8}$ of a mile. A mile is 1760 yards. A
(60) kilometer is about how many yards? 1100 yards

7. A card will be drawn from a deck of 52 playing cards and
(94) replaced. Another card will be drawn. What is the probability that both cards will be hearts? $\frac{1}{16}$

Write equations to solve problems 8 and 9.

8. What percent of $30 is $1.50? $W_P \times \$30 = \$1.50$; 5%
(77)

9. Fifty percent of what number is $2\frac{1}{2}$? $\frac{1}{2} \times W_N = 2\frac{1}{2}$; 5
(77)

10. Trinh left $5000 in an account that paid 8 percent interest
(110) compounded annually. How much interest was earned in
3 years? $1298.56

11. Use a ratio box to solve this problem. A merchant sold an
(92) item at a 20 percent discount from the regular price. If the
regular price was $12, what was the sale price of the item?
$9.60

12. The points (0, 4), (−3, 2), and (3, 2) are the vertices of an
(62) isosceles triangle. Find the area of the triangle. 6 units²

13. Use the Pythagorean theorem to find the length of one of
(112) the two congruent sides of the triangle in problem 12.
(*Hint*: First draw an altitude to form two right triangles.)
$\sqrt{13}$ units

14. Use a ratio box to solve this problem. Jessica sculptured a
(98) figurine from clay at $\frac{1}{24}$ of the actual size of the model. If
the model was 6 feet tall, how many inches tall was the
figurine? 3 inches

15. Roughly estimate the volume of a tennis ball in cubic
(113) centimeters by using 6 cm for the diameter and 3 for π.
Round the answer to the nearest ten cubic centimeters.
110 cm³

16. Multiply and write the product in scientific notation.
(83)

$$(6.3 \times 10^6)(7 \times 10^{-3})$$ 4.41 × 10⁴

17. Tim can get from point *A* to point *B*
(112) by staying on the sidewalk and
turning left at the corner *C* or he can
take the shortcut and walk straight
from point *A* to point *B*. How many
yards does he save by taking the
shortcut instead of staying on the
sidewalk? Begin by using the
Pythagorean theorem to find the
length of the shortcut. 20 yards

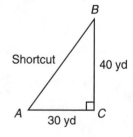

18. (a) Solve for h: $A = \frac{1}{2}bh$ $h = \frac{2A}{b}$
(108)

(b) Use the formula $A = \frac{1}{2}bh$ to find h when $A = 16$ and $b = 8$. 4

19.

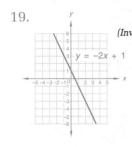

19. Make a table that shows three pairs of numbers for the
(Inv. 9,107) function $y = -2x + 1$. Then graph the number pairs on a coordinate plane and draw a line through the points to show other number pairs of the function. What is the slope of the graphed line? See student work.; −2

20. Find the volume of the pyramid.
(113) Dimensions are in meters. 16,000 m³

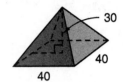

21. Find the volume of the cone. Dimen-
(113) sions are in centimeters. 6280 cm³

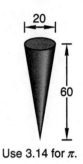

Use 3.14 for π.

22. Refer to the figure to find the measure of each angle.
(40) Dimensions are in centimeters.

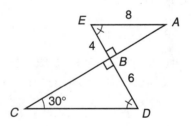

(a) $\angle D$ 60°   (b) $\angle E$ 60°   (c) $\angle A$ 30°

23. In the figure in problem 22, what is the length of $\overline{CD}$?
(97) 12 cm

Solve:

24. $\dfrac{7.5}{d} = \dfrac{25}{16}$ 4.8
(98)

25. $1\frac{3}{5}w + 17 = 49$ 20
(93)

Simplify:

26. $5^2 - \left\{ 4^2 - \left[3^2 - \left(2^2 - 1^2 \right) \right] \right\}$ 15
(63)

27.
(88)
$\dfrac{440 \text{ yd}}{1 \text{ min}} \cdot \dfrac{1 \text{ min}}{60 \text{ s}} \cdot \dfrac{3 \text{ ft}}{1 \text{ yd}}$ $22\frac{\text{ft}}{\text{s}}$

28.
(30)
$1\dfrac{3}{4} + 2\dfrac{2}{3} - 3\dfrac{5}{6}$ $\frac{7}{12}$

29.
(26)
$\left(1\dfrac{3}{4}\right)\left(2\dfrac{2}{3}\right) \div 3\dfrac{5}{6}$ $1\frac{5}{23}$

30.
(85)
$(-7) + |-3| - (2)(-3) + (-4) - (-3)(-2)(-1)$ 4

LESSON 114

Negative Exponents

Facts Practice: Multiplying and Dividing in Scientific Notation
(Test W in Test Masters)

Mental Math:

a. $(-3)^3 + (-3)^2$ **b.** $(4 \times 10^8)^2$

c. $10m - m = 9^2$ **d.** Convert 60°C to degrees Fahrenheit.

e. 150% of $3000   **f.** 150% more than $3000

g. Find 25% of 40, -1, $\times 5$, -1, $\div 2$, -1, $\div 3$, $\times 10$, $+ 2$, $\div 9$, $\div 2$, $\sqrt{\ }$.

Problem Solving:

Four blocks marked X, a 250-g mass, and a 500-g mass were balanced on a scale as shown. Write an equation to represent this balanced scale and find the mass of each block marked X.

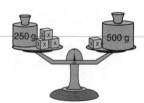

We have used negative exponents to express small numbers in scientific notation.

$$0.00025 = 2.5 \times 10^{-4}$$

We stated that the negative sign on the exponent indicates that the decimal point should be moved to the left when the number is written in standard form. In this lesson we will further explain the meaning of negative exponents.

Study the following sequences. Notice in sequence (a) that the exponent of each term is 1 less than the exponent of the preceding term.

(a) ..., 10^3, 10^2, 10^1, 10^0, 10^{-1}, 10^{-2}, 10^{-3}, ...

(b) ..., 1000, 100, 10, 1, $\dfrac{1}{10}$, $\dfrac{1}{100}$, $\dfrac{1}{1000}$, ...

In sequence (b) the value of each term is one tenth the value of the preceding term. Sequences (a) and (b) show two ways to write the same numbers. Can you find pairs of numbers that are reciprocals in each sequence? You will see that the terms to the right of 10^0 and 1 are reciprocals of the terms to the left of 10^0 and 1. For example, 10^{-3} $\left(\frac{1}{1000}\right)$ is the reciprocal of 10^3 (1000). Likewise, 10^{-4} is the reciprocal of 10^4. Since 10^4 equals 10,000, we find that

$$10^{-4} = \frac{1}{10,000}$$

So the expression 2.5×10^{-4} means $2.5 \times \frac{1}{10,000}$.

$$2.5 \times \frac{1}{10,000} = \frac{2.5}{10,000}$$
$$= 0.00025$$

Example 1 Show why 1.5×10^{-3} equals 0.0015.

Solution The expression 10^{-3} means $\frac{1}{1000}$. So 1.5×10^{-3} means $1.5 \times \frac{1}{1000}$, which we simplify.

$$1.5 \times 10^{-3} = 1.5 \times \frac{1}{1000} \qquad \text{replaced } 10^{-3} \text{ with } \frac{1}{1000}$$

$$1.5 \times 10^{-3} = \frac{1.5}{1000} \qquad \text{multiplied}$$

$$\mathbf{1.5 \times 10^{-3} = 0.0015} \qquad \text{divided}$$

Example 2 Simplify: 2^{-3}

Solution The negative exponent means that 2^{-3} is the reciprocal of 2^3. We find that 2^3 is 8.

$$2^3 = 2 \cdot 2 \cdot 2 = 8$$

So 2^{-3} is the reciprocal of 8 which is $\frac{1}{8}$.

$$2^{-3} = \frac{1}{8}$$

Example 3 Write 10^{-3} as a decimal number.

Solution Since 10^3 equals 1000, its reciprocal, 10^{-3}, equals $\frac{1}{1000}$. We write $\frac{1}{1000}$ as the decimal **0.001.**

Practice*   Simplify:

     a. 5^{-2} $\frac{1}{25}$
            b. 3^{-4} $\frac{1}{81}$
            c. 2^{-5} $\frac{1}{32}$

     d. 10^{-2} $\frac{1}{100}$
            e. $2^3 \cdot 2^{-3}$ 1
            f. $2^{-2} + 2^{-3}$ $\frac{3}{8}$

     g. Write 10^{-2} as a decimal number.   0.01

     h. Show why 7.5×10^{-4} equals 0.00075. (See Example 1.)
        $7.5 \times 10^{-4} = 7.5 \times \frac{1}{10,000} = \frac{7.5}{10,000} = 0.00075$

Problem set   **1.** The regular price was $72.50, but it was on sale for 20%
114   *(46,92)*   off. What was the total sale price including 7% sales tax?
           Use a ratio box to find the sale price. Then find the sales
           tax and total price. $62.06

     2. On his first 4 tests, Eric's average score was 87. What
     (55)   score does he need to average on his next 2 tests to have a
        6-test average of 90?   96

     3. In a bag there are 6 red marbles, 9 green marbles, and 12
     (Inv. 10)   blue marbles. One marble is to be drawn from the bag.

        (a) What is the probability that the marble will be blue? $\frac{4}{9}$

        (b) What is the chance that the marble will be green? $33\frac{1}{3}\%$

        (c) What are the odds that the marble will not be red?
           7 to 2

     4. If a box of 12 dozen pencils costs $10.80, then what is the
     (46)   cost per pencil? $7\frac{1}{2}$¢ per pencil

     5. How much interest is earned on $5000 at 8 percent
     (110)   simple interest in 6 months? $200

     6. One fourth of the students in the class earned an A on the
     (Inv. 5)   test. One third of the students earned a B. The rest of the
           students earned C's.

6.(a)   Class Test Scores

        (a) Sketch a circle graph that displays this information.

        (b) If 6 students earned an A, then how many students
           earned a grade lower than a B?   10 students

7. The ratio of cars to trucks passing by the checkpoint was
(65) 5 to 2. If 3500 cars and trucks passed by the checkpoint,
how many were cars? 2500 cars

8. The snowball grew in size as it rolled down the hill. By
(113) the time it came to a stop, its diameter was about four feet.
Using 3 in place of π, roughly estimate the number of
cubic feet of snow in the snowball. 32 ft^3

Write equations to solve problems 9 and 10.

9. What is 120% of $240? $W_N = 1.2 \times \$240; \$288$
(60)

10. Sixty is what percent of 150? $60 = W_P \times 150; 40\%$
(77)

11. The points (3, 2), (6, –2), (–2, –2), and (–2, 2) are the
(75,99) vertices of a trapezoid.

(a) Find the area of the trapezoid. 26 units^2

(b) Find the perimeter of the trapezoid. 22 units

12. (a) Arrange these numbers in order from least to greatest.
(100)

$$\sqrt{6}, 6^2, -6, 0.6 \quad -6, 0.6, \sqrt{6}, 6^2$$

(b) Which of the numbers in (a) are rational numbers?
$6^2, -6, 0.6$

13. Complete the table.
(48)

FRACTION	DECIMAL	PERCENT
$1\frac{4}{5}$	(a) 1.8	(b) 180%

14. Divide and write each quotient in scientific notation.
(111)

(a) $\dfrac{5 \times 10^{-9}}{2 \times 10^{-6}}$ 2.5×10^{-3} (b) $\dfrac{2 \times 10^{-6}}{5 \times 10^{-9}}$ 4×10^2

15. What is the product of answers (a) and (b) in problem 14?
(83) 1

16. Convert 12 inches to centimeters. 30.48 centimeters
(50)

17. (a) Solve for d: $C = \pi d$ $d = \dfrac{C}{\pi}$
(108)

(b) Use the formula $C = \pi d$ to find d when C is 62.8.
(Use 3.14 for π.) 20

18.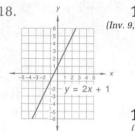

18. Find three pairs of numbers for the function $y = 2x + 1$.
(Inv. 9,107) Then graph the number pairs on a coordinate plane and draw a line through the points to show other number pairs of the function. What is the slope of the graphed line?
See student work.; 2

19. Find the perimeter of this figure. Dimensions are in centimeters. (Use 3.14 for π.) 27.42 cm
(104)

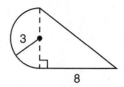

20. (a) Find the surface area of this cube. Dimensions are in feet. 54 ft^2
(105,113)

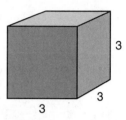

(b) If this cube is a box that contains the largest pyramid it can hold, what is the volume of the pyramid? 9 ft^3

21. Find the volume of this cylinder. Dimensions are in meters. 235.5 m^3
(95)

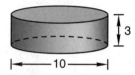

22. Refer to this figure to find (a)–(c).
(40)

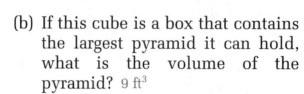

(a) m∠ACB 50°   (b) m∠CAB 40°   (c) m∠CDE 80°

23. An aquarium that is 40 cm long, 10 cm wide, and 20 cm deep is filled with water. Find the volume of the water in the aquarium. 8000 cm^3
(70)

24. Solve: $0.8m - 1.2 = 6$ 9
(93)

25. Solve and graph: $3(x - 4) < x - 8$
(93)

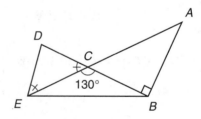

Simplify:

26. $4^2 \cdot 2^{-3} \cdot 2^{-1}$ 1
(114)

27. 1 kilogram − 50 grams
(32) 950 grams

28. $(1.2)\left(3\dfrac{3}{4}\right) \div 4\dfrac{1}{2}$ 1
_(43)_

29. $2\dfrac{3}{4} - 1.5 - \dfrac{1}{6}$ $1\frac{1}{12}$
_(43)_

30. $(-3)(-2) - (2)(-3) - (-8) + (-2)(-3) + |-5|$ 31
_(85)_

LESSON
115

Mental Math:
a. $\frac{1}{100}$
b. 1
c. 1
d. 2.5 m
e. $800
f. $800
g. 100¢
Problem Solving:
$\frac{2}{3}$ (See Lesson 113)

Volume, Capacity, and Mass in the Metric System

Facts Practice: $+ - \times \div$ Algebraic Terms (Test V in Test Masters)

Mental Math:

a. 10^{-2}

b. $\left(4 \times 10^{8}\right) \div \left(4 \times 10^{8}\right)$

c. $\dfrac{1.44}{1.2} = \dfrac{1.2}{g}$

d. Convert 250 cm to m.

e. $\frac{2}{3}$ of $1200

f. $1200 reduced $\frac{1}{3}$

g. How many cents is a nickel less than 3 dimes and 3 quarters?

Problem Solving:

Three tennis balls just fit into a cylindrical container. What fraction of the volume of the container is occupied by the tennis balls?

Metric units of volume, capacity, and mass are related. The relationship describes the volume and the masses of a quantity of water under certain standard conditions. There are two commonly used references.

> **One milliliter of water has a volume of 1 cubic centimeter and a mass of 1 gram.**

One cubic centimeter can contain 1 milliliter of water, which has a mass of 1 gram.

> **One liter of water has a volume of 1000 cubic centimeters and a mass of 1 kilogram.**

One thousand cubic centimeters can contain 1 liter of water, which has a mass of 1 kilogram.

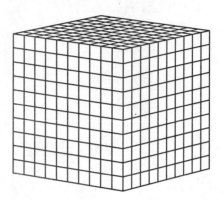

Example 1 Ray has a fish aquarium that is 50 cm long and 20 cm wide. If the aquarium is filled with water to a depth of 30 cm,

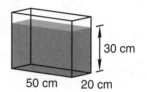

(a) how many liters of water would be in the aquarium?

(b) what would be the mass of the water in the aquarium?

Solution First we find the volume of the water in the aquarium.

$$(50 \text{ cm})(20 \text{ cm})(30 \text{ cm}) = 30{,}000 \text{ cm}^3$$

(a) Each cubic centimeter of water is 1 milliliter. Thirty thousand milliliters is **30 liters.**

(b) Each liter of water has a mass of 1 kilogram, so the mass of the water in the aquarium is **30 kilograms.** (Since a 1-kilogram mass has a weight on Earth of about 2.2 pounds, the water in the aquarium has a weight of about 66 pounds.)

Example 2 Jan wanted to find the volume of a vase. She filled a 1-liter beaker with water and then used all but 240 milliliters to fill the vase.

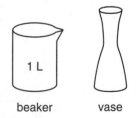

(a) What was the capacity of the vase?

(b) If the mass of the vase was 640 grams, what was the mass of the vase filled with water?

Solution (a) The 1-liter beaker contains 1000 mL of water. Since Jan used 760 mL (1000 mL − 240 mL), the volume of the inside of the vase was **760 cm³.**

(b) The mass of the water (760 g) plus the mass of the vase (640 g) was **1400 g.**

Practice   **a.** What is the mass of 2 liters of water? 2 kg

b. What is the volume of 3 liters of water? 3000 cm³

c. When the bottle was filled with water, the mass increased by 1 kilogram. How many milliliters of water were added? 1000 milliliters

d. A tank that is 25 cm long, 10 cm wide, and 8 cm deep can hold how many liters of water? 2 liters

Problem set 115

1. How much interest is earned in 9 months on a deposit of $7000 at 8 percent simple interest? $420
(110)

2. With two tosses of a coin,
(Inv. 10)

(a) what is the probability of getting two heads? $\frac{1}{4}$

(b) what is the chance of getting two tails? 25%

(c) what are the odds of getting heads, then tails? 1 to 3

3. On the first 4 days of their trip the Schmidts averaged 410 miles per day. On the fifth day they traveled 600 miles. How many miles per day did they average for the first 5 days of their trip? $448\frac{mi}{day}$
(55)

4. The 18-ounce container cost $2.16. The one-quart container cost $3.36. The smaller container cost how much more per ounce than the larger container? $1\frac{1}{2}$¢ more per ounce
(46)

Use ratio boxes to solve problems 5 and 6.

5. Adam typed 160 words in 5 minutes on his typing test. At that rate, how long would it take him to type an 800-word essay? 25 minutes
(72)

6. The ratio of guinea pigs to rats running the maze was 7 to 5. Of the 120 guinea pigs and rats running the maze, how many were guinea pigs? 70 guinea pigs
(65)

7. Kelly was thinking of a certain number. If $\frac{3}{4}$ of the number was 48, then what was $\frac{5}{8}$ of the number? 40
(74)

8. A used car dealer bought a car for $1500 and sold the car at a 40% markup. If the purchaser paid a sales tax of 8%, what was the total price of the car including tax? $2268
(92)

9. What is the sale price of an $80 skateboard after successive
(110) discounts of 25% and 20%? $48

10. The points (−3, 4), (5, −2), and (−3, −2) are the vertices of
(99) a triangle.

  (a) Find the area of the triangle. 24 units²

  (b) Find the perimeter of the triangle. 24 units

11. A glass aquarium with the dimensions
(115) shown has a mass of 5 kg when empty.
What is the mass of the aquarium
when it is half full of water? 10 kg

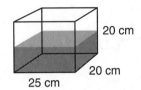

20 cm
20 cm
25 cm

12. Complete the table.
(48)

FRACTION	DECIMAL	PERCENT
(a) $\frac{7}{8}$	0.875	(b) $87\frac{1}{2}\%$

13. Compare $a \div b \enspace \textcircled{<} \enspace a - b$ if a is positive and b is
(79) negative

14. Simplify and express each answer in scientific notation.
(83,111)

  (a) $\left(6.4 \times 10^6\right)\left(8 \times 10^{-8}\right)$ 5.12 × 10⁻¹

  (b) $\dfrac{6.4 \times 10^6}{8 \times 10^{-8}}$ 8 × 10¹³

15. Convert 36 inches to centimeters. 91.44 centimeters
(50)

16. (a) Solve for b: $A = \frac{1}{2}bh$ $b = \frac{2A}{h}$
(108)

  (b) Use the formula $A = \frac{1}{2}bh$ to find b when A is 24 and
   h is 6. 8

17.
(Inv. 9,107)

17.

$y = -2x$

17. Find three pairs of numbers for the function $y = -2x$.
Then graph the number pairs on a coordinate plane and
draw a line through the points to show other number pairs
of the function. What is the slope of the graphed line?
See student work.; −2

18. Find the area of this figure. Dimensions
(104) are in millimeters. (Use 3.14 for π.)
29.72 mm²

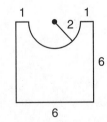

1   1
2

6

6

19. (a) Find the surface area of the cube.
(95,105)   60,000 cm²
     (b) Find the volume of the cube.
         1,000,000 cm³
     (c) How many meters long is each
         edge of the cube? 1 m

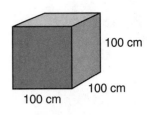
100 cm
100 cm
100 cm

20. (a) Find the volume of the cylinder.
(95,113)   Dimensions are in inches.
         6750π in.³
     (b) If within the cylinder is the largest
         sphere it can contain, what is the
         volume of the sphere? 4500π in.³

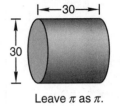
|←—30—→|
30
Leave π as π.

21. Refer to the figure to find (a)–(c).
(40)

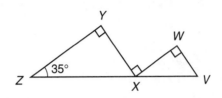

Y
W
35°
Z
X
V

   (a) m∠YXZ 55°   (b) m∠WXV 35°   (c) m∠WVX 55°

22. In the figure in problem 21, ZX is 21 cm, YX is 12 cm,
(97) and XV is 14 cm. Write a proportion to find WV. 8 cm

23. A pyramid is cut out of a cube of
(113) plastic with dimensions as shown.
     What is the volume of the pyramid?
     72 in.³

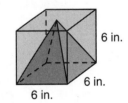
6 in.
6 in.
6 in.

Solve:

24. 0.4n + 5.2 = 12 17
(93)

25. $\dfrac{18}{y} = \dfrac{36}{28}$ 14
(98)

Simplify:

26. $\sqrt{5^2 - 3^2} + \sqrt{5^2 - 4^2}$ 7
(20)

27. 3 yd − 2 ft, 1 in.
(56) 2 yd, 11 in.

28. $3.5 \div \left(1\dfrac{2}{5} \div 3\right)$ $7\frac{1}{2}$ or 7.5
(43)

29. 3.5 + 2⁻² − 2⁻³
(114) $3\frac{5}{8}$ or 3.625

30. $\dfrac{(3)(-2)(4)}{(-6)(2)} + (-8) + (-4)(+5) - (2)(-3)$ −20
(85)

LESSON
116

Factoring Algebraic Expressions

Mental Math:
a. $4\frac{1}{4}$

b. 2.5×10^3

c. 0.4

d. 10,000 cm²

e. $500

f. $500

g. $3.60

Problem Solving:

Facts Practice: Multiplying and Dividing in Scientific Notation (Test W in Test Masters)

Mental Math:

a. $(-2)^2 + 2^{-2}$

b. $(5 \times 10^5) \div (2 \times 10^2)$

c. $3x + 1.2 = 2.4$

d. Convert 1 m^2 to cm^2.

e. 125% of $400

f. $400 increased 25%

g. Estimate an $8\frac{3}{4}$% sales tax on a $41.19 purchase.

Problem Solving:

Here is a front, top, and side view of an object. Sketch a three-dimensional view of the object from the perspective of the upper right front.

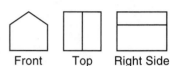

Front   Top   Right Side

Algebraic expressions are classified as **monomials** and **polynomials.** Monomials are single-term expressions such as the following three examples:

$$6x^2y^3 \qquad \frac{5xy}{2w} \qquad -6$$

Polynomials are composed of two or more terms. All of the following algebraic expressions are polynomials:

$$3x^2y + 6xy^2 \qquad x^2 + 2x + 1 \qquad 3a + 4b + 5c + d$$

Polynomials may be further classified as binomials, expressions with two terms, and trinomials, expressions with three terms. So $3x^2y + 6xy^2$ is a binomial, and $x^2 + 2x + 1$ is a trinomial.

Recall that to factor a monomial, we express the numerical part of the term as a product of prime factors, and we express the literal (letter) part of the term as a product of factors instead of using exponents. Here we factor $6x^2y^3$.

$$6x^2y^3 \qquad \text{original form}$$

$$(2)(3)xxyyy \qquad \text{factored form}$$

Some polynomials can also be factored. To factor a polynomial we first find the greatest common factor of the terms of the polynomial. Then we use the distributive property to write the expression as a product of the GCF and the remaining polynomial.

To factor $3x^2y + 6xy^2$ we first find the greatest common factor of $3x^2y$ and $6xy^2$. With practice we may find the GCF visually. This time we will factor both terms and circle the common factors.

$$3x^2y \quad + \quad 6xy^2$$
$$\textcircled{3} \cdot \textcircled{x} \cdot x \cdot \textcircled{y} + 2 \cdot \textcircled{3} \cdot \textcircled{x} \cdot y \cdot \textcircled{y}$$

We find that the GCF of $3x^2y$ and $6xy^2$ is $3xy$. Notice that removing $3xy$ from $3x^2y$ by division leaves x. Removing $3xy$ from $6xy^2$ by division leaves $2y$.

$$\frac{3x^2y}{3xy} + \frac{6xy^2}{3xy} \qquad 3xy \text{ removed by division}$$

$$x + 2y \qquad \text{remaining binomial}$$

We write the factored form of $3x^2y + 6xy^2$ this way.

$$3xy(x + 2y) \qquad \text{factored form}$$

Notice that we began with a binomial and ended with the GCF of its terms times a binomial.

Example 1 Factor the monomial: $12a^2b^3c$

Solution We factor 12 as $(2)(2)(3)$, and we factor a^2b^3c as $aabbbc$.

$$12a^2b^3c = (2)(2)(3)aabbbc$$

Example 2 Factor the trinomial: $6a^2b + 4ab^2 + 2ab$

Solution First we find the greatest common factor of the three terms. Often we can do this visually. Notice that each term has 2 as a factor, a as a factor, and b as a factor. So the GCF is $2ab$. Next we divide each term of the trinomial by $2ab$ to find what remains of each term after $2ab$ is factored out of the expression.

$$\frac{6a^2b}{2ab} + \frac{4ab^2}{2ab} + \frac{2ab}{2ab} \qquad 2ab \text{ removed by division}$$

$$3a + 2b + 1 \qquad \text{remaining trinomial}$$

Notice that the third term is 1 and not zero because we divided $2ab$ by $2ab$; we did not subtract.

Now we write the factored expression in this form.

$$\text{GCF(remaining polynomial)}$$

The GCF is $2ab$ and the remaining trinomial is $3a + 2b + 1$.

$$2ab(3a + 2b + 1)$$

Practice   Factor each algebraic expression.

a. $8m^2n$ $(2)(2)(2)mmn$

b. $12mn^2$ $(2)(2)(3)mnn$

c. $18x^3y^2$ $(2)(3)(3)xxxyy$

d. $8m^2n + 12mn^2$
   $4mn(2m + 3n)$

e. $8xy^2 - 4xy$ $4xy(2y - 1)$

f. $6a^2b^3 + 9a^3b^2 + 3a^2b^2$
   $3a^2b^2(2b + 3a + 1)$

**Problem set
116** $^{(Inv.\ 10)}$

1. With one roll of a pair of dice,

    (a) what is the probability of rolling a 5 (expressed as a decimal rounded to two decimal places)?   0.11

    (b) what is the chance of rolling either a 4 or a 7?   25%

    (c) what are the odds of rolling a 12?   1 to 35

2. $^{(20)}$ A kilobyte of memory is 2^{10} bytes. Express the number of bytes in a kilobyte in standard form.   1024 bytes

3. The better sale seems to be the "40% of" sale which is 60% off the regular price instead of 40% off the regular price.

3. $^{(92)}$ Which sign seems to advertise the better sale? Explain your choice.

Sale!
40% off the
regular price!

Sale!
40% of the
regular price!

4. $^{(48)}$ Complete the table.

Fraction	Decimal	Percent
(a) $1\frac{3}{4}$	(b) 1.75	175%
$\frac{1}{12}$	(c) $0.08\overline{3}$	(d) $8\frac{1}{3}\%$

5. $^{(80)}$ Triangle ABC with vertices $A\ (0, 3)$, $B\ (0, 0)$, and $C\ (4, 0)$ is rotated 180° about the origin to $\triangle A'B'C'$. What are the coordinates of the vertices of $\triangle A'B'C'$?
  $A'\ (0, -3)$, $B'\ (0, 0)$, $C'\ (-4, 0)$

6. $^{(89)}$ What is the measure of each exterior angle and each interior angle of a regular 20-gon?   18°; 162°

7. $^{(92)}$ At a 30%-off sale Rob bought a jacket for \$42. How much money did Rob save by buying the jacket on sale instead of at the regular price?   \$18

8. The figure illustrates an aquarium
(115) with interior dimensions as shown.

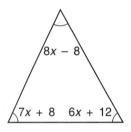

30 cm

20 cm

40 cm

(a) The aquarium has a maximum
capacity of how many liters?
24 liters

(b) If the aquarium is filled with water, what would be
the mass of the water in the aquarium? 24 kg

9. Use a unit multiplier to convert 24 kg to lb using the
(50) approximation 1 kg ≈ 2.2 lb. 52.8 lb

10. Write and solve an equation for the following sentence:
(101) $2x - 6 = 48$; 27

Six less than twice what number is 48?

11. Find the measure of the largest angle
(101) of this triangle. 64°

$8x - 8$

$7x + 8$ $6x + 12$

12. Solve for C: $F = 1.8C + 32$ $C = \frac{F - 32}{1.8.}$
(106)

13. The inside surface of this archway
(104) will be covered with a strip of wallpaper. How long does the strip of
wallpaper need to be in order to reach
from the floor on one side of the
archway around to the floor on the
other side of the archway? Use 3.14
for π and round up to the next inch.
195 in.

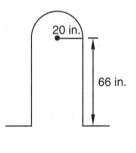

20 in.

66 in.

14. What is the total surface area of this right triangular prism?
(105) 1500 cm²

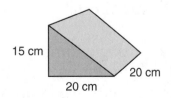

15 cm

20 cm

20 cm

15. What is the volume of the right triangular prism in
(95) problem 14? 3000 cm³

16. Find the slope of each line and the point where each line
(107) intersects the y-axis. (a) 1; (0, −2) (b) −2; (0, 4)

(a)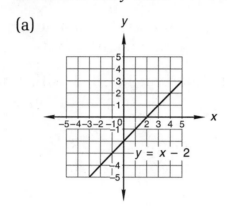

(b)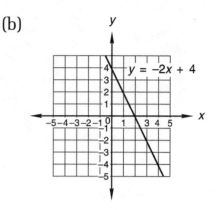

17. The following formula can be used to
(108) find the area (A) of a trapezoid. The
lengths of the parallel sides are a and b,
and the height, h, is the perpendicular
distance between the parallel sides.

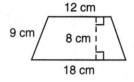

$$A = \frac{1}{2}(a + b)h$$

Use this formula to find the area of the illustrated trapezoid.
120 cm²

18. Find two solutions for $3x^2 - 5 = 40$. $\sqrt{15}, -\sqrt{15}$
(109)

19. Express each quotient in scientific notation.
(111)

   (a) $\dfrac{8 \times 10^{-4}}{4 \times 10^{8}}$ 2×10^{-12} (b) $\dfrac{4 \times 10^{8}}{8 \times 10^{-4}}$ 5×10^{11}

20. What is the product of the two quotients in problem 19?
(83) Why? The product is 1 because the numbers are reciprocals.

21. Factor each algebraic expression.
(116)

   (a) $9x^2y$ (3)(3)xxy

   (b) $10a^2b + 15a^2b^2 + 20abc$ 5ab(2a + 3ab + 4c)

22. A playground ball just fits inside of a
(113) cylinder with an interior diameter of
12 in. What is the volume of the ball?
Use 3.14 for π and round your answer
to the nearest cubic inch. 904 in.³

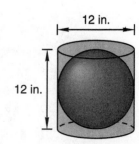

23. Refer to the figure to find
₍₄₀₎

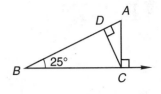

(a) m∠BCD. 65°

(b) m∠BAC. 65°

(c) m∠ACD. 25°

(d) What can you conclude about the three triangles in the figure? The three triangles are similar.

24. Refer to the figure in problem 23 to complete this
₍₉₇₎ proportion. *CD*

$$\frac{BD}{BC} = \frac{?}{CA}$$

Solve:

25. $x - 15 = x + 2x + 1$ **26.** $0.12(m - 5) = 0.96$ 13
₍₁₀₂₎ −8   ₍₁₀₂₎

Simplify:

27. $a(b - c) + b(c - a)$ **28.** $\dfrac{(8x^2 y)(12x^3 y^2)}{(4xy)(6y^2)}$ $4x^4$
₍₉₆₎ $bc - ac$ or $-ac + bc$ ₍₁₀₃₎

29. (a) $(-3)^2 + (-2)(-3) - (-2)^3$ 23
_(103,105)
     (b) $\sqrt[3]{-8} + \sqrt[3]{8}$ 0

30. If $\overline{AB}$ is 1.2 units long and $\overline{BD}$ is
_(7,35) 0.75 units long, then what is the
length of $\overline{AD}$? 0.45 units

LESSON 117

Slope-Intercept Form of an Equation

Mental Math:
a. −6
b. 3.5 × 10²
c. 5, −5
d. 212°F
e. $500
f. $3500
g. −1
Problem Solving:
   36   1-by-1
   25   2-by-2
   16   3-by-3
    9   4-by-4
    4   5-by-5
 + 1   6-by-6
   91   total

Facts Practice: $+ - \times \div$ Algebraic Terms (Test V in Test Masters)

Mental Math:

a. $\dfrac{(-9)(-4)}{-6}$ **b.** $\left(7 \times 10^{-4}\right) \div \left(2 \times 10^{-6}\right)$

c. $2a^2 = 50$ **d.** Convert 100°C to Fahrenheit.

e. $12\frac{1}{2}\%$ of $4000   **f.** $12\frac{1}{2}\%$ less than $4000

g. Find 10% of 60, + 4, × 8, + 1, $\sqrt{\ }$, × 3, + 1, ÷ 4, × 5, + 1, $\sqrt{\ }$, − 7.

Problem Solving:

In this 4-by-4 square we see sixteen 1-by-1 squares, nine 2-by-2 squares, four 3-by-3 squares, and one 4-by-4 square. How many squares of any size are in this 6-by-6 square?

The three equations below are equivalent equations. Each equation has the same graph.

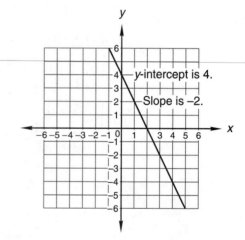

(a) $2x + y - 4 = 0$

(b) $2x + y = 4$

(c) $y = -2x + 4$

Equation (c) is in a special form called **slope-intercept form.** When an equation is written in slope-intercept form, the coefficient of x is the slope of the graph of the equation and the constant is the **y-intercept** (where the graph of the equation intersects the y-axis).

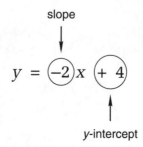

Notice the order of the terms in this equation. The equation is solved for y, and y is to the left of the equals sign. To the right of the equals sign is the x-term and then the constant term. The model for slope-intercept form is written this way.

> **Slope-Intercept Form**
> $$y = mx + b$$

In this model, m stands for the slope and b for the y-intercept.

Example 1 Transform this equation so that it is in slope-intercept form.

$$3x + y = 6$$

Solution We solve the equation for y by subtracting $3x$ from both sides of the equation.

$3x + y = 6$	equation
$3x + y - 3x = 6 - 3x$	subtracted $3x$ from both sides
$y = 6 - 3x$	simplified

Next we arrange the terms on the right side of the equals sign using the commutative property so that the order is x-term first then the constant term.

$y = 6 - 3x$	equation
$y = -3x + 6$	commutative property

Example 2 Graph $y = -3x + 6$ using slope and y-intercept.

Solution The slope of the graph is the coefficient of x, which is -3, and the y-intercept is $+6$, which is located at $+6$ on the y-axis. From this point we move to the right one unit and move down 3 units and end up at another point on the line. Continuing this pattern, we identify a series of points through which we draw the graph of the equation.

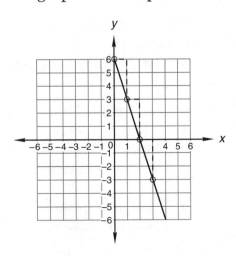

Example 3   Using only slope and y-intercept, graph $y = x - 2$.

Solution   The slope is the coefficient of x, which is $+1$. The y-intercept is -2. We begin at -2 on the y-axis and sketch a line that has a slope of $+1$.

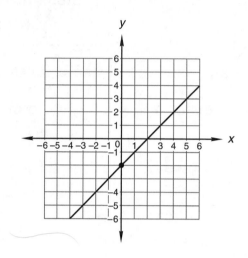

Practice   Write each equation below in slope-intercept form.

a. $2x + y = 3$
$y = -2x + 3$

b. $y - 3 = x$
$y = x + 3$

c. $2x + y - 3 = 0$
$y = -2x + 3$

d. $x + y = 4 - x$
$y = -2x + 4$

Using only slope and y-intercept, graph each of these equations.

e. $y = x - 3$

f. $y = -2x + 6$

g. $y = \dfrac{1}{2}x - 2$

h. $y = -x + 3$

Problem set 117

1. *(110)* How much interest is earned in four years on a deposit of $10,000 if it is allowed to accumulate in an account paying 7% interest compounded annually? $3107.96

2. *(Inv. 10)* In 240 at-bats Chester has 60 hits.

(a) What is the statistical probability of Chester getting a hit in his next at-bat? $\frac{1}{4}$

(b) What are the odds of Chester getting a hit in his next at-bat? 1 to 3

3. On her first four tests Monica's average score was 75%.
(55) On her next six tests Monica's average score was 85%.
What was Monica's average score on all ten tests? 81%

4. Complete the table.
(48)

Fraction	Decimal	Percent
(a) $1\frac{2}{5}$	1.4	(b) 140%
$\frac{11}{12}$	(c) $0.91\overline{6}$	(d) $91\frac{2}{3}\%$

5. The image of $\triangle ABC$ reflected in the y-axis is $\triangle A'B'C'$. If
(80) the coordinates of vertices A, B, and C are $(-1, 3)$, $(-3, 0)$,
and $(0, -2)$, respectively, then what are the coordinates of
vertices A', B', and C'? A' $(1, 3)$, B' $(3, 0)$, C' $(0, -2)$

6. The figure shows regular octagon
(89) *ABCDEFGH.*

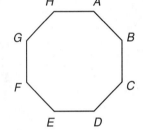

(a) What is the measure of each
exterior angle? 45°

(b) What is the measure of each
interior angle? 135°

(c) How many diagonals can be drawn from vertex A?
5 diagonals

7. In one year the population in the county surged from
(92) 1.2 million to 1.5 million. This was an increase of what
percent? 25%

8. A beaker was filled with water to the
(115) 500 mL level.

(a) What is the volume of the water in
cubic centimeters?
500 cubic centimeters

(b) What is the mass of the water in
kilograms? 0.5 kilograms

9. Use two unit multipliers to convert 540 ft² to yd². 60 yd²
(88)

10. Write and solve an equation for the following sentence:
(101)

*Six more than three times what number squared
is 81?* $3x^2 + 6 = 81$; $5, -5$

11. Find the measure of the angle
(101) marked *y*. 50°

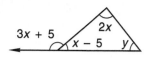
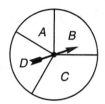

12. Solve for c^2: $c^2 - a^2 = b^2$ $c^2 = b^2 + a^2$ or $c^2 = a^2 + b^2$
(106)

13. The face of this spinner is divided
(Inv. 10) into four sectors. Sectors *B* and *D* are
90° sectors, and sector *C* is a 120°
sector. If the arrow is spun once,

    (a) what is the probability (expressed
as a decimal) that it will stop in
sector *B*? 0.25

    (b) what is the chance that it will stop in sector *C*? $33\frac{1}{3}\%$

    (c) what are the odds of the arrow stopping in sector *A*?
      1 to 5

14. The coordinates of the vertices of a square are (0, 4),
(112) (3, 0), (−1, −3), and (−4, 1).

    (a) What is the length of each side of the square? 5 units

    (b) What is the perimeter of the square? 20 units

    (c) What is the area of the square? 25 units²

15. A cylinder and cone have equal
(113) heights and diameters as shown in
the illustration.

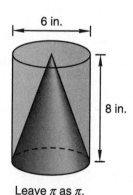

    (a) What is the volume of the
cylinder? 72π in.³

    (b) What is the volume of the cone?
      24π in.³

Leave π as π.

16. The formula for the volume of a rectangular prism is
(106)

$$V = lwh$$

    (a) Transform this formula to solve for *h*. $h = \frac{V}{lw}$

16.(b) 10 cm   (b) Find *h* when *V* is 6000 cm³, *l* is 20 cm, and *w* is 30 cm.

17. Refer to the graph to answer questions (a)–(c).
(117)

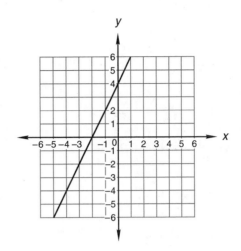

(a) What is the slope of the line? 2

(b) At what point does the line intersect the y-axis? $(0, 4)$

(c) What is the equation of the line in slope-intercept form? $y = 2x + 4$

18. Write each of these equations in slope-intercept form.
(117)

(a) $y + 5 = x$ $y = x - 5$ (b) $2x + y = 4$ $y = -2x + 4$

19. Factor each algebraic expression.
(116)

(a) $24xy^2$ $(2)(2)(2)(3)xyy$ (b) $3x^2 + 6xy - 9x$
  $3x(x + 2y - 3)$

20. What is the area of a square with sides 5×10^3 mm long?
(83)

(a) Express the area in scientific notation. 2.5×10^7 mm^2

(b) Express the area as a standard numeral.
  25,000,000 mm^2

21. Use two unit multipliers to convert the answer to problem
(88) 20(b) to square meters. 25 m^2

22. Triangle *ABC* is a right triangle and is
(97) similar to triangles *CAD* and *CBD*.

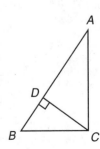

(a) Which side of △*CBD* corresponds to side *BC* of △*ABC*? side *BD*

(b) Which side of △*CAD* corresponds to side *AC* of △*ABC*? side *AD*

23. Refer to this figure to find the length of segment *BD*. $\frac{5}{12}$ in.
(7,30)

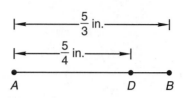

A D B

24. Solve and graph: $\frac{3}{4}x + 12 < 15$
(93)

$x < 4$

0 1 2 3 4 5

25. Solve: $6w - 3w + 18 = 9(w - 4)$ 9
(102)

Simplify:

26. $3x(x - 2y) + 2xy(x + 3)$ $3x^2 + 2x^2y$
(96)

27. $2^{-2} + 4^{-1} + \sqrt[3]{27} + (-1)^3$ $2\frac{1}{2}$
(114)

28. $(-3) + (-2)[(-3)(-2) - (+4)] - (-3)(-4)$ -19
(85)

29. $\dfrac{1.2 \times 10^{-6}}{4 \times 10^3}$ 3×10^{-10}
(111)

30. $\dfrac{36a^2b^3c}{12ab^2c}$ $3ab$
(103)

LESSON
118

Copying Angles and Triangles

Facts Practice: Multiplying and Dividing in Scientific Notation
(Test W in Test Masters)

Mental Math:

a. $(-3)^2 + 3^{-2}$
b. $(5 \times 10^{-6})(3 \times 10^2)$
c. $\frac{k}{33} = \frac{200}{300}$
d. Convert 7500 g to kg.
e. 150% of $4000
f. $4000 increased 150%
g. At an average speed of 30 mph how long will it take to drive 40 miles?

Problem Solving:

Sylvia wants to pack a 9 in. by 14 in. rectangular picture frame that is $\frac{1}{2}$ in. thick into a rectangular box with inside dimensions of 12 in. by 9 in. by 10 in. Describe why you think the frame will or will not fit in the box.

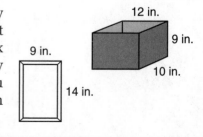

Recall from Investigations 2 and 8 that we used a compass and straight edge to construct circles, regular polygons, angle bisectors, and perpendicular bisectors of segments. We may also use a compass and straight edge to copy figures. In this lesson we will practice copying angles and triangles.

Suppose we are given this angle to copy.

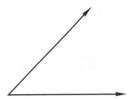

We begin by drawing a ray to form one side of the angle.

Now we need to find a point through which to draw the second ray. We find this point in two steps. For the first step we set the compass and draw an arc across both rays of the original angle from the vertex of the angle. Without resetting the compass we draw an arc of the same size from the endpoint of the ray as we show here.

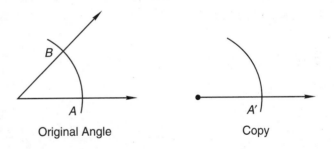

Original Angle   Copy

For the second step we reset the compass to equal the distance from A to B on the original angle. To verify the correct setting we swing a small arc through point B while the pivot point is on point A. With the compass at this setting we move the pivot point to point A' of the copy and draw an arc that intersects the first arc we drew on the copy.

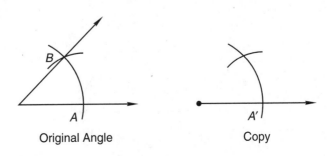

Original Angle   Copy

Where the arcs intersect on the copy is the point through which we draw the second ray of the copied angle.

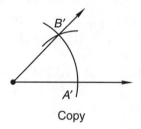

Copy

We use a similar method to copy a triangle. Suppose we are asked to copy $\triangle XYZ$.

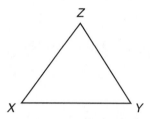

We will begin by drawing a segment equal in length to segment XY. We do this by setting the compass so that the pivot point is on X and the drawing point is on Y. We verify the setting by drawing a small arc through point Y. To copy this segment we first sketch a ray with endpoint X'. Then we locate Y' by swinging an arc with the preset compass from point X'.

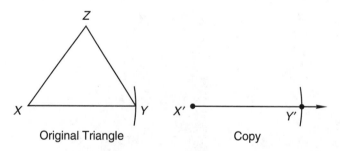

Original Triangle   Copy

To locate Z' on the copy we will need to draw two different arcs, one from point X' and one from point Y'. We set the compass on the original triangle so that the distance between its points equals XZ. With the compass at this setting we draw an arc from X' on the copy.

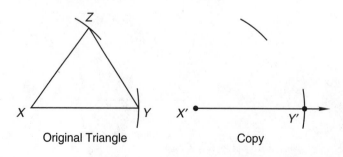

Original Triangle   Copy

Now we change the setting of the compass to equal *YZ* on the original. With this setting we draw an arc from *Y'* that intersects the other arc.

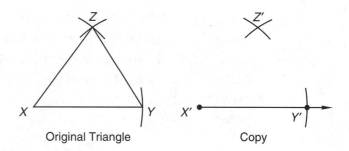

Original Triangle   Copy

The point where the arcs intersect which we have labeled *Z'* corresponds to point *Z* on the original triangle. To complete the copy we draw segments *X'Z'* and *Y'Z'*.

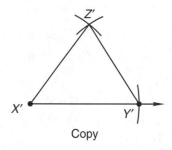

Copy

Activity: Copying Angles and Triangles

Materials needed:

- Compass and straight edge for each student

  With students working in pairs, have one student draw an angle and have the partner copy the angle. Then reverse roles. Repeat the process drawing and copying triangles.

Practice   **a.** Use a protractor to draw an 80° angle. Then use a compass and straight edge to copy the angle. See student work.

b. With a protractor draw a triangle with angles of 30°, 60°, and 90°. Then use a compass and straight edge to copy the triangle. See student work.

**Problem set
118**

1. The median home price in the county increased from
(92) $180,000 to $189,000 in one year. This was an increase of
what percent? 5%

2. To indirectly measure the height of a power pole Teddy
(97) compared the lengths of the shadows of a vertical meter
stick and of the power pole. When the shadow of the
meter stick was 40 centimeters long, the shadow of the
power pole was 6 meters long. About how tall was the
power pole? 15 meters

3. Armando can
select a
Pythagorean
triplet like 3-4-5
to verify when he
has formed a
right angle. For
example, he can
measure and
mark from a
corner 3 meters
along one line
and 4 meters
along a proposed
perpendicular
line. Then he can
check if it is 5
meters between
marks.

3. Armando is marking off a grass field for a soccer game.
(112) He has a long tape measure and chalk for lining the field.
Armando wants to be sure that the corners of the field are
right angles. How can he use the tape measure to assure
he makes right angles?

4. Convert 15 meters to feet by using the approximation
(50) 1 m ≈ 3.28 ft. Round the result to the nearest foot.
49 feet

5. The illustration shows one room of a scale drawing of a
(98) house. One inch on the drawing represents a distance of
10 feet. Use your ruler to help you calculate the actual
area of the room. 225 ft²

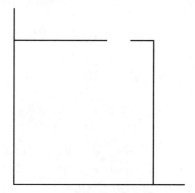

6. If a pair of dice is rolled,
(Inv. 10)

(a) what is the probability of rolling a 9? $\frac{1}{9}$

(b) what is the chance of rolling a 10? $8\frac{1}{3}\%$

(c) what are the odds of rolling an 11? 1 to 17

7. Use the Pythagorean theorem to calculate the distance
(99) from (4, 6) to (−1, −6). 13 units

8. A two-liter bottle filled with water
(115)

(a) contains how many cubic centimeters of water?
2000 cubic centimeters

(b) has a mass of how many kilograms? 2 kilograms

9. Write and solve an equation for the following sentence:
(101)

Two thirds less than half of what number is five sixths? $\frac{1}{2}x - \frac{2}{3} = \frac{5}{6}$; 3

10. In this figure lines *m* and *n* are parallel. If the sum of the measures of angles *a* and *e* is 200°, then what is the measure of $\angle g$? 80°
(102)

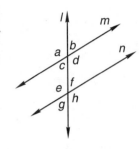

11.

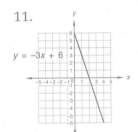

$y = -3x + 6$

11. Transform the equation $3x + y = 6$ into slope-intercept form. Then graph the equation on the coordinate plane.
(117)
$y = -3x + 6$

12. Find the measure of the smallest angle of this triangle. 50°
(101)

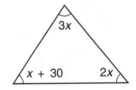

13. A cube, 12 inches on edge, is topped with a pyramid so that the total height of the cube and pyramid is 20 inches. What is the total volume of the shape?
(113)
2112 cubic inches

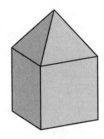

14. The length of segment *BD* is 12. The length of segment *BA* is *c*. Using 12 and *c* write an expression that indicates the length of segment *AD*.
(101)
$\overline{AD} = c - 12$

15. The three triangles in this figure are similar. The sum of *x* and *y* is 25. Use proportions to find *x* and *y*.
(97)
$x = 16$; $y = 9$

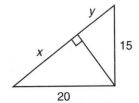

16. Sylvia cut an orange in half. (The flat surface formed is
(105) called a **cross section.**)

Sylvia knew that the surface area of a sphere is four times the greatest cross sectional area of the sphere. She estimated that the diameter of the orange was 8 cm and she used 3 in place of π. Using Sylvia's numbers calculate an estimate of the area of the orange peel of the whole orange. $A = 4\pi r^2 \approx 4 \cdot 3(4 \text{ cm})^2 \approx 192 \text{ cm}^2$

17.

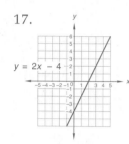

$y = 2x - 4$

17. Write the equation $y - 2x + 5 = 1$ in slope-intercept
(117) form. Then graph the equation. $y = 2x - 4$

18. Refer to the graph to answer questions (a)–(c).
(117)

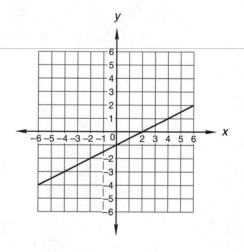

(a) What is the slope of the line? $\frac{1}{2}$

(b) What is the y-intercept of the line? -1

(c) What is the equation of the line in slope-intercept form? $y = \frac{1}{2}x - 1$

19. See student work.

19. Draw an estimate of a 60° angle and check your estimate
(96,118) with a protractor. Then set the protractor aside and use a compass and straight edge to copy the angle.

20. A 7-inch diameter semicircle was cut from a rectangular
(104) half sheet of paper. What is the perimeter of the resulting
shape? (Use $\frac{22}{7}$ for π.) $34\frac{1}{2}$ in.

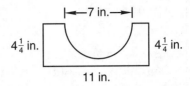

21. A dime is about 1×10^{-3} m thick. A kilometer is
(111) 1×10^3 m. How many dimes would be needed to make a
stack of dimes one kilometer high? Express your answer
in scientific notation.

21. $\dfrac{1 \times 10^3}{1 \times 10^{-3}}$

$= 1 \times 10^6$
dimes

22. Factor each algebraic expression.
(116)

    (a) $x^2 + x$ $x(x + 1)$

    (b) $12m^2n^3 + 18mn^2 - 24m^2n^2$ $6mn^2(2mn + 3 - 4m)$

Solve:

23. $-2\frac{2}{3}w - 1\frac{1}{3} = 4$ -2
(93)

24. $5x^2 + 1 = 81$ $4, -4$
(109)

25. $\left(\frac{1}{2}\right)^2 - 2^{-2}$ 0
(114)

26. $66\frac{2}{3}\%$ of $\frac{5}{6}$ of 0.144
(48)

                    0.08 or $\frac{2}{25}$

27. $[-3 + (-4)(-5)] - [-4 - (-5)(-2)]$ 31
(91)

Simplify:

28. $\dfrac{(5x^2yz)(6xy^2z)}{10xyz}$ $3x^2y^2z$
(103)

29. $x(x + 2) + 2(x + 2)$
(96) $x^2 + 4x + 4$

30. The hypotenuse of this right triangle
(100) is between which two consecutive
whole numbers of millimeters?
22 mm and 23 mm

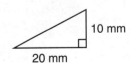

LESSON
119

Division by Zero

Facts Practice: $+ - \times \div$ Algebraic Terms (Test V in Test Masters)

Mental Math:

  a. $(2^{-2})(-2)^2$ **b.** $(1 \times 10^{-8}) \div (1 \times 10^{-4})$

  c. $2y + \frac{1}{2} = \frac{1}{2}$ **d.** Convert 5 cm^2 to mm^2.

  e. $66\frac{2}{3}\%$ of $600   **f.** $600 reduced $33\frac{1}{3}\%$

  g. What fraction of an hour is 5 minutes less than $\frac{1}{3}$ of an hour?

Problem Solving:

Figure *ABC* is an equilateral triangle whose perimeter is 6 cm. Segment *AD* bisects segment *BC* forming two congruent right triangles. Find the length of segment *AD* and leave the answer in irrational form.

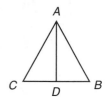

When performing algebraic operations it is necessary to guard against dividing by zero. For example, the following expression reduces to 2 only if *x* is not zero:

$$\frac{2x}{x} = 2 \quad \text{if } x \neq 0$$

What is the value of this expression if *x* is zero?

$$\frac{2x}{x} \qquad \text{expression}$$

$$\frac{2 \cdot 0}{0} \qquad \text{substituted 0 for } x$$

$$\frac{0}{0} \qquad \text{multiplied } 2 \cdot 0$$

 What is the value of $\frac{0}{0}$? How many zeros are in zero? Is the quotient 0? Is the quotient 1? Is the quotient some other number? Try the division with a calculator. What answer does the calculator display? Notice that the calculator displays an error message when division by zero is entered. The display is frozen and other calculations cannot be performed until the erroneous entry is cleared. In this lesson we will consider why division by zero is not possible.

Consider what happens to a quotient when a number is divided by numbers closer and closer to zero. As we know, zero lies on the number line between −1 and 1. Zero is also between −0.1 and 0.1, and between −0.01 and 0.01.

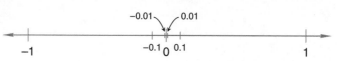

In the following example, notice the quotients we get when we divide a number by numbers closer and closer to zero.

Example 1   Find each set of quotients. As the divisors become closer to zero, do the quotients become closer to zero or farther from zero?

(a) $\dfrac{10}{1}, \dfrac{10}{0.1}, \dfrac{10}{0.01}$ (b) $\dfrac{10}{-1}, \dfrac{10}{-0.1}, \dfrac{10}{-0.01}$

Solution   (a) **10, 100, 1000**   (b) **–10, –100, –1000**

As the divisors become closer to zero the quotients become farther from zero.

Notice from Example 1 that as the divisors approach zero from the positive side, the quotients become greater and greater toward positive infinity. However, as the divisors approach zero from the negative side, the quotients become less and less toward negative infinity. In other words, as the divisors of a number approach zero from opposite sides of zero, the quotients do not become closer. Rather, the quotients grow farther and farther apart approaching infinitely far apart. We might wonder, as the divisor finally reaches zero, whether the quotient would equal positive infinity or negative infinity! Considering this growing difference in quotients as divisors approach zero from opposite sides of zero is one way to understand why division by zero is not possible. Another consideration is the relationship between multiplication and division.

Recall that multiplication and division are inverse operations. The numbers that form a multiplication fact may be arranged to form two division facts. For the multiplication fact $4 \times 5 = 20$ we may arrange the numbers to form these two division facts.

$$\frac{20}{4} = 5 \quad \text{and} \quad \frac{20}{5} = 4$$

We see that if we divide the product of two factors by either factor, the result is the other factor.

$$\frac{\text{product}}{\text{factor}_1} = \text{factor}_2 \quad \text{and} \quad \frac{\text{product}}{\text{factor}_2} = \text{factor}_1$$

This relationship between multiplication and division breaks down when zero is one of the factors as we see in Example 2.

Example 2 The numbers in the multiplication fact 2 × 3 = 6 can be arranged to form two division facts.

$$\frac{6}{3} = 2 \quad \text{and} \quad \frac{6}{2} = 3$$

If we attempt to form two division facts for the multiplication fact 2 × 0 = 0, one of the arrangements is not a fact. Which arrangement is not a fact?

Solution The product is 0, and the factors are 2 and 0. So the possible arrangements are these.

$$\frac{0}{2} = 0 \quad \text{and} \quad \frac{0}{0} = 2$$

$$\text{fact} \qquad\qquad\qquad \text{not a fact}$$

The arrangement **0 ÷ 0 = 2 is not a fact.**

The fact 2 × 0 = 0 does not imply that 0 ÷ 0 = 2 anymore than 3 × 0 = 0 implies that 0 ÷ 0 = 3. This breakdown in the inverse relationship between multiplication and division when zero is one of the factors is another indication that division by zero is not possible.

Example 3 If we were asked to graph the following equation, what number could we not use in place of x when generating a table of ordered pairs?

$$y = \frac{12}{3 + x}$$

Solution This equation involves division. Since division by zero is not possible, we need to guard against the divisor, 3 + x, being zero. When x is 0, the expression 3 + x equals 3. So we may use 0 in place of x. However, when x is −3, the expression 3 + x equals zero.

$$y = \frac{12}{3 + x} \qquad \text{equation}$$

$$y = \frac{12}{3 + (-3)} \qquad \text{replaced } x \text{ with } -3$$

$$y = \frac{12}{0} \qquad \text{not permitted}$$

Therefore, we may not use −3 in place of x in this equation. We may write our answer this way:

$$x \neq -3$$

Practice **a.** Use a calculator to divide several different numbers of your choosing by zero. Remember to clear the calculator before entering a new problem. What answers are displayed?
A typical error message display is ⌈E⎯⎯0⌋. Error messages vary.

b. The numbers in the multiplication fact 7 × 8 = 56 can be arranged to form two division facts. If we attempt to form two division facts for the multiplication fact 7 × 0 = 0, one of the arrangements is not a fact. Which arrangement is not a fact and why?
0 ÷ 0 = 7 is not a fact because division by zero is not possible.

For the following expressions, find the number or numbers that may not be used in place of the variable.

c. $\dfrac{6}{w}$ $w \neq 0$

d. $\dfrac{3}{x - 1}$ $x \neq 1$

e. $\dfrac{4}{2w}$ $w \neq 0$

f. $\dfrac{y + 3}{y - 3}$ $y \neq 3$

g. $\dfrac{8}{x^2 - 4}$ $x \neq 2, -2$

h. $\dfrac{3ab}{c}$ $c \neq 0$

Problem set 119 **1.** Robert was asked to select and hold three cards from a
$^{(Inv.\ 10)}$ normal deck of cards. If the first two cards selected were aces, what is the chance that the third card he selects will be one of the two remaining aces? 4%

2. If one saves $5.00 buying an item at a sale price of $15,
$^{(92)}$ then the regular price was reduced by what percent? 25%

3. On a number line graph all real numbers that are both
$^{(78)}$ greater than or equal to −3 and less than 2.

-4 -3 -2 -1 0 1 2 3

4. What is the sum of the measures of the interior angles of
$^{(89)}$ any quadrilateral? 360°

5. Complete the table.
(48)

Fraction	Decimal	Percent
(a) $\frac{1}{200}$	(b) 0.005	0.5%
$\frac{8}{9}$	(c) $0.\overline{8}$	(d) $88\frac{8}{9}\%$

6.(a)

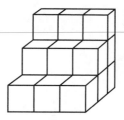
10 cm
10 cm

6. (a) Use a centimeter ruler and a protractor to draw a right
(17)   triangle with legs 10 cm long.

    (b) What is the measure of each acute angle? 45°

    (c) Measure the length of the hypotenuse to the nearest
    centimeter. 14 cm

7. Simplify and write the result in scientific notation.
(111)

$$\frac{(6 \times 10^5)(2 \times 10^6)}{(3 \times 10^4)} \quad 4 \times 10^7$$

8. Factor each expression.
(116)

    (a) $2x^2 + x$ $x(2x + 1)$ (b) $3a^2b - 12a^2 + 9ab^2$
                                             $3a(ab - 4a + 3b^2)$

The figure below was formed by stacking 1 cm cubes. Refer to
this figure to answer problems 9 and 10.

9. What is the volume of the figure? 18 cm³
(70)

10. What is the surface area of the figure? 48 cm²
(105)

11. Transform the formula $A = \frac{1}{2}bh$ to solve for h. Then use
(108) the transformed formula to find h when A is 1.44 m² and
  b is 1.6 m. $h = \frac{2A}{b}$; 1.8 m

12. If the ratio of boys to girls in a class is 3 to 5, then what
(65) percent of the students in the class are boys? $37\frac{1}{2}\%$

13. If a 10-foot ladder is leaned against a
(112) wall so that the foot of the ladder is
  6 feet from the base of the wall, how
  far up the wall will the ladder reach?
  8 ft

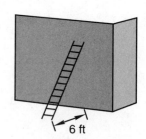
6 ft

The graph below shows line *l* perpendicular to line *m*. Refer to this graph to answer problems 14 and 15.

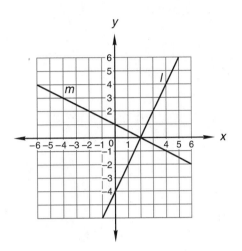

14. (a) What is the equation of line *l* in slope-intercept form?
(117) $y = 2x - 4$
     (b) What is the equation of line *m* in slope-intercept form?
        $y = -\frac{1}{2}x + 1$

15. What is the product of the slopes of line *l* and line *m*?
(107) Why? The product of the slopes is −1. The slopes are negative reciprocals.

16. If $8000 is deposited in an account paying 6% interest
(110) compounded annually, then what is the total value of the account after four years? $10,099.82

17. The Joneses are planning to carpet their home. The area
(88) to be carpeted is 1250 square feet. How many square yards of carpeting need to be installed? (Round the answer up to the next square yard.) 139 square yards

18. In the following expressions, what number may not be
(119) used for the variable?

(a) $\dfrac{12}{3w}$ $w \neq 0$ (b) $\dfrac{12}{3 + m}$ $m \neq -3$

19. If $\overline{BD}$ is *x* units long and $\overline{BA}$ is *c* units
(101) long, then using *x* and *c*, what expression indicates the length of $\overline{DA}$?
$\overline{DA} = c - x$

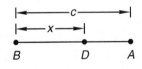

20. In this figure the three triangles are
(97) similar. Find the area of the smallest triangle. Dimensions are in inches.
54 in.²

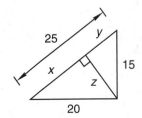

21. A sphere with a diameter of 30 cm
(113) has a volume of how many cubic
centimeters? 14,130 cm³

Use 3.14 for π.

22. Draw an estimate of a 45° angle. Then use a compass and
(96,118) straight edge to copy the angle. See student work.

Solve:

23. $\dfrac{2}{3}m + \dfrac{1}{4} = \dfrac{7}{12}$ $\frac{1}{2}$
(93)

24. $5(3 - x) = 55$ -8
(102)

25. $x + x + 12 = 5x$ 4
(102)

26. $10x^2 = 100$ $\sqrt{10}, -\sqrt{10}$
(109)

Simplify:

27. $\sqrt{90{,}000}$ 300
(20)

28. $x(x + 5) - 2(x + 5)$
(96) $x^2 + 3x - 10$

29. $\dfrac{(12xy^2z)(9x^2y^2z)}{36xyz^2}$ $3x^2y^3$
(103)

30. $33\dfrac{1}{3}\%$ of 0.12 of $3\dfrac{1}{3}$
(48) $\frac{2}{15}$ or $0.1\overline{3}$

LESSON
120

Graphing Nonlinear Equations

Facts Practice: Multiplying and Dividing in Scientific Notation
(Test W in Test Masters)

Mental Math:

a. $(10^2)(10^{-2})$
b. $(5 \times 10^{-5})^2$
c. $2x^2 = 32$
d. Convert 0°C to Fahrenheit.
e. 10% of $250
f. 10% more than $250
g. 2 × 12, + 1, $\sqrt{\ }$, × 3, + 1, $\sqrt{\ }$, × 2, + 1, $\sqrt{\ }$, + 1, $\sqrt{\ }$, − 1, $\sqrt{\ }$

Problem Solving:

A paper cone, the same height and
diameter as a cylindrical glass beaker, is
filled with water and the water is poured
into the beaker. How many cones of water
are needed to fill the beaker?

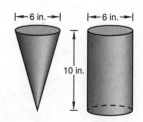

Equations whose graphs are lines are called **linear equations.** (Notice the word "line" in linear.) In this lesson we will graph some equations whose graphs are not lines but are curves. To graph each equation we will make a table of ordered pairs and plot enough points to get an idea of the path of the curve.

Example 1   Graph: $y = \dfrac{6}{x}$

Solution   We make a table of ordered pairs. For convenience we select x values that are factors of 6. We remember to select negative values as well. Note that we may not select zero for x.

$$y = \frac{6}{x}$$

x	y	(x, y)
1	6	$(1, 6)$
2	3	$(2, 3)$
3	2	$(3, 2)$
6	1	$(6, 1)$
-1	-6	$(-1, -6)$
-2	-3	$(-2, -3)$
-3	-2	$(-3, -2)$
-6	-1	$(-6, -1)$

On a coordinate plane we graph the (x, y) pairs we found that satisfy the equation.

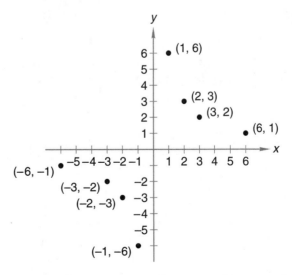

This arrangement of points on the coordinate plane suggests two curves that do not intersect.

We draw two smooth curves through the two sets of points.

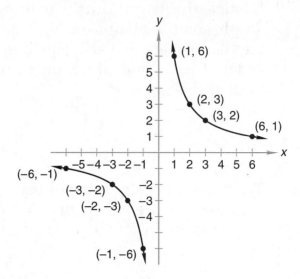

Example 2 Graph: $y = x^2$

Solution We begin by making a table of ordered pairs. We think of numbers for x and then calculate y. We replace x with negative numbers as well. Remember that squaring a negative number results in a positive number.

$$y = x^2$$

x	y	(x, y)
0	0	(0, 0)
1	1	(1, 1)
2	4	(2, 4)
3	9	(3, 9)
−1	1	(−1, 1)
−2	4	(−2, 4)
−3	9	(−3, 9)

After generating several pairs of coordinates we graph the points on a coordinate plane.

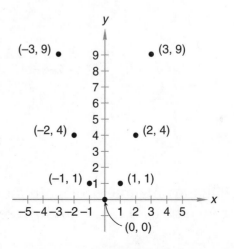

We complete the graph by drawing a smooth curve through the graphed points.

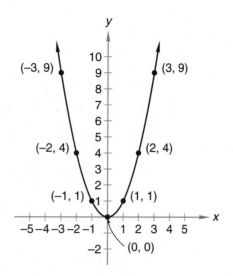

The coordinates of any point on the curve should satisfy the original equation.

Practice

a. Graph: $y = \frac{12}{x}$. Begin by creating a table of ordered pairs. Use 6, 4, 3, 2, −2, −3, −4, and −6 in place of x.
See student work.

b. Graph: $y = x^2 - 2$. Compare your graph to the graph in Example 2. See student work.

c. Graph: $y = \frac{10}{x}$. Compare your graph to the graph in Example 1. See student work.

d. Graph: $y = 2x^2$. Compare your graph to the graph in Example 2. See student work.

Problem set 120 [Inv. 10]

1. Schuster was playing a board game and rolled a 7 with a pair of dice three times in a row. What are the odds of Schuster rolling a 7 with the next roll of the dice? 1 to 5

2. [92] If the total cost of an item including 8% sales tax is $2.70, then what was the price before tax was added? $2.50

3. [79] If $x < y$ compare: $x^2 \bigcirc y^2$ insufficient information

4. [58] If a trapezoid has a line of symmetry and one of its angles measures 100°, then what is the measure of each of its other angles? 100°; 80°; 80°

5. Complete the table.
(48)

FRACTION	DECIMAL	PERCENT
(a) $\frac{1}{1000}$	(b) 0.001	0.1%
$\frac{8}{5}$	(c) 1.6	(d) 160%

6. The hypotenuse of this triangle is
(99) twice the length of the shorter leg.

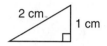

(a) Use the Pythagorean theorem to find the length of the remaining side. $\sqrt{3}$ cm

(b) Use a centimeter ruler to find the length of the unmarked side to the nearest tenth of a centimeter.
1.7 cm

7. Simplify and write the result in scientific notation.
(111)

$$\frac{(4 \times 10^{-5})(6 \times 10^{-4})}{8 \times 10^3} \quad 3 \times 10^{-12}$$

8. Factor each expression.
(116)

(a) $3y^2 - y$ $y(3y - 1)$

(b) $6w^2 + 9wx - 12w$
$3w(2w + 3x - 4)$

The figure below shows a cylinder and a cone whose heights and diameters are equal. Refer to this figure to answer problems 9 and 10.

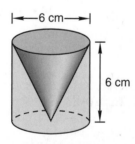

9. What is the ratio of the volume of the cone to the volume
(113) of the cylinder? $\frac{1}{3}$

10. The *lateral surface area* of a cylinder is the area of the
(105) curved side and excludes the areas of the circular ends. What is the lateral surface area of the cylinder rounded to the nearest square centimeter? 113 cm²

11. Transform the formula $E = mc^2$ to solve for *m*. $m = \frac{E}{c^2}$
(106)

12. If 60% of the students in the assembly were girls, then
(54) what was the ratio of boys to girls in the assembly? $\frac{2}{3}$

The graph below shows $m \perp n$. Refer to this graph to answer problems 13 and 14.

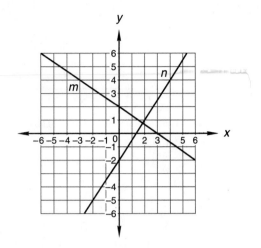

13. What is the equation of each line in slope-intercept form?
(117) line m: $y = -\frac{2}{3}x + 2$; line n: $y = \frac{3}{2}x - 2$

14. What is the product of the slopes of lines m and n? Why?
(107) The product of the slopes is -1. The slopes are negative reciprocals.

15. If a $1000 investment earns 20% interest compounded
(110) annually, then the investment will double in value in
how many years? 4 years

16. The stated size of a TV screen or
(112) computer monitor is its diagonal
measure. A screen that is 17 in. wide
and 12 in. high would be described
as what size of screen? Round your
answer to the nearest inch. 21 in.

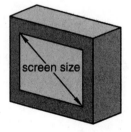

17. Already-mixed concrete is sold by the cubic yard. The
(70,88) Smiths are pouring a concrete driveway that is 36 feet
long, 21 feet wide, and one half foot thick.

(a) Find the number of cubic feet of concrete needed.
378 cubic feet

(b) Use three unit multipliers to convert answer (a) to
cubic yards. 14 cubic yards

18. In the following expressions, what number may not be
(119) used for the variable?

(a) $\dfrac{12}{4 - 2m}$ $m \neq 2$

(b) $\dfrac{y - 5}{y + 5}$ $y \neq -5$

19. Graph: $y = x^2 - 4$
(120)

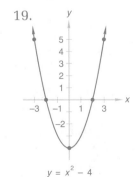

19.

$y = x^2 - 4$

20. Refer to this drawing of three similar
(97) triangles to find the letter that
completes this proportion. y

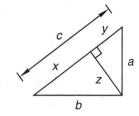

$$\frac{c}{a} = \frac{a}{?}$$

21. Recall that the surface area of a sphere is four times its
(105) greatest cross-sectional area. What is the approximate
surface area of a cantaloupe that is 6 inches in diameter?
Use 3.14 for π and round the answer to the nearest square
inch. 113 in.^{2}

22. A cup containing 250 cubic centimeters of water holds a
(115) quantity of how many liters of water? 0.25 liters

Solve:

23. $15 + x = 3x - 17$ 16
(102)

24. $3\frac{1}{3}x - 16 = 74$ 27
(93)

25. $\frac{m^2}{4} = 9$ 6, −6
(109)

26. $\frac{1.2}{m} = \frac{0.04}{8}$ 240
(98)

Simplify:

27. $x(x - 5) - 2(x - 5)$
(96) $x^2 - 7x + 10$

28. $\frac{(3xy)(4x^2y)(5x^2y^2)}{10x^3y^3}$ $6x^2y$
(103)

29. $|-8| + 3(-7) - [(-4)(-5) - 3(-2)]$ −39
(91)

30. $\dfrac{7\frac{1}{2} - \frac{2}{3}(0.9)}{0.03}$ 230
(43,45)

INVESTIGATION
12

Proof of the Pythagorean Theorem

When mathematicians want to demonstrate that a particular
idea is true they construct a **proof.** Following logical steps, a
proof describes how certain given information leads to a
certain conclusion. Indeed, virtually all of the structure of
mathematics is built upon conclusions reached by a proof. One
extremely important and useful conclusion about our world is

that the lengths of the legs (a and b) and the hypotenuse (c) of a right triangle are related in the following way:

$$a^2 + b^2 = c^2$$

Recall that this conclusion is called the Pythagorean theorem. Mathematicians have constructed literally hundreds of proofs of the Pythagorean theorem. In fact, one of America's presidents, James A. Garfield, is credited with providing an original proof of this theorem. In this investigation we will develop one of the many proofs of the Pythagorean theorem. As a whole class, work through the exercises in this investigation with the guidance of your teacher.

The following proof is based upon the characteristics of similar triangles. Recall that the corresponding angles of similar triangles are congruent and that the lengths of their corresponding sides are proportional.

1.

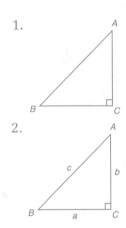

1. Begin by sketching a right triangle. For reference, name the vertices A, B, and C, with $\angle C$ being the right angle. This triangle is a "generic" right triangle, so the measures of the acute angles do not affect the outcome of the proof.

2.

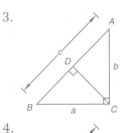

2. It is customary to refer to the lengths of the sides of a right triangle by the lowercase form of the letter of the opposite vertex. So along side AB write a lowercase c, along side BC write a lowercase a, and along side CA write a lowercase b. Remember that these lowercase letters refer to the lengths of the sides. Since this is a "generic" right triangle we do not know the lengths of the sides. However, it is not necessary to know the lengths of the sides in order to establish the relationship among the sides.

3.

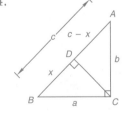

3. Next draw a segment from vertex C across the triangle to side AB so that the segment is perpendicular to $\overline{AB}$. Name the point where the segment intersects $\overline{AB}$ point D.

4.

4. Point D divides segment AB into two shorter segments. We have already labeled the distance from A to B as c. Now label the distance from B to D as x. The distance from D to A is the rest of c which can be found by subtracting x from c. So label the length of $\overline{AD}$ as $c - x$.

Check your drawing with the following description: If you have performed questions 1–4 correctly you should have drawn a right triangle ABC and divided the right triangle into two smaller right triangles, named $\triangle BCD$ and $\triangle ACD$. The hypotenuse and one leg of $\triangle BCD$ should be labeled a and x.

The hypotenuse and one leg of $\triangle ACD$ should be labeled b and $c - x$. The hypotenuse of $\triangle ABC$ should be labeled c and is equal to length x plus length $c - x$. (Note that you may need to position "c" on your drawing to indicate that it represents the entire length of $\overline{AB}$.)

We will use this figure and what we know about similar triangles to reach the conclusion that the Pythagorean theorem applies to all right triangles. Before proceeding with the algebraic proof we need to be convinced that the three triangles in the figure we have drawn are similar. If their corresponding angles are congruent, then the triangles are similar.

5. 90°; The sum of the measures of all three angles is 180°. The right angle of the triangle removes 90° from this total leaving 90° to be shared by the remaining two acute angles.

5. What is the sum of the measures of the two acute angles of a right triangle? Why?

6. If $\angle B$ of $\triangle ABC$ measures m degrees, then how many degrees is the measure of $\angle A$? $90° - m$

7. If the number of degrees in the measure of $\angle B$ is m and the number of degrees in the measure of $\angle A$ is $90° - m$, then how many degrees are in the measure of

  (a) $\angle BCD$? $90° - m$ (b) $\angle ACD$? m

8. All three triangles are similar because each triangle has degree angle measures of 90, m, and $90 - m$. Since their corresponding angle measures are equal, their angles are congruent, and the triangles are similar.

8. Can we conclude that all three triangles in the figure are similar? Why?

Since similar triangles have sides whose measures are proportional, we should be able to write proportions that relate the lengths of the sides of these triangles. Because we are referring to the lengths of the sides, we will use the lowercase letters on the diagram a, b, c, x, and $c - x$.

Recall that we began with the largest triangle, $\triangle ABC$, and that we divided this triangle into two smaller triangles. We will write two proportions. One proportion will relate the largest triangle to one of the smaller triangles. The second proportion will relate the largest triangle to the other smaller triangle.

9. Write the complete proportion that relates the given lengths of the hypotenuse and a leg of $\triangle ABC$ to the lengths of the corresponding sides of $\triangle BCD$. $\frac{c}{a} = \frac{a}{x}$

$$
\begin{array}{ccc}
 & \triangle ABC & \triangle BCD \\
\dfrac{\text{hyp}}{\text{leg}} & \dfrac{c}{a} & = \dfrac{\square}{\square}
\end{array}
$$

10. Write the complete proportion that relates the given lengths of the sides of $\triangle ABC$ to the lengths of the corresponding sides of $\triangle ACD$. $\frac{c}{b} = \frac{b}{c-x}$

$$
\begin{array}{ccc}
 & \triangle ABC & \triangle ACD \\
\dfrac{\text{hyp}}{\text{leg}} & \dfrac{c}{b} & = & \dfrac{\square}{\square}
\end{array}
$$

11. From 9:

$$\frac{c}{a} = \frac{a}{x}$$

$$cx = a^2$$

or

$$a^2 = cx$$

From 10:

$$\frac{c}{b} = \frac{b}{c-x}$$

$$c^2 - cx = b^2$$

or

$$b^2 = c^2 - cx$$

11. Cross multiply the proportions you wrote in questions 9 and 10.

12. If you have finished cross multiplying the proportions in questions 9 and 10, you should see the term "cx" in both cross products. (Check with your teacher if you do not see "cx" in both cross products.) In the first cross product we see that cx equals a^2. This means that we can replace cx with a^2 in the second cross product. Replace cx with a^2 in the second cross product and write the result. $c^2 - a^2 = b^2$ or $b^2 = c^2 - a^2$

13. Transform the equation you found for your answer to question 12 by solving for c^2. What do we call this equation? $c^2 = a^2 + b^2$ or $a^2 + b^2 = c^2$; Pythagorean theorem

This completes an algebraic proof of the Pythagorean theorem for all right triangles.

Some proofs of the Pythagorean theorem involve dividing up and rearranging areas of squares built on the sides of a right triangle. These proofs are based on the concept that a^2, b^2, and c^2 represent areas of squares as shown below.

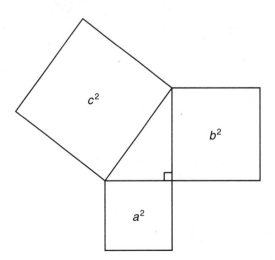

The following activity demonstrates that the combined areas of the squares labeled a^2 and b^2 in the drawing above equal the area of the square labeled c^2.

Activity: Pythagorean Puzzle

Materials needed by each student:

- Copy of "Activity Master 8" from the *Math 87 Test Masters*
- Scissors
- Envelope or plastic locking bag for each student, if desired

One solution: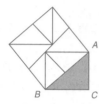

The object of the puzzle is to rearrange the pieces of the squares drawn on the legs of right triangle *ABC* to form a square on the hypotenuse of the triangle.

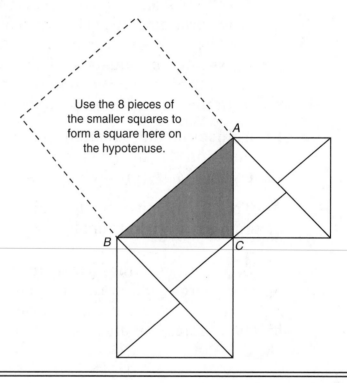

Use the 8 pieces of the smaller squares to form a square here on the hypotenuse.

Appendix

Supplemental Practice Problems for Selected Lessons

This appendix contains additional practice problems for concepts presented in selected lessons. It is very important that no problems in the regular problem sets be omitted to make room for these problems. This book is designed to produce long-term retention of concepts, therefore long-term practice of all the concepts is necessary. The practice problems in the problem sets provide enough initial exposure to concepts for most students. If a student continues to have difficulty with certain concepts, some of these problems can be assigned as remedial exercises.

Supplemental Practice for Lesson 3

Find each missing number.

1. $w + 36 = 62$ 26

2. $x - 24 = 42$ 66

3. $5y = 60$ 12

4. $z \div 8 = 16$ 128

5. $18 + m = 72$ 54

6. $24 - n = 6$ 18

7. $6p = 48$ 8

8. $144 \div q = 8$ 18

9. $36 = 4m$ 9

10. $\dfrac{a}{18} = 3$ 54

11. $\dfrac{18}{c} = 3$ 6

12.
$$\begin{array}{r} 84 \\ -\ E \\ \hline 36 \end{array}$$ 48

13. $8 + 6 + 5 + x + 4 = 30$ 7

14. $36 + 18 + 27 + w = 90$ 9

Supplemental Practice for Lesson 6

List the whole numbers from 1–10 that are factors of:

1. 36   1, 2, 3, 4, 6, 9

2. 3600   1, 2, 3, 4, 5, 6, 8, 9, 10

3. 350   1, 2, 5, 7, 10

4. 1326   1, 2, 3, 6

5. 4320   1, 2, 3, 4, 5, 6, 8, 9, 10

6. 950   1, 2, 5, 10

7. 12,000   1, 2, 3, 4, 5, 6, 8, 10

8. 35,420   1, 2, 4, 5, 7, 10

9. 36,270   1, 2, 3, 5, 6, 9, 10

10. 123,450   1, 2, 3, 5, 6, 10

11. 1,000,000   1, 2, 4, 5, 8, 10

12. 2520   1, 2, 3, 4, 5, 6, 7, 8, 9, 10

Supplemental Practice for Lesson 15

Reduce each fraction to lowest terms.

1. $\dfrac{15}{20}$ $\frac{3}{4}$

2. $\dfrac{8}{24}$ $\frac{1}{3}$

3. $\dfrac{9}{24}$ $\frac{3}{8}$

4. $\dfrac{12}{18}$ $\frac{2}{3}$

5. $\dfrac{24}{30}$ $\frac{4}{5}$

6. $\dfrac{16}{32}$ $\frac{1}{2}$

7. $\dfrac{24}{36}$ $\frac{2}{3}$

8. $\dfrac{28}{35}$ $\frac{4}{5}$

9. $3\dfrac{15}{18}$ $3\frac{5}{6}$

10. $6\dfrac{18}{24}$ $6\frac{3}{4}$

11. $8\dfrac{9}{15}$ $8\frac{3}{5}$

12. $4\dfrac{18}{32}$ $4\frac{9}{16}$

Supplemental Practice for Lesson 19

Find the perimeter of each of these polygons. Dimensions are in inches.

1.   64 in.

2.   58 in.

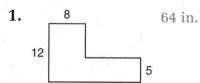

3. 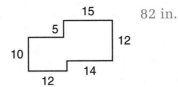 82 in. **4.** 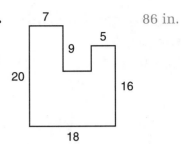 86 in.

Supplemental Practice for Lesson 20

Simplify:

1. 8^2 64   **2.** 2^6 64   **3.** 3^3 27   **4.** 10^5 100,000

5. $3^2 + 2^3$ 17   **6.** $5^2 - 4^2$ 9   **7.** 4^3 64   **8.** 15^2 225

9. $\dfrac{10^4}{10^3}$ 10   **10.** $\dfrac{8^2}{2^3}$ 8   **11.** $5^4 - 5^3$ 500   **12.** 25^2 625

13. $\sqrt{81}$ 9   **14.** $\sqrt{121}$ 11   **15.** $\sqrt{49}$ 7   **16.** $\sqrt{144}$ 12

17. $\sqrt{900}$ 30   **18.** $\sqrt{625}$ 25   **19.** $\sqrt{196}$ 14   **20.** $\sqrt{441}$ 21

Supplemental Practice for Lesson 21

Write the prime factorization of each of these numbers.

1. 81 $3 \times 3 \times 3 \times 3$ **2.** 300 $2 \times 2 \times 3 \times 5 \times 5$ **3.** 2000 $2 \times 2 \times 2 \times 2 \times 5 \times 5 \times 5$

4. 625 $5 \times 5 \times 5 \times 5$ **5.** 450 $2 \times 3 \times 3 \times 5 \times 5$ **6.** 1200 $2 \times 2 \times 2 \times 2 \times 3 \times 5 \times 5$

9. $2 \times 2 \times 2 \times 2 \times 5 \times 5 \times 5 \times 5$ **7.** 440 $2 \times 2 \times 2 \times 5 \times 11$ **8.** 750 $2 \times 3 \times 5 \times 5 \times 5$ **9.** 10,000

10. 128 $2 \times 2 \times 2 \times 2 \times 2 \times 2 \times 2$ **11.** 780 $2 \times 2 \times 3 \times 5 \times 13$ **12.** 1540 $2 \times 2 \times 5 \times 7 \times 11$

Supplemental Practice for Lesson 23

Simplify using regrouping:

1. $5\dfrac{3}{5} + 2\dfrac{4}{5}$ $8\frac{2}{5}$ **2.** $7\dfrac{3}{8} + 1\dfrac{3}{8}$ $8\frac{3}{4}$ **3.** $2\dfrac{3}{7} + 3\dfrac{4}{7}$ 6

4. $5\dfrac{3}{4} + 3\dfrac{3}{4}$ $9\frac{1}{2}$ **5.** $6\dfrac{5}{8} + 5\dfrac{7}{8}$ $12\frac{1}{2}$ **6.** $8\dfrac{5}{9} + 2\dfrac{7}{9}$ $11\frac{1}{3}$

7. $6\dfrac{7}{8} - 2\dfrac{1}{8}$ $4\frac{3}{4}$ **8.** $5 - 3\dfrac{1}{4}$ $1\frac{3}{4}$ **9.** $6 - 2\dfrac{3}{5}$ $3\frac{2}{5}$

10. $5\dfrac{1}{3} - 1\dfrac{2}{3}$ $3\frac{2}{3}$ **11.** $4\dfrac{2}{5} - 1\dfrac{4}{5}$ $2\frac{3}{5}$ **12.** $6\dfrac{1}{6} - 2\dfrac{5}{6}$ $3\frac{1}{3}$

Math 87

Supplemental Practice for Lesson 26

Simplify:

1. $3\frac{3}{4} \times \frac{2}{5}$ $1\frac{1}{2}$

2. $2\frac{1}{3} \times 3$ 7

3. $1\frac{4}{5} \times 3\frac{1}{3}$ 6

4. $7 \times 2\frac{2}{3}$ $18\frac{2}{3}$

5. $\frac{5}{8} \times 3\frac{1}{5}$ 2

6. $2\frac{1}{4} \times 1\frac{3}{5}$ $3\frac{3}{5}$

7. $3\frac{1}{2} \div 3$ $1\frac{1}{6}$

8. $2\frac{3}{4} \div \frac{3}{4}$ $3\frac{2}{3}$

9. $1\frac{1}{2} \div 2\frac{2}{3}$ $\frac{9}{16}$

10. $3\frac{1}{3} \div 1\frac{3}{4}$ $1\frac{19}{21}$

11. $6 \div 3\frac{3}{5}$ $1\frac{2}{3}$

12. $\frac{5}{8} \div 3\frac{1}{2}$ $\frac{5}{28}$

Supplemental Practice for Lesson 30

Simplify:

1. $\frac{3}{5} + \frac{3}{10}$ $\frac{9}{10}$

2. $\frac{3}{4} + \frac{1}{2} + \frac{3}{8}$ $1\frac{5}{8}$

3. $2\frac{5}{6} + 1\frac{1}{2}$ $4\frac{1}{3}$

4. $\frac{5}{6} + \frac{3}{4}$ $1\frac{7}{12}$

5. $\frac{5}{6} + \frac{3}{8} + \frac{7}{12}$ $1\frac{19}{24}$

6. $3\frac{3}{5} + 2\frac{2}{3}$ $6\frac{4}{15}$

7. $\frac{5}{8} - \frac{1}{2}$ $\frac{1}{8}$

8. $3\frac{5}{6} - 1\frac{1}{2}$ $2\frac{1}{3}$

9. $4\frac{3}{4} - 1\frac{1}{3}$ $3\frac{5}{12}$

10. $\frac{8}{12} - \frac{2}{3}$ 0

11. $6\frac{3}{5} - 3\frac{1}{3}$ $3\frac{4}{15}$

12. $5\frac{1}{4} - 1\frac{5}{6}$ $3\frac{5}{12}$

Supplemental Practice for Lesson 31

Name these decimal numbers.

1. 16.125 sixteen and one hundred twenty-five thousandths

2. 5.03 five and three hundredths

3. 105.105 one hundred five and one hundred five thousandths

4. 0.001 one thousandth

5. 160.165

6. 4000.321

5. one hundred sixty and one hundred sixty-five thousandths

6. four thousand and three hundred twenty-one thousandths

Write as decimal numerals.

7. One hundred twenty-three thousandths 0.123

8. One hundred and twenty-three thousandths 100.023

9. One hundred twenty and three thousandths 120.003

10. Five hundredths 0.05

11. Twenty and nine hundredths 20.09

12. Twenty-nine and five tenths 29.5

Supplemental Practice for Lesson 33

Round to the nearest whole number.

1. 23.459 23   **2.** 164.089 164   **3.** 86.6427 87

Round to two decimal places.

4. 12.83333 12.83   **5.** 6.0166 6.02   **6.** 0.1084 0.11

Round to the nearest thousandth.

7. 0.08333 0.083   **8.** 0.45454 0.455   **9.** 3.14159 3.142

10. Round 283.567 to the nearest hundred. 300

11. Round 283.567 to the nearest hundredth. 283.57

12. Round 126.59 to the nearest ten. 130

Supplemental Practice for Lesson 35

Simplify:

1. 45.3 + 2.64 + 3 50.94   **2.** 0.4 + 0.5 + 0.6 + 0.7 2.2

3. 3.6 + 2.75 + 0.194 + 3 9.544   **4.** 12.8 + 6.32 + 15 34.12

5. 10 + 1.0 + 0.1 + 0.01 11.11   **6.** 278.4 + 3.26 + 1.475 283.135

7. 14.327 − 6.5 7.827   **8.** 10.8 − 9.67 1.13   **9.** 6.5 − 4.321 2.179

10. 10 − 4.76 5.24   **11.** 0.1 − 0.019 0.081   **12.** 5 − 4.937 0.063

13. 0.3 × 0.12 0.036   **14.** 4.5 × 5 22.5   **15.** 8 × 0.012 0.096

16. 0.2 × 0.3 × 0.4 0.024   **17.** 1.2 × 1.2 × 100 144

18. 1.44 ÷ 12 0.12   **19.** 0.144 ÷ 8 0.018   **20.** 0.144 ÷ 16 0.009

Supplemental Practice for Lesson 37

Find the area of each triangle. Dimensions are in centimeters.

1. 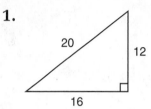 96 cm²

2. 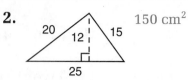 150 cm²

3. 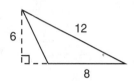 24 cm²

4. 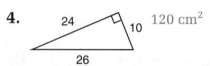 120 cm²

5. 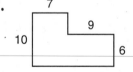 35 cm²

6. 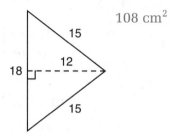 108 cm²

Find the area of each figure. Dimensions are in centimeters.

7. 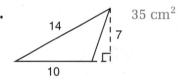 124 cm²

8. 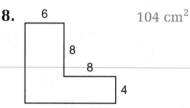 104 cm²

9. 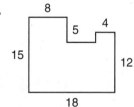 228 cm²

10. 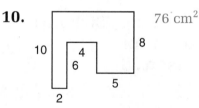 76 cm²

Supplemental Practice for Lesson 43

Change each of these decimals to a reduced fraction or mixed number.

1. 0.48 $\frac{12}{25}$

2. 3.75 $3\frac{3}{4}$

3. 0.125 $\frac{1}{8}$

4. 12.6 $12\frac{3}{5}$

5. 0.025 $\frac{1}{40}$

6. 1.08 $1\frac{2}{25}$

Change each of these fractions and mixed numbers to a decimal number.

7. $\frac{5}{8}$ 0.625

8. $\frac{1}{3}$ $0.\overline{3}$

9. $2\frac{2}{5}$ 2.4

10. $6\frac{1}{6}$ 6.1$\overline{6}$ **11.** $\frac{11}{20}$ 0.55   **12.** $5\frac{5}{9}$ 5.$\overline{5}$

Supplemental Practice for Lesson 45

Complete each division.

1. $0.15 \div 0.5$ 0.3   **2.** $14.4 \div 0.06$ 240   **3.** $18 \div 0.4$ 45

4. $5 \div 0.8$ 6.25   **5.** $12.5 \div 0.04$ 312.5   **6.** $288 \div 1.2$ 240

7. $4.3 \div 0.01$ 430   **8.** $1.5 \div 0.12$ 12.5   **9.** $9 \div 1.8$ 5

10. $4.5 \div 2.5$ 1.8   **11.** $8 \div 0.04$ 200   **12.** $12.5 \div 0.5$ 25

Supplemental Practice for Lesson 48

Copy and complete the table.

FRACTION	DECIMAL	PERCENT
$\frac{5}{6}$	**1.** $0.8\overline{3}$	**2.** $83\frac{1}{3}\%$
3. $1\frac{1}{5}$	1.2	**4.** 120%
5. $\frac{2}{25}$	**6.** 0.08	8%
$1\frac{3}{5}$	**7.** 1.6	**8.** 160%
9. $\frac{3}{40}$	0.075	**10.** $7\frac{1}{2}\%$
11. $1\frac{1}{4}$	**12.** 1.25	125%

Supplemental Practice for Lesson 49

Change:

1. 40 inches to feet and inches 3 feet, 4 inches

2. 200 seconds to minutes and seconds 3 minutes, 20 seconds

Simplify:

3. 3 ft, 21 in. 4 ft, 9 in.   **4.** 2 hr, 90 min 3 hr, 30 min

Add and simplify:

5.   3 yd 2 ft 7 in.
      + 1 yd 1 ft 8 in.
      _____
       5 yd   1 ft   3 in.

6.   5 hr 18 min 23 s
      + 2 hr 45 min 48 s
      _____
       8 hr   4 min   11 s

7.   5 lb 10 oz
      + 6 lb   8 oz
      _____
       12 lb   2 oz

8.   2 gal 3 qt 1 pt
      + 3 gal 2 qt 1 pt
      _____
       6 gal   2 qt

Supplemental Practice for Lesson 50

Use unit multipliers to convert.

1. 24 ft to in. 288 in.
2. 24 ft to yd 8 yd
3. 300 min to hr 5 hr
4. 300 min to s 18,000 s
5. 500 cm to m 5 m
6. 500 cm to mm 5000 mm
7. 100 lb to oz 1600 oz
8. 100 pounds to tons $\frac{1}{20}$ ton

Supplemental Practice for Lesson 52

Simplify:

1. $4 + 4 \times 4 - 4 \div 4$ 19
2. $40 - 20 \div 10 - 5$ 33
3. $5 + 6 \times 7 + 8$ 55
4. $3^2 + 4^2 - 5 \times 2$ 15
5. $\dfrac{10 + 10 \times 10}{10}$ 11
6. $\dfrac{5 + 5 \times 5 \div 5 - 5}{5}$ 1

Evaluate:

7. $ab - bc + abc$ if $a = 5$, $b = 4$, and $c = 2$ 52

8. $xy + \dfrac{x}{y} - 5$ if $x = 8$ and $y = 4$ 29

9. $abc - ab - \dfrac{a}{c}$ if $a = 6$, $b = 4$, and $c = 3$ 46

10. $m - mn$ if $m = \dfrac{3}{4}$ and $n = \dfrac{1}{2}$ $\frac{3}{8}$

11. $wx + xz - z$ if $w = 1.2$, $x = 0.5$, and $z = 0.1$ 0.55

12. $ab - ac - \dfrac{ab}{c}$ if $a = 4$, $b = 3$, and $c = 2$ –2

Supplemental Practice for Lesson 56

Subtract:

1. 5 ft, 7 in. − 3 ft, 10 in. 1 ft, 9 in.

2. 10 min, 13 s − 3 min, 28 s 6 min, 45 s

3. 4 yd, 6 in. − 2 ft, 8 in. 3 yd, 10 in.

4. 1 hr, 10 min − 24 min, 40 s 45 min, 20 s

5.   8 yd   2 ft   4 in.
     − 1 yd   2 ft   9 in.

       6 yd   2 ft   7 in.

6.   3 hr   17 min   30 s
     − 2 hr   48 min   43 s

           28 min   47 s

Supplemental Practice for Lesson 60

Write an equation to solve each problem.

1. What number is $\frac{3}{4}$ of 24? $W_N = \frac{3}{4} \times 24$; 18

2. Three fifths of 60 is what number? $\frac{3}{5} \times 60 = W_N$; 36

3. What number is 0.4 of 80? $W_N = 0.4 \times 80$; 32

4. Six tenths of 60 is what number? $0.6 \times 60 = W_N$; 36

5. What number is 30% of 120? $W_N = 0.3 \times 120$; 36

6. Six percent of 250 is what number? $0.06 \times 250 = W_N$; 15

7. What number is $\frac{5}{6}$ of 300? $W_N = \frac{5}{6} \times 300$; 250

8. Two thirds of 90 is what number? $\frac{2}{3} \times 90 = W_N$; 60

9. What number is 0.5 of 50? $W_N = 0.5 \times 50$; 25

10. Seven tenths of 140 is what number? $0.7 \times 140 = W_N$; 98

11. What number is 75% of 400? $W_N = 0.75 \times 400$; 300

12. Eighty percent of 400 is what number?
    $0.8 \times 400 = W_N$; 320

Supplemental Practice for Lesson 64

Find each sum.

1. $(-36) + (+54)$ 18   **2.** $(-15) + (-26)$ −41

3. $(-6) + (-12) + (+15)$ −3   **4.** $(+4) + (-12) + (+21)$ 13

5. $(-6) + (-8) + (-7) + (-2)$ −23

6. $(-9) + (-15) + (+50)$ 26

7. $(+42) + (-23) + (-19)$ 0   **8.** $(-54) + (+76) + (-17)$ 5

9. $\left(-3\frac{1}{2}\right) + \left(-2\frac{1}{4}\right)$ $-5\frac{3}{4}$ **10.** $\left(-1\frac{1}{3}\right) + \left(+2\frac{5}{6}\right)$ $1\frac{1}{2}$

−6.7   **11.** $(-1.7) + (-3.2) + (-1.8)$ **12.** $(-4.3) + (+2.63)$ −1.67

Supplemental Practice for Lesson 66

Find the circumference of each circle. Dimensions are in centimeters.

1.

Use 3.14 for π.
125.6 cm

2.

Use $\frac{22}{7}$ for π.
44 cm

3.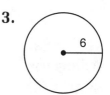

Leave π as π.
12π cm

4.

Use 3.14 for π.
31.4 cm

5.

Use $\frac{22}{7}$ for π.
88 cm

6.

Leave π as π.
15π cm

Supplemental Practice for Lesson 68

Simplify:

1. $(-3) - (-8)$ 5

2. $(-12) + (+20)$ 8

3. $(+8) - (-15)$ 23

4. $(+6) - (18)$ −12

5. $(-3) + (-4) - (-5)$ −2

6. $(+3) - (-4) - (+5)$ 2

7. $(-2) - (-3) - (-4)$ 5

8. $(+2) - (3) - (-4)$ 3

9. $(-6) - (-7) + (8)$ 9

10. $(+8) - (+9) - (-12)$ 11

11. $(-3) - (-1) - (-8) - (2)$ 4

12. $(-9) - (10) - (-11)$ −8

Supplemental Practice for Lesson 69

Express in the customary form of scientific notation.

1. 0.15×10^7 1.5×10^6

2. 48×10^{-8} 4.8×10^{-7}

3. 20×10^5 2×10^6

4. 0.72×10^{-4} 7.2×10^{-5}

5. 0.125×10^{12} 1.25×10^{11}

6. 22.5×10^{-6} 2.25×10^{-5}

7. 17.5×10^{10} 1.75×10^{11}

8. 0.375×10^{-8} 3.75×10^{-9}

Supplemental Practice for Lesson 75

Find each area. Dimensions are in centimeters.

1. 94 cm²

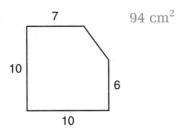

2. 108 cm²

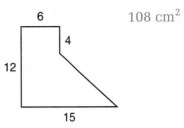

3. 160 cm²

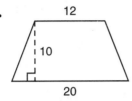

4. 168 cm²

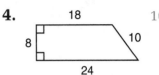

Supplemental Practice for Lesson 77

Translate and solve:

1. What percent of 75 is 60? $W_P \times 75 = 60$; 80%

2. Sixty is 75% of what number? $60 = 0.75 \times W_N$; 80

3. Thirty is what percent of 90? $30 = W_P \times 90$; $33\frac{1}{3}$%

4. Thirty is 150% of what number? $30 = 1.5 \times W_N$; 20

5. What percent of 40 is 50? $W_P \times 40 = 50$; 125%

6. Twenty percent of what number is 50? $0.2 \times W_N = 50$; 250

7. What percent of $5.00 is $3.50? $W_P \times \$5.00 = \$3.50$; 70%

8. Twelve is $66\frac{2}{3}$% of what number? $12 = \frac{2}{3} \times W_N$; 18

Supplemental Practice for Lesson 82

Find the area of each circle. Dimensions are in centimeters.

1.

Use 3.14 for π.
1256 cm²

2.

Use $\frac{22}{7}$ for π.
616 cm²

3.

Leave π as π.
16π cm²

4.

Use 3.14 for π.
314 cm²

5.

Use $\frac{22}{7}$ for π. 154 cm²

6.

Leave π as π.
64π cm²

Supplemental Practice for Lesson 83

Write each product in scientific notation.

1. $(1.2 \times 10^5)(3 \times 10^6)$
   3.6×10^{11}

2. $(3 \times 10^6)(6 \times 10^3)$
   1.8×10^{10}

3. $(4.2 \times 10^8)(2.5 \times 10^{12})$
   1.05×10^{21}

4. $(2.5 \times 10^5)(4 \times 10^7)$
   1.0×10^{13}

5. $(4 \times 10^{-3})(2 \times 10^{-8})$
   8×10^{-11}

6. $(6 \times 10^{-7})(4 \times 10^{-5})$
   2.4×10^{-11}

7. $(2 \times 10^{-4})(6.5 \times 10^{-8})$
   1.3×10^{-11}

8. $(6 \times 10^{-4})(4 \times 10^8)$
   2.4×10^5

9. $(1.6 \times 10^{-5})(7 \times 10^{-7})$
   1.12×10^{-11}

10. $(7 \times 10^{-9})(3 \times 10^5)$
    2.1×10^{-3}

11. $(1.4 \times 10^7)(8 \times 10^{-5})$
    1.12×10^3

12. $(7.5 \times 10^{-8})(4 \times 10^6)$
    3×10^{-1}

Supplemental Practice for Lesson 93

Solve:

1. $3x - 5 = 40$ 15

2. $15 = 2x - 19$ 17

3. $12 + 2x = 60$ 24

4. $80 = 4x - 16$ 24

5. $8x - 16 = 56$ 9

6. $3x + 12 = 54$ 14

7. $0.8x - 1 = 1.4$ 3

8. $0.3w + 1.2 = 3$ 6

9. $\frac{3}{4}w - 12 = 60$ 96

10. $3\frac{1}{3}m + 30 = 120$ 27

11. $-4w + 20 = 8$ 3

12. $-0.2y + 1.4 = 3.2$ −9

Supplemental Practice for Lesson 101

Write and solve an equation for each problem.

1. Six more than twice what number is 72? $2n + 6 = 72$; 33

2. Five less than the product of 8 and what number is 27?
   $8n - 5 = 27$; 4

3. Ten less than half of what number is 50?
   $\frac{1}{2}n - 10 = 50$; 120

4. What number is 12 more than the product of 6 and 4?
   $n = (6 \times 4) + 12$; 36

5. The sum of what number and 6 is 5 less than 12?
   $n + 6 = 12 - 5$; 1

$\frac{3}{4}n = 60 - 12$; 64 6. Three fourths of what number is 12 less than 60?

Supplemental Practice for Lesson 102

Simplify and solve:

1. $5m + 6 + m - 18 = 60$
12

2. $3x + 20 = x + 80$ 30

3. $3(x - 4) = 36$ 16

4. $x + 2(x - 4) = 24 - x$
8

5. What is the measure of the smallest angle in this figure?
$2x + 3x + 4x = 180$; $9x = 180$;
$x = 20$; So, $2x = 40$;
The smallest angle measures 40°.

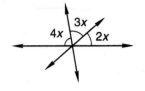

6. Find the measure of the largest angle in this triangle.
$2x + x + 20 + x - 20 = 180$;
$4x = 180$; $x = 45$; So, $2x = 90$;
The largest angle measures 90°.

Supplemental Practice for Lesson 111

Write each quotient in scientific notation.

1. $\dfrac{8 \times 10^8}{4 \times 10^4}$
2×10^4

2. $\dfrac{6 \times 10^3}{3 \times 10^6}$
2×10^{-3}

3. $\dfrac{3.6 \times 10^6}{2 \times 10^{12}}$
1.8×10^{-6}

4. $\dfrac{1.2 \times 10^8}{3 \times 10^4}$
4×10^3

5. $\dfrac{2.4 \times 10^{12}}{8 \times 10^7}$
3×10^4

6. $\dfrac{3 \times 10^7}{4 \times 10^5}$
7.5×10^1

7. $\dfrac{4.2 \times 10^6}{7 \times 10^9}$
6×10^{-4}

8. $\dfrac{1 \times 10^8}{2 \times 10^{12}}$
5×10^{-5}

9. $\dfrac{1.8 \times 10^7}{6 \times 10^{11}}$
3×10^{-5}

10. $\dfrac{7.5 \times 10^{12}}{5 \times 10^7}$
1.5×10^5

11. $\dfrac{6.3 \times 10^8}{9 \times 10^4}$
7×10^3

12. $\dfrac{4 \times 10^6}{5 \times 10^{10}}$
8×10^{-5}

Supplemental Practice for Lesson 114

Simplify:

1. 4^{-2} $\frac{1}{16}$

2. 2^{-3} $\frac{1}{8}$

3. $4^2 \times 4^{-2}$ 1

4. $3^3 \times 3^{-2}$ 3

5. $2^{-2} \times 2^{-3}$ $\frac{1}{32}$

6. $2^{-2} + 2^{-2}$ $\frac{1}{2}$

7. $10^{-2} \times 10$ $\frac{1}{10}$

8. $3(3^{-3})$ $\frac{1}{9}$

9. Write 10^{-3} as a decimal number.   0.001

10. What is the reciprocal of 2^{-2}? 2^2 or 4

Glossary

absolute value The quality of a number that equals the distance of the graph of the number from the origin (zero mark). Since the graphs of −3 and +3 are both 3 units from the origin, the absolute value of both numbers is 3. Absolute value is symbolized by writing a vertical bar on each side of a numeral, e.g., $|-3| = 3$.

acute angle An angle whose measure is greater than 0° and less than 90°.

acute triangle A triangle in which all three angles are acute angles.

addend One of two or more numbers that are to be added to find a sum.

adjacent angles Two angles that have a common side and a common vertex. The angles lie on opposite sides of their common side.

algebraic addition The combining of positive and/or negative numbers to form a sum.

algorithm A particular process for solving a certain type of problem. Often the process is repetitive, as in the long division algorithm.

altitude In a triangle, the distance from the base to the opposite vertex; also called the *height* of the triangle.

angle In geometry, the figure formed by two rays called sides that have a common endpoint called the *vertex*.

arc Part of the circumference of a circle.

area The number of square units of a certain size needed to cover the surface of a figure.

average The sum of a group of numbers divided by the number of numbers in the group; also called the *mean*.

base   (1) A designated side (or a face) of a geometric figure. (2) The lower number in an exponential expression. In the exponential expression 2^5, the number 2 is the base and the number 5 is the exponent.

bisect   To divide a segment or angle into two congruent parts.

centimeter   One hundredth of a meter.

central angle   An angle whose vertex is the center of a circle.

chance   A way of expressing the likelihood of an event; the probability of an event expressed as a percent.

chord   A segment through a circle whose endpoints are on the circle.

circumference   The perimeter of a circle.

common factors   Identical factors of two or more indicated products.

complementary angles   Two angles whose sum is 90°.

complex fraction   A fraction that contains one or more fractions as the numerator or denominator of the fraction.

composite number   A counting number that is the product of two counting numbers, neither of which is the number 1.

concentric circles   Two or more circles with a common center.

congruent figures   Figures that have the same shape and size.

constant   A number whose value does not change. In the expression $2\pi r$, the numbers 2 and π are constants while r is a variable.

coordinate(s)   (1) The number associated with a point on a number line. (2) The ordered pair of numbers associated with a point in the coordinate plane.

coordinate plane   A plane, every point of which can be designated by two numbers representing positions relative to the x-axis and y-axis of the plane.

corresponding parts   Sides or angles of similar polygons that occupy the same relative positions.

counting numbers   Sometimes called the *natural numbers*, these numbers are of the set {1, 2, 3, 4, 5, …}.

decimal fraction   A decimal number.

decimal number   A numeral that contains a decimal point.

decimal point   A dot placed in a decimal number to use as a place value reference point. The place to the left of the decimal point is always the units' (ones') place.

denominator   The bottom term in a fraction.

diagonal   Of a polygon, a segment with endpoints on non-consecutive vertices of the polygon.

diameter   The distance across a circle through its center.

difference   The result of subtraction.

digit   Any of the symbols 0, 1, 2, 3, 4, 5, 6, 7, 8, or 9.

directed numbers   *See* **signed numbers.**

dividend   The number to be divided. In the expression 10 ÷ 2, the dividend is 10 and the divisor is 2.

divisible   If one whole number is divided by another whole number and the quotient is a whole number (the remainder is zero), we say that the first whole number is *divisible* by the second whole number: 10 is divisible by 2.

divisor   The number by which another number is divided. In the expression 10 ÷ 2, the divisor is 2 and the dividend is 10. Also called a *factor* of a number. Both 2 and 5 are divisors of 10.

edge   A line segment of a polyhedron where two faces intersect.

equation   A statement that two quantities are equal.

equilateral triangle   A triangle whose sides all have the same length.

equivalent fractions   Fractions that have the same value.

estimate   To determine an approximate value.

evaluate   To find the value of an expression when its variables are replaced by numbers.

expanded notation   A way of writing a number as the sum of the products of the digits and the place values of the digits.

exponent   The upper number in an exponential expression which shows how many times the base number is to be used as a factor. In the expression 2^5, 5 is the exponent and 2 is the base.

exponential expression   An expression that indicates that one number is to be used as a factor a given number of times. The expression 4^3 tells us that 4 is to be used as a factor 3 times. The value of 4^3 is 64.

face   A flat surface of a geometric solid.

factor   (1) Noun: One of two or more numbers that are to be multiplied. In the expression $3xy$, the factors are 3, x, and y. (2) Verb: To write as a product of factors. We can factor the number 6 by writing it as 2×3.

fraction   A part of a whole or the indicated division of two numbers, such as $\frac{4}{5}$.

function   A set of number pairs related by a certain rule so that for every number to which the rule may be applied, there is exactly one resulting number.

geometric solid   A three-dimensional geometric figure. Spheres, cones, and prisms are examples of geometric solids. *See also* the chart inside the back cover for the names of some geometric solids.

gram   The basic unit of mass in the metric system.

greatest common factor (GCF)   The largest number that is a factor of two or more indicated numbers.

height   The perpendicular distance from the base to the opposite side of a parallelogram or trapezoid, or from the base to the opposite face of a prism or cylinder, or from the base to the opposite vertex of a triangle, pyramid, or cone. *See also* **altitude**.

hypotenuse   The side of a right triangle that is opposite the right angle. Thus, the longest side of a right triangle.

improper fraction   A fraction whose numerator is equal to or greater than the denominator. Thus, a fraction equal to or greater than 1.

independent events   Two events are said to be *independent* if the outcome of one event does not affect the probability that the other event will happen. If a dime is tossed twice, the outcome (heads or tails) of the first toss does not affect the probability of getting heads or tails on the second toss.

inscribed angle   An angle whose vertex is on a circle and whose sides include chords of the circle.

integers   The whole numbers and the opposites of the positive whole numbers. The members of the set {..., −2, −1, 0, 1, 2, ...}.

intersect   To share a common point or points. Lines that intersect meet at a common point.

inverse operation   Two operations are *inverse operations* if one operation will "undo" the other operation. If we begin with 3 and multiply by 2, the product is 6. If we divide 6 by 2, we will undo the multiplication by 2, and the answer will be 3, the original number.

invert   When said of a fraction, to interchange the numerator and denominator.

irrational numbers   The family of numbers that cannot be expressed as a ratio of two integers and that can be represented by points on the number line, e.g., π and $\sqrt{2}$.

isosceles triangle   A triangle with at least two sides of equal length.

kilogram   One thousand grams.

kilometer   One thousand meters.

least common denominator (LCD)   Of two or more fractions, a denominator that is the least common multiple of the denominators of the fractions.

least common multiple (LCM)   The smallest number that is a common multiple of two or more given numbers.

line   A straight collection of points extending without end.

linear equation   An equation whose graph is a line.

liter   The basic unit of capacity in the metric system.

lowest terms   In reference to a fraction, when the numerator and denominator contain no common factors.

mean   *See* **average.**

median   The middle number when a set of numbers is arranged in order from the least to the greatest.

meter   The basic unit of length in the metric system.

milligram   One thousandth of a gram.

milliliter   One thousandth of a liter.

millimeter   One thousandth of a meter.

mixed number   A numerical expression composed of a whole number and a fraction, such as $2\frac{1}{2}$.

mode   The number in a set of numbers that appears the most often.

monomial   An algebraic expression composed of a single term.

multiple   A product of a selected counting number and another counting number. Multiples of 3 include 3, 6, 9, and 12.

multiplier   One of two numbers that are to be multiplied; a factor.

natural numbers   *See* **counting numbers.**

negative numbers   Numbers to the left of zero on the number line.

numeral   Symbol or groups of symbols used to represent a number.

numerator   The top term of a fraction.

obtuse angle   An angle whose measure is greater than 90° and less than 180°.

obtuse triangle   A triangle that contains one obtuse angle.

odds   A way of describing the likelihood of an event; the ratio of favorable outcomes to unfavorable outcomes.

opposites   Two numbers whose sum is 0. Thus, a positive number and a negative number whose absolute values are equal. The numbers −3 and +3 are a pair of opposite numbers.

origin   The point on a number line with which the number zero is associated.

outlier   A number in a set of numbers that is distant from the other numbers in the set.

parallel lines   Lines in the same plane that do not intersect.

parallelogram   A quadrilateral that has two pairs of parallel sides.

percent   (1) Per hundred. Forty percent is 40 per hundred. (2) Hundredth. Forty percent is forty hundredths.

perimeter   Of a plane geometric figure, the distance around the figure.

perpendicular lines   Two lines that intersect and form right angles.

pi (π)   The number of diameters equal to the circumference of a circle. Approximate values of pi are 3.14 and $\frac{22}{7}$.

plane   In mathematics, a flat surface that has no boundaries.

point   A location on a line, on a plane, or in space with no size.

polygon   A closed, plane geometric figure whose sides are line segments. *See also* chart inside back cover for names of polygons.

polyhedron   A geometric solid whose faces are polygons.

polynomial An algebraic expression composed of two or more terms.

positive numbers Numbers to the right of zero on the number line.

power The value of an exponential expression. The expression 2^4 is read as "2 to the fourth power" and has a value of 16. Thus, 16 is the fourth power of 2. The word *power* is also used to describe the exponent.

prime factorization The expression of a composite number as a product of its prime factors.

prime factors The factors of a number that are prime numbers.

prime number A whole number greater than 1 whose only whole number divisors are 1 and the number itself.

prism A polyhedron with two congruent parallel bases.

probability A way of describing the likelihood of an event; the ratio of favorable outcomes to all possible outcomes.

product The result of multiplication.

proper fraction A fraction whose numerator is less than the denominator.

proportion Two equivalent ratios.

Pythagorean theorem A description of a characteristic of right triangles that states that the area of a square constructed on the longest side of a right triangle is equal to the sum of the areas of the squares constructed on the other two sides of the right triangle.

quadrant Any one of the four regions of a rectangular coordinate system, which is formed by two perpendicular number lines that intersect at the origins of both number lines.

quotient The result of division.

radical expression An expression that contains radical signs, such as $\sqrt{x}$, $\sqrt[3]{16}$, and $\sqrt[4]{xy}$, which indicate roots of a number.

radius   The distance from the center of a circle to a point on the circle. Plural: *radii*.

range   The difference between the largest and smallest numbers in a set of numbers.

rate   A ratio of two measures.

ratio   A comparison of two numbers by division. The ratio of a to b is written $\frac{a}{b}$.

rational numbers   The number family that includes all numbers that can be written as a fraction (or ratio) of two integers.

ray   A part of a line that begins at a point and continues without end in one direction.

real numbers   All the numbers that can be represented by points on a number line. Composed of rational and irrational numbers.

reciprocals   Two numbers whose product is 1. The reciprocal of $\frac{4}{3}$ is $\frac{3}{4}$ since $\frac{4}{3} \times \frac{3}{4} = 1$.

rectangle   A parallelogram that has four right angles.

regular polygon   A polygon in which all sides have equal lengths and all angles have equal measures.

repetend   The repeating digits of a decimal number often indicated by a bar. In the number $0.08\overline{3}$ the repetend is 3.

rhombus   A parallelogram with all four sides of equal length.

right angle   One of the angles formed at the intersection of two perpendicular lines. A right angle has a measure of 90°.

right triangle   A triangle that contains one right angle.

root   (1) The solution to an equation. (2) The value of a radical expression.

scale factor   The number that relates corresponding sides of similar geometric figures.

scalene triangle   A triangle whose three sides are of different lengths.

scientific notation   A method of writing a number as a product of a decimal number and a power of 10.

sector   A portion of a circle including its interior, bound by a central angle of the circle and its included arc.

segment   A part of a line with two distinct endpoints.

semicircle   A half circle.

sequence   An ordered list of numbers arranged according to a certain rule.

signed numbers   Numbers that are either positive numbers or negative numbers.

similar polygons   Two polygons that have the same shape but that may not be the same size. The corresponding angles of similar polygons are equal in measure and the lengths of the corresponding sides are proportional.

slope   The number (ratio of rise to run) that indicates the slant of the graph of an equation or function at a particular location.

solid   *See* **geometric solid.**

square   (1) A rectangle with all four sides of equal length. (2) The product of a number and itself. The square of 3 is 9.

square root   One of two equal factors of a number. A square root of 49 is 7 because $7 \cdot 7 = 49$. The principal or positive square root of a number is indicated by the radical symbol $\sqrt{}$.

straight angle   An angle whose measure is 180°.

sum   The result of addition.

supplementary angles   Two angles whose sum is 180°.

surface area   The total area of the surface of a geometric solid.

term (1) Of a fraction, a number that serves as a numerator or denominator. (2) Of a sequence, one of the numbers of the sequence. (3) Of an algebraic expression, a constant or variable expression composed of one or more factors. The expression $2x + 3xyz$ has two terms.

trapezoid A quadrilateral with exactly one pair of parallel sides.

unit conversion The process of changing a number to an equivalent number that has different units.

unit multiplier A ratio equal to 1 composed of two equivalent measures.

unit price The price of one unit of measure of a product.

variable A letter used to represent a number that has not been designated.

vertex A point of an angle, polygon, or polyhedron where two or more lines, rays, or segments meet. Plural: *vertices*.

vertical angles A pair of non-adjacent angles formed by a pair of intersecting lines.

volume The number of cubic units of a certain size that equals the space occupied by a geometric solid.

whole numbers The numbers of the set {0, 1, 2, 3, 4, ...}.

***x*-axis** Horizontal number line of a coordinate plane.

***y*-axis** Vertical number line of a coordinate plane.

***y*-intercept** The point on the *y*-axis of a coordinate plane where the graph of an equation intersects the *y*-axis.

Index

Symbols

| | (absolute value), 352, 384
∠ (angle), 36
≈ (approximately equals sign), 402
{ } (braces), 1, 383
[ ] (brackets), 383
¢ (cent sign), 1
. (decimal point), 2
° (degree symbol), 84, 87
⌐ (division box), 3
— (division or fraction bar), 3, 39, 317, 384
÷ (division sign), 3
$ (dollar sign), 1
= (equals sign), 2, 19
<> (greater than/less than sign), 19
≥ (greater than or equal to sign), 470
≤ (less than or equal to sign), 470
$\overleftrightarrow{AB}$ (line), 33
$\overline{AB}$ (line segment), 34
— (minus sign), 2
× (multiplication sign), 3
· (multiplication sign), 3
≠ (not equal to sign), 7
|| (parallel lines), 35
( ) (parentheses), 3, 8, 316
% (percent), 39
⊥ (perpendicular lines), 35
π (pi), 401-402
+ (plus sign), 2
$\overrightarrow{AB}$ (ray), 34
∟ (right angle), 35
√ (square root), 106, 656-657

A

Absolute value, 352
  in addition of signed numbers, 389-390
  as symbols of inclusion, 384
Absolute zero, 192
Acute angle, 36, 88. *See also* Angle(s)
Acute triangle, 377. *See also* Triangle(s)
Addend(s), 2
  missing, 13
Addition
  algebraic, 414, 511
  associative property of, 8
  commutative property of, 6

Addition (cont.)
  of decimal numbers, 206
  of exponents when multiplying powers
    of 10, 286, 506
  of fractions
    with common denominators, 45
    with different denominators, 172
    using prime factorization, 174
  identity property of, 7
  of integers, 353
  with missing numbers, 13-14
  of mixed measures, 297
  of mixed numbers
    with common denominators, 45
    with different denominators, 172
  of money, 2
  on a number line, 20, 353
  pattern, 58, 72
  of signed numbers, 353, 389-390
Additive identity, 7
Adjacent angles, 241, 372
  of a parallelogram, 372
Algebraic addition, 414, 511
Algebraic expressions, 510
  factoring, 728-729
Algebraic-logic, 318
Altitude, 219. *See also* Height
Angle(s), 35-36
  acute, 36
    degree measure of, 87-90
  adjacent, 241, 372
  alternate exterior, 636
  alternate interior, 636
  bisector, 492
  central, 114
  classification of, 36, 88
  complementary, 241
  congruent, 595
  copying, 741-742
  corresponding, 94, 596, 636
  exterior, 541-542
  inscribing, 113
  interior, 541
  measuring, 88
    by estimation, 588-589
  naming, 35

Place Value Chart

			Whole Numbers Places												Decimal Places					

hundred trillions	ten trillions	trillions	hundred billions	ten billions	billions	hundred millions	ten millions	millions	hundred thousands	ten thousands	thousands	hundreds	tens	ones	tenths	hundredths	thousandths	ten thousandths	hundred thousandths	millionths
10^{14}	10^{13}	10^{12} ,	10^{11}	10^{10}	10^{9} ,	10^{8}	10^{7}	10^{6} ,	10^{5}	10^{4}	10^{3} ,	10^{2}	10^{1}	10^{0} .	10^{-1}	10^{-2}	10^{-3}	10^{-4}	10^{-5}	10^{-6}

Time

60 seconds	= 1 minute
60 minutes	= 1 hour
24 hours	= 1 day
7 days	= 1 week
365 days	= 1 common year
366 days	= 1 leap year
10 years	= 1 decade
100 years	= 1 century

Probability, Chance, Odds

Probability	Ratio of $\dfrac{favorable}{possible}$
Chance	Probability expressed as a percent
Odds	Ratio of favorable:unfavorable

Equivalence Table for Units

Length	
U.S. Customary	**Metric**
12 in. = 1 ft 3 ft = 1 yd 5280 ft = 1 mi 1760 yd = 1 mi	10 mm = 1 cm 1000 mm = 1 m 100 cm = 1 m 1000 m = 1 km
Weight	**Mass**
U.S. Customary	**Metric**
16 oz = 1lb 2000 lb = 1 ton	1000 mg = 1 g 1000 g = 1 kg
Liquid Measure	
U.S. Customary	**Metric**
16 oz = 1 pt 2 pt = 1 qt 4 qt = 1 gal	1000 mL = 1 L

Classification of Quadrilaterals

Shape	Characteristic	Name
	No sides parallel	Trapezium
	Exactly one pair of parallel sides	Trapezoid
	Two pairs of parallel sides	Parallelogram
	Parallelogram with congruent sides	Rhombus
	Parallelogram with right angles	Rectangle
	Rectangle with congruent sides	Square

Note that squares, rectangles, and rhombuses are types of parallelograms and that a square is a type of rectangle and a type of rhombus.

Regular and Irregular Polygons

Name	Regular	Irregular
Triangle		
Quadrilateral		
Pentagon		
Hexagon		
Octagon		

Geometric Solids

Type		Examples
Polyhedron	Cube	
	Rectangular prism	
	Triangular prism	
	Pyramid	
Cylinder		
Sphere		
Cone		